FRANKLIN D. ROOSEVELT

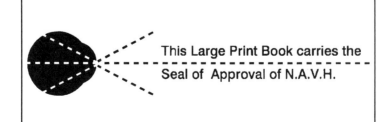

This Large Print Book carries the
Seal of Approval of N.A.V.H.

FRANKLIN D. ROOSEVELT

A POLITICAL LIFE

ROBERT DALLEK

THORNDIKE PRESS

A part of Gale, a Cengage Company

Farmington Hills, Mich • San Francisco • New York • Waterville, Maine
Meriden, Conn • Mason, Ohio • Chicago

LIBRARY OF CONGRESS CIP DATA ON FILE.
CATALOGUING IN PUBLICATION FOR THIS BOOK
IS AVAILABLE FROM THE LIBRARY OF CONGRESS

ISBN-13: 978-1-4328-4642-8 (hardcover)
ISBN-10: 1-4328-4642-6 (hardcover)

Published in 2018 by arrangement with Viking, an imprint of Penguin Publishing Group, a division of Penguin Random House LLC

Printed in the United States of America
1 2 3 4 5 6 7 22 21 20 19 18

To our grandchildren,
Hannah, Ethan, Sammy, and Eli,
and my sister-in-law and brother-in-law,
Ellie and Bob Topolovac

CONTENTS

PREFACE

In April 1945, soon after Franklin Roosevelt died, the *New York Times,* never an uncritical fan, declared, "Men will thank God on their knees a hundred years from now, that Franklin D. Roosevelt was in the White House."

It was an unusual tribute to a president. As a rule, Americans are not drawn to politicians and politics but see the men and women seeking elected office as more self-serving than advocates of the public interest. In a system that puts personal gain above social reform, it's little wonder that they view officeholders as primarily out for themselves. Every scandal or hint of malfeasance only deepens that conviction. Although numerous officials genuinely do work to advance the country's well-being, all too often their efforts are lost on the public. In 2016 national cynicism expressed itself in an initial low turnout at the polls. Only 9 percent of potential voters participated in both parties' primary elections. Distrust of the 2016 presidential aspirants, Republican Donald Trump and Democrat Hillary Clinton, marked a surge of disgust about the parties and their chiefs that raised doubts about the genius of American politics.

In this time of demoralization, it seems well to remind Americans that the system has been capable of generating candidates for high office whose commitment to the national interest exceeded their flaws and ambitions. In 1952, for example, mindful of the public's discontent with current events, Harry Truman stood aside and Dwight Eisenhower, a man unquestionably devoted to the country's well-being, restored confidence in democracy's ability to provide a well-regarded leader. Between 1961 and 1963, John F. Kennedy struck similar notes of faith in the government. Hubert Humphrey, who lost the presidency to Richard Nixon in 1968, has won retrospective regard by refusing to blow the whistle on Nixon's wrongdoing during the campaign for fear it would provoke a constitutional crisis. Sadly, Humphrey's reluctance to reveal Nixon's violation of the Logan Act — which forbids a private citizen's interference in diplomatic negotiations — was a measure of decency that opened the way to Nixon's presidency and the Watergate crisis. Ronald Reagan's Iran-contra scandal and Bill Clinton's impeachment over the Monica Lewinsky affair only deepened the growing disillusionment with politics.

Few political leaders in the country's history have commanded as much respect as Franklin D. Roosevelt, but more than seventy years after his passing, he has become a remote figure to most Americans. It seems well, then, despite the large body of fine existing biographies, histories, and documentary collections, to remind people, especially a younger generation with limited knowledge of American history, of what great presidential leadership looks like.

The central argument of this book is that Roosevelt, like his cousin Theodore, was an instinctively brilliant politician; he certainly consulted polls, after they came into vogue in the mid-thirties, but he principally relied on his feel for public mood to guide him in leading the country. I believe that my emphasis on his political judgment goes far to set my book apart from other biographies. I also revisit Roosevelt's health problems and argue that his decline began earlier than customarily described.

I have no wish to suggest that Roosevelt was an unqualified success. But then, what president has been above criticism? At the close of his two terms, George Washington complained of " 'unmerited censures' of the vilest kind." And Abraham Lincoln, probably our greatest chief executive, suffered under a barrage of attacks too numerous to recount. But grounded in his conviction that he was serving the country's best interest, he used humor to counter public hostility. Responding to assertions that he was a two-faced liar, he said, Do you think I would keep this face if I could substitute another?

Roosevelt kept his counsel on most of the criticism that dogged him through his twelve years, though in private he was anything but passive about it. He took special exception to assertions that he wished to be a dictator — an American Hitler, Mussolini, or Stalin. Yet however much he fell short in his presidency, I especially hope that revisiting the extraordinary challenges Roosevelt faced, personally and publicly, will help rekindle faith that great political leadership is not out of reach and that the country's finest institutions he did so much to preserve remain a source of national strength.

RD
Washington, D.C.
Fall 2016

Let us here assembled constitute ourselves prophets of a new order.

Franklin D. Roosevelt, July 2, 1932

There is nothing so exciting as creating a new social order.

Eleanor Roosevelt, December 29, 1933

PROLOGUE:
EVERYTHING TO FEAR

March 4, 1933, Inauguration Day for the thirty-second president of the United States, defied the usual temper of national renewal. Cold, overcast weather matched the country's bleak mood. The weeks leading up to Franklin Roosevelt's induction into the White House were a nightmare, as an unprecedented economic collapse had quieted the cheerleading about America's future that business leaders, the press, and politicians had made a hallmark of the 1920s. Optimism was in short supply; voices of despair crowded out the promise of American life. In January 1933, Calvin Coolidge, the retired Republican president, said: "In other periods of depression it has always been possible to see some things that were solid and upon which you could base hope. But as I look about, I now see nothing to give ground for hope, nothing of man." Herbert Hoover, the defeated incumbent, described "the state of the public mind" as suffering from "a steadily degenerating confidence in the future which had reached the height of general alarm. . . . We are in a pitiful position," he said on his last day in office. ". . . The whole economy [is] in jeopardy. . . . We are at the end of our string." Two months before, in a

New York Times article, James Truslow Adams, a writer of popular histories, lamented the passing of the American belief in ending famine and poverty. "It is this dream," he asserted, "in its various aspects, which to many today appears to lie shattered under the debris of the economic crash of the past three years."

From a listening post in the Soviet Union in Riga, Latvia, George F. Kennan, a twenty-eight-year-old Foreign Service officer, foresaw nothing but disaster for the United States: "There it [i.e., the United States] lies now," he recorded in a diary, ". . . in all its ignorance and all its sordidness, a society conceived in selfishness and dedicated to the proposition that one man's suffering is no other man's business, incapable of regulating its own public life, waiting stupidly for the advent of catastrophe." Two months later, a "pall of gloom and anxiety" that gave resonance to Kennan's prediction shadowed Roosevelt's arrival in the capital. New York's mayor, Fiorello LaGuardia, warned that unless there were reforms that gave people some kind of economic safety net, there would be "chaos and disorder, and something worse. There is something peculiar about human beings," he added. "They just simply refuse to go hungry." Looking back on the days leading up to Franklin Roosevelt's inauguration, a historian declared: "The Republic had virtually ceased to function as a vital organism and lay prostrate, paralyzed, seemingly moribund in the fearful cold."

Opinion leaders across the nation appeared to be bankrupt for ideas that might bring a recovery. Walter Lippmann, the country's most distinguished journalist, observed that "the fixed points

16

by which our fathers steered the ship of state have vanished." The head of the American Bar Association told a Senate committee calling upon America's best and brightest to propose solutions that he had "nothing to offer, either of fact or theory." The president of the Pennsylvania Railroad saw "no panacea," while William Gibbs McAdoo, Wilson's secretary of the treasury and U.S. senator from California, complained in March 1933 that America's collapsing banking system "does credit to a collection of imbeciles."

Many saw Roosevelt as the last chance to rescue the country from a collapse that could permanently alter its economic and political systems. A New York Republican congressman told him that Congress should "give you any power that you may need." The truth is that Roosevelt had no more idea of how he would restore the country's prosperity than Abraham Lincoln had in trying to persuade the rebellious Southern states to remain in the Union. Though Lincoln and Roosevelt faced crises more threatening to the national well-being than any since George Washington had launched the Republic, they shared common ground with other presidents in uncertainty about the course of their administrations. Warren G. Harding, the least effective of Roosevelt's recent predecessors, lamented the absence of a book that could tell him how to manage the national economy, and, he confessed, even if there were one, he doubted that he could understand it. John F. Kennedy, the most candid of Roosevelt's successors about how he would take charge of the country's considerable difficulties at home and abroad, privately acknowledged that he had no clue about the path ahead.

17

For Roosevelt, who believed that his initial task was not to advance an economic program, which was certain to generate demoralizing debate, but to regenerate the country's trust in its institutions and leaders or, more specifically, in his own leadership, by publicly appealing to a higher authority for guidance in combating the Depression.

Roosevelt, who was a nominally religious man, took refuge in his faith when considering the national crisis facing him as president. As he traveled by train from New York to Washington, symbolically following the route Lincoln had taken to his own first inaugural, Roosevelt asked Jim Farley, a New York political ally and devout Catholic who had been instrumental in assuring his election, to join him in his compartment. He told Farley, who listened with mounting appreciation, that no particular economic plan would save the country, but rather its religious convictions — its attachment to a belief in divine guidance or the expectation that Providence would bring the nation through the crisis. Roosevelt said that he planned to begin his administration with a well-publicized visit to Washington's St. John's Episcopal Church, where he would ask for the Lord's intervention. He would use the opening line of his inaugural speech to ask Americans to follow his lead and make March 4 "a day of national consecration."

Roosevelt's conversation with Farley rested on the assumption that his words would reach a large audience and stimulate the hope essential to a national revival. He instinctively understood that in times of strife and uncertainty, symbols could be more compelling than any substantive executive or legislative act. Eventually, presidential initiatives that could buoy the economy and reduce suffering and unemployment would be necessary. But in the first days of his presidency, these could not counter the almost universal despair and launch the national restoration that would be the foundation for a successful presidential term.

Roosevelt faced a variety of problems that even the staunchest advocates of positive thinking could not confront without doubts about the nation's future. The most immediate and gravest of these was the economy: the speed and depth of the turn from prosperity to depression that began in 1930.

When Hoover entered the White House in March 1929, he confidently declared, "I have no fears for the future of our country. It is bright with hope." A year later, the descent into economic disarray was painfully evident, and Hoover's optimism seemed like empty rhetoric. In a matter of weeks, beginning in late October, stocks on the New York exchange had fallen more than 40 percent in value, a loss of $26 billion, equivalent to a fourth of the country's gross domestic product. Over the next three years the U.S. economy shrank by 27.8 percent, and the GDP was a little more than half its 1929 value. Deflation matched the drop in stocks and national output, with prices falling between 6 and 10 percent in each of the next three years. Between 1930 and 1933, five thousand banks — 20 percent of all the country's financial institutions — failed, wiping out ninety thousand savings accounts, the loss for many of lifetime investments that generated fears of destitute retirements. As the banks collapsed, hordes of terrified depositors rushed to withdraw their holdings from the institutions one senator described as nothing more than "pawn shops." The bulk of these banks, which were unaffiliated with the Federal Reserve System (which counted only a third of the country's banks as members), had nowhere to turn for the on-hand cash that could keep them solvent and assure customers that they would not close their doors. At the end of 1930, when the Federal Reserve System failed to rescue New York's Bank of United States, the largest private bank in America, the entire national banking system seemed to be in jeopardy.

When Roosevelt took office in March 1933, unemployment stood at an unprecedented 25 percent of the labor force. Prospects of finding work were so bleak that some among the nearly thirteen million jobless had given up looking. Workers' wages, which stood at $50 billion in 1929, had plummeted to $30 billion by the end of 1932. Desperate for any employment at any sort of wage, men, women, and children accepted as little as two to five cents an hour for as many hours as they could get. Sharecroppers across the southern United States survived on one dollar a day, an income that allowed for a diet more suited to domestic animals. "Emaciated children who never tasted milk," one newspaper description reads, "wandered the streets, some shoeless in winter, too poorly clad to go to school." National birth rates declined, as few people wanted to bring children into a world where they would face privation.

Stories of hunger and even starvation haunted the land: Late at night, men kept vigil at restaurants waiting for clean-up crews to throw leftover food in garbage cans, while some hungry families searched city dumps for something to eat. Accounts of former middle-class citizens selling apples on street corners to eke out a living coupled with tales of homelessness, and cities and towns unable to provide the pittance of relief that could sustain the needy through hard times abounded. More than a million desperate Americans — men, women, and children — roamed the country in search of jobs, food, and shelter.

No one could ignore the suffering that reached into every city and rural county across the nation. "Below Riverside Drive in New York City, an encampment of squatters lined the shores of the Hudson from 72nd Street to 110th Street," the historian William Leuchtenburg writes. ". . . Along the banks of the Tennessee in Knoxville, in the mudflats under the Pulaski Skyway in New Jersey, in abandoned ovens in Pennsylvania's coal counties, in the huge dumps off Blue Island Avenue in Chicago, the dispossessed took their last stand." In West Virginia and Kentucky evicted families found shelter in unheated tents in the dead of winter, and stories of people slowly starving amid disintegrating families in New York, Philadelphia, and Salt Lake City added to the growing sense of desperation.

American abundance, the conviction that no one in the United States need be impoverished if he was willing to work, was no longer a widespread article of faith. Angry citizens puzzled over the national plenty in food and housing and clothing that was suddenly beyond the reach of honest folks who were humiliated by their dependence and loss of respectability. Franklin Roosevelt captured the national dilemma when he said in his inaugural address that the country's distress came "from no failure of substance. We are stricken by no plague of locusts," he declared, invoking the religious imagery that he saw as vital to a national revival. ". . . Plenty is at our doorstep, but a generous use of it languishes in the very sight of the supply."

Some of the anger found an outlet in jokes at Herbert Hoover's expense. In one, Hoover says to his treasury secretary, Andrew Mellon, "Lend me a nickel, I want to call a friend." "Here's a dime, call all your friends," Mellon replies. Hoover, who kept insisting that prosperity was right around the corner, became the butt of vaudeville comedians: They would tell their audiences that business was supposedly improving, and then ask "Is Hoover dead?," or describe the president as the greatest engineer in history, since in just two years he had "drained, ditched, and damned the United States." His name became synonymous with the worst features of the Depression: "Hoovervilles" for shantytowns; "Hoover blankets" for newspapers used as covering against the cold; "Hoover flags" for "empty pockets turned inside out." A man with little play of mind and a rigid temperament, Hoover deepened the gulf between him and his critics by accusing them of "unpatriotic" behavior. He understood that the country needed a joke, a song, or story of some kind that would relieve the national despair. But wounded pride prevented him from accepting that presidents were always convenient targets in hard times. No one would compose a rousing anthem to a president leading a nation burdened by a failing economy.

Franklin Roosevelt, refusing to downplay what

he called "the dark realities of the moment," declared in his inaugural that he would address his fellow Americans "with a candor . . . which the present situation of our people impel. Values have shrunken to fantastic levels . . . the means of exchange are frozen in the currents of trade; the withered leaves of industrial enterprise lie on every side; farmers find no markets for their produce; the savings of many years in thousands of families are gone. Most important, a host of unemployed citizens face the grim problem of existence, and an equally great number toil with little return. Only a foolish optimist," he added, implicitly reminding people of Hoover's unconvincing cheerleading, would ignore the disaster that had descended on the nation.

Was the country, then, on the verge of revolution? With the worst economic downturn in U.S. history and no national programs to help the unemployed, sustain the elderly through lifetime pensions, or save banks by guaranteeing the savings of their depositors, millions of Americans felt abandoned by a system of savage capitalism. The head of a national farm bureau federation predicted that without prompt government aid, the countryside would soon erupt in rebellion. A Los Angeles banker warned against a coming upheaval: "The farmers will rise up. So will labor. The Reds will run the country — or maybe the Fascists. Unless, of course, Roosevelt does something."

For all the talk of upheaval, little militancy actually existed among the country's unemployed and impoverished. To be sure, there was a rising resentment and anger against the comfortably privileged's decrying calls for public relief as

23

calculated to encourage sloth and dependency among the needy. But this anger did not translate into demands for organized action that would redistribute wealth. Instead, afflicted Americans were more apathetic than rebellious, more docile and stoic than indignant with rage at the failure of free enterprise to sustain opportunities for work and prosperity.

However difficult conditions were in 1932–33, they had not been bad enough for long enough to persuade a majority of Americans to abandon the American dream — the idea that national progress was inevitable and that they and their children would enjoy greater creature comforts. In addition, for a country with a dominant tradition of individualism, the unemployed were reluctant to engage in organized group action. If they were out of work, they believed it was their fault. After all, millions of Americans still had work; the unemployed chided themselves for not being among them. And so, jobless men and women clung to the belief that individual initiative remained the best path to the good life. The wisest response to the Depression was not radical change but determined efforts to make ends meet and outdo competitors in the search for a job.

As historian Lawrence Levine has argued, the popular culture of the 1930s continued to reflect traditional views about the virtues of free enterprise by self-made men. The magazine, newspaper, and radio advertisements of the time, for example, emphasized not group action of any kind but individual improvement through using products that could improve your life: "Magazine ads in the early 1930s were filled with pictures of anxious men and women," Levine writes, "plagued by lack of sleep, lack of confidence, lack of financial means, lack of foresight and planning; beset by the scourge of halitosis, flawed skin, yellow teeth, bad English, caffeine addiction; worried by every fear imaginable." The path to success was through controlling or ending all these problems with readily available products like Milk of Magnesia (with its appealing acronym, MOM) or particular food and hygiene merchandise. "Jobs could be kept, lovers won, social acceptance assured by bathing with Lifebuoy Soap, shaving with Gillette Razor Blades, drinking Ovaltine [free of caffeine], using Listerine Mouth Wash."

In the first years of the Depression, the country's role models were not rebels calling for revolutionary change to replace outdated economic and political habits, but traditional business leaders counseling renewed faith in the virtues of hard work and frugality. "Thrift and prudence," the president of the National Association of Manufacturers told Americans, were practices that would assure every man's well-being. Automobile titan Henry Ford decried people's tendency to shun tough jobs: "There is plenty to do, if people would do it." The popular 1932 book *Cheer Up!* condemned the habits of "dishonesty, inefficiency, and general carelessness" that had taken hold in the twenties. Good times would come again with the revival of "moral character," but only if people had the "courage" to rectify their mistakes through the stoutness of heart it would take to conquer bad habits. And John D. Rockefeller, whose name was synonymous with success and wealth, urged: "Work! Persevere! Be Honest! Save!"

The rhetoric was not lost on millions of suffering Americans. The most popular films and publications of the time embraced the opinion leaders' advice. The hugely successful Walt Disney film cartoon of 1933, *The Three Little Pigs,* had audiences singing along with the eldest pig, "Who's Afraid of the Big Bad Wolf?" Building his house of stones and bricks, he prevented the wolf's attempt to blow it down. But his younger self-indulgent brothers, who spent their time singing and dancing and took the easier path of building straw houses, learned that there was no defense against the wolf without forethought and "perseverance."

Similarly, *Amos 'n' Andy,* the most popular radio show of 1932–33, with a devoted audience of some forty million Americans, echoed the themes of hard work and frugal living. For fifteen minutes nightly from 7:00 to 7:15, the two black main characters, who had come to Chicago from Georgia, entertained listeners with episodes contrasting the industrious Amos's life lessons about the virtues of hard work with Andy's affinity for indolence and quick-rich schemes.

Franklin Roosevelt's greatest challenge on assuming office was finding ways to combat the Great Depression with effective federal programs that would not agitate public fears of a swing toward collectivism and away from individualism by a president reaching for too much power. As the novelist John Dos Passos described it, "In times of change and danger when there is a quicksand of fear under men's reasoning, a sense of continuity with generations gone before can stretch like a lifeline across the scary present." The unsettling events of World War I had opened the way to Warren G. Harding's candidacy, which rested on the promise of "healing," "normalcy," and "restoration." A general national preference for comfortable habits over untried solutions, however, was not the only test of Roosevelt's political skills. Other enduring problems at home and emerging ones abroad competed for his attention along with the economic crisis.

Not the least of these was the deep cultural divide between urban and rural Americans, or modernists and fundamentalists, as they were described in the 1920s. As some social scientists asserted, the coming economic collapse was partly the result of an imbalance between the farm and urban industrial economies. Instead of a belief in shared prosperity, each side saw themselves benefitting at the expense of the other; they were locked in a contest over whose special interest would be served. If Roosevelt was to find the means to overcome the nation's crisis, it would have to rest on shared support from every region and every ethnic, religious, and racial group. But tensions across geographic locales and among these many clusters of diverse Americans, who in hard times clung more tenaciously than ever to their group identities, made any prospect of unifying the nation behind White House initiatives especially difficult.

During the 1920s, for the first time in the country's history, more Americans began living in cities of populations of 100,000 or more than in small towns and on farms. The transformation of the nation into a primarily urban society threatened rural folks who aggressively supported ideas and traditions largely in harmony with their established way of life. The adoption of the Eighteenth Amendment in 1919 was as much a rejection of city habits as it was of demon liquor. As the historian Richard Hofstadter observed, Prohibition "was linked not merely to an aversion to drunkenness and to the evils that accompanied it, but to the immigrant drinking masses, to the pleasures and amenities of city life. . . . It was carried about America by the rural-evangelical virus."

Millions of immigrants had flooded into the country since the 1870s and taken up residence in northern and midwestern cities. Prohibition was a prelude to the 1924 National Origins Act, which threw up barriers to a continued influx of the southern and Eastern European migrants who had made up the bulk of the roughly twelve million newcomers entering the United States during the previous fifty years. Many of them were Catholics and Jews — Italians, Greeks, Poles, Russians, Hungarians, and other Slavs, to mention just the most prominent nationalities — with religious affiliations and alien languages that made them indigestible masses. They defied the ideal of an American melting pot: Many in the United States doubted that the newcomers could shed old ways or abandon "un-American" habits, as had the northern and western Europeans who had preceded them. To be sure, fears of political radicalism and a competition for jobs in the aftermath of a postwar recession also animated the resistance to allowing more of these immigrants into the country. But the belief that these groups could never be turned into citizens who fully accepted Anglo-Saxon economic and political traditions made them antagonists of assimilated Americans.

If Roosevelt was to give Americans a New Deal, as his presidential campaign promised, he needed to reconcile the urban and rural wings of his

Democratic Party. The experience of the 1920s gave little hope that the two sides could find common ground. In 1924, the party had sharply divided over a presidential nominee: The rural wing favored William Gibbs McAdoo, Woodrow Wilson's son-in-law, while the urbanites embraced Governor Al Smith of New York, a Catholic with an unmistakable New York accent. A deadlocked convention took 103 ballots before it could settle on John W. Davis, a West Virginia native and Wall Street lawyer. Although the party would nominate Smith in 1928, he suffered an overwhelming defeat in the national election, signaling the extent to which the country remained split between cities and towns, Catholics and Protestants, southern and Eastern Europeans and assimilated voters. For "the older America," a Southern newspaper editor wrote, Smith's defeat meant that the country's "Anglo-Saxon stock" would not be "overturned and humiliated." The "small communities and rural regions" had "risen up in wrath" against the country's "great cities."

No group in the America of the 1920s reflected the antimodern side of the divide more clearly than the Ku Klux Klan. By that decade the Southern, anti-black Klansmen of the post–Civil War era had morphed into a national movement not only in rural communities but in cities as well, where economic imperatives had driven numerous Americans from the countryside. The Klansmen were no longer just a society of vigilantes fighting to preserve Southern racial purity, but a movement fighting to preserve traditional American mores against the social and political disruptions of a polyglot, more materialist, and less spiritual nation abandoning its old-time religion.

Hiram Wesley Evans, the Klan's leader, spoke for millions of Americans when he complained that Nordic Americans had become strangers in their own land: "The sacredness of our Sabbath, of our homes, of chastity, and finally even of our right to teach our own children in our own schools fundamental facts and truths were torn away from us. Those who maintained the old standards did so only in the face of constant ridicule." Evans advocated a return of power to "the everyday, not highly cultured . . . but entirely unspoiled and not de-Americanized, average citizen of the old stock."

The depths and extent of the national divide facing Roosevelt had registered on the nation in 1925 when the state of Tennessee took John T. Scopes, a biology teacher, into court for violating a statute against teaching evolution. Clarence Darrow, a prominent Chicago attorney who spoke for urban America, came to Dayton, Tennessee, to defend Scopes from the "rubes," "hicks," and "yokels," as sophisticates dubbed them, who seemed hopelessly opposed to the realities of a changing world. William Jennings Bryan, the Nebraska Populist and three-time Democratic presidential nominee, who defended Tennessee's attempt to preserve biblical wisdom from the "anti-religious, immoral teachings" of modernists like Scopes and Darrow, was ridiculed for his pronouncements during testimony on the state's behalf. The national press coverage of the trial, which ended in a one-dollar fine of Scopes, deepened the impression that America was two irreconcilable countries. Muting the resentments of the fundamentalists and convincing urban leaders that helping farmers and small towns was essential to the national well-being was an imposing challenge to a new president in the darkest days of the Depression.

For all their devotion to traditional habits, however, modernizing influences did have some appeal to rural Americans. As Lawrence Levine has shown, 1920s popular culture reveals a nation that was drawn in two directions at once. No national figure reflected popular ambivalence more clearly than Charles Lindbergh, the "lone eagle," whose solo flight across the Atlantic to Paris in 1925 had made him a universally admired hero. For Americans from every walk of life, he represented the "self-sufficient individual of the past," a pioneer like the timeless folk heroes Daniel Boone and Davey Crockett. Lindbergh was the product "not of the city but of the farm, not of schools and formal training but of individual initiative and self-contained genius." At the same time, though, he demonstrated the triumph of the new technology that provided the wherewithal for his successful flight. Lindbergh gave simultaneous expression to the popular affinity for "the past and the present, the individual and society."

Clues to the state of the popular mind can be found as well in the films and comic strips of the decade. Movies that reached millions of Americans and dramatized "the new woman [flapper], the new morality, the new youth, the new consumption" also celebrated traditional American virtues. Films like *Forbidden Fruit, Flapper Wives, Madness of Youth, Modern Maidens,* and *Love Mart* titillated audiences with risqué portrayals, but they consistently ended with the triumph of familiar moral standards. Flappers invariably entered lives of "middle-class respectability." The hugely popular *The Ten Commandments* (1923), for example, was divided between the story of Moses and one in a modern setting in which the commandments were tested in a competition between brothers. Although the wayward brother would eventually come to disaster, his gains along the way were enough to satisfy audiences attracted both to the hedonism of the 1920s and traditional moral verities. As for comic strips, which also reached a vast national audience, Levine points out that they emphasized old-fashioned "steadiness" and celebrated "the average." But they were featured in newspapers that "heralded the new . . . and called for change and progress." These were the two halves of "the cultural equation that characterized the United States throughout the decade."

In 1933 the stalled domestic economy demanded Washington's primary attention, but rumblings of trouble abroad could also not escape the attention of a president responsible for America's long-term safety.

After World War I, the failure of Woodrow Wilson's inspiring promises — a peace without victors, a war to end all wars, and a war to make the world safe for democracy — frustrated the millions of Americans who had assented to the bloodletting as a great crusade. But the horrors of trench warfare, which cost ten million lives, including fifty thousand Americans in just eighteen months, and was brilliantly captured in the 1930 film version of Erich Maria Remarque's novel *All Quiet on the Western Front,* fueled American isolationism and antimilitarism. The arms manufacturers and bankers who profited from the war became known as "merchants of death." The fighting and vindictive peace convinced a majority of the population that European and Asian conflicts were of little consequence to the United States and certainly not worth the sacrifice of blood and treasure. The failure of the Associated Powers, as they were called, to pay their war debts to the United States further incensed Americans, who now wished to avoid future overseas involvements. In an era when the Atlantic and Pacific oceans and weak neighbors to the north and south seemed to ensure safety from armed assaults, the country remained convinced that isolationism best served the national interest. Although Britain and France did not enjoy similar geographical advantages in assuring their security, their wartime losses generated a shared affinity for pacifism.

The hope that the 1914–18 conflict had convinced people everywhere of the futility of war found clear expression in the 1928 Kellogg-Briand pact negotiated by U.S. Secretary of State Frank B. Kellogg and French Foreign Secretary Aristide Briand. The agreement outlawed war, but without any enforcement provisions, it was no more than a symbolic bow to Wilson's idealism. Some contemporary critics dismissed it as a harmless international kiss or a greeting card from Santa Claus. The nationally syndicated columnist Walter Lippmann predicted that "the effort to abolish war can come to nothing unless there are created international institutions, an international public opinion, an international conscience which will play the part which war has always played in human affairs."

Nothing initially gave the lie to the pacifist impulse more clearly than developments in East Asia. In 1921–22, Secretary of State Charles

Evans Hughes, seeing Asia as the likely battleground for another world conflict, presided over a Washington Arms Conference that agreed to Nine-Power, Five-Power, and Four-Power treaties. These agreements endorsed naval arms limitations and the preservation of China's territorial integrity, and pledged Britain, France, Japan, and the United States to consult one another in response to any East Asian crisis.

None of these commitments, however, deterred Japan from seizing control of China's resource-rich province of Manchuria and setting up the puppet state of Manchukuo in 1931–32. The League of Nations, which had been established as a collective security deterrent to aggression, refused to impose meaningful sanctions on Japan, and the United States was equally lax in punishing Tokyo for treaty violations. The closest Washington came to a protest was Secretary of State Henry L. Stimson's doctrine refusing to recognize Japan's conquest. Reluctant to undermine Japan's position as a bulwark against Soviet Communist expansion in East Asia or to provoke a crisis that might lead to war, Hoover and Stimson confined themselves to a verbal rebuke of the Japanese. Their caution reflected the widespread opposition in the United States to anything threatening another overseas conflict and acknowledged America's focus on its economic collapse: "The President is so absorbed with the domestic situation," Stimson noted in a diary, "that he told me frankly that he can't think very much now of foreign affairs."

Yet some Americans worried that the country was blinding itself to the dangers that unchecked aggression in Asia or Europe represented. In 1933, however, U.S. opinion leaders worried less about an attack on American soil than the likelihood that authoritarian regimes would command the future. Events in Russia, Italy, Germany, and across Asia and Latin America suggested that the world was becoming unsafe for democracy. The economic collapse that had circled the globe by 1933 demonstrated the limitations of free enterprise in dealing with the Depression. Benito Mussolini, Italy's Fascist dictator, famously made the trains run on time, and Russia's state-managed economy seemed more productive than America's private markets. In January, when the *New York Times* reported that Joseph Stalin, Soviet Russia's Communist dictator, told his Central Committee that a Five-Year Plan had tripled Soviet industrial output by 219 percent compared with a downturn in the United States of 56 percent, it gave advocates of centralized economic control a compelling argument.

Nothing was more troubling to democracy's advocates in Britain, France, and the United States than the 1933 collapse of the Weimar Republic, Germany's experiment with democracy, and the rise to power of Adolph Hitler and the Nazi or National Socialist Party. Exploiting a decade of resentment toward the Allies, who had imposed a punitive treaty on Germany, Hitler had convinced millions of Germans that Weimar's republican leaders had betrayed the German army by agreeing to an unnecessary surrender. He further appealed to German national pride with denunciations of the despised Versailles Treaty, which had placed the blame for World War I on Germany, compelling reparation payments that had led to runaway inflation in 1923. France's occupation of the Rhineland dictated by the treaty, coupled with lost territories in the East, created a witch's brew of rage that Hitler took advantage of in bringing himself to power. His appeal to ancient antagonisms to Jews as the architects of German miseries gave him an additional hold on public support.

Weimar's fall deepened convictions in the United States that only "a strong executive making unpopular decisions" could rescue the country from its current plight. "Popular government," Walter Lippmann wrote in a column, "is unworkable except under the leadership and discipline of a strong national executive. Any group of 500 men, whether they are called congressmen or anything else, is an unruly mob unless it comes under the strict control of a single will." Others shared his belief. The conservative American Legion declared "existing political methods" insufficient to deal with the national crisis. Columbia University president Nicholas Murray Butler praised the greater effectiveness of "totalitarian societies," which he believed had leaders of "far greater intelligence, far stronger character and far more courage" than electoral systems.

At the start of 1933, there was little to give Americans eager to preserve traditional habits of mind and action hope that the country could avoid radical change. If Herbert Hoover, the man many saw as the greatest economic manager of their lifetimes, could not restore the national economy to sustained growth, what could succeed except some untried reform experiment?

The prospect of a Franklin Roosevelt presidency presiding over a period of uncertain change generated little optimism among some of America's most astute observers. Although the ninety-one-year-old justice Oliver Wendell Holmes had said that Theodore Roosevelt had a first-class temperament but a second-class mind, the observation had entered into the popular discussion as applying to his distant cousin Franklin, as well. Hoover dismissed his rival for the highest office as a "chameleon on plaid," and *New York Times* journalist Elmer Davis observed that Franklin Roosevelt was the kind of "man who thinks that the shortest distance between two points is not a straight line but a corkscrew." Lippmann as well complained of Roosevelt's equivocating, decrying his efforts "to be such different things to such different men." In addition, he belittled Roosevelt's intellectual limitations, simply saying he didn't "have a very good mind." He had never come to grips with the great issues of the day and was no more than a "kind of amiable boy scout."

Mindful of his critics' complaints, Roosevelt would take much future pleasure in confounding his harshest detractors. They could not foresee the political mastery and competence he would bring to bear in dealing with the Great Depression and world crisis that shadowed his coming years in office. When he promised that he and the Democrats would become prophets of a new order, no one could imagine the extent to which they would transform the federal government over the next twelve years by creating a welfare state and making the United States into the world's greatest power.

CHAPTER 1
THE MAKING OF A PATRICIAN

In the two-hundred-and-thirty-year history of the United States, forty-five Americans have become president. Unlike in royal kingdoms, no noble family line anoints the men who enter the highest office, and no common characteristics distinguish them from millions and millions of their fellow native-born citizens. They have come from every corner of the country — south and north, east and west — and have included a variety of ethnicities, religious denominations (including a Catholic), and, most surprisingly, given the country's long history of racism and segregation, an African American.

The story of each president's rise to the White House is sui generis, and explaining the achievement of each in achieving the highest office is a puzzle unto itself. The earliest occupants of the post — Washington, Adams, Jefferson, Madison, Monroe, and Adams, members of the founding generation — seemed to be natural candidates for national leadership. But once Andrew Jackson won the presidency in 1828 and Vice President John Tyler took office after the death of William Henry Harrison in 1841, no one could confidently predict who might take the prize. Abraham Lin-

39

coln, a self-taught lawyer of the most humble origins, further confounded president watchers by becoming one of the country's three greatest chief executives.

The success of Franklin Roosevelt, arguably the third of America's greatest presidents, and surely the most important of the twenty-nine since Lincoln, only adds to the puzzle. There was little about Roosevelt that moved contemporaries to see him as a logical candidate for the White House, let alone one who would be accorded the exalted status of being judged a great president. True, he was a Roosevelt, and the name meant so much after Theodore, Franklin's distant cousin, and then uncle after he married Eleanor, served seven plus years as chief executive with great distinction and popular approval. Membership in the country's Northeast elite gave Franklin additional advantages. But others of his generation also came from favored families and enjoyed greater wealth and better academic records than his, and though they were no less ambitious for public distinction, they never matched Franklin's political accomplishments. Some contemporary competitors ascribed Franklin's rise to high office to dumb luck and a charming disposition, echoing Anthony Trollope's observation that "The capacity of a man . . . [to be prime minister] does not depend on any power of intellect or indomitable courage, or far-seeing cunning. The man is competent simply because he is believed to be so."

Considering Franklin's life almost seventy-five years after it ended allows us the distance to weigh dispassionately the influences that facilitated his reach for and use of power. As the British historian

A. J. P. Taylor said, "The politician performs upon the stage; the historian looks behind the scenery." There was much about Franklin Roosevelt that still seems unremarkable, but some attributes — supreme self-confidence and unfailing self-reliance — distinguished him from earlier and later aspirants and help explain why he stands apart from almost all of America's other leaders.

Like anyone intent on becoming president, an elevated sense of self-importance, if not uniqueness, was a constant in Franklin's life. From an early age, he knew he was special or deserved to think of himself as worthy of high regard. He came from a storied family that not only had amassed considerable wealth but had contributed to the building of a great, singular nation.

Franklin's knowledge of his family's history was a source of pride and satisfaction, as it was for his parents, whose identities were inextricably bound up with an appreciation of their forebears. Their ancestors, who had been in the New World since the 1650s, had prospered in Manhattan real estate and the West Indian sugar trade. Franklin's great-great grandfather, who was lauded in family recollections as "Isaac the Patriot," had backed the American Revolution, helped draft New York's first constitution, and served a five-year term as president of the Bank of New York from 1786 to 1791. A Gilbert Stuart painting of him conveys his stature as an eighteenth-century American patrician. In the first half of the nineteenth century, subsequent Roosevelts attended Princeton University and established a landed estate along the banks of the Hudson River. James Roosevelt, Franklin's father, was the offspring of a

41

Roosevelt and an Aspinwall, a New England family that dominated New York's shipping industry.

Franklin loved to regale listeners with stories of his father's early life. James's grand tour of Europe between 1847 and 1849 as a twenty-year-old was grist for Franklin's lifelong attraction to youthful adventure. Even if some of his father's exploits were more legend than reality, Franklin took pleasure in recounting throughout his career James's walking tour of Italy with a mendicant priest and an alleged brief term of service in Giuseppe Garibaldi's red-shirt army, fighting to liberate Italy from foreign and papal rule. Franklin's fascination with family history included writing an account of the Roosevelts' Hyde Park estate.

He was no less admiring of the maternal side of the family, the Delanos. His mother, Sara Delano, was a snob who overlooked no opportunity to cite her family's heritage. The *"grande dame,"* as one biographer described her, was "serene in her confidence that she and hers had been from birth at the apex of all the world that counted." The Delano pedigree dated from ancient times and included centuries in France and the first Delano arriving in the New World in 1621 on the *Mayflower.* Eventually settling in Bedford, Massachusetts, what was in the seventeenth century the world's greatest whaling port, the family became wealthy mariners and shipbuilders. Sara was no less proud of her mother's line, which included revolutionary soldiers, clergymen, and elected Massachusetts officeholders. Franklin took special pride in his maternal grandfather, Warren Delano, who accumulated a fortune in the China trade. A wooden replica of the clipper *Surprise,* which carried his seven-year-old mother and her family to China in 1862, adorned a table in the Oval Office during Franklin's presidency, as did two paintings of the ship on a wall of his study at Hyde Park.

Franklin's life as a child on the banks of the Hudson gave new meaning to the word *indulgence.* His healthy, youthful twenty-seven-year-old mother was in the prime of her childbearing years, but a difficult birth discouraged her from risking additional pregnancies. His fifty-three-year-old father, delighted at having a male heir, was content with a son on whom he could lavish all his parental attention. But as an only child in a cloistered world, Franklin found particular satisfaction and strength in his own company. Companionship was certainly pleasing, but he learned to feel that he could master daily challenges by himself.

Despite an America agitated by farmer-labor-industrial strife, urbanization featuring concentrated communities of recent unassimilated migrants from Eastern and southern Europe, and political corruption spawning radical demands for reform, Franklin later recalled a placid boyhood in the 1880s and 1890s with nannies and tutors and a "regularity of . . . places and people" that insulated him from the outside world's unsettling events. As he matured, his father was his regular companion in hunting, horseback riding, fishing, and sailing, especially off Canada's Campobello Island in the Bay of Fundy, where his parents often retreated in the summer months. It was in these coastal waters that Franklin developed a lifelong love of seafaring, and here also that he developed a firsthand acquaintance with class differences. The presence of cooks, servants, and tutors in his Hyde Park home didn't register on him as evidence of his family's elevated position, but on Campobello, British class lines governed the island's permanent residents and the community of wealthy Americans who purchased property and summered there. They were regarded by the locals as landed aristocrats, and the sense of privilege became fully apparent to Franklin.

Annual trips to Europe, especially Germany, where Sara had attended school for several years in the 1860s as a teenager, opened a larger world to Franklin. Having been tutored in German and French, he had more than passable command of both languages by the time he was nine, so Sara enrolled Franklin in a local school at Bad Nauheim during their stay in Germany in 1891. "I go to the public school with a lot of little mickies," he wrote some cousins. "I like it very much," he added, despite being surrounded by children he obviously considered his inferiors. Although the "mickies" had no command of English, he could read about their history and compute arithmetic problems in their language. His feelings of dominance echoed what one biographer called his father's "invincible belief in his personal and class superiority to most of mankind." Never revealing that he viewed these provincials as inferior, Franklin displayed his proper breeding by treating them with a politeness and warmth that won their approval and made him one of the most popular boys in the class. It was an early demonstration of his capacity to charm people he wished to befriend, whatever his real feelings about them. Others registered his sense of superiority not as the behavior of a dismissive snob but rather as supportive benevolence — a winning asset for an ambitious politician.

His view of his German classmates may have come partly from his favorite tutor, Jeanne Sandoz, a French-speaking, Francophile young woman from Switzerland, of whom Franklin told his parents: "I like her. She smiles all the time." In the over two years she was his tutor, she heightened his interest in Europe, which his mother had already stimulated when he was nine by encouraging him to collect stamps, a hobby she had developed as a child. Partly to please his mother but also from a genuine curiosity about the larger world than the slice of America he knew, Franklin became an avid collector, simultaneously teaching himself geography and history. By 1896, when he was fourteen, he had visited Britain and the Continent eight times. That fall he was sent to a private boys' school in Massachusetts, where he could receive a fuller education than anything his parents could provide at home and he could prepare himself for the competitive world he would eventually face by measuring himself against other boys his age.

Groton, a preparatory school founded in 1883 by the Reverend Endicott Peabody, its headmaster, was designed to accommodate the desire of wealthy families to endow their sons with "manly Christian" virtues. Peabody, who had studied in England and wished to establish a school like those serving Britain's aristocratic families, launched Groton with the financial support of some of America's most affluent men, including the banking titan J. P. Morgan and the leaders of the Massachusetts Episcopal church. Located thirty-five miles northwest of Boston on ninety acres of farmland, the school was limited to six forms, in the British tradition, with no more than twenty boys in each class, starting at age twelve. Peabody's mission was to shape the boys' minds and bodies by instilling a sense of Christian charity in his privileged charges and stressing physical development with athletic contests that encouraged competition and fair play. The academic side of their schooling was a necessary but secondary consideration.

By 1896, when Franklin arrived at Groton, the school had already established itself as the premier preparatory institution in America. At a cost of $500 a year — twice the average American family's annual income — only wealthy, and chiefly Northeast, Episcopalians could afford to compete for the limited places in Peabody's academy.

Groton was a great testing ground for the fourteen-year-old Franklin. Joining the third form, a group that had already spent two years together and developed well-defined cliques and friendships, Franklin faced the challenge of fitting in. As outsiders, he and another new boy entered into a self-protective bond. Two weeks into the term, he assured his parents — or perhaps more himself — "I am getting on very well with the fellows, although I do not know them all yet."

His assimilation at Groton was not always easy. On his arrival at the school, he became the object of some ridicule. His father's son from a first marriage, the forty-two-year-old James Roosevelt Roosevelt, had a son at Groton, James Roosevelt Roosevelt, Jr. (Taddy), who was two years older than Franklin and in the fourth form. He was an awkward, ungainly teenager described as "a queer

sort of boy" who was "much made fun of."
Mocked as "Uncle Frank," Franklin had to live
down his nephew's negative reputation. He kept
Taddy at arm's length, telling his parents, "I see
very little of him."

Franklin's small size and unimpressive athletic
skills also added to his initial difficulties at the
school. At five foot three and a little over one
hundred pounds, with no experience in competitive sports, he gave little promise of contributing
much to the form's football or baseball teams.
True, he displayed rapid physical growth between
fifteen and eighteen, but it was never enough to
make him a force on Groton's playing fields. Nor
did he have any special athletic skills to make him
anything other than a second- or third-string
player. In addition, the school's Swedish gym
teacher, a Mr. Skarstrom, whom the boys playfully dubbed "Herr Cigar Stump," cautioned
Franklin against overly strenuous exercise, warning that his heart might not support the exertion
and that he should avoid rowing and limit his
participation in football. Although Skarstrom's assertion rested on no conclusive evidence and
eventually faded from Franklin's initial concern, it
was enough to discourage him from trying to
outdo his classmates in the school's most popular
sports. Because athletics were so important in
establishing each boy's standing, however, Franklin did take on the job of assistant manager and
then manager of the school's baseball team, which
made him responsible for equipment and uniforms
and the condition of the home playing field. It did
not match the prestige of being one of the starting
nine or even a place on the bench, but it gave him
standing as a team player willing to take on less

glamorous assignments. Peabody later summed up Franklin's athletic record at the school by saying, "He was rather too slight for success."

Another social obstacle was the fact that his earlier schooling put him academically ahead of most of the other eighteen boys in his form, which was unlikely to sit well with teenagers resentful of a newcomer's underscoring their scholastic shortcomings. His classmates were not especially appreciative of his end-of-the-year standing as number four in the form. Peabody's own view of him as a boy without fault added to Franklin's strained relations. Most of the boys received black marks for failing to follow all the school's rules. An infraction as minor as speaking in study hall or as serious as missing chapel could cause a boy to receive from one to five demerits. Challenging school standards and bearing the consequences with a penalty of designated chores like cleaning campus grounds or suffering some kind of physical punishment was regarded as a demonstration of masculine courage. Franklin's untarnished record opened him to accusations of lacking "school spirit."

His remaining three years at Groton were more an exercise in winning approval than accumulating the academic knowledge that might serve him well in college studies or his later life's work. Since graduation from so prestigious a school as Groton seemed sufficient to ensure admission to a fine college, academic distinction was generally considered of secondary consequence. As for a future career, it was of little concern to privileged boys, who had the family wealth and connections to assure them of a comfortable living.

Seeking to win the regard of his classmates and

endear himself to boys in the higher and lower forms as well required a balancing act that provided a glimpse into Franklin's later talent as a "juggler" of opposing interests and values and as a masterful political artist who understood how to appeal to people with different outlooks.

Being one of the boys meant occasionally defying authority by acting as something of a cutup. "I managed to get three or four black marks this week," he wrote his parents in October 1897, at the start of his second school year, "but I had good fun, quite worth them." When a Mr. Coolidge, a new teacher (or "new duck," as Franklin derisively called him), took charge of the third and fourth forms for a day, he could not control them. Franklin wished his parents "could have heard the noise we made. Some musical gentlemen in the far end of the room had a whistling concert, while I amused myself by singing Yankee Doodle in a high falsetto key. Old Coolidge made the whole form stand up. That did not do much good, & . . . then paper & ink & nutshells flew thick and fast, & the old man got perfectly wild." Coolidge began yelling at the wrong boy, "while he really wanted me, but the end of the period came just in time to save me from a large number of Black-marks." As he reached the upper grades, Franklin became more self-confident about his place in the school and "developed an independent, cocky manner and at times became very argumentative and sarcastic," a classmate recalled. It "irritated the other boys considerably," but never enough to jeopardize his standing with them, especially when he directed it at higher authority.

By contrast with his ability to escape punishments, or to manage his rowdiness, Franklin felt sorry for his cousin, Warren Delano Robbins, who entered the third form in 1897 and suffered repeated punishments for misbehavior. "Poor Warren has five more [black marks] this week," Franklin wrote his parents, "and I know how hard it is for him to keep from getting them." Warren's lack of self-control and ineptness in turning aside penalties for bad behavior heightened Franklin's affinity for mastering situations and people he wished to control.

At the same time Franklin navigated the school's disciplinary system, he ingratiated himself with Peabody by performing the sort of manly Christian duties the headmaster considered the greatest good the school could instill in its charges. In January 1899, in Franklin's third year, the local Missionary Society appointed him and a classmate "special missionaries to look after Mrs. Freeman an old woman near the school. She is an old coloured [sic] lady, living all alone and 84 years old. We payed [sic] our first visit to her today, right after church, and talked and gave her the latest news, for nearly an hour. We are to visit her a couple of times a week, see that she has coal water, etc, feed her hens . . . and in case of a snowstorm we are to dig her out. . . . It will be very pleasant as she is a dear old thing, and it will be a good occupation for us."

Years later, in 1932, as Franklin ran for president, Peabody told another Groton graduate: "There has been a good deal written about Franklin Roosevelt when he was a boy at Groton, more than I should have thought justified by the impression that he left at the school. He was a quiet, satisfactory boy of more than ordinary intel-

50

ligence, taking a good position in his form but not brilliant. . . . We all liked him. So far as I know that is true of the masters and boys alike."

Few things gave Franklin more standing at Groton than his ties to his cousin Theodore Roosevelt. In June 1897, when TR was assistant secretary of the navy, he gave an evening presentation at the school focused on his earlier service as police commissioner in New York City. "After supper tonight," Franklin wrote his parents, "Cousin Theodore gave us a splendid talk on his adventures when he was on the Police Board. He kept the whole room in an uproar for over an hour, by telling us killing stories about policemen and their doings in New York." When TR returned to the school in October 1898, he was even more popular: His standing as a Spanish-American War hero who had led his regiment of Rough Riders in successful battles in Cuba and his campaign for governor of New York, which was coming to an obvious victory, made him an idol to teenage boys fascinated by his adventures. His emphasis on what he called the strenuous life made him a model for how every schoolboy thought he should behave. The following month, after TR's victory, Franklin told his parents: "We were all wild with delight when we heard of Teddy's election." In January 1900, when TR's picture appeared on a screen at an evening lecture by the social reformer Jacob Riis, "the whole school cheered."

Perhaps the most striking feature of Franklin's four years at Groton was his competitive energy. Before arriving at the school, he had enjoyed a cloistered life with no siblings or rivals for his parents' attention. Once he entered Groton, however, he was a teenager simultaneously vying

51

with peers for adult approval and finding his own voice by rebelling against authority. Above all, he was a young man intent on outdoing his classmates and establishing himself as the best at whatever he did. Peabody set the standard for him in a sermon Franklin took special note of: "For life — which is in any way worthy," Peabody said, "is like ascending a mountain. When you have climbed to the first shoulder of the hill, you find another rise above you, and that achieved there is another, and another still, and yet another peak, and then height to be achieved seems infinity: but you find as you ascend that the air becomes purer and more bracing, that the clouds gather more frequently below than above, that the sun is warmer than before and that you not only get a clearer view of Heaven, but that you gain a wider and wider view of earth, and that your horizon is perpetually growing larger."

Franklin's ambition was more focused, more grandiose than what most teenage boys manifest in their formative years. While his parents had instilled in him the conviction that his ancestry and wealth distinguished him from the great majority of cohorts, this was insufficient to satisfy his desire to attain special standing among his peers. A need to prove himself, to justify his worthiness, and to live up to his cousin Theodore's high standard may have sparked his competitiveness. Peabody reinforced Franklin's determination with his metaphor comparing a young man's drive as an ascent into Heaven, which justified an impulse to eclipse rivals as an unconditional good. We will never know exactly what was driving Franklin to be the best, but his affinity to come out on top, to stand apart from everyone, was a motive force throughout the rest of his life.

In September 1900, Franklin made a seamless transition to Harvard University. Although admission to the college required taking tests, wealthy private-school graduates, especially the offspring of alumni, were favored applicants. Groton boys had an almost perfect record: Sixteen of the eighteen seniors in Franklin's class won acceptance to the Cambridge school. They lived together in $400-a-year suites in Westmorly Court, one of four "Gold Coast" dormitories, as they were called, on Mount Auburn Street. Among the principal attractions of Harvard for these privileged students was the university's commitment to segregating them from aspiring middle-class boys. The Groton graduates ate all their meals together and socialized only with one another or with alumni of elite Northeast prep schools who lived in the three adjacent dormitories. The less affluent boys were housed in more austere university quarters in Harvard Yard. Were it not for classes and team sports, the two groups would have seen little of one another. The housing arrangements spoke volumes about the rise of the elites, who by 1900 had become "robber barons" holding sway in corporate trusts and dominating national and local politics along with ethnic political bosses.

The curriculum developed by Charles Eliot, the school's president since 1869, left students free to elect any courses they preferred. It also largely freed the faculty to concentrate on their research and writing rather than on classroom and laboratory instruction. Harvard made no pretense of being a great teaching institution. In Eliot's view, the faculty was composed of some of the country's best minds, and students had the opportunity of taking advantage of their presence at the school. Many undergraduates, especially those whose social status had brought them to Cambridge, were indifferent to the educational opportunities the university offered and saw themselves living in a different sphere from the faculty. They were content to simply pass their examinations with the help of tutors and earn enough credits to receive a bachelor's degree. Devoting too much attention to developing one's intellect was suspect as unmanly.

Although Franklin was conscientious about not missing classes and repeatedly noted his determination not to record "cuts," he had, like the great majority of his closest classmates, limited interest in the intellectual riches of the university. The elective course system left students free to identify the least rigorous classes taught by professors who preferred to keep their distance from undergraduates.

At the start of the fall term of his freshman year, Franklin mapped out a program of study with the help of history professor Archibald Cary Coolidge. Although Franklin signed on for elementary geology, it was only a nod in the direction of science. His focus was on English, French, and Latin literature; medieval and modern European history; and constitutional government. Like all his Groton classmates, he did not have to take Harvard's first-year courses, as he had already met this requirement in preparatory school, and consequently was able to complete his degree in three years.

Franklin's interest in his college studies was

distinctly limited, and while he was not neglectful of his academic work, it was never his highest priority. His letters home testify to his concentration on social life and extracurricular affairs. "I have such a lot to write about," he told his parents a week into the term: football practice; recreation at Sanborn's, a billiard parlor in Cambridge, where the preppies often gathered in the evening; the furnishings for his rooms; and a visit to family friends in Boston. An unforgettable return visit to Groton the following week for a Consecration Service filled the pages of a second letter. On October 19, he reported on a "Beer-Night in a senior's room" that brought upperclassmen together with freshmen; his undiminished determination to play football despite being only on a scrub team — whimsically called the Missing Links — of which he was proud to be captain; and interviews with the *Harvard Crimson,* the college newspaper, where he was in competition with eighty-five other undergraduates for a coveted staff position. "If I work hard for two years," he told his parents, "I may be made an editor." He was excited about a weekend at Newburyport, a coastal resort thirty-five miles northeast of Boston, where he and a Groton friend would go duck shooting. In a follow-up note he reported that his companion had shot two ducks; "I none but had a splendid time." He also took notice of the bad publicity his half nephew Taddy was getting in the press for marrying a woman with a questionable background. Embarrassed by news stories that were tarnishing the Roosevelt name, he wrote his parents, "It would be well for him . . . to go to parts unknown . . . and begin life anew."

Through the rest of the fall term, he was occupied with football — his scrub team and Harvard varsity games; invitations to afternoon teas from Boston Brahmins; dining at the Touraine, Boston's finest hotel restaurant; and a torchlight parade from Cambridge through Boston marking the coming presidential election, which Franklin allegedly covered for the *Crimson* with a headline report that President Eliot would vote for President McKinley and vice-presidential nominee Theodore Roosevelt. Because Eliot had been in sharp public disagreement with TR over his "Jingoism [and] chip-on-the-shoulder attitude . . . of a ruffian and a bully," his support of the candidate was a national news story. (Thirty-one years later Franklin acknowledged that another *Crimson* reporter actually deserved credit for the scoop.) In a November 6 letter, Franklin excitedly described his attendance at a play, where students "roughhoused" the performance by throwing "missiles . . . all over the place" and forcing the theater to lower the curtain half a dozen times; an evening of heavy drinking by "9/10 of Cambridge," though he remained sober; sleeping till noon on Sunday; squash games most of the afternoon; and a quiet election day.

A constant note of anxiety ran through all his fall letters about his father's failing health. Heart problems that repeatedly forced James to curtail his activities moved Franklin to counsel against a parental trip to New York in favor of a retreat to Aiken, South Carolina, where he hoped "Papa can have absolute rest." By the beginning of December, he was "too distressed about Papa and cannot understand why he does not improve more quickly." But at seventy-two James was in the final stages of heart failure. On December 8, after

Franklin joined his parents in New York, James died with Sara and Franklin at his bedside. Franklin remained with his mother through a gloomy holiday season.

Aside from mentions of midyear examinations and grades, including a B in history and a D+ in Latin, which "I got thro' better than I expected," his letters home continued to focus on his extracurricular activities, which kept him "awfully busy": skating, sledding, hockey, rowing in hopes of winning a place on the crew team, Freshman Glee Club rehearsals, and time-consuming *Crimson* assignments that occupied him three or four hours a day. Dinners, and visits to relatives and friends in the Boston area and to Groton, where he enjoyed reunions with other recent graduates, filled his evenings and weekends. He was so busy, he told his mother, that he could not find time for his stamp collection, which he preferred to keep in Hyde Park. He also remained absorbed with furnishing his residence: rugs, a piano, a bookcase, and wall hangings made his rooms "perfect." "I haven't had 1/4 second to myself," he complained to Sara on April 27. His work at the *Crimson* had grown to six hours a day, which he described as "quite a strain." A "scoop" he published about cousin Theodore's appearance on campus to lecture in the introductory government course about his experience as governor of New York made Franklin a fixture at the paper. As summer holiday beckoned, he and Sara made plans for a European trip that included a North Cape cruise through the Norwegian fjords.

When Franklin and Sara returned from Europe in September 1901, they learned that President McKinley had been assassinated in Buffalo, New

York, where he had gone to attend a Pan American Exposition. Franklin's family connection to the new president, cousin Theodore, added to his existing luster as a patrician with access to most of Boston's, New York's, and Washington's elite social circles. The highlight of his year was a visit to Washington and attendance at a January 1902 White House coming-out party for TR's daughter, Alice. The day began with an afternoon tea at a Washington socialite's home, "which was interesting and filled with New Yorkers whom I knew"; continued with a dinner for forty distinguished guests at another home; and concluded with a White House dance, "which was most glorious fun . . . from start to finish." He went to bed at 2 a.m. and slept until noon. An afternoon tea at the White House that day, a quiet dinner, and a 10 p.m. reception at the Austrian ambassador's residence, where members of the diplomatic corps gathered, ended his memorable visit.

Yet Franklin was not focused only on college and off-campus frivolity. An academic assignment to write a serious paper about the Roosevelts in prerevolutionary New Amsterdam commanded his attention, as it presented an opportunity to reflect on what shaped a family's success and decline. His conclusion about the fate of the well-to-do in colonial America echoed what he had been taught by Peabody about the obligations of the privileged and the values that cousin Theodore represented as a progressive leader. Franklin ascribed the waning of some of the country's early elite families to a "lack [of] progressiveness and the true democratic spirit." The "very democratic spirit" of the Roosevelts, in contrast, had given them enduring "virility. . . . They have never felt that they were born in a good position they could put their hands in their pockets and succeed. They have felt, rather, that being born in a good position, there was no excuse for them if they did not do their duty by the community." The conclusion was a window into Franklin's thinking about his own future: He hoped to use his social standing to launch a successful career that included some form of public service.

Franklin put his rhetoric into action by organizing a fund drive for South Africa's Boers, whom he viewed as abused and oppressed by the British during and after their defeat in the Boer War. He also devoted time to helping poor youths in boys' clubs organized by the Episcopal Church. Helping the dependent and less advantaged was not Franklin's foremost activity or interest at this time, but it did form enough of his early outlook that under changed circumstances it could become a major part of his life's work. In a more oblique way, he developed a greater sensitivity to these issues through his evolving relations with his mother. After James's death, Sara became increasingly reliant upon Franklin, counting on him for companionship. She spent parts of his remaining Harvard years in Boston, where she could see him more often, as she felt isolated and lonely in Hyde Park. In 1903 Franklin agonized over whether he should travel to Europe without her. "I don't want to be away from you for four weeks in the summer; also that I don't want to go unless you could make up your mind not to care at all," he wrote her in April. As his ship left New York on July 24, he told her: "Goodbye dear Mummy. I am longing for Aug. 25 [when he would return]. Don't worry about me — I always land on my feet —

but wish so much you were with me." A profusion of letters to her during his month-long trip aimed to fill the void in her life and appease whatever guilt he felt for abandoning her.

During his second year at Harvard he had experienced a major disappointment that heightened his ambivalence about his overly indulged patrician classmates, whom Franklin considered insufficiently appreciative of their advantages, and strengthened his conviction that he could not rely strictly on his pedigree to ensure his success.

A highlight of their college years for Harvard patricians was election to membership in one of the campus clubs. An invitation to the most prestigious of these societies was considered a mark of distinction one carried for life. Like his cousin Theodore, Franklin hoped to win acceptance to Porcellian, considered the most prominent and desirable of these groups. But in the winter of 1902, one or more of the sixteen Porcellian members vetoed his admission. It was, he recalled later, the "greatest disappointment of my life." With no explanation or account of why the club rejected him, he was left to speculate on his defeat. Was it something he had done to offend a current member? Some classmates thought him smug and too cocky, especially since they viewed him as shallow and no more than a "featherduster." Was it the public embarrassment Taddy had caused with his scandalous marriage? Was it anything cousin Theodore was doing as president that offended a conservative member who wanted no part of another Roosevelt in Porcellian? Whatever the reason, the snub left a lasting wound. Acceptance in Alpha Delta Phi, popularly known as the Fly Club, the second-highest-rated fraternity, was some solace, but it was insufficient to erase the stigma of not being acknowledged as among the most elite of the elite.

Rather than accept this reversal as a blot on his college life, he became more engaged and determined to show himself as worthy of the greatest possible regard from classmates and faculty. Over the next two years, he became something of a specialist in rare book collecting, serving as librarian of the Fly and subsequently of the Hasty Pudding Club, buying books and manuscripts for their libraries and for himself, with a concentration on American naval history. His work as a bibliophile, which echoed his earlier stamp collecting, won him election to Signet, the campus literature club, and to the Memorial Society, which preserved the university's history with particular attention to "the great men who have been students or teachers here." In time, Franklin would be counted among the most distinguished of the university's graduates; his living quarters became a place of remembrance.

But his principal campus activity became editing the *Crimson*. In the spring of his junior year, he was named managing editor with the assurance that in the fall of 1903 he would become the editor in chief. Because he would receive his B.A. in June, he needed a reason to remain on campus for a fourth year, so he signed on for a master's degree in history. He had no intention of completing the required courses or writing a thesis, as his work for the *Crimson* was all-consuming. It included composing editorials on a variety of topics, which included counseling entering students to stay off probation — hardly a call for work toward academic distinction — and most of all to demonstrate the greatest possible school spirit, especially in support of the football team. Although others of his editorials were devoted to campus and broader local and national politics, his *Crimson* editorship showed little originality or promise of journalistic distinction, but rather displayed a conventional mind preaching homilies about service in support of the public well-being. The distinguishing feature of his editorial term was a "geniality" that his managing editor described as "a kind of frictionless command." His forte was not bold, imaginative thinking about campus or wider current events but rather a degree of personal charm that made for good relations with friends and subordinates.

As Franklin's college career came to a close, his mind turned to the future. Since he had no plan to use his family connections to start a business career, he decided to attend law school at Columbia University. He had no clear idea of what he might do with such training, but it would take him to New York and allow him more time to consider what his true life's work might be, assured that his background and Harvard degree would guarantee success in whatever field he chose. Photos of him at this time testify to his secure place in turn-of-the-century America. At six feet tall and a slender 150 pounds, the twenty-two-year-old Franklin stares out from a graduation photograph without the pince-nez that would famously become a fixture in many later photos. He has a full head of hair parted in the middle and wears a dark double-breasted suit, high collar, silk tie with pearl stickpin, vest, and handkerchief in the breast pocket. He has the appropriately serious countenance of a handsome, young, self-confident patrician. Another photo of him seated in the middle of eleven seniors, *Crimson* board members dressed in well-tailored dark suits, bespeaks American royalty prepared to take the world under their command.

Franklin's preoccupation at this time was a coming marriage to Eleanor Hall Roosevelt. To some among his friends and family, especially his mother, it was a surprising match. But it was not that Eleanor lacked the social standing Sara considered essential for her son's mate, as her heritage was every bit as aristocratic as Franklin's. She was the daughter of Theodore's younger brother, Elliott, and on her mother's side she was a descendant of the Halls, who were landed gentry; the Livingstons, who signed the Declaration of Independence and administered the oath of office to George Washington; and the Ludlows, who had prospered as merchants and realtors in New York City. At her coming out in 1902, the eighteen-year-old Eleanor was a prominent debutante.

Yet she was also a shy, socially awkward girl with a troubled family history that made her not quite the best match for the ebullient Franklin. Although family and social ties threw them together, Eleanor's unhappy early life experience and retiring personality seemed unlikely to attract so dynamic a young man. Her mother had wounded Eleanor's pride as a child by calling her "granny," as her seriousness made her seem old before her time. "I wanted to sink through the floor," Eleanor recalled later in describing how she felt about her mother's unflattering nickname. Such childhood memories continued to distress her even as late as her forties, when she remembered herself as "an ugly little thing, keenly conscious of her deficiencies, and her father, the only person who really cared for her, was away much of the time." Her mother's death when she was eight years old strengthened her attachment to her father, but he was an alcoholic who was lost to Eleanor when he died two months before her tenth birthday.

The orphaned child became the ward of her stern grandmother Hall, who could never fill the void left by her parents' passing. But rescue of sorts came when Eleanor turned fifteen and her grandmother sent her to Allenswood, an English boarding school on the outskirts of London. She flourished there under the direction of a French headmistress, Marie Souvestre. Souvestre remembered that this bright but needy American girl singled herself out from the forty students in her charge by "the perfect quality of her soul." Eleanor was "full of regard for others" with "a fineness of feeling truly exquisite." Eleanor's classmates shared this view of her and reciprocated her kindness toward them. "She was 'everything' at the school," a cousin who visited her there said. "She was beloved by everybody." Eleanor recalled the three years she spent at Allenswood as "the happiest years of my life." Yet the sadness of her earlier years continued to shadow her, and she remained a serious, even dour, young woman. Mlle Souvestre would describe all her virtues but conclude regretfully, "Mais elle n'est pas gaie."

After her return from England in 1902 for her December coming out, Eleanor and Franklin began seeing each other at various social events. By all accounts, she was plain in appearance with "overly prominent" teeth. Franklin, moreover, teased her that she was "grandmotherly" when she gave him sober advice about preserving his health. Nonetheless, Franklin found her irresistible and asked her to marry him. "Why me?" she is supposed to have replied. "I am plain. I have little to bring you." Sara certainly agreed. She thought them too young: He was twenty-one and Eleanor eighteen, and neither had a clear life plan. Moreover, Sara had hoped for "a more worldly and social match" for her adored son, the sort of vivacious debutante Sara assumed Franklin would wed after he had matured into an establishment figure like her late husband.

It may well be, as one biographer has speculated, that Franklin saw in Eleanor someone who could help him fulfill his life's ambitions — "a helpmate . . . to bring them to fruition." But that is hindsight. At the time neither of them saw the road ahead.

But there were more immediate and compelling reasons that accounted for Franklin's attraction to Eleanor. No one should discount the extent to which he had genuinely fallen in love and was fulfilling the role of a young man eager for a longterm union. But he was also determined to escape the control of his overly protective mother. Marrying Eleanor represented an escape from Sara's dominance and establishing his own family apart from her. There was no question that Sara would remain the family matriarch, but she would have to share her son with a wife and any future children. Fully cognizant of how resistant Sara might be to his detaching himself from her, Franklin hid his courtship and decision to marry until he had proposed and Eleanor had accepted. It was partly an act of defiance or a way to create distance from a mother whose life was excessively bound up with his. It was a more pronounced way of separating himself from "Mummy" than his decision to tour Europe without her in the summer of 1903. But in choosing Eleanor, he was also very much his mother's son. Like Sara, he would become the dominant figure in his closest relationship. In marrying Eleanor, he was choosing a woman who believed her physical and emotional limits might leave her a spinster. "I hope that I shall always prove worthy of the love that you have given me," she wrote him gratefully after agreeing to their union. "I have never known before what it was to be absolutely happy."

Unsurprisingly, Sara was less than pleased to receive her son's startling news and urged Franklin to wait a year before announcing his engagement and to separate himself from Eleanor to give himself a chance to reflect on his decision. "She was an indulgent mother but would not let her son call his soul his own," a friend of Eleanor's said. "I know what pain I must have caused you," Franklin wrote Sara. "You know that nothing can ever change what we have always been & always will be to each other." He agreed to Sara's proposal that he accompany her on a Caribbean cruise and delay making news of the engagement public. Eleanor weighed in with a solicitous letter to Sara as well: "I know . . . how hard it must be, but I do so want you to learn to love me a little."

Franklin's secret courtship of Eleanor, which blunted Sara's resistance to their marriage, became a model for how he later dealt with political associates and opponents. "Never let the left hand know what the right is doing" was a tactic he would use effectively in dealings with officials who were unsympathetic to a plan of action he believed essential. By keeping them in the dark, Franklin was repeatedly able to advance controversial policies that adversaries found difficult to counter when ignorance of his aims gave them limited time and opportunity to defeat him.

One unspoken consideration in taking Sara's feelings into account, if not conforming to her wishes, was the financial hold she had over them. Franklin and Eleanor each had trust funds that gave them a combined annual income of about $12,000 — a tidy sum equivalent to over a quarter of a million dollars today, but one that was not sufficient to support the lifestyle to which they were accustomed. Sara controlled the principal in Franklin's trust and enjoyed an income that allowed her to ensure her son's creature comforts — New York City and Hyde Park houses, servants, extensive travel, yachts and automobiles, and membership in fashionable clubs. James Roosevelt, Franklin and Eleanor's second child, later said that "Granny's ace in the hole . . . was the fact that she held the purse strings in the family. For years she squeezed all of us — Father included — in this golden loop."

In November 1904 Franklin and Eleanor announced their engagement and set March 17, 1905, for their wedding. The date accommodated TR, who was inaugurated for four more years on March 4, and agreed to Eleanor's request that he stand in for her deceased father and give her away. The engaged couple sat behind TR on the capitol steps as he took the oath of office, enjoyed lunch with the presidential party at the White House, sat with the president on the reviewing stand during the traditional parade, and danced away the evening at an inaugural ball. TR arrived at the wedding, which was held at a Ludlow mansion on East 76th Street between Madison and Fifth Avenues, from a St. Patrick Day's parade, and was more the center of attention than the bride and groom. "Well, Franklin," he exclaimed after the vows had been exchanged, "there's nothing like keeping the name in the family." As the two hundred guests followed the president into a dining room for refreshments, the couple found themselves standing alone. Only when TR, who seemed to enjoy himself hugely telling stories and performing for the audience, left did Franklin and Eleanor regain the notice of the assembled party.

After a week to themselves at Hyde Park, the couple returned to the city, where they took up residence for three months in an apartment in the Hotel Webster within walking distance of Sara's house at 200 Madison Avenue. His law studies had never been his highest priority, as he doubted that legal practice would be his life's calling, and throughout the spring he remained more focused on the social engagements and preparations for their summer honeymoon in Europe. The extensive socializing with the Delano and Roosevelt clans took their toll on Franklin's schoolwork. He failed two of his four courses, and only scored B's in the two he passed. The failures did not surprise him, but refusing to let them stand, he planned to retake the exams in contracts and pleadings in September so that he could take a full schedule of second-year classes. Pride dictated that he not flunk out of or quit law school — at least not yet.

The summer honeymoon was the typical Grand Tour of privileged Americans, who socialized with their counterparts across Europe. Crossing on the

Oceanic, a British liner, the couple dined each evening with the ship's captain, who led them on a tour of the vessel. Eleanor thought the ship "overwhelming" in size, and her heart went out to the steerage passengers, for whom she was "more sorry than ever." Although Franklin and, especially, Eleanor, had glimpsed the underside of life through charitable work, they had never before lived at such close hand to it.

The couple sent Sara almost daily accounts of their doings in England, Scotland, France, Italy, Germany, and Switzerland, faithfully recording the names of the elites who welcomed them into their homes and the pleasure of visiting or revisiting Europe's most storied sights. The cost of the trip was prodigious: They stayed in the $1,000-a-night Royal Suite in London's Brown's Hotel. Undoubtedly, the honeymoon couple had received some kind of discount, but Franklin enjoyed teasing Sara, who was financing the trip: "We have ordered thousands of dollars worth of clothes," he wrote at the start of the tour, "and I am going to send you several cases of champagne, as I know it is needed in Hyde Park." They were delighted, but not surprised, by the regard shown them as representatives of an America currently taking a prominent place on the world scene. With Uncle Ted much in the news in the summer of 1905 as the world leader who was facilitating a peace agreement in Portsmouth, New Hampshire, to end the Russo-Japanese War, Eleanor and Franklin took special pride in their country's newfound standing, fostered by their kinsman.

For the five years after they returned to the United States in September 1905, Eleanor found that her wealth and social standing could not

69

insulate her from the terrors of everyday life. Her material well-being was never in jeopardy: Initially they lived in a house at 125 East Thirty-Sixth Street, three blocks from her mother-in-law. Three years later, Sara moved them all to 49 East Sixty-Fifth Street, where they lived in adjoining houses with a common vestibule and doors giving access to their respective drawing and dining rooms. Franklin's household had a cook, maid, and butler, and as soon as children came along, nurses and nannies. None of this, however, could counter the emotional turmoil Eleanor experienced as a new mother with a domineering mother-in-law who made her feel like a child incapable of assuming adult responsibilities. The birth of a daughter, Anna, in May 1906, followed by a son, James, in December 1907, and another son, Franklin, Jr., in April 1909, largely overwhelmed her. Dealing with the usual sibling rivalries among her children, with James on the family yacht refusing to sit still and Anna kicking him and James biting her on the arm, leaving a blue welt, were trials enough. But the death of seven-month-old Franklin, Jr., from a flu that put too much strain on a weak heart filled Eleanor with grief and self-recrimination for having failed to give him proper care. Sara's omnipresence, coupled with that of the nurses and nannies, some of whom she considered incompetent, was a rebuke of sorts, a reminder that she could manage neither her household nor her children.

Franklin's self-centeredness and insensitivity to his wife's struggles only exacerbated her tensions. In 1908, after they had moved into their Sixty-Fifth-Street house, which Sara had largely designed and furnished, Eleanor was unhappy with the new arrangements, which made her mother-in-law a more immediate member of the household. "You were never quite sure when she would appear, day or night," Eleanor recalled later. She complained to Franklin that this was not their own home and dissolved in tears, saying that she didn't want to live this way. Franklin dismissed her complaint, telling her that she should have objected sooner, and then walked out of the room, refusing to confront the situation. He had his tensions with "mamma" as well. When Eleanor felt unwell and went home early from a New Year's Eve party in Hyde Park, Franklin stayed until three or four in the morning. Sara was incensed at his insensitivity to Eleanor but insisted nonetheless that he come to breakfast at 8 a.m. A cousin staying with them remembered how furious he was at Sara, but he would not risk a break with her by resisting her demands to be so central a part of their lives. In addition to his genuine love for so attentive a parent, she made their lives too comfortable for him to consider striking out against her. However appealing the life she made possible, though, he was determined to move beyond acquiescing to her.

In September 1905, he passed the exams he had failed the previous spring. He remained less than enthusiastic about the law but persevered at Columbia through the spring of 1907, when he took and passed the New York bar exam. Once admitted to the bar, he abandoned plans to complete his law studies and earn a degree. Instead he spent the spring and summer at Hyde Park and Campobello with Eleanor and the children before beginning work as an unpaid clerk for a year at the Wall Street law firm of Carter,

Ledyard and Milburn. It specialized, among other areas, in admiralty law, but however much his interest in seafaring made this a welcome prospect, Franklin was less than excited about spending a career settling maritime disputes, and complained to Sara of becoming "a full-fledged office boy." He saw nothing glamorous in his clerkship, mockingly describing himself as a " 'counselor at law' who specialized in 'unpaid bills,' the chloroforming of 'small dogs,' the preparation of 'briefs on the liquor question' for ladies, the prosecution of 'race suicides,' and the care of babies 'under advice of expert grandmother.' " His apprenticeship included research for senior members of the firm in its law library, carrying property deeds to the county clerk's office for notarization, running various other errands, and a bit of law training handling municipal court cases.

His duties over the next two years in the firm's admiralty division, where he was assigned, became more consistent with associates making their way up the corporate ladder toward partner. But he was unenthusiastic about what he saw as the duties of a work-a-day lawyer. In a conversation made famous by a fellow clerk who reported it later, Franklin told five other aspiring associates that he had no intention of becoming a practicing lawyer. Rather, he planned to follow in his uncle Ted's footsteps, standing first for a New York State Assembly seat, then winning appointment as assistant secretary of the navy, then running for governor, and if that succeeded, setting his sights on the White House. It may well be that Franklin prophesized his future with uncanny accuracy or that his fellow clerk conveniently remembered what later served Franklin's public image. But what is indisputable is that Franklin wanted something more challenging and grander than a life in a staid Wall Street law firm transferring money from one rich client to another.

Yet his few years in law practice were not without value. As his son Elliott observed later, "A listing in the Social Register and four years at Harvard had not provided F.D.R. with direct knowledge of how most men lived and thought; his life prior to September 1907 had been a thoroughly sheltered one. The actualities of law, which not infrequently required him to meet, interview, and advise all kinds of people with all kinds of problems, brought F.D.R. at least partly out from under the shelter. The three years spent with Carter, Ledyard and Milburn constituted F.D.R.'s first immediate and real contact with the world that existed beyond Hyde Park, Campobello, Cambridge, and 65th Street. In view of the social and political philosophy he evolved in later years, this first contact cannot be regarded lightly, refined and negligible as it may have been." Much else would shape Franklin's later political thinking and career, but the brief stop at Carter, Ledyard and Milburn would set him on a path that no one could foresee in 1910.

CHAPTER 2
THE MAKING OF A POLITICIAN

In the summer of 1910, almost three years after he had entered law practice, Franklin decided to run for political office. The allure of a potential law partner's income compared to the relatively small salary of a New York State officeholder was no deterrent. To be sure, he had a wife, two children, and a third, another son, Elliott, about to be born in November, but his and Eleanor's trusts and Sara's largess freed him from concern about earning his keep.

His law work and an "upper-class life of suitable affability, conventionality, and vacancy" bored him. It was not as if he was prepared to forsake his privileged status, but "the chatter, the snobbery, the pomposity, the absorption in money" left him feeling unfulfilled. TR, who shared Franklin's amenities as a comfortable patrician, had already set an example by not abandoning his privileges when joining the political fray. He had become the most successful president since Lincoln, convincing most Americans that his Square Deal and New Nationalism were wise responses to the domestic maladies of the time. Under his aegis a new activism abroad in support of peace and prosperity had temporarily eclipsed traditional isolationism. Despite complaints from some on the left in Norway that TR was a "mad imperialist" who had seized the Panama Canal, the Nobel committee awarded him the 1906 Peace Prize for mediating an end to the Russo-Japanese War.

For Franklin, entering the public arena had the allure of exciting challenges — running a campaign, winning an election, and outdoing other officeholders. Moreover, it was an opportunity to take control from men TR and he considered less worthy of leadership than they were. The two Roosevelts viewed themselves as among the country's natural-born leaders — men from families that had governed the nation for generations and were better suited to assessing and defending the national interest than the arrivistes who had taken control in recent decades. They judged these newcomers, chiefly ethnic Catholics, as too self-serving to put the public well-being ahead of themselves and their political machines, which had become the dominant influence in state and local politics.

With the instincts of a seasoned statesman, Franklin understood that to state his views about contemporary politicians and politics too openly might brand him as an undemocratic snob. Moreover, if he was going to run for something, he needed the endorsement of the men he considered unworthy of public influence. It was not much of a reach for him to keep his own counsel, for he was already well versed in hiding his views from people he wished not to offend, especially his mother. As Franklin entered politics, the historian Arthur Schlesinger, Jr., observed, "The habit of masquerade remained. The public face could never be relied on to express the private man."

In the spring of 1910, John Mack, the Dutchess County district attorney, invited Franklin to run for the Assembly seat representing Poughkeepsie, the city closest to Hyde Park. Louis Chandler, former New York Democratic lieutenant governor and the party's defeated gubernatorial nominee in 1908, had won the seat in 1909 but was thinking of retiring. Although Franklin would need to finance the race himself, it would likely give him a successful start in politics. Poughkeepsie was a Democratic stronghold, with a Democratic mayor and district attorney, and 1910 would likely be a promising year for Democrats. The Republican Party was divided into progressive and conservative factions, and William Howard Taft, TR's handpicked successor as president, had alienated Roosevelt supporters and was unpopular with a majority of Americans.

The proposal to Franklin did not come unexpectedly, as he had clearly signaled his interest in running for office. Despite his undisguised enthusiasm for TR, he identified himself as a Democrat. His father, James, had been a staunch supporter of the party and had had a personal relationship with former New York governor and then president Grover Cleveland. James's financial backing for Cleveland's successful 1884 campaign had led to the offer of an ambassadorship, which he refused. In 1887, James took five-year-old Franklin to meet Cleveland in the Oval Office. In what later became a remarkable irony, Cleveland, who was struggling with Congress and faced an unsuccessful battle for reelection in 1888, patted Franklin on the head and said, "I hope, young man, that you will never be president of the United States."

Franklin was happy to accept Mack's invitation, but then Chandler decided against retiring and rejected a suggestion that he instead run for a New York Senate opening representing Columbia, Dutchess, and Putnam Counties. Unlike the Assembly seat, the Senate office seemed out of reach for a Democrat. The three counties had a long history of electing Republicans to the state Senate, and the incumbent, who had won his last election by a landslide, was committed to running again. That left Franklin with the choice of either running as a Senate candidate himself, with only a one-in-five chance of success, or waiting until the Assembly seat became available. Always the optimist and convinced that 1910 was a winning year for Democrats, he accepted the Senate challenge. Even if he lost, he would have earned the gratitude of party chiefs for having taken on a thankless assignment and could look forward to their backing for the Assembly race when Chandler finally stepped down.

Franklin's greatest concern in making the Senate bid was that TR might effectively oppose his candidacy by campaigning in the district in support of the Republican candidate. But when one of TR's sisters, prodded by his niece Eleanor, asked if he would speak against Franklin, TR urged Franklin to get into politics without worrying about his intentions, signaling that he would not undermine his nephew's chances. TR regretted that Franklin identified himself as a Democrat, but saw his nephew as "a fine fellow" and had no interest in joining a fight over an issue as minor as a New York Senate seat.

For his part, Edward Perkins, the Democratic

Party's Dutchess County chairman and ally of the party's Tammany machine, was unenthusiastic about backing a candidate whom he expected to keep his distance from Tammany's Catholic bosses. Franklin's wealth gave him independence from party sachems, and should he become an officeholder, he might prove to be the sort of upstart his cousin Ted had been in the Republican camp. On the other hand, assigning Franklin the seemingly hopeless task of running for a Senate seat raised the likelihood that he would be a reliable source of party money. And if by some miracle he should win, Perkins saw him as a naive novice who could be given some minor committee assignments and replaced by a more reliable nominee in the next election.

When Franklin showed up in riding breeches and boots before the Dutchess County party's committee confirming his nomination, Perkins regarded him as thumbing his nose at professional politicians. Perkins made his distaste for the young country gentleman obvious by dismissively advising him to dress appropriately in the future. But Franklin, who consciously chose his appearance to draw a clear line between himself and these nouveau party officials, refused to be intimidated. When he spoke before the party's nominating convention after receiving their blessing, his words left no doubt that he intended to be his own man. "I accept this nomination with absolute independence," he announced, "I am pledged to no man; I am influenced by no special interests." In 1910, this was the standard language of progressives on both sides of the aisle who had declared war on political machines and their allies, self-serving robber barons and trusts. The progressives, many of them middle-class or older-school Americans, saw themselves as putting the upstart politicos in their place: These newcomers needed to accept that incorruptible men like TR and Franklin were better suited to ensure the preservation of honest government and equal opportunity, which had served the nation so well in the past.

In a monthlong campaign preceding the November 8 election, Franklin made his progressive idealism abundantly clear, quoting Lincoln, "I am not bound to win, but I am bound to be true. . . . I'm bound to live up to what light I have. I must stand with anybody that stands right, and part with him when he goes wrong." If honesty and forthrightness as well as assurances to farmers, who made up the majority of district voters, that he would be attentive to their economic interests were part of a winning strategy, so was Franklin's candor.

He made every effort to identify himself with Uncle Ted. In 1910, TR, who remained the most popular public figure in America, added to his luster by battling New York's machine Republicans. He attacked them as corrupt political bosses lining their pockets through favors to corporate interests. Franklin picked up on the theme by criticizing local Republicans with the same rhetoric. Eager to show voters that he shared more than a name with the former president, Franklin started campaign speeches with the disarming declaration, "I'm not Teddy. A little shaver said to me the other day that he knew I wasn't Teddy — I asked him 'why' and he replied: 'Because you don't show your teeth.' " Audiences loved it and immediately made the connection between the two of them.

A majority of district voters also found considerable appeal in Franklin's unapologetically playing the part of a well-off country gentleman. Some Democratic Party hands counseled him against renting a red Maxwell touring car to travel the county's country roads, where the automobile might frighten horses and farmers might regard him as a self-satisfied rich man who, once in office, would not represent his constituents. In fact, the car resonated with farmers as the honest expression of a modern young man bringing fresh ideas and openness to current affairs. Franklin had accurately read the public's mood. Voters sought a change, or more to the point, a return to an idealized version of democracy, one in which selfless officeholders promoted the public good, but they also wanted someone whom they saw as forward-looking or in sync with the times and receptive to modern technologies that improved people's lives. Franklin seemed to embody both: He was a well-spoken advocate of traditional ideals who relied on the latest innovations to transmit his message.

Because the Democrats seemed more likely than a divided Republican Party to advance reforms restoring national values, they won control in New York State and across the country. To the surprise of local political pundits, Franklin scored a decisive victory. His 1,140-vote margin over the Republican incumbent was almost twice what the Democratic candidate for governor won in Franklin's Senate district. It instantly raised his profile as a rising star and promising progressive statewide candidate.

As he took the oath of office in Albany on January 4, 1911, the twenty-eight-year-old Franklin was the picture of mannered eloquence. Alongside the mainly middle-class Irish lawyers who made up the 114 Democratic Party's majority in both statehouses, the "tall and lithe Franklin" with his gold-bowed pince-nez spectacles had the appearance of a matinee idol. One journalist said that he "could make a fortune on the stage and set the matinee girl's heart throbbing." He looked to some like "a Roman patrician" and to others, an ancient Greek solon. He enjoyed the favorable publicity and the implicit suggestion that, like TR, he was an aristocrat at odds with the bosses. It did not escape Democratic Party leaders that they might have a rebel in their midst. Big Tim Sullivan, the senator representing New York City's Bowery district and a Tammany stalwart, astutely predicted that "this kid is likely to do for us what the Colonel [TR] is going to do for the Republican Party [in 1912], split it wide open."

Franklin gave prompt meaning to Sullivan's calculation. In January 1911, he rented a large house a few blocks from the state capitol, removing Eleanor and the children from Sara's shadow and giving notice to those who suspected he might be a dilettante passing through town on his way to Washington. But as Franklin understood, if he made headlines in New York — the most populous and richest state, and one that had given the country two presidents over the previous twenty-five years — he would project himself onto the national scene.

In 1911, two years before the Seventeenth Amendment to the Constitution mandated popular elections of U.S. senators, New York's legislature had an open seat to fill. Democratic majorities in both houses ensured the selection of

81

someone from their party. Under the command of Tammany boss Charles F. Murphy, a majority of Democrats supported "Blue-eyed Billy" Sheehan, a Buffalo business mogul who had gained party favor with generous financial contributions. Sheehan was the perfect target of progressive reformers, who complained that the party was beholden to wealthy donors rather than the needs of the people. Supported by nineteen other party insurgents, Franklin led a revolt against Murphy's backing of Sheehan. When the twenty insurgents denied Murphy the 101 votes Sheehan needed, the dispute lasted more than two months into March, generating national newspaper stories that made Franklin an overnight political celebrity. The end result, however, was a compromise that diminished Franklin's standing as a good-government leader determined only to support antimachine politicians. While the reformers were able to block Sheehan, they could not put someone of their choosing in place. If they were to send a Democrat to the U.S. Senate, he and the dissidents would have to settle for State Supreme Court Justice James A. O'Gorman, another Tammany associate, who, if anything, was closer to Murphy than Sheehan.

Because he wasn't able to affect the outcome of the Senate contest and in fact himself voted for O'Gorman, Franklin was forced to defend his reputation as a principled politician genuinely committed to progressive reform. His opponents in the legislature and outside Albany attacked him as anti-Irish and anti-Catholic. Fellow legislators, angry at being held in session for so long over an issue with a foreseeable outcome, savaged him. His appearance at the vote on O'Gorman provoked jeers and derision. With pointed contempt for Franklin, the Republican minority leader complained of how the mountain had yielded a mouse. However discomfiting, the battle taught Franklin a useful political lesson — namely, that he could claim a victory if his public face belied the reality of his defeat and the public saw him as true to his beliefs. When he spoke about the fight to his legislative colleagues and to public audiences, he characterized his efforts as a victory for good government: He dwelled not on O'Gorman's appointment but Sheehan's defeat. To his satisfaction, the public accepted his version of events, not because his assessment was so believable, but because voters were so eager for another progressive hero like TR and hoped that political change was succeeding.

In the spring of 1911, after the Sheehan fight ended, Franklin found ample opportunity to promote other progressive causes. He fought successfully for New York state approval of the Seventeenth Amendment. He also argued the case for direct primaries, which was a progressive nostrum in states across the country for preventing political machines from controlling nominations for local and national offices. When a revised charter for New York City governance came up for consideration, Franklin initially opposed it as a machine instrument that would expand boss rule. He reversed himself, however, when Tammany threatened to reapportion Dutchess County in a way that would undermine Franklin and his allies, but when progressives took him to task for playing politics, he reversed himself again.

Reformers were less than happy with him when, during the remainder of the 1911 session, he refused to come out for a woman suffrage bill or to back labor measures limiting the working hours of women and children. Nor did he show much interest in legislative investigations of the tragic Triangle Shirtwaist Company fire in New York City that killed 148 sweatshop workers, most of them immigrant women and children trapped in a building with inadequate escape routes. He understood that the farmers who had made the difference in electing him were unsympathetic to certain progressive reforms and the plight of poor newcomers to the United States.

Frances Perkins, a socialite who frequented the same elite circles as Franklin, met him in 1910 at a party on the east side of Manhattan. She remembered that "there was nothing particularly interesting about the tall, thin young man with the high collar and pince-nez." She encountered him again the following year in Albany, where she was a social worker representing the Consumers' League. He impressed her then as a supercilious snob who "really didn't like people very much. . . . He had a youthful lack of humility, a streak of self-righteousness, and a deafness to the hopes, fears, and aspirations which are the common lot." She shared Tim Sullivan's view of him as an "awful, arrogant fellow." Roosevelt himself told her years later, "You know, I was an awfully mean cuss when I first went into politics."

His arrogance was less a reflection of his feelings of superiority than of the defensiveness of a novice politician trying to master the political challenge of serving his own moral imperatives and the practical considerations at odds with them. This came home most forcefully to him in November when Assembly elections resulted in a

Democratic defeat: The party lost 37 seats, which turned a 24-member majority into a 13-seat deficit. Franklin put the best possible face on the loss by describing it as a setback for party bosses whose corruption had alienated voters: "Murphy and his kind must, like the noxious weed, be plucked out, root and branch." But he understood that the party's defeat rested partly on public perceptions of the Democrats as a divided organization incapable of effective governance. While reformers denounced Tammany as corrupt, the "bosses" dismissed the progressives as "political prigs" who lacked "human sympathy, human interest, and human ties."

The party's sudden reversal of fortune pushed Franklin in two different directions. For one, he became more attentive to the needs of his farm constituents and to assuring that they would be aware of his advocacy on their behalf. His genuine interest in conservation and position as chairman of the Senate's committee on Forest, Fish, and Game enabled him to press for measures that served his district as well as the Hudson River Valley environment he wished to preserve. When Tammany senators blocked a bill appropriating money for forest fire protection and Roosevelt verbally attacked them for "a criminal neglect of the public interest," the chamber's presiding officer cut him off, insisting that the senator had made his point: "What he wants is a headline in the newspapers."

At the same time, however, believing that backing progressive causes would best serve the country and his long-term political future, he now joined reformers in supporting woman suffrage and regulations limiting working hours and mandating conditions that protected young people, including women, from exploitation by factory and mine operators. He also advocated state financing of hydroelectric plants, which could reduce utilities costs to consumers, and which he hoped would appeal both to opponents of exploitive trusts and farmers happy to pay lower rates.

As he looked toward his reelection campaign in 1912, he articulated a political position he thought might reconcile the opposing interests he was trying to serve. He chose Troy as the venue for a speech to reach a statewide audience and even win attention outside of New York. The home of Rensselaer Polytechnic Institute, a training ground for modern engineers, as well as a thriving farmer's market, the city, which stood eight miles north of Albany at the juncture of the Hudson River, Erie Canal, and railway lines that carried the city's manufactured goods to every region of the country, Troy was a powerful symbol of the harmonious existence of the old and new in early twentieth-century America.

Troy was an ideal backdrop for what Franklin wanted to say — namely that America's traditional affinity for individual freedom needed to be balanced against the interests of the larger community or society in a changing country.

Hoping that his formulation would impress itself on reformers and farm constituents alike, he announced a "new theory," which he called "the struggle for the liberty of the community rather than the liberty of the individual." Competition, as the country had known it, had been useful in building America, but cooperation must now define its future. He understood that his "theory" might come under attack as "un-American" or a "dangerous" flirtation with socialism, but he was convinced that calling it cooperation would disarm any conservative objections. There was nothing new in Franklin's pronouncement; populists and progressives had been talking about the general interest as opposed to special interests for almost thirty years. His "theory" spoke more to his search for a way through his own political dilemma than to any compelling prescription for how the country should conduct its public affairs.

In the fall of 1911 when Franklin traveled to Trenton, New Jersey, to meet with the state's fifty-four-year-old progressive governor, Woodrow Wilson, he was making a bet on his own and the country's political future. The former president of Princeton University was a newcomer to politics, and his election signaled public receptivity to men who represented themselves as Democrats determined to replace corrupt political bosses and their party machines with leadership serving majorities rather than special economic interests. Wilson, who was already focused on running for president after less than a year as governor, was eager to know if Roosevelt could help bring the New York delegation to his side in the Democratic convention, which was to be held in Baltimore in June 1912. Franklin doubted that he could persuade Tammany's bosses to support Wilson, but he made clear that he intended to try. While as many as 30 of New York's 90 delegates to the convention might be Wilson men, the state party's unit rule dictated that the majority would control all the convention votes. Wilson had little hope of commanding the party's largest bloc of delegates.

When New York's Democrats met in April to

select convention representatives, Franklin's efforts on Wilson's behalf came to naught. Charlie Murphy's men dominated the proceedings, choosing anti-Wilson delegates, and refusing to make Franklin, Wilson's principal advocate, one of their number. In response, Franklin helped organize a "New York State Wilson Conference" that demanded an end to the unit rule so that Wilson's backers could make their influence felt at the Baltimore convention. Murphy saw no reason to accommodate the dissidents. Although Franklin did attend the national meeting, where he lobbied for Wilson to anyone who would listen, he could not influence the New York vote. When Wilson won the nomination on the convention's forty-sixth ballot despite Murphy's opposition, Franklin was exhilarated. It was a "splendid triumph," he wired Eleanor, who was in Campobello. He saw Wilson's victory as opening undefined possibilities for him, telling her, "All my plans vague."

He may have been vague about what a Wilson presidency might mean for him, but not about his immediate future. He hoped to play a central role in advancing Wilson's candidacy and to ensure his own reelection to the state Senate. Winning New York for Wilson, however, proved to be a great challenge. With TR heading a Progressive Party that would take votes from Taft and divide the Republican majority, it seemed possible to put New York in Wilson's column, but New York Democrats were also divided by Tammany's continuing hostility toward Wilson. In July, Murphy's opponents, including Franklin, established the Empire State Democracy to contest Tammany candidates at the New York State Democratic convention in Syracuse in October.

Franklin threatened that the reformers had a "club" with which to bludgeon Tammany, but hoped they wouldn't have to use it. Because Murphy's self-interest dictated that they hold the party together and carry the state for Wilson, they agreed to a gubernatorial and a number of congressional candidates who were more acceptable to the progressives.

Franklin's success in helping unify the state party for Wilson gave no assurance of his reelection to the Senate. He had made some powerful party enemies during the Sheehan fight who were accusing him of being an agent of "discord." At the end of July, he told Eleanor that "Tammany and the 'Interests' are really making an effort to prevent my re-nomination." His success depended on party operatives in Dutchess County, and he once again hired a motorcar to tour the county byways. A month's campaigning and the backing of several local newspapers secured his goal. "It seems hardly possible that the local Democratic bosses can be in earnest in their efforts to turn down Senator Franklin D. Roosevelt," an editorial that ran in several of the papers declared. ". . . His record has been an extraordinarily good one for a young man in his first term." Understanding that denying Franklin his re-nomination would be unpopular, all the party factions lined up behind him.

His reelection, however, remained uncertain and was put in jeopardy by his contracting typhoid fever at the end of September after brushing his teeth with contaminated water, leaving him largely bedridden for all of October, the height of the campaign season. However positive an impression he had made on voters over the previous two years, Franklin could not assume that they would automatically favor a sitting senator who was absent, whatever the reason. Tammany had no interest in helping him through the crisis. They were content to see a regular Republican reclaim the seat, though a TR progressive had also entered the race and put the outcome in doubt. Franklin clearly needed a stand-in, someone who could replace him as a speaker and handshaker at the country crossroads and keep his name and record before voters.

To save his political career he turned to the forty-one-year-old Louis McHenry Howe, an Albany journalist with an unmatched reputation for political savvy. The two first met when Howe, who shared Franklin's progressive bias and antagonism to Sheehan's election, interviewed the novice senator for the Empire State Democracy, and they took an immediate liking to each other. Pint-size, emaciated — he weighed under 100 pounds — and pockmarked, Howe was known as "the gnome of Albany," and as he liked to think of himself, a slayer of political giants. He prided himself on his distinction as one of the four ugliest men in the city. No one ever identified the other three, and one observer considered his appearance beyond comparison in off-putting looks. It wasn't just his physical attributes that offended anyone who studied him; it was also his cultivated slovenliness, as he would typically be dressed in unpressed baggy pants and food-stained jackets, shirts, and ties. He was a chain-smoker, and his nicotine-stained hands attested to his constant tobacco use.

The first meeting between Franklin and Howe was like the beginning of a courtship. Howe was drawn to the young patrician, who was everything he wasn't — handsome, well groomed, a prep school and Ivy League graduate; Howe himself had never finished college. Roosevelt was a cosmopolite with a presence that Howe instantly admired. Howe had a history of performing in amateur theater and could imagine himself on a world stage or, at least after meeting Franklin, he could imagine himself behind the scenes of a universally famous public figure. He also had a fascination with Thomas Carlyle's idea of the hero in history, believing that great men were the driving force behind seminal events. Not long after developing an association with Franklin as a publicist he addressed him as "Beloved and Revered Future president."

Eleanor disliked the disheveled little man, but Franklin sized him up as a very smart student of politics with an affinity for the irreverent. His attitude seemed to say, Yes, I'm ugly and small, but I tower over you establishment folks — the rich, the famous, the up-from-the-bootstraps power brokers — because I see through you and around the corner on current events and future political trends. Howe's defiance of convention resonated with Franklin, outwardly the most conventional of patricians but one who quietly questioned the accepted standards by which the worlds of economics and politics and international relations currently operated. As Franklin would say later, everything he learned about economics at Harvard was wrong.

Howe and Franklin shared a competitive urge to be the best, and prove themselves worthy, in Franklin's case, to those Porcellian snobs who rejected him and those workaday politicians who dismissed him as an amateur, and in Howe's case, to the whole world that looked down on someone with such an unprepossessing appearance. Neither man was so rebellious that he couldn't function within the existing system of politics and power, but both were sufficiently detached from it, and could see its abundant flaws, that they could effectively become establishment rebels — men who would counter accepted wisdoms from the inside.

In turning to Howe to rescue his rerun for the Senate, Franklin had made the right choice. Howe was out of work and relished the $50-a-week salary Franklin agreed to pay him. Moreover, he was eager to put fresh ideas into action on how to run a winning campaign. These included sending voters "personal" letters, or at least ones that appeared to have Roosevelt's original signature. He asked farmers, the biggest swing bloc in the district, to respond in writing about legislation Franklin proposed to introduce in 1913 that would increase the return on their produce. He used the same tactic in reaching out to fisherman unhappy about increased licensing fees, and to organized labor to ask if they wanted the senator to advocate at the upcoming session for a workmen's compensation law. Enclosing self-addressed stamped envelopes helped facilitate the "flood of letters" that soon arrived at campaign headquarters. Howe did not neglect women's issues, nor did he ignore the prevailing antibossism mood in the district, running full-page newspaper ads that promised Roosevelt's support for suffrage and attacked Republican, but not Tammany, bosses. "I am having more fun than a goat," Howe wrote Franklin, signing himself "Your slave and servant." The result he achieved was spectacular: At a cost of $3,000, Howe managed a Roosevelt victory by almost 2,000 out of 29,000 votes cast. His margin in the district exceeded the majorities won by Wilson and the Democratic candidate for governor.

Franklin was pleased at his reelection, but did not look forward to fresh fights he expected to erupt in the legislature, where few anti-Tammany Democrats remained. Battling with dozens of other legislators was far less appealing to him than serving in an executive position with the greater freedom to act on his beliefs. In mid-January, then, he was excited by an invitation from President-elect Wilson to come to Trenton to discuss appointments, including his own, in the new administration. He knew exactly what position he wanted: TR's old job as assistant secretary of the Navy. Although the United States had the third-largest navy in the world — it was a third the size of Great Britain's and half the size of Germany's — it was a formidable fighting force capable of defending American possessions in the Western Hemisphere and the Pacific. As the department's only assistant secretary he would assume substantial administrative responsibilities and have a measure of authority far beyond anything he could exercise as a second-term New York state senator. The lure of national visibility added to the attraction of moving to Washington.

Wilson made no specific commitment to him at their meeting, but in March, William Gibbs McAdoo, Wilson's choice as treasury secretary, invited Franklin to become either an assistant secretary in his department, or the collector of the port of New York. Franklin, however, wanted neither post. Economics had never been a particular interest of his, and becoming collector would mean future conflicts with Tammany over patronage jobs and a reputation as more of a political operative than a public official serving the national cause.

Wilson had already decided to name Josephus Daniels, the editor of the North Carolina *Raleigh News and Observer* and an early, effective supporter of his presidential bid, as secretary of the Navy, though his only credential for the position was that his father, who was killed in the Civil War when Josephus was three, had built ships for the Confederate Navy. Daniels's appointment spoke volumes about Wilson's own limited concern with defense or international diplomacy, as did his choice of the fifty-two-year-old William Jennings Bryan as secretary of state. Bryan, who had run for president three times, knew little about external affairs. During a trip to Europe and the Near East in 1908, he had revealed his ignorance of the outside world when the mention of the Balkans by a diplomat evoked the response: "What are the Balkans?" Bryan's appointment spoke loudly about Wilson's limited concern with overseas challenges. At the start of his term, Wilson observed, "It would be the irony of fate if my administration had to deal chiefly with foreign affairs." While Bryan and Daniels shared Wilson's pacifist outlook and moralistic assumptions about international relations, their cabinet posts were largely rewards for helping Wilson become president.

Wilson and Daniels both agreed that Franklin should be appointed Daniels's second in command. They had warm feelings for Franklin after his enthusiastic support for Wilson's candidacy during the convention and the campaign. Moreover, they were confident that his interest in seafaring and naval history, and his family connection to TR, would make him a most suitable assistant. Franklin at once replied that it was "the one place, above all others, I would love to hold." When, as a courtesy to New York's U.S. senators, Daniels discussed Franklin's appointment with them, Republican Elihu Root, who had had extensive dealings with TR, said, "You know the Roosevelts, don't you? Whenever a Roosevelt rides, he wishes to ride in front."

Sworn in as assistant secretary of the Navy on March 17, 1913, Franklin, who had moved to Washington, D.C., with his family, wrote Sara, "I'm baptized, confirmed, sworn in, vaccinated — and somewhat at sea." He was signing lots of papers "on faith — but I hope luck will keep me out of jail," he joked. "I will have to work like a new turbine to master this job," he added, "— but it will be done even if it takes all summer." Two days later, with Daniels away, Franklin served as acting secretary "and up to my ears. I must have signed three or four hundred papers today and am *beginning* to catch on." However daunting the responsibilities for the thirty-one–year-old novice (he was the youngest man ever to become assistant secretary) to Washington administration and politics, he could not have been happier at his good fortune in landing the post: "I now find my vocation combined with my avocation," he wrote his mother. It was no idle boast. He was a skilled seaman, as he soon demonstrated to a skeptical destroyer captain when Franklin took the helm of his ship, navigating it through the narrow channel between Campobello and the Canadian coast.

Franklin's new position at once raised expectations about his future: "Battleship man — or mad — though you be I am truly glad of your appointment to Washington," Oswald Garrison Villard, the pacifist editor of the *Nation,* wrote him. "May it lead straight onward for you as it did for TR — but not by means of that barbarism known as war." Daniels likewise imagined a similar path for the two Roosevelts: "His distinguished cousin TR went from this place to the Presidency," Daniels noted in a diary. "May history repeat itself."

It was clear to anyone who knew Franklin and his association with Uncle Ted that he would be an impassioned promoter of the Navy. But this had not troubled Wilson or Daniels, whose affinity for pacifism promised to put them at odds with the young man. Moreover, Franklin might likewise prove to be an unmanageable subordinate. His self-confidence, born of his privileged background and associations, instantly made him a comfortable participant in Washington's rich social life. Because he needed no introduction to the influential people in and out of government who frequented the capitol, his voice would be heard in high places and might lead to conflicts with the White House. He was a handsome, charming, delightful young man of whom it was later said that meeting him for the first time was like uncorking a bottle of champagne. The savvy Daniels, however, liked Franklin's youthful spirit and felt he could handle any insubordination. He was therefore more amused than angered when Franklin as acting secretary indiscreetly told reporters: "There's another Roosevelt on the job today. . . . You remember what happened the last time a Roosevelt occupied a similar position?" The reference was not lost on the journalists who recalled that TR had defied administration policy in 1898 by ordering the U.S. fleet from Hong Kong to Manila as a step toward war with Spain.

From the first, Franklin was diplomatic in deferring to his boss, though in private he was condescending toward the man he called "the funniest looking hillbilly I had ever seen." He was especially critical of Daniels's ignorance about ships and sailing and had great fun entertaining friends with imitations of the fifty-year-old Southerner, with his receding hairline, old-fashioned string tie, long black coat, and North Carolina twang. Franklin shared Daniels's progressive distrust of business moguls, but he had his doubts about Bryan's and Daniels's support of government ownership of telephone-telegraph lines and railroads. Nor did he have much sympathy with his boss's outspoken advocacy of white supremacy and the South's Jim Crow laws, or his backing of Prohibition. Franklin's disrespect for Daniels was so overt among friends that Interior Secretary Franklin K. Lane reprimanded him, telling him that he should either be respectful or resign his office. He finally curbed his sarcasm.

Franklin thoroughly enjoyed the deference shown him as assistant secretary, as well as the seventeen-gun salutes and ruffles when he boarded a ship with its crew in freshly pressed whites and officers in dress uniforms saluting the civilian chief. He was less fond of the daily bureaucratic minutiae of navy yard problems generated by labor-business conflicts or the supervision of the department's civilian personnel. Howe, whom Roosevelt made his personal assistant, eased Franklin's administrative duties by tirelessly managing them. Where Franklin was the charming model gentleman, always elegantly dressed, well spoken, and correct in manners, Howe remained the abrasive, gruff, ill-mannered subordinate who gave Roosevelt's critics a convenient target. "I am hated by everybody," Howe bragged. "I always have been hated by everybody, and I want to be hated by everybody."

Franklin was drawn to the job by more than just the ceremonial attractions of the office, however, for he viewed himself as a vital voice for national defense to counter the pacifist sentiments of Wilson, Bryan, and Daniels. In the spring of 1913, a Japanese-American crisis erupted over Tokyo's protests against a California statute barring Japanese ownership of farmland as being at odds with existing treaties and accepted standards of international relations, and an insult to Japan's national pride. Its objections convinced America's military chiefs that Japan would stage a surprise strike against U.S. forces in the Philippines, as it had in 1904 against Russia's fleet in Port Arthur, Manchuria. When a debate erupted between American naval and army officers who urged movement of reinforcements to Manila and a resistant White House, Franklin privately echoed the military's views. "I did all in my power" to encourage the deployment of ships, Franklin later wrote America's most influential naval strategist, Admiral Alfred Thayer Mahan. In public, however, sensitive to the political fallout from an open dispute with his superiors, Franklin opposed mobilizing forces and supported efforts to calm the war scare. Although the crisis quickly passed, Franklin thought that Daniels and the White House were too passive in preparing for a possible conflict.

A situation with Mexico the following year strengthened Franklin's conviction that the Navy Department needed his more militant voice to manage foreign troubles. In February 1913, General Victoriano Huerta staged a coup during which Francisco Madero, the head of the elected government, was assassinated. Contrary to the accepted practice of recognizing governments regardless of how they came to power, Wilson refused to deal with Huerta's regime, stating, "I will not recognize a government of butchers." Determined to compel America's southern neighbor to act on constitutional scruples and the rule of law, Wilson further announced that he wanted to "teach the South American republics to elect good men."

In April 1914, to force Huerta's abdication, Wilson seized upon an incident in Vera Cruz, where Mexican authorities had arrested three U.S. sailors who had come ashore to load supplies on their warship. The American commander of the flotilla in port demanded that the Mexicans not only release the sailors but also fire a twenty-one-gun salute to the American flag. The Mexicans' refusal to comply with the order to salute allowed Wilson to win congressional approval for action to compel Huerta's resignation. The president ordered naval blockades of Mexico's east and west coast ports and the occupation of Vera Cruz to prevent a German cargo ship from delivering a shipment of arms.

Franklin, who was on an inspection tour of West Coast bases, spoke out in support of Wilson's actions. He expected a war to follow and hoped to direct operations against Mexico's Pacific ports. Distrustful of his aggressive subordinate, who he suspected might attempt to get ahead of the White House by initiating unauthorized military actions, Daniels ordered him back to Washington. During his train trip across the country, Franklin spoke to reporters at several station stops about the likelihood of a U.S.-Mexican war, telling them, "Sooner or later, it seems, the United States must go down there and clean up the Mexican political mess." By the time Franklin reached the capital, however, Wilson had pulled back from his aggressive stance. Embarrassed by the resistance of Mexican forces in Vera Cruz, which cost nineteen American lives; a German protest against the illegal U.S. seizure of its ship; and ridicule from European and Latin American capitals of the administration's professed pacifism and contradictory assault on a weak neighbor, Wilson followed the advice of Bryan and Daniels to withdraw U.S. forces from Mexico and accept a mediation initiative led by Argentina, Brazil, and Chile. Daniels made it clear to Franklin that the White House did not want to go to war and that his overheated rhetoric was not appreciated.

By July 1914, Franklin's frustration over the Wilson administration's stance toward Mexico moved him to consider a proposal that he run for a U.S. Senate seat in New York. He complained to Eleanor that he saw "no *definite* policy of construction" on Mexico. We drift on from day to day as usual . . . the time has come for a concrete program." The want of a decisive Mexican policy wasn't the only factor motivating him to leave the Navy Department. Treasury Secretary William G. McAdoo encouraged him to get in the race as a way to build an anti-Tammany organization in New York. Defeating Tammany greatly appealed to Franklin, but the prospect of holding greater influence in national affairs than he had in his subcabinet post was even more compelling. "I *might* declare myself a candidate for U.S. Senator in the Democratic and Progressive Primaries," he wrote Eleanor on July 19. "The Governorship is, thank God, out of the question." Since his arrival in Washington, he had "been every day struck by the fact that the standards of Albany and of Harrisburg [Pennsylvania]," where honesty and efficiency were in short supply, "are by no means the standards of Washington, for in the national capital I have found on the part of the administration a sincere and successful desire to manage and maintain the government of the nation for the sole benefit of the people."

The outbreak of World War I at the beginning of August strengthened Franklin's belief in the need for aggressive leadership by the Navy Department, which he feared Daniels would not provide. "A complete smash up is inevitable," he wrote Eleanor on August 1, "and there are a great many problems for us to consider. . . . These are history-making days. It will be the greatest war in the world's history." He wanted to contribute whatever he could to leading the country through these tumultuous times, but he had substantial doubts that he could make much of a difference as second in command under a passive secretary. On August 2, returning to Washington from Massachusetts, where he had presided at the opening of the Cape Cod Canal, he "found everything asleep and apparently oblivious to the fact that the most terrible drama in history was about to be enacted. . . . To my astonishment on reaching the Dept. nobody seemed the least bit excited about the

European crisis — Mr. Daniels feeling chiefly very sad that his faith in human nature and civilization and similar idealistic nonsense was receiving such a rude shock. . . . These dear good people like W.J.B. and J.D. have as much conception of what a general European war means as [three-year-old] Elliott has of higher mathematics." The failure to ready the U.S. fleet for the many challenges Franklin perceived would confront the nation made him angry. "I nearly boil over when I see the cheery 'manana' way of doing business. . . . I am *running* the real work, although Josephus is here," he reported to Eleanor on August 5. "He is bewildered by it all, very sweet but very sad."

Wilson's pronouncement that "The United States must be neutral in fact as well as in name during these times that try men's souls" fell short of what Franklin believed essential to America's security and influence in world affairs. He left little doubt about his own preference for an Anglo-French victory in the war or about his eagerness for an American role in defeating "the Huns": "I feel hurt because the Emperor William has left the U.S. out — he has declared war against everybody else," he told Eleanor only half joking. "The Belgians are putting up a glorious and unexpected resistance. . . . Everybody here feels that this country as a whole sympathizes with the allies against Germany." When Great Britain entered the war, he "thank[ed] God England has gone in in earnest. . . . I've been disappointed that England has been unable to force a naval action." As the conflict came to a standstill in the fall, he grew all the more frustrated by the administration's passivity. "The country needs the truth," he told Eleanor, "about the Army and the Navy instead of a lot of soft mush about everlasting peace which so many statesmen are handing out to a gullible public."

His discontent with the administration's response to the war made him all the more inclined to accept McAdoo's invitation to run in the New York State primary for the Senate nomination. McAdoo gave Roosevelt the false impression that Wilson would support his candidacy as a test of progressive strength against Tammany. Mindful that Wilson was trying to reach some kind of accord with New York's Democratic machine in order to present a united front in the November congressional elections, however, Daniels counseled Franklin against entering the race. But ever the optimist and convinced that Howe could work more of the political magic he had brought to the successful 1912 campaign, Franklin ignored Daniels's advice. When Franklin announced his candidacy on August 13, no other Democrat had entered the lists, and Tammany's Charlie Murphy gave no indication that he would back anyone else. With no challenge to his candidacy, Franklin spent the rest of August in Campobello resting up for a September speaking tour. In the meantime, Howe, who had private doubts about the wisdom of Franklin's decision, loyally mounted an August blitz in his behalf.

Early in September, as Franklin launched his campaign, Murphy surprisingly announced his support of James W. Gerard, Wilson's ambassador to Germany. Understanding that he might well be no more than a sacrificial lamb against a united Republican Party, Gerard agreed to enter the primary on the condition that he remain in Berlin.

This left Franklin to compete against an absent opponent whose service in a war zone gave him immunity from criticism. Eager to avoid tensions with Murphy over the Senate contest, Wilson refused to take sides in the primary. Left on his own against Tammany's ability to turn out a large Gerard vote in New York City and with no compelling message that brought upstate Democrats to his side, Franklin took an embarrassing almost three-to-one beating in the election. Refusing to acknowledge his "hurt," however, he declared the contest a step on the road to a greater progressive advance. He cabled Gerard that he would campaign for him in the fall if the ambassador would repudiate Murphy and "all he stands for." Gerard's diplomatic reply that, should he become senator, he intended to represent everyone, was enough to win Franklin's endorsement. Franklin saw no gain from continuing the intraparty squabble that Wilson shunned and could only benefit Republicans in November.

For Franklin, meanwhile, the war increasingly underscored the importance of an American Navy that could ensure control of the seas. Echoing Admiral Mahan and TR, he declared, "Our national defense must extend all over the western hemisphere, must go out a thousand miles into the sea, must embrace the Philippines and over the seas wherever our commerce may be. To hold the Panama Canal, Alaska, American Samoa, Guam, Porto Rico [sic], the naval base at Guantanamo and the Philippines, we must have battleships." In addition, he believed that a prudent American response to the conflict required universal military training. He made no secret of his views, speaking in public forums and at congressional hearings as a representative not of the president, secretary of state, or Daniels, but of the admirals: "Let us learn to trust the judgment of the real experts, the naval officers," he said at a Navy league banquet in New York in May 1915.

When Bryan resigned as secretary of state the following month over a dispute with Wilson about how the administration's defense of neutral rights might provoke a war with Germany, Franklin exulted in the departure of someone he considered a deterrent to wise defense policies. "I can only say I'm disgusted clear through," he told Eleanor about Bryan. He secretly hoped that Daniels might resign as well, but the Navy secretary remained confident that Wilson was determined to keep the United States out of the fighting. Wilson's refusal to agree to compulsory training or to ask Congress to increase naval spending for possible involvement in the war effectively left Franklin on the fringes of the administration. Like TR, he decried Wilson's declaration that "There is such a thing as a man being too proud to fight." America could best serve the world, Wilson insisted, by standing as an example of peace. He viewed the conflict as "a war with which we had nothing to do, whose causes cannot touch us," a statement he issued as a rebuke to "some amongst us [who] are nervous and excited."

Franklin recognized himself as one of the war hawks to whom Wilson's comment was addressed. But unlike Republicans who openly attacked the president's shortsightedness, Franklin tried to criticize Wilson's pacifism by more subtle means. In the fall of 1915, as acting secretary, he announced the establishment of a 50,000-man Naval Reserve. He worried that having "pulled the trigger" on a plan that Daniels had "failed for a year . . . to take any action [on] . . . the bullet may bounce back on me." But eager not to lose his place in the administration from which he could exert pressure for preparedness, or to end a political career that had already suffered a setback in 1914, he did no more than publicly outline a plan for the reserves, rather than affirmatively declare it a new Navy Department entity.

As the 1916 presidential election approached, the gap between Wilson and preparedness advocates diminished. In the summer of 1915, the president agreed to larger appropriations for the nation's defense. His firm response to the sinking of the British liner *Arabic* with the loss of two American lives also heartened Franklin, though he doubted that he himself would have been "quite so polite" as Wilson if he were managing the diplomatic exchange. Moreover, when he pressed the president to establish a Council of National Defense, he was pleased that Wilson seemed willing to "take it up soon." Although Germany agreed to the "*Arabic* Pledge," promising not to sink liners without regard for the safety of their passengers, Wilson, mindful that progressive Republicans believed that only a strong America could compel the world to follow its lead toward high ideals, asked Congress in 1916 to increase military spending. TR declared Wilson's request too small to ensure a proper role for America in foreign affairs, but pacifists opposed it as moving the country toward involvement in the war.

Franklin understood that Wilson's actions were those of an official trying to hold on to his office, but he was pleased nonetheless that Wilson was moving in the right direction and might come to see the need for U.S. participation in a war he believed could ultimately imperil America's well-being and limit its capacity to move the world toward a higher moral ground. In the spring of 1916, after a U-boat torpedoed the *Sussex,* a French ship, with the loss of two more U.S. lives, Wilson threatened a break with Germany if it did not reaffirm its pledge to avoid sinking liners with Americans aboard. Still reluctant to drive America into the war, Berlin declared its determination not to sink passenger vessels "without warning and without saving human lives." Wilson described Germany's latest commitment as a diplomatic triumph, and his supporters introduced the campaign slogan, "He kept us out of war." The agreement strengthened Wilson's hold on majority opinion favoring an America at peace, but it also satisfied many preparedness proponents who believed that the president's call for larger military budgets had forced Berlin to accept America's civilized definition of neutral rights.

In 1916 Franklin made the case to voters for Wilson's realistic approach to America's defense needs and the unhelpful complaints of Republicans about his leadership. "Every minute of time taken up in perfectly futile and useless arguments about mistakes in the past slows up [naval] construction," he declared. "Worse than that it blinds and befogs the public as to the real situation and the imperative necessity for prompt action. How would you expect the public to be convinced that a dangerous fire was in progress, requiring every citizen's aid for its extinguishment, if they saw the members of the volunteer fire department stop in their headlong rush towards the conflagration and indulge in a slanging match as to who was responsible for the rotten hose or the lack of water at the fire." Franklin's pronouncement was a shrewd use of a homey analogy that made a policy dispute more understandable to ordinary citizens. It would not be the last time he used such language to bring the public to his side.

To Roosevelt's satisfaction, Wilson won reelection in November, though by the slimmest of margins. Franklin exulted over the continued sway of progressive advance, telling Eleanor that he would wire his conservative uncle Warren Delano III: "The Republican party has proved to its own satisfaction I hope that the American people cannot always be bought. I hope to God I don't grow reactionary with advancing years." His joy at Wilson's victory rested as much, if not more, from his confidence that he would remain at the center of national events.

With Wilson safely back in the White House, Franklin quietly pressed the case for U.S. involvement in the fighting. "We've got to get into this war!" he repeatedly told Daniels, who consistently responded, "I hope not." In the New Year, after Berlin announced plans for unrestricted submarine warfare, a measure that seemed to guarantee that the United States would enter the conflict, Franklin urged Wilson to prepare the fleet for quick action. The president refused to take any actions that might be seen as provocative, however, telling Roosevelt: "I want history to show not only that we have tried every diplomatic means to keep out of the war; to show that war has been forced upon us deliberately by Germany; but also that we have come into the court of history with clean hands." Franklin, for his part, took a more dispassionate view of the military: "We in the navy committed acts for which we could be and may be sent to jail for 999 years," he said later.

Wilson's request to Congress on April 2 for a declaration of war, triggered by German attacks on U.S. ships, vindicated Franklin's conviction that America's only correct course was to join the Allies in what Wilson felicitously called a fight to make the world safe for democracy. In the nearly three years that Franklin had been at odds with the administration over the country's response to the war, however, his differences with Daniels and Wilson had been less pronounced than he thought. The president and Daniels were not unmindful of Franklin's divergence from their pacifism, but his presence in the administration served an unspoken political end by easing Wilson's political problems with preparedness opponents. Having TR's nephew in the Navy Department echoing his uncle's views gave preparedness advocates some hope that their demands for a military buildup might not be entirely out of reach.

Yet for all Franklin's impatience with Wilson's and Daniels's reluctance to take a stand against Germany, he shared with them the conviction that German aggression represented a threat to America's overseas possessions and commerce and, more important, the democratic values America had in common with Britain and France. They all believed that the war was an uncertain contest between autocracy and representative government and that, despite its professions of neutrality, the United States favored the Allies. Although Franklin believed it essential for the United States to ensure a Franco-British victory through direct involvement, while Wilson hoped that American loans and materiel supplies would be enough to secure that outcome, in the end they agreed that a British-French defeat was unacceptable. They all recognized the potential of the war to change the world forever, as the stakes were ultimately democratic systems of law and order pitted against illiberal militaristic governance.

Wilson reluctantly came around to Franklin's means to their shared ends, because, as he saw it, he had no choice: Germany was forcing him to take sides. Equally important was the fact that by April 1917, the conflict had already taken millions of lives and strained every nation's treasury. Wilson and most Americans had come to believe that the United States could not only bring the suffering to a close but also persuade the belligerents — victors and vanquished — that autocratic rule and traditional power politics were root causes of human misery. Wilson would shortly call for a peace without victors or at least a peace that would not be vindictive and that would draw Germany and all the nations of the world into a community of shared progressive values. Franklin put a premium on a German defeat as essential to preserving America's global commerce and future economic well-being. But like Wilson and Daniels, he understood that Americans needed some larger goal beyond national self-interest to ennoble the sacrifice of thousands of American lives. He accepted that it was not enough to speak of the nation's defeat of German aggression, and that progressives, which represented majority opinion in 1917, took comfort in Wilson's insistence that the conflict bring a permanent end to war and a universal commitment to self-determination.

"Missionary diplomacy," as Wilson's biographer Arthur Link called it, was almost as much a reflection of Franklin's thinking as it was Wilson's. In January and February 1917, Franklin had traveled to Haiti and Santo Domingo with other U.S. officials to assess conditions on the island. American Marines had been sent to Hispaniola in 1915 to end periodic eruptions of political and financial turmoil there. Although strategic and economic considerations were uppermost in shaping U.S. actions, idealistic pronouncements gave a patina of justification to America's presence. Franklin had no problem with an occupation serving what he saw as U.S. interests, but he also deluded himself into believing that Marines bringing progress to backward countries was an example of American altruism. Franklin applauded road building, improved public health, support for elementary education, and a new rule of law under a written constitution: "Ninety-nine percent of the inhabitants were not only satisfied with what has been done for them," he told a reporter on his return to Washington, "but . . . would look with terror on an abandonment by this country of its interest in their welfare." He ignored the repression and abuses of power that had marked the occupation, less because he wished to whitewash the behavior of the Marines, whose contempt for the locals matched Southern contempt for American Negroes, than because he'd convinced himself that despite any misdeeds by the troops the Haitians and Dominicans were far better off under American control.

Franklin's romantic view of expansive American action abroad extended to involvement in what was now being called the Great War. Where Wilson regarded American belligerency as a tragedy and feared that domestic tolerance and constitutional restraints might not survive the fighting and make it impossible for the United States to arrange a peace without victors, Franklin, watching from the House gallery as Wilson asked for a declaration of war, joined in the thunderous applause at the president's description of Germany's rulers as ruthless power brokers indifferent to justice and freedom. It was not Wilson's concern that participation in the fighting might undermine American democracy that registered most strongly, but his description of a postwar world with universal self-determination and an enduring peace. That image thrilled his congressional audience and aroused the enthusiasm of Americans as well as Europeans who were desperate to find some justification for additional sacrifices. No words, Franklin told the press, could have better expressed the high purposes for which American blood and treasure would now be expended. It was rhetoric powerful enough to inspire an isolationist America to fight, despite the growing awareness that in 1916 as many as two million men, on both sides of the line, had been killed or wounded in northern France at Verdun and the Somme. For Americans the trench warfare represented a collapse of civilized standards, which a U.S. involvement in the fighting was meant to restore.

Franklin was not oblivious to the war's terrible toll, but he was as naively idealistic as the millions of doughboys who rushed to join Wilson's crusade for worldwide progress and a chance at battlefield heroism. He immediately lobbied Daniels and

Wilson for permission to become a naval officer. Following in Uncle Ted's footsteps — resign as assistant secretary, become a war hero, and then run for higher office — was a compelling fantasy that TR encouraged Franklin to embrace. "You must get into uniform at once," he urged Franklin. Not content to leave the fighting to younger men, the fifty-eight-year-old TR, despite failing health that would end his life in January 1919, asked Wilson to let him organize a volunteer division for combat in France. He was confident that thousands of patriots would flock to his standard. Sensing that his days were numbered, he thought he "could do this country most good by dying in a reasonably honorable fashion at the head of my division in the European War." Wilson refused, telling TR, "The Western Front was no 'Charge of the Light Brigade.' " Wilson also rejected Franklin's request, arguing that he would be called upon for invaluable war work in his current position. "Neither you nor I nor Franklin Roosevelt have the right to select the place of service to which our country has assigned us," Wilson told Daniels.

For over a year after the United States entered the war, Franklin remained in Washington working feverishly to mobilize, supply, and deploy American naval forces. His letters to Eleanor during her retreats to Campobello and Hyde Park during the summer and fall of 1917 are a record of the active social life of a patrician on the make. In that correspondence he did not, however, express any concern about the political repression that became part of the domestic wartime policy aimed against dissenting voices and German ethnics suspected of sympathy for the fatherland. Shutting down German language courses in high schools, renaming sauerkraut "liberty cabbage" and frankfurters "hot dogs" did nothing to promote battlefield success, but Franklin was an uncomplaining advocate of the need for unqualified patriotism. If he had doubts about the wisdom of such knee-jerk censorship, he wasn't going to risk the political criticism a dissent would provoke. He also supported a 1917 Espionage Act barring any promotion of disloyalty — however vaguely defined that term was — and a 1918 law against sedition forbidding "disloyal, profane, scurrilous, or abusive language" attacking the U.S. government or its Constitution. As with the abuses the Marines committed in Haiti, he offered no objections to the suppression of civil liberties and occasional violence by vigilantes.

Although he found himself "so rushed" that he couldn't find time "to think quietly," and "inexpressibly busy" with "something new turning up every minute," his inability to significantly affect the war effort greatly frustrated him. He worried that German submarines would cross the Atlantic and attack East Coast harbors with the loss of essential ships. In July, he wrote Eleanor, who was in Campobello, "If by any perfectly wild chance a German submarine should come into the bay and start to shell Eastport or Pool, I want you to grab the children and beat it into the woods. . . . I am not joking about this, for while it is 500 to 1 against the possibility, still there is just that one chance that the Bosch will do the fool and unexpected thing." He argued for the rapid building of fifty-foot patrol boats to meet this cross-Atlantic threat. But Daniels and Navy admirals refused to make Franklin's proposal a high priority. They did not share his sense of urgency about potential attacks and preferred allotting scarce resources to the construction of destroyers and 110-foot boats that could be of greater service than the smaller crafts.

Franklin's greater frustration, however, was his inability to persuade American and British naval authorities to adopt a plan for a North Sea mine barrier that might bottle up German subs in their home ports. Franklin wanted the British to seed a 240-mile area between the northeastern tip of Scotland and Norway with mines that would prevent the subs from entry to the Atlantic, where in the opening months of 1917 they had taken a frightful toll on Allied shipping. The losses were so severe that British chiefs feared that left unchecked, they could cost them the war, but still viewed Roosevelt's proposal as too impractical to work at an acceptable cost. Instead, they opted to deploy convoys: concentrations of merchant vessels escorted by destroyers prepared to counter sub attacks, which in fact greatly reduced Allied losses. In the fall of 1917, however, Roosevelt's persistence in pressing the case for the mines paid off when British and American chiefs agreed to test the idea. A functioning system of mines, however, did not become fully operational until October 1918, a month before the end of the war.

Because war work in Washington couldn't satisfy his yearning for action, Franklin persuaded Daniels in the summer of 1918 to let him inspect the fighting fronts. The tour was intended as much to advance his political ambitions as it was the combat effort, and for him it was the high point of the war. Daniels instructed him to examine the financial aspects of all U.S. naval activities, including leases and contracts with local authorities; to coordinate all naval activities with British and French officials; report on general conditions abroad as they applied to the Navy; and investigate anything else he considered advisable. Franklin's presence may have raised the morale of the military and civilian authorities he met in Britain and France, but the tour was ultimately more an indulgence of his own desire to get close to the fighting than anything that added significantly to the war effort.

For the crossing to Europe, Franklin chose a newly commissioned destroyer on convoy duty and watched with keen interest as the crew assumed battle stations during drills and one false sighting of a submarine. In Britain, he met with the highest U.S. and British naval officers, King George V, British prime minister Lloyd George, and other members of the war cabinet, who urged him to go to Rome to persuade the Italians to coordinate naval operations in the Mediterranean with their British and French counterparts. It was during this trip that he also met Winston Churchill, who was then minister of munitions. Later Churchill didn't recall their meeting, which annoyed Franklin, who nevertheless understood that, as a relatively minor official, he made no particular impression on the British leader.

Crossing the Channel to France brought him in direct contact with the battlefields, which were the most exciting moments of his trip. French officialdom was no less welcoming than the British of TR's relative, but meetings with President Raymond Poincaré, Premier Georges Clemenceau, Marshall Joseph Joffre, and General Ferdinand Foch could not exceed the thrill of visiting the battlefronts at Château-Thierry and Belleau

Wood, where "villages had been badly wrecked by artillery fire." He threaded his "way past water-filled shell holes" into a field with "rusty bayonets, broken guns, emergency ration tins, hand grenades, discarded overcoats, rain-stained love-letters, crawling lines of ants and many mounds," the final resting place of fallen troops, "some wholly unmarked, some with a rifle stuck bayonet down in the earth, some with a helmet, and some, too, with a whittled cross with a tag of wood or wrapping paper hung over it and in pencil scrawl an American name." He saw "a number of dead Boche in the fields and in one place a little pile of them awaiting burial." He was close enough to the retreating German forces to fire one of the French 155 batteries at them. For him, it was "a thoroughly successful day."

Franklin returned home in September, exhausted and ill with double pneumonia and the Spanish flu. He had to be carried from the ship on a stretcher when he arrived in New York and was lucky to survive the pandemic, which took millions of lives. He remained in New York convalescing at his mother's home until mid-October. During that time he wrote a report that validated his lengthy trip to Europe by suggestions for improved operations abroad; Daniels pronounced it illuminating and passed it along to Wilson.

Shortly after his return to the States, a personal crisis threatened his marriage and political future. For perhaps two years beginning in 1916, he had been engaged in an extramarital affair with twenty-five-year-old Lucy Mercer, Eleanor's social secretary. A beautiful, poised, engaging young woman from a Social Register family, Lucy apparently offered Franklin an escape from dealing with a demanding mother, a somewhat joyless marriage, and five children between the ages of ten and a few months.

Alice Roosevelt Longworth, TR's daughter and a prominent Washington presence known for her caustic humor, was privy to Franklin's secret, and he didn't hesitate to bring Lucy with him to dinners at her home. Alice took special pleasure in discovering the foibles of Washington's high and mighty: "If you haven't got anything good to say about anyone, come sit by me," she would tell guests. No fan of Eleanor's, she did more than hint publicly at Franklin's affair, telling close friends, Franklin "deserved a good time. He was married to Eleanor." When Alice, who had a terrible marriage herself and maliciously enjoyed making Eleanor uncomfortable, tried to tell her Franklin's secret, Eleanor refused to listen. "She inquired if you had told me," Eleanor wrote Franklin, "and I said no and that I did not believe in knowing things which your husband did not wish you to know so I think I will be spared any mysterious secrets!" But Eleanor had her suspicions, and in July 1917, when Franklin insisted that she go to Campobello without him, she protested that he wanted her out of town. "You were a goosy girl to think or even pretend to think that I don't want you here *all* the summer, because you know I do!" he wrote her.

Franklin's "secret" became evident to Eleanor in September 1918, when while unpacking his baggage, she found a cache of love letters between him and Lucy exchanged during his time abroad. Was he so careless in the midst of his debilitated state as to forget the letters, or was he eager that

118

Eleanor learn the truth so that he might free himself to marry Lucy? Hurt and furious, Eleanor angrily offered Franklin a divorce, but both Sara and Louis Howe warned him that taking such a step could mean a bleak future. Sara threatened to withhold the subsidies she had been providing, and Howe predicted that it would mean the end of his political career. Howe also attempted to convince Eleanor to understand that Franklin would be bereft without her. Reasoned calculation prevailed: Franklin promised to cut off all contacts with Lucy (a promise he broke toward the end of his life) and to be more attentive to her and the children. Eleanor apparently also refused to have future intimacy with her husband. It was a terrible punishment for the thirty-six-year-old Franklin, but he accepted it, at least for the time being, as the price of reclaiming his family and career. Eleanor would never again speak the name Lucy, even if it belonged to someone other than Franklin's lover.

As part of the reconciliation and to discourage gossip about their strained marriage, Franklin invited Eleanor to join him on a trip to Europe in January 1919. With the war over in November, Daniels sent Franklin to administer the return and/or distribution of U.S. naval stores in Britain and France. The trip served as a kind of second honeymoon for the Roosevelts, a chance to renew the affection of their relations fourteen years earlier. To the friends and relatives they saw in London and Paris, they "had never seemed so gay together." But as Eleanor's biographer Blanche Wiesen Cook explains, between 1918 and 1920, the marriage problems had triggered depression and bulimia in Eleanor. She had little appetite, frequently vomited after eating, and struggled with loose teeth and sore gums. "She felt profoundly tired, suffered headaches, and had days when she wondered about her will to live," Cook writes. In the midst of her suffering, however, she resolved to forge a more independent life in which she devoted herself to larger causes like the League of Nations than to herself or her family.

Franklin had his share of difficulties as well. A downturn in Wilson's standing, marked by his party's loss of Congress in 1918 and Republican opposition to his peace settlement and the League of Nations, cast a shadow over the entire administration. The collapse of Wilson's health in the fall from a disabling stroke only added to the sense that Democrats would lose control of the White House and Republican majorities in Congress would be very likely in 1920. More directly, a scandal involving the entrapment of homosexual sailors threatened Franklin's political ambitions. Reports that commanders at the Newport, Rhode Island, naval base had court-martialed the sailors moved Franklin to set up an investigative unit to lure other homosexuals into revealing their "lewd behavior." When a Navy chaplain was caught in the trap and a trial followed in which the unit's actions were revealed, Episcopal Church authorities in the state demanded that the official responsible for the entrapment policy be dismissed. Although Franklin denied knowledge of the unit's methods, a Navy court reprimanded him for an "ill-advised" initiative.

Other problems dogged him as well. In the winter of 1919–20, he suffered lingering effects from the flu, accompanied by sinusitis and tonsillitis. He also clashed with Daniels. When Admiral

William S. Sims testified before a Republican-controlled congressional subcommittee on the Navy Department's faulty war preparations, Franklin chimed in with a speech largely confirming Sims's complaints. Daniels felt betrayed, and the White House also took notice of Franklin's criticism. His open friendship with British Ambassador Lord Grey, who had enraged the ailing president and Mrs. Wilson by refusing to dismiss an embassy official they claimed had slandered the president's wife, made Franklin the object of their animus as well. Mrs. Wilson told Daniels that she "hated" Franklin Roosevelt.

Franklin became so convinced that his career in public office had come to an end that in March 1920 he agreed to set up a law practice with two friends, Langdon Marvin and Grenville T. Emmet. His participation as a full partner in the firm, however, would have to wait a year until he left the Navy Department. But whether he would actually join the practice at all came into question as a result of political developments in the summer of 1920.

Despite diminished Democratic prospects in 1919–20, Franklin foresaw a return of progressive reform after a cycle of conservative rule. If he were to advance his career, he realized, he would have to position himself at the forefront of his party as a sort of heir to the throne in waiting. In 1918 Wilson and Daniels had encouraged him to run for the governorship of New York, advice he and Howe had then rejected — and not because they feared Tammany's opposition, which had undermined his Senate bid in 1914. After that defeat, he and Howe had agreed that Tammany's support would best serve his path forward. In

1917, he had spoken at Tammany's July 4 annual Independence Day celebration, where to the delight of his audience, he had announced that "if Tammany could stand to have him, he could stand to come." He further cemented his ties to Tammany by endorsing Al Smith, a machine mainstay, for governor. Franklin's actual reluctance to put himself forward for the governorship in 1918 rested on a concern that he would be attacked for abandoning his Navy post and that a gubernatorial campaign would prevent him from making the tour of the battlefields that could underscore his war service. In addition, he anticipated Republican gains that year and did not want to risk entering a losing race. Although Smith, running against a Republican tide, won the office, Franklin did not regret his decision. He considered his tour of the fighting fronts invaluable.

By 1919, his Navy work and presence in Paris at the Versailles Conference had generated enough national visibility and positive publicity to make him a potential vice-presidential nominee. In May, he had boosted his standing with a fiery attack on Republican conservatism in a speech before the Democratic National Committee in Chicago. The 1920 contest, he declared, would be between "conservatism, special privilege, partisanship, destruction on the one hand — liberalism, commonsense idealism, constructiveness, progress on the other." Although this progressive rallying cry had enjoyed popular support for almost twenty years, dating back to TR's presidency, it no longer resonated with the public: Disappointed hopes of a peace without victors and a brave new world without war had soured Americans on reform crusades. The popular impulse encouraging civic participation was giving way to national apathy.

Nonetheless, Franklin struck resonant chords with faithful Wilsonians, who for the moment continued to shape the party's platform. The boss-run Republican nominating convention in June, with the so-called "smoke-filled room" deal that resulted in the bland senator Warren G. Harding of Ohio being named its presidential nominee, was effectively a repudiation of TR's progressivism, which made Franklin's appeal within the Democratic Party more compelling. Mindful that Roosevelt, who had made his peace with Tammany, could be instrumental in gaining New York's essential electoral votes for Ohio's progressive governor James M. Cox, the party's presidential nominee, the convention made Franklin its vice-presidential standard-bearer.

Franklin's nomination received mixed reviews. Some, like the prominent journalist Walter Lippmann, praised the choice as giving politics a better name and "a decent future." It was an effective answer to cynics who were asking, "What is the use?" Herbert Hoover, the millionaire mining engineer and philanthropist, who had established a reputation as a progressive Republican, called Franklin's selection "a contribution to the good of the country." But other Republicans were not as generous. The young "boyish" Franklin seemed "a little silly in his exuberance," one of them wrote Massachusetts senator Henry Cabot Lodge. "He is a well-meaning, nice young fellow, but light," Lodge replied. "His head [is] evidently turned and the effect upon a not very strong man is obvious."

Wilson, who despite his physical collapse wanted a third-term nomination, also judged the Cox-

Roosevelt ticket to be without much merit. Told of the convention's choices, he erupted in "a stream of obscenities and profanities," calling the fifty-year-old former newspaper publisher and three-time governor of Ohio "a nonentity and a mediocrity." He regarded thirty-eight-year-old Roosevelt as "affable and deferential but also a bit bumptious." Wilson believed that they would shun him in the campaign as an unpopular failure and electoral liability: Economic dislocations at home and disarray abroad had created "bitterness toward Wilson . . . everywhere. He hasn't a friend," an aide told Roosevelt. But disregarding his diminished standing, Cox asked to meet with him, which he and Franklin did on the south lawn of the White House on July 18. The president, paralyzed on his left side, sat in a wheelchair. A shawl covered his left shoulder and arm and the left side of his face "leaned slack-jawed upon his chest." When Cox, who was moved to tears by Wilson's appearance, told him that they were "a million percent with you and your Administration, and that means the League of Nations," Wilson whispered his appreciation. "I am very grateful. I am very grateful."

Vice-presidential campaigns typically command limited attention, and Franklin's was no exception. With not even a wire service reporting on him, Franklin's appearances produced only local news stories, but this did not discourage him from traveling widely across the Northeast, Midwest, and West, where in three months he gave as many as a thousand speeches. When an aide "asked him if he had any illusions that he might be elected," Franklin replied, "Nary an illusion." Nonetheless, the campaign for him was exciting: Traveling on a private railway car, meeting Democratic Party officials across the country who could help him in any future elections, speaking to enthusiastic crowds that cheered him, and enjoying the camaraderie of associates with whom he shared long days and evenings, often playing poker, was fun. One press aide dismissed him as a playboy on a lark.

Whatever the results, the campaign gave him an excellent schooling in national politics: He learned how to read public mood and how to conduct future political races. Most of all, he successfully presented himself to the public as a party leader who would be counted as a future presidential candidate, especially because having another Roosevelt in the White House had widespread appeal. An engineer on his campaign train said, "That lad's got 'a million vote smile' — and mine's going to be one of them." The campaign also schooled Eleanor in the art of politics and heightened her respect for Howe, who took pains to include her in the day-to-day work of the speech-making and appeals to voters as they traveled together on a cross-country train.

Harding's victory did not surprise Roosevelt, and only the degree of the defeat shocked him: 61 percent of the popular vote for so undynamic an individual. Franklin ascribed it to the "materialism and conservatism" that follow every war. "People tire quickly of ideals and we are now repeating history," he observed. He told Cox that another Democrat would not win the White House until the country faced a fairly serious economic downturn. He could not know how prophetic his words were.

CHAPTER 3
POLIO

In 1921, a future run for high office was the primary focus of Franklin's long-term ambitions. Because it might be several years before times favored another electoral bid, he had to take on intermediate work that would ease the financial burdens of a lavish lifestyle and educating his now five children: Upkeep on the East 65th Street mansion in Manhattan, the Hyde Park estate, and the Campobello home; payments to servants who helped Eleanor manage a household with children between the ages of five and fifteen; and private school fees that required more than trust fund payments and Sara's generosity could provide. But he also needed a job that would leave time for activities ensuring public visibility. He spent half-days in the law firm he had formed with Langdon Marvin and Grenville Emmet, and the other half as vice president in charge of the New York office of the Fidelity and Deposit Company of Maryland, a surety and bonding corporation. While these positions largely satisfied his financial requirements, he took on his new assignments with limited enthusiasm. Neither law practice nor insurance sales excited his interest or served as a platform for making a lasting mark on the country.

He took greater satisfaction from a host of civic activities that gave him standing as a Good Samaritan eager to serve the public well-being. Working with the Boy Scout Foundation of Greater New York, Lighthouses for the Blind, the National Civic Foundation, the Harvard University Board of Overseers, and the Woodrow Wilson Memorial Foundation gave him continuing visibility as a civic-minded patrician devoted to worthy causes.

His choice of groups was revealing. He could have identified himself with any number of charitable or nonprofit organizations, all of which would have kept his name before the public as a prelude to another run for office and would also have satisfied his sense of noblesse oblige. The charitable work he did select was a window on his inner life: Like TR, Franklin saw the Boy Scouts as a training ground for manly activities — learning self-reliance and preparing oneself for the competition so central to American life. Communing with nature and conserving the environment were other passions he shared with Uncle Ted and were part of the Scouts' credo. Lighthouses was an organization devoted to severely impaired citizens. Helping the blind meant serving those least able to make their way in the world, and Franklin's compassion for victims of so severe a disability was testimony to his priorities. The country, especially its most advantaged citizens, should be attentive to people in greatest need.

His service to Harvard gave him credentials as a loyal alumnus who could turn to other elite Harvard graduates for support in future political campaigns and as a civic-minded backer of higher education. As for the Wilson Memorial Foundation, Franklin's chairmanship secured his credentials as a loyal Democrat. Although Wilson objected to the word "memorial," which suggested he was already deceased (he would pass away in February 1924), Franklin viewed it as a tacit acknowledgment that Wilson's progressivism and universalism were now passé. By including the word "Memorial," he was not implying that Wilsonian idealism had been permanently abandoned, but that for the moment it was out of sync with the public's mood. He and the party would have to bide their time until Americans became receptive to another round of reform.

All of Franklin's recent activities demonstrated his keen reading of the current national sentiment. In the 1920s, standing as a lawyer and financier resonated with the affinity for private gain. The value of philanthropy, rather than government largess, was also in keeping with the public mood. Few in America believed that Soviet Communism, which many in Europe saw as a model for a more humane society and a better future, was a worthy competitor to free enterprise. Franklin didn't need polls, which did not come into vogue until the mid-1930s, to assess the contemporary political climate. He instinctively understood that popular sentiment was a blend of many impulses and was like the atmosphere: You couldn't touch, see, hear, taste, or smell it, but it was part of the national landscape, which could change at any time. One of Franklin's later prodigies, Lyndon B. Johnson, Texas congressman, senator, vice president, and president after John F. Kennedy's assassination, reflected Franklin's understanding when, in his characteristically crude way, he told a reporter that "in politics, overnight chicken shit can turn to chicken salad." Johnson's language was never Roosevelt's, but by 1921, Franklin recognized what a successful career in American politics required.

In the spring and summer of 1921, although Franklin and Howe were considering a possible 1922 U.S. Senate campaign, high office was a mirage on the horizon. Settling into his new work routine and blunting an ongoing Senate subcommittee attack on his part in the Navy's response to the Newport scandal commanded his attention. In the middle of July, he returned to Washington to refute committee accusations that he had organized and directed the entrapment of homosexual sailors by "disgraceful" actions. Although the allegations ended up as one-day newspaper stories having little resonance, the anxiety of having to deal with such unpleasantness drained his energies. At the end of July, he welcomed the opportunity to escape a steamy Manhattan for a Boy Scout outing in upstate New York at Bear Mountain, where he acted as a toastmaster. When he arrived at Hyde Park on July 29, his secretary Marguerite (Missy) LeHand thought he seemed exhausted, worn down by the tensions over the Newport case, the summer heat, and the demands of performing at the Boy Scout conclave. He was more than ready to escape to Campobello on August 5 by sailing to Maine with friends on a 140-foot power yacht docked in New York harbor. As the most experienced sailor aboard, Franklin took the helm to steer the yacht through treacherous crosscurrents along the Maine coast — an exhilarating but exhausting task that brought the crew safely into harbor on August 8.

When he woke early on the morning of August 9, he faced another day of nonstop activity that further tested his reserves of energy. Deep-sea fishing with his friends on the power yacht occupied the hours from dawn to late afternoon, and during the outing, he slipped overboard while moving back and forth on the slippery deck and had to be helped back onto the boat. The water was "so cold," he said, "it seemed paralyzing." It was an apt metaphor, for apparently at some point in the previous two weeks, the incubation period for poliovirus, he had contracted the potentially crippling disease. At that time, less than 1 percent of infected adults the age of thirty and older suffered lasting damage. The thirty-nine-year-old Roosevelt was one of the unlucky few.

Today our much greater understanding of the disease suggests that Franklin's weariness had weakened his immune system and facilitated the virus's path through his body. On August 10, despite feeling "oddly depleted," he began another day of nonstop physical activity: sailing with Eleanor and the older children on his twenty-five-foot yacht; joining volunteers to beat back a fire on a nearby island; and trotting a mile and a half from the Roosevelts' home across the three-mile-wide Campobello to a swimming hole, followed by another run to a beach for a dip in the ocean, and a final run back to the house. Feeling totally spent, achy and chilled, Franklin skipped dinner and went to bed.

A devotee of cousin Theodore's "Strenuous Life," Franklin, despite periodic bouts of illness, prided himself on his physical stamina and healthy living, which allowed him to follow a regimen of hard work and rigorous exercise. He could not imagine a life without sailing, fishing, golfing, horseback riding, and hiking. Surely, he was suffering from nothing more than a bad cold or flu and would recover as quickly as he had from past afflictions.

On the morning of August 11, he was running a 102-degree temperature and complained of severe pain in the back of both legs. The doctor from the nearby village of Lubec, Maine, thought he was dealing with "a nasty summer cold." By the next morning, though, the pain was worse, and by evening, Franklin had lost the ability to stand; he was paralyzed from the waist down. Louis Howe, who had agreed to work for Franklin again after ending his Navy Department service, was living with his family on Campobello. Franklin's worsening condition alarmed him and Eleanor. Accurately guessing that he could find a specialist vacationing in one of Maine's coastal cities, which were a magnet for wealthy northeastern businessmen and professionals, Howe reached a Dr. William Keen, an eighty-four-year-old surgeon and faculty member of Philadelphia's Jefferson Medical College, who had performed surgery on President Grover Cleveland. Keen readily agreed to make the 101-mile trip from Bar Harbor to see Franklin.

Arriving on Saturday evening, August 13, Keen performed a close examination, which persuaded him that a blood clot had formed in Franklin's lower spine. The good news, however, was that it would dissolve in time, though it might take several months, after which Franklin could expect to be as mobile as ever. In the meantime, Keen instructed Eleanor and Howe to massage Franklin's legs vigorously to help dissolve the clot. In a 2013 book that persuasively reconstructs the onset and course of Roosevelt's illness, James Tobin concludes that "Keen's judgment was wrong in every detail." The massaging caused "excruciating" pain and may have further damaged Franklin's leg muscles, though it could also have averted life-threatening clots. Less than a week after his visit, Keen changed his diagnosis, writing Eleanor that the problem was probably not a clot but an inflammation of the spinal cord that would take many months to subside. He was mistaken about this as well.

In the meantime, Howe, who had a variety of health problems and whose own experience with many physicians had made him a skeptic about medical judgments, saw the need for another opinion. Keen, after all, was a surgeon, not a diagnostician. Howe wisely viewed Keen's assessment as vague and was concerned that he had already changed his diagnosis. Howe reached out to Fred Delano, Franklin's uncle, who immediately got in touch with a Dr. Parker in Washington, D.C. Parker thought that the illness might be infantile paralysis, a disease that normally afflicted children, but was not unknown in adults. He advised Delano to consult with specialists on poliomyelitis at Boston's Peter Bent Brigham Hospital. Delano rushed to Boston, where he met with Dr. Samuel Levine, a young physician who had observed numerous polio cases. Levine recommended an immediate spinal tap, which could clarify the diagnosis.

When Eleanor told Keen of Levine's advice, he "very strenuously" objected to the proposal for a lumbar puncture, though he called Dr. Robert Lovett, one of the medical directors of the Brigham Infantile Paralysis Clinic, who agreed to travel to Campobello. His examination of Franklin on August 24 convinced him of the need for the spinal tap, almost two weeks after Franklin had first manifested symptoms of illness. The results — cloudy spinal fluid signaling a concentration of white blood cells and an infection — made it "perfectly clear" that Franklin's paralysis was caused by poliomyelitis. Could Franklin regain the use of his legs? Would he ever walk again unaided or would he face a life of immobility? Lovett explained that no one could give definitive answers to these questions so early in the course of the illness, but his experience with the disease indicated that Franklin did not have the "severest type" and that "disability was not to be feared," apparently meaning that Franklin would somehow be able to get around. Whether out of dogged optimism in response to Lovett's assessment or a desire to put on a brave face to the world so that he would not be out of consideration as a future officeholder, Franklin wrote his law partner Langdon Marvin: "I am almost wholly out of commission as to my legs but the doctors say that there is no question that I will get their use back again though this means several months of treatment in New York."

On September 14 a crew of six carried Franklin on a stretcher to a waiting boat for the trip across Passamaquoddy Bay to Eastport, Maine, where he was transferred to a baggage cart and wheeled to a waiting train. Passed through a window that had been removed and then reinstalled before reporters could catch a view of the smiling Franklin lying in a compartment, the patient gave the impression, reinforced by the comments of the physician accompanying him, that he was temporarily immobilized and would make a full recovery from his current affliction. The overnight journey of approximately 550 miles brought Franklin into Grand Central Station on the afternoon of September 15. As Tom Lynch, a Poughkeepsie friend and supporter of Franklin's past campaigns, watched porters transfer him to a waiting ambulance for the brief thirty-seven-block ride to Presbyterian Hospital at Madison Avenue and 70th Street, he marveled at the patient's cheerfulness — smiling and calling out to Lynch to ride with him uptown. It was all part of an orchestrated effort to hide the full extent of Franklin's disability.

Because he was a defeated vice-presidential candidate who seemed intent on following in his uncle Ted's path to the White House, the press had a keen interest in Franklin's health. The day after he returned to New York, the *New York Times* ran a front-page story under the headline: "F.D. ROOSEVELT ILL OF POLIOMYELITIS . . . Patient stricken by Infantile Paralysis A Month Ago and Use of Legs Affected." The article cited Dr. George Draper, Roosevelt's Harvard classmate and expert on polio, as the lead physician on the case. Draper told the *Times* that Franklin was "recovering" and "definitely . . . will not be crippled." There would be no "permanent injury from this attack." While in the hospital, Franklin wrote *Times* publisher Adolph S. Ochs that he was on his way to a full recovery and was already taking "up part of my somewhat varied interests." When Josephus Daniels came to visit him and reached out to shake Franklin's hand, Franklin delivered a blow to his chest. "You thought you were coming to see an invalid," Franklin exclaimed. "But I can knock you out in any bout." Whatever his actual condition, he was determined to create the impression that he was only temporarily laid low.

Although Draper felt it was important to buoy Franklin's spirits with rosy predictions that would keep the seriousness of his condition from the public, he worried privately that Franklin was deluding himself. Doing so was fine for the time being as a defense against despair that his political career was finished, but eventually he would have to face the reality of his disability. The hard truth became more evident over the next six weeks when Franklin showed little improvement during his hospital stay. At the end of October, his legs were as paralyzed as when he arrived. Because there was no benefit from remaining in the hospital and the prescribed physical therapy could be administered at home, he was moved by ambulance to his 65th Street residence, where he was carried to a second-floor bedroom, the quietest part of the house.

During his six weeks in the hospital, Draper, Eleanor, Howe, and Sara feared that Franklin might never be able to sit up, and if he managed to get past that hurdle, he would still have to accept that he would never walk again without the aid of crutches and would need a wheelchair to get around. Draper told Lovett, "He has such courage, such ambition, and yet at the same time such an extraordinary sensitive emotional mechanism that it will take all the skill we can muster to lead him successfully to a recognition of what he really faces without crushing him." To his doctors' relief, however, by the time he returned home Franklin had skirted the worst outcome: He had regained the ability to sit up. Though he remained paralyzed from the waist down, his doctors assured him that he could have an erection and was capable of intercourse. Still, they worried that when he understood how damaged his legs actually were, he would fall into a deep depression.

Over the next few months, as the extent of Franklin's disability became increasingly apparent, he instead devoted himself to regaining some measure of mobility. In January 1922, he began a regimen of crawling around the floor of his bedroom or up the one flight from the dining room to his bedroom while dragging his lifeless legs behind him. But this small expedient was temporarily lost when his leg muscles became so atrophied that they bent backward. To stretch the tendons and straighten the legs, his doctors put them in plaster casts at the cost of excruciating pain. Two weeks of this torture, which he bore stoically, produced the needed change. But the episode clearly demonstrated to the doctors, Eleanor, and Howe, who now lived with them at 65th Street, that his legs were permanently damaged. Only fourteen-pound steel braces on each of his lower limbs and the use of crutches would enable him to walk unassisted, and mastering these devices would require substantial practice.

A conflict soon erupted between Eleanor and Sara about Franklin's future. Eleanor believed that "his very life depended . . . on his ability to remain active, interested, and ambitious in public life." She did everything possible to keep him abreast of current events before him, inviting former political associates to visit and discuss the news of the day. She brought newspaper stories to his attention and looked for editorials that might stimulate his interest. She strongly supported a decision to make New York rather than Hyde Park their principal residence and encouraged Franklin's intention to resume his business activities. In Campobello, she had slept on a couch in his bedroom, partly to allay his understandable fears of a fire that would leave him trapped in his bed. While she performed nursing duties — giving sponge baths, shifting his positions to prevent bed sores, administering catheters and enemas, massaging his back and legs, shaving him, and brushing his teeth — she would discuss national and international developments to distract him from the humiliation he felt at having lost his physical independence. Her attentiveness restored some of the affection that had marked the start of their relationship, and the focus on public affairs formed something of an education that would transform her future.

By contrast with Eleanor, Sara was determined to guard Franklin from additional health problems and future disappointments in trying to resume his political career. Insensitive to everyone else's perception that a life of inactivity would devastate her son, she tried to persuade him to retire to Hyde Park and lead the life of a country gentleman. After all, she argued, he already had a record of accomplishment in the New York State Senate, the Navy Department, and in a run for the vice presidency. He had his hobbies, money would not be a problem, and he would not lack for social exchange among the many rich and famous people he knew, who would all be welcome guests

137

at the Hudson River retreat.

In her determination to protect Franklin from the perils of trying to resume a normal life, Sara only added to Eleanor's already heavy burdens of buoying Franklin's spirits and managing their large household. "That old lady with all her charm and distinction and kindliness hides a primitive jealousy of her daughter-in-law which is sometimes startling in its crudity," a family friend recalled. Eleanor later said of Sara: "She dominated me for years," but Franklin's illness "made me stand on my own two feet in regard to my husband's life, my own life, and my children's training." Without the crisis, "I might have stayed a weak character forever."

Eleanor urged Sara to see how essential Franklin's business, philanthropic, and political activities in New York were to his well-being. But Sara believed that she knew better than either Eleanor or Howe — who, as in the 1920 campaign, was Eleanor's ally in the battle over Franklin's future — what was best for her son. She thought that if she could remove Howe, who disgusted her, from the household, she would have one less obstacle to settling Franklin in Hyde Park. She urged Franklin to take his distance from "that ugly, dirty little man," a remark that angered Franklin, who shared Eleanor's view that he had been a godsend during the most trying days of his illness. "Thank heavens [Louis] is here," Eleanor said during the initial siege at Campobello, "for he has been the greatest help." Sara also stirred up trouble between Eleanor and Anna, the oldest Roosevelt child, now fifteen, by enlisting Anna in her campaign against Howe.

Sara could not dispute that Howe was devoted

to Franklin: He had turned down lucrative job offers after leaving the Navy Department to continue working for the man he believed would someday become America's president. She recognized that Howe's devotion to Franklin rested on his own self-interest. Howe was no altruist, but a tough-minded realist. His ambition for Franklin expressed his deep personal need, but it was never at odds with Franklin's own strivings. While the work of advancing Franklin's career would simultaneously boost Howe, his astuteness about New York and national politics was vital to Franklin's bid for high office.

Sara complained of Howe's "exploitive ambition" and intrusion by accepting Franklin and Eleanor's invitation to live in the 65th Street mansion. But for Franklin the arrangement was a way to compensate Howe for the larger salaries offered him by a New York newspaper and an oil company. His presence in the household also continued to be a help to Eleanor, who relied on him not only for some of the physical chores involved in caring for Franklin but also in keeping Franklin's hopes alive for a future in politics. For his part Franklin described Howe as "my go-between" in his dealings with his law firm and the surety company. He greatly enjoyed Howe's irreverence, and his sense of humor brightened Franklin's days. A note, for example, from Howe reporting that Eleanor had directed him to go to Tiffany's to buy a watch put a smile on Franklin's face: "Lord knows," Howe wrote, "I have acted as your alter-ego in many weird commissions, but I must refuse to risk my judgment on neckties, watches or pajamas."

■ ■ ■ ■

Howe, who continued to think of himself as uniquely ugly, validated psychologist Alfred Adler's description of the "inferiority complex." Adler explained that an individual like Howe compensated for his physical imperfections with grandiose ambitions or "superiority striving" to be a kingmaker if not a king. Howe could never see himself standing before an audience as himself. Acting in amateur theater productions or taking a part at center stage in some other venture, however, had special appeal, as there he could be the heroic figure he could never be in real life. Franklin, the handsome patrician whose appearance and standing could bring millions of voters to his side, was the ideal man for Howe to make the object of his ambition, mentoring him to facilitate a crowning achievement.

Howe devoted himself to keeping news and images of Franklin's disability to a minimum. He shared with Franklin the conviction that their joint aspirations meant maintaining the public view of Franklin as physically strong and youthful. Even before he left the hospital, he began dictating letters to Missy LeHand to keep up contacts around the country, especially with leaders of the Democratic Party. No one reading these missives would think that he was the slightest bit downcast or was anything but optimistic about planning a prompt return to public affairs. Both he and Howe sensed that exposing his condition might generate a certain amount of voter sympathy, but was more likely to turn electors toward a leader who seemed more physically capable of meeting any and every challenge. They believed they needed to appeal to American enchantment with good-looking matinee idols like Warren G. Harding, who had won the White House in 1920 in spite of questions about his intelligence and capacity to lead the nation.

Ultimately, though, decisions about Franklin's future rested with him. Supported by Eleanor and Howe and encouraged by his physicians to lead as normal a life as possible, in December 1921, he started a daily exercise program with a physical therapist, who told his doctor that Franklin was "a wonderful patient, very cheerful, and works awfully hard." He rejected suggestions, however, that he begin the arduous challenge of walking with crutches, almost as if that would be an implicit acceptance of the fact that he would never walk again unaided. Three months later, though, in March 1922, he acknowledged that he needed steel braces on his lower limbs to help him stand, and crutches to move forward. He continued to hold out hope of regaining feeling in his legs below the knees, but he now embraced the freedom that crutches gave him to move unassisted. He also accepted the need for a wheelchair as another means of regaining mobility but rejected the conventional models. Instead, he designed his own conveyance, an armless kitchen chair mounted on wheels, which was easier to get into and lacked the large side wheels that revealed the user's immobility. Although he could not propel himself with just the rollers beneath the chair's legs, and had to rely on someone to push him, the image of him sitting on a straight-backed chair served his and Howe's efforts to mask his disability.

During the summer of 1922, he fled the city's

heat for Hyde Park, where he launched a new exercise regime to build up his upper torso and create the impression of a middle-aged man in robust good health. Using rings suspended above his bed and parallel bars on the lawn, he practiced pull-ups to develop sufficient arm strength to walk on crutches down the quarter-mile driveway to the main Albany Post road running by the house. The strenuous routine soon gave him the appearance of a practiced weightlifter.

In October he returned to his office at the Fidelity and Deposit Company, where he insisted on walking from his chauffeured car to the building's elevators. He was overly optimistic about his mastery of the crutches, and while moving across the lobby, he slipped on the marble floor and landed on his back. Some of the onlookers rushed to help him sit up, but he waved them off with a smile and assurances that he was fine. Determined to maintain some semblance of independence, he righted himself and only then asked for assistance to stand and resume his labored walk.

For the next two years, he continued to serve as a nominal partner at Fidelity. Bored by his association with the Emmett-Marvin law firm, he started his own law office with Basil O'Connor, a brilliant young man with a Harvard law degree who agreed to a partnership. O'Connor would do most of the work, while Franklin would be the rainmaker attracting clients. His business activities, however, were overshadowed by continuing efforts to restore his legs, even though it became increasingly clear that his exercise programs would never restore his muscles sufficiently to enable him to stand and walk on his own or without braces and crutches or possibly a cane. He turned to heated water therapies in pools where he could swim and even feel some sensation in his toes. These gave him buoyancy and even some ability to stand, and seemed to be the miracle cure he coveted. "The water got me into this fix," he liked to say, "and the water will get me out." Wintering off the Florida Keys in houseboats where he fished with friends in the sun raised his spirits. The days on the houseboat, he told Sara, were a constant pleasure or what he called a "somewhat negligee existence. All wander around in pajamas, nighties, and bathing suits." But Missy LeHand, who accompanied him as secretary and hostess to the guests aboard, recalled days "when it was noon before he could pull himself out of depression and greet his guests wearing his lighthearted facade." Although he was grateful for the assistance of LeRoy Jones, a black caregiver, to help him with bathing and dressing, Jones's appearance at his cabin each morning signaled anew his loss of the physical independence that had allowed him to relish walking, running, swimming, sailing, and bird watching.

As Franklin became more attached to the temporary restorative power of thermal waters, in October 1924 he decided to visit Warm Springs, Georgia, located in the Appalachian foothills between Atlanta and Columbus. He wanted "to try out a remarkable swimming pool of natural highly mineralized water . . . at a temperature of 90 degrees." He was taking his cue from George Foster Peabody, a Wall Street banker and New York Democrat, who owned an inn and a spring there that Peabody assured him could relieve various ills. He forwarded to Franklin a letter from a paralyzed teenage boy who, after three summers swimming in the spring waters, was able to walk with a cane. Franklin's visit to Warm Springs made him a convert, for after an hour in the pool, he marveled at the "wonderful" effects the mineral-laced waters had on him. Although he was advised that it would take "three weeks to show the effects," he was eager to believe that the treatment would do him "great good." He had "no doubt that I've got to do it some more," and concluded that "a great 'cure' for infantile paralysis and kindred diseases could well be established here."

His enchantment with the salutary effects of Warm Springs was so great that he decided to purchase it from Peabody and turn it into a rehabilitation center for polio sufferers. In the spring of 1926, he bought the property: the 1,200 acres of land on which the springs were situated, a group of dilapidated cottages, and a largely abandoned resort inn. Investing $200,000, or two-thirds of his fortune, in the enterprise, he now devoted himself to persuading leading orthopedic surgeons (who worried that Roosevelt was advocating medical quackery) and wealthy investors that Warm Springs could become a successful site for the healing of paraplegics. He convinced a group of physicians to test his assertions about the beneficial effects of the thermal waters on their patients. Although the chief of New York State's public health service, the principal physician reviewing the treatment of twenty-four young adults, did not attest to any miracle cures, he did believe that the springs' waters resulted in significant improvement in patient mobility and especially psychological outlook. The report gave Franklin the wherewithal to sway several philanthropists to support a Warm Springs Foundation, which began modernizing the facilities. The renovation and the health gains achieved by patients put Warm Springs on the map as the country's leading center for polio victims. Franklin's success as a more than capable executive in this venture was an early demonstration of his political and philanthropic talents.

The Warm Springs enterprise served not only the patients flocking there but also Franklin's determination to resume his political career. What motivated him to take up so daunting a challenge seems close to inexplicable. "We can never, even by the strictest examination, get completely behind the secret springs of action," Immanuel Kant observed of men's motives. Nonetheless, there are telltale indications of what drove Franklin to take on what those knowledgeable about the current political scene would have considered an impossible task. In the 1920s it was inconceivable that someone who had suffered so debilitating an illness could imagine himself assuming the burdens of high, and certainly not the highest, office. Even at that time, when presidential power was a pale image of what it would later become, the idea of a "crippled" man at the head of the American government was a step too far.

As FDR biographer James Tobin explained, Franklin's work on behalf of Warm Springs testified to his competence in achieving big goals. But nothing he accomplished at that time could quiet his "feelings of revulsion, pity, and embarrassment that his body provoked in others." If he were to run again for office, he would have to hide his disability or at a minimum distract voters from opinions many held about "cripples," whom they viewed as inferior, tragic, and maybe "even evil," a recipient of God's wrath for sinful actions.

Under the influence of his uncle Theodore, Franklin had considered a bid to become a U.S. senator or New York's governor, and ultimately president. His track record as a New York State senator, assistant secretary of the Navy, unsuccessful candidate for a U.S. Senate nomination, and a vice-presidential nominee before he was forty had established him as a Democrat with a bright political future. Encouraged by Louis Howe, whose personal desire for prominence animated his very being, Franklin clung to hopes of gaining the greatest political prize. In fact, the polio heightened his ambitions, as once it struck, he no longer needed Howe's or Eleanor's prodding to continue his career; it became an impulse or motive force in itself. "I'm not going to be conquered by a childish disease," he said repeatedly. Like Howe's physical appearance, Franklin's polio intensified his determination to achieve goals of power and superiority. His life, as Alfred Adler would have described it, became "the expectation of a great triumph" as partial compensation for the loss of his lower limbs or his sense of inferiority to others who enjoyed normal mobility.

Within weeks after polio had laid him low, he, Howe, and Eleanor began a concerted campaign to revive and advance his political career. Franklin's early letters following his illness bespoke not his suffering and potential permanent disability but expectations of recovery. Howe's effort to keep reporters from learning the extent of Franklin's disability on the trip back to New York and the *New York Times* story predicting his recovery were all part of an initial campaign to maintain the image of the youthful, vibrant Franklin intact.

His fortunes received a needed boost in December 1922, when Al Smith asked his help in running for a second term as governor. After serving in that position from 1918 to 1920, he had lost a reelection bid in the 1920 national Republican landslide. By 1922, New York voters seemed ready to reelect a progressive Democrat. But Smith, who had meanwhile become a successful business executive making substantial money for the first time in his life, was initially hesitant to enter the race again. Because he had hopes of one day becoming president, however, and understood that in order to be nominated he would have to serve another term as governor, he agreed to run. Eager to ensure the support of upstate voters, Smith turned to Franklin for an open endorsement. Having been at peace with Tammany since 1918 and regarding Smith as genuinely committed to the well-being of the state's least advantaged citizens, as well as a fine counter to the Republican Party's identification with big business and selfish interests, Franklin was ready to lend his assistance. He replied to Smith's private request for public backing in a letter that did as much to announce his own viability as a politician of consequence as to advance Smith's candidacy. "We realize that years of public service make it most desirable that you think now of your family's needs," Franklin wrote him. Shrewdly bringing himself into focus as on a par with Smith, he added: "I am in the same boat myself — yet this call for service must come first." In short, *when the time is right, I will be ready to make the same sacrifice.*

While Franklin developed the stamina to travel

and stand before audiences without appearing physically incapable of discharging the duties of office, Eleanor became a stand-in for her husband. As Blanche Wiesen Cook, her biographer, explained, in 1919, after the rejection and humiliation she suffered from Franklin's betrayal, "she felt abandoned and unlovely." She struggled to find an identity that would enable her to feel indispensable and productive. She did not want to repeat her grandmother Hall's experience of sacrificing personal fulfillment to serve her children and grandchildren. "I determined that I would never be dependent on my children by allowing all my interests to center in them," she said. Moreover, with Sara — who competed with her for the children's affection — nannies, and tutors available to assume childcare duties, she had the freedom to turn to public affairs for an arena of activity in which to seek fulfillment.

Her initial foray into politics came in the fall of 1919 on behalf of women's rights. Attending a weeklong Congress of Working Women in Washington, she had a sense of exhilaration at aligning herself with what was then considered a subversive movement. With women battling for the right to vote, which they obtained only with the ratification of the Nineteenth Amendment in August 1920, conventional views of women's subordinate place remained very much the standard. As late as 1925, when Eleanor spoke about the abuse of workingwomen with some like-minded activists, her sons listened to their conversation with indifference, if not hostility. "At lunch," Eleanor wrote Marion Dickerman, a feminist friend, "We had a discussion on trade unions. I was left, as I always am with the boys, (James, 18, Elliott, 15, Franklin, Jr., 11, and John, 9) feeling quite impotent to make a dent. . . . [They] regard me as a woman . . . [with] queer opinions [that] can't be considered seriously as against those of their usual male environment."

Eleanor's inauguration into national politics had come with her taking part in Franklin's 1920 vice-presidential campaign. Although he asked her to keep a diary on a cross-country four-week train tour from New York to Colorado, he principally wanted her at his side as an emblem of marital fidelity, certifying Franklin as an ideal family man who would appeal to the newly minted women's vote. Between stops on the trip Eleanor kept to herself, reading and looking out at the scenery. During the evenings, Franklin left her alone when he played cards and drank with his staff and the reporters covering his campaign. One day, though, Louis Howe, who was writing Franklin's speeches, chatting up the press, and advising him on all manner of subjects, invited Eleanor into the discussions. He asked her advice on speech drafts, how to persuade reporters to write favorable stories, and how to reach the greatest number of voters. For the first time, she enjoyed the political give and take of a run for office.

After polio disabled Franklin, a duality of purpose characterized Eleanor's political activities. Beginning in 1922, the excitement and satisfaction of participation in progressive causes moved her to become an active member of the League of Women Voters, the Women's Trade Union League, the Women's Division of the New York State Democratic Committee, and the Women's City Club of New York. Fund-raising, panel discussions, and campaigning for New York

Democrats also filled her days. She became an outspoken advocate of Al Smith in his bid to unseat Nathan I. Miller, the sitting governor. She led Dutchess County Democrats in nominating Smith at the state party convention. During the campaign, she told the press that Miller suffered from "hopeless moral blindness" and called him a "standpatter," which she compared to crookedness. He was no less than "a stumbling block in the march of civilization." She urged progressive Republicans to understand that Miller was antagonistic to everything for which they stood. Louis Howe doubtless had a hand in preparing her remarks, but the statement reflected her understanding that hyperbole was an acceptable mainstay of American politics.

At the same time that she became a political activist in her own right, she also consciously assumed the part of Franklin's surrogate. Howe made clear that she "had to become actively involved in Democratic politics in order to keep alive Franklin's interest in the party and the party's interest in him." He urged her to keep the Roosevelt name before the public by speaking at Democratic Party functions and at the meetings of the women's organizations she had joined. She took up the challenge with considerable trepidation, for the very idea of standing before an audience terrified her. At her first speech, she recalled, "I trembled so much that I did not know whether I could stand up." She was sure her "voice could not be heard." Howe tutored her, advising her to take deep breaths when she felt panicky, to grip the lectern when her hands trembled, to keep eye contact with her audience, to speak more slowly, to stand up straight instead of slouching, and to suppress the inappropriate giggles that made her discomfort obvious. She was soon in command of herself, following Howe's injunction: "Have something to say. Say it. And sit down."

Nothing put Eleanor or the Roosevelt name before the public more visibly than her involvement in the Bok Peace Award, established in 1923. The $50,000 prize for the best plan by which the United States could "do its share toward preserving world peace" stimulated universal interest and generated more than twenty-two thousand submissions. Eleanor served as a member of the jury and drew fire from Senate Republicans when she and her fellow jurors chose as the winning idea American participation in the World Court. Isolationists denounced them as proponents of "communistic internationalism," and Eleanor herself was identified as one of several "unscrupulous women" who were subversives "influenced by foreign radicals." The FBI opened a file on her that would swell in later years as a result of her associations with "known radicals" and "fellow travelers." However controversial, her Bok service deepened the Roosevelt association with progressive causes.

But Eleanor could only do so much on her own to restore Franklin's political standing, as he could remain on the sidelines for only so long before he lost momentum as a future gubernatorial or presidential candidate. His 1922 endorsement of Smith helped, but he had to come forward in the 1924 Democratic Party contest for the presidential nomination — not as a candidate himself, but as a prominent voice at the convention.

Charlie Murphy, Tammany leader and Smith's close friend, who was planning Smith's 1924

151

presidential nomination, was eager to give Franklin the public spotlight. Smith had retaken the governorship in 1922 and had the support of "ethnics" and urban bosses, but a prominent Protestant patrician serving as a booster would be a great advantage. It was already clear that the fight for the nomination at the convention in Madison Square Garden in New York would be between traditional party Protestants, now led by William Gibbs McAdoo, Woodrow Wilson's son-in-law and treasury secretary, and the city ethnics, led by Murphy and Smith.

Franklin was delighted with the chance to join the fray and play as large a role as possible in choosing the party's nominee. To bolster Smith's standing with ethnics, he persuaded Babe Ruth, baseball's most prominent celebrity, to endorse him. More significantly, Franklin accepted Murphy's invitation to be national chairman of Smith's campaign and to put Smith's name in nomination for the presidency. Smith was reluctant to give Roosevelt the position: "For God's sake why?" Smith asked Judge Joseph Proskauer, who had suggested the idea to him. The judge bluntly replied: "Because you're a Bowery mick and he's a Protestant patrician and he'd take some of the curse off you."

On June 26, a steamy summer's day in New York, Roosevelt, aided by crutches and his oldest son, sixteen-year-old James, made his way from his seat in the New York delegation to the convention platform, where he would speak not only to 1,400 delegates on the floor and hundreds more convention attendees in the galleries but also to the first radio audience ever tuned in to a national political convention. Franklin had practiced repeatedly walking the distance across the platform to the lectern to appear in command of himself as he took the stage. Bathed in sweat and barely able to stand without clutching the sides of the speaker's podium, he seized the moment to extol Smith's virtues in a nominating address made memorable by Roosevelt's description of Smith as "the Happy Warrior of the political battlefield."

Ironically, Franklin thought the quote, taken from a William Wordsworth poem, too literary for a mass political audience, but the author of his speech, Judge Proskauer, insisted that it not be stricken. None of Roosevelt's several references to Smith as the "guiding hand" behind numerous progressive measures in New York resonated as powerfully as the "Happy Warrior" image. Combined with the visual of Roosevelt himself smiling at center stage with no overt regard for his disability, it gave Franklin greater popular appeal than Smith, for it was the partly paralyzed Roosevelt who was the true Happy Warrior. Franklin knew that he had hit a home run with respect to his political future. Resting in the privacy of his bedroom afterward, he exulted to a friend, "Marion, I did it." A typical newspaper assessment of his performance declared: "There was nothing at the Democratic Convention more inspiring than the heroism of Franklin D. Roosevelt. It was the nominator that loomed large in the picture, an invalid on crutches, perhaps in pain, who conquered the frailties of body by sheer power of will." Another columnist concluded that "the convention would make no mistake if it should name Roosevelt himself." Yet another journalist believed that Roosevelt "would stampede the convention were he put in nomination." With his speech, this writer concluded, Roosevelt had "done for himself what he could not do for his candidate."

In resisting the use of the "warrior" reference, Roosevelt was hesitant to accede to the party's yearning for a new hero, one who could speak to its eagerness for another round of bold reform. He understood how utopian such enthusiasm was in 1924, when standpat Republicanism carried the day and it was unlikely that any Democrat could win back the White House. Calvin Coolidge, who had become president in 1923 after Harding died suddenly on a West Coast trip, did not strike Franklin as a "world beater" but was clever enough to take advantage of the current conservative mood to win the 1924 election.

As for the Democratic nomination, Howe and Roosevelt saw little likelihood that either Smith or McAdoo would emerge as the victor. In April, Howe had told a fellow Democrat that he foresaw a multi-ballot contest, one that would end when the convention bosses would choose "some unguessable John Smith." Still, Howe could not have imagined that the fight would go on for fourteen days and 103 ballots, and that the "John Smith" would be John W. Davis. A one-term West Virginia representative in the House, a prominent Wall Street attorney who had argued 140 cases before the Supreme Court, solicitor general of the United States under Wilson, and then Wilson's ambassador to the United Kingdom, Davis was a safe compromise choice for a sharply divided Democratic Party with little chance of regaining control of the White House. Franklin understood that as long as the party remained split over issues like

154

Prohibition; the Ku Klux Klan, which had re-gained national standing in the twenties with at-tacks on blacks, Catholics, Jews, and immigrants more generally; and teaching evolution in public school biology classes, the Democrats could not win the presidency.

To no avail, Roosevelt had made an eloquent appeal in his nominating address for party unity: "You equally," he had declared, "who come from the great cities of the East and the plains and hills of the West, from the slopes of the Pacific and from the homes and the fields of the Southland, I ask you in all sincerity . . . to keep first in your hearts and minds the words of Abraham Lincoln: 'With Malice toward none, with charity to all.' " His prophetic insight was that the path to political power for the party depended on its unifying around a progressive agenda.

However much Roosevelt promoted Smith in public, he had his doubts about Smith's capacity for the presidency. After the convention, Franklin privately expressed his frustration with Smith, who he thought was too unbending in his opposition to the McAdoo side of the party and too insensi-tive to its antagonism to a New York ethnic constituency openly indifferent to the concerns of voters in the South and the West. He ultimately regarded Smith as a well-intentioned but crude politico. Roosevelt's true feelings about him were not lost on Smith and remained a source of antagonism between the two that would finally break into the open when neither man was politi-cally useful to the other.

In the period from 1925 to 1928, though, they had a shared interest in keeping the growing competition between them muted. To that end,

Franklin encouraged Eleanor to campaign for Smith in his successful 1924 race for a third gubernatorial term in New York. Smith's opponent was Theodore Roosevelt, Jr., Eleanor's cousin, whom she charged with being supported by "stupid or dishonest public servants." She crisscrossed the state in an automobile with "a steam-spouting teapot" that reminded voters of the Republican's Teapot Dome scandal, in which she had few qualms about suggesting TR, Jr.'s, involvement. Eleanor later acknowledged that her teapot-adorned auto was a "rough stunt," but she had no regrets about her cousin's decisive defeat. Her role in the campaign went far to quiet talk of a Roosevelt-Smith divide. Like Franklin, she also genuinely admired Smith's progressivism.

Although she took pleasure in becoming an influential voice in electoral politics and helping establish the large part women could play in what had been strictly a man's domain just four years before, she was also sensitive to Franklin's reluctance to cede her center stage. "You need not be proud of me, dear," she told him. "I'm only being active till you can be again — it isn't such a great desire on my part to serve the world and I'll fall back into habits of sloth quite easily! Hurry up for as you know my ever present sense of the uselessness of all things will overwhelm me sooner or later!" Actually, her note was more an exercise in ego-massaging than a truthful account of how she felt about her involvement in politics. She loved her newfound role as a voice for women in public life and for reforms serving the least advantaged at home and promoting peace abroad.

In the two-year period after the Happy Warrior speech raised his profile, Franklin and Howe saw every reason to confine his political ambitions to the future, or more specifically, to the 1930s. When Louis B. Wehle, an old Harvard friend and co-worker on labor problems during World War I, suggested that Franklin allow him to organize support for a 1928 presidential nomination and campaign, Franklin discouraged him. He said that choosing a nominee or organizing support for any one candidate should wait at least until the end of 1927. Moreover, as for himself, he couldn't imagine making such an effort until he had shown greater progress in regaining the use of his legs. He hoped to be walking without braces in another year. He foresaw a time after that when he would replace crutches with canes and eventually have the ability to walk free of all these devices.

Although he told Wehle that his expectations were principally based on hope, he and Howe were focused on making a visual case for Roosevelt's increasing mobility. The pictures they released for public consumption showed a man standing erect with nothing more than a cane for support. As James Tobin, the closest student of Franklin's disability, wrote, "In conversations with reporters or anyone else, neither of them would claim that FDR was more mobile than he really was. But the photographs delivered a powerful message — simply that he didn't look 'crippled.' He was up and around. He appeared to be all right after all." Tobin, who tracked the stories about FDR in the 1920s released by the Smith and Roosevelt camps, detected a distinct difference in the ways each portrayed Franklin's physical condition. The Smith accounts made mention of Roosevelt's handicap and dependence on crutches; the reports originating with Howe emphasized Franklin's steady recovery from polio and expectation of a return to full mobility.

Privately, Franklin doubted that he would ever again walk unaided. His aim, he told one physical therapist, was to avoid the pity and revulsion people seemed to feel toward someone as disabled as he was. He hoped to make people "forget that he was a cripple." He was determined to develop a way of walking that at a minimum gave the appearance of normal movement. In the two years after 1926, with the help of a physical therapist, Franklin hit upon the technique of gripping someone's arm with one hand and propelling himself forward with a cane in the other. The maneuver gave the impression of someone who had overcome his paralysis and had enough leg strength to walk with a minimum of help.

Howe, with Franklin's consent, was clearly building toward the day when Roosevelt would launch a presidential campaign. The operation began in the aftermath of the 1924 convention with a circular letter inviting Democratic convention delegates to suggest ways in which the party could reunify around progressive ideas and, implicitly, around a candidate eager to win the support of party members from every section of the country. The letter evoked a substantial response, but little that offered a path toward party harmony. Consequently, in February 1925, Franklin followed up with an appeal to party leaders to agree to a national conference over which he would preside. The gathering would aim to put the Democrats' divisions aside by committing the party to progressive principles and underscoring its opposition to the dominant conservative impulses of the Republicans. Although Roosevelt gained political standing among Democrats with his call for unity, too many of their leaders believed that a conference would result in acrimony for them to follow Franklin's lead, and the idea came to naught. In August 1925, when thousands of hooded Klansmen, mainly from the South, marched in Washington, D.C., flaunting their support of racial segregation and animus toward immigrants and minorities in the Northeast who voted for Democratic nominees, it only underscored the continuing divide in the party.

The Roosevelt-Howe initiatives increased concerns among Smith's advocates that they faced a potentially powerful competitor for the presidential nomination in 1928. They understood that the Happy Warrior speech had greatly increased Franklin's popularity and that the radio had become a prime ally in expanding his political reach. Unlike Smith, whose New York accent grated on folks across the South and the West, Franklin's rich tenor voice and sensitivity to his diverse national audience made him a serious challenger for the top spot in the Democratic Party in 1928.

While the Smith camp could not afford overtly to antagonize Roosevelt, it could try to sidetrack his reach for the Oval Office by prodding him to run for a U.S. Senate seat for New York. They arranged accordingly to have Franklin nominate Smith for a fourth gubernatorial term at the New York State convention in Syracuse in September 1926. There were rumors that Franklin's nominating speech would not only touch off a rally for Smith but also one urging Roosevelt to become the party's Senate nominee for the seat currently held by Republican James W. Wadsworth. The likelihood that Franklin would defeat Wadsworth and then as a senator be forced to vote on issues that would alienate voters in one section or another of the country could help undermine his larger plans for 1928.

Franklin and Howe, however, refused to be taken in by the Smith ploy. Franklin had genuine resistance to becoming a senator, and had made it clear that his preference for government service would always be in an executive capacity rather than as one of many legislators. His experience in the New York upper house had left him with a lasting bias against serving in Congress. He also did not think he was far enough along in his rehabilitation to take on the rigors of a campaign — statewide or national. Half jokingly, Howe told him: "Please try to look pallid and worn and weary when you address the convention so it will not be too exceedingly difficult to get by with the statement that your health will not permit you to run for anything for two more years."

Finally, a run for office in 1928 would play havoc with Franklin's commitment to Warm Springs. Having invested $200,000 of his wealth in turning it into the country's premier treatment facility for polio sufferers, he refused to abandon or reduce his involvement in the project with an all-consuming political race. He also had sound political reasons for continuing to keep Warm Springs as a top priority, for his identification with a national facility in the foothills of western Georgia could ultimately raise his political standing across the South, a vital consideration in winning the White House. In the spring of 1927, when the worst Mississippi River floods to that date wrought damage across part of the South, Roosevelt urged a special congressional session be held to deal with the crisis. Howe had accurately predicted that such a public appeal would "go grand in the South and make you the fair-haired boy."

In 1927–28, as tensions between Smith and Roosevelt grew over how to win the White House and restore the party to greater power, reasons for keeping their differences under wraps became greater than ever. Although Smith admired Franklin and his courageous fight to overcome his disability, he also didn't trust him, remarking to a friend, he "just isn't the kind of man you can take into the pissroom and talk intimately with." Roosevelt reciprocated the wariness. For all his progressive actions as governor in support of women, children, the least advantaged, and public power, Smith also showed an affinity for self-made millionaires like John J. Raskob of General Motors, arguing that Raskob's association with the party would help the Democrats win votes in the "big industrial states."

Franklin accurately predicted that Smith would get the party's 1928 presidential nomination. After the Harding scandals tainted McAdoo, who had taken legal fees from an oil executive involved in Teapot Dome, he said that he would not run again. To appease McAdoo's Southern supporters, Smith accepted Houston, Texas, as the party's 1928 convention site. It was the first time since the Civil War that the Democrats held their presidential nominating convention in a Southern city. Franklin did not think that Smith's gesture would rescue him from a lopsided defeat by millionaire businessman and Secretary of Commerce Herbert Hoover, the likely Republican nominee.

For the sake of his own political future, though, Franklin and Howe believed it essential to give Smith their all-out backing. Smith, at least, shared their progressive outlook, while Hoover was the darling of corporate America, which saw one of their own in the White House as an effective barrier to Democratic expansion of federal programs.

While Smith could count on urban ethnic support, the majority of Southern, Midwestern, and Western voters remained convinced that a Catholic from the sidewalks of New York was unsuited to join the ranks of earlier Protestant presidents. Hoover's engineering and business background and record of public service closely aligned with the current national mood. The prosperity of the Roaring Twenties, as many dubbed the decade, seemed to be the product of exactly what Hoover and his Republican Party offered the country: a chicken in every pot, a car in every garage. Hoover was the beau ideal of the time. A Stanford graduate with a degree as a mining engineer, he had made a fortune in Australia and China extracting gold, silver, lead, and zinc from their untapped mines. A millionaire before the age of forty, he was a paragon of the American belief in success gained through skill and hard work. His humanitarian service during World War I in Belgian food relief added to his standing as a Theodore Roosevelt progressive who built a private fortune and devoted himself to the public good.

Roosevelt's decision to avoid a clash with Smith over the nomination also rested on the fact that he was only forty-six in 1928 and could run for governor in 1932 when he was fifty. Since he assumed that Hoover would serve two terms, he looked to 1936, when there would be no incumbent president to contest for the highest office. Roosevelt's political passivity in 1928 pleased Smith, up to a point. He was delighted that Franklin made no effort to capture the presidential nomination, but he was now eager to have Franklin become the Democratic nominee for New York governor. With the Republicans planning to nominate the state attorney general, Albert Ottinger, a Jew from New York City with impeccable credentials, they had a serious prospect of winning control of the state and putting New York's 45 electoral votes, the largest of any state, in Hoover's column. It would ensure Smith's defeat in the presidential election. Smith was convinced that Roosevelt was the most likely Democrat to hold the state for him and the party. Roosevelt, however, believed that in a Republican year, Ottinger could beat him and effectively end his political career.

Franklin did everything he could to deter Smith from urging his candidacy. He went to Houston for the convention, where, as in 1924, he gave the nominating address for Smith. Focused on the estimated 15 million Americans listening on the radio, Franklin lauded Smith as a great humanitarian, and the *New York Times* reported, "It is seldom that a political speech attains this kind of eloquence." But Roosevelt's speech and effective use of his new technique in walking to the podium only made him all the more desirable as the party's candidate for governor. When Smith reached Franklin on the phone in Warm Springs on September 30, 1928, the day before the New York State nominating convention, he included on the call John J. Raskob, the corporate millionaire and chairman of the party's national committee, and the investment banker Herbert Lehman to persuade Franklin to run. Raskob met Franklin's objections about the financial hardship of a candidacy with promises of money to support Warm Springs. Lehman countered Franklin's concerns about the limitations imposed by his health by promising to run with him as lieutenant governor and relieve him of all duties that over-taxed his physical capacity.

When Smith came back on the phone and asked if he would run if the convention nominated him, Franklin refused to answer, which convinced him that Franklin would indeed accept the challenge. "Thanks, Frank," Smith said. "I won't ask you any more questions." After they hung up, an observer who had heard the call asked Roosevelt if he did intend to run. "When you're in politics," Franklin replied, "you've got to play the game." Part of his calculation involved the political consequences he might suffer if he refused Smith's repeated requests. Should Smith lose New York and the election, Franklin could be held account-able for facilitating Smith's defeat. His acceptance of the nomination antagonized Howe, who thought he should wait until 1932, but once Franklin was unanimously chosen by the del-egates, Howe threw himself wholeheartedly into the campaign.

Although Franklin and Howe flirted with the idea of purposely losing in a noble fight that would put him in good standing for a future campaign, Roosevelt's nature dictated that he battle to win, and so the campaign became an all-out sprint to capture every possible vote across the state. Eager to refute any suggestions that he was too disabled to serve as governor, Franklin joked: People run for governor, but in my case, "I am counting on my friends all over the state to make it possible for me to walk in." Roosevelt assembled a formidable team of astute politicians led by Howe and supported by Eleanor, who mobilized Democratic women across the state. From his own campaign Smith deputized to assist Franklin Bronx Democratic boss Edward J. Flynn, a descendant of what are called in Boston "lace curtain" Irish immigrants. A graduate of the Fordham law school, Flynn was as savvy as Howe about appealing to voters across political lines. They persuaded Raymond A. Moley, a Columbia University political science professor, to write some of Roosevelt's speeches and suggest issues that could win over urban and upstate voters. They turned to James A. Farley, another member of the Tammany Irish Catholic cohort, to mobilize Democratic voters in upstate counties, where the party's candidates usually polled poorly. They invited Henry Morgenthau, Jr., Franklin and Eleanor's Dutchess County neighbor and friend, owner of a large farm himself, and publisher of the weekly *American Agriculturalist,* to map out strategies for winning the farm vote. Finally, they brought thirty-two-year-old Samuel I. Rosenman into the mix as a speechwriter and expert on legislative matters. A brilliant graduate of Columbia University Law School, an elected member of the Assembly for five years, and a leading authority on drafting bills, he became part of Roosevelt's traveling group — always available to answer questions about current legislative affairs and to turn Franklin's ideas into compelling public talks.

During the four-week campaign, Roosevelt's aides served him effectively. But no one did more to win voter and press approval than Franklin himself. Initially moving about the state by train, he quickly shifted to automobiles, which gave him more visibility to voters and promoted greater interaction with crowds and anyone on the streets of the many towns and villages through which the campaign progressed. By the end of October, Ottinger's two-to-one odds of winning shifted in favor of Roosevelt. He had won over many voters by the appeal of a man who was overcoming a crippling disability and was speaking for the public interest over the private gain of selfish businessmen. He injected his personal narrative into the discussion by urging an end to a law that neglected the health problems of old and young. Imagine where I might have been without my private resources to rehabilitate myself? he asked. It touched a responsive chord in thousands of voters who had direct experience of or knew of less fortunate people who were forced to cope unsuccessfully with debilitating health problems. At the same time, Franklin made the case for public control of water power and electric utilities over private companies lining their pockets with profits at the public's expense.

When the election was held on November 6, Hoover outran Smith by over 6 million votes out of 36 million nationwide. Smith lost his home state of New York by over 100,000 votes and won only five of the eleven Deep South states that normally voted Democratic. By contrast, Roosevelt bested Ottinger by a little over 25,000 ballots out of a total of 4.23 million. On the night of the voting, however, the result remained in doubt — so much so that Roosevelt finally left his election headquarters at the Biltmore Hotel on Madi-

son Avenue to go home to sleep. With upstate ballots coming in slowly, Howe and Flynn assumed
that the Republican machines in the upstate counties were preparing to manipulate the final tally. A
public threat to ensure an honest count by arranging for county sheriffs and a hundred lawyers
to oversee the returns brought a quick result favoring Roosevelt. Ottinger, however, wouldn't concede defeat until November 19, when he concluded that "the final count of the official canvas"
made Roosevelt the governor-elect.

It was a remarkable achievement — not just
because Franklin won New York State's highest
elected office in a Republican year but because he
had overcome a disability that seemed to put such
a successful campaign out of reach. It was also
the beginning of an extraordinary seventeen-year
political career that defied all odds.

CHAPTER 4
"CHAMELEON ON PLAID"

Franklin's election to the governorship in November 1928 instantly made him a prominent Democratic candidate for the presidency. In the sixty-year period since 1868, half of all the party's choices for the Oval Office had come from New York, and all but one of these candidates, Judge Alton B. Parker in 1904, had served as governor.

The prospect of a presidential run was exactly what Roosevelt and Howe hoped would follow Franklin's service in Albany. But there were many hurdles to overcome before that could happen. First, Roosevelt would have to demonstrate success in Albany, proving that his disability did not impede his effectiveness as a chief executive. Second, he would need to chart a reform agenda that would resonate with New Yorkers and win legislative approval. Third, he would have to find a way to delay his candidacy until 1936, when no incumbent would block his path to the White House. No one could have foreseen the results of Hoover's first term, but Roosevelt and Howe expected him to enjoy four years of national prosperity that would make him difficult to defeat in 1932. Moreover, by 1936, Roosevelt believed that the good times would have run their course

168

and the electorate would be ready for the return of a progressive Democratic administration.

Roosevelt's immediate challenge as he took the oath of office on January 1, 1929, was to keep his predecessor from turning Franklin's governorship into Smith's fifth term. In December, Smith had visited Roosevelt at his 65th Street home in New York and all but declared his intention to hold on to power through his two principal subordinates: Belle Moskowitz, his secretary, and Robert Moses, New York secretary of state. Smith urged Franklin to keep them in place and advised him that Mrs. Moskowitz was ready to draft his inaugural address and his legislative agenda. Smith rationalized his maintaining control by privately predicting that Franklin's precarious health would not allow him to serve out a year in office. Smith reserved a suite of rooms in an Albany hotel, where he would reside and be available for consultations. Whether he expected to control Herbert Lehman, the lieutenant governor, who would succeed Roosevelt, if he expired, as Smith predicted, was never discussed. Smith was less than subtle in trying to elbow Franklin aside. "Well, Frank, you won't have to worry about being governor," he told him. "You can come to Albany for the inauguration and stay around for a while and get the hang of things, and when you get a chance you can hop back to Warm Springs. And we'll be here to see that things go all right."

Eleanor had warned Franklin that Moskowitz and Moses were hoping to take over his administration and do Smith's bidding. Whatever her own convictions about Franklin's capacity to perform his duties as governor, she had no interest in fending off the Smith alliance's threat by becoming

Franklin's surrogate. She was busy with "a range of social initiatives aimed at strengthening government protection for women and children," the international peace movement, a leading role in Democratic Party politics, teaching at the Todhunter School for Girls in Manhattan, and making her political opinions known through magazine articles, newspaper columns, and lectures. When asked by reporters how she felt about Franklin's election, she replied: "No, I am not excited about my husband's election. I don't care. What difference can it make to me?" She wished to make clear her determination not to become a traditional first lady and abandon her own rewarding activities as a public figure.

Roosevelt, for his part, had no intention of letting Smith turn him into a messenger boy or a stand-in for his predecessor's behind-the-scenes control of the state government. He was determined to hold Smith at arm's length without offending him, if possible, and viewed the challenge as an initial test of his political skills. He told Smith that the inaugural speech and legislative message were already being completed and proposed showing them to Moskowitz and Smith when they were completed. But that was nothing more than a delaying action, as he never shared the documents with either of them. As for Moses, he made clear that he wanted no part of working with Franklin in the governor's office for, as he told Smith, "He rubs me the wrong way." Franklin then finessed the issue by promising to keep him on as parks commissioner. Finally, he rejected Smith's suggestion to leave Albany by asking: "Did *you* ever leave Albany for any extended stay during a legislative session?" "No," Smith replied.

"Then I won't either," Franklin answered.

Anyone eager to learn Roosevelt's plans for his administration could gain some insight by looking to whom he selected as his closest advisers. While he reappointed sixteen of Smith's eighteen department heads, his inner circle consisted of people close to him, not Smith. Howe replaced Moskowitz as the governor's principal aide and adviser; Ed Flynn replaced Moses as the secretary of state, who oversaw most of the state's operations; Samuel Rosenman wrote speeches and offered counsel on legislative affairs; Henry Morgenthau became the principal official on agriculture and conservation; and Frances Perkins was the administration's voice on industrial and labor matters.

With his Smith problem more or less resolved, Franklin saw two other, more significant ways to persuade the press and the public that he was as much a fully functioning governor as anyone who had preceded him in office. To that end he gave newspaper reporters greater access to him with press conferences than Smith had provided during his four terms. He also took pains to address any concerns the journalists may have had about his disability. He made a point of joking about "walking, running, and jumping." He ended interviews with the cheery explanation: "Well boys, I have to run," and anything that amused him, he described to reporters as "funny as a crutch." He was especially sensitive to convincing a larger public that he was an active governor, overseeing the needs of all New Yorkers. He never forgot that he had won the governorship by a fraction of the popular vote.

The best way to reach constituents across the state was not through its many newspapers that reported on events in Albany. Most were in Republican hands and would not be especially sympathetic to a Democratic governor, and in any case, stories from the state capitol often went unread and had limited impact on public thinking about a governor. People increasingly were getting their news from radio broadcasts. "It seems to me," Franklin said in 1929, "that radio is gradually bringing to the ears of our people matters of interest concerning their country which they refused to consider in the daily press with their eyes." He was convinced that in the previous five years, the number of politically interested citizens who had taken their guidance from newspaper editorials had been halved, with many of them now relying on radio to inform and guide them. As a consequence, in the spring of 1929, he gave the first of what eventually became famous as Fireside Chats. He broadcast on Sunday nights, when the radio audience was largest, and made every effort to establish an intimacy with his audience. As Perkins, who watched him give some of these talks, recalled, "His head would nod and his hands would move in simple, natural, comfortable gestures. His face would smile and light up as though he were actually sitting on the front porch or in the parlor with them." He tried to imagine himself sitting with a friend in his living room by the fireside talking over a family matter. Many of his listeners had the feeling that they were holding a conversation with him.

The radio was a wonderful medium for lobbying people across the state to pressure their legislative representatives to enact Roosevelt's progressive agenda promoting conservation, regulations of utilities, and the welfare of farmers and labor.

In fact, after each talk, letters flooded into the governor's office supporting his initiatives. The success of his radio talks pleased Roosevelt, but he did not see them as a substitute for more direct contact with constituents. He took advantage of the state's many rivers and canals to travel by houseboat to some of New York's more remote towns like "Aurora or Watertown or Saranac Lake," which had never been visited by a governor, let alone one supposedly immobilized by polio.

By the end of the 1929–30 legislative session, William Green, the head of the American Federation of Labor, told Roosevelt, "Labor has very seldom secured the enactment of so many measures which so favorably affect their economic, social and industrial welfare during a single session of a legislative body." Franklin's success rested partly on the country's changed economic conditions, as the stock market crash in October 1929 and the rising unemployment and general economic downturn in 1930 gave the state government a larger role in people's lives. Roosevelt's advocacy of cheaper electric power through the construction of hydroelectric plants on the Saint Lawrence River; help to farmers through tax reductions, flood control, farm-to-market roads, and reduced agricultural surpluses; and aid to the growing ranks of jobless citizens through unemployment insurance resonated with New Yorkers upstate as well as in the five boroughs of New York City. In speeches and radio talks, he attacked the country's "robber barons" profiting from Hoover's pro-business policies that favored large corporations and, according to Roosevelt, threatened to turn working-class Americans into modern-day serfs. Just as the Constitution endorsed separation of church and state, Roosevelt said, so the country needed to have "a complete separation of business and government." Roosevelt understood that a total division was an unrealistic proposal, but at a time when businessmen were losing their standing with the millions of Americans affected by the economic downturn, it was smart politics. As Joseph Kennedy, an enormously wealthy business mogul, told his three sons, the big men in America in the coming decade would be in government, not business.

As the economy sank in 1930, and Hoover tried to cheer up demoralized Americans with pronouncements that "the fundamental business of the country . . . is on a sound and prosperous basis" and his vice president declared that prosperity was "just around the corner," Roosevelt's appeal as a humane governor trying to enact measures that actually relieved the suffering of those impoverished by the economic collapse soared. By the fall of 1930, when Roosevelt ran for reelection, the contrast with Hoover could not have been more pronounced. Although Roosevelt's Republican opponent in the governor's race, Charles H. Tuttle, the U.S. attorney for the Southern District of New York, attacked his opponent's passive response to charges of corruption against New York mayor Jimmy Walker, Franklin fixed his attention on Hoover's tepid reaction to the Depression. "Never let your opponent pick the battleground on which to fight," he told Rosenman.

While the columnist Walter Lippmann declared "this squalid mess [in New York City] is due to nothing but Governor Roosevelt's own weakness and timidity," Franklin hammered Hoover for his refusal to make the federal government the prime combatant against the economic collapse. Hoover, who believed that private charity rather than government should be the principal agent in easing economic distress, refused to commit his administration to undertaking any measures he thought would destroy the initiative of the unemployed. "Aid to jobless citizens must be extended by Government," Roosevelt said, "not as a matter of charity, but as a matter of social duty." Such action was essential if the country was "to preserve our democratic form of government." He told the New York legislature that "modern society, acting through its Government, owes the definite obligation to prevent the starvation or dire waste of any of its fellow men and women who try to maintain themselves but cannot" because of conditions beyond their control. When a supporter of Hoover's restrained policy toward the unemployed told Roosevelt "that the only hope was to let the system strike bottom," he dismissed the suggestion as coldhearted, saying, "People aren't cattle, you know."

Joseph Alsop, Franklin and Eleanor's cousin and a national columnist, wrote that Roosevelt was "humane, liberal, efficient, and so popular that he won reelection by an impressive majority." Roosevelt himself made his campaign a referendum on what his administration had done for labor and seniors, and for the state's "hospitals, public works, cheap electricity, regulation of public utilities [and] prisons." It promoted his reputation as a governor who put people first, and it led to a 725,000-vote margin of victory, the greatest landslide in a statewide election in New York history. His triumph was the result of a 91 percent turnout in New York City and an unprecedented forty-one upstate counties out of fifty-seven voting for a Democratic governor. Franklin's success extended to Democratic victories in races for all statewide offices and Democratic majorities in both legislative houses. The sweep was not only an endorsement of Roosevelt's policies but also of the governor himself. Rosenman ascribed the outcome to "the warmth of the man and the orator, who knew how to convey his personality and charm to the people he met and to the people he talked with over the air." As consequential, the victory made him the front-runner for the Democratic nomination in 1932.

Louis Howe and James Farley, who had chaired the state's Democratic committee during 1930, began regular consultations with Roosevelt about the upcoming presidential race. Farley, a heavyset, bald Irishman with an incomparable capacity for political management, issued a statement after Franklin's reelection, saying, "I do not see how Mr. Roosevelt can escape becoming the next presidential nominee of his party." Charming and genial, Farley was brilliant at courting Democratic politicos, whose names he never forgot. Everyone of importance in the party found his way onto a list Farley kept in green ink. Trusting Farley's political instincts, Roosevelt told him, "Whatever you said, Jim, is alright with me." For three weeks at the end of June, Farley traveled across the country on his way to Seattle conferring with Democratic leaders in nineteen states about the feasibility of Roosevelt's candidacy. His reports to Franklin strengthened their optimism regarding his presidential prospects. At the same time that they promoted Franklin's national standing, though, they understood that they could not ignore state issues over the following two years without jeopardizing his greater goals. It was clear to them that anything Roosevelt did in New York would now resonate nationally.

During 1931, as the Depression deepened and four million additional Americans lost their jobs, bringing the total in the spring of that year to eight million, or about 15 percent of the workforce, Roosevelt saw it as essential for state governments to relieve the misery of the unemployed. He remembered that at the end of the nineteenth century and in the first years of the twentieth, progressive officials, led by Wisconsin, had made their respective states testing grounds for innovative reforms. They launched programs that they hoped could improve the living standards of children, women, seniors, immigrants, and the indigent. Roosevelt believed that in the midst of the current economic crisis, when the Hoover administration shunned bold initiatives, measures originating in Albany could make a difference in the lives of many of New York's twelve million citizens. His proposed reforms might also persuade other governors to follow his lead as well as boost his national standing.

In March 1931, he asked the legislature to create a commission that would investigate a state program of unemployment insurance. He opposed anything that could be described as a public dole, which would be sure to draw Hoover's ire as a program bound to make New Yorkers permanent wards of the state. In his opposition to government handouts, Hoover preached the virtues of "local responsibility and mutual self-help." Roosevelt called for state money to finance public works that would provide jobs for the unemployed, and if this fell short of providing sufficient financial support, he wanted appropriations to pay for food, clothing, and shelters that could rescue the destitute from their poverty.

In June, Roosevelt seized the chance to speak to the annual national Governors Conference to promote the idea of the states as "48 laboratories" of social experimentation that could alleviate the economic collapse that had descended on the country. The government needed to "protect its citizens from disaster [with] the better planning of our social and economic life," he said. "State and national planning is an essential to the future prosperity, happiness and the very existence of the American people." Roosevelt's call for government activism challenged Hoover's faith in free enterprise. From Hoover's perspective, Roosevelt was charting a course that could lead to socialism or the sort of state planning and control used by Soviet Russia. Roosevelt welcomed the clash of opinions with the White House and the conservative business interests in the Democratic Party, led by Alfred DuPont, the multimillionaire industrialist, and General Motors chief John J. Raskob.

In August, Roosevelt put a request before the state legislature for $20 million (worth $275 million in 2016) to pay for the jobless program he had discussed in the spring. To emphasize his commitment to the effort, he personally delivered the message to the legislature. The Republicans initially rejected his request, but the pressure to do something was so great, including Roosevelt's threat to call them back into another special session, that it forced their capitulation. As Rosenman recalled, "Their actions in first opposing

Roosevelt and then yielding to him increased his national stature and prestige almost as much as the merits of the legislation itself." The establishment of the Temporary Emergency Relief Administration (TERA) established Roosevelt as the model of the humane leader whom people wanted in hard times. It was not lost on him that Hoover's refusal to adopt policies to help needy Americans in the Depression eclipsed his reputation as the man who saved Belgium with food relief in World War I.

To ensure the success of the relief agency, Roosevelt persuaded Jesse Straus, a businessman known for his integrity and successful management of Macy's department store, to become its director. The appointment refuted suggestions from the White House that Roosevelt was a closet socialist who favored antibusiness policies as the way out of the country's economic crisis. Straus gave some credence to that conviction when he named forty-one-year-old Harry Hopkins, a social worker, as TERA's executive administrator. A graduate of Grinnell College in Iowa, where he had grown up, Hopkins had come to New York in 1912, where he built a reputation as a brilliant administrator of programs for the poor and disabled, including leadership of the New York Tuberculosis and Health Association, his last job before coming to TERA. His effectiveness at running TERA persuaded Roosevelt to make him head of the agency when Straus left in the spring of 1932. Hopkins's almost emaciated appearance, the result of stomach problems and nervous energy that kept him in perpetual motion, made an instant impression on Roosevelt. He saw in Hopkins qualities similar to his own in defying a physical disability and never allowing it to impede his life's work. He also viewed Hopkins's crusade against tuberculosis as comparable to his own against polio.

In the winter of 1931–32, Farley may have regarded Roosevelt as the Democratic Party's surefire presidential nominee, but others in the party were not as ready to concede the outcome of the June-July convention. Despite his impressive performance as governor, some believed that his disability would prevent him from mastering the larger job of the presidency, especially in the midst of a crisis as severe as the Great Depression. A Democratic Party two-thirds rule for the nomination convinced Roosevelt's opponents that he could be stopped from winning the 770 delegates he needed.

The impulse to resist the apparent inevitability of a Roosevelt nomination rested on the Democrats' belief that Hoover would be an easy mark in 1932 and that the presidency would be theirs to win. The collapse of almost 2,300 banks during the year deepened Hoover's unpopularity. White House denials that unemployment was all that serious a problem and Hoover's assertion that "Federal aid would be a disservice to the unemployed" made him seem heartless and indifferent.

The widespread antagonism to Hoover found expression in the jokes and sarcasm that now attached themselves to his public image. "A thousand bitter jokes" aimed at a president who seemed helpless in response to the country's economic collapse were the only humor Americans could find in the national disaster. Circumstances had so undermined and depressed Hoover that, in the words of one observer, a rose would wilt in his hand. After a White House meeting, Secretary of State Henry Stimson noted in a diary, "The President . . . went through all the blackest surmises. . . . It was like sitting in a bath of ink to sit in his room." Historian Arthur Schlesinger, Jr., wrote later, "The very word 'Hoover' became a prefix charged with hate."

The anger directed toward Hoover took on new dimensions in the winter of 1931–32 when he urgently called for congressional commitment of $2 billion for the Reconstruction Finance Corporation (RFC), which was intended to help banks and other industries get through the crisis. Bankers had "the honor of being the first group to go on the dole," Will Rogers, the humorist, social commentator, and popular movie star of the 1930s, declared. It was acceptable to help banks and railroads, one senator announced, but nothing was provided for "that forlorn American, in every village and every city of the United States, who has been without wages since 1929." Although Congress endorsed Hoover's proposal, the measure did little to combat the Depression. In fact, the slump accelerated: During 1932, the steel industry, a contemporary marker of any advanced nation's economic health, operated at only 11 percent capacity. In a country of 123 million people, some 45 million were now unable to earn an income. "If the election was held tomorrow," a former governor of Oregon said, "any Democratic candidate who had not been convicted of anything more than rape or murder would defeat Mr. Hoover."

Even so, the cast of candidates competing for the chance to run against Hoover was not especially impressive. While all of Roosevelt's aides

181

were confident that he could prevail, they could not forget the miserable divide of 1924 and lived with the fear that the party could enter into another self-defeating contest that would destroy its chances of recapturing the White House. They took small comfort from Will Rogers, who said, "I belong to no organized political party. I am a Democrat." He raised the party's popular appeal, however, with cracks about the current failings of Hoover's administration, telling audiences, "Be thankful we're not getting all the government we're paying for." His most popular in 1931–32 was: "On account of being a democracy and run by the people, we are the only nation in the world that has to keep a government for four years, no matter what it does." In another he wisecracked: "I don't make jokes. I just watch the government and report the facts."

However much Franklin enjoyed front-runner status, becoming the party's choice required the closest possible political maneuvering. An initial test of Roosevelt's fight to become the nominee came in January 1932 when the Democratic National Committee had to choose between four cities vying for the summer convention. Franklin wanted no part of Atlantic City, where New Jersey's boss Frank Hague, an ally of Al Smith's, could pack the galleries with an anti-Roosevelt crowd, or San Francisco, where newspaper publisher William Randolph Hearst, another Roosevelt opponent, could do the same. Roosevelt preferred Kansas City, where Tom Pendergast, the local boss and Franklin ally, could reliably produce a Roosevelt cheering section, but he was content to settle for Chicago, where he did not foresee a local organized stop-Roosevelt movement.

Although they were optimistic about the outcome, Roosevelt and his aides appreciated that the path to his selection by two-thirds of the delegates was hardly a foregone conclusion. One concern was Eleanor's reluctance to see Franklin as the nominee. The thought of being first lady with all its ceremonial duties and an end to activities she enjoyed made her cool to Franklin's campaign. With her many Democratic Party contacts and earlier work encouraging women's participation in politics, Eleanor would have been an ideal surrogate for Franklin for the women's vote. But Farley and Howe had to rely on Mary Dewson, a social worker and advocate for Smith in 1928, to take on the assignment. However competent she was, especially in advocating minimum wage and maximum work hours for women and children, her serving in that role was bound to raise unwanted issues about Eleanor's absence in the campaign. Was she in fact too worried about the strain on Franklin's health to become a leading voice in support of her husband? It was a question no one in Roosevelt's camp wanted asked.

When Howe read a letter Eleanor wrote expressing her anguish about becoming first lady, he tore it to pieces and told Marion Dickerman, who had shown it to him, "You are not to breathe a word of this to anyone, understand? Not to *anyone.*" According to some accounts, Eleanor considered a divorce to escape a burden she anticipated as making her "a prisoner in the White House, forced onto a narrow treadmill of formal receptions." But if she ever seriously contemplated so drastic a step, she came to understand that it would not only destroy Franklin's chance of becoming president but would also make her an outcast in Democratic circles and end her political role as the party's leading women's advocate. It seemed better to let events take their course, and should Franklin become president, she could turn her potential duties as first lady in new directions.

On January 21, 1932, Roosevelt abandoned the traditional coy expressions of reluctance to run and made an announcement that he hoped to win the nomination. On February 6, Al Smith told backers who were urging him to make himself available that he would not campaign for the nomination, but if the Democratic Convention chose him, he would "make the fight."

Smith's supporters welcomed the candidacies of several favorite sons that could result in a deadlocked convention, which they hoped would block Roosevelt and open the way for Smith. Newton D. Baker was a prominent figure in this group. His record of private and public service appealed to progressives and conservatives alike. He had a distinguished career as a corporate lawyer, representing the interests of utilities; he had been a progressive mayor of Cleveland, Ohio; and had distinguished himself as Woodrow Wilson's secretary of war and a leading advocate of the League of Nations. In January 1932, however, he was favored by isolationists, and particularly William Randolph Hearst, the most influential newspaper publisher in America and a leading antagonist of internationalists, by announcing that majority opposition to the League had converted him to their position.

Other potential rivals for the candidacy were two prominent governors. Albert Richie had been a popular Maryland governor since 1920. A lawyer who had served as general counsel on the War Industries Board, Richie, at fifty-six, seemed sufficiently schooled in executive experience to serve effectively as president. His greatest drawback was a rigid adherence to Jeffersonian states' rights. He was fiercely critical of Hoover's centralization of control, and while acknowledging that unemployment was a daunting current problem, favored a laissez-faire approach: He wanted "natural forces [to] take their course, as free and untrammeled as possible." His advocacy of less intervention than even Hoover favored should have been a prescription for defeat in a national campaign, but his good looks, personal charm, and long government service made him a favorite son to be taken seriously.

Sixty-two-year-old Oklahoma governor Alfalfa Bill Murray had a regional appeal to Southern and Western voters. As Arthur Schlesinger wrote, "He was a creation of America's last frontier, a figure out of an earlier America, tall and raw boned, with wavy gray hair, a gaunt and weathered face, and seedy mustachios." He had an up-from-his-bootstraps life story, and carefully cultivated a rustic appearance, dressing in "an old dirty frock coat over unpressed trousers that showed a shank of thin hairy leg, with wrinkled white socks hanging over the top of his shoes." He ran Oklahoma as a personal fiefdom, and his gruff manner and high-handed administration of the state's offices gave him a reputation for getting things done. His slogan of "Bread, Butter, Bacon, Beans" gave him standing as a governor who in hard times aimed above all to feed his people. It was difficult to imagine him winning the support of urban voters across the country, but he could tie up some of the Western delegations, which Roosevelt needed to reach the winning two-thirds margin.

The most formidable of these dark-horse candidates was John Nance Garner, a thirty-year east Texas congressman from Uvalde and Speaker of the House of Representatives since 1931. Nicknamed "Cactus Jack" for his opposition to a cactus as the Texas state flower, his down-home qualities made him popular in his district and with other congressional Democrats. His isolationist advocacy of "America First" won him the backing of Hearst, and he also enjoyed the support of McAdoo, who was more opposed to Roosevelt than committed to Garner. McAdoo had predicted that Franklin's poor health would make him "a dead man on the ticket," and should he survive and win the White House, he would "Tammanize the United States." With Hearst and McAdoo's help Garner won the California primary, and when combined with his lock on Texas, he commanded the 90 delegate votes of the two states.

But Garner had his share of enemies. He was a crusty conservative, whom John L. Lewis, president of the United Mine Workers union, later dismissed as "a labor-baiting, poker-playing, whiskey-drinking, evil old man." In 1940, *Time* magazine described Garner as "a hickory conservative who does not represent the Old South of magnolias [and] hoopskirts . . . but the New South: money-making, industrial, hardboiled . . . He stands for oil derricks, sheriffs . . . mechanized farms, $100 Stetson hats." Whatever his personal attributes, he seemed capable of blocking or even defeating Franklin, which gave him a claim on the vice-presidential nomination.

During the first half of 1932, in the run-up to the convention, a war of words between Smith and Roosevelt made it clear who the principal contestants for the nomination were and that Smith's earlier refusal to make an active campaign was an empty promise. In April, Roosevelt declared in a radio talk, "No nation can long endure half bankrupt. . . . These unhappy times call for the building of plans that rest upon the forgotten, the unorganized . . . for plans of those like 1917 that build from the bottom up and not from the top down, that put their faith once more in the forgotten man at the bottom of the economic pyramid." Smith, who had moved into the conservative camp, denounced the "forgotten man" concept to a Democratic Party Jefferson Day dinner in Washington, D.C., as an invitation to "class warfare. I will take off my coat and fight to the end against any candidate who persists in any demagogic appeal to the masses of the working people of this country to destroy themselves by setting class against class and rich against poor!"

Roosevelt answered his charges in a May commencement talk at Oglethorpe University in Atlanta, Georgia. Convinced that Smith was now outdoing Hoover as a rigid laissez-faire conservative, Roosevelt announced his conviction that the country needed more "planning" and less free enterprise. Above all, he decried "foolish consistency," privately repeated that everything he learned about economics at Harvard was wrong, and memorably stated that a "gigantic waste," including "the profligate waste of natural resources," had accompanied the country's "industrial advance." The time had come for less devotion to "an individualistic society" and greater commitment to "social planning." Specifically, "the country needs and, unless I mistake its temper, the country demands bold, persistent experimentation. It is common sense to take a method and try it: If it fails, admit it and try another. But above all try something."

Roosevelt's call for experimentation was in reality more of a rousing campaign slogan than an actual policy that could end the Depression. Before he could restore the American economy, he told Rosenman, he had "to get elected." Roosevelt believed that settling on decisive economic actions during the campaign was a formula for political defeat. No one knew for certain what would ensure economic recovery, and to assert that he had found the answer was certain to alienate one interest group or another. A striking example of his prevarication resonated in his response to a policy battle over protective tariffs. When asked whether he was a protectionist — that is, an economic nationalist determined to defend particular interests — he refused to answer. Although he attacked Hoover's high tariff protectionism, he trimmed sail so often on what tariffs he would eliminate or at least reduce that his policies ultimately seemed little different from Hoover's. When an aide assigned the thankless task of writing a coherent speech on the topic presented Roosevelt with "competing drafts," Franklin "read the two through with seeming care. And then he left me speechless by announcing that I had better 'weave the two together.' "

In avoiding committing himself on the tariff question, it was not as if Franklin had no preference: He was firmly on the side of the internationalists, as he was of U.S. participation in the

League of Nations. He had been a staunch advocate of Wilson's universalism during his days as assistant navy secretary and in the 1920 presidential campaign, when he and James Cox endorsed Wilson's League formula for preventing another world war and the slaughter of millions on the battlefields and at home. Indeed, his conviction that another conflict would wreak devastation on cities and innocent civilians through merciless air raids heightened his desire for some kind of international arrangement to preserve future peace. The realities of the 1932 campaign, however, made it clear that most Americans viewed international affairs as a distraction from domestic troubles which, in the midst of the Depression, Washington needed to make its only priority. In January 1932, after Newton Baker abandoned the League, Roosevelt felt he had no choice but to follow suit and appease Hearst, who was demanding that he state his current position on this compelling issue. In February, Franklin said that the League was no longer the organization Wilson had envisioned and so, "in present circumstances, I do not favor American participation."

When an outraged Wilsonian wrote to complain about Franklin's betrayal of progressive idealism, he replied: "Can't you see that loyalty to the ideals of Woodrow Wilson is just as strong in my heart as in yours — but have you ever stopped to consider that there is a difference between ideals and the methods of obtaining them?" He justified the shift in his public position by saying, "I am looking for the best modern vehicle to reach the goal of an ideal while they [my critics] insist on a vehicle which was brand new and in good running order twelve years ago. Think it over! And for heaven's sake have a little faith."

If that letter had been just a random complaint about his chameleon-like shifting about, Franklin might have set the matter aside, but a *New York Times* editorial in May following the Oglethorpe address stung him. The *Times* complained that he was a candidate with no fixed position and that his call for action — "above all try something" — was a prescription for a possible disaster. Past experience, the *Times* said, shows that "the man most to be avoided in a time of crisis is the one who goes about wringing his hands and demanding that something be done without explaining or knowing what can or ought to be done."

No commentator was more critical of Roosevelt's perceived opportunism than Walter Lippmann, the country's leading journalist. He complained that Roosevelt belonged "to the new postwar school of politicians who do not believe in stating their views unless and until there is no avoiding it. . . . Where, for example, does he stand on the tariff, on reparations and debts, on farm relief, on taxation, on banking reform, on the railroad perceived problem?" Roosevelt's political game, Lippmann asserted, "consists in gathering delegates first and adopting policies afterward to hold them together." In Lippmann's opinion, Roosevelt had developed "the art of carrying water on both shoulders." The columnist did take issue with a congressman who said that Roosevelt is "the most dangerous enemy of evil influences," as Lippmann saw him as no more than "an amiable man with many philanthropic impulses, but . . . not the dangerous enemy of anything. He is too eager to please." He was especially passive, Lippmann added, in response to Tammany corruption, because Roosevelt "is no crusader. He is no tribune of the people. He is no enemy of entrenched privilege. He is a pleasant man who, without any important qualifications for the office, would very much like to be President."

Roosevelt did not, in fact, avoid proposing clear answers or firm solutions to the country's economic crisis. He recalled Wilson's decision in September 1917, five months after the United States had entered World War I, to call upon academics to prepare the administration for future peace negotiations by writing papers on the geographical, historical, economic, and political issues relevant to the territories and peoples likely to be affected by postwar policies. More than 150 of the country's best scholars had worked for the Inquiry, as Wilson's group was called, but only twenty-three of them had accompanied him and Colonel Edward House, Wilson's principal White House adviser, to Paris for the peace talks.

In March 1932, Rosenman urged Roosevelt to gather information on what to do about the "the worst danger spots" in the economy. If he was asked to address these questions anytime soon, Rosenman said, they would "be in an awful fix," as they would be "without a well-defined and thought-out affirmative program." Roosevelt "was interested at once." Rosenman advised against inviting "successful industrialists, some big financiers, and some national political leaders" to participate, as none of those men had come up with "anything constructive to solve the mess we're in today." Instead, he thought they should turn to the country's universities. "You have been having some good experience with college professors," Rosenman reminded him. They would be eager "to strike out on new paths," and would "get away from all the old fuzzy thinking on many subjects."

Roosevelt told him to go ahead with his plan but wanted assurances that the "whole thing" would be kept "pretty quiet." Although he didn't explain why, he was guarding against the public's antipathy toward intellectuals, who had "tied themselves to Wilson and the war" and the failed promises of a new world order. "The public [had] turned on the intellectuals as the prophets of false and needless reforms," the historian Richard Hofstadter explained, "as architects of the administrative state, as supporters of the war, even as ur-Bolsheviks; the intellectuals [had] turned on America as a nation of boobs, Babbits, and fanatics." While Roosevelt was "deeply interested" in setting up what he jokingly called his "privy council," he wanted to get nominated and elected — that was the important thing — and he was not sure whether this kind of group would help or hinder.

Rosenman; Basil O'Connor, Roosevelt's law partner; and three Columbia University professors — Raymond A. Moley, Rexford G. Tugwell, and Adolph A. Berle, Jr. — formed the core of Roosevelt's advisory group. In September 1932, when a *New York Times* journalist reported on the academics who had been invited to help identify ways of combating the Depression, he called them "The Brains Trust" and then "The Brain Trust."

The forty-five-year-old Moley was a native of Ohio with an undergraduate degree from Oberlin College and a Ph.D. from Columbia, which he received in 1918. He returned to Columbia as a professor of government at Barnard College in 1923. Five years later, he joined Columbia's Law School faculty, where he specialized in criminal justice and criminal-law administration. His acquaintance with Roosevelt began that year when he helped with speechwriting for the gubernatorial campaign. Although he flirted with running for public office, Moley recognized that he was too stiff a personality to appeal to voters, and so he satisfied his fascination with politics by becoming an adviser and speechwriter. With his extensive academic contacts, Moley was considered by Rosenman to be the perfect choice to organize Roosevelt's advisory group. His professorial demeanor, underscored by the constant presence of a heavy, dark pipe, gave him the authority Roosevelt and Rosenman sought to create and lead the Brain Trust. Moley was more than happy to take on the assignment. He prided himself on a tough-minded realism that would enable him to choose members for the trust who had the academic expertise that could help end the Depression. "I feel no call to remedy evils," he liked to say. "I have not the slightest urge to be a reformer. . . . I am essentially a conservative fellow. I tilt at no windmills." According to Schlesinger, he became a "tactful ringmaster of the experts and, as middleman for their ideas, judicious and sensible. Roosevelt found his efficiency of great value."

The forty-one-year-old Tugwell, who Moley thought could be especially helpful to address the farm economy, held advanced degrees in economics from the University of Pennsylvania's Wharton School of Finance and Commerce and Columbia's economics department. He joined the Columbia faculty in 1920 after teaching at Pennsylvania and the University of Washington. He was an advocate of planning as a way to bring order to America's chaotic free-enterprise Depression economy, especially in agriculture, where technology had caused overproduction and sharply reduced farm income. Tugwell was a handsome man with thick wavy hair and a buoyant personality. His enthusiasm for shocking people with talk of making America over made him the antithesis of the unromantic Moley.

When Moley took him to Albany to meet Roosevelt in late March, Tugwell held forth for almost two hours after dinner on the "relationship of agriculture to the general economic situation." He only called a halt at midnight when Eleanor insisted that they let the governor go to sleep. "I never saw Roosevelt listen to anyone as long as he did to you," Moley told Tugwell afterward. Troubled at the thought that he might have made a fool of himself in front of the potential next president of the United States, Tugwell was relieved to be invited into Roosevelt's bedroom the following morning to continue the conversation. No doubt influenced by the subsequent events that made Roosevelt into a larger-than-life figure, Tugwell later recalled that his first meeting with Roosevelt was "somewhat like coming into contact with destiny itself."

At the time, Moley was no less impressed with Roosevelt. "You ask what he is like," Moley wrote his sister in April 1932. "The idea people get from his charming manner — that he is soft or flabby in disposition and character — is far from true. . . . When crossed he is hard, stubborn, resourceful, relentless." Moley dismissed speculations about

Roosevelt's having been weakened by his illness as "bunk. Nobody in public life since T.R. has been so robust, so buoyantly and blatantly healthy. . . ." he reported. "I've been amazed with his interest in things. It skips and bounces through . . . intricate subjects." Although Moley soon realized that Roosevelt was little acquainted with current economic thinking, he did not believe that would be a problem. On the contrary, he believed it would give Roosevelt "complete freedom from dogmatism . . . a virtue at this stage of the game." Moley worried, however, about what he saw as the governor's uncritical acceptance of what the experts said. "He makes no effort to check up on anything that I or anybody else has told him," Moley observed.

The thirty-seven-year-old Adolf A. Berle, Jr., was the most brilliant and accomplished member of the "Privy Council." The son of a Boston Protestant minister, Berle was a child prodigy who entered Harvard College at the age of fourteen. Winning high honors during his undergraduate studies, he then attended Harvard Law School, where he earned a masters and a law degree, again with high honors. At twenty-one, he joined one of Boston's most prestigious firms, Brandeis, Dunbar, & Nutter. Service as a second lieutenant in the Great War, with an assignment to duty in the Dominican Republic to help increase the country's sugar production and then as an expert on Russia's economy, won him a place on the Inquiry and among the handful of experts who went to the Paris peace talks. At the close of the war, he briefly joined a New York law firm before establishing a firm of his own in 1924. For all his brilliance, his contemporaries complained that his personal manner was arrogant and curt, and he had few social skills. He was an infant prodigy, one critic said, "who remained an infant long after he ceased to be a prodigy."

In 1925, Berle began teaching a course at the Harvard Business School and publishing articles critical of the structure of America's largest corporations. He was convinced that the United States was becoming an oligarchy, which he argued threatened American democracy by accumulating too much wealth in too few hands. A grant from the newly established Social Science Research Council and an appointment as a professor at the Columbia Law School gave him the time to work on a book, *The Modern Corporation and Private Property,* which he published in the fall of 1932 with Gardiner Means, a Harvard Ph.D. in economics. The book was a searing indictment of concentrated wealth and its impact on America's free enterprise system. Although Berle favored Newton Baker for the presidency, he was pleased to share his ideas about the economy and monetary policy with Roosevelt beginning in April 1932.

Roosevelt valued the Privy Council, as he enjoyed calling them, well aware that historically the term referred to a monarch's secret advisory group. He would chuckle every time he used the term, amused that he was playing the part of a king being counseled by tribunes. But whether he was ready to follow their lead on any of the advice they were offering was another matter. It was good to have a storehouse of ideas for the day he would have to make policy decisions, but, as he would say after he became president, first things first, and what remained unsettled was getting to the

White House.

Initially, Roosevelt seemed like an unstoppable candidate. His progressive record as governor, combined with the efforts of Howe and Farley to promote him to party leaders, put many of the Midwestern states in Roosevelt's column. His residence in Georgia and courting of Southern politicians, meanwhile, had drawn the South to his standard. Although his backers arrived at the convention in Chicago in late June with a majority of delegates, and Chicago's mayor packed the galleries with Roosevelt supporters, Roosevelt remained 104 delegates short of the two-thirds necessary for the nomination. A surge of support for Al Smith in the Northeast, where only Maine, New Hampshire, and Vermont favored Roosevelt; Roosevelt's defeat by Garner in the California primary in May; and favorite-son votes in Virginia, Ohio, and Illinois threatened a deadlocked convention. An abortive attempt to abolish the two-thirds rule only weakened Roosevelt's appeal, irritating Southern delegates who believed that the rule had served their minority standing since their return to regular party status in the late nineteenth century.

When the nominating votes started in the early morning hours of July 1, Roosevelt, who listened in on the telephone from the governor's mansion in Albany, worried that his support might not hold beyond initial ballots. But his first-ballot vote of 666 delegates gave him a commanding lead over Smith, who had only 201 delegates behind him. Garner's 90 delegates put him in third place, but, most important, they represented the key to an early nominating decision. Although Roosevelt gained 11 votes on a second ballot and another 5 when a third ballot was cast that morning, bringing his total to 682, he remained 90 votes short of victory. The exhausted delegates agreed to an adjournment until that evening, giving Roosevelt's deputies time to swing a deal with the Garner camp. The negotiations were conducted through McAdoo, who led the California delegation. If Roosevelt would accept Garner as his vice president and give assurances that he would appoint progressive secretaries of state and treasury, the California and Texas delegations would vote for him on the fourth ballot. Roosevelt and Garner were both only too happy to agree, and that evening Roosevelt won the nomination with 945 votes. A bitter Smith refused to make the vote unanimous, retaining the remaining 190 delegates.

In choosing Garner as his vice president, Roosevelt was not only clinching the nomination but also fixing his sights on Southern electoral votes. In 1928, Hoover had broken the Democratic Party's long-term hold on the South by winning five states in Dixie, running from Virginia through North Carolina, Tennessee, Florida, and Texas. Roosevelt was mindful of Southern antagonism to a Democratic Party tied to urban ethnics who were disdainful of a region identified with fundamentalism. If he was to win in 1932 and build a reliable coalition, he would have to ensure Southern support. While his Warm Springs ties would be helpful, healing the great divide between the North and South would mean convincing Southerners that a Democratic Party headed by a New York governor would not be hostile to their concerns. Beyond that, Roosevelt saw the presidency as a vehicle to reintegrate the nation and serve a larger ideal. In September, he told *New*

York Times reporter Anne O'Hare McCormick that the nation needed someone in the White House who could "understand and treat with the country as a whole. For as much as anything it needs to be reaffirmed at this juncture that the United States is one organic entity, that no interest, no class, no section, is either separate or supreme above the interests of all."

Although he was now the nominee, Roosevelt's selection left many rifts within the party. First, Louisiana's Huey Long had helped turn aside efforts to seat anti-Roosevelt Louisiana, Minnesota, and Puerto Rico delegations that would have sunk his candidacy. Jim Farley said later that it was "the most vital moment of the Convention." Second, a battle over a platform plank supporting the repeal of Prohibition, largely provoked by stop-Roosevelt forces, had almost deadlocked the convention. Roosevelt had refused to take a stance on the issue, which had caused an unbridgeable divide at the 1924 Convention and undermined them in the subsequent campaign. It threatened to weaken the Democrats' appeal again. Third, the effort to shift Texas to Roosevelt from Garner almost failed. Strong-minded Texan delegates, who had come to Chicago to make Garner the nominee, refused to give up their goal. Sam Rayburn, Garner's House colleague from Texas, who was arranging the move to Roosevelt, persuaded only 54 delegates out of 107 to make the switch. Fortunately for Roosevelt and Rayburn, several anti-Roosevelt delegates were absent from the caucus, trying to persuade other delegations to make Garner the nominee. Fourth, if the convention had gone beyond the fourth ballot, Roosevelt, Farley, and Howe believed it would have defeated

Franklin's candidacy.

Finally, there was a considerable number of delegates who considered Roosevelt, in the words of H. L. Mencken, as "one of the most charming men, but like many another very charming man he leaves on the beholder the impression that he is also somewhat shallow and futile." His response to Tammany corruption in New York during his governorship gave him a reputation as a political temporizer who would sacrifice his principles for political harmony and votes. One Texas delegate, unhappy with Roosevelt's nomination, said that the party had "a kangaroo ticket, stronger in hind end than the front." After Roosevelt's victory, Chicago bookies were posting 5-to-1 odds that Hoover would defeat him.

Roosevelt's charm and apparent superficiality were partly a defense against establishing close contacts — a technique for bringing people to his side without allowing them to know the full man. But in 1932, mindful of the need to develop a plan that would bring relief, recovery, and reform to the country, he wasn't sure exactly what such a program would consist of and so opted for a realpolitik. He understood that he would need the support of the Southern congressmen and senators, whose seniority gave them control of crucial legislative committees. Likewise, he was not prepared to introduce policies that would draw immediate opposition. The campaign he was about to launch needed to keep its focus on Hoover. Most voters were less inclined to vote for someone than against Hoover, who had failed them so badly. Roosevelt judged that his candidacy needed principally to spark hope and a belief that he could do better than a president who had fallen so short in countering the Depression.

For his part, Hoover recognized that people would favor anyone who made them more optimistic about the country's future. He told Rudy Vallee, a popular star of stage, screen, and radio, that he would give him a medal if he could sing a song that would make people forget their troubles and the Depression. To chase away the gloom, gatherings of businessmen sang, "Pack up your troubles in your old kit bag and smile, smile, smile." Nothing, however, could dispel Hoover's dourness, which only added to the grim national temper and put him at a great disadvantage against someone with the charm and upbeat demeanor of a Roosevelt. Mindful of how important establishing positive associations with Roosevelt were, Ed Flynn persuaded Howe to switch the campaign song from "Anchors Away" to "Happy Days Are Here Again," which was the finale of the 1930 film *Chasing Rainbows*.

As he prepared to launch his national campaign, Roosevelt concluded that no policy proposal would resonate as deeply with voters as the belief that he represented change — a break with the immediate past and the restoration of national economic well-being. How would he generate a national feeling of excitement, of hopeful expectations? He could point to his progressive policies as governor, but he realized that no particular policy would give rise to renewed hope as much as a general enthusiasm for a new president with an affinity for innovation.

He believed that his campaign would need to sustain the confident mood identified with his candidacy during the four months leading up to the election. He saw that he could make an immediate gain by breaking the custom of how a candidate was informed of his nomination. Instead of "the absurd tradition that the candidate should remain in professed ignorance of what has happened . . . until he is formally notified of that event," Roosevelt announced that he would fly to Chicago to speak to the convention and accept the nomination, an arduous eight-hour flight made worse by bad weather that would allay any doubts about his physical capacity to serve as president.

In his speech on July 2 before the cheering delegates and galleries, he apologized for arriving late and underscored the peril he had faced in traveling to be with them. "I have no control over the winds of Heaven and could only be thankful for my Navy training," he declared. He wanted his presence to stand as a "symbol of my intention to be honest and to avoid all hypocrisy or sham, to avoid all silly shutting of the eyes to the truth in this campaign." He followed with praise of Wilson and the Democratic Party's faith in progressive advance. He complimented the country on remaining "orderly and hopeful" despite "these days of crushing want. . . . To fail to offer them a new chance is not only to betray their hopes, but to misunderstand their patience." The current economic disaster, he said, was the consequence of the business community's and the current administration's failure to address the nation's problems in a constructive and compassionate way. He promised to relieve the suffering of the unemployed and farmers whose incomes had shriveled and whose homesteads were lost while the Republicans in Washington waited passively for the economy to self-correct.

In a peroration meant to assure his constituents that he would not disappoint, Roosevelt declared, "I pledge you, I pledge myself, to a new deal for the American people. Let us all here assembled constitute ourselves prophets of a new order." Mindful of the country's long history of religious evangelism, he described his campaign as a "crusade to restore America to its own people." Neither he nor Sam Rosenman, who had drafted the speech, foresaw the extent to which the words "new deal" would become emblematic of the administration.

Since defeating Hoover seemed like a foregone conclusion, Democratic senators urged Roosevelt to avoid excessive exposure, which could leave him vulnerable to attacks favoring the Republicans. They urged him to stay close to home, and speak only occasionally on radio and at a few carefully staged rallies on the East Coast. Garner echoed the point and warned against putting forward any "wild-eyed ideas" that would allow Hoover "to kick the shit out of us." Speaking tours would be a mistake. "All you have got to do," Garner told Roosevelt, "is to stay alive until election day."

In July, Hoover's unpopularity deepened when he mishandled a veterans' march on Washington. Dubbed the Bonus Army or Bonus Expeditionary Force (BEF), as the veterans called themselves, the 20,000 men, some with their families, had come to the Capitol in June to press their case for an early payment of bonuses that had been promised to be issued in 1945. On June 15, a sympathetic majority in the House of Representatives had voted to support the measure, but two days later the Senate, reluctant to further unbalance the federal budget with payments totaling $2.4 billion, rejected the House bill by a vote of 62 to 18. About a third of the veterans then returned home, but several thousand, already residing in makeshift quarters on Anacostia Flats outside of the capital, announced their intention to "stay till 1945." Although the district chief of police, a brigadier general in the wartime army, sympathized with the unemployed veterans asking for nothing more than what they had earned by their service, he could not ensure a peaceable end to their encampment.

On July 28, when the D.C. police tried to evict some veterans from abandoned buildings on Pennsylvania Avenue, violence erupted, and two veterans were killed. District commissioners now asked the White House for federal troops, which Hoover was only too happy to provide. An astonishingly large force of cavalry with drawn swords, a column of infantry brandishing bayonets, and six tanks led by General Douglas MacArthur attired in a dress uniform with medals and ribbons on his tunic and accompanied by his chief aides, Majors Dwight D. Eisenhower and George S. Patton, ousted the veterans from the abandoned buildings and then from the Flats, where they burned the shacks as they drove the men, women, and children before them under a hail of tear gas.

The administration tried to justify the armed action against the BEF as a necessary response to a potential rebellion by communists and criminals, but millions of Americans sided with the veterans. The Washington *News,* a Republican paper, spoke for White House critics when it declared, "What a pitiful spectacle is that of the great American Government, mightiest in the world, chasing unarmed men, women and children with Army tanks. . . . If the Army must be called out to make war on unarmed citizens, this is no longer America." Newsreel footage of the assault refuted claims that the troops were dealing with an unruly and dangerous mob. Roosevelt, who opposed paying the bonus, but shared the indignation so many felt toward the administration for its abuse of war veterans, now viewed Douglas MacArthur as the proverbial man on horseback and the most dangerous man in America. "There's a potential Mussolini for you," Roosevelt said. "Right here at home."

The Bonus episode gave Roosevelt an even greater sense of urgency about winning the White House. And however much Hoover appeared to effectively be a defeated incumbent, Roosevelt discounted all predictions that he was already beaten and resisted advice urging a low-key campaign. He was determined to get out on the hustings and refute all lingering doubts about his physical capacity to shoulder the burdens of the presidency. In addition, with less than a third of registered voters identified as Democrats, Roosevelt thought it a mistake to take anything for granted about the outcome of the election. Progressive Republican Harold Ickes in Chicago warned him that "while many independents and Republicans are favorably inclined toward you at this time I find that they are not prepared to make up their minds finally until you have passed upon the case of [New York City] Mayor [Jimmy] Walker."

For two weeks in August, Roosevelt responded to the Walker problem by holding hearings on the mayor's acceptance of bribes. Earlier investigation had made Walker's corruption clear, but in deciding whether he should compel Walker's resignation or simply reprimand him, Roosevelt faced a political conundrum. Warned that he would lose votes in the South and West if he let Walker off easy and that he would jeopardize support in New York, New Jersey, Massachusetts, Connecticut, and Illinois if he removed him from office, Roosevelt struggled to present himself as judicious and fair. Winning praise for his evenhandedness during the proceedings, he ultimately escaped having to make the difficult decision when Walker resigned on September 1 and left the country for a European tour.

Roosevelt began a post–Labor Day cross-country speaking tour of cities in the Midwest and West. During the next eight weeks, he logged over 13,000 miles, mostly by train, and gave twenty-five major speeches in cities between Boston and the West Coast. He also gave impromptu talks from the back of his campaign train, but he fostered the impression of a candidate focused on every major issue facing the country by speaking in strategically chosen cities on specific topics: In Topeka, Kansas, he addressed the farm problem; in Salt Lake City, Utah, he spoke about the plight of the railroads; in Portland, Oregon, he discussed public utilities; in San Francisco, California, at the Commonwealth Club, he waxed philosophical about the dilemmas of an industrial America with no frontier and the need to prevent economic oligarchy; in Seattle, Washington, and Sioux City, Iowa, he straddled the tariff issue; in Detroit, Michigan, he promised "social justice" to the millions who had fallen into poverty (but avoided saying how he would do so);

in Sioux City and Pittsburgh, he decried Hoover's deficits and pledged reduced federal expenditures and balanced budgets; and in Baltimore and Boston, as the campaign came to a close, he pilloried Hoover and the "Four Horsemen of the present Republican leadership — the Horsemen of Destruction, Delay, Deceit, Despair" — and the desperate need for unemployment relief and jobs that could sustain family life.

Hoover initially believed that Roosevelt's radicalism would alienate the business community and lead to his defeat. Soon, however, the president began complaining that his challenger was winning support by being "a chameleon on plaid." He charged that Roosevelt's speeches revealed a consummate political opportunist intent on capturing the White House by making contradictory appeals calculated not to end the Depression but to win votes. Hoover's argument was not without merit. The journalist Elmer Davis, who followed Roosevelt across the country, discerned few coherent pronouncements on what voters could expect from a Roosevelt administration. "You could not quarrel with a single one of his generalities; you seldom can," Davis wrote. "But what they mean (if anything) is known only to Franklin D. Roosevelt and his God." For example, at the same time that Roosevelt blasted Hoover for piling up unbalanced budgets and massive federal debt, he promised to practice deficit spending if he had to feed and clothe starving, homeless citizens. A Roosevelt ally said later that "the campaign speeches often read like a giant misprint, in which Roosevelt and Hoover speak each other's lines."

As the campaign moved toward November,

Hoover realized that attacking Roosevelt as an unprincipled political chameleon was not enough to beat him. In the final days of the campaign he replaced his plan to give only a few speeches with a crowded schedule of strident talks. The crowds' reactions to him — boos, catcalls, threats of violence that had his Secret Service escorts on edge — made clear how unpopular he had become. But instead of driving him to the sidelines, it strengthened his determination to warn against the consequences of a Roosevelt presidency and a Democratic Congress. He denounced Roosevelt and the Democrats as zealots under the spell of "the same philosophy of government which has poisoned all of Europe . . . the fumes of the witch's cauldron which boiled in Russia." Roosevelt's proposed new deal "would destroy the very foundations of our American system." The Democrats were "the party of the mob." But as long as he and the Republicans remained in Washington, they would know "how to deal with the mob." But his invoking memories of the military's action against the Bonus Marchers only deepened the rage voters felt against a president and an administration denying the realities of the Depression by saying that "many people have left their jobs for the more profitable one of selling apples." Exhausted by and furious at the public's overt rejection of his appeal for another term, Hoover seemed on the verge of a nervous collapse.

In his vagueness about how he intended to end the Depression if he became president, Roosevelt consciously hoped to deflect criticism of his capacity to do so. He also understood that voters were less attentive to what he said than how he said it. "If Roosevelt's program lacked substance," William Leuchtenburg says, "his blithe spirit — his infectious smile, his warm mellow voice, his obvious ease with crowds — contrasted sharply with Hoover's glumness." When the Roosevelt campaign struck up "Happy Days Are Here Again," people wanted to believe that he had the cures to the country's woes. Optimism was the one thing, above all, that Hoover couldn't offer, and it was an attribute Roosevelt maintained throughout the twelve additional years in his political career.

Roosevelt won a landmark victory on November 8. Mindful that the election was going to be a landslide, someone sent Hoover a telegram that read: "Vote for Roosevelt and make it unanimous." Almost forty million voters went to the polls, four million more than in 1928. Roosevelt bested Hoover by over seven million popular votes and captured forty-two of the forty-eight states, winning 472 electoral ballots to Hoover's 59 from only six states. The Democratic margins in Congress were as expected — nearly three to one in the House and almost two to one in the Senate.

By contrast with Franklin, Howe, Farley, and Flynn, who were ecstatic about the runaway victory, Eleanor Roosevelt continued to have mixed feelings. She shared in her husband's joy at having overcome the terrible blow polio had dealt him to become president. But she rued what her new status could mean for her, having had firsthand knowledge of the burdens that TR's presidency had inflicted on his wife, Edith. The turmoil in my heart and mind," she wrote later, "was rather great that night, and the next few months were not to make any clearer what the road ahead would be."

If Franklin had his own share of uncertainties about the challenges he would face as president in such dismal times, he never revealed them. Masking his private feelings was something he believed essential to managing the office and maintaining public confidence. Harold Ickes, who became Roosevelt's secretary of the interior, complained about the difficulty of working with him. "Because I get too hard at times?" Roosevelt asked. "No," Ickes said, "because you . . . keep your cards close up against your belly. You never put them on the table." Tugwell saw Roosevelt's reticence as a way to deny "any agony of indecision." A more practical explanation would be that he kept his counsel because it served his political options or freedom to wait until the last moment to choose a course of action.

During the four-month interregnum between his election and inauguration on March 4, Roosevelt remained flexible about the details of his administration. Few could doubt that progressive measures would be central features, as so much of his rhetoric addressed federal programs rescuing the indigent and conserving the country's natural resources. But Roosevelt was not ready to commit to a legislative agenda in any detail. Huey Long, the Kingfish from Louisiana, who urged him to adopt aggressive radical actions, complained that when he put his views before Roosevelt, the president-elect would respond: "Fine! Fine! Fine!" When Joe Robinson, a conservative Democratic senator from Arkansas, would counsel restraint, Roosevelt would likewise say: "Fine! Fine! Fine!" "Maybe he says 'Fine!' to everybody," Long complained. It was part of what Tugwell described as Roosevelt's "almost impenetrable concealment of intention," leading him to conclude shrewdly that "there was another Roosevelt behind the one we saw and talked with. I was baffled, unable to make out what he was like, that other man." What was clear to him and Moley, however, was Roosevelt's talent for being an actor on a world stage. He had spent a lifetime preparing himself to assume the roles of governor and president. He was a master performer who, we can assume, had rehearsed the part he would play innumerable times, and it was evident that he greatly enjoyed doing so. In time, those closest to him concluded that Franklin Roosevelt's idea of the presidency was himself as president.

Roosevelt biographer Jonathan Alter believes that Roosevelt's response to polio included the development of a keen acting ability. Eager to blunt the discomfort at the sight of his withered legs beneath his muscular torso, Roosevelt "joke[d] and reminisce[d], so that friends were amused and distracted from the invalid they were seeing." He honed "his theatricality — the way he tuned his voice and planned his entrances and exits for maximum effect, because he could no longer dominate a room with his physical size and presence." In time, delighted with the effectiveness of his public posturing, he would tell Orson Welles, the iconic Hollywood figure, "Orson, you and I are the two greatest actors in America."

On one matter, however, Roosevelt wished to leave little doubt: He wanted no association with Hoover's policies in the closing days of his term. For all his evasiveness, Roosevelt made it clear that he regarded the Depression as the product not of international events, as Hoover believed, but of domestic ones. When Hoover tried to enlist Roosevelt in a war debt repayment plan and an international economic conference, Roosevelt rejected the initiatives. "He did not get it at all," Hoover complained after a November 22 meeting at the White House. He described Roosevelt as "a very ignorant and well-meaning young man." "You can't trust him," Hoover added, labeling him "a very dangerous and contrary man." Roosevelt not only viewed Hoover's policies as shortsighted but considered any association with him as potentially damaging. While he had compassion for so un-popular a leader and wanted to give him respect-ful credit at the close of his term, he did not want to undermine the surge of confidence voters had accorded to him as the only official who could restore prosperity and preserve the country's political institutions.

With the economy worsening and banks col-lapsing during the four-month winter hiatus before Roosevelt assumed office, the prospect of a new administration wasn't sufficient to maintain public confidence in a revival. Misery in America that winter, FDR biographer Jean Edward Smith says, was widespread: "Fifteen million workers, one out of every three, had lost their jobs." The hungry haunted city garbage dumps, and, Tugwell observed, America never knew "such moving distress from sheer hunger and cold." The price of a bushel of wheat stood at a three-hundred-year low, which was ruinous to wheat farmers. Malnu-trition afflicted almost every family in the coal-mining regions of West Virginia and Kentucky. Foreclosures on homes and farms were rampant. And Roosevelt, who explained that he had no power to act, "refused to issue statements on the sharpening economic crisis or to announce his plans. He merely waited. All his actions were in slow waltz time."

The one thing he could not avoid, which would give some indication of the direction of his administration, was the appointment of cabinet officers. Even here, however, he provided no clear evidence about how he intended to end the Depression. The eight men and one woman he chose represented a collection of political outlooks and geographical regions. His selections had the familiar feel of a clever politician striking a balance among competing interests. There was nothing dramatically out of the ordinary about his choices, except for including the first woman cabinet appointee in the group, as to suggest the arrival of a "new order."

The secretary of state was the sixty-one-year-old Cordell Hull, a Tennessee senator, conservative Grover Cleveland Democrat, and Wilsonian free trader opposed to high tariffs, representing the Southern and business wings of the Party. Sixty-four-year-old William Woodin was secretary of treasury. An industrialist with an engineering degree, like Hoover, and the president of the American Car and Foundry Company, Woodin was a Republican who had helped finance Roosevelt's campaign. His selection gave the country's business leaders reassurance that Roosevelt was not an enemy of free enterprise. Daniel C. Roper, the secretary of commerce, was a South Carolinian with a long career in government and political ties to Wilson and the business community, another choice that reinforced Roosevelt's effort to refute Hoover's warnings of his radicalism.

213

Having made assurances of his traditionalism, Roosevelt appeased supporters on the left with his Agriculture, Labor, Interior, and Justice department appointments. The forty-four-year-old Henry A. Wallace was the son of Harding's secretary of agriculture and a progressive Iowa Republican. His innovations in corn production and success in starting Hi-Bred Corn Company, which made him wealthy, gave him credibility as an agribusinessman. His rhetoric was that of a TR New Nationalist, of government policies to restore the farm economy and preserve the rural way of life, a position that gave him standing with Roosevelt.

Similarly, the fifty-two-year-old Frances Perkins, who had long-term associations with Al Smith and Roosevelt during their governorships, had helped make New York the most progressive state in the Union with liberal advances in child labor laws and women's working conditions. The fifty-eight-year-old Harold L. Ickes, a journalist, lawyer, and Progressive Republican from Chicago with a reputation as a vocal opponent of corrupt politicians and an affinity for social causes, including black rights, became the secretary of the interior and a voice for maintaining TR's conservationism. Roosevelt's choice for attorney general of Senator Thomas A. Walsh of Montana, the driving force behind the investigation of the Teapot Dome scandal, boosted the president-elect's appeal in the Mountain West. Naming Jim Farley as the postmaster general ensured that Roosevelt supporters would receive the many patronage jobs a first-term president commanded.

If Roosevelt's cabinet raised doubts about the likely boldness of his leadership in striking out on new paths to counter the Depression, his response to an assassination attempt revived and strengthened public faith in his courage to meet and overcome the national crisis.

On February 15, Roosevelt arrived in Miami on a yacht from an eleven-day Caribbean vacation to speak to the annual gathering of the American Legion. Seated in an open car at Bay Front Park, where the legionnaires were meeting, he was an open target for Giuseppe Zangara, an unemployed bricklayer, who had purchased a revolver in a Miami pawnshop with the intention of killing the president-elect. As Roosevelt sat chatting with Chicago mayor Anton Cermak, who stood outside the car next to a Secret Service agent, Zangara got off five shots, hitting five bystanders, including Cermak, but not Roosevelt. A woman standing next to the gunman had saved Roosevelt from injury by hitting Zangara with her handbag. Cermak would die two weeks later from his injuries and the thirty-two-year-old Zangara, who said that he was out to get all capitalists, and anyone who was "rich and powerful," especially any president, was tried and executed.

All reports of Roosevelt's response to the shooting emphasized his composure and even his disdain at his brush with death. He insisted that Cermak be transported in his car to the nearest hospital, where he waited until the mayor was out of the emergency room and he could speak with him. Moley recorded that after Roosevelt returned that night to the yacht "there was nothing — not so much as the twitching of a muscle, the mopping of a brow, or even the hint of false gaiety — to indicate that it wasn't any other evening in any other place. Roosevelt was simply himself — easy, confident, poised, to all appearance unmoved." His grace under fire "brought a surge of national confidence in him as had none of his other actions since the election." For his part, Franklin viewed the assassination attempt as a blessing in disguise — a postelection rallying event carrying him into the presidency on a wave of sympathy and approval that he believed would greatly serve his initial presidential actions in the coming struggle with the Great Depression.

CHAPTER 5
"INSTRUMENT OF THEIR WISHES"

Was there any precedent for what was happening to the economy in the four-month interregnum before Franklin could replace Hoover? When British economist John Maynard Keynes was asked this question, he replied yes: "It lasted four hundred years and was called the Dark Ages." In February, during a meeting with the president-elect in Warm Springs, Walter Lippmann told Roosevelt, "The situation is critical, Franklin. You may have no alternative but to assume dictatorial powers." Readers of Lippmann's column would not have been surprised by his advice. He had been beating the drum for "a strong national executive. Any group of 500 men," he had told readers, "whether they are called congressmen or anything else, is an unruly mob unless it comes under the strict control of a single will."

Lippmann was not the only one urging assertive presidential leadership. David Reed, Pennsylvania's Republican senator, publicly declared the need for an American Mussolini. "Leave it to Congress," he said, "we will fiddle around here all summer trying to satisfy every lobbyist, and we will get nowhere. The country does not want that. The country wants stern action, and action taken quickly." Kansas's Republican governor, Alf Landon, echoed the point: "Even the iron hand of a dictator is in preference to a paralytic stroke." The publisher William Randolph Hearst was producing and advising on a prescriptive Hollywood film, *Gabriel Over the White House,* which depicted a president who "dissolves Congress, creates an army of the unemployed, and lines up his enemies before a firing squad." A draft of a five-minute speech Roosevelt was to deliver to World War I veterans in the American Legion included a closing paragraph that he deleted from his talk: It asserted that the troops under the president's command would remain so "in any phase of the situation that now confronts us."

Roosevelt resisted any suggestions that could undermine America's democratic traditions. When Eleanor suggested that the country might benefit from a benevolent dictator "who could force through reforms," Franklin "looked at her quizzically and remarked that one could not count upon a dictator staying benevolent." While he was eager to take the lead in ending the national crisis, he had no intention of trying to imitate Mussolini, Stalin, or Hitler, who had become Germany's chancellor on January 30. He asked his friend Felix Frankfurter, a law professor at Harvard, to discourage Lippmann's talk of expanding presidential control at the expense of Congress. "This constant harping on the inadequacies and obstructions of Congress fits in with the misdirection on that subject for the last ten years," Frankfurter wrote Lippmann, "and gives impulse to . . . the fascist forces."

Lippmann had no desire to abandon democratic customs permanently, and Roosevelt was intent on not doing so even temporarily. Representative government was a precious tradition he was intent on preserving. He believed that the United States had the flexibility to find its way through the current crisis with its institutions intact. Because circumstances had made him the focus of mass hopes to preserve America's constitutional order, he appreciated that he would have a central role in the process. But he wanted a recovery that could be achieved without destroying what set America apart from other countries around the globe.

He relished his emerging role on the world stage, and approached the presidency with the excitement of a born leader who was about to make a lasting mark on the country's political history. To be sure, the challenge would test his skills as a politician, but he appreciated the chance to lead a transformational administration with the cunning a successful leader needed to use if he were to buoy the economy and put institutions in place that would make America more humane and less vulnerable to future economic downturns.

Roosevelt choreographed every detail of his first days in Washington. When he and Eleanor and the rest of his family detrained at Union Station on the evening of March 2, a large crowd awaited them. Many were convinced that Roosevelt no longer suffered the effects of polio and expected him to walk through the station, but a car arrived for the family, so his supporters' assumptions about his mobility were not challenged. After the assassination attempt in Miami, it seemed best to limit his exposure to crowds. But mindful of how important symbolism was in leading the nation, Roosevelt and his family stayed at the Mayflower

Hotel on Connecticut Avenue instead of the more upscale Willard, which was known as the residence of presidents. He also wanted to cancel the customary ball on inaugural night, which he thought would be in bad taste when so many in the country were suffering. But convinced that a festive dance party would brighten people's spirits, Eleanor insisted that it go on as planned. Franklin, however, refused to attend, avoiding any overt display of his disability.

The Mayflower, like the Willard, was close to the White House, where he planned to go the following day to pay a traditional call on the departing president. The meeting on the afternoon of March 3 generated new tensions with Hoover. With depositors everywhere eager to preserve their savings by withdrawing funds from failing banks, their operations were suspended by thirty-two state governments to head off a collapse. Most banks in the other sixteen states voluntarily closed their doors or limited withdrawals. When Hoover received a report that Roosevelt and his advisers would do nothing to forestall bank failures before the change of administrations, he decided to use the ceremonial visit to press the president-elect into a joint response to the crisis. Roosevelt's continuing refusal to cooperate struck Hoover as "infamous politics devoid of every atom of patriotism." Roosevelt had no interest in further tarring Hoover with accusations of failed leadership, but he remained determined to shun any demonstration of ties to Hoover that could suggest continuity with his administration instead of a fresh start.

As the meeting came to an end, Roosevelt told Hoover that in light of the current situation in the nation, he would fully understand if Hoover did

not feel compelled to honor the custom of returning his call. "Mr. Roosevelt," Hoover contemptuously replied, "when you are in Washington as
long as I have been, you will learn that the
President of the United States calls on nobody."
James Roosevelt, who had accompanied his
parents to the White House, said that he had never
seen his father so angry as when they departed.
But believing that it would be an unproductive
distraction from the constructive notes he wished
to strike at the start of his term, Roosevelt gave
no public evidence of his ire. Hoover, for his part,
remained an aggrieved party. On March 4, as he
and Roosevelt rode from the White House to
Capitol Hill for the inaugural ceremony, he was
sullen and unsmiling. Roosevelt tried to make
small talk, but Hoover was unresponsive. Roosevelt eventually gave up and focused on the
crowd lining Pennsylvania Avenue, waving his silk
hat and smiling at his supporters, who were
"shouting, cheering, and singing 'Happy Days Are
here Again.' " A Harvard classmate of Franklin's,
watching from a grandstand, said that Roosevelt
seemed "full of cheer and confidence." By contrast, Hoover's face was "like a lump of dough
before it goes into the oven, puffy and expressionless."

That morning, accompanied by all his cabinet
choices, except Thomas Walsh, attorney general
nominee, who had died on the way to the inauguration, Roosevelt had attended a prayer service at
St. John's Episcopal Church presided over by
Groton's seventy-six-year-old headmaster, Endicott Peabody. Whether or not Franklin genuinely
believed that his presence at the service could
inspire a heavenly intervention to help him ease

the country's troubles, he knew it would resonate with millions of Americans, regardless of religious denomination.

Roosevelt also understood that the first step toward national recovery would be his greatly awaited inaugural address. The speech was a masterful use of language to ease current fears and encourage positive thinking about the future. Roosevelt, coatless and hatless despite a cold March wind, began his speech before a crowd of over a hundred thousand gathered on the east front of the capitol by describing the inaugural ritual as "a day of national consecration." He followed with a declaration that "the present situation of our Nation" impelled him "to speak the truth, the whole truth, frankly and boldly" about the nation's plight. But while he saw no need to "shrink from honestly facing conditions in our country today," he immediately offered assurances that "this great Nation will endure as it has endured, will revive and will prosper. So, first of all, let me assert my firm belief that the only thing we have to fear is fear itself — nameless, unreasoning unjustified terror which paralyzes needed efforts to convert retreat into advance." But, Roosevelt reminded the crowd again, "Only a foolish optimist can deny the dark realities of the moment."

Who was to blame for the current state of the nation? Roosevelt knew that identifying the perpetrators of the country's economic collapse would put conservative opponents of any of his legislative measures to restore prosperity on the defensive. The culprits, he said, were the country's business leaders, "a generation of self-seekers . . . the money changers" who valued riches more than the country's "ancient truths," and in the midst of the crisis had "fled from their high seats in the temple of our civilization." In short, they had caused a disaster and refused to take responsibility for it.

The challenge now was to "apply social values more noble than mere monetary profit." But "restoration calls . . . not for changes in ethics alone." The nation cried out for "action, and action now." The first priority was "to put people to work," partly by creating government jobs that would "stimulate and reorganize the use of our natural resources." This necessitated a shift of part of the population from America's "industrial centers" to the land, where the value of agricultural products had to be increased "and with this the power to purchase the output of our cities." He echoed William Jennings Bryan's memorable assertion that if farms were destroyed, grass would grow in every city in the country. Foreclosures on "small homes and our farms" had to end. National planning to address these dislocations was essential, as was supervision of banks and "an end to speculation with other people's money." He promised to urge these measures upon a special congressional session as a means of putting "our national house in order." And although international trade was "vastly important," he believed in "putting first things first": The "emergency at home cannot wait on" economic readjustment abroad.

Because so many voices had been raised in support of centralized presidential authority to combat the crisis, Roosevelt felt compelled to end his address with a reassurance that he intended to act "under the form of government which we have inherited from our ancestors. Our Constitution is so simple and practical that it is possible always to meet extraordinary needs by changes in emphasis and arrangement without loss of essential form. . . . It is to be hoped that the normal balance of executive and legislative authority may be wholly adequate to meet the unprecedented task before us. But it may be that an unprecedented demand and need for un-delayed action may call for temporary departure from that normal balance of public procedure." He warned that if Congress failed to act and the national emergency continued, he would not shirk his duty to ask Congress for "broad Executive power to wage a war against the emergency, as great as the power that would be given to me if we were in fact invaded by a foreign foe. . . . We do not distrust the future of essential democracy," he concluded. But he acknowledged that the public wanted "direct, vigorous action. They have asked for discipline and direction under leadership. They have made me the present instrument of their wishes. In the spirit of the gift I take it."

The public reception to his speech was all that Roosevelt could have wished. In the days immediately after March 4, close to half a million people sent messages of support and thanks for restoring their faith in America. The country was so starved for inspired leadership after Hoover's desultory performance that Roosevelt could have said almost anything and found an enthusiastic audience. Just the promise of action now by a leader brimming with confidence was enough to excite popular approval and expectations of a rising economy.

A cartoon in the *Philadelphia Record* titled

"Finis" captured the spirit of the day: In front of the White House a smiling Roosevelt with rolled-up shirt sleeves and no hint of his disability carries a large garbage can packed with an empty chicken pot, a flat tire, and other symbols of Republicans' and Hoover's many unfulfilled promises. Hoover is pictured carrying a satchel and reading a railroad timetable as he departs. A *Kansas City Star* cartoon titled "Looks as If the New Leadership Was Really Going to Lead" depicts a smiling Roosevelt pulling a donkey hitched to a cart labeled "Congress" carrying Uncle Sam and two other unnamed occupants, followed by two elephants and an endless line of people. Again there is no indication of Roosevelt's disability; indeed, the cartoon features a robust Roosevelt walking briskly. In the *Richmond Times-Dispatch* "Uncle Sam's Day and Night Nursery," and subtitled "Tending Another Tough One," a Dr. Roosevelt is portrayed as rushing to help a crying baby in a crib with "Unemployment" lettered on its side; a bawling infant in another crib marked "Farm Relief" is offset by three other contented babies in "Economy," "Banks," and "Beer" cribs.

A common thread running through all these editorial cartoons is that of a new, powerful president whom Ed Hill, a popular radio broadcaster of the time, described as someone with the courage to lift himself from "the bed of invalidism," with "the determination and patience to make himself walk." They suggested that he had "the qualities to lead the nation to recovery." The cartoons reinforced the decision Roosevelt and Howe had made at the onset of his illness in 1921 to encourage the belief that he had largely recovered from his paralysis.

While no one could doubt that the new president was prepared to use the government to ease the suffering of those who had fallen on hard times and restore traditional opportunities for ambitious men and women seeking the good life, his speech offered no details on how he intended to achieve this transformation or how to implement a New Deal, the description that now attached itself to his administration. To sustain the upsurge in hope, just days after taking office Roosevelt issued two presidential proclamations that conveyed a message of political momentum. He directed Congress to meet in a special session beginning March 9 and announced a bank holiday, closing the banks as a prelude to a banking bill. The directive to Congress underscored his inaugural promise to preserve the country's democratic norms — bank reform would not be the product of some autocratic action by the White House, but the result of a legislative initiative undertaken by the people's representatives in cooperation with the president. "I cannot too strongly urge upon the Congress the clear necessity for immediate action," Roosevelt told the legislators.

Congress was only too glad to comply. The bill Roosevelt sent to the House on March 9 proposed not the nationalization of the country's financial institutions, which his verbal attack on bankers in his inaugural speech suggested, but a set of reforms that could stabilize the banks with support from the federal government. After less than forty minutes of debate, the House, many of whose members had not read the bill, and amid shouts of "Vote, Vote," passed the president's law. The Senate followed that evening with 73 in favor and only 7 against. Roosevelt promptly signed the measure, which had become law after only eight hours of discussion.

No one could complain about the bill's introducing radical reform. On the contrary, some progressives were disappointed at the president's failure to seize the chance to nationalize the banks, an action that a New Mexico senator thought could have been done "without a word of protest." One congressman, who also thought Roosevelt had squandered an opportunity to bring the country's Wall Street moguls under control, declared: "The President drove the money-changers out of the Capitol on March 4th — and they were all back on the 9th."

Because he understood that most Americans would not grasp the details of the banking bill, and because he wished to put an exclamation point on the end of the crisis and use his ability to win popular support through public discussion, he held a press conference on March 8 and gave a radio talk on March 12. His well-honed skills as a public speaker who could make powerful personal connections with his audiences were on display in both venues. The press conference took place in the Oval Office, where Roosevelt, seated at his desk, shook hands with all hundred and twenty-five reporters who were present. The journalists appreciated the informality of the setting, which stood in sharp contrast to Hoover's stiff, formal weekly press gatherings, at which he stood at a lectern and enforced strict time limits.

Unlike Hoover, Roosevelt shunned advance written questions and expanded the meetings to twice a week — on Wednesday mornings, to reach afternoon newspapers, and on Friday afternoons, to appear in Saturday morning papers. The sessions were more like extended conversations with intimates than confrontational clashes with reporters eager to extract headlines from a guarded politician. At the first meeting Roosevelt told the press pool, "These conferences are going to be merely enlarged editions of the kind of very delightful family conferences I have been holding in Albany for the last four years." But he did set a number of conditions: He would not answer "if questions," nor would he respond to those he did not wish to discuss or those that "I do not know anything about." Moreover, he did not want to be quoted. Most of what they heard at these meetings would be off the record or for background use without attribution. For the reporters, the meetings represented an opportunity to get inside information on administration actions. For Roosevelt, they were a useful vehicle for getting his agenda before the public. In time, it became clear that Roosevelt had a talent for "surpassing charm," one of the reporters observed, while saying "almost nothing." His engaging manner routinely disarmed the journalists, and as early as the end of the first conference, in an unprecedented expression of appreciation for his effectiveness in drawing the country back from the brink of disaster and the civility he showed the press, the reporters applauded his performance.

Roosevelt's warm reception from the press was matched by a radio talk that generated widespread public approval. Before he spoke, he tried to picture the audience that would be listening to him: "A mason at work on a new building, a girl behind a counter, a farmer in his field." On the evening of March 12, after he was introduced by

CBS newsman Robert Trout — "The President wants to come into your home and sit at your fireside for a little fireside chat" — he spoke for some twenty minutes from the White House to an estimated sixty million Americans, almost half the country's population. "I want to talk for a few minutes to the people of the United States about banking," he began. His presentation was aimed more at the "overwhelming majority who use banks for the making of deposits and the drawing of checks" than at "the comparatively few who understand the mechanics of banking." He thanked the public for its "good temper" during the "inconvenience" of the bank holiday, and the fact that he had described the bank closures as a "holiday" rather than as a crisis had put a positive face on the action and provoked no organized protest. He praised Congress — Democrats and Republicans alike — for supporting the rehabilitative bank bill they had enacted. He assured his listeners that the banks would reopen in the coming week on a sound basis, and for those that did remain on shaky ground, the government was working to make them whole.

The response to Roosevelt's address was overwhelmingly positive. Although he couldn't see his audience, he spoke as if they were sitting directly before him: "He grimace[d] or nod[ded] toward the microphone as if he were on stage." His audience, in turn, responded as if they were taking advice from a paterfamilias who had only their well-being at heart. When banks opened on the following Monday, the president's assurances resulted in a rush of depositors taking their money from under their mattresses, as Roosevelt urged them to do, and putting it back in reopened banks.

Will Rogers voiced the national mood when he said that Americans "know they got a man in there who is wise to Congress, wise to our so-called big men. The whole country is with him, just so he does something. If he burned down the Capitol we would cheer and say, 'Well, we at least got a fire started.' " "I guess at your next election we will make it unanimous," William Randolph Hearst remarked. Walter Lippmann observed that Roosevelt had converted national confusion and "desperation" into renewed "confidence in the government and in itself." For Raymond Moley, "Capitalism was saved in eight days." And Roosevelt, Boston's Cardinal William O'Connell declared, "was a God-sent man."

Roosevelt's popularity rested not only on his personal appeal but also on the basic conventionality of his program: Banks were being made safe by limited reforms rather than by nationalization or public ownership. Similarly, the nation was being encouraged to balance its books. Declaring that "liberal governments have been wrecked on rocks of loose fiscal policy," Roosevelt asked Congress to pass an economy bill that cut government benefits for veterans and salaries for federal employees and avoided what he predicted could become a federal bankruptcy. Although bringing Congress along on a bill that alienated many Democrats with its 30 percent cut in federal spending was harder than enacting the bank law, Roosevelt prevailed — as he did on a request for legislation legalizing 3.2 percent beer and light wines.

Mindful that budget cuts had only limited value, he acknowledged that he had done nothing yet to restore the country's economic health. He told

Wilson adviser Colonel Edward House that "while things look superficially rosy, I realize well that thus far we have actually given more of deflation than inflation. . . . It is simply inevitable that we must inflate and though my banker friends may be horrified, I still am seeking an inflation which will not wholly be based on additional government debt." While he had no intention of bypassing Congress and concentrating power in the White House, he reluctantly concluded that he would have to move beyond accepted wisdom on how economic recovery would be managed.

He was particularly eager to address the unemployment problem and the need for higher agricultural prices. He hoped "to put people to work in the national forests and on other government and state properties," envisioning that some two hundred thousand men on the dole could cut down trees for lumber and build breaks to prevent forest fires in the West. As for increasing the value of farm products, his notion was to take acreage out of production. He cautioned, though, that none of these proposed programs was set in concrete; he considered them experimental, and acknowledged that additional thinking about these issues might be necessary.

The more tangible news was his decision to hold Congress in session in order to enact a New Deal agenda. Although he publicly lamented the absence of "constructive" economic actions, his bank and budget measures were in fact essential preludes to progressive New Deal initiatives. This is not to suggest that he planned a series of conservative measures as prerequisites for being able to put the New Deal into effect. But he judged intuitively that initial policies that echoed

231

traditional means and ends would do more to advance subsequent progressive actions than bold strokes at the outset. Exactly what he would do, however, was as much a mystery to him as to outside observers. Because no one had surefire remedies for the Depression, he signed on to a program of experimentation or trial and error. During the campaign, he had said, "The country demands bold, persistent experimentation. It is common sense to take a method and try it. If it fails, admit it frankly and try another. But above all try something." He compared himself to the quarterback on a football team who cannot predict future plays, because his choice of action depended on the results of current ones. And in a Fireside Chat, he said, "I have no expectation of making a hit every time I come to bat. What I seek is the highest possible batting average, not only for myself but for the team."

It was politics and policy by no set rules, except Roosevelt's uncanny, inexplicable feel for what might work and what would stimulate public approval. Reading his press interviews from that time deepens the impression that he had no larger philosophy or grand design — only a commitment to restoring American prosperity by whatever means would ease suffering and blunt talk of replacing established economic and political institutions. "I am told that what I am about to do will become impossible," Roosevelt declared at his first press conference. "But I am going to try it." The historian Richard Hofstadter wrote, "The nation was confronted with a completely novel situation for which the traditional, commonly accepted philosophies offered no guide. An era of fumbling and muddling-through was inevitable.

Only a leader with an experimental temper could have made the New Deal possible."

The experiment began on March 16 when Roosevelt announced an agricultural initiative, launching a search for a program that would reflect a consensus of farm interests, but more important, that would address the collapse of the farm economy. The fundamental point on which all the farm groups could agree was a provision in the existing law that promoted inflation or the restoration of commodity prices that sustained farm families. When Roosevelt signed on to a Thomas Amendment, named after Oklahoma senator Elmer Thomas, a soft-money advocate, that echoed William Jennings Bryan's Populist call for cheaper dollars, Lewis Douglas, a former conservative congressman from Arizona, Roosevelt's budget director, and architect of the administration's austerity budget, declared it "the end of Western civilization." The administration's abandonment of a gold-backed dollar was condemned by conservative economists as a reckless departure from the economic standards that had made America stable and prosperous. Because the gold standard and ways of boosting agricultural income provoked such strong reactions, Roosevelt gave himself political cover by pressing farm organizations into agreeing to a compromise law.

The final version of the farm bill reflected Roosevelt's belief that national well-being greatly depended on finding common ground among diverse opinions. The 1924 divide in the Democratic Party convinced him that compromise and consensus were essential to a functioning nation. As in his campaign, when he worked to minimize the split between the modernists or urban resi-

dents and fundamentalists or Southern evange-
lists, in 1933 he considered consensus or national
unity to be invaluable in restoring public confidence. Restoring bank stability, he told his radio
audience on March 12, "is your problem no less
than it is mine. Together we cannot fail." As in
wartime, a country unified around national goals
was more likely to succeed than one divided by
factionalism. As for inflation, the congressional
commitment to cheaper dollars allowed Roosevelt
to take the dollar off the gold standard. Although
conservatives complained about the triumph of
"mob rule," Roosevelt understood a majority in
the country was far more interested in economic
revival and higher prices than any theoretical argument about ratios of gold and silver to the dollar.

The Agricultural Adjustment Act became law
on May 12, and the separate creation of a Farm
Credit Administration (FCA) to refinance farm
mortgages defused tensions across the Midwest
and the South, where farmers were rescued from
losing their homes and livelihoods, however
diminished they may have been. In response to
the FCA, a *New York Herald Tribune* cartoon of
May 17 depicted FDR on a stage before the
footlights rescuing a farm family from the villain-
ous banker threatening to foreclose "on the old
homestead." The novelist Saul Bellow said, "The
secret of his political genius was that he knew
exactly what the people needed to hear."

In the first Hundred Days of his administration,
Roosevelt famously signed fifteen major bills into
law. But the greatest importance of these measures
was less what people believed each would achieve
in righting the country's economic balance than
in creating a sense of movement that would

somehow restore national prosperity. Raymond Moley said later that Roosevelt had no coherent plan in pressing all these measures on Congress. To think otherwise would be "to believe that the accumulation of stuffed snakes, baseball pictures, school flags, old tennis shoes, carpenter's tools, geometry books and chemistry sets in a boy's bedroom could have been put there by an interior decorator."

Yet each of these laws had specific consequences — some more long lasting than others. The Agricultural Adjustment Administration (AAA) was established as an all-purpose agency representing a variety of farm interests. Most of all it aimed to raise farm prices and income as a guard against turmoil across the farm belt. The key voice in Roosevelt's inner circle arguing for farming's centrality to national prosperity was Agriculture Secretary Henry A. Wallace. A successful agribusinessman with an encyclopedic knowledge of farm practices, Wallace was also a brilliantly effective evangelist for rural America. With an unpretentious manner and openness that led some to think of him as another Lincoln or as a more serious Will Rogers, Wallace enjoyed his public image as a model of American individualism and frontier strength. He also believed in the power of Eastern religions and mystical thinking in advancing world peace and individual health. He was a White House curiosity, but Roosevelt's attraction to the unorthodox gave him a unique standing, and Wallace's determination to fight for the agricultural sector made him a valuable agent in Roosevelt's struggle to save the storied yeoman farmers who had overcome past hardships in carving out a living on the American frontier and laid the roots of American democracy.

As Jonathan Alter says of the farm initiative, though, "the idea was action, any action, with little or no thought given to the long-term consequences." The main provision of the law was a domestic allotment plan that paid farmers for reduced production, defraying the cost with a tax on processors of agricultural commodities. But untilled land and the planned destruction of crops and livestock that could feed hungry Americans struck some as simply "wicked," a perversion of the centuries-old human struggle to sustain life. One spokesman for farm groups described the AAA's scarcity program as "idiotic . . . and one which makes a laughing stock of our genius as a people."

Opponents of restricted production favored a program for exporting surpluses or "dumping" the excess harvest abroad. Because some members of Congress, led by South Carolina senator "Cotton Ed" Smith, criticized the AAA as a radical experiment or as an imitation of a Soviet communist agency, Roosevelt agreed to make George Peek, a conservative associate of the storied sixty-two-year-old millionaire Bernard Baruch and president of the Moline Plow Company, the head of the AAA. That appointment, however, instantly created a left-right struggle within the Agriculture Department and did little to restore farm prosperity to the idealized levels before World War I.

In setting up the AAA, Roosevelt had been under the misconception that farm prosperity was the key to a national economic rebound. As historian David Kennedy points out, while farmers made up 30 percent of the country's workforce, "the New Dealers' faith in agricultural revival as the master key to general prosperity" was "quaintly anachronistic." Roosevelt would have done better in 1933 to focus on the urban industrial centers as the mainstay of any revival. "But nostalgia, intellectual inertia, and political pressure beckoned the New Dealers backward, to the cornfields and hay-meadows and pastoral idylls of national mythology — and into the welcoming arms of a lean and hungry agricultural lobby . . . The agricultural sector [became] a virtual ward of the state. . . . No members of American society would emerge from the New Deal more tenderly coddled than farmers, especially those large-scale commercial growers to whom most New Deal agricultural benefits accrued."

In signing on to a farm program that aimed to bring supply and demand into greater balance by restricting production, Roosevelt sacrificed long-term improvements for short-term gains. While farm prices did begin an upward spiral in the first months of his term, their rise was more the consequence of a shift in attitude than the result of the voluntary domestic allotment plan reducing crops. In addition, as farm production fell, the reduced need for farmworkers drove many of them into the cities, where they swelled the ranks of the urban unemployed. Yet Roosevelt remained convinced that the AAA quieted some of the agitation in agricultural areas, where "violence has become so widespread that these measures are necessary to prevent revolution."

No group suffered more from the domestic allotment programs than the sharecroppers and tenants, who were also the most powerless and least likely to rebel. The acreage most readily removed from production was that tilled by tenants, the men who leased land and lived from hand to mouth in servitude to their landlords. A million and a half families across the cotton South — two-thirds of them white and one-third black — labored under these conditions of peonage. By transferring little, if any, of the payments they received from the AAA for keeping their acreage uncultivated, the landowners only compounded the poverty of these near-destitute tenants.

Protests against this new economic deprivation were met with severe repression. For black tenants, especially, open objection to the measure invited beatings and possible lynching. Twenty-eight blacks were killed across the South in 1933. When Senate liberals tried to advance an anti-lynching law that might counter antiblack violence by federal statute, Roosevelt balked at pressure to take up the cause, convinced that Southerners, who controlled crucial congressional committees, would respond by blocking his many other proposed reforms. Pressed by Socialist Party leader Norman Thomas to do the right thing, Roosevelt replied, "I know the South, and there is arising a new generation of leaders, and we've got to be patient." Eleanor, who viewed such criminality as barbaric, nonetheless echoed her husband's recommendation of patience. As she told Walter White, a black civil rights advocate, "The President feels that lynching is a question of education in the states, rallying good citizens, and creating public opinion so that the localities themselves wipe it out. However, if it were done by a Northerner, it will have an antagonistic effect." Both Roosevelts had hope that the South would eventually become a liberal mainstay in the Democratic

Party. "The young people in the South, and the women, they are thinking about economic problems," FDR confided to a Party progressive, "and will be part of a liberal group." (Thirty years later, President John F. Kennedy, who, like FDR, held back on civil rights legislation in order to advance his domestic reforms, gave up on changing the South. The segregationists, he said, are "hopeless, they'll never reform." They hadn't "done anything about integration for a hundred years." Kennedy was echoing civil rights leader Martin Luther King's conclusion that "wait has almost always meant never.")

Roosevelt was likewise determined to create work for young men between the ages of eighteen and twenty-five through conservation of the country's forests. Eager to take youngsters off relief before they became habituated to being on the dole, the president believed that work in the great outdoors would not only be productive in preserving the environment but would also foster the physical well-being of men in their formative years. As President Lyndon Johnson, echoing FDR in the 1960s, would phrase it, the object was to give people a hand up, not a handout.

On March 21, Roosevelt asked Congress to finance a Civilian Conservation Corps (CCC), which it approved on March 31. He directed Wallace, Perkins, and Ickes to put 250,000 unmarried men between the ages of eighteen and twenty-five from impoverished families to work as quickly as possible. They were to "build dams, drain marshlands, fight forest fires, and plant trees." With thirteen million Americans searching for work, young men from all over the country — most of whom had never set foot in a forest before

— rushed to join the Corps. Although the dollar-a-day wage paid to volunteers provoked complaints that the government was depressing wages and creating forced labor camps like those in Nazi Germany and Soviet Russia, the chance to work outdoors and send home twenty-five of the thirty dollars a month they earned to their struggling families, as required by the CCC, was irresistible.

The CCC was also a magnet for World War I veterans, including some of those who had been part of the Bonus Army routed by Hoover. When these men returned to Washington, some of them older than the twenty-five-year-old age limit for CCC recruits, Roosevelt upped the age restriction and took pains to ensure that the veterans were provided with hot food and surplus Army clothing. The vets were a welcome addition to what became known as Roosevelt's "Tree Army."

In the nine-year history of the CCC, close to three million men served in 2,500 camps for between six months and a year, making an invaluable contribution to the national environment: three billion trees planted, eight hundred state parks created, thousands of miles of trails cleared, a billion fish stocked in rivers and streams, thiry thousand wildlife shelters established, historic battlefields restored, and scores of forest fires contained at the cost of forty-nine corps members' lives. In the words of one historian, "the CCC left its monuments in the preservation and purification of the land, the water, the forests, and the young men of America."

It was Roosevelt himself who may have described the accomplishments of the CCC best when he pointed to "the prevention of floods and the erosion of our agricultural fields, the prevention of forest fires, the diversification of farming and the distribution of industry." He dismissed as "utter rubbish" complaints about the Army's role in running the camps as "militarization" and insisted that its involvement was simply a way to establish some kind of normal order. He lauded the program as contributing to a greater sense of nationhood: a growing acceptance "that the East has a stake in the West and the West has a stake in the East, that the nation must and shall be considered as a whole and not as an aggregate of disjointed groups." What Roosevelt could not foresee was the degree to which the CCC would establish a tradition of national service that presidents Kennedy and Johnson replicated when they established the Peace Corps and Volunteers in Service to America (VISTA) thirty years later.

At its heart, the CCC was an expression of Roosevelt's personal affinity for the land and conservation of the country's forests and waterways, which he wished to preserve for generations to come. The CCC was a lineal deployment of his own use of Hyde Park as a laboratory and a preserve, where he had planted five thousand trees. His presidency would see the creation of national and state forests, national and state parks, national monuments, wildlife sanctuaries, and historic sites throughout the country. In sponsoring these efforts he left a legacy as great as that of his cousin Theodore.

Saving the farm community and conserving the forests appealed to romantic ideals about America's special place among nations, but it did relatively little to end the Depression or relieve the suffering of the unemployed and their families. As Frances Perkins recalled, "It is hard . . . to

241

reconstruct the atmosphere of 1933 and to evoke the terror caused by unrelieved poverty and prolonged unemployment." By now most of the states and localities had run out of funds to ease the misery of the indigent, and suggestions that the federal government step in provoked cries of opposition from some in Congress, who warned that it would lead to the demise of the federal system and the introduction of socialism or communism. "God save the people of the United States," a Maine Republican congressman said in response to proposals for federal welfare grants.

Opposition to such measures in Congress, however, was represented by only a small minority. Roosevelt's more serious problem was finding the best means to help the impoverished as quickly as possible. Perkins had over two thousand plans on her desk, but she and the president rejected any that might turn the needy into permanent wards of the state. In March, after Harry Hopkins and William Hodson, New York City's chief of welfare services, presented an idea to Perkins at the crowded Women's University Club of D.C., where they spoke under a stairwell, Perkins arranged an appointment for them with the president. Persuaded by their proposal, Roosevelt asked senators Wagner, La Follette, and Costigan, from New York, Wisconsin, and Colorado, respectively, to draw up a bill that appropriated $500 million for relief. Half the money was to go to states that could put up matching grants, with the other $250 million earmarked for states too poor to match the federal largess. The proposal not only gave the administration standing as a Good Samaritan, it also scored political points in states outside the South, where the Democrats were less popular.

The bill sailed through Congress by the end of April, and in May Roosevelt appointed Hopkins the director of the new Federal Emergency Relief Administration (FERA). The president had developed a good opinion of Hopkins in Albany when he served as chairman of New York's relief agency. Roosevelt was impressed not only with his compassion for the needy, but, even more important, with his lack of reverence for standard methods and social norms regarding welfare, his impatience with bureaucratic hurdles, and his insistence on quick, effective action. "Every dollar entrusted to us for lessening of distress," Hopkins said, "the maximum amount humanly possible was put into the people's hands. The money, spent honestly and with constant remembrance of its purpose, bought more of courage than it ever bought of goods."

The journalist Raymond Clapper believed that Roosevelt valued Hopkins not just for his administrative skills in managing hundreds of millions of dollars but because he was "quick, alert, shrewd, bold" and carried things off "with a bright Hell's bells air" or devil-may-care attitude. Hopkins's offbeat personality also appealed to Roosevelt: His passion for horse racing, where he cultivated friendships with touts; his delight in low-stakes poker games; his hyperactive mannerisms, fueled by gallons of coffee and chain-smoking; and his disheveled appearance, making him a rival to Louis Howe as worst-dressed man in government, made him an unforgettable character. He was brusque, sarcastic, profane, and a workaholic, and his personal excesses jeopardized his health. Ross McIntire, Roosevelt's physician, said, "Our biggest job is to keep Harry from ever feeling completely well. When he thinks he's restored to health, he goes out on the town — and from there to the Mayo Clinic," where doctors would deal with intestinal problems that produced a variety of symptoms and kept him undernourished and disturbingly thin.

Hopkins also had an unforgettable aide in Aubrey Williams. The forty-two-year-old Alabaman was an up-from-the-bootstraps Southerner who knew poverty firsthand and was an evangelist for using federal relief programs to aid struggling men and women of all races and religions. He and Hopkins made a compatible team: Like Hopkins, Williams was "taut and sharp, intolerant of cant, contemptuous of red tape and 'channels.' " Williams regarded Hopkins as "the only man in Washington who was really whole souled in his concern for human welfare." He shared Hopkins's distaste for projects that promised relief in the long run, repeating his boss's observation that "people don't eat in the long run — they eat every day."

Hopkins felt such urgency about getting relief to the poor that he gave $5 million to state relief agencies during his first two hours as head of FERA. Mineworkers — who, according to John L. Lewis, their union president, subsisted on a diet "actually below domestic animal standards" — were among the first in line to receive this help. But Hopkins quickly developed a passion to end these payments as strong as his ardor to feed, clothe, and house the needy. He viewed impoverishment as a great disaster not only for its victims, but for the entire country, but the reports he received about the demoralizing effects of poverty on former members of the middle class persuaded him that welfare should be no more than a temporary expedient. The mayor of Toledo, Ohio, reinforced his conviction, saying, "I have seen thousands of these defeated, discouraged, hopeless men and women, cringing and fawning as they come to ask for public aid."

No one made Hopkins and Roosevelt more aware of indigent suffering than the forty-year-old Lorena Hickok, a former journalist with a brilliant capacity for close in-depth reporting. Born in Wisconsin and raised in the Midwest, Hickok suffered through an unhappy childhood with a father who beat her regularly and maliciously killed the family dog and cat. The misery of living with so violent a parent and her mother's death moved Hick, as most everyone called her, to flee her home at the age of fourteen. Working as a maid and taken in by an aunt, she finished high school with high honors. At five foot eight, she stood out among women and more than held her own among men. "She looked and acted like one of the boys," Doris Kearns Goodwin says, "with her flannel shirt and trousers loosely covering her two-hundred-pound frame, and a cigar hanging from her mouth."

Despite failing out of college, Hickok pursued a dream of becoming a writer like the novelist Edna Ferber. Her ambition and talent won her jobs as a reporter at the *Milwaukee Sentinel* and *Minneapolis Tribune,* and in 1928 she landed in New York, where she worked for the Associated Press and won an award for her coverage of the Lindbergh baby kidnapping. In 1932, as the country's leading female journalist, she was assigned by the AP to cover Eleanor Roosevelt during the presidential campaign. Her contact with Eleanor blossomed into an affectionate relationship that, combined with the onset of her diabetes, persuaded her to give up journalism for a job as FERA's chief investigator.

Hickok's relationship with Eleanor has drawn considerable attention from biographers and historians. It has been richly reconstructed from a substantial correspondence in which they exchanged expressions of love, and Hickok lamented their time apart: "I remember your eyes, with a kind of teasing smile in them and the feeling of that soft spot just northeast of the corner of your mouth against my lips." Eleanor pledged her love to Hick and "wished she could lie down beside Hick and take her in her arms." "The essential question for the biographer," Goodwin says, "is not whether Hick and Eleanor went beyond kisses and hugs, a question there is absolutely no way we can answer with certainty." The more relevant concern is what role their relationship played in their respective lives during the 1930s.

What is most interesting in their relationship is not whether it was a lesbian episode in Eleanor's life but rather how it set Eleanor and Franklin apart from accepted standards during their time in the White House. In a 1905 photograph of the well-dressed Roosevelts seated on the steps of the Hyde Park house, they playfully displayed their attraction to unconventional behavior: In a kind of role reversal, Franklin is knitting and Eleanor holds a wine glass. Likewise, their mutual affinity for offbeat people like Louis Howe, Harry Hopkins, and Hickok is a window on the administration's unconventionality.

No one in the White House circle reflected the

spirit of noncomformity more than Laura Delano, a Roosevelt cousin who was described as "a law unto herself" or "years ahead of her time." She typically appeared in red nail polish, hair dyed "blue, then purple," "a silk blouse open to the waist, gold bracelets clattering up and down each arm," provoking wonder "how she could lift it — a ring with a huge stone on every finger, and brooches everywhere — in her hair at her hip, on her bosom. She also wore masses of rouge and lipstick, which she replenished constantly in mid-conversation no matter where she was." Unmarried but in "a lifelong liaison with her large, good-natured, mostly silent chauffeur," she bred dogs — "Irish setters first, then long-haired dachshunds. . . . She could be incredibly rude if the company bored her," a family member recalled. But "she adored FDR," and he reciprocated her affection, and "delighted in her lively, unpredictable company," his cousin Margaret Daisy Suckley said.

None of Roosevelt's affinity for unusual or even eccentric individuals is to suggest that the Roosevelt White House was a center of radical thought or action. But there was also a measure of personal unorthodoxy that translated into the experimental temperament of the New Deal, which enabled someone like Hickok, with her unusual qualities and empathy for the disadvantaged borne of her own life experience, to have a significant impact on policy. Her reporting from the field described the misery of needy people on relief in a way that called into question FERA's efforts to rescue them. As a consequence, relief administrators and recipients developed an uncomfortable relationship that was not lost on Hopkins. He understood that someone unemployed and destitute had become a social outcast who was "made to feel his pauperism. Every help which was given him was to be given in a way to intensify his sense of shame." Hopkins concluded: "I don't think anybody can go year after year, month after month, accepting relief without affecting his character in some way unfavorably. It is probably going to undermine the independence of hundreds of thousands of families. . . . I look upon this as a great disaster." As David Kennedy points out, "The Depression . . . revealed one of the perverse implications of American society's vaunted celebration of individualism. In a culture that ascribed all success to individual striving, it seemed to follow axiomatically that failure was due to individual inadequacy." To most Americans, then, unemployment was less the product of social ills or a flawed national economy than the personal shortcomings of the men and women who had fallen on hard times.

The indignities of welfare and the self-contempt generated by unemployment made Hopkins into an advocate of work relief, though he worried that Roosevelt would resist a proposal that seemed certain to be costly and counter the president's own desire for a balanced budget. Roosevelt's higher priority, however, was to put people to work — any kind of work — that would generate self-respect and stimulate economic growth. Work relief gave birth to a Civil Works Administration in November 1933: It pumped a billion dollars into the economy (the equivalent of 16.2 billion 2016 dollars) during its five months in existence. By the beginning of 1934, over four million jobless men and women had found a place on the

CWA rolls digging ditches, laying pipes, and building and repairing roads, schools, playgrounds, athletic fields, hospitals, airports, and municipal structures. Teachers, artists, actors, and needy college students enjoyed the benefits of this federal largess. Some critics of the CWA denounced these projects as "boondoggles" — "pointless, unnecessary, time-wasting work." For example, women who were hired to make mattresses from surplus cotton, which were given to destitute families, were criticized as doing make-work that undermined actual bedding manufacturers.

Roosevelt himself decried the unproductive "few hours of weekly work cutting grass, raking leaves or picking up papers in the public parks" as "a narcotic, a subtle destroyer of the human spirit." He considered make-work to be another form of the dole, which sapped "the vitality of our people." He echoed the concerns of social workers, who said that some of the unemployed were "beginning to regard CWA as their due — [they feel] that the Government actually owes it to them. And they want more." The CWA lasted only eight months, as Roosevelt ultimately judged it to be too expensive and too likely to create expectations about an unending supply of federal jobs. He also feared that it would encourage a growing conviction that "we are going to have permanent Depression in this country."

While accepting that temporary relief of the jobless was essential, Roosevelt hoped that a National (Industrial) Recovery Act could, in combination with the AAA, end the Depression. Initially he believed that the AAA and the FERA would be sufficient to restore prosperity, but after two months in office, marked by some hectoring from Moley and Tugwell, and a proposal in Congress to increase jobs by mandating a thirty-hour work week, he accepted the need to enact an industrial recovery program that would also advance the rights of labor to organize and receive a living wage.

The act that Roosevelt put before Congress in June represented a dramatic break with past government-business relations. Its objective was to rebuild the economy and restore the belief in America as a land of opportunity — a nation that gave men and women of all stripes the chance to prosper. Of course, blacks and people of color were less favored. Ensuring the crucial support of Southern congressmen and senators, who had the power to block a major recovery measure, required deferring to their racial bias. The administration's goal was primarily to revive white, middle-class America's well-being. There were some in the White House who hoped to spread the economic benefits to the least fortunate and least favored, but as the president said about foreign affairs in his inaugural, "first things first."

Roosevelt confronted a plethora of proposals on how to revive American industry. Clearly, Hoover's laissez-faire approach had been discredited, state socialism was denounced as un-American, and a scheme of government cooperation with big business seemed the best solution. When Raymond Moley cautioned Roosevelt to understand that he was "taking an enormous step away from the philosophy of equalitarianism and laissez-faire," Roosevelt replied: "If that philosophy hadn't proved to be bankrupt, Herbert Hoover would be sitting here right now." Roosevelt, always intent on making government action understandable to the general public, urged business "to prevent over-production, to prevent unfair wages, [and] to eliminate improper working conditions." No one could be opposed to so transparently fair and productive a proposal, but turning these appealing concepts into a detailed plan was another matter. Roosevelt ordered several of his advisers with competing views to lock themselves in a room until they came up with a workable solution.

By May 15, the group presented the president with a bill that he agreed to send to Congress. It included two principal parts: The first section proposed cooperation among trade groups, with codes of fair competition aimed at curbing overproduction by loosening antitrust regulations. Industries embracing the codes were also obligated to raise workers' wages, with the increased costs of production underwritten by industrywide agreements on higher prices under a code of "fair competition." Clause 7(a) famously established labor's right to collective bargaining: the freedom to negotiate wages and hours in pursuit of a decent living. Section two established a Public Works Administration (PWA) backed by $3.3 billion to finance countrywide infrastructure projects that would modernize the nation and reduce unemployment. Raymond Moley later described the National Industrial Recovery Act as "a thorough hodge-podge of provisions" that nobody was certain would work. It was, he added, a "confused, two-headed experiment."

Roosevelt believed that if anyone could bring order and action to the National Recovery Administration (NRA) it was fifty-one-year-old Hugh Johnson. A West Point graduate who had risen to the rank of brigadier general in World War I, Johnson had established a reputation for effectiveness implementing the draft and serving as the Army's liaison to the War Industries Board, where he became associated with Bernard Baruch. After resigning from the Army and serving as an executive at the Moline Plow Company, he became Baruch's principal assistant. A gruff, combative martinet with an affinity for heavy drinking, Johnson approached his new job at the NRA as another exercise in military command. He understood that he was taking on an impossible assignment, especially when Roosevelt mandated that Harold Ickes run the WPA from the Interior Department and divided authority for administering the program. "This is just like mounting the guillotine on the infinitesimal gamble that the ax won't work," Johnson said.

Although Baruch warned that Johnson was "a born dictator" and couldn't be trusted, Roosevelt, who thought that "every administration needed a Peck's Bad Boy," dismissed such criticism by insisting that Johnson's outbursts — his "intemperate ballyhoo and frenetic pace," his "fusillade of insults, wisecracks, and picturesque phrases" — amused him. More to the point, Johnson served Roosevelt's purposes: If the NRA proved to be a failure, the blame would be laid on Johnson, the imperious take-charge general, and not on a White House experimenting with an untested means of stimulating industrial recovery. To underscore Johnson's responsibility for NRA actions, Roosevelt described him as madly rushing from the White House "for points unknown" after obtaining his signature on agency codes. "He hasn't been seen since," Roosevelt said, reinforcing the image of Johnson as a runaway train.

Despite the challenges of making the NRA an effective economic instrument, Johnson threw himself into the job with unflagging energy. Working eighteen-hour days and presiding over industry code hearings, he mounted a campaign to pressure the country's major corporations into accepting the plan's provisions. Overnight "NRA Member" signs, with a symbolic blue eagle and the words "WE DO OUR PART," began appearing in shop windows across the country. NRA membership became a testament of every business's patriotism. Two million employers promised to support economic revival through cooperation with the NRA and enthusiastically participated in a parade along New York's Fifth Avenue, which drew a quarter of a million marchers and two million observers. A Pennsylvania family made the news when it named a newborn daughter "Nira," and the president sent the parents a note of congratulation. Seizing on the popular enthusiasm for the NRA, Johnson denounced the "slackers" and "chiselers" who refused to cooperate with it, saying, "May God have mercy on the man or group of men who attempt to trifle with this bird."

Although Johnson understood that the surge of support would wane and tempt industries to abandon their commitments to the NRA in search of larger profits, he hoped that a reviving economy and a reluctance to dishonor their good names would sustain the agreements he had extracted from business chiefs for as long as possible. "You may have been Captains of Industry once," he told a group of Atlanta businessmen with the high-handedness of a commanding officer speaking to a group of inductees, "but you are Corporals of Disaster now."

Although Johnson would keep the reins of power until the fall of 1934, the NRA never lived up to expectations. Indeed, by the end of 1933 it was awash in complaints that it was destroying free enterprise by fostering monopolies, serving the interests of large corporations over small businesses, failing to protect labor from exploitative managers, promoting a massive government bureaucracy akin to that of Fascist rule in Italy, and most of all, doing little to actually expand the economy. Its failure could ultimately be attributed to its fundamentally mistaken assumption that reducing supply and raising prices would be adequate to foster prosperity. Moreover, the WPA under Ickes operated with such extreme caution against boondoggles that could embarrass him and the administration that it fell short of expectations on reducing joblessness.

Although the NRA did add almost two million workers to payrolls, set precedents for minimum wages and maximum hours, and kept the economy on an even keel — or at least from descending into further deflation — it did not come close to ending the Depression. Instead, it gained a reputation for promoting "excessive centralization and the dictatorial spirit." Its performance, marked by government codes that micromanaged everything from hardware stores to burlesque theaters, gave credence to Louisiana senator Huey Long's warning that the NRA contained "every crime and fault of both monarchy and socialism," exceeding the worst controls in the Soviet Union. Others, like Frances Perkins, saw in Johnson's behavior an echo of Mussolini's support for the corporate state. Still, as the historian Arthur Schlesinger wrote, the "NRA gave the American people for a fleeting moment a tremendous sense of national solidarity. . . . For all its defects, [the] NRA represented an essential continuity that in the midst of crisis helped preserve American unity."

Not only did Roosevelt want to dodge any criticism for the NRA's failure by placing the blame for it on Johnson, he also sought to assure the public that in no respect was he using it to abandon the country's democratic institutions or to make himself into a dictator like those commanding power in Europe. When critics attacked the New Deal as socialistic, he declared that it was simply multiplying "the number of American shareholders" or expanding the middle class. In his second Fireside Chat on May 7, he told a radio audience, "Our policies are wholly within purposes for which our American Constitutional Government was established 150 years ago." He added: "It is wholly wrong to call the measures that we have taken Government control of farming, industry, and transportation. It is rather a partnership between Government and farming and industry and transportation, not partnership in profits, for the profits still go to the citizens, but rather a partnership in planning, and a partnership to see that the plans are carried out."

Where electric power was concerned, however, Roosevelt saw government ownership as a national benefit that did not violate economic freedom but advanced it. In his inaugural, Roosevelt, borrowing from the Bible, had said that, "Where there is no vision, the people perish." In the Tennessee Valley, which encompassed seven Southern states — Tennessee, Alabama, Georgia, Mississippi, North Carolina, Kentucky, and Virginia — people

255

were indeed perishing. Seasonal floods exacerbated by denuded forests swept away topsoil and destroyed crops; failing farms, 98 percent lacking electricity, forced thousands of Valley families onto the welfare rolls; and "flood, fire, and erosion" consigned Valley residents to a lifetime of poverty.

Senator George Norris of Nebraska had battled unsuccessfully throughout the 1920s to improve living conditions in the Valley by urging construction of dams on the Tennessee River at Muscle Shoals, Alabama. A number of dams had been constructed there during the war as a way to generate power for nitrates needed for explosives and fertilizers. After the war ended, however, the government had lost interest in the productive capacity of the Muscle Shoals dams, and Norris's efforts to promote appropriations for hydroelectric plants met with unqualified opposition from presidents Coolidge and Hoover, who saw such efforts as socialism or an attack on free enterprise.

Roosevelt, who wished to create some measure of prosperity for the Valley's impoverished farmers — partly as an incentive for keeping rural residents from crowding into cities — championed Norris's cause. He asked Congress to create a Tennessee Valley Authority (TVA) that could produce cheap electricity for the Valley's farmers as well as provide services for flood control, soil conservation, and reforestation. A congressional supporter of Roosevelt's vision observed that "TVA is not primarily a dam-building job, a fertilizer job or power-transmission job," but an operation that could serve the Valley's "physical, social, and economic condition." Opponents again charged the proposal with being "an attempt to graft onto our American system the Russian idea," and the

New York Times dismissed "the enactment of any such bill at this time . . . [as] the 'low' of Congressional folly." Roosevelt considered such orthodoxy a failure of imagination. When asked by Norris how he would respond when asked about "the political philosophy behind TVA," he replied: "I'll tell them it's neither fish nor fowl, but whatever it is, it will taste awfully good to the people of the Tennessee Valley." In the heady Hundred Days of the new administration, both houses of Congress gave bipartisan approval to TVA, and Roosevelt signed the law on May 18.

Despite Roosevelt's focus on America's domestic crisis and his concession to isolationists during the campaign by opposing membership in the League of Nations, he counseled the public on the enduring importance of international affairs. In his May 7 radio talk, he emphasized the significance of foreign relations for long-term U.S. prosperity and the country's stake in promoting world peace. "Hand in hand with the domestic situation which, of course, is our first concern is the world situation," he declared. He urged his audience to understand that "the domestic situation is inevitably and deeply tied in with the conditions in all of the other Nations of the world." He explained that "permanent" prosperity depended on "prosperity all over the world." He described the four objectives of U.S. participation in current and future international conferences as a general reduction of armaments, which curtailed fear of armed attacks and unbalanced budgets; a reduction of trade barriers that could advance international trade; a stabilization of currencies to facilitate trade; and better relations between all nations. "The international conference that lies before us [in London this summer]," he added, "must succeed. The future of the world demands it and we have each of us pledged ourselves to the best joint efforts to this end."

The May 7 talk was a window on his hopes of moving the country toward a greater involvement overseas. He was well aware of the loss of political support he could suffer if he ran counter to current isolationist sentiment, but by identifying disarmament as a leading objective of his foreign policy, he was advocating a goal hardly anyone opposed. The problem he faced, though, was promoting arms reduction without becoming party to commitments that might involve the United States in European conflicts that Americans considered of limited relevance to the country's future.

Advocates of U.S. military strength were not without a voice in the discussion. When General Douglas MacArthur, the Army chief of staff, discussed the Army's budget with Roosevelt, he exploded in anger at the president's plan to reduce the already small Army of 140,000 men as a way to free up money for relief. MacArthur contemptuously declared, "When we lost the next war, and an American boy, lying in the mud with an enemy bayonet through his belly and enemy foot on his dying throat spat out his last curse, I wanted the name not to be MacArthur but Roosevelt." Roosevelt responded angrily: "You must not talk that way to the President." MacArthur apologized and offered to resign, but Roosevelt would not hear of it, and told the general to work out a compromise budget. "You've saved the Army," Secretary of War George Dern told Mac-

Arthur as they left the Oval Office. But seeing his life's work in jeopardy, MacArthur later recalled that he "vomited on the steps of the White House."

Tensions over U.S. engagement in foreign affairs also erupted over Adolf Hitler's treatment of Germany's Jews, which became all too evident in the opening months of 1933. Roosevelt came under pressure from liberal groups to protest the Nazis' exclusion of Jews from the government, professions, and universities and their campaign to boycott Jewish businesses. He was also urged to support reduced barriers to Jewish migration to the United States. But State Department warnings that any public condemnation of Nazi measures would amount to interference in Germany's domestic affairs discouraged Roosevelt from taking overt action. He was also reluctant to antagonize labor leaders, who predicted that relaxed immigration standards were likely to worsen the country's unemployment problem. When Hjalmar Schacht, the president of Germany's Reichsbank, came to the White House in May to discuss the coming London Economic Conference, Roosevelt impressed him as sympathetic to Hitler's efficiency in dealing with Germany's economic problems and assured him that "this hurdle [of tensions over Jewish persecution] would be cleared even if its importance should not be underestimated."

Roosevelt's desire for an arms reduction formula likewise fell victim to isolationist pressures. To advance disarmament talks being held in Geneva, Switzerland, on May 15, Roosevelt decided to put a negotiating formula before the delegates. With Hitler slated to speak two days later on foreign affairs, which threatened to provoke a European crisis, Roosevelt hoped to head off Nazi belligerency with calming arms control proposals. He sent a letter to the heads of the fifty-four government participants at the Geneva talks urging the elimination of aggressive weapons and commitment to a nonaggression pact that would reduce fears of invasions. Hitler responded by praising Roosevelt's "magnanimous proposal . . . as a guarantor of peace." British prime minister Ramsay MacDonald saw the president's message as an opportunity for Great Britain to cooperate "with the United States in everything relating to peace, world prosperity and human progress." Because the French viewed Hitler's response as nothing more than rhetoric to mask German militancy and because American isolationists objected to a presidential pronouncement that might be interpreted as committing the United States to the security of its former allies, Roosevelt felt compelled to deny U.S. readiness to guarantee any other nation's safety or to do more than consult with them if they came under attack. In short, the White House made it clear that the administration would do nothing to reverse America's determination to isolate itself from conflicts abroad.

The diminished prospects for an arms control agreement heightened hopes of making the London Economic Conference, scheduled for the summer, a step toward renewed international prosperity and peace. But America's isolationism and economic nationalism left its role in facilitating a successful meeting an open question. Roosevelt's choice of delegates seemed to provide a clue to his intentions. Eager to encourage expectations of U.S. backing for productive talks, Roosevelt named Secretary of State Cordell Hull, his highest-ranking foreign affairs official, head of the American delegation. Mindful of the Senate's influence in blocking Wilson's foreign policy goals, Roosevelt also appointed Key Pittman, Nevada Democrat and chairman of the Foreign Relations Committee, as well as Republican senator James Couzens from Michigan, a midwestern isolationist state. Tennessee congressman Samuel McReynolds, Democratic chairman of the House Foreign Affairs Committee; Roosevelt's former running mate, James Cox; and Ralph Morrison, a Texas Democratic Party donor, filled out the delegation. On the surface, it was an impressive group of men, but in choosing representatives who had never attended an international meeting and held contrary views on economic and financial policies, the president was effectively ensuring that a divided delegation would rely on him for guidance in reaching final conference agreements.

Roosevelt's machinations were all too evident to close observers. Before appointing Couzens, for example, he had tried to persuade California's isolationist senator Hiram Johnson to join the delegation. The chance to visit London for the first time tempted the sixty-five-year-old Johnson, but convinced that Roosevelt would use the appointment to undermine his isolationism, Johnson declined the offer. Similarly, despite his satisfaction at being selected chief of the delegation, Hull distrusted Roosevelt's commitment to reduced tariffs and increased trade as a response to the Depression. The selection of high-tariff advocates Pittman and Couzens suggested that Roosevelt was torn between economic nationalism and free trade. With his slight lisp, Hull complained about

261

"that man across the street who never tells me anything."

British ambassador Ronald Lindsay also saw through Roosevelt's rhetoric as anything but a commitment to international cooperation: "What his intentions are," Lindsay cabled London before the opening of the conference, "is wrapped in complete obscurity and every statement of them, whether by himself or by his spokesmen, is evasive." British chargé d'affaires D'Arcy Osborne weighed in with the warning that the "situation here is so incalculable and President himself so mercurial and his policies so admittedly empirical that all estimates and forecasts are dangerous."

Despite the president's May 7 pronouncement that the future of the world demanded a productive meeting, he read British-French pressure during negotiations for currency stabilization as an impermissible bar to price rises in the United States, and thus to successful talks. With the dollar falling to lows against the pound and the franc, the British and French worried about a flood of inexpensive American imports; for Roosevelt, the cheap dollar was stimulating the American economy. He had in fact agreed to currency stability in earlier discussions with British prime minister Ramsay MacDonald and French premier Edouard Herriot, but ever the pragmatist who rejected orthodox solutions to an unprecedented crisis, he viewed their intransigence on the currency issue as further evidence that the European statesmen, as he told Morgenthau, were "a bunch of [self-serving] bastards."

In a July 3 message that essentially ended the conference, Roosevelt declared: "I would regard it as a catastrophe amounting to a world tragedy if the great Conference of Nations" allowed "itself to be diverted by the proposal of a purely artificial and temporary experiment affecting the monetary exchange of a few nations only," and so, he declared stabilization a secondary matter that diverted the conference from its "main objectives." MacDonald complained that Roosevelt's obsession with raising prices was the real diversion and that the president was no longer the man he had earlier spoken with in Washington. Pro-stabilization delegates dismissed any continuance of the talks as a "pure waste of time."

In fact, on the American side, the conference had been something of a fiasco from the start, as the delegates were largely at sea as to what Roosevelt expected of them. Pittman's sole concern was serving the silver interests of Nevada. An alcoholic who went on drunken sprees in London, shooting out street lamps with a six-shooter and chasing a technical adviser critical of Pittman's silver obsession down the halls of Claridge's very staid hotel with a Bowie knife, Pittman made the local press with his antics and embarrassed the delegation. Warren Robbins, the protocol officer, who was supposed to ensure the representatives' regard for the niceties of diplomatic discourse, added to the embarrassment by wearing a monocle, enjoying publicity as "the mystery man" of the delegation, and showing off a wife with dyed purple hair. Walter Lippmann declared, "Mr. Roosevelt's purposes may be excellent, but he has completely failed to organize a diplomatic instrument to express them"

Ironically, the conference wound up advancing Roosevelt's standing with isolationists suspicious of his internationalism. It also gave him the opportunity to keep ambitious aides under control. As head of the delegation, Hull bore the brunt of the dismay that Roosevelt's domestic preoccupation and the U.S. delegation's behavior provoked. Immobilized by conflicts among "the collection of difficult personalities" and frustrated by the president's muddled instructions, Hull refused to pronounce on any topic in public. From the beginning of his presidency, Roosevelt had shown limited regard for Hull, who seemed more useful as a prominent ex-senator who could keep the upper house in check than as a valuable foreign policy adviser. At the same time, Roosevelt was able to check Raymond Moley's rising influence, which seemed to threaten his own standing. As assistant secretary of state, Moley had gained prominence during the first months of the administration as Roosevelt's most significant adviser, to the point that *Time* featured him on its cover. Joseph P. Kennedy, wealthy businessman and FDR financial backer, warned Moley that Roosevelt was becoming unhappy with his celebrity. Commentators joked that Roosevelt had become Moley's appointments secretary, and one administration insider said that Moley "acted as if he was running the Government and that Roosevelt was carrying out Moley's suggestions."

As Roosevelt moved to counter Anglo-French pressure for stabilization, he also opened the way to Moley's eclipse. As the conference moved toward a stabilization agreement, Roosevelt instructed Moley to go to London to arrange a compromise on raising world price levels. Moley's assignment registered in the press as a mission that could save the proceedings: "Moley, Moley, Moley, Lord God Almighty" ran one headline.

Roosevelt's July 3 announcement not only destroyed prospects for a conference accord but also, to Hull's satisfaction, weakened Moley's standing. Hull had made his antagonism to Moley clear to the president, describing him as usurping his authority and diminishing his own capacity to act as the president's representative. In down-home Tennessee language, he complained to intimates of "that piss-ant Moley" who "curled up at mah feet and let me stroke his head like a huntin' dog and then he goes and bites me in the ass!" The conference's failure put an end to any talk of Moley as the wonder man of the administration. Moreover, his falling out with Hull made him a liability Roosevelt thought to deal with by sending Moley to study conditions in Hawaii. Since it would be too obvious that he was being ostracized, Roosevelt agreed to keep him on for several weeks while he prepared a report on crime for the attorney general. Although he would continue to work on FDR speeches for two more years, his overreach, failed London mission, and increasingly conservative bent alienated him from Roosevelt and turned him into a leading New Deal critic.

Commentators in 1933 and since have excoriated Roosevelt for having destroyed hopes of economic cooperation among democratic nations, which undercut their ability to counter the militancy of Hitler and Mussolini. Unquestionably, Roosevelt's economic nationalism fueled in turn self-serving attitudes toward internationalism in former allies. But the principal culprit in undermining cooperation against Nazi aggression was not the failure of the democracies jointly to fight the Depression, but the legacy of World

War I. The war had strengthened isolationist convictions in the United States and aroused pacifist passions across Europe in response to the pointlessness of the fighting that had cost eighteen million lives for no constructive purpose. Even if the London conference had resulted in harmony among the democracies, including the United States, it is more than doubtful that it would have deterred Nazi aggression, made Hitler and the Nazis any less aggressive, or made his British and French foes any quicker to take up arms against Germany.

For Roosevelt, the failure in London only added to his standing in the United States as the country's best hope of overcoming the Depression. The opening Hundred Days of his presidency had made him an esteemed leader, even though no one could discern a precise pattern in the fifteen major bills that he saw through Congress, which included a securities act that regulated Wall Street and the Glass-Steagall law, which separated investment and commercial banking and created the Federal Deposit Insurance Corporation (FDIC) guaranteeing the safety of bank deposits. No one who took full measure of the economic and unemployment measures in June 1933 was ready to declare the Depression over. But the decisive actions of the new administration had given millions of Americans relief and reason to hope for better days.

As William Leuchtenburg summed it up, Roosevelt's New Deal "had written into the laws of the land the most extraordinary series of reforms in the nation's history." They bolstered farmers, the unemployed, homeowners, bank depositors, union laborers, conservationists, and advocates of an improved national infrastructure. Moreover, they bridged the divide between cities, towns, and rural areas that had turned the country against itself in the 1920s. "At the end of February [1933]," Walter Lippmann said, "We were a congeries of disorderly panic-stricken mobs and factions. In the Hundred Days from March to June, we became again an organized nation confident of our power to provide for our own security and to control our own destiny." You saved capitalism, Moley told Roosevelt, while others marveled at his transformation from an amiable, attractive man and governor with a "beguiling smile" into a dynamo with poise, courage, and empathy for the country's least fortunate citizens and a commitment to help them.

Few incidents caught the spirit of change from Hoover to Roosevelt better than the new administration's response to a second Bonus Army march, which descended on Washington in May. Instead of being met with tanks and troops with fixed bayonets, the bedraggled veterans were "killed with kindness." Roosevelt "offered the veterans an Army camp, three meals a day, endless supplies of coffee, and a large convention tent, where leaders could orate to their hearts' content." He agreed to confer with their representatives, and Mrs. Roosevelt visited them on a rainy day, walking through ankle-deep mud to lead the vets in singing "There's a long trail a-winding." As one observer noted, "Hoover sent the Army. Roosevelt sent his wife." Arthur Schlesinger summed up the end of the demonstration perfectly: After "two weeks, most of the veterans went affably into the Civilian Conservation Corps, and the second Bonus Epeditionary Force had met a painless Waterloo."

267

CHAPTER 6
"TRUSTEE OF THE EXISTING SOCIAL SYSTEM"

By the summer of 1933, Franklin and Eleanor had settled into comfortable patterns of behavior that not only suited them but also inspired public confidence in the president and first lady. Yet for all his eagerness to experiment, Roosevelt was a creature of habit whose personal routine gave assurances that he was grounded in familiar American customs. Each day began at approximately 8 a.m. with breakfast in bed of orange juice, scrambled eggs, toast, and coffee. As he ate, he read six leading newspapers from New York, Baltimore, and Washington. Press publications from the Midwest would not reach him until later in the day, but each morning Howe presented a digest of the previous day's papers from beyond the East Coast. While still in bed or shaving or dressing with the help of his valet, Roosevelt consulted with Howe and Missy LeHand, both of whom lived in the White House and were available at any time of day. In addition, Ray Moley, budget director Lewis Douglas, and any cabinet officer who had pressing business often joined the meeting.

Marvin McIntyre, Roosevelt's appointments secretary, and Steve Early, the press secretary, saw the president at about 10 a.m. to go over the day's schedule, which was crowded with fifteen-minute meetings that invariably exceeded the allotted time. Demands on the president's attention outran his capacity to engage fully with the many requests for consideration of pressing issues. Briefed beforehand about each visitor's agenda, Roosevelt developed a technique for blunting or sidetracking unwanted requests. When, for example, Texas congressman Lyndon Johnson urged that the Rural Electrification Administration (REA) string transmission lines across his district, the south central Texas Hill Country, where population density fell short of a federal standard, Roosevelt diverted him by asking if he had ever seen a Russian woman naked. He then filled Johnson's allotted fifteen minutes with a description of Harry Hopkins's impressions of the women he met during a recent visit to Moscow. Whisked out of the Oval Office by LeHand, Johnson had to wait weeks for another appointment to renew his request. Louisiana senator Huey Long, who prided himself on outtalking everyone, complained that "I go to that office intending to give that fellow [FDR] a lecture which he needs. Then after a while I find myself leaving without speaking my piece. He's hard to talk to."

Presidential business was primarily conducted in the White House's west wing Oval Office, where Roosevelt sat behind a large desk covered with selected memorabilia. Moved from his bedroom to the office in a wheelchair from which two Secret Service agents transferred him to a desk chair, he greeted each day's work with enthusiasm, never overtly conceding anything to his disability.

To observers, taken aback by his need to be scooped up like a child when being moved from one chair to another, he seemed unself-conscious about what one onlooker called his "ghastly invalidism." For roughly eight hours between 10 a.m. and 6 p.m., he sat behind his desk, usually eating lunch there while he discussed current events with anyone he wanted to see about existing challenges and listened to summaries from the flood of letters from ordinary citizens to the White House. A swim in the White House pool; a health exam by Dr. Ross T. McIntire, the Navy's chief physician; and an occasional drive through the Virginia countryside, where he could enjoy the great outdoors reminiscent of the bucolic Hyde Park environs, often filled out his workday.

Two packs of Camel cigarettes daily helped relieve the unrelenting pressure of the office. The "children's hour," a gathering of White House aides and anyone else he wanted to see for pre-dinner martinis or bourbon old-fashioneds; Hollywood films with happy endings; stamp collecting, for which he had an enduring passion and which deepened his knowledge of geography; and poker evenings with "the boys" punctuated by much banter provided end-of-day recreation from the burdens of the day. But the back-and-forth over drinks and poker was also a vehicle for gathering information on conditions in the country and abroad and learning more about the people in his administration.

Dinner was invariably at 8 p.m., informally in the Oval Office study, or formally in a dining room where more guests could be accommodated. The White House State Dining Room was reserved for special occasions, including visits from foreign dignitaries. Dinner guests uniformly testified that the food was atrocious. White House secretary Grace Tully described it as boardinghouse fare, while novelist Ernest Hemingway said the meals were "the worst I've ever eaten," complaining about "rainwater soup . . . rubber squab . . . wilted salad and a cake some admirer had sent in." The actress Tallulah Bankhead recalled that she steeled herself against White House dinners by eating a full meal beforehand. Even Harold Ickes, who described himself as "not very fussy about my food," complained about the uninspiring meals he sat through, and thought it "a little out of proportion to use a solid-gold knife and fork on ordinary roast mutton." For Roosevelt, "The quality of the conversations more than made up for the mediocre quality of the food."

Such household matters were, in any case, Eleanor's responsibility, and Franklin respected the fact that she had quickly developed broader concerns as first lady than the mundane business of planning menus or, as she put it, standing in long lines greeting White House guests and hosting official dinners. Eleanor, forty-eight at the time, was determined to do more as first lady than manage the White House social life. She signaled her intentions when she came to Washington at Mrs. Hoover's invitation five weeks before the inauguration to discuss family arrangements. She took the night train and hailed a cab to take her to the Mayflower for breakfast. She had refused the offer to be met by a White House car and a military aide who could be either in uniform or civilian garb, as she wished. After breakfast, she walked to the White House accompanied by Lorena Hickok, dismissing a warning from the State

Department's chief protocol officer that she would be mobbed.

She also defied convention by working on two books that would give her some distance from White House duties: A celebration of her father, *Hunting Big Game in the Eighties: The Letters of Elliott Roosevelt, Sportsman,* and *It's Up to the Women,* an appeal to the country's women to fight for reforms that could relieve suffering during the Depression. Her policy book demonstrated her determination to move beyond symbolic gestures associated with first ladies and gave support to the president's promise of a New Deal that would free the country, and women in particular, from the burdens of the era. She advised readers on how to manage households on limited budgets and urged them to fight the good fight for social justice. When Vice President Jack Garner's wife, Mariette, asked Eleanor if she thought she could continue working as his secretary, as she had for several years, including when he was Speaker of the House, Eleanor exclaimed, "I most certainly do!"

Her encouragement to Mariette Garner to continue productive work reflected her own search for a constructive role in the administration. She wanted to identify a way to advance presidential actions that not only ended the Depression but also put permanent social change in place and gave new meaning to the first lady's role. She hoped to serve these purposes partly by helping Franklin stay in touch with the public sentiment. She feared that White House aides would give him an excessively rosy picture of national conditions that blunted the need for immediate and far-reaching reforms. Her daily letters revealed suffering across the country, which she put before him as an inducement to prompt action. She urged him to read White House mail that was not cherry-picked to include only laudatory praise. She asked Franklin if she could serve as a "listening post," and read and respond to some of his mail. Looking at her "quizzically," he replied that Missy LeHand would consider it "interference" and turned aside her proposal, as he was opposed to having Eleanor so closely involved with his day-to-day administration of affairs.

Perhaps more to the point was the fact that tensions between them moved Franklin to maintain some distance in their daily contact. Differences dating from at least the Lucy Mercer episode found expression in an anecdote Ben Cohen liked to tell. Entering the Oval Office one day around noon, he observed a chuckling president. "Would you mind sharing the amusement with me?" Cohen asked. Roosevelt responded: "Eleanor was just in here after a morning appointment with her doctor. 'So, what did he say about that big ass of yours?' " Franklin reported himself as asking. "Oh, Franklin," she replied, "He had nothing at all to say about you."

But Franklin's resistance to her suggestion that she become a sounding board did not discourage her from expanding the bounds of a first lady's role. His rejection spurred her to find meaningful activities outside of his control, which he quickly came to regard as a valuable part of his administration. She seized on her prominence to speak on the radio and in person about the importance of government programs serving the needy. She held unprecedented press conferences for women reporters, where she made the case for government activism to ease the distress of the unemployed. "At the President's press conference, all the world's a stage;" a wire service reporter observed, "at Mrs. Roosevelt's, all the world's a school." She persuaded CCC administrators to set up a camp for women and convinced Harry Hopkins to commit some of his CWA budget to jobs for as many as a hundred thousand women. She signed a contract to write a monthly column for the North American Newspaper Alliance and another featured in *Women's Home Companion* in which she urged women to write to her. The historian Mary R. Beard observed that Eleanor's columns gave "inspiration to the married, solace to the lovelorn, assistance to the homemaker, menus to the cook, help to the educator, direction to the employer, caution to the warrior, and deeper awareness of its primordial force to the 'weaker sex.' " Beard added that people were accustomed to "the Great White Father in the White House . . . now the Great White Mother emerges as a personality in her own right and starts an independent course of instruction on her own account."

Eleanor's refusal to have Secret Service agents at her side, and her insistence on traveling on buses, trains, and planes as an ordinary citizen endeared her to millions of Americans who appreciated her democratic values, including "seven-cent luncheons" of eggs, potatoes, and puddings. Her appearance at the Bonus Army encampment was of a piece with her growing stature as a humanist. One of the reporters who regularly covered her wrote Eleanor to tell her that she had refuted some of her cynicism about powerful officeholders. Most politicians "lost the human touch if they ever had it," she declared. "To have been able to see you at close hand, demonstrating the exact contrary, means truly a great deal to me."

Yet for all the admiration and warm support that Eleanor's activities generated, she also faced criticism for them. One journalist saw her as governed by "a ruthless craving for personal publicity." A tour Eleanor led of Washington's inner-city black neighborhoods, followed by pressure for legislation that could ease the poverty of slum dwellers, was initially judged to be nothing more than self-serving. But her sincerity of purpose and genuine commitment to serving the disadvantaged eventually overcame the hostility of even some of her harshest critics. In September 1933, when she spoke at a conference discussing how to help the needy get through the coming winter, Eleanor impressed the audience with "the spontaneous outpouring of her heart." She recounted the misery of a mother who had lost a child because she lacked the material resources to keep him well, and insisted that people who say that "the poor do not suffer, . . . just don't think and don't know."

Her frustration at insurmountable challenges was never greater than in her attempts to address the poverty of mining communities in northern West Virginia, where, one observer said, "Only slavery exceeded the coal industry in degradation of human beings." In response to pleadings from Lorena Hickok, Eleanor visited mining areas in Pennsylvania and West Virginia, and she could not believe that such a "cesspool of human misery" existed in America. Ninety-five percent of the "children in West Virginia's Monongalia County suffered from various curable but intense blights: malnutrition, defective vision, rickets, rotten teeth." In Morgantown, the main street was awash in "stagnant, filthy water, which the inhabitants used for drinking, cooking, washing, and everything else imaginable." In houses covered with black coal dust, hungry children slept on "bug infested rags, spread out on the floor." Eleanor wrote that in one home, six hungry children were fed scraps of "the kind that you or I might give to a dog."

To better the lives of miners and their families, Eleanor, with Franklin's enthusiastic support, helped establish Arthurdale, a model community or subsidized homestead near Reedsville in the northeast corner of West Virginia, which was named for Richard Arthur, from whom the land was purchased. The goal was to settle families in newly constructed homes, with plans to employ the men in a post office or furniture factory or, when the latter did not pan out, a vacuum cleaner assembly plant. Unfortunately, plans for that, too, were abandoned, as were proposed factories for shirt making and building radio cabinets. The want of demand for the products of these facilities in a depressed economy worked havoc on the reputation of the Subsistence Homestead Division of the NIRA, the agency responsible for Arthurdale, which was then transferred to the Department of the Interior.

After witnessing the wretched poverty of these West Virginia enclaves, Eleanor believed that federal interventions to rescue them were not failed experiments in socialism or communism, as vocal critics on the right asserted, but rather humane attempts to restore a measure of dignity to suffering people and head off the social unrest that such hopeless conditions bred. Although Eleanor clung to hope that planned communities could foster a measure of prosperity among formerly destitute peoples in coal mining towns or city slums, they fell short of expectations. Nonetheless, she spent considerable time at Arthurdale, commuting from Washington and establishing special relations with the 165 families settled there, especially keeping track of the children's progress and joining in town activities, including dancing the Virginia reel with the homesteaders on an entertainment night in the community center.

Because the stumbling performance of Arthurdale took awhile to become evident, it did little to undermine Eleanor's growing popularity. By the summer of 1933, seventy-four-year-old Carrie Chapman Catt, the leading architect of the 1920 women's voting rights amendment, told Eleanor that "I have had a collection of statesmen hanging upon my wall, but under the new administration, I have been obliged to start a new collection and that is one of stateswomen. Now it is ready and you are the very center of it all." In 1933 alone, Eleanor received over three hundred thousand pieces of mail asking her help, soliciting advice, and making her the most recognizable first lady in the country's history since Martha Washington. In 1935, Louis Howe asked Eleanor if she would like him to begin organizing a 1940 presidential campaign for her. The suggestion pleased Eleanor, who also believed that a woman president was possible in the future, but did not think that the country was ready for one yet, and so put Howe off by saying that one politician in a family was enough.

Besides, in the closing months of 1933 and the first half of 1934, it was not clear whether the Roosevelt New Deal would stand the test of time. Although the index of business activity had jumped 50 percent in the first months of the new administration, much of those gains were lost by the fall in a recession that seemed to make no more sense than the broader collapse that defied national faith in traditional free enterprise. Roosevelt saw the need to give a Fireside Chat on October 22 to reinforce hopes for the economic revival that had been spurred by his inaugural speech and initial New Deal measures. The talk recounted the administration's gains in providing relief to the destitute, reducing unemployment, limiting foreclosures on family farms and homes, insuring bank savings accounts, and raising prices on agricultural and industrial goods. Acknowledging that the Depression was far from ended and that the administration was aiming to make additional economic advances in the coming months, Roosevelt urged the country to take heart in the fact that "our troubles will not be over tomorrow, but at least we are on our way and we are headed in the right direction."

To give substance to his rhetoric, Roosevelt undertook a fresh experiment to trigger an upward surge in the economy. With farmers particularly in full-throated complaint, he decided to test out a theory that buying gold on the world market would devalue the dollar, increase American exports, and raise domestic commodity prices, especially including farm produce. When conservative Wall Street bankers attacked the president's exercise in manipulating the dollar, it provoked an angry defense from farmers and other advocates of inflation who shared the administration's anger toward bankers and businessmen, whom they viewed as stewards only of their own interests.

By the end of 1933, the failure of that experiment gave resonance to British economist John Maynard Keynes's observation that "the gyrations of the dollar looked . . . more like a gold standard on the booze than the ideal managed currency of my dreams." Keynes correctly suspected that Roosevelt's manipulation of gold prices was based on a set of random decisions that would have shocked economists devoted to scientific calculations of market forces. When Roosevelt told Morgenthau one morning that they would increase the price of gold by twenty-one cents and Morgenthau asked for an explanation, the president replied, "Because 'three times seven' is a lucky number." Morgenthau discreetly kept the president's insouciance to himself, as it would only have confirmed conservative assessments of how reckless his actions were. In January 1934, Roosevelt signed a Gold Reserve Act that fixed the value of the dollar at 59 percent of its earlier gold measure and brought a halt to what Keynes dismissed as "puerile" economics unworthy of an undergraduate. Roosevelt rationalized the administration's gold program by saying that "if we continued a week or so longer without my having made this move on gold, we would have had an agrarian revolution in this country."

The pressure on the administration from farm organizations faced with crop prices falling below the cost of production was palpable. "The West is seething with unrest," Roosevelt wrote his mother in the fall of 1933, "and must have higher values to pay off their debts." Reports from Lorena

Hickok describing the poverty and suffering in the agricultural sector reached his desk and alerted him to communist agitation trying to provoke an "agrarian revolution." At a minimum, farmers were threatening a million-man protest in Washington: "If wheat and cotton prices did not move forward," Roosevelt told a financial adviser opposed to inflationary policies, Washington would see "marching farmers." As it was, farmers were taking the law into their own hands, disrupting foreclosure sales and assaulting sheriffs and judges who tried to enforce them. Across Iowa, Minnesota, Wisconsin, and the Dakotas, farmers led by Milo Reno, the head of the radical Farmers Holiday Association, demanded price supports, inflation, and an embargo on produce priced below costs. The governors of the five farm states came to Washington to warn the White House and Congress that upheaval was imminent without immediate help, and predicted that the goodwill Roosevelt enjoyed among farmers would crumble soon unless they saw an economic upsurge.

By 1934, across the Great Plains running from Texas through Kansas, Oklahoma, Nebraska, and New Mexico to the Dakotas, a combination of destructive farming practices and a severe drought turned the area into a dust bowl from which 3.5 million people migrated to California and other states during the decade. The misery of these displaced families — generally known as "Okies" after the thousands who had fled Oklahoma — was captured brilliantly in John Steinbeck's 1939 novel *The Grapes of Wrath* and the 1940 feature film based on the book. The dust storms that swept across the region and sent their thick clouds as far east as Chicago, Cleveland, Washington,

D.C., New York, and Boston added to the economic misery of farmers. In response to the disaster the Roosevelt administration set up soil erosion divisions in the departments of Agriculture and Interior, but at the time, these were little more than Band-Aids placed on terrible wounds.

Conditions improved as the result of AAA programs and the Farm Credit Administration's refinancing mortgages, combined with a Roosevelt charm offensive in two meetings with Western governors in the first half of 1934 to calm farm protests. The president remained stymied, though, about how to restore lasting prosperity to small farmers and agribusinesses through rising commodity prices. A federal silver-buying program was introduced to increase the returns on their crops, but instead of raising prices on farm produce, as advocates predicted, it did little more than enrich silver-mining interests in western states.

By the spring of 1934 there was an undercurrent of feeling that Roosevelt had no clearer idea of how to restore the country's capitalist system to its vaunted standing as an engine of mass prosperity than the many other voices offering economic solutions. The popular English writer H. G. Wells, a socialist, saw America at this time as agitated by "a widespread discontent and discomfort. . . . The actual New Deal has not gone far enough and fast enough for the great masses of the American population." Some on the left urged radical departures from traditional remedies as the necessary alternatives to the president's stumbling program. "Nothing but failure can be expected from the New Deal," the editors of *Common Sense,* a leftist periodical, declared in September of that year. Conservatives, meanwhile, warned against abandoning familiar policies for untried nostrums. Keynes's ideas about deficit spending impressed traditionalist economists as a desperate attempt to find some novel way to end the Depression. Budget director Lewis Douglas, who in August 1934 resigned in protest against Roosevelt's fiscal excesses, wrote to convince him that unbalanced budgets threatened "not only your place in history but conceivably the immediate fate of Western civilization."

Roosevelt, however, refused to give up on the New Deal, for doing so would have meant conceding not only the loss of hope that he had raised so effectively during his year in office but the failure of his presidency. It was certainly true that in 1934, the economy was hardly robust: Over ten million Americans — about 20 percent of the workforce — were still without jobs, while national income, which had gained about 25 percent in a year, was still only half of what it had been in 1931. But passage of the Securities Exchange Act in June, setting up the Securities and Exchange Commission (SEC) to regulate the stock market, and of the Federal Communications Commission law (FCC) in the summer to control the airways by licensing radio stations, were seen as solid gains for New Deal reform. Investors were assured of greater protection from fraudulent Wall Street operators, and liberal Democrats could balance conservative control of newspapers, which Roosevelt complained published half-truths about him and the New Deal, by winning radio licenses that gave the mass public more balanced news reports.

Keynes also encouraged Roosevelt to maintain his bold stance in pursuit of recovery. "You have made yourself the trustee for those in every country who seek to mend the evils of our condition by reasoned experiment within the framework of the existing social system," he wrote in a letter to the *New York Times* on December 31, 1933. "If you fail, rational change will be gravely prejudiced throughout the world, leaving orthodox and revolution to fight it out. But if you succeed, new and bolder methods will be tried, and we may date the first chapter of a new economic era from your accession to office."

Keynes's reassurance heartened Roosevelt, though he remained skeptical of all economists, telling Adolph Berle that "no two or three hundred or two thousand economists, businessmen, or politicians" could agree on much of anything. And after Keynes paid a visit to the White House at the end of May, Roosevelt told Frances Perkins, "I saw your friend Keynes. He left a whole rigmarole of figures. He must be a mathematician rather than a political economist." Keynes reciprocated the president's misgivings, complaining to Perkins that he had "supposed the President was more literate, economically speaking." Keynes urged the president to engage in deficit spending as the quickest and surest route to prompt recovery — "I lay overwhelming emphasis on the increase of national purchasing power resulting from governmental expenditure which is financed by loans" — rather than tax increases, which drew money out of the economy. His prescription was "the only sure means of obtaining quickly a rising output at rising prices." With extraordinary insight into what would eventually restore American prosperity, as it was already doing for the German economy through Hitler's program of rearmament, Keynes added, "That is why a war has always caused intense industrial activity." Why not spend on infrastructure in a time of peace instead of arms? Keynes asked.

Roosevelt could only go so far in finding money for infrastructure projects, he explained to Keynes: "There is a practical limit to what the Government can borrow — especially because the banks are offering passive resistance in most of the large centers." His observation was testimony to the limited faith he had in Keynes's affinity for deficit spending, though he was certainly intent on taking action of his own. In May 1934, he told Colonel House that "many new manifestations of the New Deal" were in the works, "even though the orthodox protest and the heathen roar! . . . We must keep the sheer momentum from slacking up too much," he added, "and I have no intention of relinquishing the offensive in favor of defensive tactics." His steadfastness rested partly on his recognition that forces on the left and the right were waiting and eager to fill the vacuum if and when the New Deal ground to a halt.

In a speech at Gettysburg, Pennsylvania, in May 1934, a site notable for such history-making events as the 1863 Civil War battle and Lincoln's most famous address, Roosevelt issued a call for a definitive end to regionalism, declaring, "The selfishness of sectionalism has no place in our national life." The address aimed to rally all Americans around his administration's efforts to forge a more prosperous united nation devoid of class and regional struggles. "It has been left to us of this generation to see the healing made permanent" between the sections, he said, recalling not only the Civil War but also the more recent ten-

sions between urban modernists and rural fundamentalists that had split the Democratic Party
and made the 1925 Scopes trial in Tennessee such
a national cause célèbre. "In our planning to lift
industry to normal prosperity," he added, "the
farmer upholds our efforts. And as we seek to give
the farmers of the United States a long-sought
equality, the city worker understands and helps.
All of us, among all the States, share in whatever
of good comes to the average man. We know that
we all have a stake — a partnership in this
Government of our country." Evoking the symbolism of the setting in which he spoke, he concluded,
"Here, here at Gettysburg, here in the presence of
the spirits of those who fell on this ground, we
give renewed assurance that the passions of war
are moldering in the tombs of Time and the
purposes of peace are flowing today in the hearts
of a united people." The speech was an attempt
not only to tamp down domestic divisions but
also to caution Europeans against their own local
antagonisms, especially those generated by Nazi
Germany's resurgent nationalism, which threatened as early as 1934 to explode in another conti-
nentwide war.

While isolationist sentiment sharply limited any
contributions Roosevelt could make to peacekeeping abroad, he was under few constraints in aiming to counter divisive voices at home assailing
him and the New Deal from conservatives to his
right and radicals on the left. In the summer of
1934, he counseled administration aides to keep
to the center in the political debates informing
the November congressional elections. He believed the New Deal held the political high ground
with a majority of Americans, but he was con-

cerned that 10 to 15 percent of voters were "at the extreme right of modern philosophy," while another 10 to 15 percent were committed to the "extreme left."

By 1934, conservatives, led by representatives of big business, had come to believe that Roosevelt's New Deal threatened "property interests" and that the foundation of a new organization prepared to defend the Constitution and "the faith of the [founding] fathers" had become essential. In their view the Republican Party, which was depicted in an August 1934 cartoon as a disheveled old man carrying signs "Roosevelt is a Red" and "Back to 1929," was in poor standing after Herbert Hoover's failed administration and the party's 1932 defeat. Moreover, conservative Democrats Jouett Shouse, John J. Raskob, Al Smith, and John W. Davis along with prominent businessmen Pierre S. du Pont, Sewell L. Avery of Montgomery Ward, and Alfred P. Sloan of General Motors preferred to back a group that could present itself as being above politics and devoted to fundamental American principles. The preference for an apolitical stand grew out of a realization that an economically depressed America had grown unsympathetic to businessmen and conservative homilies that offered no immediate relief from economic problems.

Although Shouse, who would head the American Liberty League, informed Roosevelt that the organization's goal was to educate Americans about property rights and free enterprise, the president had no illusions that it aimed to mount an attack against the New Deal and inflict political defeats on him in the coming elections by arguing that he was subverting the Constitution with the intention of imposing socialism or Soviet-style communism on America. League members complained that government handouts were discouraging workers from taking jobs with private industry and that the president was restricting free speech in order to hide the truth about the administration's anti-business philosophy. In a speech at Washington's Mayflower Hotel before two thousand of the wealthiest people in America, Al Smith, who had joined their ranks, denounced the president and his administration for promoting class warfare: The Brain Trusters were socialists, he charged, and the New Deal was communism in disguise. *Time* magazine reported, "With few exceptions, members of the so-called Upper Class frankly hate Franklin Roosevelt." In one of the most famous cartoons of the Roosevelt era, Peter Arno in the *New Yorker* magazine portrayed tuxedo- and fur-clad socialites inviting two other members of their crowd to "Come along. We're going to the Trans-Lux [a movie theater] to hiss Roosevelt."

Roosevelt understood that such conservative pronouncements were unlikely to have any more appeal now than they had when Hoover made them in 1932. In response, he launched a speaking campaign to remind Americans that he was not sponsoring an "all-embracing government" resembling any of those in Europe, but rather an administration that aimed to help free enterprise throw off the shackles of the Depression. The objective, he explained, was not to advance the well-being of the "privileged few," as had been the case under the Republican administrations of the 1920s, but to promote "greater security for the average man than he has ever known before in the history of America." As he told a press conference, the Liberty League was like the man or organization that endorsed two or three of the Ten Commandments, but ignored the other seven or eight. Their omission, he asserted, spoke volumes about the League's indifference to destructive exploitation by unprincipled entrepreneurs or the obligation of government to help unemployed citizens find jobs. Roosevelt took greatest offense at the League's claims about the loss of individual liberties. In a Fireside Chat, he asked, "Have you lost any of your rights or liberty or constitutional freedom of action and choice?" Was there any evidence that the New Deal had in any way diminished the Bill of Rights? "Ask yourself," he told listeners, "whether you personally have suffered the impairment of a single jot of these great assurances."

Other voices came to Roosevelt's defense. How, they asked, could the business architects of the Great Depression, which had robbed so many Americans of their freedom — the liberty that came with a decent living — dare to decry the government's attempt to restore the unemployed and ruined farmers to a condition of independence? Liberty was lost, one New Dealer insisted, not when government did too much, but when it did too little. Winston Churchill denounced conservative comparisons of Roosevelt and Hitler as authoritarian leaders as an insult to civilization. Hitler's regime would have little positive resonance in history, Churchill declared with impressive foresight, while Roosevelt's would be remembered for a "renaissance of creative effort." Donald Richberg at the NRA scoffed at the Liberty League's attack on the Brain Trust as the advance wave of totalitarianism. "When any man ventures to scoff at the use of brains in government," Richberg said, "he should be asked to explain by what part of the anatomy he believes human affairs should be conducted." Walter Lippmann rejected League assertions that only a return of business confidence and not government meddling would repair the economy. He asked whether people should be left to suffer "like Chinese coolies in a famine until, for some mysterious reason, the warm blood of confidence rises once more in the veins of bank directors and corporation executives?" Attacks by the wealthy against the New Deal only deepened feeling in the country that business moguls were essentially "stupid and greedy" and fully deserved the appellation "economic royalists."

The enlightened business journal *Fortune* opined that "disinterested critics" understood that Roosevelt's New Deal "has had the preservation of capitalism at all times in view." Indeed, conservative commentators who denounced Roosevelt as "a traitor to his class" misread the president's determination to maintain traditional economic opportunities. While Roosevelt did believe it essential to create a structure of security that would prevent distress in any future economic downturn, he was as devoted to free enterprise as any successful businessman and as a majority of Americans, who shared the conviction that hard work and innate talent should be cherished as the stepping stones to a better life.

At the same time that Roosevelt dismissed conservative complaints about big government and diminished individualism as the protests of selfish men lacking compassion, he also felt compelled to defend his administration from left-ists who urged the nationalization of industries and a redistribution of wealth through confisca-tory taxes on the rich. Three demagogues on the left gave Roosevelt special concern: Louisiana governor and, beginning in 1932, senator Huey P. Long; Detroit radio priest Father Charles Cough-lin; and California's Dr. Francis E. Townsend. Each in his own way and collectively presented a threat to the president's hold on the mass public by promising far more than they could deliver.

The forty-one-year-old Long was the most for-midable of Roosevelt's leftist foes. Born in a log cabin in Winn Parish in north central Louisiana, Long grew up on a farm, the seventh of nine children subjected to "the drudgery of country life," which he hated and wished to escape in any way possible. Exceptionally intelligent, he worked his way through college as a salesman hawking "furniture, soap, groceries, [and] patent medicines for 'women's sickness.' " Studying law at Tulane University, where he completed a three-year course in eight months, he passed the state bar at twenty-one and launched a political career as a spokesman for impoverished Louisianans, a majority of whom had been too poor to attend school and were illiterate. At five foot eleven and 160 pounds, he was not an imposing figure. With a bulbous nose, heavy jowls, unruly reddish brown hair, and "a pixielike mien," he was, his biographer says, "a cartoonist's delight."

Long's campaign carried him to the governor-ship at the age of thirty-five in 1928. A brilliant orator who railed against the 2 percent of the state's population that owned 70 percent of its wealth (especially the corporations led by the

Rockefeller Standard Oil Company, Louisiana's dominant business group), Long campaigned on the slogan: "Every man a king, but no one wears a crown." Unwilling to compromise with opponents, Huey said, "I used to try to get things done by saying 'please.' That didn't work and now I'm a dynamiter. I dynamite 'em out of my path." When one of his critics asked if he had heard of the state constitution, he replied: "I'm the Constitution around here now." His rule in the state, his brother Julius said, was "an administration of ego and pomposity [unsurpassed] since the days of Nero." His brother Earl added, "I did not know how they hold elections in Mexico or Russia or anywhere else, but I do not think they could surpass what was going on in Louisiana." The conservative columnist Westbrook Pegler dubbed Long "Der Kingfish." In retrospect, he wrote, "Long resembled, not a Hitler or a Mussolini, but a Latin American dictator . . . in revolt against economic colonialism, against the oligarchy." Despite a record of helping the needy, he fell victim to "his own arrogance and cupidity, his weakness for soft living and rage for personal power."

Although elected to the U.S. Senate in 1930, Long refused to give up the governorship until he secured his legacy in the state, and held both offices simultaneously. He took up his Senate post exclusively in January 1932, where he continued to pronounce on the evils of corporate wealth and the need to give suffering Americans their fair share of the nation's abundance. Despite his calls for social justice that resonated with fellow senators, he antagonized them with displays of arrogance and nastiness, describing them as "shoeless rabble at a lynching" and "dime-a-dozen punks." He was a "perpetually erupting volcano," one Roosevelt aide said, who alienated Senate colleagues with harsh rhetoric that ignored traditional regard for restrained language in the upper house. Senator Alben Barkley of Kentucky told him, "You are the smartest lunatic I ever saw in my whole life." Virginia's Democratic senator Carter Glass called Long a "demagogic screech owl from the swamps of Louisiana."

In 1933, in a meeting at the White House, he attacked the president as an ingrate for having given patronage to Long's Louisiana political enemies, who favored the establishment over needy Louisianans. Getting no satisfaction from Roosevelt, Long began criticizing him and his associates as privileged Americans: Roosevelt was Prince Franklin, Knight of the *Nourmahal,* the yacht the wealthy Vincent Astor lent him, and Agriculture Secretary Henry Wallace was "Lord Corn Wallace." Roosevelt retaliated the following year by unleashing an IRS investigation of Long and his associates, four of whom were later indicted for tax evasion. By 1935, Roosevelt told White House aides, "Don't help anybody that is working for Huey Long or his crowd. That is 100 percent!" Mindful of Roosevelt's antipathy to him, Long laid plans to strike back, telling the mayor of New Orleans, "I have something on that SOB cripple in the White House that will keep him from doing anything against me. I know that he tours around in a boat with a degenerate and that if I ever spring that he can't touch me."

"A clash of wills between the two men was inevitable," Long's biographer T. Harry Williams concludes. "Each was so constituted that he had

292

to dominate other and lesser men. Neither could yield to the other without submerging himself and dimming his destiny."

Roosevelt's anti-Long injunction reflected his concern that the Louisianan was becoming a significant political threat. Long, in historian David Kennedy's words, was the "shrewdest operator and the most thoroughly professional politician" of the three radicals challenging the president. Before Long got to the Senate, Roosevelt had already identified him, along with General Douglas MacArthur, as the most dangerous man in America, adding "We shall have to do something about him." "He had brains, money, ambition, extravagant oratorical skills, a gift for political theater, and a lupine instinct for the nation's political jugular," Kennedy adds. "He was the radical most likely to succeed."

A classic narcissist and exhibitionist whose red hair, cherubic face, and pug nose joined with "pongee suits . . . orchid colored shirts . . . striped straw hats, watermelon pink ties, and brown and white sport shoes" to make him an unforgettable presence in every setting. "The only sincerity there was in him," brother Julius said, "was for himself." Determined to make an indelible impression wherever he went, Long never removed his straw hat during a meeting with Roosevelt at the White House except "to tap it against the President's [lifeless] knee to drive home a point." Mindful of the opposing opinions he would face constantly as president and convinced that open combativeness would serve little purpose, Roosevelt consistently responded to the sort of hostility Long displayed with good humor, never letting on in public that he was angry at him. Behind the scenes, however, he was prepared in time to strike back at aggressive opponents like Long.

In January 1934, Long launched a national campaign to make every man a king through the Share Our Wealth Society, a fantastic scheme promising to give every family a home, an automobile, and a radio. In addition, there were to be guaranteed payments for college, old-age pensions, and shorter work weeks. All this would be achieved through the "simple" redistribution of the national wealth. Although Walter Lippmann dismissed Long's scheme as "not bread for the hungry, but a stone. . . . not water for the thirsty, but a mirage," three million Americans rushed to join his Share Our Wealth clubs. In 1934, more Americans wrote him "than all other senators combined, more even than the president." When the Senate resisted legislation enacting his scheme, he declared a "mob is coming to hang the other ninety-five of you damn scoundrels, and I'm undecided whether to stick here with you or go out and lead them." Tennessee senator Cordell Hull replied, "Let the mob hang the ninety-five of us, and then, if you want to do complete justice, go out and commit suicide yourself."

But Long was less interested in justice with the Share Our Wealth campaign than using it for a run for the presidency. As early as June 1933, when the Hundred Days wrapped up with White House and congressional paeans praising New Deal gains, Long refused to "participate in the Democratic victory." In a prelude to his Share Our Wealth promotion, he said, "I do not care for my share in a victory that means that the poor and the downtrodden, the blind, the helpless, the orphaned, the bleeding, the wounded, the hungry and the distressed, will be the victims."

When Share Our Wealth began to gain traction in 1934, Long turned to Gerald L. K. Smith, a Protestant minister and brilliant demagogue, to rally poor Southerners to join the cause. The thirty-year-old Smith had arrived in Shreveport in 1928 from Wisconsin and Indiana, where he had grown up and gone to college. He watched Huey's rise to power with unbounded admiration, calling him a "superman," who "can do as much in one day as any ten men." A handsome six-footer with eye-catching features, Smith had a way with words that captivated audiences wherever he spoke. H. L. Mencken described him as the "gustiest and goriest, the deadliest and damnedest orator ever heard on this or any other earth — the champion boob bumper of all epochs." Mencken regarded Smith as an even greater crowd pleaser than William Jennings Bryan: "A flashing eye, a hairy chest, a rubescent complexion, large fists, a voice both loud and mellow, terrifying and re-assuring . . . and, finally, an unearthly capacity for distending the superficial blood vessels of his temples and neck, as if they were biceps — and you have the makings of a boob-bumper worth going miles to see."

Huey made Smith his principal spokesman for Share Our Wealth. Like Long, Smith excoriated the rich and sang the virtues of the poor, demanding that the disadvantaged get their fair cut of the national abundance: "Pull down those huge piles of gold," he cried, "until there should be a real job [and] not a little old sow-belly, black-eyed pea job but a real spending money, beefsteak and gravy, Chevrolet, Ford in the garage, a new suit, Thomas Jefferson, Jesus Christ, red, white, and blue job for every man." As people across the South rallied to the Share Our Wealth message, Smith described Long as America's savior: "Rally us under this young man who came out of the woods of north Louisiana, who leads us like a Moses out of the land of bondage into the land of milk and honey where every man is a king but no one wears a crown." In praising Long, Smith said, "No great movement has ever succeeded unless it has deified some one man."

Coughlin was not far behind Long as a threat to Roosevelt's hold on the public, or at least Roosevelt believed so. Because Coughlin was born in Canada in 1891 and was a Catholic, he could never become a rival for the presidency, but he did command Roosevelt's attention with radio sermons that attracted a huge audience. The president was impressed by Coughlin's imaginative outreach through the relatively new electronic mass medium, so much so that it may even have inspired Roosevelt's own initial interest as governor in using radio for political purposes. In 1926, the thirty-five-year-old Coughlin had turned to radio as a source of revenue for his small congregation in Royal Oak, Michigan, where he had come to escape the overly restrictive rules of the Basilian Catholic order to which he belonged in Canada. An only child with a mother who insisted that the priesthood be his life's calling, Coughlin accepted her order with little protest. But an aversion to a cloistered orthodoxy and a passion for some kind of activism in which he would reach a large audience drew him to radio, where he could make greatest use of his impressive talents as a public speaker.

His initial radio ventures were religious homilies

that appealed first to audiences in Detroit and then across the Midwest, especially in Chicago and Cincinnati, cities with large Catholic populations. With the onset of the Depression in 1930, however, politics began to take center stage in his radio talks. Convinced that he had a responsibility to help needy Americans suffering in the Depression, Coughlin focused his message more and more on current events. With his sonorous voice — "a voice," historian Alan Brinkley writes, "resonant with strength and anger and hope and promise" — and a talent for graphic imagery that enlivened his radio sermons, Coughlin warned against the dangers of communism posed by the indifference of Hoover and corporate America to the distress of the unemployed. As the Depression deepened, Coughlin became more vocal and strident in attacks on the corporations and millionaires whose greed he said stood in the way of economic and social justice. He invoked Catholic teachings to promote policies opposed to Soviet-style collectivism or the "laissez-faire individualism" that built family fortunes. Instead, like Long after him, he argued that the wealthiest were obliged to help the needy by sharing some of their riches, as their fortunes were as much the product of those who worked for them as their own ingenuity as business moguls.

Because an emphasis on Catholic doctrine seemed as likely to alienate Protestant Americans as draw them to his reform agenda, Coughlin became the voice of a modern secular populism — a program of change reminiscent of that espoused by William Jennings Bryan and the Populist Party of the 1890s. Declaring his opposition to "modern capitalism," which he said international bankers controlled, Coughlin railed against "modern Shylocks" who, as Bryan had declared, were crucifying "us upon a cross of gold . . . the filthy gold standard which from time immemorial has been the breeder of hate . . . and the destroyer of mankind." Like Bryan, Coughlin called for the "revaluation of gold" and "the remonetization of silver." The federal government had to nationalize the banks if the gold and silver policies he promoted and a resulting inflation were to end the Depression and revitalize the economy. While Roosevelt shared Coughlin's desire for price increases, especially for produce that could benefit farmers, Coughlin's prescription for prosperity was no less flawed than the Populist nostrums in the previous century. Like that of earlier radicals, his rhetoric outran his economic understanding.

But Roosevelt and congressional Democrats could not afford to ignore Coughlin or denounce him as a promoter of false solutions. As early as 1931, a Roosevelt ally had advised him that Coughlin had "a following just about equal to that of Mr. Gandhi," and that he could be a valuable supporter in a run for the presidency. By 1934, he was the most listened to voice on radio, and his popular reach, as demonstrated by newspaper and magazine articles about his sermons and the prodigious piles of mail sent to him each week, exceeded that of the White House. However much his reform agenda appealed to audiences, it was his radio presence, with "a voice of such mellow richness, such manly heart-warming, confidential intimacy, such emotional and ingratiating charm," as the writer Wallace Stegner, a regular listener, described it, that captivated audiences yearning for economic change.

During his campaign for the White House and in the first months of the New Deal, Roosevelt had welcomed Coughlin's expressions of regard: "The New Deal is Christ's deal," the *New York Times* reported Coughlin saying in April 1934. The choice was between "Roosevelt and ruin," the priest also declared. But, as with the clash between Roosevelt and Long, relations between the president and Coughlin soon became a rivalry of competing policies and egos. Roosevelt was warned that Coughlin was "difficult to handle" and that the chain-smoking, peripatetic cleric "might be full of dynamite," and the president never lost sight of the problems Coughlin's reductionist program and grandiose ambitions presented. By 1934, the disadvantages of the relationship exceeded the benefits. Roosevelt saw Coughlin as mostly self-serving, untrustworthy, and "dangerous." He refused to sign on to Coughlin's monolithic silver policy and dismissed his reform agenda as little more than a smokescreen for personal control.

Roosevelt's distance angered and frustrated Coughlin. He feared a break with the president, but also felt compelled to criticize him for refusing to support his vision of how to end the Depression. In response, Coughlin alternated between praising and denouncing him. In one radio broadcast, he compared the New Deal to "the policies of a Hitler, the suggestion of a Mussolini, and the dogma of a Stalin more honored in our midst than the ideas of a Washington or a Jefferson"; in another, he lauded "the courage of our President" and the "uprightness and integrity" of Treasury Secretary Henry Morgenthau. The contradictions in his ideas soon began to undermine public faith in Coughlin as a reliable source of economic reform.

In November 1934, in an attempt to regain consistency in his message, Coughlin gave up on Roosevelt and his administration. He had also discovered that Roosevelt was encouraging aides to use government agencies to look into his finances, including revelations that he or his private secretary was a speculator in silver futures; to persuade networks to limit his airtime; and to ask Catholic Church prelates to rein him in. His hostility to Roosevelt and the New Deal now largely morphed into a clash of personalities that undermined Coughlin's appeal. As a Catholic priest who over time could not command the sort of majority support Roosevelt enjoyed, Coughlin was at a distinct disadvantage. But "a strain of megalomania that wore away his self-restraint," Alan Brinkley says, played him false. Prevented by current political standards that barred the organization of a political party led by a priest, he focused his opposition in the establishment of the National Union for Social Justice — a group lobbying for Coughlin's banking and silver policies and explicitly against Jews, whom it freely associated with gold and banking interests. Roosevelt's New Deal was no longer Christ's deal, Coughlin said, but the "Jew deal," in which prominent Jews like Morgenthau, Ben Cohen, and Sam Rosenman were shaping policy to serve the country's moneyed men. Too radical to attract the sort of national support Coughlin yearned for, the Union inadvertently consigned itself to a minor role in American politics.

However appealing the Long and Coughlin remedies were to the victims of the Depression disappointed in the New Deal, they faced competition from continuing hope that Roosevelt might yet find better answers to the collapse and a movement of senior citizens taking their cue from Dr. Francis E. Townsend, a physician in Long Beach, California. In the fall of 1934, the sixty-seven-year-old physician had gained national notoriety with a proposal to rescue everyone over sixty from poverty with what he called the Townsend Old Age Revolving Pension Plan (OARP).

A late bloomer who didn't attend medical school in Nebraska until he was thirty and then worked as a general practitioner for seventeen years in the Black Hills of South Dakota, Townsend developed his OARP idea after watching three elderly women rummaging for food in a garbage can outside his home. His scheme called for $200-a-month federal payments to all citizens over sixty on the condition that they give up whatever work they had, leaving job openings for younger people, and that they spend their allotment within thirty days, thereby boosting economic activity across the country. The funding for the program was to come from a national transaction tax on all sales. In fact the proposal did nothing to expand the economy or increase purchasing power and effectively only redistributed existing wealth. Walter Lippmann described Townsend's error as "forgetting the simple truth that someone must produce the wealth which is consumed by the nonproducers, be they infants, old people, sick people, the unemployed, the idle rich, or the criminal classes. If Dr. Townsend's scheme was a good remedy, the more people the country could find to support in idleness," Lippmann dismissively declared, "the better off it would be." Nine percent of the population, Lippmann might have added, would command half the country's output. The proposal nonetheless had great appeal to the millions of seniors who had lost their jobs and bank savings and faced destitution at the end of once productive lives.

What had begun as a letter to the *Long Beach Press-Telegram* in September 1933 had by January 1934 begun to burgeon into a national movement of white Anglo-Saxon lower-middle-class citizens, some of whom associated Townsend with Jesus Christ, and hailed him as "the man God raised up to do this job." Meetings of Townsend clubs resembled more old-time religious gatherings, punctuated by hymns and shouts of "amen," than political caucuses organizing for congressional election campaigns. The assemblies often ended with members singing "Onward Townsend soldiers, marching as to war." Roosevelt never took any interest in the Townsend scheme, but as with Long and Coughlin, he could not simply dismiss a movement led by a man some of his followers said would one day be spoken of in the same breath as "George Washington and Alexander Hamilton or Abraham Lincoln and General Grant."

If the rise of Long, Coughlin, Smith, and Townsend to prominence wasn't sufficient to test Roosevelt's patience and challenge his popularity, the emergence in 1934 of Upton Sinclair as a political phenomenon added an additional burden that brought Roosevelt to the limits of his self-confidence.

Sinclair was a well-known radical who had achieved notoriety with his 1906 book *The Jungle,* which documented the horrors of the meat processing industry. A socialist and muckraker who, in H. L. Mencken's description, had embraced every good cause in the world, Sinclair was at the forefront of California's affinity for innovative schemes to end the economic disaster. Declaring that "Capitalism has served its time and is passing from the face of the earth," Sinclair added, "A new system must be found to take its place." His plan, End Poverty in California (EPIC), called for the shift of idle land and factories to farmers' and workers' cooperatives that would produce goods for purchase with money or scrip printed and traded strictly within the state. However impractical an idea, "production for use," as it was called, raised Sinclair's political popularity in California where, after switching from Socialist to Democratic Party registration, he won a lopsided victory in the Democratic primary for governor in August 1934, amassing over 400,000 votes to his eight rivals' 377,000.

Roosevelt had no desire to either endorse or discredit Sinclair, but smart politics dictated that he give him a cordial welcome at the White House and broad hints of backing for his idealized reforms. After a two-hour meeting with the president, Sinclair came away singing his praises as "one of the kindest and most genial and frank and open-minded and lovable men I have ever met." Sinclair told reporters, "I've been taken into the family," though in fact it was all a White House smokescreen for placating Californians. When Frances Perkins returned from a West Coast trip to report that Sinclair was a "fanatic" and that EPIC might "ruin the California banking system," Roosevelt shrugged her concerns off, telling her that if the plan failed in California, it would have no appeal in other states, and if it succeeded, it would be copied. Roosevelt's determined neutrality was put to the test when Sinclair pressed him for an endorsement, and he took refuge in the policy, "I cannot take part in any state campaign."

Alarmed by Sinclair's ideas, Ray Moley warned in a magazine article that the "production-for-use program" was "a call for blessed retreat — back beyond industrial civilization, back beyond the established national financial structure, back beyond the use of gold and silver and currency, back to barter, back to nature." Moley's analysis of the impracticality of EPIC frightened enough people in the state to contribute to the defeat of Sinclair's bid for the governorship, which he lost by a quarter million votes. The outcome enhanced Roosevelt's reputation as a shrewd politician who resisted identification with a poor idea and a losing political cause. At the same time his refusal to criticize publicly a proposal as transparently flawed as EPIC also revealed his uncertainty about the capacity of New Deal plans to restore prosperity and his conviction that he might need to experiment with even the most unorthodox of economic schemes to get out of the Depression.

In 1934, at the same time that Roosevelt was maneuvering around dissenting voices in the country, he was struggling to keep his own house in order. By the fall, fissures had opened in the administration that threatened to disrupt the effective application of New Deal programs and raised questions about the president's capacity to govern or manage ambitious and strong-minded subordinates. "Most of his major appointments to the cabinet and to the various New Deal . . . agencies were peculiarly violent, quarrelsome, recalcitrant men," speechwriter Robert Sherwood observed. After almost two years in office, the Roosevelt administration was awash in personal tensions between Eleanor, cabinet officers, and the many subcabinet and agency officials trying to make sense of the relief, recovery, and reform agenda the White House and Congress had rushed to put in place.

Interior Secretary Harold Ickes was at the center of the administration's infighting. He regarded Eleanor's advocacy of subsistence homesteads like Arthurdale as unworkable and a huge waste of money. "We are spending money there like drunken sailors," Ickes confided to his diary in October, and lamented the bad publicity the project was generating in magazines and newspapers. Although he did little to rein in Eleanor, Roosevelt appeased Ickes by telling him: "My Missus, unlike most women, hasn't any sense about money." His words, typically, were an exercise in soothing jangled nerves or convincing an angry complainant that he was on his side.

Ickes's principal fight was with Henry Morgenthau, who had become undersecretary of the treasury in 1933. In January 1934, after William Woodin resigned because of poor health, Morgenthau replaced him as secretary. Ickes saw a deep divide in the administration between conservatives, like Morgenthau, and progressives, like himself, and complained to Roosevelt in March 1934 that "a well-conceived conspiracy was in process of being carried out to make my position in the Cabinet untenable." Ickes's complaint was more a product of his imagination than of an actual plot to drive him from office, but it was a revealing expression of his contempt for a despised rival. He confided his "low opinion of Morgenthau" to his diary, describing him as full of "childish objections" and as "somewhat stupid." It was difficult for him to contain his temper with Morgenthau, adding that he distrusted anything the secretary said.

By January 1934, the bickering between the two men had come to so annoy Roosevelt that he urged cabinet members "to go away for a rest. . . . He said he didn't want any members of the Cabinet to break down and he especially wanted Henry and me to go away for a week or two," Ickes noted. ". . . He was quite insistent about it. He told me that it was beginning to worry him just to look at me and that if I didn't go away he would get mad." The tensions were worrisome enough to convince Roosevelt that he needed a grand strategy for bringing temperamental characters like Ickes and Morgenthau under control. His usual solution was to appease both antagonists by pretending to favor in turn one of them over the other. After a particularly heated argument between Morgenthau and Ickes, he privately called each of them with harsh comments on his opponent and soothing words of sympathy for his plight in having to put up with so trying an adversary.

But Roosevelt's most serious concern in 1934 was the outcome of the upcoming midterm congressional elections. He hoped the traditional loss of seats by the party in power in the White House could be avoided, but no one in the administration was ready to make such a calculation. Jim Farley, who was as smart a political prognosticator as anyone, thought that they might be lucky enough to break even, which would effectively amount to a great victory. Roosevelt had little confidence that they would do that well, and thought that the best way to help their cause was to stay as far as possible from involvement in state and local contests. He was, in any case, unenthusiastic about backing all of the Democrats on the ballot. In some cases he preferred progressive Republicans, like Bob and Phil La Follette, running, respectively, for a U.S. Senate seat and the statehouse in Wisconsin, and Farmer-Laborite candidates in Minnesota, who were more committed to the New Deal than their Democratic opponents. He was eager for people to share his belief that "the government is being run less for political purposes and more for the general good than it has been in some time." He hoped they understood that "we are trying to do service regardless of mere party" or politics. "The party label does not mean so very much," he announced at a press conference, but then told the amused reporters to keep that off the record. In fact, "he was less a sincere bipartisan leader in this period than he was a man working astutely under the guise of bipartisanship toward a national liberal party" that would include progressive Republicans.

Although he assumed an agnostic public posture of detachment from the contests, the elections were as much a referendum on Roosevelt as they were on local candidates. In the end they produced a stunning victory for those Democrats who had campaigned on a New Deal platform. They increased their advantage in the Senate from 59 to 69 seats, while expanding their control of the House to a 322-to-103 margin. It was only the second time in the country's history that a sitting majority had boosted its control in a midterm election. All the criticism throughout the year from critics on both the right and the left about Roosevelt and the New Deal ultimately had little impact on the president's popularity. Ickes was correct when he noted in his diary, "I have never had contact with a man who was as loved as he is." James MacGregor Burns captured Roosevelt's appeal perfectly when he explained his grip on the American public as the product of "timely action, unfailing cheerfulness in public and private, and a masterly grasp of public opinion. Millions sat by their radios to hear his warm, reassuring words," and "businessmen, labor chiefs, bankers, newspaper editors, farm leaders" who saw him in the White House reported that they were "cheered, impressed, relieved." As for the elections, the journalist William Allen White said, "He has been all but crowned by the people."

In September 1934, when Roosevelt met with Upton Sinclair at the White House, he had told him, "I cannot go any faster than the people will let me." But the election results demonstrated that the president was as much the leader of public feeling as the follower. He had an almost uncanny sense of how Americans would respond to the administration's various initiatives and how to explain clearly what he was doing. Before Ronald Reagan inherited the title, it was Roosevelt who was the Great Communicator. His skillful public performances, however, could not conceal the reality of continuing economic distress nor could it deter the Liberty League or Long, Coughlin, Townsend, and Sinclair from proposing alternative solutions to the Depression. His response to the demagogues, however, largely contained their appeal.

As with his doubts about the New Deal's economic effectiveness, his management of foreign affairs was even more frustrating for him than his control over domestic affairs. Still the TR-Wilson internationalist of his earlier years in the Navy Department and after, when he saw a muscular United States playing a major role abroad, he was unable to counter the isolationist sentiment that had followed World War I. The rise of Japanese aggression in Asia in the 1920s and 1930s confirmed Americans' belief that detachment from external conflicts best served the national interest. By 1933, the country had returned to its traditional foreign policy roots. Arms manufacturers were known as merchants of death and pacifism was as powerful a creed as orthodox religion.

Despite giving in to isolationist pressures during the 1932 campaign, Roosevelt remained devoted to his conviction that the United States should play a meaningful role abroad. Although the failure of the London Economic Conference had frustrated him, he did not lose sight of American influence to promote international trade, reduce armaments, and avoid war. After London, his principal foreign goals were to rekindle Wilson's idealism by implementing a Good Neighbor policy in the Western Hemisphere and promoting international commerce and peace in Asia by reestablishing relations with the Soviet Union. In his brief remarks on foreign affairs in his inaugural speech, he had promised "the policy of the good neighbor . . . who resolutely respects . . . the rights of others." On Pan-American Day in April 1933, he had given substance to his pledge by committing himself to equality among the American republics. His refusal to send troops to quiet turmoil in Cuba in 1933, and a May 1934 treaty repealing the Platt Amendment, which sanctioned America's right to intervene in the island, made believers of Latinos who had dismissed his words as political rhetoric. In the summer of 1933, when he cruised the Caribbean with stops in Haiti, Puerto Rico, the Virgin Islands, Colombia, and Panama, and became the first president ever to visit South America and cross the Panama Canal, he generated good will and challenged the traditional anti-Americanism that served local communists and fascists. At the same time, his actions resonated with the current mood of antimilitarism and isolationism in the United States. A friendly noninterventionist policy toward Latin America was widely regarded as a wise way to exert U.S. influence abroad.

Similarly, his resumption of relations with Soviet Russia was accepted as a benign advance toward reinstating economic exchange and a gesture toward world peace. Ever mindful of public sentiment, Roosevelt was careful to orchestrate the decision as one that principally served the national interest. Public antipathy toward an antireligious, undemocratic regime had kept the two countries apart since the communist takeover in 1918. But Roosevelt believed that a renewed diplomacy could not only open markets to U.S. goods but send a signal to Tokyo that the United States was aligning itself with the Soviet Union against any further Japanese aggression, which had already led to the invasion and control of Manchuria. He told Margaret (Daisy) Suckley, his distant cousin with whom he maintained a warm friendship, that he worried that Japan had plans to fight "a European nation to show that they could beat them" and to increase its reach in Asia to the borders of India. The Japanese, he believed, also planned "a *foothold* . . . in Central America." He reported a conversation with British prime minister Ramsay MacDonald about Japan's aggression in which they agreed to bar it from gaining "Naval parity."

Selling Americans on the prospect of a trade-promoting economic measure was relatively easy, as they were receptive to almost anything that promised jobs and commerce. But convincing the public that Joseph Stalin's government was not hostile to organized religion and that aligning the country with Russia against Japan would not draw us into an Asian war was more problematic. The adjective "godless" was indelibly attached to any mention of communism, and the idea of allying America with any other nation against Tokyo seemed to risk tensions that could lead to an unwanted conflict.

But Roosevelt was in a period where he could do no wrong. A survey of the country's newspapers revealed that a large majority of the population favored recognition of Russia, and a conversation Roosevelt had with Father Edmund A. Walsh, a leading opponent of the new policy, disarmed potential Catholic resistance to an exchange of ambassadors. Roosevelt made the case for the benefits of the resumption of relations, but Walsh also remembered their meeting as a charm offensive, which the president carried out "with that disarming assurance so characteristic of his technique in dealing with visitors."

Roosevelt insisted that Maxim Litvinov, Soviet

commissar for foreign affairs, pay a high-visibility visit to the White House, during which the president could publicize his demands for concessions and show Americans that it was the Soviets who were courting him, and who would pay a healthy price for U.S. recognition. Hull had warned him that without concessions on religious freedom, in particular, he could lose the 1936 election. Roosevelt accordingly won agreements from Litvinov on Russia's not carrying out subversive actions and propaganda in the United States.

Because he saw religious concerns as the most controversial issue troubling a majority of Americans, Roosevelt trumped up a story certain to reach the press about how he had also convinced Litvinov to concede freedom of worship to Americans in the Soviet Union. Confident that what he reported in a cabinet meeting would reach a wider audience, he described how he told Litvinov that everyone ultimately believes there is a God. "You know, Max," he added, "your good old father and mother, pious Jewish people, always said their prayers. I know they must have taught you to say prayers. . . . By this time Max was as red as a beet and I said to him, 'Now you may think you're an atheist. . . . But I tell you, Max, when you come to die . . . you're going to be thinking about what your father and mother taught you.' . . . Max blustered and puffed and said all kinds of things, laughed and was very embarrassed, but I had him. I was sure from the expression of his face and his actions that he knew what I meant and that he knew I was right."

It was a wonderful fictionalization of what he had actually said, but it served his purpose in

312

ensuring that Soviet recognition would receive a warm greeting. And no one in the press was inclined to challenge his account of what transpired between him and Litvinov. They shared Roosevelt's hopes of expanded trade and diminished prospects of war from his diplomatic initiative, but they had also developed a special affection for a president who, despite his disability, was a model of good cheer and optimism. They regarded siding with Roosevelt as nothing less than an act of patriotism.

With the congressional victory in 1934, some members of Roosevelt's circle were ready to endow him with indecipherable political talents. He was "the most complicated human being I ever knew," Frances Perkins said. Morgenthau described him as someone "extraordinarily difficult . . . to describe . . . a man of bewildering complexity of moods and motives." Robert Sherwood said, " 'Amen!' to their statements on his complexity." In trying "to look beyond his charming and amusing and warmly affectionate surface into his heavily forested interior," Sherwood concluded that "his character was not only multiplex, it was contradictory to a bewildering degree. He was hard and he was soft," vindictive and forgiving, "a ruthless politician" who prided himself on his "practical, down-to-earth, horse-sense" realism, but also a champion of doubtful causes that were "political liabilities" that risked "political suicide." A progressive who was "condemned as a 'traitor to his class' " and "that Red in the White House," he "was in truth a profoundly old-fashioned person with an incurable nostalgia for the very 'horse and buggy era' on which he publicly heaped so much scorn." And yet he made himself "easily understandable to his countrymen and to the world at large."

Much of the rhetoric about Roosevelt's complexity can be discounted as the sort of hero worship that is often the product of people whom a president has brought into the center of national politics being given the chance to play out their greatest ambitions and fervently held ideals on the world stage. For the men and women around Roosevelt, he was larger than life, another Washington or Lincoln in the making.

As early as 1934, Roosevelt's unprecedented reforms and hold on the public gave him lofty standing, especially after the lackluster presidents of the 1920s and the yearning to recapture the exciting leadership of Theodore Roosevelt and Woodrow Wilson. But what made Roosevelt so remarkable was not some mystical capacity to hide his inner thoughts and plans, or his multilayered personality. True, he was an enormously charming man: As Winston Churchill later recalled, meeting him for the first time as president was an exciting and memorable occasion. Moreover, Roosevelt encouraged the view of himself as someone larger than life, an impenetrable character standing apart from ordinary mortals. When he told Morgenthau, "Never let your left hand know what your right is doing," it prompted Morgenthau to ask: "Which hand am I, Mr. President?" Having drawn Morgenthau into the exchange, Roosevelt replied: "My right hand, but I keep my left under the table." When Tommy Corcoran, a prominent lawyer and architect of New Deal laws, took exception to Franklin's identification with Theodore Roosevelt, saying "The difference between you and T.R. is that you never fake," the president exclaimed, "Oh, but Tommy, at times I do, I do!"

The key to Roosevelt's success was ultimately less his complexity or capacity to keep his own counsel than his brilliant political instincts: his intuitive sense of timing, his ability to read and articulate the public mood, and his skill in manipulating the people around him through charm and guile. In short, he was an extraordinarily democratic politician. Yet he was never just a mirror of public mood. He had firm convictions about both domestic and foreign affairs, but he understood from early in his presidency never to get too far ahead of public opinion in reaching for a policy goal. To him, politics was an art, and he was an exceptional practitioner of the craft that underlay it. Conditions in the country certainly provided him with an uncommon opportunity for dynamic leadership. But Hoover, who faced the same conditions as Roosevelt, lacked the political skills to take advantage of the public's yearning for bold direction. At the close of 1934, it could have been said that Roosevelt was the right man, at the right time, in the right place. The country wanted a Svengali, a Houdini, or a compelling leader with magical solutions to daunting problems that defied ordinary men with conventional remedies. It wouldn't always be that way, but for the moment Roosevelt was a president above reproach.

Chapter 7
Mastering Washington
"Bedlam"

Despite his popularity reflected in the congressional elections, Roosevelt understood that unless he maintained a sense of forward momentum in 1935, calls for alternatives to the New Deal would erode his standing and jeopardize his reelection in 1936. "The legend of invulnerability fades fast," *New York Times* columnist Arthur Krock declared in February of the new year.

By the end of 1934, Roosevelt had begun to find the demands of being president in a time of unrelieved crisis exhausting. Earlier that year, his cousin Daisy Suckley paid him a visit during which he acknowledged that "he *does* get mentally tired and that it is terrifying to realize the responsibility that rests on him." He added that he would admit that to very few, and that "it was not for quotation."

His readiness to confide in Daisy spoke volumes about his need for a nonpolitical friend with whom he could be candid about his struggles with daily pressures. He felt compelled to hide even the slightest sign of exhaustion lest people think he lacked the stamina to shoulder the burdens of office. He also feared that any suggestion that the presidency was overwhelming him would dispirit the country and retard its recovery. While the public's impressions of him as upbeat and buoyant accurately reflected his general demeanor and mood, he also believed that a degree of role playing was essential to his political success, and that this role playing included a steady display of cheerful confidence that better days were ahead. But mindful of Hoover's mistake in promising a quick return to prosperity, he understood the political value of striking a proper balance between hope and reality.

Eleanor said that Franklin "had no confidants . . . not even me," but in fact it was Daisy who served as a sounding board and trusted companion with whom he could speak frankly. Ten years his junior, Daisy and he had first become close in 1922 during Franklin's recuperation from polio. Sara had asked her to pay a call on him, explaining that her son "was lonely and needed company." Daisy's visits provided a welcome respite from his medical preoccupations and a chance to build a warm relationship with a fellow patrician and Hyde Park neighbor. For Daisy, who never married, Franklin filled her life with interesting talk. For Franklin, whose relationship with Eleanor lacked much marital intimacy, Daisy was an undemanding companion with whom he could share his feelings or speak freely without fear of embarrassment or political consequence. "He might have been happier with a wife who was completely uncritical," Eleanor wrote later. He would certainly have been happier with a spouse who was less unrelentingly serious: "All her life," a niece of Eleanor's recalled, "Eleanor yearned to be more spontaneous, to relax more readily, but in the end how can one force oneself to be spontaneous?"

After the congressional victory, Roosevelt told Daisy, "Yes — the election was surprisingly good — but — well — I suppose it means more work." Early in 1935, he added that developments were making him "piss cross" and that "I need either to swear at somebody or to have a long suffering ear like yours to tell it to quietly!" He was disappointed that a favorable Supreme Court decision on gold had deterred him from "delivering an impassioned plea on the air that night if it had gone the other way." He was spoiling for an open fight with conservatives, who were easy marks at the start of 1935, but striking out against them or openly denouncing Long, Coughlin, Townsend, or Sinclair would shatter the image of an inclusive administration focused on serving all Americans.

He found some relief from the White House pressures in visits to Hyde Park and Warm Springs. He especially enjoyed the relaxed atmosphere of his upstate New York retreat, where he could drive a specially designed car with hand controls and luxuriate in the greenery of his beloved Hudson River Valley. "I hope to have a real four days without political thoughts," he told Daisy in October 1934, "— isn't that a grand idea for the period immediately preceding an important election?" At the end of his stay, he looked forward to another visit "to rediscover more of our County." He was grateful for her undemanding companionship on his drives around the countryside: "I think you added several years to my life & much to my happiness," he told her.

Despite his weariness at the time, his political instincts remained as keen as ever. He judged that his continued success with the public and an upward swing in the economy depended on persuading Congress to enact additional reforms. Although he had demonstrated impressive leadership in the Hundred Days and since, he remained mindful that obtaining majority votes from 533 egotistical legislators was a bit like herding cats. Although he had large Democratic majorities in both houses after the November elections, congressmen and senators who had won votes by emphasizing their White House ties could be more independent until the next election, as they did not feel compelled to give the president unqualified backing — at least for the immediate future.

Congressional support rested not only on a unified response to the national crisis Roosevelt had inherited but also on the shrewd techniques he employed to corral votes from its often demanding, self-centered members. "Every Senator [is] a law unto himself," Roosevelt told Colonel Edward House. "Every one seeking the spotlight." Handing out patronage was one such time-tested method, but Roosevelt had expanded upon the mere granting of favors by enlisting congressmen to become partners with him in the initiation and passage of laws. It was his way of sharing the glory and making them more popular in their districts and states. "Individual legislators were drawn into the executive policy-making process not as representatives of Congress nor of their constituencies, but as members of the administration," James Burns explained. Yet it wasn't all friendly teamwork, as the variety of conflicting interests in Congress had made some of its members sporadically uncooperative. Roosevelt responded by withholding favors. Returning from a fishing trip in 1934, he told a group of them that he had learned something during his vacation about swimming with barracudas and sharks.

At the start of 1935, with the economy still less than robust with 10.6 million workers unemployed — 20 percent of the workforce — and so many voices calling for radical measures to end the Depression, Roosevelt felt compelled to reinforce public support with promises of additional action. On January 4 he delivered his State of the Union address before a joint congressional session with a description of his agenda for the coming term. A written message would have been an acceptable option, but a personal appearance registered more forcefully on Congress, and with the magic of radio, he was able to reach a large national audience. He offered a fresh celebration of the "new order of things . . . under the framework and in the spirit and intent of the American Constitution." It was a reiteration of his inaugural appeal for hope: He reminded the country that a "new economic order [was] rising from the disintegration of the old," and that the New Deal was an "evident restoration of that spirit of confidence and faith" in the country's progress.

Mindful that he could not ignore dissenting voices decrying the limits of his reforms, he tried to blunt attacks on the administration's achievements by warning that the critics threatened "to disturb or dispel" or "slow our onward steps." He took particular aim at share-the-wealth schemes that he disparaged as going too far in upending traditional economic arrangements. He acknowledged that his administration had not yet "weeded out the over privileged and . . . lifted up the underprivileged" and that more remained to be done if they were to reach the promised land of shared prosperity. Yet he cautioned about dispensing with free enterprise or removing "the profit motive." "By the profit motive," he added, "we mean the right by work to earn a decent livelihood for ourselves and for our families." He had no desire to "destroy ambition, nor do we seek to divide our wealth into equal shares." Nonetheless, he hoped within the existing framework of capitalism to promote "a proper security" for every family. It was "an ambition to be preferred to the appetite for great wealth and great power."

With the Gross Domestic Product (GDP) still at only 75 percent of where it had been in 1929, he fixed greatest attention on "where we can do still better." His first concern was to confront "the stark fact before us that great numbers still remain unemployed," and had been forced onto relief rolls, where it would be wrong to let them languish. Some in the administration were doubtful that a remedy could be found: "We are probably going to keep on providing relief — probably permanently," Ray Moley said. "It looks as though we are in this relief business for a long, long time," a Hopkins aide declared. Always the optimist, Roosevelt rejected such demoralizing conclusions. "The Federal Government must and shall quit this business of relief," he told his audience, because this dependence "induces a spiritual and moral disintegration fundamentally destructive to the national fiber." Stressing a point that should have brought comfort to every conservative in the country, Roosevelt added: "To dole out relief in this way is to administer a narcotic, a subtle destroyer of the human spirit. It is inimical to the dictates of sound policy. It is in violation of the traditions of America. Work must be found for able-bodied but destitute workers."

Roosevelt proposed establishing a single agency that could arrange employment for the jobless on projects that would provide long-term benefits to the country. "I am not willing that the vitality of our people be further sapped by the giving of cash, of market baskets, of a few hours of weekly work cutting grass, raking leaves or picking up papers in the public parks. We must preserve not only the bodies of the unemployed from destitution but also their self-respect, their self-reliance and cour-age and determination." The work itself was to include slum clearance, rural housing and electri-fication, reforestation, soil conservation, improv-ing existing roads, construction of national highways "designed to handle modern traffic," and "many other projects which the Nation needs and cannot afford to neglect." While he promised that none of these efforts would be unproductive make-work, he also pledged to support them only until the private sector revived sufficiently to end the Depression.

As for those unable to work or incapacitated by old age or infirmities, it was the responsibility of the federal government to take up the burden of assuring their security. "Such people, in the days before the great Depression, were cared for by lo-cal efforts — by States, by counties, by towns, by cities, by churches and by private welfare agen-cies," he said. "It is my thought that in the future they must be cared for as they were before. I stand ready through my own personal efforts, and through the public influence of the office that I hold, to help these local agencies to get the means necessary to assume this burden."

He ended his message by challenging isolationist sentiment with a call for a U.S. contribution to peacekeeping. "I cannot with candor tell you that general international relationships outside the borders of the United States are improved," he said. "On the surface of things many old jealousies are resurrected, old passions aroused; new strivings for armament and power, in more than one land, rear their ugly heads. . . . I believe, however, that our own peaceful and neighborly attitude toward other Nations is coming to be understood and appreciated. The maintenance of international peace is a matter in which we are deeply and unselfishly concerned." He reassured Americans, however, that he was not about to take any steps that could lead the country into war.

The president's discussion of foreign affairs while the country still struggled with dispiriting domestic problems carried political risks, but he was willing to spend some of his political capital on a peace initiative. On January 16, he asked the Senate to endorse a proposal for U.S. entrance into the World Court, a League agency designed to adjudicate international disputes that could lead to wars. Because nations could bring cases before the Court without formal membership, Roosevelt's initiative was essentially a symbolic gesture promoting the rule of law and world peace, a sentiment that could meet with little opposition.

But Roosevelt's political instincts failed him, and his idealism obscured his reading of the public mood. Vice President Garner, Ickes, and Farley thought it a mistake to challenge what they viewed as overwhelming popular sentiment against membership in the international tribunal, even if it seemed in keeping with widespread pacifist sentiment. They were surprised that Roosevelt was willing to put his reputation behind such a questionable maneuver. For his part, the president found it hard to believe that the Senate and the country more generally would turn aside as innocuous a commitment as joining a Court promoting the rule of law over militarism. But hostility to anything even hinting at involvements abroad, however much they might promote world peace, was far more intense than Roosevelt and advocates of American internationalism understood.

In the two weeks after he put his request before the Senate, a groundswell of opposition emerged. A default on war debts by America's Associated Powers, the suspicion that any sort of involvement with Europe would eventually drag the United States into another war, and the conviction, fostered in 1934 by Senate hearings led by Gerald Nye of North Dakota, that entrance into World War I and foreign affairs in general served the selfish interests of bankers and munitions makers all contributed to influencing popular sentiment about foreign affairs.

The Senate, which initially seemed certain to provide a two-thirds vote in favor of Court membership, became a battleground over Roosevelt's request. Progressive senators Hiram Johnson of California, William Borah of Idaho, and Huey Long denounced the Court as controlled by sinister forces that could destroy U.S. sovereignty. Senator Homer T. Bone of Washington declared Europe a breeding ground of war and warned that participation in the Court would mean exposing the United States to the "poisonous mess" being created by Hitler and Mussolini.

"To hell with Europe and the rest of those nations," Minnesota senator Thomas D. Schall declared. The loudest voice in the country against the Court proposal was Father Coughlin's. He turned his radio broadcasts into a forum for paranoid warnings about the evil men — bankers and "plutocrats" — behind the League and the Court, and cautioned that joining the latter would do nothing less than destroy "our American way of life." Supported by Hearst's national chain of newspapers, the opposition generated thousands of telegrams and letters to senators, which persuaded 44 of them to side with the isolationists by either voting against the proposal or absenting themselves from the Chamber. Roosevelt's supporters could muster only 52 votes — seven short of what was needed for approval.

The defeat stunned and angered Roosevelt. Ickes "thought the President distinctly showed that the defeat of the World Court protocol had cut pretty deeply. At times there seemed to be a bitter twinge to his laughter and good humor and perhaps a little showing of willingness to hurt those who brought about his defeat." Roosevelt, who rarely spoke or wrote openly about his feelings on political controversies, told former secretary of war Elihu Root that "the deluge of letters, telegrams, Resolutions of Legislatures, and the radio talks of people like Coughlin turned the trick against us." "In normal times," he wrote former secretary of state Henry Stimson, "the radio and other appeals . . . would not have been effective. However, these are not normal times; people are jumpy and very ready to run after strange gods. This is so in every other country as well as our own." He complained that Court opponents "are willing to see a city burn down just so long as their own houses remain standing in the ruins." "As to the 36 Gentlemen who voted against the principle of a world Court," Roosevelt wrote Senate Majority Leader Joe Robinson, "I am inclined to think that if they ever get to Heaven they will be doing a great deal of apologizing for a very long time — that is if God is against war — and I think He is." The primary issue that Roosevelt wanted everyone to consider in the matter was not U.S. autonomy but world peace.

The defeat of the World Court initiative proved to be a prelude to further demoralizing developments over the next three months. The collapse of disarmament talks in Geneva spurred by the British refusal to accept international armament inspections left Roosevelt feeling "much discouraged," as he told Cordell Hull. Hitler's announcement on March 16 that, to facilitate German rearmament, he would introduce conscription with a half-million-man army provoked further unease. William E. Dodd, the University of Chicago history professor Roosevelt had made ambassador to Berlin, added to the president's concern by telling him: "There has not been so terrible a social and economic situation for Western Civilization since the collapse of the Roman empire. . . . From Rome to Tokyo governments of the dictatorial type are in power . . . [and] with all newspapers, radio, armies, churches and universities at their command, they are apt to remain in power and finally subordinate modern civilization, returning the next generation . . . to the medievalism" of the thirteenth century. Dodd thought that only a revolution in U.S. foreign policy could address the crisis.

Roosevelt hoped that a conference at Stresa, Italy, in April of British, French, and Italian representatives could agree on "a complete blockade of Germany" to punish its violation of the Versailles Treaty clauses on armaments. He told Colonel House that he was reluctant to weigh in with any suggestions before the meeting for fear they "would meet with the same kind of chilly, half-contemptuous reception . . . as an appeal would have met in July or August 1914." When the conference came to a quick and unproductive end, Roosevelt wrote Dodd: "We are naturally much concerned here over the results at Stresa. . . . I feel very helpless to render any particular service to immediate or permanent peace at this time." In light of the Senate's Court rejection, Roosevelt saw no political gain at home or abroad from sending "special missions" to Europe to promote the peace. In any case, he believed that "no European Capitol in the present confusion cares a continental damn what the United States thinks or does. They are very unwise in this attitude." But for the time being, political reality dictated that he do nothing.

In the first months of 1935, Roosevelt also faced daunting domestic difficulties. His two principal proposals in the new congressional session — a $4.8 billion measure for work relief to get three and a half million unemployed off the dole and into public works jobs, and a Social Security bill to provide people over sixty-five with old-age pensions — ran into immediate opposition from the right and the left. Conservatives saw the biggest appropriation in the history of any nation as a budget buster and a move toward Soviet-style welfare state control. Critics on the left complained about the "security wage" Roosevelt wished to pay public employees, which was twice what they could receive on welfare, but still well below private sector salaries. Liberals joined by Huey Long and Father Coughlin warned that the lower-paying government jobs would force general wages down and prevent private-sector workers from earning a decent living. Under pressure from organized labor, the Senate passed a "prevailing wage" amendment to the work relief bill.

As for the Social Security law, "It is difficult now to understand fully the doubts and confusions in which we were planning this great new enterprise," Frances Perkins noted later. In a conversation with Supreme Court Associate Justice Harlan Stone, Perkins, whom Roosevelt had tasked with designing the program, confided her uncertainty about how to make it work within constitutional bounds. Stone in reply whispered, "The taxing power of the Federal Government, my dear; the taxing power is sufficient for everything you want and need."

Legislators and other voices on the left, however, objected to a system that withheld taxes from current wages to fund future pension payments instead of expanding the economy through federal largess. Moreover, it made no provisions for farmworkers, domestics, or workers in small businesses with less than ten employees. Those who were already past sixty-five were also left out of the plan; their support was assigned to a combination of federal and state payments. The same formula of joint federal-state responsibility applied to unemployment insurance and aid for the incapacitated, as well as single mothers with dependent children. Roosevelt was not unmindful of the economic drawbacks to his bill, but he believed that they were essential to preserve its fundamental goals. "We put those payroll contributions there," he explained, "so as to give contributors a legal, moral, and political right to collect their pensions and their unemployment benefits. With those taxes in there, no damn politician can ever scrap my social security program."

Although the opposition at the start of 1935 to his latest New Deal reforms frustrated and angered him, he adopted a patient outlook. In early March, he told Daisy Suckley, "It's a little hurricane we're passing through down here and rather risky to the future of the country — but it's worse in other countries & I'm trying to keep a very tight rein on myself — for the time has not come yet to speak out." However, he assured Ray Stannard Baker, Wilson's biographer, that his reticence was only temporary. The public, he explained, was unreceptive to "a constant repetition of the highest note on the scale. . . . People tire of seeing the same name day after day in the important headlines of the papers, and the same voice night after night on the radio. For example, if since last November I had tried to keep up the pace of 1933 and 1934, the inevitable histrionics of the new actors, Long and Coughlin and [Senator Hiram] Johnson, would have turned the eyes of the audience away from the main drama itself." Nonetheless, he thought that "the time is soon at hand for a new stimulation of united American action. I am proposing that very thing before the year is out." For the moment he was content to let "the diversion by the trinity of Long, Coughlin and Johnson" run on. "It is vastly better to have this free sideshow presented to the public at this

329

time than later on when the main performance starts."

Despite his assurances, though, the opposition was taking a toll on Roosevelt. Always putting the best possible face on his conduct of affairs, he encouraged a view of himself as unflappable. "He was one of the most alive men I ever met," Jim Farley recalled. "He never gave me the impression he was tired or bored." But Farley saw beyond the mask and observed, "He would have been a great actor." "It was part of his conception of his role," Rex Tugwell said, "that he should never show exhaustion, boredom, or irritation." He wanted "posterity [to] believe that decision was simple for him, that he selected goals with careless ease and pursued them with serenity." He refused "to admit to [any] misgiving or foreboding." Whatever the day's travails, Roosevelt insisted, when his head hit the pillow at night, he went right to sleep.

In fact, he struggled with the tensions generated by his responsibilities and the political crosscurrents constantly descending on him. In the fall of 1934, Louis Howe struggled with respiratory problems born of a lifetime of smoking, and shortness of breath confined him to bed. In January, he succumbed to pneumonia and in March, he fell into a coma. Although he awoke after several days, exhibiting his caustic humor by demanding a cigarette, Roosevelt was told that he could die at any time within the next several weeks.

The public and private pressures on Roosevelt compelled him to leave the White House temporarily for more relaxed surroundings. He told Colonel House that he might escape to Hyde Park for a few days in May, "as I find from experience that getting away from Washington for a short time every month or six weeks is excellent for perspective as well as for temper." A ten-day fishing cruise in the Caribbean with a stop in the Bahamas at the end of March had convinced him that such a break was essential to restoring his energy for political combat. He found it impossible, however, to detach himself entirely from the job. Although he was "having a grand cruise," he wrote his mother, "much sun and fishing and a splendid rest in these delightful waters," he complained to Eleanor that "the news from Washington about the Big [relief] Bill is most confusing, and I get long contradictory appeals for all kinds of action by me! It is well to let them try to work it out themselves I think." He told McIntyre: "It was a grand cruise," and he was "bursting with health, except the U.S. Senate — They continue to give us all a headache."

Left to itself, Congress did pass the Social Security and work relief bills. Roosevelt's unwitting allies in his victory were conservatives who generated support for his reforms by overstating the case against them. Business leaders warned of the coming apocalypse from the enactment of Social Security, which they predicted would bring financial collapse and "ultimate socialistic control of life and industry." It would destroy "initiative," discourage "thrift," and stifle "individual responsibility," the head of General Motors argued, and capitalism would ultimately fail: "With unemployment insurance no one would work; with old age and survivors insurance no one would save; the result would be moral decay, financial bankruptcy and the collapse of the republic." Republicans in the House foresaw the enslavement of workers, with one member cautioning that "the lash of a dictator will be felt." Another saw nothing but "calamity ahead: This bill opens the door and invites the entrance into the political field of a power so vast, so powerful as to threaten the integrity of our institutions and to pull the pillars of the temple down upon the heads of our descendants."

The Republicans would have had a more effective argument in pointing out the law's shortcomings in setting up an imperfect organization, especially on the state-by-state "crazy-quilt unemployment compensation system." Their scare tactics ultimately failed to deter the Democratic majority from mustering 371 votes in the House and 76 in the Senate for Roosevelt's somewhat revised proposal, and the bill became law. In the end, most of the Republicans, reluctant to oppose majority opinion, voted for the measure. "After all the howls and squawks," Roosevelt told William Bullitt, his ambassador to Moscow, "the Social Security bill passed the House with only thirty-three votes against it." Confident the Senate would follow suit, he said, "Even senators can become nationally unpopular!"

The Republicans were no more effective in contesting work relief, which not only won congressional approval but also gave Roosevelt discretion over how to spend the nearly five-billion-dollar appropriation tied to it. The passage of these bills helped change the way millions of Americans perceived the role of the federal government in protecting people from the uncertainties of industrial life.

Roosevelt's biggest challenge after Congress signed off on work relief was how to allot the funds that were now available. He created an elaborate bureaucratic smokescreen of three divisions that largely hid the concentration of power in Harry Hopkins's hands. It was Roosevelt's way of silencing complaints from Ickes, who accurately saw Roosevelt pushing him aside and subordinating the PWA to allow Hopkins and the new Works Progress Administration (WPA) to disburse its windfall funding. Ickes was livid that newspaper accounts described Hopkins as "the big man in the new work-relief organization" and "would emerge as cock of the walk." He shared the view of Daisy Suckley, who said that Hopkins was "one of the most unattractive people I've ever met . . . A strange, weak-looking face, thin, slouching, untidy — impossible socially." Ickes also took satisfaction from Vice President Garner's conviction that "Hopkins had done more harm to the country than any man in history." And now, Ickes believed, Hopkins planned to arrogate to himself power "that normally would belong to the President." He saw Hopkins as little more than "an unprincipled schemer," and the best that he could bring himself to say about Hopkins was that "Harry was an agreeable scoundrel when he wanted to be."

Hopkins reciprocated Ickes's antipathy. When Chicago mayor Ed Kelly complained to Hopkins about Ickes, Hopkins told him: "Ickes wants to get a lot more of this money and by implication take it away from me, which would mean . . . that the President would be left in a hell of a jam." Ickes's preference for long-term projects, Hopkins added, meant that "you never get anybody to work." In May 1935, Hopkins recorded in a diary, "All day planning the work program, which would be a great deal easier if Ickes would play ball —

but he is stubborn and righteous which is a hard combination — he is the 'great resigner' — anything doesn't go his way, he threatens to quit. He bores me."

Although he would never say so openly, the president largely sided with Hopkins, but not because, as Hopkins's biographer George McJimsey argues, Roosevelt "was attracted to his personality or his liberalism." Rather, it was because Ickes's track record at the PWA convinced Roosevelt that Hopkins would be much more effective in getting the unemployed on the job rolls. "Ickes was a very careful deliberate administrator, who took pains to examine personally every detail of every project and the disposition of every nickel that it cost. . . . This is hardly to his discredit," Hopkins biographer Robert Sherwood wrote. It was the approach of "a conscientious public servant," who thought about "the return on the taxpayers' investment. Hopkins [by contrast] did not give a damn about the return," and instead focused on "getting relief to the miserable and getting it there quickly. . . . Ickes thought primarily of the finished job — Hopkins of the numbers of unemployed who could be put on the job immediately."

The conflict took a toll on both men, and on Roosevelt as well, who had to work assiduously to appease Ickes by repeatedly assuring him how important he was to the administration. As a progressive Republican from Chicago, Ickes was a major link to Midwestern liberals and as such a valuable counter to Detroit's Father Coughlin. Nevertheless, the growth of Hopkins's influence at Ickes's expense triggered a steady barrage of complaints. The conflict "fed his always hungry insecurities," Ickes's biographer T. H. Watkins asserts, "robbed him of sleep, and once again drove him to the edge of clinical paranoia." As for Hopkins, he suffered "wrenching inner tensions" from their battles and "developed a dangerous duodenal ulcer."

Given the accomplishments of the WPA, Roosevelt made the right call. Because it was inhibited by congressional rules from undertaking projects preserved for private industry or traditional government assignments like building military bases, many WPA efforts were denounced as having no lasting value. Still, as William Leuchtenburg points out, Hopkins "displayed remarkable ingenuity in much that he did": building medical, educational, recreational, and airport facilities, and financing theater productions, scholarly publications, and artwork adorning public buildings. He employed thousands of men and women who had reached a dead end in the Depression, who represented the coming together of diverse cultures and ethnicities that had previously been shunned by mainstream society. Among the projects the WPA helped fund were New York City's LaGuardia Airport; Chicago's Outer Bridge Drive (also known as Lake Shore Drive Bridge), which was completed in 1937 and at 356 feet long and 100 feet wide was the first twentieth-century bridge to span the Chicago River; Shangri-La, the presidential retreat in Maryland, later renamed Camp David; and upgrades to Doubleday Field in Cooperstown, New York, all of which are still standing today.

The Federal Writers' Project hired six thousand writers, including Saul Bellow and Ralph Ellison, to produce guides to every state (and Washington,

D.C.) in the country, to celebrate the country's regional differences. The Mathematical Tables Project produced twenty-eight volumes of useful information, including navigation tables used by the Navy in World War II. The WPA funded Jackson Pollock, and George Stanley, who built the Art Deco–style Muse of Drama and Dance sculpture at a cost of $100,000, which still adorns the entrance to the Hollywood Bowl.

The great sculptor Gutzon Borglum, who chiseled Mount Rushmore, had inspired Hopkins to support the arts. Borglum had told him: "Hoover was . . . dead from the top down. His heart seemed to have ceased beating to the call of laughter, to music, the charm of letters. . . . Everything seemed to die in his hands." He urged Hopkins to "concentrate on the schools, the poor schools, the little schools, the public schools . . . start with the children; make their classrooms, study rooms, and halls pleasant, with color and design, fairytales and history, home life. You are not after masterpieces . . . the real success will be in the interest, the human interest, which you will awaken; and what that does to the Nation's mind." Hopkins complained at a press conference that all some people thought about was repairing streets, but he wouldn't apologize for putting money into worthwhile research projects that "dumb people criticize. . . . God damn it," he said. "Here are a lot of people broke and we are putting them to work making researches of one kind or another. . . . We have projects up there to make Jewish dictionaries. There are rabbis who are broke and on the relief rolls. One hundred and fifty projects . . . deal with pure science. What of it? . . . We are not backing down on any of these projects."

Hopkins's key effort, in response to Borglum's advocacy, was setting up a National Youth Administration to help the more than four million youngsters between the ages of sixteen and twenty-five find work or stay in school long enough to develop marketable skills. Eleanor Roosevelt, who feared that without federal intervention these young people would become a lost generation drawn to political extremes, was the driving force behind this rescue operation. She had no patience with bureaucratic rigmarole that stood in the way of progressive advance and once facetiously suggested dynamiting a supervising official when he invoked rules holding up a WPA program. She was as critical of conservatives who complained that the 1930s' generation of youngsters lacked the initiative and spirit to find work. She told one of them that her mail was filled with pleas for help from desperate youngsters, and urged him to understand that "a civilization which does not provide young people with a way to earn a living is pretty poor."

For months she had "badgered, cajoled and grown cold" trying to persuade Franklin to issue an executive order establishing the NYA as an arm of the WPA. He finally gave in when she convinced him that a program focused on the young would not only help revive the economy by preparing them for productive work but also go a long way toward making them lifelong Democrats. Just as he saw the political advantages in bringing minorities into his administration and advancing their group status, so he saw "a good deal" in what Eleanor argued about helping the young. "I have determined that we shall do something for the

Nation's unemployed youth," he announced in June 1935, "because we can ill afford to lose the skill and energy of these young men and women. They must have their chance in school, their turn as apprentices and their opportunity for jobs — a chance to work and earn for themselves." The NYA not only opened avenues of possibility for young people, Blanche Wiesen Cook wrote, it also "represented a critical turning point in ER's independent role as First Lady and as her husband's partner in an increasingly difficult political climate."

Roosevelt named the forty-four-year-old Aubrey Williams as the NYA's director, a logical choice to head the organization, given the impressive work Williams had done under Hopkins as director of state relief for the PWA. An Alabaman with firsthand knowledge of poverty, Williams had the intelligence and ambition to earn a doctorate at the University of Bordeaux after Army service in France during World War I and began a successful career as a social worker. As much as poverty itself he despised the racial segregation that pervaded the Southern states. "If I sound bitter in describing life and liberty in the Union," he wrote in 1934, "I make no apology for it. It is time for us to be bitter." Described as "radical by temperament, hard-working, relentlessly honest, relentlessly idealistic," Williams was eager to take on an assignment that some saw as a thankless effort, one that involved not only improving the lot of young people but disarming the hostility toward the administration of communist and socialist youths who had given up on the country's economic and political traditions.

Hopkins and Williams saw the new agency as a

golden opportunity to make a difference in the lives of needy youngsters who were out of school, on relief, and adrift in the country with little hope for the future. Because Williams valued the input of local reformers close to the cities and towns where young men and women wrestled with daily survival, and because Roosevelt was sensitive to potential charges of excessive federal control and potential comparisons to Hitler's mobilization of Nazi youth, they appointed forty-eight state directors to oversee the administration of the WPA funds distributed to the NYA.

In his search for talented administrators, Williams was drawn to relatively young men who could make easy connections with their cohorts. He was especially sensitive to finding liberal Southerners who would include blacks in their efforts to provide jobs and training. No one satisfied such requirements more suitably than a twenty-six-year-old aide to Texas congressman Richard Kleberg, Lyndon B. Johnson. "A tornado in pants," as someone called him, Johnson had been serving as a virtual congressman during his more than three years with Kleberg, a self-indulgent playboy with little interest in his congressional duties or the larger affairs of state. The ambitious Johnson solicited the support of several Texas congressmen for the NYA job, including Sam Rayburn, who had become a mentor, as well as liberal Maury Maverick and conservative Martin Dies. Williams recalled that it was the only time that "bastard" Dies ever called him, and since so broad a spectrum of Texans were recommending Johnson, including the state's U.S. senators, Williams endorsed his candidacy to Roosevelt. As the youngest of the forty-eight directors,

Johnson would test the idea that NYA enrollees would be more comfortable with someone close to their own age group.

Johnson exceeded all their expectations, operating what Williams called "the best NYA program in all of the states." When news of Johnson's work reached Mrs. Roosevelt, she wrote to congratulate him and then visited Texas to investigate why he was "doing such an effective job." Johnson took her to an Austin vocational training center for girls and accompanied her to college campuses running NYA programs. Nothing elevated Johnson in Eleanor's and Williams's estimate more than his efforts to help indigent African Americans. Pressed by Eleanor, who saw blacks as "America's most neglected people," Roosevelt had signed an executive order barring discrimination against them in WPA programs. Three hundred thousand black youngsters across the country seized the chance for NYA training that might lead to gainful employment. Johnson, defying Southern bias against spending federal funds on black poverty, quietly gave meaning to Roosevelt's directive by making helping African Americans a priority. While he could conceive of no way to meet NAACP demands for "a qualified Negro appointed as a Deputy Administrator" in Texas, he saw no bar to quietly helping ambitious black youngsters with jobs or money to stay in school.

Mary McLeod Bethune, the leading black official at the NYA, who headed an Office of Minority Affairs, described Johnson as the best director in the South and "a very outstanding young man," who was "going to go places." Beatrice Denmark, another black NYA administrator, had effusive praise for Johnson's work on behalf of young women: "I have found what I have been hoping to find for colored girls," she said after a visit to Texas. "I believe I know the Negro condition in the southern states, and no one would be more delighted to see them have the kind of training that Mr. Johnson is setting up in Texas. The Texas Director is doing what we are talking."

Although the NYA gave part-time jobs to 2 million high school and college students and full-time work to another 2.6 million just out of school, it fell well short of ensuring the long-term economic futures of these young people. Radicals at an American Youth Congress insisted that permanent solutions to their economic problems would require $3.5 billion a year for seven years. "You don't have to tell me that the Youth Administration doesn't touch the whole problem," Eleanor told a gathering of the Youth Congress. "I know that." So did the president, but both he and Eleanor saw their funding demands, among others, as unrealistic. While appreciative of her willingness to hear them out, leaders of the group dismissed her and the president's good intentions as gestures that would never solve the country's ills. "She thinks she can reform capitalists . . . by inviting them to the White House for dinner and a good talking-to," one of them wrote. "I'm convinced . . . that she as well as her husband would go much further if they'd have support. But every time they take an even mildly progressive stand they antagonize some group or other," which Roosevelt feared would threaten his reelection.

That young critic misjudged what were in fact the New Deal's greatest problems: its own limitations, its flawed programs, and the uncertainties within its ranks about what direction to take. By

1935, with the economy still struggling to revive and Roosevelt continuing to search for answers, he had lost the momentum that was so evident in 1933–34 and had been given new life with the November congressional returns. The historian Charles Beard marveled at "the disintegration of Roosevelt's prestige . . . with staggering rapidity" in the first months of the year.

Conservative Democrats like Moley and Baruch saw the road to full recovery through faith in business, or what the economist Paul Krugman many years later would call dismissively the "confidence fairy." Tugwell and liberal allies insisted that the New Deal would have to do much more if the economy was to make an enduring upturn. The left was badly divided about the direction to take and made headlines with its internal sniping. In April, when Ickes told a press conference that Huey Long suffered from "halitosis of the intellect," it "made a great hit with the correspondents," and Roosevelt praised it as "the best thing that had been said about Huey Long." But the rifts within the administration left insiders depressed and the thirty-five-year-old Tommy Corcoran, an assistant general counsel and principal drafter of New Deal laws, fearful that it might be ten or twelve years before a liberal agenda could find fulfillment.

Doubts about Roosevelt's leadership were now being raised on every side. Long went after "Prince Franklin's" court: Jim Farley, "the Nabob of New York"; Ickes, "the Chinchbug of Chicago"; Henry Wallace, "the ignoramus of Iowa"; and Hugh Johnson, "the Oo-la-la of Oklahoma." Liberals, the *New Republic*'s Bruce Bliven reported, are "a sad lot, shivering in the wintry wind. . . . They do believe that the President has let them down badly. I do not think that anything he might do now could restore their confidence in him." At the *New York Times* Francis Brown observed that faith in Roosevelt had been shattered. Liberals, fondly recalling the first days of the administration, when "it seemed certain that a new America could be created," now cynically described the Hundred Days as "only a bitter joke." "Once more," Walter Lippmann exclaimed, "we have come to a period of discouragement after a few months of buoyant hope. Pollyanna is silenced and Cassandra is doing all the talking."

Contributing to the disillusionment with Roosevelt and the New Deal were the struggles of its principal vehicle for recovery, the National Industrial Recovery Act. The NRA was already under attack publicly as the "National Run Around," from Huey Long as the "National Racketeers Association," "National Ruin Administration," "Nuts Running America," and "Never Roosevelt Again," and from blacks, who said it stood for "Negroes Ruined Again." Even Roosevelt himself had begun to have doubts about its viability and wondered whether the country was simply not "ready to function as an integrated economy on the basis of national planning." When he raised this question with Rex Tugwell, he "knew that NRA was done for; and I hardly expected to see another attempt of the sort in my lifetime."

But it was the Supreme Court that ultimately put an end to the program. Roosevelt had been fearful that the Court would rule against New Deal innovations as executive and federal overreach. Four conservative justices and three liberals effectively put Court decisions in the hands of seventy-two-year-old former New York governor, 1916 Republican presidential nominee, secretary of state, and chief justice Charles Evans Hughes, and Hoover appointee, sixty-year-old Owen Roberts, the youngest member of the Court. In 1933–34, five-to-four decisions had given New Dealers initial hope that the Court would see the economic collapse as a basis for backing remedial legislation. Early in his term, when Roosevelt asked a group of senators about the legality of an action, Oklahoma's Thomas Gore told him: "Mr. President, you could go on the street right now, knock down an old man, drag him into the White House, and take his clothes. . . . It would be just about as legal as what you are planning to do. But that doesn't matter. You can do it anyway."

Despite his amusement at Gore's assertion and Hughes's pronouncement in a favorable ruling for the New Deal that "emergency does not create power, [but] emergency may furnish the occasion for the exercise of power" and "justify temporary expedients," Roosevelt worried that the Court's tolerance for "expedients" would not be limitless. Yet in 1934, the Court issued decisions that encouraged liberals to conclude that a Court majority had abandoned its earlier conservative predilections and that "a new era has dawned," in the words of the *New York World Telegram*. But the Court was not about to give up its role as a defender of constitutional protections from excessive government intrusion into individual rights and the free workings of the economy.

Consequently, Roosevelt was not entirely surprised in May 1935 when the Court unanimously overturned the NIRA as exceeding what the

Constitution's commerce clause allowed. In ten of nineteen earlier federal district court cases, judges had ruled against the NRA as breaching constitutional limits. All nine Supreme Court justices now agreed that the law delegated unlawful powers to the president and that the A.L.A. Schechter Poultry Corporation, the plaintiff in the case under review, was not engaged in interstate commerce, and therefore its activities could not be regulated by the NRA, including its employees' hours and wages. The Act had given the federal government unlimited power and sanctioned "a completely centralized government," the Court declared. Privately, Justice Louis Brandeis told Roosevelt aides Tommy Corcoran and Ben Cohen that Roosevelt "has been living in a fool's paradise" and instructed them to "go back and tell the President that we're not going to let this government centralize everything. It's come to an end."

Roosevelt, Jeff Shesol reveals in his study of the president and the Court, "was stunned — if not by the decision, then by the defection of the Court's liberals," and asked, "Where was old Isaiah?" the name he used for Brandeis, before Corcoran and Cohen shared what the most reliable liberal voice on the Court had told them. Attorney General Homer Cummings protested the Court's action as "an ultra–states right decision" that turned "the clock back a great many years." Conservatives, by contrast, celebrated the end of what they called Roosevelt's reign of terror, the restoration of the Constitution, and the preservation of fundamental law. Progressive Republican Senator Hiram Johnson said that conservative state rights Democrats were "as gleeful as the stand-pat Republicans. . . . Every rat seems to have come out of his hole and is making faces at the White House."

Roosevelt regarded the Court's decision as an assault not only on the NRA, but the entire New Deal and his leadership, and on May 31 struck back in a press conference. When a reporter asked him to comment on the NRA decision, Roosevelt, concealing his anger toward the Court with a characteristic show of humor, replied: "That's an awful thing to put up to a fellow at this hour of the morning, just out of bed." After reading out loud several telegrams from businessmen around the country urging him to save them by rescuing the program, Roosevelt described the Court's ruling as the most important since the Dred Scott case. Taking issue with the its assertion that a national crisis had never given the government license "to enlarge constitutional power," he pointed to laws passed in the first months of 1917 after the United States became involved in World War I that were "far more violative of the strict interpretation of the Constitution than any legislation that was passed in 1933." The nub of the issue, Roosevelt said, was the interstate commerce clause and the need to view it "in the light of present-day civilization" and not "in the horse-and-buggy age when that clause was written. But the understanding of that clause has changed with the change in interstate commerce. Does this decision mean that the United States Government has no control over any national economic [or social] problem?" he asked rhetorically. By limiting the federal government's capacity to address these issues, Roosevelt added, we have been "relegated to the horse-and-buggy definition of interstate commerce."

Ickes thought they had reached a crossroads: "We have to meet this issue or abandon any effort to better the social and economic conditions of the people," a sentiment with which Roosevelt agreed. He was determined not to "compromise and temporize. . . . I am inclined to fight," he told Tugwell. "The principles of NRA must be carried on in some way," he wrote Bill Bullitt in Moscow. He found the "dictum in the Schechter case . . . disturbing," he told Henry Stimson, because "the Court would probably find only ten percent of actual transactions to be directly in interstate commerce," and would drastically limit the power of the federal government in managing or, more to the point, boosting the economy. Norman Davis, a millionaire financier and foreign affairs expert who had served Roosevelt as an observer at the Geneva Disarmament Conference, warned against trying constitutional reform to overcome the Schechter decision: "The opposition would yell so loud about dictatorship . . . and they would do to you what they did to Wilson and the League." Roosevelt responded that "things are not as well economically and socially as they appear on the surface — on the other hand, they are better politically than they appear to be. . . . These are reasons why a campaign of inaction would be bad for the country as well as for the party!"

A conservative Republican in Hyde Park, New York, had told Franklin's cousin Daisy, "F.D.R. has gone to pieces and is having a regular breakdown and will probably have to resign!" But Daisy knew better: "F. has such a buoyant nature," she confided to her diary. "He could not survive without it." Moreover, as Roosevelt had told Colonel House earlier in the year, "This 'rumor factory' called Washington almost gets under my skin — but a long as it does not actually do so, we are all right." On June 4, he gave substance to his fighting spirit and determination to give renewed life to the New Deal by sending a message to Congress listing nine measures that "I must get this session." After a refreshing break at Hyde Park, where he and Daisy spent the afternoon of June 11 driving on back roads and exploring the countryside, and a graduation address to West Point cadets urging world peace, he returned to Washington, which he "found . . . as usual a bedlam."

The "bedlam" partly revolved around a struggle to provide electric power to the 90 percent of farms — some twenty-seven million farmers — that lacked this modern amenity. On May 11, 1935, Roosevelt had issued an executive order creating the Rural Electrification Administration (REA) as an arm of the work relief act. The costs of electric power that was available in rural areas were as high as four times the price in urban centers. Moreover, utility companies saw little profit in electrifying the countryside and had no incentive to string lines there. Despite its good intentions, the REA had little initial impact on unserved parts of the country. Using the relief act as a vehicle to establish the agency had created insurmountable problems: The law required that 25 percent of the money earmarked for REA be spent on labor and that 90 percent of the laborers had to be drawn from relief rolls. Morris Cooke, a Pennsylvania management engineer whom Roosevelt made head of REA, advised him that using work relief funds to build electric lines meant spending far too much on unemployed laborers lacking the necessary skills for building transmission lines. Cooke persuaded the president to let him loan REA money to private utility companies to do the necessary work. But the companies themselves had no interest in taking part in operations they believed would be unprofitable. The alternative was to add legislation that would allow loans to be made to nonprofit farmer co-operatives, but the utilities were dead set against the idea, and lobbied Congress not to finance them.

So, by the summer of 1935, Roosevelt had a new, unwelcome legislative fight on his hands. "I do hope 'Things' will get wound up soon in Washington, so that you can get a real vacation — You must need it," Daisy wrote him in July. "Reading all the hot-headed explosions in the paper these days; it is a blessing to be a little aloof from it all — the wonder to me is that you seem able to keep an 'aerial' view." Daisy urged him not to "let them get you angry by what they say in the papers! It takes half the wind out of their sails if you don't answer back." She thought that the people "expect[ed] just about *perfection* of you, and don't want you to be even capable of losing your temper! It's pretty hard on you," Daisy conceded, but she was "quite certain" that she was "right." "You are so very right about not answering attacks no matter how provoking," he replied. Confiding in her continued to give him an outlet for emotions he kept hidden from others: "You alone have known that I was a bit 'down cast' these past weeks," he added. "I *couldn't* let anyone else know it — but somehow I seem to tell you all those things and what I don't happen to tell you, you seem to know anyway!"

A letter Lincoln had written during the darkest days of the Civil War, when he had come under repeated attacks, also gave Roosevelt solace. Lincoln had refused to respond to his critics, reasoning that to do so would close him off from attending to all other business. FDR identified with Lincoln's reflections on his efforts to "do the best I know how, the very best I can; and I mean to keep on doing it to the end. If the end brings me out all right, what is said against me will not amount to anything. If the end brings me out all *wrong,* then angels swearing I was right would make no difference." Roosevelt believed that Lincoln, like himself, "no matter how philosophic he was in public," was hurt by these attacks. But his predecessor had "kept his peace — that was and is the great lesson," Roosevelt told Daisy. "You won't always be right," he remarked to Tugwell, "but you mustn't suffer from being wrong. That's what kills people like us." Given the backgrounds and knowledge of public affairs and history of his advisers, he believed that they were likely to be right much of the time.

Much too much has been made of Roosevelt's inscrutability by historians and critics. As his exchanges with Daisy indicate, he struggled with the uncertainties of his decisions while making every effort to shield his intentions and emotions from an observing, prying world. His public image of buoyant hopefulness was a mask he believed essential to his political mastery. Almost everything he said and did aimed to serve political ends — whether it was giving a speech before an audience, speaking to the press, conferring with aides, wooing congressmen who visited him in the Oval Office, or even at rest with his stamp collection or fishing in a rumpled sweater while on vacation, or giving out news about his family and dog Fala. And like TR before him, he was exceptionally adept doing so, especially because he had the added advantage of being able to communicate by radio, which enabled him to speak directly to millions of Americans.

And, like Lincoln, Roosevelt ultimately succeeded. In the period from June through August, he won congressional approval for five major laws — above all the final draft of Social Security and labor's right to collective bargaining. His determination to bend Congress to his will was as much a matter of establishing a record of strong leadership in preparation for the following year's presidential reelection campaign as it was of preserving and advancing the New Deal. The passage of the Social Security law in August was a major priority that had stood at the top of his reform agenda since at least March and could be traced back to key concerns in his governorship. But the Wagner National Labor Relations bill was an issue that had come to his attention only recently.

Roosevelt had been more interested in reducing jobless numbers and increasing wage scales than in supporting collective bargaining and unions. The array of liberal measures identified with him had certainly given him standing with industrial workers, for as one of them remarked, "Mr. Roosevelt is the only man we ever had in the White House who would understand that my boss is a sonofabitch." But he was not the architect of the National Labor Relations Act (NLRA). Labor Secretary Frances Perkins recalled that he had no "part in developing" the law, "and, in fact, was hardly consulted about it. It was not a part of the president's program. It did not particularly appeal to him when it was described to him. All the credit for it belongs to [New York Senator Robert] Wagner, who had been advocating workers' rights for years. After the Senate passed Wagner's bill in mid-May, Roosevelt remained lukewarm to the measure, which rejected traditional objections to collective bargaining and strikes as violations of antitrust laws opposing restraint of trade. However, when the Supreme Court's Schechter ruling at the end of May weakened the NRA's 7A proviso on workers' rights, Roosevelt took up the cause for Wagner's bill, and the House approved it at the end of June. On July 5, Roosevelt's signature made it law.

Roosevelt's popular standing as a president fighting for public over corporate interests found additional resonance in his 1935 battle against thirteen holding companies that controlled three-quarters of the electric utility providers in the country. He had been at odds with the companies since his governorship, describing them as "a corporate invention, which can give a few corporate insiders unwarranted and intolerable powers over other people's money." He shared the progressive view that electrical power was a public utility and a necessity that should be available to Americans at reasonable rates. The only objective of the holding companies, which siphoned off money from the providers, was to fatten their bank accounts rather than delivering electric power to economically hard-pressed consumers. "The holding company system," Judge Robert E. Healy, counsel to the Federal Trade Commission, said, "is to a degree more or less of a parasite and

352

excrescence on the actual operating companies." The FTC described these businesses as engaged in "fraud, deceit, misrepresentation, dishonesty, breach of trust and oppression," all in their unapologetic self-interest.

The holding-company bill Roosevelt put before Congress included a "death sentence" clause that would eliminate these entities within five years. It was attacked by corporate executives as a prelude to socialism, national paralysis, and "nationalization of the industry," and by lobbyists who wooed congressmen and senators with campaign contributions and a well-orchestrated barrage of letters and telegrams "ostensibly from ordinary people who held utility stock" and feared the loss of lifetime savings.

Roosevelt had tried to counter the fear tactics of the bill's opponents by denouncing industry advocates as "the most powerful, dangerous lobby . . . that has ever been created by any organization in this country," and by declaring, "I am against private socialism of concentrated economic power as thoroughly as I am against governmental socialism." He also asserted that "regulation [alone] has small chance of ultimate success against the kind of concentrated wealth and economic power which holding companies have shown the ability to acquire in the utility field." But he could not combat entirely a campaign of rumors that he was losing his mind and was beset by "violent fit[s] of hysterics," or assertions that his bill was a threat to free enterprise and Americanism. In the end, he had to abandon the death sentence and settle for a regulatory law that broke up the holding companies into smaller units required to operate in an undefined public interest.

At the same time, however, the administration was busy building huge dams across the West to join the Tennessee Valley Authority in generating cheap electric power provided by public utilities. As early as his first gubernatorial term in 1929–30, Roosevelt had favored such multipurpose flood control dams. As president, he remained an enthusiastic advocate of these government-sponsored projects. By the close of 1935, "nearly twenty major dams were under construction": Bonneville and Grand Coulee, the largest man-made structure in history, on the Columbia River; Boulder on the Colorado; and Fort Peck on the Missouri. "We are working toward no less a goal than the electrification of America," TVA director David Lilienthal announced.

Where Roosevelt viewed the holding-company bill as a necessary advance against corporate greed and toward middle-class security, he saw tax legislation as largely a political alternative to radical attacks on the country's existing economic system. A wealth tax act he put before Congress on June 19, he said, would "throw to the wolves the forty-six men who are reported to have incomes in excess of one million dollars a year," a princely sum in 1935. Although Mississippi's Pat Harrison, the conservative chairman of the Senate Finance Committee, would "have kittens on the spot" when he read the bill, Roosevelt said, he was determined to "steal [Huey] Long's thunder." He sent a placating message to William Randolph Hearst, one of the millionaires in question, to head off his likely opposition by explaining that he was "fighting Communism, Huey Longism, Coughlin-

354

ism, Townsendism. I want to save our system, the capitalistic system. . . . I want to equalize the distribution of wealth." The tax was, he added, his way of combating "crackpot ideas." The inheritance tax feature of the measure aimed to limit the accumulation of excessive wealth that assured "the perpetuation of great and undesirable concentration of control in a relatively few individuals over the employment and welfare of many, many others."

At the same time, he told Henry Morgenthau that the message he was "sending up is more or less a campaign document laying down the principles as to where he stands. He does not expect any action on this but gives the people a year to think it over." When Ickes warned him that "we wouldn't have anything substantial to show the people for the expenditure of their money" on WPA programs and expressed concern about "the effect . . . on the President's political fortunes next year," Roosevelt read him the tax message he had just sent to Congress, saying that "he thought it was the best thing that he had done as President. . . . At one place in the message he looked up at me with a smile and said, 'That is for Hearst.' " Ickes took Roosevelt's point, recording that the tax proposal "will go far to strengthen his position with the average man and woman."

Hearst responded as Roosevelt had apparently expected him to: by denouncing the tax message as "essentially Communism," and the president as "Stalin Delano Roosevelt." Hearst directed his editors to label the measure as "the soak-the-successful" bill and to dismiss Roosevelt's New Deal as the "Raw Deal." Roosevelt told Ickes that "there was no man in the whole United States who was as vicious an influence as Hearst," adding "that he had never had very much of an opinion of Hearst." In fact, Franklin needed an opponent, a whipping boy for his coming presidential campaign, and as he had Hoover in 1932, he expected Hearst to provide a compelling reason to vote for Roosevelt and the Democrats in 1936.

In the end, the tax bill was more symbol than substance. Gleeful that Roosevelt was apparently following his lead toward a Share the Wealth model, Huey Long marched around the Senate floor, thumping his chest in celebration as the clerk read the bill, and taking the microphone afterward to shout, "Amen." But when he saw the final result he realized it was little more than posturing. As the amended bill, stripped of the inheritance tax and with a token graduated corporate income tax, made its way toward passage with passive acceptance by Roosevelt, Long denounced the president as "a liar and a faker," who was doing no more than "copying my share-the-wealth speeches that I was writing when I was fourteen years old." As Long anticipated, the final bill had little impact on the redistribution of wealth or, most important, in combating the Depression, "the transfer [of] money from those who would save it to those who would spend it." Moreover, it generated little revenue to help balance the budget. With the political implications of the bill in mind, one congressman said of the legislation, "This is a hell raiser, not a revenue raiser."

In accepting a limited tax reform law, Roosevelt was again focused primarily on the coming presidential election and his chances of a second term. He was eager for a measure that would appeal to most voters but was reluctant to go too far in alienating well-off businessmen and undermining Republican support. In July 1935, when he heard about a "Republicans-for-Roosevelt League," he asked Jim Farley to "have someone check on the whole set up. . . . This is a field which may well be explored intensely." Remembering that Walter Lippmann had criticized him in 1932 as "no enemy of entrenched privilege," Roosevelt's tax bill gave him the bona fides as a reformer trying to right the balance between privilege and poverty.

While he took satisfaction from the legislative gains Congress had voted for in the extended session between June and August — what many were now calling the second Hundred Days or the second New Deal — the push toward the left had, despite his careful balancing of competing interests, also provoked businessmen and opened up a political divide in the country that gave Roosevelt pause. The publisher Roy Howard wrote to tell him that "many business men who once gave you sincere support are now, not merely hostile, they are frightened." They viewed the tax bill as an act of "revenge on business." Howard predicted "that there can be no real recovery until the fears of business have been allayed through the granting of a breathing spell to industry." There needed to be "a recess from further experimentation until the country can recover its losses."

Roosevelt felt compelled not only to answer Howard, but also to publicize their exchange. Although he had told Tugwell that "public life takes a lot of sweat, but it doesn't need to worry you," the opposition troubled him. A Gallup poll asking whether Roosevelt supporters in 1932 would vote for him again in 1936 showed that while he maintained a healthy majority backing, he faced a decline in support in every region of the country of between 4 and 13 percent, except in the Mountain states, where he had a 5 percent gain. In a public defense of the New Deal, he told Howard that he was seeking "a wise balance in American economic life, to restore our banking system to public confidence, to protect investors in the security market, to give labor freedom to organize and protection from exploitation, to safeguard and develop our national resources, to set up protection against the vicissitudes incident to old age and unemployment, to relieve destitution and suffering and to relieve investors and consumers from the burden of unnecessary corporate machinery." There could be no question that he thoroughly favored the more humane society that the New Deal had fostered, but he wanted to disarm the fears his reforms had stirred up. To that end he assured Howard that his program of change "has now reached substantial completion and the 'breathing spell' of which you speak is here — very decidedly so."

In introducing reforms that effectively created a welfare state, Roosevelt was thinking not only about the well-being of Americans but also the competition for what would later be called hearts and minds abroad. Communism in Russia, Fascism in Italy, and Nazism in Germany represented a challenge to democracy. Which system of governance could best serve the needs of their peoples? Roosevelt was especially concerned about Latin America, where poverty and instability might enable one of the competing ideologies to make significant inroads. In August, after Daisy Suckley received a letter from him "corroborat-

[ing] what I think you think," she answered him: "You are trying to do, something to this effect: these extraordinary changes are taking place all over the world, with Communism, Fascism, Dictatorship, etc. as the natural results — You are trying to meet these changes, and to go along with them, and to control them so that *this* country will not have to live through some of the horrors that others have had."

Roosevelt's greatest challenge in foreign affairs remained managing domestic opinion. How could he have an impact abroad when the great majority of Americans was still largely indifferent to overseas conflicts? They saw another war in the making in Europe and did not want to become involved, especially because hearings by North Dakota senator Gerald Nye had convinced many that self-serving bankers and munitions makers had orchestrated the country's involvement in 1917. They were equally determined to steer clear of the Sino-Japanese tensions that might erupt into a general Asian conflict. In a Gallup poll of twenty-two key issues facing America, including employment, ending the Depression, redistributing wealth, and preserving the Constitution, neutrality in international affairs ranked third in importance, and increased national defense stood next to last. On top of that, 75 percent of the country favored a national referendum before it entered another war.

Popular disfavor to involvements abroad greatly concerned Roosevelt. In 1935, advancing the national economy remained his highest priority, but he also wished to give more attention to foreign conflicts than the country would allow. With Mussolini increasing Italian troop strength in East Africa in response to a border dispute with Ethiopia, and Hitler announcing German rearmament, including building air forces and raising a half-million-man army, Roosevelt wrote Breckinridge Long, his ambassador in Rome, "These are without doubt the most hair-trigger times the world has gone through in your lifetime or mine. I do not even exclude June and July 1914," the eve of World War I. In August, the president wrote William E. Dodd, his ambassador in Berlin, "A year ago I was fairly optimistic — today I am the opposite."

Roosevelt wanted to do what he could to preserve the peace, but was reluctant to do anything that might be interpreted as an intentional provocation that would both anger Americans and add to tensions abroad. In August, when Secretary of War George Dern scheduled a trip to the Philippines to attend the inauguration of a new government, Roosevelt instructed him to avoid going to Australia, the Dutch East Indies, or Indo-China "because of the very ticklish situation in the Pacific." A visit to those countries by a cabinet member traveling on a cruiser or any warship "would not be understood."

Nothing was more illustrative of Roosevelt's sensitivity to domestic attitudes than his response to congressional pressure to enact a neutrality law that would ensure that the United States would not take part in any future conflict abroad. Antiwar demonstrations in the first half of 1935 in Washington and on university campuses across the country underscored public cynicism about World War I and opposition to any military engagement.

Roosevelt was not unsympathetic to these

pacifist sentiments, but he believed that they went too far in urging against taking a role in world affairs. "We face a large misinformed public opinion," he told a friend, and in April had written Colonel House, "I am, of course, greatly disturbed by events on the other side." He wished he could find some way "by which the weight of America could be thrown in to the scale of peace and stopping the armament race." As he wrote Dodd in Berlin later in the year, "I do not know that the United States can save civilization but at least by our example we can make people think and give them the opportunity of saving themselves." It was a thin reed to lean on, as the dictators in Italy, Germany, Russia, and Japan had little regard for an economically depressed America preaching homilies about peace. Nonetheless, Roosevelt hoped that the world's powers would not totally discount the United States' potential influence.

In the meantime, he tried to satisfy isolationists by proposing that Congress enact a neutrality law that suspended shipment of munitions to warring nations. At the same time, however, he asked for approval of a $1.1 billion military appropriation, the largest peacetime defense budget in the country's history. In addition, he wanted any neutrality statute to include a provision for discretionary presidential power to exempt a victim of aggression from the ban. It quickly became clear that the Senate Foreign Relations Committee, which seized the initiative in drafting such a law, wanted impartial neutrality, a ban on loans and arms to all belligerents, and a prohibition against Americans traveling in war zones. Because he realized that any ensuing debate over neutrality legislation would sidetrack his domestic initiatives, Roosevelt asked Senator Pittman, the committee's chairman, to set aside the neutrality bill.

But when organized public pressure for an impartial neutrality law became too strong, and with the Senate ignoring his request to drop neutrality from its current agenda, Roosevelt reverted to proposals for discretionary embargoes. Congress, however, remained opposed to any executive action that could position the United States on one side in a conflict and possibly draw it into a war. Under these circumstances the best Roosevelt could hope for was a law that targeted a likely Italo-Ethiopian conflict. Although it would technically apply to both countries, it would in fact be strictly enforced only against Italy, which in the event of a war would lose access to U.S. loans and arms and passengers on its trans-Atlantic ships. Roosevelt also urged that a time limit of six months be placed on the mandatory arms embargo, when a change in public mood might give him the freedom to side with victims of aggression in future wars.

The law Roosevelt signed on August 31 gave him the freedom to punish Italy and required a review in January of what best served the national interest. He hoped he could then convince Congress to restore his freedom to invoke discretionary embargoes. "The President should have some discretion," he told William E. Dodd. "If some European power were to seek, by force of arms, a raw material source in South America, we should have to take sides and might, without going to war ourselves, assist the South American nation with supplies of one kind or another."

But the national conviction that Wilson had

mistakenly labeled Germany as the culprit in bringing on the Great War and had used his executive powers to defend neutral rights and lead the country into a pointless conflict made Roosevelt's expectations about what he might accomplish overseas too optimistic. The isolationist mood that had given birth to the 1935 neutrality law effectively deprived the United States of any significant influence abroad: An America that posed no threat of directly aiding Ethiopia to fight Italy or any other country under attack was an irrelevancy in the calculations of Mussolini, Hitler, and Japanese military leaders plotting new acts of aggression.

Coming events would demonstrate how unsatisfactory congressional control of foreign policy was. Roosevelt's judgment on every phase of overseas affairs was certainly not perfect, but his grasp of the danger that threats from abroad posed to national security greatly exceeded public and congressional understanding in the mid-1930s and beyond. As a politician, however, keenly aware that effective foreign policy leadership depended on majority opinion, he gave voice to public sentiments he never fully shared. In time, he expected the harsh realities about the dangers to America of uncontested military aggression to be acknowledged by the public and allow him to steer the ship of state along a more realistic course. But for the moment, he was a foreign policy leader without a following.

CHAPTER 8
TRIUMPH OF THE NEW ORDER

By September 1935, although early Gallup polls showed 53 percent of voters favoring him, Roosevelt approached the campaign for the coming presidential election with caution. He knew that only nine of his thirty-one predecessors had managed to win a second term, and the assassinations of Lincoln and McKinley had reduced to seven the number who had actually served eight full years. Even Theodore Roosevelt, for all his popularity, had resisted running again in 1908 and exceeding the tradition of an eight-year limit. Roosevelt had been concerned about a challenge from Huey Long since as early as February 1935, as he suspected that various "Republican elements are flirting with Huey Long and probably financing him." These factions believed that "a third Progressive Republican ticket and a fourth 'Share the Wealth' ticket . . . would crush us and that then a free for all would result in which case anything might happen."

If Long allied himself with Father Coughlin's National Union for Social Justice, Roosevelt feared, he could conceivably form a third party that could attract enough Democratic votes to return a Republican to the White House. Across the South and Middle West, Long and Coughlin turned out huge audiences to hear them speak in person and on the radio. Long's dramatics also won him considerable press attention, including being featured on the cover of *Time* magazine in April. He was quoted in the *New York Times* as claiming, "I can take this Roosevelt. He's scared of me. . . . I can out-promise him and he knows it." He also told a *Times* reporter, "Your next President will be Huey Long," if Roosevelt ran again against Hoover. In September, Long signed a contract for a book to be titled *My First Days in the White House,* and although he did not seriously believe that he could win enough electoral votes in 1936 to gain the presidency, he did think that if he could unseat Roosevelt, a Republican administration would open the way to his election in 1940.

But on September 8, 1935, thirty-year-old Carl Weiss, a Baton Rouge physician, assassinated the Kingfish. Because Long's guards killed Weiss after the shooting outside the governor's offices in the Baton Rouge capitol building, we will never know his motive for the assassination. Long himself certainly didn't know, for as he stumbled away, mortally wounded, he exclaimed, "I wonder why he shot me."

At press conferences the following week, Roosevelt said that he knew nothing about the assassination until Joe Kennedy and Father Coughlin informed him of it during a visit to the Oval Office. Beyond stating that he had sent a telegram of condolence to Mrs. Long and that the Coughlin-Kennedy meeting was strictly a "social" exchange with no discussion of politics, Roosevelt responded publicly to Long's demise with decorous silence. Jim Farley, however, cited to Ickes several states that "Roosevelt would have lost if Long had lived and had been a candidate." Although conspiracy buffs had no grounds for alleging a Roosevelt hand in the assassination, they found a basis for their suspicions in the elimination of someone who seemed to pose a serious threat to Roosevelt's reelection, and, at a minimum, was an irritant to the administration.

The Roosevelt press conferences in which he gave only passing mention to Long's death focused primarily on WPA and PWA spending and the Ickes-Hopkins rivalry, which had recently become a news item, and which Roosevelt hoped to solve during a deep-sea fishing vacation the three would take in the Pacific. By the beginning of September, the pressures of the recent congressional session had left the president drained. While he had won most of the fights, or at least achieved partial victories, in the battles over his second New Deal laws and the dispute over the neutrality bill, the clash of wills involved had strained his emotional reserves. Walter Lippmann, who interviewed him on September 16, found him "on edge" and "dangerously tired" and thought, "his judgment couldn't be depended on and that [his condition] might lead to a severe nervous breakdown." Lippmann's observation partly rested on an uncharacteristic outburst or show of true feeling by Roosevelt when Eleanor joined the conversation with remarks he considered inane: "Oh, Eleanor," he shouted at her, "Shut up. You never understand these things anyway." When Daisy Suckley wrote Franklin on September 12 that "I have worried a good deal over your being depressed during those last weeks in Washington," he replied: "You alone have known that I was a bit 'cast down' these past weeks." But given Lippmann's impression, his mood was less of a secret than Roosevelt suspected.

His tensions were also the product of personal ambivalence about his most intimate relationships. Eleanor was little comfort to him, not because she did anything particular to make his life difficult, but simply because the passage of time had revealed that they were two very different people. He was fundamentally a political animal, self-centered and always alert to what might constitute a political advantage. She was more idealistic and saw his pursuit of high office as eclipsing or at least distracting from his interest in advancing good causes. The more she pressed him to speak out for politically progressive causes, the more he withdrew from confiding in her about public affairs. He was not indifferent to her idealism, and in fact regarded it as a noble attribute. But her insensitivity to realpolitik made him reluctant to trust her judgment and reinforced his natural inclination to hide his feelings behind a mask of amiability, or apparent but often feigned agreement.

Franklin's advocates saw Eleanor as much too insensitive to the pressures playing on him. "She could be a crashing bore," her grandson Curtis Dall Roosevelt said. "She was very judgmental. . . . The human irregularities, the off-color jokes he loved, she couldn't take. He would tell his stories, many of them made to fit a point, and she would say, 'No, no, Franklin, that's not how it happened.' " Their son Elliott also perceived his father's problems with Eleanor: "If only Mother could have learned to ease up, things would have been so different with Father, for he needed relaxation more than anything in the world." Daisy believed that Franklin and Eleanor had "deep & lasting" feelings for each other. But "the fact that they could not relax together, or play together, is the tragedy of their joint lives, for I believe, from everything I have seen of them, that they had everything else in common. It was probably a matter of personalities, of a certain lack of humor on her part — I cannot blame either of them. They are both remarkable people — sky-high above the average."

Franklin found surcease in his poker games with his cronies and in the warm, relaxed affection of Missy LeHand and Daisy. Missy served as his girl Friday: She was a kind of surrogate wife — if not sexually than certainly as one who attended to his daily needs at work and play. Whatever the truth about any physical intimacy they shared, they were strongly attached to each other — so much so that it might have triggered the same anger in Eleanor that she felt when Franklin's affair with Lucy Mercer threatened to displace her. But, as Doris Goodwin says, "Eleanor knew that without Missy to attend to Franklin's personal needs, the independent life she had labored to create for herself would be impossible to maintain." Elliott Roosevelt believed that "knowing Missy was always there allowed Mother to come and go as she pleased without worrying about Father or feeling she was neglecting her wifely duties."

Similarly, Daisy Suckley's closeness to Franklin was unconcerning for Eleanor. Was Daisy Franklin's lover? Again, no one can speak authoritatively on the matter, and no evidence has been found to support the existence of a sexual relationship. There is no question, however, that they were strongly attached to each other, and from the letters exchanged between them, it seems fair to conclude that she was indispensable to him. He not only greatly enjoyed her as a companion but also valued her as a confidante. Occasionally, he would call her in the middle of the night merely to hear her calming voice. Daisy understood that what she had "been able to contribute was a complete lack of 'strain.' He told me once that there was no one else with whom he could be completely himself. . . . He would have me around half the time paying no attention to me, working on his stamps, reading or working. I was somebody nearby, so he wouldn't be alone — And we understood each other." Their meetings during his frequent visits to Hyde Park provoked gossip to which Daisy took exception: "On the subject of petty gossips," she wrote him after an August get-together, "I should like to say that it isn't of any importance *what* they say, . . . and I certainly can laugh them all off. . . . But the real point is that it wouldn't be wise or *fair* to you and your 'madam' to give them any kind of a handle to use against you both."

As a result, when Roosevelt asked Daisy to join him on his cross-country trip to dedicate Boulder Dam, followed by a fishing holiday in the Pacific off Baja California, she turned him down. On September 22, as he was about to leave for his journey, she asked Franklin: "Do you realize the amount of will power that was necessary to refuse a certain invitation this past week?" Geoffrey Ward, the editor of Daisy's diaries and letters, believes that at their last meeting they may have "confessed to each other the loneliness they felt. Certainly they talked of a special bond of friendship and agreed to share some of their secret thoughts, by letter and long-distance telephone and in person whenever they could arrange to be together." They kept up their correspondence during Franklin's four-week trip, with him confiding, "There is no reason why I should not tell you that I miss you *very* much. . . . I look forward so to my letter [she had sent him] on the ship."

Despite Daisy's absence, the trip was a restorative, giving him "a mental peace and a sense of proportion which is much needed." "I have been sleeping much and have begun to get very brown," he told Daisy. "I have been getting an honest to goodness rest. . . . I have longed to have you with me," he pined. As the trip ended, he wrote: "Today we are back to the same time as NY so I can think of you as keeping the same hours as I do — Don't forget to take very good care of a very special person — because it means a great deal to lots of people — but I think most [to] — Your affec F."

The return of Roosevelt's good humor was the product not just of getting away from Washington's political combat, but also of the enthusiastic greetings he received along the way from crowds that gathered to see him, and the pleasure he took at visiting the spectacular Boulder Dam, bordering Arizona and Nevada on the Colorado River. On September 30, at a dedication ceremony overlooking the 726-foot high structure, he celebrated "this great feat of mankind" that had turned a barren landscape into a "twentieth-century marvel," the "greatest dam in the world" that could generate nearly two million horse-power units of electric energy. The project had provided work to four thousand men, contributed to the health and comfort of millions living across the Southwest, and increased the wealth of the entire country. It was, he believed, compelling testimony to the success of his administration and the wisdom of using the government to build a better America.

A triumphal tour of Los Angeles in an open automobile on October 1, during which an estimated one million people greeted him, concluded with a speech to an audience of seventy-five thousand in the Los Angeles Coliseum. He told them that the expressions on people's faces across the nation had heartened him and convinced him that the country was emerging from the Depression. At a talk the next day in San Diego before boarding the heavy cruiser *Houston,* he touted the economic advances of the last two and a half years. But with Italy on the verge of attacking Ethiopia, he could not resist mentioning foreign affairs. In the last paragraphs of his talk, he assured the audience that America would remain at peace, but in a thinly veiled reference to Mussolini's Italy, he voiced the hope that other nations would follow America's lead and act like a "good neighbor." It was evidence of his concern about foreign affairs and his understanding that it inhibited him from proposing direct involvement by the United States.

He did not need polls to tell him that he was striking all the right chords with a majority of Americans. As Harry Hopkins observed, "The President got a great reception wherever he went and unless the Republicans can trot out somebody better than any I have seen suggested, I think there is no question but that he will be reelected." Ickes saw the crowds as "proof of the President's personal popularity."

Almost three weeks at sea, during which he took special satisfaction in promoting improved relations between Ickes and Hopkins, added to Roosevelt's reviving sense of serenity. Their daily shipboard interactions, including a competition over who could catch the largest fish, diverted them from the acrimony over PWA versus WPA projects. Roosevelt eased their tensions with an amusing item he wrote for the ship's newsletter titled "Buried at Sea": "The feud between Hopkins and Ickes was given a decent burial today," he reported. "The President officiated at the solemn ceremony which we trust will take these two babes off the front page for all time." He described Hopkins as "dressed in his immaculate blues, browns and whites," while Ickes "wore his conventional faded grays, Mona Lisa smile and carried his stamp collection. . . . Hopkins expressed regret at the unkind things Ickes had said about him and Ickes on his part promised to make it stronger — only more so — as soon as they could get a stenographer. . . ."

Ickes, who made a detailed record of the trip, "marveled again and again at his [FDR's] high cheer and at his disposition. Never once did he act self-conscious; on no occasion did he seem to be nervous or irritated. Cheerfully he submitted to being wheeled up and down the special ramps that had been installed on the *Houston* for his use, or to being carried up and down like a helpless child when he went fishing." Roosevelt greatly enjoyed the outings in whaleboats to catch a variety of fish, including 109-pound and 134-pound sailfish, and delighted in the two-hour-and-twenty-minute battle that tested the strength of his muscular shoulders and arms to land the larger of these fish. But it was ultimately the congeniality of everyone on the trip that made it so pleasant an outing. Ickes, who had been reluctant to go, said that Hopkins, with whom he had been battling so hard, "fitted in well with his easy manners and quick wit," and the president was a model host.

The *Houston* landed at Charleston, South Carolina, on October 23, and within weeks Roosevelt was writing to Robert Bingham, his ambassador in London, "I am . . . heir to manifold problems and difficulties of a somewhat burdensome nature." Although he believed that a political hiatus was essential to restrain partisan strife in the coming election year and had no intention of proposing a substantial legislative program, he was determined to launch a rhetorical campaign that made clear the differences between himself and his opponents on the right, whom he saw as his greatest threat. He believed that he had largely neutralized significant opposition from the left with his second Hundred Days, especially the Social Security and National Labor Relations acts, and he was genuinely in sync with much of the its desire for a social safety net and infrastructure projects reducing unemployment. Above all, he aimed to command the broad middle ground, where he believed most of the voters, who favored government activism, but within limits, stood.

Hardly anyone, including himself, was betting against Roosevelt's reelection. "Economic conditions are vastly better," he told Josephus Daniels, and "people are getting tired of the attitude of Hearst, the Republican leaders and the old Wall Street crowd." At a cabinet meeting on November

8, Roosevelt announced, "We will win easily next year but we are going to make it a crusade." He hoped not only to win reelection but also to receive an endorsement so resounding that it would make the New Deal a permanent part of the country's life.

But as in every election, doubts were expressed; some unseen event could unseat an incumbent. *New York Times* columnist Arthur Krock imagined a possible wave of unpopularity that could defeat him, and Daisy Suckley shuddered at the thought that "in six months he may be the most hated man in the country." She "pray[ed] he may not have to suffer that — For a cripple, who can't even pace the floor of his own room," she said, "it would be just so much harder to bear." Moreover, opinion polls showing that 70 percent of Americans favored a balanced budget and reduced national debt, and preferred a conservative to a liberal political party by a 53 to 47 margin, raised questions about the president's drift to the left in the previous six months.

The emerging foreign crisis in Africa between Italy and Ethiopia proved to be something of a godsend for Roosevelt — not because he had any sympathy with Mussolini's aggression or believed that he could involve the United States in the conflict, but because it allowed him to deemphasize domestic concerns and fix greater public attention on foreign affairs. He viewed overseas tensions as far more threatening to the nation's long-term well-being than did most Americans. He regarded Italy's assault on a people "in very much the stage of civilization as the small Kings & Barons were in Europe in the 12th Century" or "six centuries behind us" as inexcusable and wished to do all he could to punish it. But he understood that his eagerness to penalize the Italians was a policy that the American people would not support. "If a foreign nation insists on attacking another," a Gallup poll asked in early October, "should the United States join with other nations to compel it to stop?" Seventy-one percent said no; only 29 percent endorsed an internationalist involvement. So, whatever steps Roosevelt did take would have to strike a balance between reprimand and restraint, and in no way suggest an activist involvement that might draw America into the conflict.

When Mussolini launched his attack on Ethiopia, Roosevelt wanted to immediately invoke the neutrality law, but the State Department counseled patience until the League of Nations took a position. Roosevelt rejected Secretary of State Hull's advice, however, arguing, "They are dropping bombs on Ethiopia and that is war. Why wait for Mussolini to say so?" He knew that most Americans sided with the African nation after reading newspaper accounts describing Emperor Haile Selassie's people being subjected to the cruelty of Mussolini's forces, which used air power against troops of Ethiopian horsemen. Vittorio Mussolini, the dictator's son, added to the outrage by his sadistic descriptions of bombing attacks as "magnificent sport" in which he had "the impression of a budding rose unfolding as a bomb fell in the midst [of a group of horsemen] and blew them up."

Since the neutrality law would only deprive Italy of arms and financial gain from Americans traveling on cross-Atlantic transports, Roosevelt saw no political drawback from a prompt introduction of congressionally mandated neutrality. Moreover, he relished the opportunity to weigh in on the side of a hapless people fighting a dictator. He also saw the value in schooling Americans in how the United States could back the rule of law and anti-Fascism abroad. But he faced limits that made his intervention ineffective and deepened American convictions about the pointlessness of U.S. involvement. The neutrality law did not limit the sale of oil, copper, scrap iron, and scrap steel, which were as much implements of war as actual armaments. In fact, U.S. exports of these commodities to Italy, and especially oil, increased threefold in the final three months of 1935. When the League of Nations rejected a call for an oil embargo by stating that American exports made it pointless, and the British and French, eager not to drive Mussolini into an alliance with Hitler's Germany, proposed Ethiopian territorial concessions to Italy, Roosevelt condemned these decisions as an outrageous abuse of "world ethics." The president's efforts on behalf of Ethiopia came to naught.

He was not unmindful of the difficulty he faced in trying to lead a nation that feared excessive concentration of government power. The undemocratic regimes in Italy, Germany, and Japan had made Americans leery of anything resembling a dictatorship in the United States. "I know I'm walking a tightrope," Roosevelt told Jim Farley in November 1935, "and I'm thoroughly aware of the gravity of the situation. I realize the seriousness of this from an international as well as a domestic point of view."

Nonetheless, he was determined to show that America would not stand by passively in the face of acts of aggression. In January, his State of the Union message emphasized foreign dangers. Noting how little attention he had given foreign affairs in his inaugural in 1933, he now declared it time to redress that imbalance. America was devoted to peace, as were all the republics in the Americas, he said, where the spirit of the good neighbor was the established norm. As for "the rest of the world. Ah! There is the rub." Since "the temper and the purposes of the rulers of many of the great populations of Europe and Asia" had become so belligerent, he believed it necessary for the people of the Americas to take "cognizance of growing ill-will, of marked trends toward aggression, of increasing armaments, of shortening tempers — a situation which has in it many of the elements that lead to the tragedy of general war."

He hoped that the world was not on the threshold of another mad scramble for power. "But if face it we must, then the United States and the rest of the Americas can play but one role: through a well-ordered neutrality to do naught to encourage the contest, through adequate defense to save ourselves from embroilment and attack, and through example and all legitimate encouragement and assistance to persuade other Nations to return to the ways of peace and good-will."

In domestic affairs, Roosevelt envisioned a continuing struggle as well — one to assure against "the rise of autocratic institutions that beget slavery at home and aggression abroad. Within our borders, as in the world at large, popular opinion is at war with a power-seeking minority," he asserted. In the battle against this small, but influential group of financial and industrial interests, he and his congressional allies had "earned the hatred of entrenched greed." Despite the gains of the last three years, the fight was not over: These men sought "the restoration of their selfish power . . . power for themselves, enslavement for the public." Roosevelt's overheated rhetoric on this topic not only reflected the public's current mood of fear but also aimed to counter accusations that he had designs on untrammeled power. It was also a sop to his party's left since he had made clear that major domestic reforms were not in the offing. He closed with an appeal to Congress for continued advance toward a more just, equitable, democratic society.

Roosevelt was a little fearful that his message "might cause a great deal of bitterness in Japan, Germany and Italy but apparently it was taken very calmly," which relieved his concern that he might be provoking an international crisis that would put him at odds with domestic attitudes. In giving voice to America's disapproval of Italy's aggression, he hoped it might help "solidify the forces of non-aggression." Moreover, he thought that things were "going well in spite of Supreme Court majority opinion and Hearst and Alfred E. Smith, and an 85 percent newspaper opposition. I still worry about world affairs more than domestic problems which includes election," he told Norman Davis, his ambassador in London. "The whole European panorama is fundamentally blacker than at any time in your life time or mine," he wrote his ambassador in France. He feared they might be in "the last days of the period of peace before a long chaos." He worried that some day soon Europe would erupt in "a major explosion." Although there were those who remained optimistic, confident that the horrors of the Great War would deter the powers from entering into another conflict, Roosevelt did not share their belief. "The armaments race means bankruptcy or war," he said, "— there is no possible out from that statement."

In the meantime, he hoped to persuade Congress to revise the neutrality law, which was about to expire. He urged a restoration of his power to distinguish between aggressors and victims of aggression in denying war implements to belligerents. But Roosevelt's proposal provoked an isolationist outcry and a counterproposal denying the White House any say in when and how embargoes would be applied. The clash of opinions led to a quick deadlock in the House and Senate and persuaded Roosevelt to accept a compromise that extended the existing law for sixteen months until April 1937. Undersecretary of State William Phillips said, "Out of the mountain of discussion and turmoil has come, in fact, a mouse." When the Italian campaign ended predictably in Ethiopian defeat in mid-1936, Roosevelt could only privately lament American passivity and its implications for responding to future attacks abroad.

German aggression particularly worried him. Although a member of the U.S. Olympic committee sent Roosevelt a laudatory note about Hitler after a 1936 interview with him during the games, it did not alter Roosevelt's negative impressions. On March 8, the day after Hitler had overturned the Versailles peace agreement and the Locarno Treaty of 1925 reaffirming Versailles by sending German troops to reoccupy the demilitarized Rhineland, Roosevelt confided to Daisy, "The

Tragedy — the deepest part of it — is that a nation's words and signatures are no longer good — if France had a leader whom the nation would follow their only course would be to occupy all Germany up to the Rhine — no further — They can do it today — in another year or two Germany will be stronger than they are — & the world cannot trust a fully rearmed Germany to stay at peace." More immediately, he did not trust the opinion of "my official people," who assured him that "there is no danger of actual war[.] I always remember their saying all the same things in July '14." He told Dodd in Berlin, "In those days I believed the experts. Today I have my tongue in my cheek. This does not mean I have become cynical; but as President I have to be ready just like a Fire Department!" With Hitler tempering his action with a proposal for a European nonaggression pact, Roosevelt added: "If in the days to come the absolutely unpredictable events should . . . get to the point where a gesture, an offer or a formal statement by me would, in your judgment, make for peace, be sure to send me immediate word. But the peace must be not only peace with justice but the kind of peace which will endure without threat for more than a week or two."

In the meantime, Roosevelt focused on domestic affairs. Escaping Washington at the end of March for a trip to central Florida, where he received an honorary degree from Rollins, the state's oldest college, Roosevelt told Daisy, "I sometimes think that each time I get a new degree I know less — Perhaps Doctorates are merely a symptom of an inquiring and receptive nature." He then took a train to the coast for a stay in the Bahamas. On the way, he met with General Johnson Hapgood, who had been dismissed from his post in Texas for describing WPA spending as "stage money" that was easier to get than appropriations for Army supplies. Although Roosevelt reinstated him in response to Republican complaints that he was "muzzling dissent," Roosevelt privately described him as "an awful bumptious unbalanced idiot who should *never* have been a general — perhaps a South Carolina Congressman — not even a Senator."

After he returned to the White House in April, he complained to Daisy, whom he described as "MM, My Margaret," "What a week — why did I come back — why this endless task — why run again — why see the endless streams of people — why the damned old basket of mail which is either full & hanging over my head or just emptied and ready to be filled?" He also told Daisy, "I sometimes feel in Washington like murdering some of my official family — they want to 'grab' or 'bite' or ridicule."

Ickes was "struck with the change in [Roosevelt's] appearance . . . particularly as compared with the way he looked when he was sworn in on March 4, 1933. He looks many years older and his face looked drawn and tired. Moreover, he seems to be much more nervous than formerly." In October, after several weeks campaigning for reelection, Roosevelt told Ickes that he was "standing the campaign well," though he did concede that he had gotten "all worked up so that he could not sleep for a week."

During that period Roosevelt gave an interview to *New York Times* journalist Anne O'Hare McCormick in which he managed to create the entirely different impression of a man seemingly unscathed by his time in office: "He is a little heavier, a shade grayer; otherwise he looks harder and in better health than on the day of his inauguration." Despite "four grilling years since the last campaign" his eyes were "as keen, curious, friendly and impenetrable as ever." It was a tribute to his acting skills that he could present himself so convincingly to a reporter as well, robust, and ready for another campaign. After almost four years in office, Roosevelt had managed to turn the controversial issue of his health into an asset. In William Leuchtenburg's words, he wore his disability "with a wonderfully nonchalant air. . . . Indeed, so vigorous did he seem that most Americans never knew he remained a cripple in a wheelchair. Frequently, in fact, writers gave the impression that Roosevelt had fully conquered his infirmity." The country, in turn, was able to view him as capable of leading it to a recovery comparable to his own return to health. In Press Secretary Steve Early's judgment, Roosevelt's affliction had had a huge positive influence on his political career. Before the polio, Early dismissed him as a lightweight who had cruised through his 1920 vice-presidential campaign. The illness, however, had turned Roosevelt into a serious and informed student of politics.

Roosevelt and Eleanor were especially distressed at this time due to the death of Louis Howe on April 18. Although he had been ill for quite a while, he remained active in politics until he passed away, helping to organize the 1936 campaign. He developed A Good Neighbor League to work with independents supporting Roosevelt as well as plans for drawing in businessmen, speech material, the writing and distribution of pamphlets, and radio promotion. His contributions had been made in the midst of severe physical suffering. "While we all feel a sense of great personal loss," Roosevelt said after Howe died, "we know that for him it must be a blessed release." Howe's passing not only left a gap in Roosevelt's inner political circle but also added to the strains in relations between Franklin and Eleanor. He had been unique in being able to be candidly honest to both of them. As Blanche Wiesen Cook wrote, he "was the one friend who had consistently served their partnership . . . no one else spoke the kind of blunt truth to power they both relied upon." He "considered ER essential to FDR's success," and "once on their own, ER and FDR began to fly apart." When differences erupted between them, Howe, more often than not, had sided with Eleanor and persuaded Franklin to see the wisdom in her pleadings on behalf of liberal causes. Howe never minced words, going so far as to tell Roosevelt directly when he felt the president was being an "idiot," "damned fool," or "stupid." Howe's passing deprived them of a mediator who often settled differences between them in a productive way. His absence would open the way to political blunders by Roosevelt that Howe might have been able to prevent.

In the spring of 1936, for all the confirmation that he enjoyed strong election prospects, recent Supreme Court decisions had convinced him that the New Deal was in jeopardy, and that even if he did win a second term, his administration would fall short in its domestic goals. At a December 27, 1935, cabinet meeting, Roosevelt, recalling the

Court's ruling in the Schechter case the previous May, had predicted that "all of the New Deal bills will be declared unconstitutional by the Supreme Court. This will mean that everything that this Administration has done of any moment will be nullified." Roosevelt then added that "if all the New Deal legislation is thrown out, there will be marching farmers and marching miners and marching workingmen throughout the land."

On January 6, when the Court had ruled by six to three that the AAA exceeded the government's authority to manage agricultural production and specifically declared the use of its taxing powers to transfer money from one group to another beyond what the Constitution allowed, it seemed to confirm Roosevelt's fears about the collapse of the New Deal. Conservatives were overjoyed at the prospect of the program's demise. "Constitutionalism" had triumphed over "Hitlerism," the *Chicago Tribune* declared, while the *Philadelphia Inquirer* called the decision the reemergence of "plain old fashioned Americanism." James McReynolds, the most conservative justice on the Court, said gleefully, "The New Deal is on the rocks." Arthur Krock saw the Court's ruling as "so broad that few New Deal acts before the Court now seem to have any chance of being upheld." Conservative columnist Mark Sullivan believed that the New Deal was "to America what the early phase of Nazism was to Germany" and predicted that unless Roosevelt and his reach for power were reined in, 1936 could mark the country's last presidential election. The Republican National Committee echoed Sullivan's warning and announced that the country was facing its worst crisis since the Civil War. Unless Roosevelt was ousted in 1936, America would become "a socialistic state honey-combed with waste and extravagance and ruled by a dictatorship that mocks at the rights of the States and the liberty of the citizen."

Angry liberals in Iowa, whom the conservative press called "Bolshevistic hoodlums," reacted to the Court's decision by burning cardboard images of the six justices who had voted on the ruling. The dissenting jurists, led by Harlan Fiske Stone, slammed the majority as out of control and usurping presidential and congressional power. Others complained that a politicized Court was operating as a "judicial dictatorship." The dean of the University of Wisconsin Law School wondered whether the government still had the capacity to govern, noting that "Our national problems appear to have outrun our constitutional capacity to deal with them."

As for Roosevelt, he initially viewed the Court's ruling as a compelling campaign issue, for if the farm economy should suffer a downturn in the coming months, it would encourage negative feelings from voters toward the justices. "If the Court does send the AAA flying like the NRA," Roosevelt had predicted before the decision, "there might even be a revolution." But he was reluctant to mount a direct attack on the judiciary and so publicly maintained a detached attitude on its decision. In response to reporters' questions at a press conference on January 7, he said only that he was still studying the majority and minority opinions. In any case, the Department of Agriculture countered the reduced payments made to farmers as a result of the Court's decision with a program under a Soil Conservation Act to pay them for "taking land out of soil-depleting crops and putting it into soil-conserving crops." This was simply an alternative method for reimbursing farmers who had reduced production of wheat, corn, cotton, and tobacco, the surplus crops AAA had been most determined to control. The maneuver incensed conservatives, who complained that it was nothing other than a political ploy to win votes in the coming election.

Despite his public posture, Roosevelt told the cabinet at the end of January that the Supreme Court was "dictating what it believed should be the social philosophy of the nation, without reference either to the law or the Constitution." After that meeting, Ickes said, "It is plain to see from what the President said today . . . that he is not at all averse to the Supreme Court declaring one New Deal statute after another unconstitutional. . . . He believes that the Court will find itself pretty far out on a limb before it is through with it and that a real issue will be joined on which he can go to the country." Ickes thought that the country would eventually have to confront the question of whether America was comfortable with "a judicial tyranny."

Roosevelt believed that in time historians would look back on the Court's decision as at odds with current conditions, which required the president and Congress to regulate commerce and agriculture. He viewed their conflict as a contest for control of public policy and complained privately that "nine appointed members of the Supreme Court" were imposing their "private, social philosophy on the country." He saw three possible means of reining in the judiciary: Packing the Court by adding liberal justices, which he initially rejected as "a distasteful idea"; amending the Constitution to limit the Court's powers; or amending the Constitution to give Congress the wherewithal to overturn Court rulings.

When Roosevelt finally commented on the Court at a press conference in June, he said that it had put the country in a "no-man's land where no Government — state or federal — can function." When a reporter asked, "How can you meet that situation?" Roosevelt answered, "I think that is about all there is to say on it." Still, he could not let the political attacks go unchallenged.

In a speech on January 8 honoring Andrew Jackson, he observed that the same issue that had confronted Jackson over a hundred years earlier beset the nation now: "The right of the average man and woman to lead a finer, a better and a happier life." To disarm any assertions that he was playing partisan politics, he added that his remarks applied to every citizen, regardless of political affiliation, as he sought to counter what he regarded as the distorted attacks of his opponents with a plea for national unity in a struggle to restore prosperity and traditional freedoms. Nonetheless, it was clear to commentators that he was invoking Jackson's legacy in a fight for "social justice" or what he called "his many battles to protect the people against autocratic or oligarchic aggression." Jackson's enemies had pursued him with "relentless hatred," Roosevelt said. ". . . But the people of his day were not deceived. They loved him for the enemies he had made." Drawing an unmistakable parallel, Roosevelt declared, "An overwhelming proportion of the material power of the Nation was arrayed against him. The great media for the dissemination of information and the molding of public opinion fought him. . . . Musty reaction disapproved him. Hollow and outworn traditionalism shook a trembling finger at him. It seemed sometimes that all were against him — all but the people of the United States." History was repeating itself, Roosevelt observed, as in Jackson's day, the government was proving itself dedicated to "the recovery and well-being" of the citizenry. Like Jackson, he was intent on the preservation of popular government and the path to that noble objective depended on truth telling — a recounting of the facts hidden behind "the smoke screen of charges and countercharges."

Roosevelt's January State of the Union and Jackson Day speeches were opening salvos in the 1936 election campaign. Al Smith set a nasty tone for the contest with a January 25 dinner speech before American Liberty League supporters at Washington's Mayflower Hotel. The audience, the *New York Times* said, represented "a large portion of the capital wealth of the country." Smith regaled them for over an hour with an attack on Roosevelt and the New Deal that exceeded any sense of proportion. Roosevelt, he said, had abandoned the "fresh air of free America" for "the foul air of communistic Russia." While the speech may have thrilled the assembled titans of business and corporate America, it opened Smith and his allies to ridicule. Senate Majority Leader Joe Robinson snidely replied in a radio talk, "It was the swellest party ever given by the du Ponts." Smith was now the "unhappy warrior," who had abandoned Third Avenue for Park Avenue. Roosevelt told Daisy that he thought Al had done "himself little good . . . but it is a queer thing that I can't hate him in spite of the things he has said & done." After listening to Al's speech, Franklin had diverted himself by staying up until 1:30 in the morning playing poker.

Daisy thought it was a good thing that Franklin couldn't bring himself to get angry at Smith, but she thought that he was one of the many people in the country who had "cataracts over their minds." Franklin hoped she would "not worry about all the horrid and unnecessary things of this political year. You are so right about them — but *we* must bear with them & while we try not to add to them still we must get the truth brought out — And if we carry on and lose at least we will have tried honorably — And there are lots & lots of other thrilling things to do in this life." Losing the White House, however, would have been a terrible psychological blow to him. He talked bravely about an alternative life, and at the age of fifty-six he was anything but ready to retire to Hyde Park and collect stamps. The presidency had enlarged his world beyond any imaginable work he could perform.

For all his talk of restraint, Roosevelt enjoyed political combat and was eager to give as good as he got or strike notes that would throw his opponents on the defensive and win votes. He found additional reason to hit hard at his political enemies in response to their ugly assault on him. Daisy told him of a conversation with a "Wall Street . . . Bankers Group" gentleman who "says it was incredible to hear those men, who are our 'best people,' educated, charming socially, etc., saying the most awful personal things against F.D.R., the kind of things you expect from a slum dweller who has *no* education!" He took special satisfaction from Daisy's report of "one of those boys on the street, who rush and wipe off your car when there's a red light," who said, "There's no one like President Roosevelt — He's the *first* one who has ever given a thought to people like me." However thick-skinned he was about the personal attacks on him as a radical "traitor to his class" aiming to overthrow traditional institutions, he saw the coming election as a battle between self-satisfied plutocrats and progressive leaders fighting to humanize the country's industrial system. In his speech at Rollins College, he had said that "every great benefit to the human race . . . has been bitterly fought in every stage leading up to its final acceptance." As David Kennedy points out, Roosevelt's objective was not only economic recovery but also "lasting social reform and durable political realignment."

Because he was anticipating a campaign that pitted the have-nots he favored against the haves, Roosevelt asked some of his wealthy ambassadors, including William Bullitt in Moscow, Anthony J. Drexel Biddle in Oslo, Robert Bingham in London, John Cudahy in Warsaw, Breckinridge Long in Rome, Ruth Bryan Owens in Copenhagen, and Jesse Straus in Paris, to resign and return home, where they would speak out on his behalf, demonstrating that some well-off Americans eagerly supported his reelection. The temporary absence of these ambassadors from their posts was also intended to allay isolationist fears of involvement in Europe's rising tensions. As Roosevelt told Jim Farley, these diplomats "could bring out forcefully the fact that this country is a peaceful nation and that all others in North and South America are living together in a peaceful manner, while the governments in Europe are crumbling. They could go on to say these governments are looking to this country as the savior of the world." Roosevelt thought this tactic "could be most effective."

Joseph P. Kennedy and Tom Watson, IBM's chief executive, were also on display as wealthy businessmen who were in favor of Roosevelt's return to the White House. Kennedy "bore the principal responsibility for interpreting the President's purposes to the business community." He organized dinner meetings that made the case for Franklin, published a book titled *I Am for Roosevelt,* and at the height of the campaign gave a nationwide radio talk aimed at businessmen. In 1938, after turning down an appointment as secretary of commerce, he would be rewarded with the job he preferred, as the first Irish American ambassador to Great Britain.

Roosevelt greatly valued having Kennedy's and Watson's support in the campaign, which represented one valuable counter to serious concerns about unbalanced budgets and national debt. Norman Hapgood, a *Harper's Weekly* editor and a crusading Wilsonian liberal, had advised Roosevelt that he would win a big victory in November "if there is not a big scare about solvency." The Hearst press, meanwhile, was beating the drum about the need for an "economizer and budget balancer" in the White House. Tom Watson urged Roosevelt to control the national debt by encouraging "self-liquidating projects" and the issuance of bonds to pay the two-billion-dollar outlay for veterans' bonus payments approved by Congress in 1936. Roosevelt's veto of the bonus bill had given him little coverage from complaints about reckless federal debt, as the congressional override left a yawning hole in the federal budget that conservatives blamed on the president. Joe Kennedy's book was primarily a response to these "Anti-Spenders," but dissatisfaction with the country's debt ran so high that "Kennedy could not even scare up a quorum of businessmen for the businessmen's dinners." He complained that "friends in the business and financial world have told me . . . I have had my last job from anyone in the business world."

The complaints about his administration's overspending worried and bothered Roosevelt. During the campaign, he sarcastically told Joe Robinson, "I am going . . . to Wilmington, Delaware, just to assure myself that the du Ponts are not broke." He instructed Henry Morgenthau and Aubrey Williams to make lists of material assets that the government had acquired as a result of New Deal programs and to promote understanding that "the Federal Relief program had prevented a further burden upon . . . County and State taxes."

But Roosevelt needed more dramatic evidence of his determination to bring the federal budget into greater balance, and so in March of 1936 he proposed a tax on undistributed corporate profits. The bill had three advantages: It would reduce deficits; it would make his harshest business critics pay down the debt about which they were complaining; and it would further raise Roosevelt's standing with the left, which viewed corporate chiefs as posturing in their concern about the national well-being. At the worst, this legislation would encourage corporations to invest their surplus funds in new facilities, with the expenditures promoting additional economic expansion, or to distribute their profits to shareholders, who would have to pay taxes on their capital gains. The proposal provoked a further outcry from the business community, but Roosevelt was able to silence them by arguing for its effectiveness in reducing the national debt. Although Roosevelt predicted that the bill would generate $1.3 billion, its final version yielded only about 60 percent of that — $785 million. Still, It scored political points for the president, who described it as a victory.

As he moved into the 1936 election campaign, Roosevelt's only political certainty was his nomination. In 1912, even so unpopular a sitting president as William Howard Taft had been able to overcome a challenge from Theodore Roosevelt, a very popular ex-president, and any conservative Democrats, like Al Smith, had not the slightest chance of unseating someone as admired as Franklin. As for dissenters like Father Coughlin and Francis Townsend, any hope they had of affecting the election's outcome was through a third party. Neither wanted any part of the Republicans, who offered nothing but reaction. The Towndsenites considered Roosevelt to be too tied up with conservative interests ever to bring them to heel. As one complained, "If only he [FDR] would spend as much time looking after the welfare of the people as he does playing on his yacht, he might be of some help." They argued that Roosevelt's Social Security law was a watered-down version of the Townsend plan: It took current income from workers, promised nothing to the elderly for years, and ignored the needs of millions on the fringes. If it should collapse, it would leave people who had paid into the system with nothing.

When Democrats and Republicans in the House decided that Townsend posed a sufficient political threat to some of their members, they launched a congressional investigation of his organization. Gerald Smith joined Townsend in declaring this a witch hunt; promised to bring Huey Long's Share the Wealth clubs, whose support he had inherited, to Townsend's side; and urged him to unite in establishing a third party. The key to such a development, however, rested with Father Coughlin and his organization, the National Union for Social Justice.

Coughlin had been promoting Congressman William Lemke of North Dakota, an advocate of the farmer and proponent of an $8 billion greenback farm-refinancing plan, as an alternative for the White House, so he, Townsend, and Smith joined forces and declared themselves in favor of a Lemke candidacy, sponsored by the Union Party. The fifty-eight-year-old Lemke was a prairie state populist with a Yale law degree and a record of having supported the New Deal, especially its measures serving the needs of North Dakota farmers. But when Roosevelt rejected a Lemke-sponsored law to save farmers from bank foreclosures, Lemke broke with him as a "bewildered" puppet of undefined interests. It was a better description of Lemke himself. Physically unremarkable, with a pockmarked face and a disheveled appearance, Lemke had a high-pitched voice with which he delivered interminable speeches citing questionable statistics, which appealed to few outside of his home-state constituents.

Since they regarded Roosevelt and the Republicans as little more than tools of Wall Street money changers and the Roosevelt presidency as having produced little more than "ruin," the Union Party group called for an end to Roosevelt's communistic experiment and a true American administration devoted to the interests of the people. Lemke himself said, "I do not charge that the President of this nation is a Communist, but I do charge that [Earl] Browder [Communist Party head], [David] Dubinsky [head of the International Ladies Garment Workers Union, ILGWU], and other Communist leaders have laid their cuckoo eggs in his Democratic nest and that he is hatching them." No one in the Union Party could explain how the president could be the tool of Wall Street while also advancing Communist ideas, but its anti-Roosevelt appeal rested not on logic but on raw emotion and a hunger for power.

Roosevelt dismissed Lemke as the author of some "wild legislation" that could wreck the recovery, and the head of a ticket that wouldn't "cut into our vote any more than it will into the Republican vote." Lemke indeed had no chance of winning a national contest or even commanding any electoral votes, and was further undermined by personality clashes between Coughlin, Townsend, and Smith and conflicts over the party's programs. "When it comes to a showdown," Roosevelt said, "these fellows cannot all lie in the same bed and will fight among themselves with almost absolute certainty," which, in fact, they did. Townsend was no match for Coughlin and Smith as a firebrand, and each of them refused to be overshadowed by the other. Coughlin made every effort to keep Smith off the platform when he spoke, and when he did have to cede center stage to Smith, he would pretend to fall asleep while Smith spoke.

Although Coughlin, Townsend, and Smith did retain the loyalty of their devoted followers, none of them was a match for Roosevelt on the campaign trail or was able to propose a general program that could serve as a viable alternative to the New Deal. H. L. Mencken described Smith's speeches as "a magnificent amalgam of each and every American species of rabble-rousing, with embellishments borrowed from the Algonquin Indians and the Cossacks of the Don," but when he finished "no one could remember what he said." As for Coughlin, he descended into attacks on Jews as closet communists, denounced international bankers as driven by communistic tendencies, declared Roosevelt "anti-God" and "the dumbest man ever to occupy the White House," and failed even to mention Lemke in speeches supposedly in favor of his election. When voters were asked if Father Coughlin's endorsement of a candidate would make a difference in their decision at the polls, only 7 percent said it would do so, while 20 percent said it would turn them against the candidate, and 73 percent said it would make no difference. Dr. Townsend fared no better in the poll: 68 percent declared their indifference to anyone Townsend preferred. In largely ignoring Lemke and the Union Party, Roosevelt effectively consigned them to the minor role a third party had usually played in recent presidential elections.

Roosevelt's focus needed to be on the Republican candidate, who would be the only one with any hope of unseating him. His popularity posed a great challenge to the G.O.P. Could they find a nominee who was capable of turning majority opinion away from the president? Progressive

Republicans were convinced that a victory in 1936 was out of reach unless they stole some of Roosevelt's thunder. The key to success was to imitate what Wilson had done after the 1912 election: As president, he had appropriated much of TR's New Nationalism. The Republican Party now had to jettison its image as the preserve of "private moneybags" and align itself with some of the New Deal ideas about helping the common man with government programs. As Idaho senator William Borah argued, offering the people the homilies of the Founding Fathers and the Constitution was a prescription for failure, as "People can't eat the Constitution." H. L. Mencken urged Republicans to attack Roosevelt as the ultimate opportunist: "If he became convinced tomorrow that coming out for cannibalism would get him votes," Mencken wrote, ". . . he would begin fattening a missionary in the White House backyard."

Herbert Hoover, however, rejected the cry for a progressive new party outlook and returned to the campaign trail in 1935 with a reiteration of his 1932 messages and an attack on the New Deal. He depicted Roosevelt's programs as warmed-over Soviet formulas, declaring that if the White House ran out of letters for its alphabet agencies, it could turn to the Russian language with its thirty-four letters. He denounced Roosevelt's reforms as the road to federal regimentation, but his call for individualism, local control, and balanced budgets were all familiar antidotes to the president's activism. Republican progressives were certain that another Hoover candidacy would only guarantee a decisive defeat. "His embrace, they believed, meant political death."

There was no question that the Republicans

faced an uphill battle: 89 percent of the public favored government old-age pensions for the needy, and by a 56 to 44 percent margin, Americans preferred concentrated power in Washington rather than in state capitals. In December 1935, a Gallup sampling of voter opinion on the presidential race identified between twenty-seven and thirty "definitely Democratic states" and only between six and eight "definitely Republican" ones. Although many Americans shared some of Hoover's concerns about New Deal policies — 60 percent of participants in one poll considered expenditures by the government for relief and recovery as excessive, 70 percent thought it necessary to start balancing the budget and reducing the national debt, and 73 percent opposed currency inflation as a cure for the Depression — Hoover showed little strength in assessments of his potential candidacy. At the end of 1935 and in early 1936, when pitted against seven other Republican hopefuls, including Governor Alf Landon of Kansas and Senator William Borah of Idaho, Hoover managed to win only 12 to 17 percent of the vote. He could not command a top finish in any region of the country.

The clear choice of most Republicans was the forty-eight-year-old Alf Landon, the only proven vote-getter in the Republican camp. A successful businessman who had made a small fortune in the oil and gas industry, he had taken the governorship of Kansas from a Democratic incumbent in 1932, a decisive Democratic year, and in 1934, when he was reelected, he was the only Republican in the country to win a statewide contest. A series of Gallup straw polls in the first three months of 1936 made Landon, with 55 percent backing, the odds-on favorite for his party's presidential nomination. A Progressive who had supported TR's candidacy in 1912, Landon was a fiscal conservative who had won public approval by balancing his state's budget while also reducing taxes. He enjoyed the support of Republicans who opposed Hoover's unqualified opposition to New Deal policies. Landon preached a form of "compassionate conservatism," including a Social Security law that was under state control, but included benefits for the needy who had been left out of Roosevelt's measure. In June, the Republican convention meeting in Cleveland gave him a first-ballot nomination and made Frank Knox, the publisher of the *Chicago Daily News* and another TR progressive, his running mate.

Landon was no match, however, for Roosevelt as a national political candidate. For two months after winning the nomination, he largely disappeared from public view. Conservative columnist Westbrook Pegler sarcastically urged anyone with information on the whereabouts of the missing governor to inform the Republican National Committee. In Kenneth Davis's description, Landon was a thoroughly decent "mild-mannered small-town Middle-American businessman" notable for his bland appearance and demeanor.

Harold Ickes thought Landon would have done better to stay in Topeka, Kansas, sitting on his front porch than to speak to audiences on the campaign trail or over the radio. Ickes described listening to a national broadcast of Landon's speech accepting his nomination as being comparable to one delivered by a college freshman or sophomore. "The effect was very drab," Ickes recorded in his diary. "There was no vigor or spirit or inspiration at any point. . . . If this is the best that Landon can do, the Democratic Campaign Committee ought to spend all the money it can raise to send him out to make speeches." A Kansas acquaintance of Landon's told Ickes that Landon was "a slow thinker" who had "only about one good speech in him every three months." Moreover, in Ickes's view, he was "mediocre in ability and on every account a poor man to put in charge of the affairs of the nation at this time." Ickes wanted the president to let him and others go after Landon as lacking the experience to be an effective president. He would be another Harding, Ickes said, who would be managed by the "big interests."

Roosevelt believed it would be a mistake to attack Landon, and instructed Ickes not to make public comments about him. When Jim Farley derisively described him in public as "a typical prairie state" governor, it touched off a heated response from his supporters, including comparisons to Lincoln as fitting that description. Roosevelt told Farley: "I thought we had decided that any reference to Landon or any other Republican candidate was inadvisable." Coming from a New York Irish Catholic, Farley's comment seemed certain to revive the sort of divide in the country that had plagued Democrats in the 1920s.

"There's one issue in this campaign," Roosevelt told Ray Moley. "It's myself and people must be either for me or against me." Moley viewed the president's statement as a demonstration of his "megalomania." To be sure, it reflected the grandiosity of someone who had risen from the ashes of his disability to win the ultimate political prize. But Roosevelt himself would have acknowledged that, in the heat of the moment while arguing with Moley (whose conservative predilections had led him to break with the president), he was overstating his own case. Voters would cast ballots not only for someone they liked or considered most sympathetic to their needs, but also for someone who had put actual reforms in place that addressed their economic problems and seemed most likely to continue fighting for their welfare in the next four years.

Roosevelt's acceptance speech at the Democratic convention in Philadelphia in June was a response to what he saw as public support for the New Deal. Since there was no question that he would receive the nomination, the focus of the convention was the substance of Roosevelt's remarks defending his first-term record and his intention to sustain and expand upon welfare reforms in the following four years. On his way to the platform in Franklin Field, where one hundred thousand people had gathered to hear him, Roosevelt was reminded of his vulnerability and limitations when one of his leg braces opened and he tumbled. A Secret Service agent broke his fall, but he still hit the ground, and the pages of his speech went flying. He recalled it as "the most frightful five minutes of my life."

Quickly collecting himself, he went on to deliver one of the memorable speeches of his presidency. He began not on a partisan note but on one of national unity by thanking all Americans for their fortitude in weathering the Depression. "The rescue," he said, "was not a mere party task. It was the concern of all of us. . . . We rose together, rallied our energies together . . . and together survived." Invoking the fight for freedom against

British tyranny by the nation's founders, he declared that modern developments had rekindled a battle against an "industrial dictatorship" by the "economic royalists" of our day. "They created a new despotism" and, echoing the complaint of Senator Alben Barkley, the convention's keynote speaker, who had blasted the Supreme Court's assault on the New Deal, Roosevelt said that the attack on his reforms had been "wrapped in the robes of judicial sanction."

The only recourse against this "economic tyranny" he saw was "the organized power of government. . . . These economic royalists complain that we seek to overthrow the institutions of America. What they really complain of is that we seek to take away their power. . . . They seek to hide behind the flag and the Constitution," but these were symbols of democracy and freedom that oppose a dictatorship by the overprivileged. And this had been the business of his administration: "Governments can err, presidents do make mistakes," he admitted, but "better the occasional faults of a government that lives in a spirit of charity than the consistent omissions of a government frozen in the ice of its own indifference. There is a mysterious cycle in human events," he concluded. "To some generations much is given. Of other generations much is expected. This generation of Americans has a rendezvous with destiny." Adding a cautionary note about the victory of tyrannies abroad, he asserted that "here in America we are waging a great and successful war . . . for the survival of democracy." Invoking Lincoln, he ended: "We are fighting to save a great and precious form of government for ourselves and for the world."

The speech was an appeal to America's better angels as well as a fine exercise in campaign rhetoric. But it was also a study in contradictions. Beginning with a call for national unity, or at least a bow toward bipartisanship by thanking all Americans for pulling together to overcome the economic crisis, he focused the rest of the speech on the administration's clash with the country's moneyed selfish interests. He vilified economic royalists as enemies of democracy, exploiting the current animus toward corporate chiefs, who were being blamed for the Depression. Since he himself was constantly criticized as being a radical or a closet communist intent on destroying free enterprise, he considered it only fair game to attack business interests as heirs to eighteenth-century British royalists trying to reimpose tyranny on Americans.

Although Roosevelt told Jim Farley, "I think we ought to conduct a very aggressive campaign," and Farley remembered their launching the drive for votes "at the first of the year and never let up until the polls closed ten months later," in fact, Roosevelt believed it wisest to begin slowly. In mid-July, two weeks after his nomination, he underscored his political neutrality by taking a two-week fishing holiday off New England. "I expect to have a campaignless August and September," he said to Josephus Daniels. He thought that the Republicans, who were already on the attack, were "shooting off all their ammunition too soon and that people will be rather sick of their same old story by the end of September." During those months, he planned to travel around the country inspecting flood areas of the Connecticut Valley, Pennsylvania, and western New York as well the drought areas of the Dakotas, ending with a trip down the Mississippi, where he would give "short talks on the flood problems, the drought problem, the soil erosion problem, etc., etc." In October, he would give four or five major political speeches. His aim was to appear presidential by emphasizing not the campaign but his commitment to helping those in need. Moreover, rather than turn the contest into a national conflict between liberals and conservatives, he tried to put a unifying face on his appeal. He told Farley to invite a Catholic priest, a Baptist minster, a Presbyterian minister, an Episcopalian minister, and a rabbi to join the campaign. (When Farley asked, "What about the Methodists?" Roosevelt instructed him to replace the Episcopalian with a representative of the more numerous Methodists.)

Although Roosevelt believed that an early poll showing him and Landon in a close race was "doctored" and a ploy "to indicate a tight race," his closest aides were more concerned and feared he was being much too passive. As Ickes told Farley, "We are in grave danger of losing the election. . . . Landon's supporters are taking full advantage of a wonderful opportunity to continue to build him up while we do absolutely nothing. . . . Meanwhile, the President smiles and sails and fishes and the rest of us worry and fume." Ickes worried that the president was "too sure of himself, too certain of his own judgment," and Steve Early only reinforced his apprehension by pointing out that "there were no campaign plans and no budget."

Eleanor was "aghast and angry" at the president's nonchalant attitude. She called the Democratic National Committee's "publicity . . . a disgrace to their organization!" She saw Landon as embarked on a crusade relying on advertisers and radio scriptwriters. She sent the president an eight-point memo asking who was in charge of publicity, speechwriting, radio talks, research, fact-checking Landon's claims, with particular attention to "doubtful and Republican states." She believed that Franklin's reelection "depended on the votes of blacks, Southern race radicals, youth, and the left-labor coalition" and was delighted when Farley answered her queries with a ten-page single-spaced reply.

When polls in August and September showed Roosevelt ahead by between four and five points and with a lead of only seventeen electoral votes, Landon began campaigning aggressively. He criticized not Roosevelt himself but the fumbling nature of the New Deal, which had failed "to unshackle initiative and free the spirit of American enterprise." Landon's advisers believed that his qualities as an "everyday American" would contrast favorably with Roosevelt's "evasiveness" and "showmanship." They considered Landon's lack of polished delivery in speeches to be a great asset and urged him to make as many personal appearances as possible. Roosevelt himself thought that Landon would be best served by separating himself from the Republican Party's fat cats, supporting Social Security and work relief, and attacking New Deal inefficiency, especially in the WPA. While Landon spoke with restraint and maintained a respectful attitude toward the president, others in his campaign, led by Knox, accused Roosevelt of "leading us toward Moscow" and the "makings of a dictatorship." Landon did not help himself, however, when he declared,

"Wherever I have gone in this country, I have found Americans."

Despite a prediction by columnist Arthur Krock that Landon would do much better than Hoover had in 1932, by the end of the campaign Landon felt compelled to echo his campaign staff's charges that Roosevelt's stewardship had brought the republic to "the verge of collapse." Yet at the same time he decried Roosevelt's radicalism, he promised government benefits to farmers, the elderly, and numerous other groups, creating confusion about what his actual program as president would be. The venerable Kansas newspaper editor William Allen White wrote that the campaign had turned into a "nightmare. It had neither logical sequence in its conception and execution nor any touch of reality."

Despite Landon's faltering, Roosevelt was troubled by what he had begun to see as "a German parallel" in how the election was being covered in the media. "If the Republicans could win or make enormous gains, it would prove that an 85 percent control of the Press and a very definite campaign of misinformation can be effective here just as it was in the early days of the Hitler rise to power," he told Dodd in Berlin. "Democracy is verily on trial." He thought the press should "confine itself to the actual facts in its news" columns and have the freedom to say whatever it chose to in its editorials. He was especially worried about the "close States," where so "hostile" a press could tip them to Landon. At the same time, he said nothing about the Federal Communication Commission (FCC), which he had established in 1934 and was busy handing out radio licenses to Democrats. He judged the news stories on the radio that favored him as striking a balance with the Republican print media. In a Fireside Chat almost a year after the election, Roosevelt said, "Five years of fierce discussion and debate, five years of information through the radio and the motion picture have taken the whole nation to school in the nation's business." Nor would he comment publicly in 1936 on what he thought of his critics, such as the syndicated columnist Mark Sullivan, who had added his voice to those accusing Roosevelt of bringing Nazism to the United States: "I hate Mark Sullivan because he is such a solemn patronizing idiot," Franklin confided to Daisy in November.

While Roosevelt continued to shun an active speaking campaign until October, he was busy promoting an aggressive role by surrogates between June and September. He was especially eager for progressive senators like Burton K. Wheeler, a Montana Democrat, and George W. Norris, a Nebraska Republican, to support his reelection in their home states as well as in Iowa, Kansas, and Wyoming. "Please beg Senator Wheeler to start speeches key places at once," Roosevelt wrote Farley on September 17. After a national radio talk in which Norris denounced the "bogus cry" of "bolshevism" and "dictatorship" leveled by Republicans against Roosevelt and praised his fight "to put some humanity on our statute books," Roosevelt promised to come to Nebraska in October to support his reelection. Similarly, when progressive Republican James Couzens of Michigan came out for Roosevelt, the president praised his "very deep courage" in leaving himself vulnerable to a defeat, which in fact occurred in a September primary. Other Progressive Republicans, like Hiram Johnson of California and Wisconsin's La Follettes (Governor Phillip and Senator Robert, Jr.), actively spoke out as well for Roosevelt. In the fall of 1936, the *New Republic* found few Progressive Republicans who would say that they were prepared to vote for Landon. Meanwhile, Roosevelt had turned Ickes loose to assault the Republican platform, making appearances in New England and the Middle West, and striking out at Landon in a radio talk Roosevelt praised as "a great Phillipic."

For all Roosevelt's eagerness to minimize his direct role in the campaign, he could not realistically confine himself to behind-the-scenes manipulations until October. On July 17, when Francisco Franco led an Army from Morocco into Spain to topple the Republican government, Roosevelt faced a foreign policy issue that might jeopardize his reelection, or so some in the administration believed. With Franco calling on Hitler and Mussolini to support his Fascist coup and France under Leon Blum's Popular Front government poised to help Madrid, a European war seemed all too likely. Ickes believed that the president needed to "give out a statement pointing to the peace record of my administration and assuring the country that I could not conceive of any circumstances which would make me favor this country intervening in another European war." Ickes thought that if Roosevelt could "impress the country with his sincerity on this issue, it would go a long way toward assuring his reelection." With the president on a fishing holiday until August 10, Hull issued a statement pledging noninterference in Spain's civil strife. Mindful of how important the peace question was for so many Americans, Roosevelt decided to make a speech on August 14 in Chautauqua, New York, a site notable for its famous lectures, which would be certain to command national attention.

Peace was the subject of his talk, he told his audience, "because in the hurly-burly of domestic politics it is important that our people should not overlook problems and issues that lie beyond our borders" and seemed likely to "have a vital influence on the United States of the future." But he hoped that in turn the United States could exert its influence around the world by its example of being a good neighbor to Canada to the north and the Latin republics to the south. "The twenty-one American Republics," Roosevelt said, "are not only living together in friendship and in peace; they are united in their determination so to remain." He looked forward to the day when they "will banish wars forever from this vast portion of the earth." Turning to the principal point of his talk, Roosevelt declared, "We are not isolationist except in so far as we seek to isolate ourselves completely from war." Yet "so long as war exists . . . there will be some danger" of U.S. involvement in a conflict. Echoing the anguish of pacifists everywhere, he added, "I have seen war. . . . I have seen blood running from the wounded. I have seen men coughing out their gassed lungs. I have seen the dead in the mud. I have seen cities destroyed. . . . I have seen children starving. I have seen the agony of mothers and wives. I hate war. . . . I shall pass unnumbered hours, thinking and planning how war may be kept from this Nation." His promise to preserve the peace, and especially to favor peace over profits by bankers and munitions makers, which Senator Nye had targeted in his Senate hearings, was calculated to win votes at home rather than influence events abroad.

Roosevelt underscored his pacifist objectives in a conversation with Arthur Krock that the journalist featured in a *New York Times* column at the end of August. Krock explained that while preserving peace or isolating the United States from a European war was a vital part of any candidate's appeal in 1936, domestic challenges, led by prosperity and protecting Americans from unemployment and economic losses, remained the chief goal. Kentucky senator Alben Barkley had captured the central concern of Americans in June when he said in his keynote address at the Democratic convention, "While anxious farmers ponder their fate, and laboring men scan the heavens for a rainbow of hope, and women and children look in vain for preservation of their lives and health," Republicans, led by Herbert Hoover and five conservative Supreme Court justices, sought to preserve constitutional principles that ignored the human suffering inflicted by the Depression. While Roosevelt supported Barkley's anti-Court rhetoric, he did not want to make the Court a central issue in the campaign, fearing that it would open him to charges of trying to undermine a coequal branch of government with the intent of becoming a dictator.

On September 29, Roosevelt took to the road for a month, beginning in Syracuse, New York, where he spoke to the state Democratic convention. Adopting a presidential posture that he would maintain throughout the remainder of the campaign, he declared his fidelity to "Americanism." Charges of communism hurled at his administration were a red herring that should be entirely and permanently cast aside. Instead, he hoped voters would recall the fact that over the previous four years "starvation was averted, homes and farms were saved, banks were reopened, crop prices rose, and industry revived. . . . The dangerous forces subversive of our form of government was turned aside." The reason the economic crisis had passed without disaster could be found in "the record of what we did." Roosevelt reminded his audience of Hoover's failures to address the crisis. As every wise conservative understood, he ended, "reform if you would preserve. I am that kind of conservative because I am that kind of liberal."

Confident of support in the South and the West, for the next four weeks Roosevelt traveled back and forth across the Midwest and Northeast, areas he believed contained contested states. He made stops in Iowa, Minnesota, Nebraska, Wyoming, Colorado, Kansas, Michigan, Ohio, Rhode Island, Massachusetts, Connecticut, Pennsylvania, and New York, and reached voters everywhere through the radio. His consistent message was that the Republicans were sponsoring the very outworn ideas that had caused the Depression and lacked a plan to restore prosperity. By contrast, his administration had attended to the suffering of millions across the country, who now had a safety net to sustain them. With variations on that theme dictated by the locale in which he spoke, Roosevelt berated the Republicans for their failures and praised all progressive leaders for their receptivity to the humane reforms that were making a difference in people's lives. Everywhere he went, he found enthusiastic audiences excited by his presence and receptive to his reminders of the differences between his conservative opponents and his supporters.

On October 31, in a final campaign speech before boisterous partisans at Madison Square Garden in New York, Roosevelt had to wait for thirteen minutes until the cheering that greeted his appearance subsided before he could begin speaking. He characterized the election as a contest to preserve "the restoration of American democracy" and to extend the "crusade to restore America to its own people." Four years earlier, he reminded his audience, Americans had "sought escape from disintegration and bankruptcy in local affairs." They wanted "protection of their currency, fairer wages, the ending of long hours of toil, the abolition of child labor, the elimination of wildcat speculation." They wanted an end to the misery of "farmers whose acres yielded only bitterness, businessmen whose books were portents of disaster, homeowners who were faced with eviction, and frugal citizens whose savings were insecure." Twelve years of Republican rule had brought the country to a low point at the hands of a "hear-nothing, see-nothing, do-nothing Government." It was a "Government by organized money," which was "just as dangerous as Government by organized mob." And "never before in all our history have these forces been so united against one candidate as they stand today. They are unanimous in their hate for me — and I welcome their hatred. I should like to have it said of my administration," he shouted over the crowd roaring its approval, "that in it the forces of selfishness and of lust for power met their match. I should like to have it said of my second administration that in it these forces met their master." The applause, the *New York Times* reported, washed over Roosevelt in a series of "roars, which rose and fell like the sound of waves pounding in the surf."

Roosevelt remained confident that he would win the election, but whether he could receive a mandate seemed uncertain. On the eve of the vote, the Gallup poll identified between thirty-one and forty states likely to go for Roosevelt and only three to six for Landon; it predicted that Roosevelt would command between 54 and 56 percent of the popular vote. Yet the poll also cited fourteen New England and Midwestern states as undecided. By contrast, the *Literary Digest,* which had a track record of accurately forecasting the 1932 election, predicted a Landon victory with 57 percent of the ballots and thirty-two states. The *New York Times* did not foresee a Landon victory, but it predicted that he would win more than the 59 electoral votes Hoover received in 1932. When a wire service asked William Allen White for comments to be released if Landon won, White replied: "Why waste good telegraph tolls on a possibility so remote?" On election night, Roosevelt remained up past midnight "poring over the figures." For all his own confidence, he did harbor doubts. "What frightened you?" a reporter later asked the president. "Oh, just my well-known conservative tendencies," he answered.

Jim Farley, certain of a decisive victory, told Roosevelt that he would win forty-six states; only Maine and Vermont would remain in the Republican column. Farley had it exactly right. Roosevelt, with slightly more than 60 percent of the popular vote, enjoyed Farley's quip: "As Maine goes, so goes Vermont." Expanded congressional majorities added to Roosevelt's landslide, as the Democrats won 331 of the 420 seats in the House and had a 76 to 20 margin in the Senate.

Despite the angry barrage of rhetoric that enraged conservatives had leveled against him, Roosevelt could look upon his victory as defining another Era of Good Feeling, much like James Monroe's triumph in 1820 when he won all but one electoral vote. Roosevelt's success rested on an outpouring of support not only from the Solid South but from across the country, where farmers, laborers, small businessmen, and urban dwellers — Catholics, Jews, Irish, Italians, Poles, and Russians — voted for a president whose New Deal programs had given them jobs, saved their farms and homes, and promised to protect them from future economic disasters. And for the first time, African Americans, abandoning Lincoln's Republican Party, decisively favored a Democrat, though less because he took a stand against racism across the South than because Mrs. Roosevelt and others in the administration had reached out to help blacks, who suffered more than any other group in the Depression. Eleanor "was the Good Fairy who saw to it that in a world of pressure groups and partisan decisions, the president did not neglect people and causes that had no other voice in places of power." When the Democratic convention and other venues where Roosevelt spoke joined in singing "Happy Days Are Here Again," Americans for the first time in years felt as if there was real meaning to the words.

CHAPTER 9
SECOND-TERM CURSE

His landslide victory initially buoyed Roosevelt and encouraged him to think that it "may have made the German and Italian populace a little envious of democratic methods." He took satisfaction from "the discrediting not only of the Hearst papers, the *Chicago Tribune*, the *New York Herald Tribune*, the New York *Sun*, and the *Boston Herald*, but also of dozens of other smaller papers which aped the others in coloring every news story and crowding their editorials with every known form of misrepresentation." He thought their biased news accounts were "so obviously untrue and unfair that we were helped." "I am beginning to come up for air," he told Josephus Daniels, "after the baptism by total submersion. . . . The other fellow was the one who nearly drowned! Thank the Lord it was not a close vote or even a gain for Brother Landon over what Herbert Hoover got in 1932." If Landon had won "the 120 or 130 votes in the electoral college as most dispassionate observers . . . thought he would, the reactionary element would have used that fact everlastingly during the next two years."

Yet Roosevelt had no illusions about managing a second term, which he knew would include its share of new uncertainties and crises. He privately acknowledged that the "added responsibility on his shoulders," had "humbled" him and compelled "some very heavy thinking" about how to proceed. "It does not help one's *happiness* to think of four years more!" he told Daisy Suckley, two weeks after the election. Even after having successfully negotiated his physical limitations during his first term, he continued to privately lament his immobility, telling Senator George Norris: "George, I am chained to this chair from morning till night. . . . You sit in your chair in your office too, or if something goes wrong or you get irritated or tired, you can get up and walk around. . . . But I can't, I am tied down to this chair day after day, week after week, and month after month. And I can't stand it any longer. I can't go on with it." But he did, and he resolved to use his remaining time in office to achieve the best for the country.

He began doing so by giving an optimistic inaugural speech on January 20, 1937. Although half the country had indicated that it wanted Roosevelt to be more conservative in his second term, he interpreted his landslide as a mandate to strike innovative notes. In its first four years, he noted, his administration had written a novel chapter in the book of self-government: "By using the new materials of social justice, we have undertaken to erect on the old foundations a more enduring structure for the better use of future generations." In short, the expansion of the government's role had not undermined the country's traditional democracy but enhanced it. Still, America was far from a prosperous nation with limited unemployment. Even with its great abundance, one-third of the nation was ill housed, ill clad, and ill nourished. The task before them was not to expand "the abundance of those who have much; it is whether we provide enough for those who have too little. In taking again the oath of office," he declared, ". . . I assume the solemn obligation of leading the American people forward along the road over which they have chosen to advance."

Because the campaign had been principally a referendum on what he had accomplished since 1933, he had said little about what he intended in a second term. Although he did not identify specific programs that would meet the goal of expanding the new order, high on his agenda was consideration of "the problem created for the Nation by the Supreme Court," which he saw blocking the New Deal. "It is a mighty difficult one to solve," he told Joe Patterson, the publisher of the *New York Daily News,* "but one way or another I think it must be faced." Moreover, he believed that the lopsided victory had given him "an absolutely free hand without the danger of being charged with having broken campaign promises." At the same time, however, he did not automatically have license to propose previously undiscussed reforms without provoking some degree of opposition.

Before he could focus on domestic issues, however, he set sail for South America, where he would spend a month recuperating from the campaign, reflecting on how to advance a reform program, and demonstrating that the United States was not indifferent to foreign affairs. Eager to push forward on his Good Neighbor policy and insulate Western Hemisphere nations against threats from a possible European war, Roosevelt had urged the twenty Latin republics to join him

417

in a conference to sustain peace in the region. Argentina offered to host the meeting of American states, which was scheduled to begin on December 1. The journey to Rio de Janeiro, Buenos Aires, and Montevideo on the cruiser *Indianapolis* with his son Jimmy and some White House aides, including Ross McIntire, his physician, took two weeks and gave him "a good rest" and the enjoyment of shipboard hijinks over crossing the equator, where the uninitiated were subpoenaed for trial and initiation into King Neptune's Court.

Along the way, Roosevelt kept in touch with Eleanor and his mother with letters recounting the pleasures of being on the high seas, the sights and sounds of Latin cities, and the warmth and enthusiasm with which "enormous" crowds cheering, tossing flowers, and running alongside his car greeted him. Shouts of "*Viva la democracia!* Viva Roosevelt" upon his arrival in Rio de Janeiro embarrassed Brazil's fifty-four-year-old president Getúlio Vargas, who had come to power by a military coup in 1930 and was setting up a corporatist state like Mussolini's Italy. He whispered to Roosevelt as they drove by the mass of cheering onlookers, "Perhaps you've heard that I am a dictator." With a smile Roosevelt replied, "Perhaps you've heard that I am one, too."

No one received more detailed reports of the journey from Roosevelt than Daisy. He described the rest and relaxation he enjoyed while sunning himself on deck, fishing, sorting stamps, crossing the equator, attending church services, and seeing the sights of Rio, with its "amazing harbor" and the "fantastic" beauty of the surrounding countryside with "great hills lush with tropic trees and flowers." He recounted the "tremendously enthusiastic . . . waving, cheering crowds in Montevideo," highlighted by "a dramatic departure with 75,000 people on the quay."

His letters to Daisy during this time were as notable for their expressions of affection as for their descriptions of the landscape and people: "Why is it that I want to talk about a C[ertain] P[erson] and have to bite my tongue to stop doing it?" he wrote her. ". . . I tell stories to the stars" with messages for her. He looked forward to the time when they "start telling some of those million things we haven't got to yet. . . . Are you still going to take care of him as you always have?" he asked. When Daisy sent him a four-leaf clover, it made for "a happy day," and he placed it within five inches of his heart. He sent her a birthday present, telling her, "If you can't explain it to the family you will have to wear it on your 'undies' — So much for your Puritanical upbringing! Which I nevertheless adore — at the correct time and place! Now will you be good! . . . I must learn Spanish — Why don't you move to W. & learn it with me." As the journey ended, he told her, "It is such a long time since 3 weeks." He arrived back in Washington on a Tuesday — "too late I fear for me to telephone you — but I hope to find a letter awaiting — & I will call you up Wed. eve about 6:30."

During the trip, the sudden death of the fifty-year-old Gus Gennerich, Roosevelt's personal bodyguard dating back to his governorship, cast a pall over the journey. While in Buenos Aires he collapsed aboard ship at a dinner table and died of a heart attack or a cerebral hemorrhage within a minute and a half after falling unconscious. The hemorrhage may have been the result of an ac-

419

cidental blow to the head suffered during the initiation ceremonies crossing the equator. The loss was "a great shock" to Roosevelt, who wrote to Sara, "I especially will miss him greatly." Gennerich had been more than just a bodyguard who shadowed the president. He helped Roosevelt's butler dress him in the morning, bathe him, and undress him before bed in the evening. He assisted his every movement, getting him "in and out of cars and fishing boats, up and down stairs, onto stages." He had shielded him when the assassin felled Mayor Cermak in Florida, and helped clean him up and lock his braces back in place after the fall at the Democratic convention in 1936. He was part of the inner circle with whom Roosevelt could genuinely relax, playing the piano, singing, and joining in nighttime poker games. Roosevelt called him "my humanizer" and an "ambassador to the man in the streets." "The tragedy of poor Gus hangs over all of us," Franklin wrote Eleanor, and he could not imagine how so loyal a friend could be replaced, especially after the death of Louis Howe earlier in the year. Both men had served as sounding boards and people with whom he could be unguarded.

In addition to Gus's death, the results of the Pan American meeting disappointed Roosevelt. He had hoped to establish mechanisms for peaceful consultations among the American republics that would stand as a model for the European and Pacific nations. But the fifty-eight-year-old Argentine foreign minister, Carlos Saavedra Lamas, who had won a Nobel Peace Prize for ending the Chaco War between Paraguay and Bolivia and had become president of the League of Nations General Assembly in 1936, resisted U.S.

leadership of hemisphere affairs. He preferred working through the League rather than on a regional scale and described U.S. peace proposals as "nothing more nor less than a means by which the United States hoped to extend its power and influence over the smaller nations of the hemisphere." Hull, who negotiated with Lamas at the Buenos Aires meeting, exchanged verbal blows with him, as did Brazil's foreign minister. The reciprocal attacks by the two Latin representatives to the conference degenerated into shouting matches, with cries of "pig" and "liar."

This acrimony between the two principal Latin states frustrated hopes of hemispheric harmony and put an end to any hopes Roosevelt had of negotiating disarmament and nonaggression agreements with the group. The discord also undermined the image of him as "the miracle man" who could head off a European war. "War is inevitable and Europe is doomed to destruction unless President Roosevelt intervenes," European diplomats had told Bullitt in Paris. But Roosevelt could not see a path to effective discussions among Europe's antagonists. He remained "most pessimistic about Europe," he told James Cox, and saw "no step that we can take to improve that situation." In January 1937 he wrote Dodd in Berlin, "If five or six heads of the important governments could meet together for a week with complete inaccessibility to press or cables or radio, a definite useful agreement might result or else one or two of them would be murdered by the others! In any case it would be worthwhile from the point of view of civilization!"

In the meantime, he intended to say nothing in public about the situation in Europe, telling William Phillips, his undersecretary of state: "Sometimes it is better to appear much wiser than one really is." Moreover, he felt compelled to "keep away from anything that might result in a rebuff of an offer of help." He feared that any failed attempt at peace negotiations would only agitate isolationist attacks and distract Congress, the press, and the public from domestic reforms he believed essential to preserving the New Deal, which in turn, he believed meant saving democracy. The South American crowds shouting *Viva la democracia!* were "for me," he told Dodd, "for the simple reason that they believe I have made democracy function and keep abreast of the time and that as a system of government it is, therefore, to be preferred to Fascism or Communism."

But he was not confident that he could achieve those goals without a more supportive majority on the Supreme Court. As he had told Joe Patterson in November, Court reform was a difficult problem, but one that had to be faced by adding liberal justices to the highest court. The executive and legislative branches of government, he said in his State of the Union message on January 6, had "helped to make democracy succeed by refusing to permit unnecessary disagreement . . . between two of our branches. . . . That spirit of cooperation was able to solve difficulties of extraordinary magnitude." While he looked forward to continuing that spirit of cooperation in the next four years, he said nothing directly about the Supreme Court. Other references to the judiciary, however, suggested that Roosevelt intended "to bring legislative and judicial action into closer harmony" to meet the "present national needs of the largest progressive democracy in the modern world."

Roosevelt's earlier hints at Court reform had apparently so unnerved the justices that they absented themselves from the State of the Union address. "None of the nine highest members of our judicial branch were present for the occasion," he wrote Claude Bowers, his ambassador in Madrid, "but I have received some intimation that they at least read the remarks that pertained to them. I hope so!" His only broad statement of reform in the speech concerned alterations in the country's executive machinery, but these were to be accomplished without violating traditional practices. He believed that the judiciary could also be reformed without radical institutional revisions. As he had told Patterson, the Court problem could be met and "solved without getting away from our underlying principles." But rumors of far-reaching Court reform were already circulating among some close observers of the White House. On February 2, when he hosted an annual Supreme Court dinner, Idaho senator William Borah, watching an amiable president in conversation with two of the justices, remarked: "That reminds me of the Roman Emperor who looked around his dinner table and began to laugh when he thought how many of those heads would be rolling on the morrow."

Roosevelt was not unaware of the anxiety in the air concerning his plans, and was apprehensive that his Court proposal would touch off an unpleasant fight. On February 5, as he was about to reveal his plan to Congress, Missy LeHand observed him to be "terribly nervous about this message," and urged Sam Rosenman, who had helped draft the announcement, to remain at the White House before taking a train back to New

York. Before sending up his proposal, Roosevelt had kept his plans a closely guarded secret. Only he and Homer Cummings, his attorney general, who had worked closely with him on it, knew what was coming. Roosevelt loved to spring surprises: "Congress has convened and I have startled them —" he wrote his ambassador in Warsaw, "more startles to come." As Jeff Shesol wrote in his book on Roosevelt and the Court, "His love of the covert; his preference for the sly over the straightforward; his occasional vindictiveness; his eagerness to astonish — all these came together in the Court-packing plan."

While it was a source of amusement to him to shock people, and especially other politicians and the press, it principally gave him a sense of power and control, which was psychologically satisfying to someone who was so dependent on others for mobility. He also considered it shrewd politics to hide a bold proposal until the last minute as a way to prevent critics from mounting effective early opposition to what many would see as making a fundamental change in the High Court. His reluctance to be more open about his intentions, however, may also have sprung from his inner doubts about so bold a plan, which seemed certain to touch off a highly visible dispute.

And so, after months of thinking about how to modernize the Court or make it an instrument of the administration's drive for change, Roosevelt settled on a proposal to add up to six justices to the Court, one for every justice who had served at least ten years and failed to retire six months after turning seventy. His plan would enable him to immediately appoint six new justices, bringing the total to fifteen. While the number of Supreme

Court justices was not enshrined in the Constitution, the Court had contained nine since 1869.

Roosevelt was not entirely surprised when his special message to Congress touched off a firestorm of debate. Some, like conservative Virginia senator Carter Glass, who had suffered repeated defeats over New Deal laws, believed that Congress would do the president's bidding on whatever he proposed. "Why, if the President asked Congress to commit suicide tomorrow," Glass said, "they'd do it." But, he added, "there has been no mandate from the people to rape the Supreme Court or tamper with the Constitution."

Speaker of the House William Bankhead of Alabama, a Roosevelt ally, thought that the president had intentionally hidden his plans from Congress "because he knew that hell would break loose." Roosevelt had tried to cloak what he was doing by describing it as a way to help the Court deal with its heavy workload, but opponents recognized immediately that the reform would allow him to pack the Court with justices who would certify the New Deal. When Chief Justice Charles Evans Hughes and others rebutted Roosevelt's assertions about the competency of men over seventy and the need to relieve an overtaxed judiciary with more justices, a skeptical Daisy asked him, "Don't you mean that you are packing it [the Court]?" He responded, "I suppose you're right, Daisy! I suppose you're right!"

The opposition was also convinced that Roosevelt was showing his true colors as a politician intent on dictatorial powers, and compared him to Machiavelli, Stalin, Hitler, Mussolini, Napoleon, Nero, and Judas. Even Vice President Garner held his nose and turned thumbs down before a

Democratic caucus when they read Roosevelt's proposal. Some critics loudly complained that he was trying to foist "a revolutionary change on Congress." They screamed "dictatorship," saw "a bloodless coup d'état" that amounted to the worst crisis since Southern secession, and foresaw the "end [of] the American state." Jerome D. Green, Harvard treasurer and an old friend of Roosevelt's, wrote the *New York Times,* "For one who knows the President it is impossible to believe that he is aiming at a future dictatorship; but it is also impossible not to recognize the packing of the Supreme Court as exactly what a dictator would adopt as his first step. The President may not know where he is going but he is on his way." Only the controlled German and Italian press unanimously cheered what they described as Roosevelt's following the example of their own leaders.

The president's supporters countered by praising him as another George Washington, Thomas Jefferson, Andrew Jackson, Martin Luther, Moses, or St. Augustine. Ickes did "not recall any single issue affecting the Government that has caused the spilling of so much printer's ink or led to so many fervent discussions." He complained that critics of the plan were elevating the Court into a God-inspired institution that was obliged to contain an unalterable number of justices. Ickes confided to a correspondent, "All that is left to do now is to declare that the Supreme Court was immaculately conceived; that it is infallible; that it is the spiritual descendant of Moses and that the number Nine is three times three, and three stands for the Trinity."

The barrage of criticism, arguing that Roosevelt's plan would destroy the country's traditional balance of power between the federal branches, provoked him to fight back. He greatly resented the warnings about his reach for dictatorial powers. When he was pressed to take action against "the depredations of the wicked Bridgeport Hydraulic Company," he sarcastically told Connecticut governor Wilbur Cross, "Thank the Lord I have not decided to become a Dictator. Therefore, there still exist forty-eight sovereign states and I am able to pass this 'buck' to the Sovereign Dictator of the independent state of Connecticut."

On March 4, at a victory dinner celebrating the 1936 election results, he attacked the Court's majority opposition to New Deal reforms, saying, "We live in a Nation where there is no legal power anywhere to deal with its most difficult practical problems — a No Man's Land of final futility." The Court had created "doubts and difficulties for almost everything . . . we have promised to fight — help for the crippled, for the blind, for the mothers — insurance for the unemployed — security for the aged — protection of the consumer against monopoly and speculation — protection of the investor — the wiping out of slums — cheaper electricity for the homes and on the farms of America." Cataloging the problems that still beset the country, he declared, "If we would keep faith with those who had faith in us, if we would make democracy succeed, I say we must act — NOW!" Ickes thought the speech "the greatest he has ever made" and admired the fact that Roosevelt had committed himself to making what would be "a hard fight" when the only alternative was to "lose everything that we have

427

gained during the last four years." Ickes believed that leaving the conservative Court majority in control would set back the country at least ten years and mean making the fight for liberal reforms like the TVA and Social Security all over again in the future if democracy was to be saved.

Five days later, on March 9, Roosevelt gave his first Fireside Chat in six months. Citing the Court's five-to-four votes, which had threatened to throw "all the affairs of this great Nation back into hopeless chaos," he declared it essential "to have a government with power to prevent" a return of the conditions that had afflicted the country just four years earlier. Yet "the unanswered challenge of a Nation ill-nourished, ill-clad, ill-housed" required a change in the Court's response to the administration's economic and social reforms. It was time for it to end its role as a "policy-making body" or "third-House of the Congress," Roosevelt argued, and return to its function as a "judicial body." His proposal for change would "save the Constitution from the Court and the Court from itself. There is nothing novel or radical about this idea. It seeks to maintain the bench in full vigor." He stressed that his record as a governor and now president demonstrated his devotion to traditional liberties. "You who know me," he ended, "will accept my solemn assurance that in a world in which democracy is under attack, I seek to make American democracy succeed."

Roosevelt ultimately hoped that his sleight of hand would help him avoid a political crisis that could dramatically erode the standing he had gained through his landslide election and ability to lead the country. As he had made clear in his speech at the Democratic Party's victory celebration, he had only four more years in office, during which his influence was bound to wane. Moreover, mindful of comparisons being made between his presidency and the authoritarian regimes in Italy, Germany, and Russia, he did not want to provoke a debate over the foundations or viability of the U.S. governmental system. In confronting the Court issue, he had rejected suggestions of a constitutional amendment that would bar the Supreme Court from overturning legislative acts endorsed by the president, as that would be far more difficult to obtain than a simple congressional act. Nor did he wish to make so fundamental a change in the public face of his proposed Court reform. Arguing for a law that emphasized the need for younger members of the Highest Court seemed like a more anodyne way to put forward his proposal to guarantee the durability of his economic and social reforms.

Still, he underestimated how sensitive an issue Court reform would be. He did receive a fair amount of supporting mail, such as a March 10 note from someone in San Diego, who had written following his Fireside Chat, that especially amused and encouraged him. H. C. Brown enclosed "some nonsensical little nursery rhyme parodies I thought you might be able to put in the hands of some clever cartoonist":

"Hickery-dickery-dock
Old Age holds back the clock.
By votes of one are laws undone,
Hickery-dickery-dock

Fe-fi-fo-fum

Judges as old as Methuselum,
Cast their votes as in days gone by,
Viewing tomorrow with yesterday's eye.

Ancient Judges, sat in the Hall,
Ancient Judges, due for a fall,
Our country's Great Leader thinks some
    younger men,
Would see that the Court gave us justice again

More often, though, the responses were negative, such as one inveighing against his "scuttl[ing] the American system, destroy[ing] our checks and balances, and throw[ing] overboard the protection of a free untrammeled Supreme Court." The issue soon touched off the worst congressional conflict of his administration. Despite his large majorities, assertions that his Court reform would play havoc with the separation of powers garnered considerable support in both the House and the Senate. A Senate Judiciary Committee report declared Roosevelt's bill "an invasion of judicial power such as has never before been attempted in this country."

Opinion polls reinforced congressional reluctance, as court reform did not make the list of the top nine items the public saw as deserving the administration's attention. (Unemployment and neutrality in international affairs remained the chief matters of public concern.) Between February and July over 50 percent of Americans consistently voiced opposition to it. Roosevelt himself, however, never lost ground: Between February and August, when pollsters asked a cross section of Americans whether they would still vote for the president, 60 to 65 percent continued to say they would. As an Associated Press reporter observed,

Roosevelt had made the presidency the center of political action for the first time since the administrations of TR and Wilson. Roosevelt was "exciting. He was human. He was copy."

In June, after Roosevelt invited all Democratic congressmen and senators to a picnic on Jefferson Island in Chesapeake Bay, they responded to his enduring popularity and personal attention by agreeing to consider a revised Court bill that raised the retirement age to seventy-five and limited Roosevelt to one appointment a year. Because conservative justice Willis Van Devanter had recently decided to resign, this amended plan would allow Roosevelt to add five new justices to the Court over the next four years. But opposition to any sort of Court reform remained, and when Vice President Garner left Washington for a vacation in Texas in mid-June, it signaled a split in the administration that weakened prospects for Senate agreement to the president's modified bill. Roosevelt coaxed Garner to return to Washington by assuring him of his support for Garner's antilabor and balanced budget views. Although Garner gave lip service to Roosevelt's proposed reform, no one viewed him as anything but an opponent of it.

When the sixty-four-year-old Senate majority leader, Joe Robinson, a master of Senate rules who was leading Roosevelt's fight for the law in the mistaken belief that Roosevelt would appoint him to the Court, died suddenly of a heart attack in July, the battle was effectively lost. Roosevelt had valued Robinson's dogged efforts to promote New Deal laws, including the Court bill, but fearing that Robinson would show his true conservative colors as a justice, wanted to balance his appointment with selections to the Court of more reliably liberal jurists. Nothing came of it all, however, when the Senate by 70 to 20 sent the revised Court reform bill back to committee, where it died a quiet death. Garner, who had returned to Washington, had delivered the bad news to Roosevelt with barely disguised pleasure: Do you want to hear the bad news "with the bark on or the bark off?" he asked. Roosevelt wanted the plain truth. "You're beat," Garner announced. "You haven't got the votes." In August and September, when pollsters asked if Roosevelt should revive his effort to enlarge the Court, less than a third of voters responded positively.

As one Roosevelt scholar noted, however, "for FDR, all was not lost." Between the end of March and late May 1937, the Court handed down three 5 to 4 decisions that validated a minimum wage statute, the National Labor Relations Act, and the Social Security law. "A switch in time saved nine," became the quip of the moment. While these rulings seemed to make Court packing superfluous, the White House believed that the Court might swing back again at any time and force another fight for reform. But White House intervention became moot when events beyond Roosevelt's control satisfied his desire for a pro–New Deal Court: During the next three years, the retirements of three conservative and two liberal justices allowed Roosevelt to appoint five liberals, who assured him of the majority for which he had hoped.

But the Court's transformation did not occur without some additional Sturm und Drang. On August 12, 1937, Roosevelt selected fifty-one-year-old Alabama senator Hugo Black as Van Devanter's replacement. A small-town Alabama lawyer who had come to the Senate in 1926, Black was a surprising choice. He was hardly a distinguished jurist with much experience as a judge, but as an outspoken New Deal supporter who had voted for every one of Roosevelt's major legislative proposals as well as his Court packing plan, he was viewed by the president to be a reliable vote on disputed reforms. In addition, the deafness of Black's seven-year-old son touched a sympathetic chord in Roosevelt, who could readily identify with someone struggling with a disability in his family.

The president believed that the Senate's tradition of a quick confirmation of a sitting member to a higher position would mean a prompt approval of Black. But Roosevelt had already put the Senate on edge by a statement to the press on July 27 that he might make a recess appointment to the Court. The unconfirmed justice would then have the advantage of being a member of the High Court. Because the anger his announcement provoked might jeopardize any easy subsequent confirmation, Roosevelt decided to act while the Senate was still in session. In response, Henry Ashurst, the chairman of the judiciary committee, asked the Senate to reach a decision by the "immemorial rule" of quick confirmation. That rule had not been breached since 1888, when Grover Cleveland nominated to the Supreme Court Lucius Lamar, a former Confederate official and Mississippi senator, and the Senate held hearings and confirmed him by a narrow margin.

But Black's nomination provoked an explosion of opposition, which rested on complaints that he had almost no judicial experience and, as demonstrated by his responses to inquisitorial questioning at Senate hearings, lacked a judicial temperament. As one fellow senator remarked, "He is a prosecutor and not a judge." Critics asserted that Roosevelt could not have made a worse choice than Black. "He is a snarling, obstreperous, narrow minded and unintelligent bounder," a Hoover supporter declared. The *Washington Post,* reporting that his "lack of training on the one hand and extreme partisanship" on the other made him a poor choice, could not find a single attribute to recommend him. On August 14, an allegation surfaced that Black had been a member of the Alabama Ku Klux Klan. But with no proof of that claim and senatorial courtesy dictating that the upper house confirm one of its own, Black's appointment was approved by a 63 to 16 vote five days after Roosevelt nominated him.

On September 13, less than a month after Black's confirmation, a *Pittsburgh Post* reporter published the first of six articles proving that Black had indeed been a Klansman and held a lifetime membership in the organization. Some senators said that they would not have voted for Black had they known about his affiliation, and a renewed outcry erupted against Roosevelt for having dishonored the Court. In a Gallup poll, 57 percent said that Klan membership should disqualify someone from appointment to the Supreme Court, and 59 percent favored Black's resignation.

However embarrassing to Roosevelt, the Court fight and revelations about Black did little to undermine his popular standing. As Roosevelt told Ickes, "People did not understand this [Court] issue and were not very much interested in it." In

September, when *Liberty* magazine asked newspaper editors and business and labor leaders who they thought would be the Democratic candidate in 1940, the survey revealed "a surprising and overwhelming belief" that Roosevelt would be "the nominee and the first third-term President." Moreover, when Roosevelt made a foreign affairs speech in October focused on aggression and the dangers of war, it largely eclipsed concerns about the Court and Black's appointment.

In October, after Black defended himself in an eleven-minute radio talk by denying any serious ties to the Klan, Daisy told Franklin, "I shall from henceforth stand up for Judge Black no matter what happens!!" In a subsequent survey, 56 percent said that Black should not resign from the Court, and in November, when Gallup asked Americans if they were for or against Roosevelt, 62.8 percent answered, "For." In addition, although the debate over Roosevelt's Court reform had produced an "unrelenting public clamor" and the *Pathé* weekly newsreel had described it as "the greatest public issue since slavery," only 27.5 percent of a December survey responded that the Supreme Court fight was the topic that had interested them most during the previous year; only 16 percent said that Black's Klan affiliation commanded their greatest attention. In choosing Black, there seems little question that Roosevelt was aware of his Klan membership and that his election to the Senate had partly required Klan support. But as with his resistance to antilynching legislation, Roosevelt saw racial bias as a relatively minor issue when weighed against the appointment to the Court of a justice who would be a reliable defender of New Deal measures. Roosevelt proved right about Black's reliability on supporting his agenda. Moreover, "the Black controversy is rich in paradox and irony." During a thirty-four-year term on the Court, Black became one of the Court's "leading exponents of civil liberties." His Court tenure until the age of eighty-five made a mockery of Roosevelt's plan to retire justices at the age of seventy or, at a minimum, expand the Court's membership so that younger justices could take up some of the work of the older men.

Nonetheless, Roosevelt's effort to master the judiciary produced something of a pyrrhic victory. His expenditure of so much political capital on the Court battle forced him to approach other congressional disputes with uncharacteristic restraint. Advancing new liberal reforms became a distant hope. The Court controversy, one contemporary observer said, sidetracked "much useful legislation that otherwise might have been put through." Secretary of Agriculture Henry Wallace believed that "the whole New Deal went up in smoke as a result of the Supreme Court fight." The conflict had opened a divide in the Democratic Party that alienated Roosevelt from some of his former political allies. He was unforgiving toward congressmen and senators who had opposed him, or as a *New York Times* reporter phrased it, the dispute had given Roosevelt "a long son-of-a-bitch list." Jim Farley thought that the Court defeat was "seared into his [Roosevelt's] political soul. . . . Presidential pride was sorely scorched. For weeks and months afterward I found him fuming against the members of his own party he blamed for his bucket of bitterness." Although outwardly he remained "as gay and debonair as ever; inwardly he was seething." Privately, he made his antagonism clear to Farley. Roosevelt's simmering anger would find a convenient target in party conservatives.

The Court struggle also made adversaries of former Republican allies, especially among progressives who had bolted their party in 1936 to back him. William Allen White now feared "him as I fear no other man in our public life," while California's Hiram Johnson gloomily predicted: "We're on the road to Fascism. He will make himself an absolute dictator." George W. Norris, whom Roosevelt had worked so hard to reelect to the Senate from Nebraska, calling him "one of the major prophets of America," effectively broke with the president.

However much Roosevelt maintained a facade of good cheer, these tensions registered forcefully on him and only confirmed his expectations of a difficult second term. He understood that every officeholder's limitations become clearer the longer he remained in the public eye. He believed that by the time he left office, his power would have evaporated and Democratic Party divisions, as well as a national conservative-liberal split, would be on full display. He expected these trends to develop slowly over the course of four years, so the rapid decline in his popularity beginning in 1938 surprised him. Ickes, who saw the president in July 1937 after Robinson died and the Court bill faced an uncertain fate, told his diary: "I had lunch with the President and I was with him for a full hour and a half. I haven't seen him looking so tired and nervous at any time. It is quite evident that he has been feeling the strain under which he has been working."

As someone with a progressive temperament and an adaptive personality that enabled him to accept that changing times meant adopting fresh ways of thinking about old problems, Roosevelt was impatient with politicians who doggedly clung to the past.

While he shared with Thomas Jefferson the conviction that laws and institutions should not be subjected to "frequent and untried changes," he also subscribed to Jefferson's view that "some men look at constitutions with sanctimonious reverence, and deem them like the Ark of the Covenant, too sacred to be touched." Both Jefferson and Roosevelt dismissed such reverence as misplaced and ignored the irony that change was the only fixed rule of history. Regard for traditions needed to "go hand and hand with the progress of the human mind," Jefferson said. "As that becomes more developed, more enlightened, as new discoveries are made, new truths disclosed, and manners and opinions change with the change of circumstances, institutions must advance also, and keep pace with the times."

In 1934, Roosevelt's admiration for Jefferson's wisdom had expressed itself in urging consideration of a memorial to him to be built on Washington's Tidal Basin. It was Roosevelt's way of elevating a Democratic Party icon to a level with Washington and Lincoln, the only two presidents who had been honored with conspicuous monuments in the capital. Roosevelt had the pleasure of dedicating the completed structure in 1943 on Jefferson's two-hundredth birthday. He saw it in part as a tribute to the statesman Roosevelt believed would have endorsed his commitment to using government to humanize the nation's industrial system and advance the general welfare. Invoking Jefferson to justify the New Deal was evident in Roosevelt's 1943 dedication when he said: "Jefferson was no dreamer — for half a century he led his State and his Nation . . . I like to think that this was so because he thought in terms of the morrow as well as the day — and this was why he was hated or feared by those who thought in terms of the day and the yesterday" — as I myself have been, Roosevelt might have added.

The Court struggle inhibited not only Roosevelt's impulse to propose additional domestic reforms but also any initiative promoting world peace. By January 1937 the civil war in Spain was generating increasing fears of a Europe-wide war. The Germans and Italians, convinced that Fascist defeat in Spain would mean a victory for the Bolshevism threatening their regimes, were contributing arms and air power to Franco's fight against the Republic, while the Soviets were aiding the Madrid government in hopes of seeing a war between the British and French on one side and the Germans and Italians on the other. Because their pacifist publics were firmly opposed to becoming involved in another conflict, the British and French governments, despite having greater sympathy for the Republic than the Fascists, established a nonintervention committee promoting neutrality in response to Spain's civil strife. Although all the powers agreed to withhold aid, the Germans and Italians gave no more than lip service to their pledges, as they viewed the Spanish civil war as not only a chance to expand Fascist influence in Europe but also as an opportunity to test their air forces in actual combat. In June 1937, Pablo Picasso captured the savagery of these bombardments in his painting *Guernica,* which depicted the horrors inflicted upon women and children in the Republic's Basque town. It was transparent to anyone who cared to see that Franco was dependent on Berlin and Rome for the military support that allowed him to make gains in the fighting.

Like the British and French, Roosevelt sided with the Republic, but also like them, his highest priority was to prevent a general European conflict. Moreover, the American public continued to want no part in any engagement in what it saw not as a landmark clash between democracy and fascism but rather another traditional European power struggle. A majority of Americans believed that the factions in Spain were merely another expression of the long-established European divide between competing antidemocratic ideologies of communism and fascism. In 1937, 70 percent of Americans thought it had been a mistake to involve themselves in the First World War. At the start of that year, they viewed neutrality as only second to unemployment in importance as a national issue, and when asked if the United States could stay out of another foreign war, 62 percent, revealing as much about their hopes as their expectations, responded in the affirmative. Two-thirds of the country favored neutrality in response to Spain's conflict. A majority of Americans remained angry at the European nations for defaulting on their war debts and considered taking any part in their quarrels as resulting in further squandering of U.S. treasure. Suspicious of presidential and congressional intentions, 69 percent opposed greater discretion for the president in administering neutrality policies, while 73 percent wanted Congress to consult the electorate before declaring war.

The outbreak of renewed fighting between China and Japan left Americans equally fearful of being drawn into a conflict in Asia. Tokyo's seizure of Manchuria in 1931 deepened long-standing sympathy for the Chinese as victims of imperialism. In American eyes, Tokyo's continued aggression made Japan a bandit nation, but 95 percent of one group polled opposed lending money to the Chinese as risking participation in the conflict. A majority also wanted Roosevelt to withdraw the 2,300 troops assigned to protect U.S. citizens in China as another guarantee against becoming enmeshed in this latest war. Roosevelt, who had spoken privately in 1934 about Japan's menace to the West, was frustrated at his inability to respond to Japanese belligerence.

He did, in any case, want to prepare the United States for a potential conflict with Japan by expanding the Navy. In May, after a fishing vacation in the Gulf of Mexico, Roosevelt came ashore in Galveston, Texas, where he had arranged to meet twenty-nine-year-old Lyndon B. Johnson, a newly elected congressman who had won a special election to replace a deceased member of the House. Johnson's unqualified support for Roosevelt's Court plan had made him a potential advocate for all the items on the president's agenda as well as a loyal acolyte. Roosevelt invited Johnson to join him on a train ride from Galveston to College Station, where he was scheduled to address three thousand ROTC cadets at Texas A&M University. In his speech, Roosevelt emphasized the need for preparedness in a world in which aggressor nations were flexing their muscles.

During his conversation with Johnson on the train, Roosevelt asked his preference for a House committee assignment. Johnson's request for a seat on the appropriations committee, one of the most coveted assignments in the House, which only the most senior members commanded, amused the president, who said afterward that the young man "came on like a freight train." Instead, Roosevelt urged Johnson to join the Naval Affairs Committee, where he could help the president build a strong navy. Johnson, who feigned a lifelong interest in naval affairs, agreed to ask for that assignment and urged Roosevelt to build a naval air base at Corpus Christi. Roosevelt later said to Tommy Corcoran, "I've just met the most remarkable young man. Now I like this boy and you're going to help him with anything you can." Roosevelt also told Ickes and Harry Hopkins that in the next generation, when the country's balance of political power shifted to the South and the West, "this boy could well be the first Southern President."

The Spanish Civil War presented a greater immediate source of trouble for Roosevelt than the Asian fighting. When the Glen L. Martin Company asked permission to sell warplanes to Madrid, the administration discouraged it. The existing neutrality law said nothing about civil conflicts, and under existing diplomatic practice the United States was allowed to sell arms to a government with which it had relations. But fearful of public opposition to taking sides in the war, Roosevelt declared any such sale at odds with administration policy. Socialist Party leader Norman Thomas complained to Roosevelt that the Spanish Republicans — or Loyalists, as they were known — were "fighting against a military, fascist revolt," to which Germany and Italy were providing assistance. Thomas predicted that a Franco "victory would menace the peace of the world by the encouragement it would give to fascist aggression," and urged the export of U.S. arms to Madrid. In a reply drafted for him in the State Department, Roosevelt said that such intervention in the Spanish war would run counter to what "our people desire so deeply," would enflame European tensions, and would further threaten world peace.

To counter pressure for intervention in Spain, Roosevelt decided to ask Congress to include civil wars in the neutrality law. His request included presidential discretion for when and against whom embargoes might be applied, but Congress saw him as being too clever by half. As in 1935, he was invoking isolationist sentiments in support of a provision potentially serving internationalist action, and Congress resisted his resumption of full control over foreign affairs. Roosevelt could then have dropped the matter and simply allowed American arms manufacturers to sell munitions to the Republican government. But because he was then more concerned about British and French efforts to confine the fighting to Spain than to help ensure fascist defeat, Roosevelt agreed to extend the neutrality law's mandatory embargo on all shipments to warring parties in a civil conflict. Believing he had a larger role to play as a peacemaker in Europe as a whole, Roosevelt refused to identify himself with either side in the Spanish conflict. His neutrality policy had the added advantage of reflecting majority opinion.

Believing that he had a larger role to play as a

peacemaker in Europe as a whole, Roosevelt could not dismiss pronouncements that he alone could head off another world war. In February 1937, when Morgenthau told him, "Europe is gradually going bankrupt through preparing for war, and you are the only person who can stop it," Roosevelt replied, "I feel like throwing either a cup and saucer at you or the coffee pot." With others in the administration expressing the same opinion, Roosevelt, whether out of a grandiosity fostered by his landslide or just the belief that someone had to take responsibility for so noble a goal, decided to let Spanish events play out on their own rather than involve the United States, which would undermine his standing with most Americans and scotch whatever slim chance there was to avert a larger war. At the same time, he urged Cordell Hull to commission a study of embargoes by executive order that would reduce the flow of raw materials to Germany. In May, he told William Phillips, who had become ambassador to Rome, that economic measures or anything that "postpones war is . . . much to the good. The progress of the disease is slowed up but the disease remains — and will probably prove fatal in the next few years."

In July and August, as the Court fight wound down, Roosevelt wrote to Mussolini and British prime minister Neville Chamberlain in hopes of encouraging some movement toward long-term peace. "The drift of events," he told the Duce, "has been toward and not away from an ultimate crisis." He praised Mussolini's statements favoring reduced armaments, asserting that arms production "on its present scale" and trade barriers were "ominous to peace." He hoped that

Mussolini would consider meeting with him at some point in order to advance better relations. Roosevelt's letter expressed his conviction that, unlike Hitler, Mussolini could be drawn into "world pacification." Similarly, he hoped that Chamberlain would consider coming to Washington to advance "Anglo-American cooperation in the promotion of economic stability and peace in the world." Chamberlain rejected Roosevelt's suggestion as encouraging hopes that could not be realized at that time, as he believed that a better route to European peace was through an accommodation with Hitler. Paul van Zeeland, Belgium's prime minister, however, did accept a Roosevelt invitation to discuss the situation in Europe, and though the president had nothing dramatic to suggest that might halt the drift toward war, he did urge the prime minster "to draw the world's attention to fascist threats."

Roosevelt saw a greater possibility of influencing foreign affairs in Asia. In July, after the Japanese had used a clash with Chinese troops at a bridge near Peiping as an excuse for renewed aggression against Chiang Kai-shek's Nationalist government, Roosevelt wanted not only to expand U.S. naval forces in the Pacific but also to arrange American occupation of the uninhabited Phoenix group of islands in the central Pacific, which he thought could serve as air and naval bases to discourage Japanese expansion. Roosevelt dismissed competing British claims to the eight atolls and two coral reefs as "a sheer case of bluff." Since no nation had occupied these islands "for years and years," Roosevelt pressed Hull to take "immediate action" to bring about U.S. occupancy. At the same time, he ordered Admiral William D.

Leahy, the chief of naval operations, to assess the presence of Japanese vessels in the Bering Sea and determine what could be done to counteract their operations in the event of war.

In September, with the Court fight at an end and White House proposals for additional domestic reforms stalled in Congress, which had adjourned, Roosevelt decided to take a two-week cross-country trip to the Northwest, where he could renew contacts with grassroots America and take the political temperature of the nation ten months after his landslide. Harold Ickes thought the president badly needed a break, given that he was "punch drunk with the punishment he has suffered recently." Ickes believed that Roosevelt had "paid a heavy toll during these past four years. His face is heavily lined and inclined to be gaunt as compared to what it was when he took office in 1933, and he is distinctly more nervous." Missy LeHand shared Ickes's concern: "She didn't see how any man should want eight years of the Presidency. . . . She didn't see how anyone could stand it."

In departing Washington, Roosevelt was temporarily leaving behind other daunting challenges that were enervating him, including how to manage an aggressive labor movement and a turndown in the economy that had begun in July. Encouraged by New Deal help to the unemployed and the National Labor Relations Act in 1935, militant labor chiefs led by John L. Lewis, head of the United Mine Workers union, gave their support to Roosevelt in 1936. Lewis contributed $500,000 to Roosevelt's campaign, the largest single donation to his reelection fund, which helped produce wide margins for the president in Pennsylvania and other coal mining regions. As a consequence, in the winter of 1936–37, Lewis and labor generally expected Roosevelt to support union demands in struggles that erupted with industrial giants U.S. Steel and General Motors. Imitating French workers, General Motors' factory employees launched a series of sit-down strikes that greatly reduced production. When Democratic Michigan governor Frank Murphy refused to send troops to break the major strike action at GM's Flint factory and Roosevelt also rejected calls for halting the workers' illegal seizure of private property, the labor action became a major topic of public discussion.

Roosevelt had limited sympathy for the workers' efforts to force the steel and auto industries into settlements that strengthened their unions. He certainly wanted labor to command a living wage, which would contribute to national economic revival, but was wary of their building their organizational and political clout and their militancy, which resulted in 4,740 strikes by 1,860,000 workers in 1937. Nor did he wish to become involved in labor's internal struggles between the American Federation of Labor (AFL), which mainly represented craft workers, and the emerging Congress of Industrial Organizations (CIO), which counted unskilled workers among its principal members.

Roosevelt especially wanted to resist defying public opinion by openly backing controversial union actions. In February 1937, 56 percent of Americans favored employers over workers in the sit-down strikes, with 66 percent saying they supported GM's refusal to negotiate until the strikers left the plants. A large majority also thought that

John L. Lewis was a radical who did not represent most of the GM workers. In March and April, 67 percent of the participants in a poll favored legislation making sit-downs illegal, supported using force to remove strikers from factories, and wanted government regulation of unions to keep them from disrupting the economy. By June, antagonized by the strikes, 71 percent of a polled group described themselves as "less in favor" of unions than they had once been. In August, a plurality of Americans believed that Roosevelt's White House had been "too friendly" to the striking workers. In June and July, when police killed protesters in Illinois and Ohio supporting sit-in strikers, public anger focused not on the police overreaction but on the militant workers who were blamed for provoking the violence.

When Roosevelt was questioned at a press conference on June 8 if he saw any possibility of a federal intervention in the steel strike, he evasively declared, "I don't know." Three days later, when asked to comment on the labor violence, he said, "Nothing this morning." When the conference ended and the reporter said the customary, "Thank you, Mr. President," Roosevelt evoked much laughter by responding, "You ought to say, Thank you for nothing." Asked again on June 15 if there would be any action on the steel strike, Roosevelt evaded the issue again by saying, "We are all hopeful that it is going to straighten out." A week later, when questioned if he was speaking to Tom Girdler, a tough antiunion leader of several steel companies, Roosevelt answered that he couldn't reveal whom he was speaking to.

Finally, on June 29, Roosevelt lost patience when reporters inquired if he was going to make a speech on labor policy. "Isn't it time to assert that policy?" one reporter asked, pressing him to clarify his views on the industrial strife. Unwilling to side with labor or to come out for repressive police action, the president declared, "The majority of the people are saying just one thing. A plague on both your houses." Roosevelt's reply outraged labor leaders, once again led by Lewis, whom Ickes described as "a great, huge bull of a man. He gives the impression that nothing can stop him short of his objective." At 230 pounds, with thick white hair and heavy eyebrows, the fifty-seven-year-old Lewis had a reputation as an uncompromising demagogue who had gained standing not only as a fierce advocate of labor but also as a foe of communists, who he insisted wanted to "lay waste to our traditions and our institutions with fire and sword." Ever mindful of labor's financial contribution to Roosevelt's 1936 campaign, Lewis did not mince words in response to Roosevelt's even-handed dismissal of capital and labor: "It ill behooves one who has supped at labor's table and who has been sheltered in labor's house," Lewis declared in a Labor Day radio talk, "to curse with equal fervor and fine impartiality both labor and its adversaries when they become locked in deadly embrace."

In the second half of 1937, the economy also added to Roosevelt's distress. Between June and October, worried about federal budget deficits that greatly troubled business chiefs as threatening inflation and that seemed to discourage them from investments in new plants and operations, Roosevelt aimed to balance the federal budget by cutting WPA and PWA expenditures. Two billion dollars drawn out of the economy by Social

Security taxes, meanwhile, decreased consumer ability to spend. Stocks fell, industrial production plunged, and unemployment rose, pushing the ranks of the jobless back to double digits. Critics, recalling Hoover's ruinous identification with the collapse of the early 1930s, described the downturn as the "Roosevelt recession."

A debate arose over what had caused the reversal. Some within and outside the administration blamed it on the president's hostility to the private sector and fears of excessive government regulation of business. Roosevelt himself was inclined to believe that a conspiracy of business moguls had purposely engineered the recession as a way to discredit him and the New Deal. "I know who's responsible," he told a cabinet meeting. "Business, particularly the banking industry, has ganged up on me. They are trying to use this recession to force me to let up on some of my program. . . . They want to increase the power of wealth without government restriction in the future." He believed that they were following the lead of French business heads, who he was convinced had toppled Leon Blum's Popular Front Socialist government.

At the same time, some in the administration, evoking John Maynard Keynes's 1936 treatise on the need for deficit spending as the path to prosperity, urged Roosevelt to resume heavy doses of federal outlays on infrastructure to put men back to work and to fuel consumption. In the closing months of 1937, uncertain about which direction to take, Roosevelt seemed suspended between budget balancing and deficit spending. Most important to Roosevelt were signs that the public was not giving up on him or the New Deal. In the fall, 64 percent of a poll expected business conditions to improve in the next six months, while 74 percent of the country did not think that the stock market's downturn forecast a new depression, and only 19 percent blamed the recession entirely on FDR's policies. Only 20 percent of another year-end poll said that the "present business slump" commanded their principal attention during 1937, while a surprising 62 percent opposed increased federal deficits to get the country out of the downturn.

In September, at stops on his train trip west, and in remarks at WPA sites in Idaho, Oregon, and Washington, large enthusiastic crowds testified to his continuing popularity and reinvigorated him. "I regain strength by just meeting the American people," he told a Boise audience. He remained angry with the press, however, or more precisely, newspaper publishers, whom he perceived as unrelenting in their hostility to him. On September 29, in a letter he wrote from the train to Press Secretary Steve Early, he vented his annoyance at the press's failure to address New Deal achievements in favor of covering frivolous interactions with individuals he had met along the way: "Apparently a few members of the reportorial staff are sending news — crowds, speeches, etc., while the majority are writing columns on whether I shake hands with Mr. X with my left hand, or looked away when Mr. Y greeted me, or spent forty seconds longer talking with Mr. Z than with his colleague," he complained to Early. "It would be a lot cheaper if all your newspapers would hire [gossip columnist] Walter Winchell and save railroad fares."

The press, however, could not ignore the principal speech of the trip, which Roosevelt delivered

451

on October 5 at a WPA bridge-building site outside of Chicago. The talk grew out of his conviction that he needed to combat isolationist sentiment by giving a speech in an isolationist area, urging international non-belligerent co-operation to punish what Roosevelt privately called the "bandit nations." Roosevelt made clear that he was not proposing a collaboration with any particular nation or posing a direct challenge to Italian, Japanese, or German aggression. Instead, he hoped to persuade peace-minded countries to search out some novel ways of opposing aggressors. In short, Americans needed to comprehend that, at a time when air forces could strike distant foes, isolationism was an outdated way to think about national security. Ickes had the impression from a conversation with Roosevelt a few days before he left for his western trip that he envisioned cutting off all trade and denying raw materials to any invading country, though he intended to make clear that "so far as the present situations in Spain and China are concerned, nothing can be done." He wanted the speech to stand as "a warning to the nations that are today running amuck."

Above all, his speech emphasized the worsening political situation abroad and the dangers it posed to peaceful nations. The "present reign of lawlessness and international terror in the world," he said, has caused "a haunting fear of calamity. . . . The very foundations of civilization" are being "seriously threatened." Unprovoked aerial attacks were killing vast numbers of innocent women and children. "Innocent peoples, innocent nations, are being cruelly sacrificed to a greed for power and supremacy which is devoid of all sense of justice and humane considerations. . . . If those things come to pass in other parts of the world, let no one imagine that America will escape, that America may expect mercy, that this Western Hemisphere will not be attacked and that it will continue tranquilly and peacefully to carry on the ethics and the arts of civilization. If those days come, there will be no safety by arms, no help from authority, no answer in science. The storm will rage till every flower of culture is trampled and all human beings are leveled in a vast chaos." Nothing less was at stake than the survival of international law and morality.

Roosevelt's message of apocalypse now was meant to alarm the country into assuming leadership of an international peace initiative or at least joining with other likeminded nations to answer the threat. The epidemic of world lawlessness needed to be contained by quarantining aggressors. "There must be positive endeavors to preserve peace," he ended. "America hates war. America hopes for peace. Therefore, America actively engages in the search for peace."

While an end-of-the-year poll showed widespread interest in the fighting between China and Japan, neither it nor the president's speech translated into public eagerness to do something bold about foreign affairs. Initially, Americans were enthusiastic about Roosevelt's goal of achieving global peace, but it quickly became clear that he had nothing to offer beyond rhetoric promoting international good will or moralistic pronouncements on the evils of aggression and war. When asked at a press conference to amplify his remarks about a quarantine, he refused to expand on precisely what he meant by the term. He urged reporters to read the last line of his speech: "America engages in the search for peace." Did that represent a repudiation of neutrality? a reporter asked. Absolutely not, Roosevelt replied. He was simply looking for a new method of preserving peace, as measures like sanctions and conferences were "out of the window."

When it became clear that Roosevelt had no specific measures to propose, his speech triggered fears that he intended to put U.S. power at the disposal of antifascist forces and produced a flood of telegrams urging against overseas involvements that could lead to war. Assistant Secretary of State J. Pierrepont Moffat noted, "The press, after two days of jubilation that somebody should have expressed in clear terms what everybody has been feeling, is growing more critical and is beginning to shy away from any risk, however remote, of involvement." A *Philadelphia Inquirer* poll of Congress "showed a two-to-one opposition to common action with the League in the Far Eastern crisis." The reaction against Roosevelt's speech was "quick and violent. . . . It was condemned as warmongering and saber-rattling," Sam Rosenman said. Roosevelt complained to Colonel House that "as usual we have been bombarded by Hearst and others who say that an American search for peace means of necessity, war." He told Rosenman, "It's a terrible thing to look over your shoulder when you are trying to lead — and to find no one there."

Roosevelt's frustration was compounded in November, when the nine powers that had signed an agreement in 1922 promising to maintain China's territorial integrity met in Brussels to seek a truce in the Sino-Japanese fighting. Despite his pledge that sanctions and conferences had no place in his quarantine proposal, Roosevelt agreed to include the United States in the Brussels talks and briefly considered a muscular response to Tokyo if it resisted peace negotiations. He complained that the European states with interests in Asia were behaving like "scared rabbits." But as isolationists warned him against any kind of international collaboration, he backed off. He informed the British that U.S. public opinion limited his ability to act decisively, and that he could "not afford to be made, in popular opinion at home, a tail to the British kite, as has been charged . . . by the Hearst press and others." He further cautioned that sanctions were out of the question, and he later told Hull that "we still have not got the answer" as to how to rein in Japan's aggression without antagonizing American opinion.

In December, when Japanese planes attacked the U.S. gunboat *Panay* and three Standard Oil tankers on the Yangtze River twenty miles from Nanking, killing three Americans, Roosevelt sent an indignant message to Tokyo demanding full compensation and guarantees against future attacks. He also considered seizing Japanese assets in the United States, embargoing raw materials exported to Japan, and establishing a blockade around Japan that he believed might "bring her to her knees within a year." But as with the quarantine proposal, a majority of Americans opposed taking any actions that could lead to war. Instead of seeking retribution for the attack, they urged the administration to withdraw all naval vessels from China to keep U.S. forces out of harm's way. Senator Henry Ashurst, chairman of the Judiciary

Committee, indicated that not a single U.S. senator was prepared to vote for war with Japan.

"As you know, I am fighting against a public psychology of long standing — a psychology which comes very close to saying 'Peace at any price,' " he wrote Endicott Peabody, his Groton schoolmaster. He saw such an outlook as demoralizing and shortsighted. When a Hyde Park friend sent him a summary of radio commentator Boake Carter's criticism of his meddling in the Sino-Japanese war, he responded that half of Carter's statements were "untrue and the other half misstated."

In November, when Congress convened in special session to consider four legislative measures Roosevelt had put before it — a government reorganization plan, a farm bill, a wage and hours law, and a conservation statute built around "seven little TVAs" — he suffered further disappointments, as the session yielded no gains. Congressional conservatives tried to use the meeting to enact an anti–New Deal agenda that included reduced federal spending, and protections for private industry by placing restrictions on labor unions.

Early in December, Roosevelt decided to escape the dispiriting atmosphere in Washington with a fishing excursion off the coast of Florida. He believed that if he left Congress to its own devices, it would ultimately have to come to him. Besides, he badly needed a rest, as a tooth infection had left him with a swollen face, and continuing pain had put him out of sorts. The likelihood of large, enthusiastic crowds gathering to greet him, as they had during his earlier Western tour, promised to boost his spirits. He asked Ickes to come along "to hold his hand." Ickes observed that "He didn't seem at all like himself. He looked bad and he seemed listless. . . . I wondered whether or not his trouble was spiritual or physical. . . . A remark . . . to the effect that he was going to let Congress alone to find out whether or not it could run the Government without his help might mean a general retreat all along the line." The conversation left Ickes feeling "pretty low" and fearful that "we will very probably be engulfed in a reactionary wave and all of the benefits of the New Deal will be swept away." There was no one on the horizon "who could take the place of the President." As for Roosevelt, he had "the appearance of a man who had more or less given up."

Roosevelt's dispiritedness was a response not only to the desultory political scene, but also to distressing problems troubling his children. His four sons, thirty-year-old James, twenty-seven-year-old Elliott, twenty-three-year-old Franklin, Jr., and twenty-one-year-old John, as well as thirty-one-year-old daughter Anna, were a source of constant concern. By December 1937, Anna and Elliott were already on second marriages; Elliott had financial problems, was an outspoken opponent of the New Deal, and worked for the Hearst newspapers, which irritated Franklin no end and moved him secretly to arrange cancellation of Elliott's contract with them. In June 1937, Franklin, Jr., had married Ethel du Pont, linking the president to the du Ponts, who had been the focus of some of his harshest attacks on wealthy moguls. James was having marital problems, and had been the subject of scandalous stories in newspapers about bootlegging in collaboration with millionaire businessman Joseph P. Kennedy

457

and a politically arranged commission as a lieutenant colonel in the Marine Corps.

In addition, Franklin's marriage to Eleanor had by now largely become one of political convenience. This is not to suggest that he did not value her reform agenda or dismissed her progressive support of minorities and public actions aiding economically deprived Americans. But she was more like one among several liberal White House advocates than a first lady with ties to the president that made her his closest adviser. The distance between them left a gap in Roosevelt's life that he sought to fill with closeness to others.

On Christmas Day, for the second year in a row, Eleanor was absent from the White House, though she had told the press that she would be there. In 1936, she was at Franklin, Jr.'s, bedside in Boston, where he was hospitalized with a life-threatening throat infection, and in 1937, she had fled Washington for Seattle to visit Anna, who was ill; Anna's second husband, John Boettiger; and Anna's two children by her first marriage. On this latter occasion, Kenneth Davis asserts, Franklin had a "vague sense of loneliness, of incompletion and un-fulfillment in his personal life." One can also imagine that he had a sense of guilt about having betrayed his marriage. When Eleanor asked him to read the manuscript of her 1937 book, *This Is My Story,* he had persuaded her to delete a quote, "If you love a person, you can forgive big things. Infidelity under certain circumstances need not ruin a relationship." Whether he was concerned that it might focus press attention on his affair with Lucy Mercer, or he simply wanted Eleanor to understand that he knew that his infidelity had cost him dearly, he retained genuine affection for her. "Dearest Babs," he wrote her while on his December fishing trip, ending with "Ever so much love. Devotedly, F."

With his mastery of public affairs both at home and abroad stalled and his family relations strained, Franklin found comfort not only in his White House associates, but in his increasingly close relationship with Daisy. During the Court fight he often spent evenings in relaxation having cocktails, watching upbeat films, or playing poker, but above all in the special relationship he had developed with the forty-five-year-old Daisy. They referred to each other as C.P., "certain person," singling out their exceptional ties to each other. They marked the days when they would come together in Hyde Park or Daisy would visit him in Washington while she pretended to be there for other reasons.

At the close of his Latin American journey, Franklin had noted the almost three weeks during which they had been largely out of touch. He counted on receiving at least one, if not two, letters from her in pouches delivered to the ship and he promised to call her the first chance he had after returning to Washington. On the last days of his trip, he wrote her: "We get into the Port of Spain at 4 A.M. so I must close this — without even seeing your letter. It is such a long time since 3 weeks ago last Monday — Goodnight. AFF, F."

During the Court fight in 1937, he told her: "I am a very firm person — except that where C.P. is concerned I'm not firm at all — & I'm being very obedient . . . & I'm taking very good care of myself." In August, after spending time with her at Hyde Park, he wrote, "What a time I've come back to — My time at H.P. made all the difference and I felt so much more cheerful & rested by Sunday and perspective returned — and calm." Four days later, when he sailed down the Potomac River to escape the Washington heat, he "declined to talk to the people on board," he told her, "— & my mind has been miles away — Why, on a boat should one's *mind* be on a hill with no water in sight — only a place where one knows there is another River?" Franklin was referring to what he and Daisy called "our hill" or what they described as "O.H.": A rustic rise overlooking the Hudson River Valley that they had discovered on a drive during Franklin's visit. Daisy told him that their four hours together had been "sitting in a car next to the nicest person in the world . . . *Wasn't* O.H. lovely? And just full of dreams!" They talked about building a small stone house on the hill he called "top cottage," and Franklin drew up plans for it.

"Do you know that it is a constant wonder to me that I ever got along at all, before I came to *really* know C.P.! He is *such* a 24-hr. help in all ways," she wrote. ". . . Do you know that Happy Times really do pass more quickly than unhappy ones? It certainly seems so — and I am so worried about your overworking — please don't run any risks — for everybody's sake and specially (very selfishly!) for the sake of YM [your Margaret]. . . . That plan [for O.H.] you made has tremendous possibilities. . . . You know — you are really very bad," she added, "for you take advantage of a weak woman's yielding tendencies — but I must confess that there is no one to blame but herself & she hasn't *any* excuse to offer in her own defense! — She's just *weak*, & she's weak for the one & only reason that she wants to be

460

weak. . . . I told the family at home I was lunching with you — and I am glad *your family* was there — It is much better so, & does not raise so many eyebrows."

In October, when Franklin planned another visit to Hyde Park and a return to "our hill," she wrote him: "I wonder why it is that tomorrow promises to be one of the really nice days of the year! *Can you imagine why?*" The evening after their drive, she wrote to say: "Oh my — we *were* so happy this P.M. — but I must go to sleep — Goodnight." He had no reluctance to embrace the pleasure that their affection gave him. Given the burdens of office at home and abroad that had descended on him so quickly in his second term and the mix of joy and distress generated by his family relations, he felt entitled to some satisfaction in his private life.

On December 30, at the final cabinet meeting of the year, Roosevelt said that he was feeling better and intended "to reassert leadership." The adoring regard shown by Daisy and the steady stream of affectionate letters from ordinary Americans boosted his spirits. In addition, the encouragement of Harvard Law School professor Felix Frankfurter was a source of constant gratification to him. Viewed by Roosevelt as a brilliant lawyer and wise counselor who had helped shape the New Deal by recommending young lawyers like Benjamin Cohen, Tommy Corcoran, and Alger Hiss for administration posts, Frankfurter exerted influence that was acknowledged in Washington as genuine wisdom.

In November, Frankfurter had rekindled the president's enthusiasm for serving the nation by telling him: "Whenever, since March 4, 1933, the

461

public mind has been confused, you alone had the power to give it composure and coherence. We are again in one of those phases where the so-called leaders of business and finance, with their journalistic and legalistic echoes, are trying to infect the general public with their own panicky and shortsighted disquietude. . . . The people don't expect you to pull rabbits out of your hat. . . . They would again hear, as they were so glad to hear in the past, at firsthand and from your own lips, that you are not panicky, that you know better than any of the croakers that there are difficulties," and that Roosevelt had "a well-defined direction toward . . . the objectives of national well-being." Frankfurter thought it would not hurt Roosevelt to acknowledge that there were no surefire answers to current dilemmas, but that he would do well to counter the "negative and poisonous public atmosphere" created by business and financial leaders with a showing of his "own robust energy and good sense and contagious confidence in the working out of our difficulties."

Frankfurter's letter was a welcome counter to a display of negativism by Vice President Garner. Mindful of the president's setbacks and declining influence, Garner asked Roosevelt at the year-end cabinet meeting whether he had given up on leading the country. Roosevelt replied that he "had put it temporarily on the shelf because he was tired. The vice president retorted: 'You were afraid, Mr. President.' The president repeated that he had been tired. The vice president came back with: 'Before you went to Florida, Mr. President, you were both scared and tired.' . . . I never heard anyone talk like this to the President," Ickes recorded, "and the President did not pursue the subject any further." Garner's rudeness signaled not only his political differences with Roosevelt on his postelection attack on the Court but also his sense that the president was now "a thoroughly repudiated leader."

CHAPTER 10
THE WORST OF TIMES

Despite his assurances to the cabinet at its year-end meeting, Roosevelt continued to be tired and frustrated throughout the winter of 1937–38. The next three years of his term looked bleak. Conservative Democrats, mindful of how the Court fight, the recession (which 58 percent of a Gallup poll described as a business depression), and public resistance to hints in his quarantine speech of international intervention had weakened his political standing, which he no longer felt was under his command. With Republicans in a distinct minority after their defeats in the 1936 presidential and congressional elections, dissenting Democrats were now Roosevelt's strongest adversaries, especially across the South, which feared reformist intervention in local economic and racial affairs by White House authorities. If Roosevelt was considering running in 1940 for an unprecedented third term, party opponents believed that they could stop him with support from millions of Americans alienated by his unbalanced budgets, tacit acceptance of labor radicalism in the sit-down strikes, increased unemployment of up to ten million in the recession, and his alleged attempt at dictatorial control similar to Mussolini's and Hitler's.

Meanwhile, newspaper owners, led by William Randolph Hearst and Colonel Robert R. McCormick, the publisher of the *Chicago Tribune*, America's most "blackguard" paper, were, Ickes said, "trying to get something on any member of the Cabinet" that could be turned into "an indictable offense." Later in the year, when Roosevelt fled Washington for another fishing holiday, he told Daisy, "What a comfort to get away from the damn newspapers ('scuse me) — I wish I had enough money to start a newspaper — confined to news without interpretation, coloration, twisting or downright lying — I think it would be a financial success!"

While publishers like Hearst and McCormick were avowed Roosevelt enemies and left no doubt of their eagerness to end his political regime, most reporters admired and openly supported the president. Despite widespread editorial opposition to Roosevelt's White House, 73 percent of Americans, influenced by sympathetic portraits of the president written by reporters, thought that the press treated his administration fairly.

At the start of 1938, mindful of the growing antipathy to his presidency and exhausted by the pressures of the office, Roosevelt had no clear plan to run again. Although between 55 and 63 percent of Americans in the early months of 1938 continued to approve of his presidential performance, 70 percent said they opposed a third term. Roosevelt took solace in looking ahead to his post–White House years. He would be fifty-nine when he left office and planned to write his memoirs. Although he loved being president, he was realistic enough about his current political standing to recognize that he would be inviting defeat if he tried for another term. Memories of Theodore Roosevelt's attempt in 1912 for a third term "colored FDR's consideration of what another run for the White House could bring. Nonetheless, in the three years remaining to him, he retained some hope of advancing international cooperation or at least of expanding U.S. military power to deter aggressors and further humanizing American social relations.

In his January 1938 State of the Union address, which he delivered in person to a joint congressional session to ensure that the full Congress would take heed of his words, and on the radio to reach a large public audience, Roosevelt focused less on the actual state of the union than on the misjudgments of governments abroad and Americans at home. He delivered the speech "in a slow and deliberate voice" over the course of forty-five minutes, placing great emphasis on controversial issues like the fascist threat and antidemocratic U.S. business monopolies. This angered conservative Democrats, who were seated in the two front rows of the House facing him. Senators Josiah Bailey of North Carolina, Carter Glass of Virginia, and Millard Tydings of Maryland made their hostility to the president and his New Deal advisers like Ben Cohen, Tommy Corcoran, and Harry Hopkins all too evident by sitting on their hands during his speech and offering only the most perfunctory applause when he was introduced and concluded his speech. "Democrats, Democrats," Carter Glass exclaimed about Roosevelt's administration, "why, Thomas Jefferson would not speak to these people." Mindful of the deepening divide, Ickes confided to his diary, "The war is on fiercer than ever between the reactionaries and the liberals in the Democratic party."

Roosevelt's opening salvo in his speech warned about the hazardous state of international affairs and urged the country to keep itself "adequately strong in self-defense. . . . Peace is most greatly jeopardized," he said, ". . . by those nations where democracy has been discarded or has never developed." He reminded Americans that they could not afford to ignore fascist "disregard for treaty obligations" and attacks on other nations. "The future peace of mankind," he stressed, depended on the restoration or establishment of democracy in the lawless nations. No one with the slightest knowledge of developments abroad could miss the reference to Italy's invasion of Ethiopia; Japan's assault on China; the fascist rebellion against Spain's democratically elected government; Germany's threat to Austria, Czechoslovakia, Poland, France, and Great Britain; or the victory of fascism in Romania, where Germany had financed sixty newspapers and the king had appointed a premier whose party had won only 9 percent of the vote in a recent election. In raising concerns about foreign threats to the United States, Roosevelt countered isolationist sentiment by striking resonant chords with most Americans, who favored stronger air, land, and naval forces. Public sympathy for preparedness in case of fascist aggression against democratic countries, including the United States, had convinced Roosevelt that disputing isolationism was best accomplished by raising the threat of attack rather than idealistic appeals to preserving democracy everywhere.

As for domestic affairs, "candor," Roosevelt said, dictated that he caution against returning to "conduct of [a] national government after the practice of 1787 or 1837 or 1887." The challenges in 1938 to satisfy "human needs" were "infinitely greater . . . than in any previous period in the life of our Republic." Congress, the courts, and the country needed "to face facts" not as they wished them to be but as they were. The imperative for 1938 was effective government regulation of agriculture and industry and the assurance of a minimum wage and maximum hours for workers. Opponents of these measures, he asserted, had no viable alternatives to propose, and "that is not what you or I would call helpful citizenship." As for Congress, he reminded it that "those suffering hardship . . . have a right to call upon the Government for aid; and a government worthy of its name must make fitting response."

In the first three months of the year stock and farm prices, industrial production, and employment continued a seven-month downward slide. When neither high-profile conversations with prominent business chiefs intended to raise business confidence, which some thought was the root cause of the economic slide, nor limited expansion of government spending stemmed the downturn, Roosevelt felt stymied in his search for answers to the country's economic troubles.

By the end of February, the "appeasement" campaign of business, one historian says, was "a shambles. . . . Business leaders (and the business press) were deriding the entire affair as a 'con' designed to promote cooptation, not cooperation." It was seen as a way "to permit the administration 'to wait to see what happens this spring.' " But Roosevelt himself never had much confidence in wooing businessmen as a solution to the downturn. As he told Fred I. Kent, a prominent New York banker and businessman, who chided him for taking counsel from "impractical theorists," he and many of his associates suffered from "a form of narrowness and lack of education" about the difficulties faced by ordinary citizens and the virtue of using federal power to assist them. Yet at the same time, mindful that 63 percent of a Gallup poll opposed a big Keynesian program of deficit spending, Roosevelt was left without a way to move forward. White House inaction "served to underscore the absence of any coherent policy for confronting the recession."

Events abroad deepened Roosevelt's sense of his loss of control. Fascism seemed triumphant everywhere. Not only were the Japanese expanding across China and unrepentant for their indiscriminate bombing and conquest of Nanking, China's capital, where between two hundred and three hundred thousand civilians were massacred in January and February of 1938, but Europe seemed at the mercy of fascist aggression as well. Hitler's Germany seized Austria in a March 12 invasion and celebrated a 99 percent favorable vote for *Anschluss,* the annexation of Austria to Germany. The acquiescence of Britain and Italy in Hitler's incorporation of Austria into the Third Reich added to Roosevelt's fears of fascist gains threatening democracy. Simultaneously, British plans to recognize Italy's Ethiopian conquest, which triggered the resignation of Foreign Minister Anthony Eden from Neville Chamberlain's cabinet, moved Roosevelt to tell John Cudahy, his ambassador to Ireland, "If a Chief of Police makes a deal with the leading gangsters and the deal results in no more hold-ups, that Chief of Police will be called a great man — but if the gangsters do not live up to their word the Chief of Police will go to jail. Some people are, I think, taking very long chances — don't you?"

A constitutional amendment proposed by Indiana representative Louis Ludlow to transfer the war-making power from Congress to a national referendum, except for the case of an invasion, also distressed him. Roosevelt warned Congress that such a provision would be "impractical in its application and incompatible with our representative form of government." He saw it crippling "any president in his conduct of our foreign relations, and would encourage other nations to believe that they could violate American rights with impunity." Instead of keeping the United States out of war as intended, the amendment would make it more likely. The amendment's defeat by only 21 votes, followed by a failed attempt to revise the country's neutrality laws to restore executive control over foreign policy, left Roosevelt feeling largely powerless.

In 1938, as in 1933, at the depths of the Depression, Roosevelt believed it essential to address domestic issues first. To revive enthusiasm for reforms that could spur an expansionary surge, Roosevelt traveled to Georgia in March, where his Warm Springs retreat gave him standing as a native son and he could celebrate the revival of the small Georgia city of Gainesville after it had been devastated by a 1936 tornado. In a speech at the city center, he praised the work of the Reconstruction Finance Corporation, PWA, and WPA in rebuilding and modernizing local government structures and private homes. It was a demonstration of New Deal effectiveness in not only repair-

470

ing the city's infrastructure but also eliminating "old conditions of which you were not proud." The work of reconstruction, Roosevelt emphasized, had "national significance" and more immediately, regional implications. He urged Americans to apply the principles of generosity to national problems, as had been demonstrated in Gainesville. "National progress and national prosperity," he said, "are being held back chiefly because of selfishness on the part of a few." The current situation was, he asserted, reminiscent of what had happened in the United States between 1921 and 1933 when advocates of unlimited laissez-faire held power. Because the South was the most economically backward part of the country and the region where Roosevelt believed progressive advances could make the greatest difference, he urged an end to feudal conditions there, which he compared to fascism: "If you believe in the one, you lean to the other," he said. Progressive reforms in these states, he added, would not only bring prosperity to the least affluent members of Southern society but also would advance the well-being of more comfortable citizens as well.

Roosevelt's message found little support in the national arena. His hold on Congress, and especially conservative Southern Democrats, who saw the New Deal as destructive to "existing social-economic relations," had all but collapsed. As Virginia senator Carter Glass observed, "The South would better begin thinking whether it will continue to cast its 152 electoral votes according to the memories of the Reconstruction era of 1865 and thereafter, or will have spirit and courage enough to face the new Reconstruction era that northern so-called Democrats are menacing us with."

Congressional votes on an executive reorganization bill were painful evidence of Roosevelt's diminished political power. Attempts to reorganize executive functions to reduce government costs had a long history, dating back to at least the Taft presidency in the first decade of the century. But in 1938 the major hurdle was not opposition to making the executive branch more efficient but allegations that Roosevelt intended to use the reform to make himself a dictator by transferring congressional powers to the White House. After the Court fight had eroded the president's standing, other opponents viewed the reorganization bill as an opportunity to reduce his influence even further by exploiting public fears of a dictatorship. Michigan's Republican senator Arthur Vandenberg claimed that the president's reorganization initiative was "more sinister as a symbol than as a reality. But we are dreadfully sensitive these days to symbols — whether they be fasces or swastikas or hammers and cycles [sic] or new blue eagles over the White House."

The White House also saw symbolic importance in the reorganization debate, for as Ickes observed, "If the President is beaten on this reorganization bill, it will be another major defeat." Even some friends of the administration, including congressmen eager to preserve legislative powers, functionaries in various government agencies fretting over threats to their domains, and cabinet secretaries who feared it might eliminate some of their departments' agencies or shift them to other departments, saw reasons to go against what a mystified president considered a rather innocuous measure. Catholic prelates, who had applauded Roosevelt's appointment of Catholics and Jews to staff his administration and had been sympathetic to its government programs helping the needy, were fearful that the bill would empower the president to establish a Department of Education, which might then take control of parochial schools and eliminate their religious teachings. Conservatives, for their part, foresaw the establishment of a Department of Welfare run by Harry Hopkins, which would greatly increase the government's deficit spending and give Hopkins a launching pad for a 1940 presidential campaign.

An outpouring of newspaper ads, op-ed columns, and radio speeches, highlighted by Father Coughlin's reemergence from retirement, and what Roosevelt biographer Kenneth S. Davis describes as "deluges of more than [330,000] telegrams addressed to congressmen and senators" at a cost of $150,000, fueled a campaign against the bill. Although the Senate passed the administration's proposal by a scant 5 votes, the House, persuaded by Massachusetts senator David Walsh's assertion that approval of the bill would be tantamount "to the plunging of a dagger into the very heart of democracy," rejected Roosevelt's insistence on pushing it forward by sending it back to the rules committee by an 8-vote margin. Although Roosevelt had released a letter to the press asserting that he had no interest in becoming a dictator, he refused to dignify the opposition by attacking it in a Fireside Chat. "The President of the United States cannot engage in a radio debate with the [conservative] Boake Carters and Father Coughlins," he wrote a friend, who had urged him to refute the overheated charges against the measure in a national speech. In any case, Roosevelt believed that the attacks leveled against the bill were so overblown that the Democratic majorities in Congress would enact it. "I didn't expect the vote," Roosevelt told Jim Farley. "I can't understand it. There wasn't a chance for anyone to become a dictator under that bill."

Although the defeat meant little to the long-run viability of the New Deal, and the much more "pressing matter now" was "a measure to bring about economic recovery," Roosevelt agreed with Ickes, who told him after the bill was shelved that "his prestige and leadership were involved right up to the hilt; that if he took this defeat on the reorganization bill, he would have to expect other defeats and he wouldn't be in a position to give effective leadership in a recovery program. . . . The important question," Ickes added, "is not that of reorganization but the prestige of the Administration." It was, Ickes concluded, the culmination of an opposition campaign against the president begun by the Liberty League in 1936.

The stakes were now a renewed progressive advance in achieving national prosperity and a more just society. Roosevelt's hesitation in moving more quickly to end the recession had partly been the consequence of a divide in the administration. On one side were pro-business advocates, led by Henry Morgenthau and others in the Treasury Department, Jim Farley, and former Brain Trust adviser Aldof Berle, who urged reduced government spending and balanced budgets to promote business confidence. On the other, were left-leaning New Dealers led by Ickes, Harry Hopkins,

Ben Cohen, Tommy Corcoran, and Eleanor Roosevelt, who favored increased spending on PWA, WPA, CCC, and NYA projects; passage of a Fair Labor Standards Act (FLSA) setting minimum wages of twenty-five cents an hour and maximum forty-four-hour work weeks; and an attack on business oligarchies, which were believed responsible for triggering the recession as a way to challenge Roosevelt, increased government control of the economy, and Democratic majorities in the 1938 and 1940 elections.

The conflicting ideas about how to restore economic growth led to a nasty fight within Roosevelt's inner circle. Ickes criticized Morgenthau as a "thoroughgoing conservative" who gave the president "bad" advice on "fiscal and economic" matters. In early April, when Roosevelt informed Morgenthau that he was signing on to the "spenders" program, with $5 billion in pump priming, Morgenthau was brought to tears and told Roosevelt, "It not only frightens me it will frighten the country," or more to the point, the business community, which would shudder at the news of the increased government deficits. Roosevelt chided Morgenthau for raising the deficit issue at a meeting with congressional leaders, calling his behavior "mischievous" and "obstructionist." Convinced that Roosevelt was adopting a course that "could ruin the country," Morgenthau threatened that he was "seriously thinking of resigning." But pressed by Roosevelt to remain in office with praise for the job he was doing and warnings that his departure would undermine both the administration's current legislative program and the chances for Democrats in the upcoming elections, as well as casting a long shadow over Morgenthau's historical reputation, Morgenthau stayed on.

On April 14, Roosevelt came out swinging. He sent a message to Congress decrying the current slump that "threaten[s] the security of our people and the stability of our economic life. . . . All energies of Government and business must be directed to increasing the national income; to putting more people into private jobs; to giving security . . . to all people in all walks of life." The first order of business was not "to weaken or destroy [the administration's] great reforms." Beyond that, it was essential to maintain and increase the appropriations for agencies providing relief and expansion of credit and to consider future actions to remedy "the problems of monopolistic practices and price fixing." Appropriations to expand work projects that would quickly provide jobs for the increased ranks of the unemployed were the top priority. The fundamental issue, he added, was nothing less than the survival of democracy as a successful system of government and social organization.

That evening, Roosevelt rallied the nation to his program with his first Fireside Chat in five months. He stressed the urgency of addressing the human suffering that had been brought on by renewed economic retreat. He acknowledged that the country was not in the dire circumstances that had afflicted it in 1933, but it was in distress nonetheless. He then recounted his message to Congress calling for measures that could address the current recession and reaffirmed his allegiance to democracy and the importance of government action that addressed economic dislocations and demands for social justice.

Roosevelt's appeals did not go unanswered.

Identifying himself as a champion of democracy rather than its foe struck resonant chords with the public. When Gallup asked Americans if they favored increased government spending "to help get business out of its present slump," those who heard the president's radio talk were 9 percent more likely to favor the increase than those who hadn't heard it. In addition, only 30 percent of a survey blamed Roosevelt and New Deal policies for the turndown, while 70 percent attributed it to "business, natural economic trends, bad distribution of wealth, [and] lingering effects of the World War." Congress finally agreed to a wages and hours law and increased appropriations for public works and other New Deal programs, as Roosevelt had asked.

But Roosevelt's requests did not receive full support, and his popularity continued to wane. While 54 percent of voters still approved of his performance, 46 percent rated it as unfavorable. Another 62 percent thought he was less popular than before, and 70 percent said they opposed a third term. Additionally, 64 percent stated that they were less well off than they had been a year earlier, and when citizens were asked how they wanted Roosevelt to fight the recession, more people favored fewer "restrictions on business initiative, such as higher taxes, reduced government spending and . . . balance[d] budget[s]" than increased government spending, as Roosevelt had proposed. And troubling to the White House, 58 percent of Americans considered the current slump to be a depression, while only 42 percent regarded it as a recession. And when people were asked if they favored replacing the existing two parties with a conservative and a liberal party, an idea that had been germinating in Roosevelt's mind, a decisive 70 percent said no. Some White House mail gave voice to the vitriolic resistance he faced: "You will go down in history as the man who ruined America," a North Carolinian wrote. A man from Atlanta urged him to "try dipping your head in a pail of water three times and just bring it out twice. Then the country will really recover."

On April 30, exhausted by the battles over reorganization and remedies to combat the recession, Roosevelt fled Washington for a Caribbean vacation. His departure, with a complement of White House aides, he wrote Daisy, amounted to "a perfect day" that included sunning himself on the forward deck of the cruiser carrying him out of Charleston, South Carolina, a two-hour afternoon nap, and an evening session with his stamps and early to bed. The next day opened with Sunday services on the quarter deck followed by "a quiet P.M." with "more sun & stamps" and passed without "*any* work — one detective story nearly finished — Movies tonight and now it's bed & 10:20." Five days into the trip he felt liberated from political pressures "& official mail which I have glanced thru' with a feeling of complete boredom & laid aside . . . That proves that the trip has been a complete success for the more fit I am physically & mentally," he told Daisy, "the more I incline to put off things that should be done — & the more tired I am the more I insist on keeping up to the minute & driving myself to all the official tasks — That sounds completely 'cuckoo' as the children say but I know C.[ertain] P.[erson] will understand."

Roosevelt returned to Washington, as he invariably did, with renewed energy. Formerly cautious

Democrats who had been fretting over budget deficits that they believed undermined business confidence now signed on to Roosevelt's renewed call for spending. In an election year, when government projects providing jobs translated into support at the polls, congressmen and senators found supporting such programs advantageous.

On April 29, Roosevelt sent a request to Congress to curb monopolies. Tying his message to the rise of dictatorships abroad, Roosevelt warned against the "ownership of Government by an individual, a group, or by any other controlling private power." An unprecedented concentration of economic power in America threatened not only the country's economic well-being but its political freedom. Roosevelt asserted that the existing antimonopoly statutes were inadequate to the challenge of curbing financial and economic predators. "Business monopoly in America paralyzes the system of free enterprise . . . and is as fatal to those who manipulate it as to the people who suffer beneath its imposition." Roosevelt wanted funding not for a remedial program but for an investigation into the problem and its remedy.

Congress, mindful of the country's antimonopoly tradition reaching back to the nineteenth century with the Sherman Anti-Trust Act and the reforms of the Progressive Era, agreed to establish a Temporary National Economic Committee staffed by three senators, three congressmen, and six officials from executive departments. Although no one could determine exactly what the TNEC's mission was, it began in June with hopes that it would produce far-reaching recommendations. It was nonetheless described as "one of the most important events of our recent history," and an inquiry that could ensure that "the New Deal will go down in history as Roosevelt's revolution."

Congress's response to Roosevelt's recommendations on the economy encouraged him to mount a campaign to purge the Democratic Party of its most conservative members. He was especially focused on Southerners who had opposed Court packing, executive reorganization, and the Fair Labor Standards Act or wages and hours law. Southern congressmen and senators viewed FLSA's requirements for a minimum wage as destructive to their regional economy by forcing local businesses to pay wages comparable to those in other parts of the country and inhibiting the shift of textile and other industries to a low-wage South. Southern opponents also regarded the law as an assault on Southern racial policies that made African Americans subsist on meager incomes, keeping them in a de facto, if not de jure, condition of dependence resembling slavery.

No one around the president was more supportive of these reform measures, including FLSA, than Eleanor Roosevelt, who was especially concerned about the plight of African Americans. In April, a "White House conference on more equitable distribution of federal benefits to black women and the Negro community" pointed to "discriminatory practices in the administration of public health services, social security benefits, and federal welfare programs." As Blanche Wiesen Cook, Eleanor's biographer, recounts, the White House was warily aware of complaints that "every decent act toward racial justice, every union organized, every speech for equal rights was condemned as communist." Eleanor's support of liberal advocates of remedial action led to her being widely criticized, to which she responded, "I am accused of being a Red, as is everyone in this country who is working for better living conditions." These attacks did more to secure her place as the leading voice of liberal reform in the administration than to discourage or deter her from urging Franklin to advance progressive measures.

The outcry across the South from Eleanor's critics and especially from foes of FLSA revived regional antagonisms reminiscent of those of the 1920s. All but one member of the House Mississippi delegation, for example, took exception to the wages and hours bill, convincing Roosevelt that the opposition to the law would keep the region in penury as the most impoverished area of the country. "Those who are making the loudest noise" against the bill, one Southern liberal senator declared, "are slave drivers." But Roosevelt believed that he was in fact offering Southerners a remedy for their economic backwardness, telling a Texas audience, "You need more industries in Texas, but I know you know the importance of not trying to get industries by the route of cheap wages for industrial workers." He was pleased when he read a Birmingham, Alabama, columnist's assertion that "the South, it may be said, is looking right, left, up, down and, over — but it still loves Roosevelt."

If voter affection for him across the region was in fact as strong as the journalist claimed, Roosevelt believed that it would allow him to transform the Southern wing of the Democratic Party into a center of New Deal support, and as such become a vehicle for turning the whole party into an advocate of liberal policies and actions. At an April 21 press conference with the American Society of Newspaper Editors, Roosevelt was asked if he thought the solid Democratic South would remain that way much longer. Well, it's a "funny place," he replied and then launched into a description of the late nineteenth-century South, where the educational level was terribly low — no high school and only three or four months a year of elementary schooling. The average citizen "did not read the daily paper . . . did not read a magazine. They were getting the lowest form of pay in the entire nation, and they were therefore completely susceptible to the demagogue." But he thought that things were changing: "The South is going to remain Democratic," he said, but it would be "a more intelligent form of democracy. . . . It is going to be a liberal democracy."

Roosevelt saw "ample evidence" that the South was moving in a liberal direction. In the first months of 1938, Democratic senatorial primaries in Alabama and Florida gave victories to two Roosevelt supporters. In April, the forty-three-year-old Lister Hill, who had served in the House for fifteen years, where he had been a staunch friend of the New Deal, won a Senate primary contest against former Alabama senator Tom Heflin, whom Ickes described as a conservative, anti–New Deal windbag. At the same time, the thirty-seven-year-old Claude Pepper, whose liberal advocacy included outspoken support for the wages and hours law, won a hard-fought Senate primary in Florida with Roosevelt's backing. "The President thinks he is one of the best men who have come out of the South in a long time," Ickes recorded. To some analysts, the Hill and Pepper victories were "proof positive that progressives are gaining ground" across the South and that the "Bourbons in the Senate" stood "on pretty soggy ground."

One Indiana resident gave the president license to launch a wider campaign for additional progressive gains in the final two years of his term. "We must also purge our party of . . . demagogue Democrats," the man wrote after the Hill and Pepper victories. "These few who have not only betrayed you but the people who made it possible for them to be in Washington. It is much harder to fight back when we have members within our own party, aligning with reactionaries fighting us. The party cannot keep the confidence of the people with such traitors in the party. They all should have opposition at the primaries." Ousting conservative Democrats from office had actually been an idea that Roosevelt had been pondering since they opposed him over Court reform in 1937 and gained additional appeal when they broke with him over executive reorganization. Speechwriter Sam Rosenman, who had a close-up view of Roosevelt during this period, said, "There was no doubt of his animosity toward those who were willing to run on a liberal party platform with him and then vote against the very platform pledges on which they had been elected." The president repeatedly complained to Rosenman about such "shenanigans. . . . But even deeper was his feeling — and I believe this was the fundamental reason for the purge — that the reactionary Democrats were doing a distinct and permanent injury to the nation."

Martin Dies, a thirty-seven-year-old Texas congressman who had been in the House since 1931, was one of the Southern conservative

Democrats whom Roosevelt found most troubling. The son of a congressman and friend of John Nance Garner, who had made Dies a member of the House Rules Committee, Dies was among a handful of congressmen who enjoyed considerable national visibility. His early support of the New Deal, which Roosevelt thought had helped give his reforms legitimacy, made Dies a favorite of the White House. But after the 1937 sit-down strikes, which he believed were controlled by communists, he became a harsh White House critic. He opposed the administration's Wages and Hours bill and clashed with Roosevelt over making its provisions compulsory for the South.

In May 1938, Dies was named chairman of a Special House Committee Investigating Un-American Activities. The Dies Committee, as it was known, became the congressional face of what Ickes called one of the "periodic Red hunts" it was "addicted to." Despite the embarrassment the committee brought on itself by raising suspicions about ten-year-old movie star Shirley Temple for alleged communist affiliations and its attack on the Federal Theater Project of the WPA, accusing the Project of promoting communism by producing subversive plays, it was a disturbing reminder of how reactionary some Democrats, especially from the South, could be. Few, however, exceeded the forty-three-year-old J. Parnell Thomas, a conservative New Jersey Republican opponent of the New Deal and minority committee member, who charged that the New Deal "sabotaged the capitalist system." In 1940, he began engaging in a salary kickback arrangement that would eventually land him in prison, but well after Roosevelt was gone and could have the satisfaction of seeing so reactionary an opponent brought down.

Moved by "confidence in himself and in the public support he thought he could muster," Roosevelt tried to "purge," as opponents described it, the Democratic Party of its conservative senators and congressmen. But surveys of public opinion between June 11 and June 16 indicated limited support for his plan. Only 28 percent of a poll said that they wanted to see a more liberal Democratic Party, while 72 percent favored a more conservative party over the next two years. At the same time, asked if the White House should use primaries to defeat Democratic senators who had opposed Roosevelt's Court packing plan, 69 percent of Democratic voters said, "No"; only 31 percent saw it as a good idea.

But convinced that the survival of the New Deal and possibilities of additional reforms depended on ousting uncooperative party members, Roosevelt took to the airwaves to defeat conservative foes. On a very hot June 24 evening, in the sixth year of his presidency, he gave the thirteenth of his Fireside Chats. He began by noting the eight major achievements of the current Congress, which had just adjourned for the year. He also celebrated the shift in the Supreme Court's views on New Deal measures, saying the "lost battle" had ultimately produced a victory in a war. He reminded his listeners that the 1936 elections had demonstrated the devotion of the American people to a "sane and consistent liberalism," proving that those who were arguing that "people were getting weary of reform" were wrong. It didn't stop them, however, from "a campaign of defeatism . . . thrown at the heads of the President and . . . Senators and Congressmen." Like the

"Copperheads" during the Civil War, who favored "peace at any price," these conservatives wanted his administration to abandon government efforts to build a more prosperous and just society. Turning to the coming party elections, he said that he was "not taking part in Democratic primaries," but as head of the party he believed himself charged with "the responsibility of carrying out the definitely liberal declaration of principles set forth in the 1936 Democratic platform." He was not opposed to any candidate on personal grounds, he added, but only to a "yes but" fellow — that is, someone who professed a commitment to progressive ideas but always found ways to avoid supporting or even opposing them.

The *New York Herald Tribune* reported that Roosevelt's speech made a compelling case for continued reform: "The rich voice, the calm assurance, the adroit catchwords, the note of simple sincerity and of genial friendliness to all mankind — punctuated by neat jabs at all who oppose him — all the old magic was there without a flaw." But, in fact, as Gallup's earlier June poll indicated, public and congressional reaction was anything but uniformly sympathetic to presidential pressure for a turn toward the left. The response to his Fireside Chat was mixed, with critics complaining about being attacked as Copperheads, a Pennsylvania man saying that "you must be too intelligent to believe what you say," and an Indiana minister taking the president to task for stooping "to do what you proposed regarding your opposition . . . and certain to strengthen" it. A Birmingham, Alabama, resident felt that he had lowered "the dignity of your office and the white house by telling folks how to vote." Roosevelt was making the same mistake he had made in the Court fight: Just as his false assertion about his motive for Court packing had offended many, so his insistence that he was not telling people how to vote in the Democratic primaries, when that was exactly his intention, angered voters opposed to presidential interference in local contests and strengthened their determination to oppose him.

Meanwhile, a host of other problems was descending on him. Harry Hopkins, to whom he had become very close, had suffered a personal loss when his thirty-seven-year-old second wife died of cancer in December 1937. The following year Hopkins himself fell ill with stomach cancer and had to have surgery at the Mayo Clinic in Rochester, Minnesota. Roosevelt's son Jimmy, who had been working as his secretary, came down with gastric ulcers and also faced surgery.

As the recession continued to dog the economy, Philip La Follette, the governor of Wisconsin, threatened to divide and undermine liberal leadership in the country when on April 28, he announced the formation of a third party, the National Progressives of America. Ickes, believing that the La Follette action would fall short and that no one else could step forward to lead liberalism, began urging Roosevelt to consider running again in 1940 in order to save progressive reform: "I told him that I loved him too much to wish such a thing on him," Ickes said, but he saw no alternative. Roosevelt replied he didn't want to run again but acknowledged the difficulty of finding someone to replace him. He went through a list of possible candidates and dismissed each one as not measuring up, but he wanted no public discussion of another term for himself, convinced it would do more harm than good. As he told Eleanor, "Any President is doubly cursed in his second term by discussion of the possibility of a third term." He considered it a distraction that "keeps any President from doing his best work" and wanted it made clear that in 1938 and 1939 he would be thinking only about current troubles.

Between July 8 and July 14, when a conference Roosevelt had asked thirty-two countries to attend in France at Evian-les-Bains to find sanctuaries for Austrian and German Jews persecuted and abused by the Nazis arrived at no workable solutions, it deepened his sense of powerlessness. A critic of the proceedings complained that sympathetic pronouncements by its delegates were "a facade behind which the civilized governments could hide their inability to act." An Intergovernmental committee set up to continue monitoring the refugee crisis was no more than a gesture devoid of anything resembling a solution.

Roosevelt fled Washington again for another sea voyage in the Pacific from July 17 to August 2. Of all his vacation cruises, one biographer wrote, this "was perhaps the one he most needed for relaxation, recreation, restoration of body and spirit. . . . He took with him no one who would tax him with weighty affairs of state." In deference to his wishes, Roosevelt's companions — Press Secretary Steve Early, White House physician Ross McIntire, former law partner Basil O'Connor, military aide Pa Watson, and Fred Adams, the son-in-law of Franklin's uncle Warren Delano III — cheered him with their camaraderie and enthusiasm. Adams and O'Connor were "like children seeing the circus for the first time," he told Daisy, and the fact that they "kept off politics by common consent" was an added delight. The absence of mail, except for radio messages, was a godsend. In one message to Marvin McIntyre at the White House, Roosevelt declared, "I take it you have a screamingly funny time over primaries! Here we don't care who wins!"

But preceding the voyage, his trip across country to San Diego, where he again boarded the cruiser *Houston,* belied his claim. Banking on his personal popularity, he turned his train journey into a campaign for liberal Democrats most sympathetic to his reforms. In Maryland, Georgia, Florida, Kentucky, Nevada, Texas, Oklahoma, and other states, he gave twenty-seven speeches promoting favored candidates, and where conservatives were running without an opponent, he made his small regard for them clear. In Kentucky, for example, he heaped praise on Senate Majority Leader Alben Barkley, who had been an unqualified proponent of the president's New Deal agenda, and faced a tough contest against the state's governor, Albert B. (Happy) Chandler, whose election Roosevelt emphasized would hurt the party and administration by removing Barkley from the majority leadership. Likewise, Roosevelt warmly endorsed Oklahoma senator Elmer Thomas, an advocate of White House conservation projects, who was fighting for his political life. In supporting certain candidates, Roosevelt also effectively celebrated the gains of New Deal conservation measures that served the Southwest by preventing soil erosion, irrigating farms, ending floods, and developing waterpower. Like his cousin Theodore, he regarded conservation as an enduring concern that would form a key part of his legacy.

Along the way, whether in Texas, Colorado, or

Nevada, Roosevelt snubbed conservative Democrats who had opposed his Court packing or shown themselves unsympathetic to other reforms. Because several of these senators and congressman, mindful of the president's popularity, showed up at his appearances, Roosevelt pointedly ignored them or omitted to give them the customary mention in his talks. They were explicitly barred from being photographed with the president, and when possible he gave a shout-out to their opponents to embarrass his detractors. In Texas, for example, Roosevelt enraged Senator Tom Connally, a highly vocal foe of Court packing, by announcing an appointment to a federal judgeship of someone of whom Connally disapproved.

In addition to the appreciative crowds reinforcing his sense of satisfaction at remaining so popular after five and a half years in office, Roosevelt luxuriated in the scenic wonders of his July voyage. He sent Daisy a daily diary account of his activities and the natural wonders of the sky and islands as they proceeded along the coast of Baja California. "Tonight's sunset," he noted on the eighteenth, was "the most amazing I have ever seen." An eight-mile run from their fishing site through rough waters back to the ship left them "soaked to the skin & tired in the right way." He described places he had never seen before, marveled at islands far out to sea, "submerged mountains with only their tops showing." The discoveries of Dr. Waldo Schmitt, a "delightful" Smithsonian naturalist, who collected previously unknown specimens, intrigued Roosevelt, who shared the scientist's fascination with nature. When Schmitt discovered "a new variety of burrowing shrimp," Roosevelt couldn't resist a crack at Washington political opponents: "You & I know lots of shrimps —" he told Daisy "— tho their brain capacity was similar to the ones discovered today!" They sailed to the Galapagos, where he had the feeling of being in "the Pleistocene Period" with "the most ancient forms of animal life in the world — tortoises, iguanas etc. are the oldest living form of the animals of 15,000,000 years ago"

All too soon he was back on the West Coast of the United States and reengaged with the primary fights. On his way back to Washington, he stopped in Georgia and South Carolina to campaign against two of his most formidable congressional opponents, senators Walter George and Ellison D. "Cotton Ed" Smith. At a speech in Barnesville, Georgia, a suburb of Atlanta, where he dedicated an REA facility, Roosevelt emphasized his attachment to the state through his fourteen-year residence in Warm Springs and his concern for the South. He reported the imminent appearance of a study citing the region's enduring economic problems and his determination to use federal programs to relieve them, mentioning the successful New Deal initiative on rural electrification that his experience in Georgia had inspired. But his continuing to aid the South, he explained, depended on the cooperation of Congress, and for him to be able to do so, Georgians would have to end sixty-year-old senator Walter George's fifteen-year Senate career and replace him with U.S. Attorney Lawrence Camp, a bona fide liberal. Roosevelt praised George as a gentleman and a scholar, as well as a friend, but despite his early support of the New Deal, including REA, TVA,

AAA, and Social Security, in 1937 and 1938 George opposed the president's court reform and the Wages and Hours law.

At a brief stop in Greenville in the northwest corner of South Carolina, Roosevelt made a less overt but no less forceful case against Smith in comments from the back of the train carrying him back to Washington. An outspoken tobacco-chewing racist who declared that "Cotton is king and white is supreme," the sixty-seven-year-old Smith enjoyed only marginal popularity in South Carolina, where he had had several close run-off elections, which made him an inviting target for Roosevelt. Smith had served for twenty-nine years in the upper house, where he had alienated colleagues by calling the Senate "a cave of winds," and represented the South's old order of states' rights and black repression. When a black minister gave a benediction at the 1936 Democratic convention, Smith walked out in protest and reported that John C. Calhoun had whispered to him from the great beyond that he had done good. His enduring objective, he told voters, was "to keep the Negro down and the price of cotton up." In opposition to FSLA, he decried FDR's minimum wage as an assault on free enterprise, adding that farmers in South Carolina could live on fifty cents a day. In his remarks at Greenville, Roosevelt again told the audience that he needed the cooperation of Congress to advance the interests of the South and alluded to the uncooperative Smith by declaring that no man or family could live on fifty cents a day.

On August 16, having returned to Washington, he told a press conference, "I cannot say I am glad to be back," and continued his campaign

492

against conservative Democrats. But first he took care to remind reporters of why they liked and admired him, telling them "I am glad to see you all again" and introducing them to Dan Callaghan, his new military aide. "He can look you all over and report to me afterwards what he thinks. I can tell him now that you improve on acquaintance," he said to much laughter.

The main business of the day, though, was to resume his appeal for liberals in the primaries. He read a statement to the reporters that began with a defense of his "interference" in the elections, poking fun at the "Tory press" for decrying his meddling in such "sordid considerations." But turning serious, he justified his intervention as essential to fulfilling promises he made in his reelection campaign, and as necessary to defeat the Democrats who gave "lip-service" to him and the New Deal in 1936 and then "turned around and knifed it in Congress in 1937 and 1938. Now that election time has come around again, the hidden opposition hides the ax behind its back and prepares to give the President lip-service once more." Roosevelt said that he had no choice but to repudiate these turncoats. One he singled out was the fifty-eight-year-old Millard Tydings of Maryland, who had broken with the administration over its deficit spending and urged a balanced-budget amendment to the Constitution. "He wants to run with the Roosevelt prestige and the money of his conservative Republican friends both on his side," Roosevelt said, so it was his "duty" to express his opinion of Tydings. He then turned to Representative John J. O'Connor from New York, "one of the most effective obstructionists in the Lower House," who was devoted to tearing down the New Deal. The president concluded by telling the reporters that they were free to quote what he had said.

Roosevelt followed his press conference with additional efforts to influence primary outcomes. He wanted a Nebraska editorial praising his efforts to protect the New Deal read on a national radio broadcast; asked Breckinridge Long, an assistant secretary of state, to intervene in the Maryland primary, "both personally and financially"; and on Labor day, September 5, spent several hours in an open convertible on a two-hundred-mile drive along Maryland's eastern shore promoting Representative David Lewis's candidacy against Tydings. Despite cheering crowds along the way, a profusion of signs supporting Tydings raised doubts about the election's outcome.

The results of the primaries proved to be a massive disappointment, and only in New York, where O'Connor went down to defeat, could Roosevelt take satisfaction from the voting. "Harvard lost the schedule but won the Yale game," he told O'Connor's successful opponent. But it provided little solace in light of the victories of George, Smith, Tydings, and other anti–New Deal Democrats in Colorado, Nevada, and Connecticut. The results confronted Roosevelt with the likelihood that any further progressive legislation would be unattainable. His "political fortunes [had] reached the lowest point of his presidency," historian James MacGregor Burns wrote. "It takes a long, long time to bring the past up to the present," Roosevelt said privately.

But personal and international concerns eclipsed his political frustrations. On September 11, his son James had surgery for ulcers at the Mayo

Clinic. James's illness had sparked tensions between Franklin and Eleanor, who had opposed James's appointment as Franklin's secretary after Louis Howe's death, telling her husband that his decision to burden their oldest son with so heavy a responsibility "appalled" her. She believed that the tensions of the job had largely contributed to James's illness, which doctors feared might be producing a life-threatening malignancy. Although tension may have contributed to James's condition, more recent understanding of peptic ulcers points to a bacterial infection as a central cause of the condition, which painkillers such as aspirin may aggravate. But whatever the actual origins of his condition, the danger to James's life was a source of distracting concern to both his parents, and led them to make a rushed trip to the Minnesota clinic and to face the prospect that James could no longer serve as his father's White House chief of staff. Although James would make a rapid recovery from successful surgery and Roosevelt would be able to return to Washington on September 14, the additional likelihood that James would become the third of their children to suffer a failed marriage saddened both parents and burdened them with guilt regarding their children's shortcomings or troubled personal relations.

Roosevelt lamented his duty to return to the White House rather than travel to Hyde Park, but "the situation in Europe is full of world dynamite," as he told Daisy, "& I don't dare be off the scene because it needs hourly watching." A week later, on September 21, after returning to the Capital, he told her, "When I can leave, I don't know 'at all at all.' Things are worse abroad & while a war does not mean us in it, it does change so many

495

things — hate — all our 'economics' — industry, agriculture, etc. And I go about these hectic days with a vile cold in my nose — nearly well every morning then comes up again in the P.M. Tomorrow I'm going to stay in bed."

The source of Roosevelt's anxiety was the Czech crisis, which involved Germany, Britain, and France. After his successful seizure of Austria in March 1938, Hitler had begun moving against Czechoslovakia as part of his plan to build a greater Reich. Specifically, he demanded Czechoslovakia's cession of the Sudetenland, with its concentration of *Volksdeutsch,* or German-speaking citizens, whom Hitler falsely claimed were being oppressed by the Czechs. On September 12, in a speech before a Nazi Party Congress, he made demands for the Sudentenland's "self-determination," which put Europe on the edge of war — or so Roosevelt, who listened to the speech in his railway car parked in the Rochester train station, feared. He sensed the Führer's determination, as he told his military chiefs, to make Czechoslovakia "disappear from the map."

The widespread pacifist sentiment in the democracies, including the United States, encouraged Hitler's willingness to bully them. University students across England had signed an Oxford Pledge not to fight in another war; the Women's Strike for Peace in the United States, where gun manufacturers continued to be denounced as "merchants of death," staged well-publicized marches; and 91 percent of Americans favored a ban on bombing civilians in any future conflict. Even in Germany, Colonel Hans Oster, a member of the counterintelligence corps who was convinced that Germany would lose if it fought

Britain and France, organized a coup to strike against Hitler if he went to war. When Hitler did try to stir militancy among Berliners with a parade of motorized troops through the city, their "sullen" response amounted to what the American journalist William Shirer called "the most striking demonstration against war I've ever seen."

The fact that the British and French governments were encouraging the Czechs to reach a settlement with Berlin, including visits to Germany on September 15 and September 22 by British prime minister Neville Chamberlain to negotiate with Hitler, and a radio talk by Chamberlain in which he dismissed talk of war because of "a quarrel in a faraway country between people of whom we know nothing," convinced Hitler that, if need be, he could resort to military action without provoking a wider conflict. Despite bitter resistance among the Czechs to Nazi threats — Prague's minister to London angrily remarked that Chamberlain had yet to learn that Czechoslovakia was a country and not a disease — the Czechs found themselves abandoned to Hitler's demands.

As the crisis unfolded, Roosevelt deplored the peace-at-any-price attitude of the British and the French. He refused to respond to pressure from his ambassadors in London and Paris, Joseph Kennedy and William Bullitt, to prevent a war by pressing the Czechs to accommodate Hitler. The forty-seven-year-old Bullitt, the offspring of a prominent Philadelphia family and a Yale graduate, who had been Roosevelt's first ambassador to the Soviet Union, despised Russia's Communist government and saw Hitler as a bulwark against Soviet expansion across Europe. He urged the president to mediate the central European conflict, well aware that Roosevelt would then be accused of "selling out a small nation in order to produce another Hitler triumph," but he believed it a price worth paying to preserve the peace.

Similarly, Kennedy, a prominent businessman who had contributed generously to Roosevelt's campaigns and served as the first head of the Securities and Exchange Commission, had been sent to London to dispute Chamberlain's policy. "I'd love to see the faces of those British aristocrats when this redheaded Irishman shows up in the Court of St. James," Roosevelt remarked. But as they had for Bullitt, the Communists seemed more of a threat to Kennedy than the Nazis. When Kennedy proposed to make a speech announcing that there was nothing in the Czech situation "worth shedding blood for," Roosevelt, who made him excise the statement, said, "Who would have thought that the English could take into camp a red-headed Irishman? The young man needs his wrist slapped rather hard."

Roosevelt wanted to find ways to aid the British and French against Germany. He asked Morgenthau to develop a plan whereby London and Paris could deposit gold in the United States for use in purchasing arms and other war supplies. He considered the possibility of telling the German ambassador that if Hitler attacked Czechoslovakia, he would throw up barriers to continued trade with it. He secretly told the French ambassador, "You may count on us for everything except troops and loans." When Chamberlain went to Germany for negotiations with Hitler, Roosevelt predicted that he and the French would assent to German aggression and then "wash the blood

498

from their Judas Iscariot hands." After warning the British ambassador that the Czechs were being asked to make "the most terrible remorseless sacrifice," Roosevelt told him that if he revealed what he was about to say, it could threaten him with impeachment. He then outlined a plan for helping fight Germany, predicted that the Czechs would not give in, and if they did, other German demands would surely follow, involving "Denmark, the Polish Corridor or most likely of all a dangerous and forcible economic or physical penetration through Romania." He also expected that "somehow or other" the United States would eventually be drawn into the fighting.

Because Roosevelt viewed the British and the French as poorly prepared to compete with Germany on the battlefield, he decided to call upon all the powers to maintain the peace. In public messages to the contending countries on September 26, Roosevelt urged them "for the sake of humanity everywhere" not to go to war. The consequences of a conflict, he declared, would claim millions of lives "under circumstances of unspeakable horror. The economic system of every country involved may well be completely wrecked." He doubted, however, that his message would have any impact, and when he heard Hitler speak on the same day, it only deepened his despair. "Did you hear Hitler today?" he asked Daisy. "His shrieks, his histrionics and the effect on the huge audience — They did not applaud — they made noises like animals." William Shirer, who attended Hitler's speech, thought the German leader was "in the worst state of excitement I've ever seen him in." Despite Hitler's histrionics, or because of them, Roosevelt sent him another plea on September 27 for a peaceful resolution of the crisis. The following day, when Hitler announced that he was inviting Mussolini, Chamberlain, and French premier Edouard Daladier to meet with him in Munich, Roosevelt told Daisy, "Could anything bring a more perfect morning! — It is too early to tell but it *looks* like no war."

The settlement at Munich two days later on September 30 was a capitulation to Hitler and became famous as the hallmark of "appeasement," ceding Czechoslovakia to him. While it relieved immediate tensions and bought what Chamberlain described as "peace in our time," as Winston Churchill foresaw in a speech to the House of Commons, "You chose dishonor and you will have war."

Neither Churchill nor Roosevelt had the slightest trust in Hitler's protestations that the Czech settlement represented his last demand. In Parliament, in October, Churchill called the agreement with Hitler a "total and unmitigated defeat." It was the height of nonsense, he said, for Hitler, who had not shown the slightest tolerance for dissenting opinions and other creeds, to demand self-determination for the Sudeten Germans. It was only a matter of time, Churchill predicted, before Hitler would dismantle the entire Czech state, and Britain, which had a recent history of taking "the line of least resistance . . . five years of uninterrupted retreat of British power" and of inexcusable neglect of its air defenses, would find itself at the mercy of Nazi aggression. Britain, Churchill added, had been reduced from a position "safe and unchallenged" to one of wretched vulnerability, which represented "a disaster of the first magnitude." The transparent threat was from a merciless Nazi Germany, which, animated by "a barbarous paganism" and "the threat of murderous force," was an unqualified opponent of British democracy. The nation's only recourse now, he urged, was to hasten a program of rearmament beginning with the building of unprecedented air defenses to protect the British Isles.

Whether Roosevelt read Churchill's speech is unknown, but it is clear that he shared Churchill's concern. While he celebrated the peaceful resolution of the Czech crisis, wiring Chamberlain, "Good man," and saw no immediate threat to the United States comparable to what Britain and France faced, he was determined to expand America's defensive capacity beyond what most in an isolationist America considered essential. "The dictator threat from Europe is a good deal closer to the United States and the American Continent than it was before," he told his ambassador in Lisbon. The possibility of Germany establishing air bases in the Western Hemisphere, which could threaten attacks on the United States, haunted him. He told Canadian prime minister Mackenzie King, "I am still concerned . . . when we consider prospects for the future. I cannot help but feel that unless very soon Europe as a whole takes up important changes in two companion directions — reduction of armaments and lowering of trade barriers — a new crisis will occur." To make it clear to Fascist aggressors where America stood in any future confrontation with Britain, Roosevelt urged King George to make a formal visit to the United States in 1939 after visiting Canada.

In an October 26 radio address to the Herald Tribune Forum, Roosevelt condemned Hitler's threat of war, his use of "economic resources that ought to be devoted to social and economic reconstruction . . . to an intensified competition in armaments"; his repression of free speech; and his "dispersion all over the world of millions of helpless and persecuted wanderers with no place to lay their heads." Roosevelt added, while Americans refuse "to accept as a permanent necessity the idea of force and reject it as an ideal of life, we must be prepared to meet with success any application of force against us." Without a "general abandonment of weapons capable of aggression, ordinary rules of national prudence and common sense require that we be prepared."

Roosevelt gave substance to his concern about American preparedness in secret conversations with military leaders. In November he told Josephus Daniels that he was working on two initiatives, the foremost being "national defense, especially mass production of planes." On November 11, Armistice Day, General John J. Pershing, commander of U.S. forces in the First World War, had discussed with Roosevelt the country's "military necessities in the light of the present European situation." He endorsed the idea of "large additions to our present air force" and agreed with the view that they needed a quick response to "tremendous increases in the production of what the Government requires. . . . If we are to be prepared to extend a long and powerful air arm to the southward, we must have instantly available the means to maintain that air activity by establishing the necessary advance bases." Pershing shared Roosevelt's fear of possible Nazi airfields in South America and also saw a compelling need to address the deficiencies in equipment of U.S. ground forces. It was imperative that they not repeat the experience of World War I, when "we were literally beggars as to every important weapon, except the rifle."

Troubled by reports of German advantages over Britain and France in air power, Roosevelt was determined to right the balance. Bullitt told him that France's air force was only 10 percent the size of Hitler's and lacked a single plane that could pose an attack against the Germans. By contrast, Germany could "bomb Paris at will" and threaten "the whole future of freedom in the world." Roosevelt publicly announced an increase in arms spending of $800 million, while behind the scenes, he approved a French purchasing mission to the United States and endorsed the building of aircraft assembly plants in Canada, where the neutrality law would not apply to the manufacture of five thousand planes a year for France in the event of war. At the same time, he wanted a significant increase in airplane production in the United States to at least fifteen thousand a year. Army chief of staff General Malin Craig asked: "What are we going to do with fifteen thousand planes? Who [are] you going to fight, what [are] you going to do with them, with three thousand miles of ocean?" When the military recommended a more balanced expansion of forces, Roosevelt protested, arguing, "A well-rounded ground army of even 400,000 could not be considered a deterrent for any foreign power whereas a heavy striking force of aircraft would." He told them that Germany and Italy had a combined ten thousand planes — three times the capacity of the British and the French — and could produce fourteen thousand more a year. Roosevelt wanted at least a ten-thousand–plane U.S. air force and the ability to build as many as twenty thousand more a year, part of which would be sold to Britain and France. Because he could not imagine gaining public support for sending a large army abroad, America's defense had to be based on its air and naval power and that of democratic allies.

Because no one actually had precise information on the size and scope of German and Italian air forces — existing estimates had in fact vastly exaggerated the Fascist advantage — and U.S. military leadership saw no likelihood of an air assault on the homeland, they continued to resist Roosevelt's investment of defense funds largely in air power. However, they did share his concerns about Fascist penetration of Latin America, where the Germans and Italians had been busy promoting their influence with arms sales, military missions, propaganda, trade deals, and other forms of economic penetration.

Roosevelt was also determined to build up the Navy as quickly as possible as a deterrent to Nazi expansion in the Atlantic and Caribbean, but also as a response to Japan's Pacific ambitions. A report in December on the progress of naval construction moved him to instruct the Navy secretary to speed up the production of destroyers. The customary practice of giving priority to repairs on ships in Navy yards over the building of new vessels was delaying the completion of new destroyers by many months. "It is absolutely contrary to the best interest of the Navy," Roosevelt told the secretary, and ordered it to be stopped.

In November, nothing added to Roosevelt's worries about a European outbreak more than events in Germany on November 9 and November 10, which came to be known as *Kristallnacht* (Crystal Night), or the night of the broken glass. The alleged trigger of the pogrom was the assassination in Paris of Ernst vom Rath, a German embassy official, by Herschel Grynszpan, a Polish-Jewish student, in retaliation for Nazi anti-Semitism. "The night of horror," Hitler biographer Ian Kershaw says, "a retreat in a modern state to the savagery associated with bygone ages, laid bare to the world the barbarism of the Nazi regime." In cities across Germany, Nazi Party activists attacked Jewish houses of worship, businesses, and other places with any sort of Jewish identity and killed as many as one hundred unarmed civilians. The exclusion of Jews from many forms of economic activity, as well as the confiscation of Jewish property and wealth, followed the night of violence as part of the "aryanization" of German life, and further reduced the likelihood of Jewish survival in Germany. The all-out campaign to rid Germany of its Jews was a product of Nazi ideology's belief that they were a menace to the nation's survival and prosperity. The Jews soon became the object of a mass paranoia that would spread across Europe and become ever more lethal over the next seven years.

Roosevelt regarded *Kristallnacht* as further evidence of German ruthlessness and readiness to resort to force in its dealings with its Jewish minority and with any country that dared to stand in the way of its expansionist ambitions. "What a plight the unfortunate Jews are in," Roosevelt said in September about their persecution in Italy, where Mussolini issued decrees expelling all post-1919 Jewish migrants and barring them, as in

Germany, from participation in the country's economic life. "It gives them little comfort to remind them that they have been 'on the run' for about four thousand years." After the pogrom ended, Roosevelt told a press conference, "The news of the past few days has deeply shocked public opinion in the United States. . . . I myself could scarcely believe that such things could occur in a twentieth-century civilization." He issued a formal protest by recalling the American ambassador from Berlin and did not send him back in the coming year.

While withdrawing the ambassador was largely a symbolic gesture, it took on greater resonance when no other country followed suit. Still, Roosevelt wouldn't go beyond that and issue a direct expression of protest to Berlin, even though TR had created a precedent for such a response in 1903 and 1906 when he sent diplomatic notes to the Russian government decrying its pogroms. When reporters asked Roosevelt if there were any plans to help those fleeing Germany, he replied that the International Refugee Commission was "at work trying to extend its help to take care of an increasingly difficult situation" and added, "I have given a great deal of thought to it." He was also asked: "Can you tell us any place particularly desirable" where Jews might be welcomed? "No," Roosevelt answered, "the time is not ripe for that." He had, in any case, to honor the quotas allowed under the 1924 National Origins Act. Because the German quota had not been filled, he combined it with the Austrian allowance and permitted some of the 190,000 Jews displaced by the *Anschluss* to come to the United States. Even so, only 27,000 refugees could find their way to America under this arrangement. Roosevelt also extended the amount of time some 15,000 Austrian and German visitors to the United States could remain in the country, calling it "cruel and inhuman to compel them to leave here."

There is no doubt, as the former League of Nations high commissioner James McDonald recorded, that Roosevelt was in search of an answer to Jewish persecution, including considerations of rescuing millions of Europe's Jews from the Nazis by bringing them to ten democratic countries. He asked Isaiah Bowman, a political geographer, president of Johns Hopkins University, and former member of the U.S. delegation to the Versailles conference, to advise him on potential areas for settling displaced Jews. Moreover, Roosevelt was under some pressure from Eleanor to respond to the issue. She told Franklin that "the German-Jewish business makes me sick." Roosevelt shared her sense of outrage. Earlier that year, at a White House meeting of interfaith leaders he had held to discuss refugees, Roosevelt described Hitler as "a maniac with a mission." Eleanor's rejection of racial and religious intolerance registered most clearly in November at a Southern Conference on Human Welfare in Birmingham, Alabama, where she resisted segregation statutes by refusing to sit in an all-white section of the city's auditorium. In a Gallup poll, 67 percent approved of her actions as a model of democratic tolerance.

Mindful of the anti-immigrant sentiment in the United States and the anti-Semitism that was all too evident in the State Department among its conservative career officers, however, Roosevelt muted his objections to Nazi discrimination against Germany's Jews. His defeats in the Court packing fight, the Democratic primaries, and the congressional elections; public resistance in the United States to involvement in overseas conflicts; and transparent opposition in other countries to relaxing immigration barriers — especially in Latin America, partly fueled by fears of job competition in a tight employment market — combined to discourage Roosevelt's humanitarian impulses. The reluctance of other world leaders to take on rescue initiatives left Roosevelt largely isolated in attempting to deal with the refugee crisis, and Joseph Kennedy's collaboration with Prime Minister Chamberlain in opposing actions that they believed would antagonize Hitler especially troubled him.

Although 94 percent of Americans disapproved of Nazi persecution of the Jews, 61 percent favored a boycott of German goods, 83 percent said they hoped Russia would defeat Germany if they fought a war, and 83 percent opposed increasing quotas allowing more European immigrants into the United States. When Ickes spoke up at a cabinet meeting for opening "our doors to political refugees," Vice President Garner responded that if Congress could hold a secret vote, "all immigration would be stopped." Likewise, isolationism continued to stand in the way of unqualified support for building the country's defenses against external threats. To be sure, large majorities favored expanding the Army and Navy, but they also opposed universal military training for twenty-year-olds. A standing American army might make it easier to draw the United States into a foreign conflict, or so millions of Americans believed.

If all the news from abroad wasn't enough to

darken Roosevelt's days, the results of the November congressional elections gave him added pause, as the Democrats suffered their worst reverses since 1930. The Republicans nearly doubled their seats in the House from 88 to 169, increased their numbers in the Senate by eight to 23, and captured 13 governorships. Josephus Daniels saw the results as "unexpected and depressing," and with the Southern conservative Democrats remaining as opposed to the administration as ever, prospects for congressional cooperation seemed dim. Roosevelt blamed the defeats on "our officeholders and our candidates [who] had not measured up." Jim Farley believed they were the result of "hostility to the spending program, the fear that the C[ongress] of I[ndustrial] O[rganizations] exercised undue influence within the administration . . . low farm prices, dissatisfaction with the W.P.A., and business discontent with regimentation."

Ever the optimist, Roosevelt put the best possible face on the defeat. "I am not wholly reconciled to last Tuesday's results," he told Daniels, "but I believe that they are on the whole helpful. We have eliminated certain individuals and certain inter-party fights which were doing positive harm." Losses in Massachusetts, Rhode Island, Connecticut, New Jersey, and Pennsylvania remedied "some bad local situations." Moreover, the elections had removed "Phil LaFollette and the Farmer Labor people in the Northwest as a standing Third Party threat. They must and will come to us *if* we remain definitely the liberal party." He expected the next Congress to be "less trouble" than the previous one. Conservative Democrats would understand that they could not control the 1940 Democratic convention without administration support and would know that Roosevelt would not back any of their number for the presidential nomination. In addition, he urged Farley to organize "a special division of the National Committee to begin giving the incumbents [new Republican governors] the 'works' as soon as they take office." He was certain that they "will slide back to reactionary policies that would make them vulnerable." He saw at least eleven eastern, midwestern, and western states, where "hardships of various types" would be the norm "under these new regimes" and make them vulnerable targets for Democratic attacks.

On December 5, on his way back to Washington from a Thanksgiving holiday in Warm Springs, Roosevelt stopped at the University of North Carolina, a "representative of liberal teaching and liberal thought," to give a speech. "It is my recognition of your recognition of that [liberal] philosophy that brings me so willingly to Chapel Hill," he told the crowd. He praised the university's affinity for "thinking and acting in terms of today and tomorrow and not merely in the tradition of yesterday." He reminded the thousands of students and faculty, who made up an attentive audience, that "it is not progress, but the reverse, when a nation goes through the madness of the twenties" that brought on the Great Depression. He chided "unthinking liberals . . . who see nothing but tragedy in the slowing up or temporary stopping of liberal progress" and "unthinking conservatives who rejoice down in their hearts when a social or economic reform fails to be 100 percent successful."

He had two pieces of advice for the undergraduates assembled before him. First, for those who were seeing him for the first time and had been told by the mass media that he was "an ogre — a consorter with Communists, a destroyer of the rich, a breaker of our ancient traditions. . . . You have heard for six years that I was about to plunge the Nation into war; that you and your little brothers would be sent to the bloody fields of battle in Europe; that I was driving the Nation into bankruptcy and that I breakfasted every morning on a dish of grilled millionaire. Actually," he declared to peals of laughter, "I am an exceedingly mild mannered person — a practitioner of peace, both domestic and foreign, a believer in the capitalistic system, and for breakfast a devotee of scrambled eggs." Second, he cautioned the students against believing that the results of the recent elections meant that "the liberal forces in the United States are on their way to the cemetery — yet I ask you to remember that liberal forces in the United States have often been killed and buried, with the inevitable result that in short order they have come to life again with more strength than they had before."

To give credence to his avowed continuing liberal commitments, on December 24, Roosevelt replaced Dan Roper, a conservative Democrat, with the consummate New Dealer Harry Hopkins as secretary of commerce. After Hopkins was alleged to have said, "We will tax and tax and spend and spend and elect and elect," the conservative press declared, "Surely, this is the most incomprehensible, as well as one of the least defensible, appointments the President has made in his six and one-half years in the White House." Personally attached to Hopkins, the president also saw him as a "stalking horse" to ensure that Roosevelt or another liberal would receive the 1940 presidential nomination.

Roosevelt believed that Republican and conservative Democratic gains in 1938 would renew the antagonisms that had been prevalent in 1930–32, which eventually led to losing their hold on voters. He expected a rekindled enthusiasm for liberal measures that would serve New Deal advocates in 1940. But circumstances had changed, and the battles in 1939 and beyond would not be over conservative or liberal policies at home, but the most prudent response to tumultuous events abroad, and these were not grounds on which liberal Democrats could be confident of victories.

Franklin D. Roosevelt
at age sixteen months with
his father, James Roosevelt,
April 1883.

Portrait of Franklin D.
Roosevelt, age five,
and his mother, Sara
Delano Roosevelt,
Washington, D.C.,
1887.

A formal photo of FDR, age eighteen, at Groton School, April 1900.

Eleanor Roosevelt, age seventeen, in her coming-out portrait, taken in New York City, 1902.

Franklin D. Roosevelt, Eleanor Roosevelt, and family, Washington, D.C., June 12, 1919. *Standing, left to right*: Anna, James, Elliott; *sitting, left to right*: FDR Jr., FDR, Eleanor, Sara, John.

Franklin D. Roosevelt and
Alfred E. Smith, 1930.

Franklin D. Roosevelt taking the oath of office as governor for the second time.
With Eleanor Roosevelt *(right)*, Sara Delano Roosevelt, Lt. Gov. Herbert H.
Lehman, and Judge Irving Lehman in Albany, New York, December 31, 1930.

Franklin D. Roosevelt, campaigning, gives a speech on the back of a
train at Redding, California, with Francis Carr and daughter,
Anna Roosevelt Dall, September 22, 1932.

Franklin D. Roosevelt, Eleanor Roosevelt, and Joseph Robinson on
Inauguration Day in Washington, D.C., March 4, 1933.

Henry Morgenthau, Secretary of the Treasury.

Secretary of the Interior Harold Ickes *(left)* and Tommy Corcoran,
the administration's ace Brain Truster, leaving the White House after
a conference with President Roosevelt, December 6, 1938.

Frank Knox *(center)*, appointed as secretary of the Navy, June 19, 1940.

Harry Hopkins with Fala at Top Cottage, Hyde Park, New York, 1942.
Photographed by Margaret Suckley.

Franklin D. Roosevelt conducting a Fireside Chat on the Works Relief Program in Washington, D.C., April 28, 1935.

Civilian Conservation Corps workers cutting out dead wood, Sequoia National Park, California, June 27, 1933.

Detail from a mural in the lobby of the Granville Ohio Post Office, painted by Wendell Jones under the auspices of the Works Progress Administration.

The Works Progress Administration sponsored the New York Jewish Theatre Unit production of *It Can't Happen Here.* Federal Theatre Project, 1935.

"The sole water supply of this section of Wilder, Tennessee." Tennessee Valley Authority, 1942.

Soup kitchen sculpture at the FDR Memorial in Washington, D.C.

Franklin D. Roosevelt with *(seated from left to right)* General Paul Malone, Louis Howe, Harold Ickes, Robert Fechner, Henry Wallace, Rexford Tugwell, and *(standing)* the men of Civilian Conservation Corps Company 350 at CCC Camp Big Meadows in the Shenandoah Valley, Virginia, August 12, 1933.

Interior Secretary Ickes congratulates Marian Anderson after a concert attended by an estimated crowd of 75,000, Washington, D.C., April 9, 1939.

Margaret "Daisy" Suckley gathering information about the Roosevelt Sugar House account book in the Roosevelt Family Archives at the White House. Photo by Franklin D. Roosevelt.

FDR giving Fala his supper in the White House study, 1943.

Joseph Kennedy *(left)* takes oath as U.S. ambassador to Great Britain, in Washington, D.C., February 18, 1938. Oath given by Associate Supreme Court Justice Stanley F. Reed as FDR looks on.

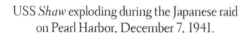

BELOW: Wendell Willkie, 1940.

USS *Shaw* exploding during the Japanese raid on Pearl Harbor, December 7, 1941.

Franklin D. Roosevelt at the Cairo conference in Cairo, Egypt, November 25, 1943. *Seated left to right:* Chiang Kai-shek, FDR, Winston Churchill, Madame Chiang Kai-shek.

Franklin D. Roosevelt, Joseph Stalin, and Winston Churchill at the Tehran conference in Tehran, Iran, November 29, 1943.

Franklin D. Roosevelt with General Dwight Eisenhower *(rear)* and General George Patton, touring the U.S. troop carrier airport in Castelvetrano, Sicily, en route home after the Cairo and Tehran conferences, December 8, 1943.

Eleanor Roosevelt on a trip to Central and South America, March 1944.

Bird's-eye view of landing craft, barrage balloons, and Allied troops landing in Normandy, France, on D-Day, June 6, 1944.

Left to right: General MacArthur, Franklin D. Roosevelt, Admiral Leahy, and Admiral Nimitz at FDR's quarters in Waikiki, Hawaii, July 28, 1944.

President Franklin D. Roosevelt and Vice President-elect Harry S. Truman riding to the White House from the railroad station upon President Roosevelt's return to Washington, D.C., November 12, 1944.

The last photograph of President Franklin D. Roosevelt, taken at Warm Springs, Georgia, on April 11, 1945, the day before he died.

CHAPTER 11
DANGERS ABROAD, UNCERTAINTIES AT HOME

On December 3, 1938, Roosevelt wrote John Boettiger, his son-in-law in Seattle, "I have been having a grand time down here at Warm Springs and hate the thought of going back next Sunday to start the long grind." For all his rhetoric about the positive results of the November elections, he knew that he would have to deal with an uncooperative Congress opposed to New Deal reforms and a national desire for isolation from overseas tensions that threatened to erupt in a European war. His understanding of the menace Hitler and the Nazis posed not only to the European democracies but to America's best interests and national security outran majority opinion and made any shift in policy a towering political obstacle.

He was also on edge about Daisy, who faced surgery at the start of the New Year to remove a "tumor, the size of a grapefruit." On January 6, after the operation in New York successfully removed what turned out to be a nonmalignant growth, Roosevelt wrote urging her to come to Washington, where she could recuperate at a niece's home. "I am sending you a [toy] watchdog," Franklin playfully told her. "He is very watchful & faithful & won't bite anyone except

513

intruders — It is grand to know that the operation is successfully over."

On his return to Washington, Roosevelt began to contemplate how he might position himself to run for an unprecedented third term as president, should external and domestic problems convince him that he remained the country's best leader to meet the difficulties of 1940 and beyond. Although he gave no overt indication that he would take up the challenge of another campaign, it seems more than likely that he was considering and even planning a run. While 69 percent of the public opposed a third term, he nonetheless remained very popular: Gallup polls in the opening months of 1939 gave him between 58 and 60 percent approval ratings. In addition, a 67 percent endorsement for Eleanor's conduct as first lady was not lost on him. Her devotion to helping America's most needy struck sympathetic chords with millions of Americans, making her an indispensable administration asset who could facilitate his reelection.

At the same time, he was also making plans for retirement. As historian Richard Moe describes it, by 1939 Roosevelt had built the Hyde Park retreat he and Daisy called "Top Cottage," because of its locale on the highest hill in Hyde Park overlooking the Hudson River. He had also signed a contract for a stunning $75,000 a year with *Colliers* magazine to write occasional pieces. He spoke to Hopkins and Rosenman about joining him in Hyde Park to help him write a memoir. All these decisions were also smart politics, for should he decide to enter the 1940 race, he could point to all his retirement plans as evidence that he had been forced into the decision to run again only in response to unpredictable events.

Roosevelt found encouragement as well in a poll that revealed that 59 percent of Democrats wanted a New Dealer to head the ticket. But Harry Hopkins, Roosevelt's chosen successor, had generated little enthusiasm. In December, Roosevelt had named him secretary of commerce — a most unlikely post for someone with a social worker's background — as a stepping stone to the 1940 presidential nomination. But the appointment did nothing to improve his political standing: 53 percent of Americans thought he had been a poor director of the WPA. Only 8 percent of Democrats favored his candidacy, and when pitted against New York Republican governor Thomas Dewey in a straw poll, Hopkins lost by a decisive 61 to 39 percent.

By backing Hopkins, Roosevelt had done more to raise his own political appeal than to give his party and the country a viable alternative. With no other appealing potential liberal candidate, the president became the best hope of New Dealers eager for additional progressive reforms. Still, he could take nothing for granted, and in the almost two years before he would face voters again, he would have to convince a majority of Americans that he remained the best choice to lead the country.

His campaign began with his State of the Union message on January 4, 1939. He reminded Congress and the public that he, above all, understood the perils facing the nation. The greatest danger, he told a skeptical Congress, was a war that could "envelop the world in flames." Such a conflict, he warned, would imperil America's religious freedom, its democracy, and its advancement of international good will, which he contrasted with "strident ambition and brute force." In a world where distances had shrunk and "weapons of attack [were] so swift," no nation anywhere was safe from aggression, and strict neutrality was no longer a feasible option. The best defense against a possible attack, Roosevelt asserted, was preparedness to meet it before it occurred. He was mindful of what Winston Churchill had asked a pro-Fascist Frenchwoman: "With Germany arming at breakneck speed, England lost in a pacifist dream, France corrupt and torn by dissension, America remote and indifferent — Madame, my dear lady, do you not tremble for your children?"

Roosevelt had chosen his cautionary words about building America's might as a shrewd way to advance its international influence. A weak, unarmed United States was a threat to no one, but a militarily strong one might cause the Germans, Italians, and Japanese to reconsider any further acts of aggression. In addition, Roosevelt's emphasis on national defense with no hint of helping other countries would make it difficult for isolationists to dispute War Department budget increases — or at least Roosevelt hoped that would be the case.

He continued his speech by warning that domestic divisions could jeopardize the country's safety, emphasizing that even robust defense forces could not preserve an America that was divided against itself. National unity, achieved by cooperation between capital and labor, and an end to "class prejudice" were essential to meeting dangers from abroad. "Our Nation's program of social and economic reform is therefore a part of defense as basic as armaments themselves," Roosevelt said. He recounted the accomplishments of the administration in forging "new tools" of government to expand the economy and to provide a social safety net insulating young and old from social ills. When he declared that government spending could be curtailed with drastic budget cuts that would keep America a $60-billion nation, "the Republican Members of Congress burst into loud applause, in effect heckling him," Ickes recorded. But Roosevelt responded by insisting that only with government investment could the country become an $80-billion nation, which in turn brought shouts of approval from some of the assembled Democrats.

Should Congress reduce government spending and functions by a third, he declared, it, and not he, would "have to accept the responsibility for such reduction; and the Congress will have to determine which activities are to be reduced." He wished to leave no doubt about the impact of cuts on "agriculture and soil conservation, veterans' pensions, flood control, highways, waterways, and other public works, grants for social and health security, Civilian Conservation Corps activities, relief for the unemployed, or national defense."

The speech was effectively a call to arms to all those who had benefitted from the New Deal, and Ickes judged it "a great address, one of the best of his career." Although Roosevelt met what Ickes called the Republican heckling during it with a gracious smile, he viewed his opponents as "antediluvian" advocates of policies that would ill serve the country. "They had every legal right to go their own way," Roosevelt wrote Herbert C. Pell, his representative in Lisbon, reiterating, "but

517

if they did, they would bear the full responsibility! After a good deal of conversation on their part, I think the session will settle down and be comparatively quiet — that is if you can keep the peace in Europe."

Despite his constitutional optimism, Roosevelt could not help but be apprehensive about the reactionaries on the other side of the aisle and in his own party. The Republicans, who had many new congressional members, were led in the Senate by Ohio's forty-nine-year-old Robert Taft, the eldest son of former president William Howard Taft, and an avowed isolationist and principled opponent of government constraints on free enterprise. In conjunction with Southern Democrats, he seemed likely to become a formidable obstacle to any expansion of the New Deal. Ickes described Taft as overtly "friendly and agreeable," but doubted "whether he has many human emotions." Roosevelt had no hope that leading Democrats like Cordell Hull, Jim Farley, and Vice President Garner, all of whom were prominently discussed as potential White House successors, would be much more supportive of liberal initiatives than Taft. Garner and Farley were openly hostile to sustaining New Deal government programs, and Hull impressed both Roosevelt and Ickes as a "somber" character with a "one-track mind." The trade agreements he favored were "all right so far as they go," but gave little hope of solving "our own economic problems," Ickes said, "let alone the grave international problems that exist today."

Roosevelt had revealed his limited faith in Hull as a 1940 candidate or even an effective foreign policy leader in 1937 when he had appointed the forty-five-year-old Sumner Welles undersecretary of state, an old friend with a direct line to the president. Welles also held credentials as a foreign policy expert, especially on Latin America, where he had served in various posts. Although he came across as "a man of almost preternatural solemnity and great dignity," who rarely smiled and seemed to carry the weight of the world on his shoulders, Roosevelt greatly valued him as a wise counselor with standing across the Americas who served as an esteemed representative of the administration's Good Neighbor policy.

Roosevelt faced an additional challenge from Texas congressman Martin Dies's special committee investigating un-American activities, which the president regarded as making reckless charges about communist influence in the administration. When Alabama congressman Joe Starnes asserted that "the Committee was interested only in facts with reference to un-American and subversive activities," Roosevelt scolded him: "Neither you nor I — nor for that matter the American public — ought to be willing to give to the name 'facts' to hundreds of pages of testimony which under every rule of Anglo-Saxon evidence is only opinion or hearsay evidence. Such evidence, I believe, is admitted in investigations in Germany and Russia but I am sorry to see it beginning in my own country." Dies's role in defeating Michigan Democratic governor Frank Murphy with charges of treason for his response to the sit-down strikes particularly inflamed Roosevelt, who sarcastically told Garner, "The Democratic Party felt lonely during the past few years but now all is well, for it has its Hamilton Dies to match the Republican's Martin Fish" — intentionally conflating their first names as a way of implying that Dies was replicating Hamilton Fish's distorted attacks on New Deal Democrats.

Because 74 percent of the public who were aware of Dies's findings believed them important enough for Congress to continue funding his investigations, Roosevelt was reluctant to take him on. In January, Ickes was about to attack Dies in a radio speech, "Playing with Loaded Dies," when Roosevelt directed him not to do it. Moreover, he directed Frank Murphy, whom he had just appointed attorney general, to investigate the organizations Dies had been attacking. When Garner pressed Roosevelt to block any further investigations, the president protested that no one in the administration could "do anything about it."

Because he was more focused on larger issues, Roosevelt refused to support congressional battles against funding the Dies committee or for increased immigration quotas allowing greater numbers of displaced Austrian and German Jews access to the United States. He did, however, press the case for Jewish sanctuaries in Africa and Palestine. He discussed with Bernard M. Baruch a resettlement of Jews in a United States of Africa, and Baruch had agreed to raise $500 million for the project "if Hitler and Mussolini do not slam the door in our faces!" When the British issued a White Paper stating that the Palestine Mandate of 1917 — the Balfour Declaration — did not sanction the conversion of Palestine into a Jewish state, Roosevelt argued against their interpretation and directed Hull to protest against any limits on Jewish migration to Palestine.

In his January budget message to Congress,

Roosevelt asked for an increase of $309 million for defense over the previous year's $1 billion. It was considered "an enormous outlay for armaments" and triggered a war scare among isolationists. To quiet such fears, and counter complaints from congressmen and senators predicting dire consequences from deficit spending, Roosevelt told a press conference, "I see no reason why, since things are moving so fast in the world, we should lay down an enormous five-year or ten-year program for national defense. . . . All this talk about a huge ten-year program is a lot of bunk."

But Roosevelt's assurances that he was not embarked on a long-range military build-up came into immediate question when he made a supplemental request on January 12 for a half-billion dollars to finance fighter planes. Shortly after, the relocation of the American fleet from the Pacific to the Atlantic for maneuvers in the Caribbean in February, which Roosevelt observed aboard a cruiser, touched off an uproar about White House intentions.

Nothing agitated Roosevelt's isolationist critics more than the crash in the Mojave Desert of an experimental American bomber with a French air force officer aboard. Eager to sell these planes to France not only as good business but also as a way to deter German aggression, Roosevelt had ordered Morgenthau, over the objections of the War Department, to facilitate the transaction. Morgenthau told his staff: "The President of the United States says that we consider the Maginot line our first line of defense and for that reason we want these people to have this thing." Although the Senate Committee on Military Affairs, led by

Missouri's isolationist Democrat Bennett Clark and supported by North Dakota's Gerald Nye and Minnesota's Ernst Lundeen, raised a firestorm over the directive, Roosevelt told Morgenthau "to go right ahead with the French . . . and let them buy what they want."

He also tried to address the senators' concerns in a White House meeting on January 31, during which he told them that Hitler aimed to expand his control of Europe beyond Austria and the Sudetenland, a move that would jeopardize America's own peace and security. "If the Rhine frontiers are threatened the rest of world is, too," he explained. "Once they have fallen before Hitler, the German sphere of action will be unlimited." Breaching a pledge of secrecy, the senators told the press that the president painted a "truly alarming" picture of world affairs. "America's frontier lay on the Rhine," the papers reported him as saying. Outraged at this breach of confidence, Roosevelt denied having said anything of the kind and attacked the leaks as complete fabrications, declaring his fealty to isolationism. "I never of course mentioned frontiers on the Rhine or in France," he told his ambassador to Ireland "but I did point out that there are fifteen or sixteen independent nations in Europe whose . . . political and economic existence is of actual moment to the ultimate defense of the United States."

Roosevelt's denial of his Rhine comments convinced no one, as those who had heard his private concerns about the Nazi threat or his public condemnations of Fascist-Nazi-Japanese aggression had little doubt about his true sentiments. When Britain's Lord Lothian, an old friend, urged him to understand that "no one could talk to Hitler" and that it was up to the United States to bear the burden of defending democratic nations, Roosevelt responded that "he was willing to help all that he could," but he was deterred by public opinion and by the fact that Britain had thrown itself "into the arms of Nazism." When Ickes implored him "to educate our own people . . . he said that it would be absolutely impossible for him or me to go on the air and talk to the world as we are talking. The people simply would not believe him." Roosevelt told Admiral Harold R. Stark, whom he was about to make chief naval officer, that "if we get into a war," he did not want him to remain "a desk Admiral." But he saw any such talk of entering the conflict as domestic political poison.

His greatest hope for the present was that an explosion of animus toward him in the Italian and German press — what he called "the howls and curses" — might be doing some good. "The charming Italian press which was 'spitting upon' the French has apparently substituted me as the target," he wrote his ambassador in Rome. "Perhaps the events in Washington . . . may have caused the Fascists and Nazis to 'Stop. Look, and Listen.' " But they had no such immediate effect, as the aggressor nations were fully cognizant that antiwar, isolationist sentiment in the United States limited what Roosevelt could do to help the democracies. What they overlooked, however, was that the French plane orders, as Edward R. Stettinius, the chairman of U.S. Steel, understood, "were almost revolutionary in their effect upon our aviation industry, and laid the groundwork for the great expansion that was to come."

Roosevelt's speaking out on foreign affairs,

meanwhile, only increased the antagonism between him and the isolationists and weakened him politically. While he was aboard the cruiser monitoring Atlantic fleet maneuvers, South Carolina senator James F. Byrnes, a supporter, cabled him, "Sorry I cannot be in Charleston to welcome you. For ten days the Senate has been debating war but formal declaration has been withheld because of inability to agree on whom we will fight. Know you have not spent two weeks studying war tactics . . . for nothing and possibly your return may solve the question." With senators denouncing Roosevelt's presence at the maneuvers as "warmongering" that would help provoke a conflict, the president sarcastically replied to Byrnes, "Sincerely hope Nye, [Arthur] Vandenberg, and Borah will not force us into war before I get back. Charleston Navy Yard needs three or four days' notice before any actual declaration."

Oswald Garrison Villard, the editor of the liberal *Nation* magazine, which opposed any form of militarism, complained: "We shall be extremely fortunate if Roosevelt does not put us into war. . . . FDR now realizes that the New Deal is stopped, that he is not making a dent on the unemployment situation, that the present tremendous spending is doing very little to restore prosperity, and that he has lost control of Congress."

Roosevelt had no intention of challenging overwhelming public opinion against war, but Villard was right about Congress and its resistance to additional New Deal measures. As Alan Brinkley explains, in 1939, a coalition of Republicans and Southern Democrats joined together to

524

scuttle Roosevelt's request for a $3 billion public works appropriation. Roosevelt's congressional allies complained that special interests were regaining the control they had lost during the Depression, and the Roosevelt contingent's protests against this reversal of fortunes proved to be ineffective. William Allen White, the Kansas progressive Republican editor who had supported much of the New Deal, declared Roosevelt's days as a great leader at an end. The president was now no more than "a crippled leader of the liberal faction of the Democratic party."

In January 1939, Roosevelt was more than mindful of the deterrents to further New Deal advance. Unconvinced by Keynes's arguments for deficit spending, he could not see how additional reforms could be financed. When Eleanor sent him a copy of a speech she had given to a gathering of the liberal American Student Union, "Keep Democracy Working by Keeping It Moving Forward," Roosevelt replied; "If you want to start a discussion among the young people some day, get them to . . . answer the following question" — namely, how to reduce the country's $3 billion annual deficit. "Such a deficit obviously cannot go on forever — expenditures $9 billion, receipts from taxes $6 billion." He then went through a list of projects on which they could easily spend another $5 billion, ranging from health facilities across the South to soil protection, flood prevention, old age security, youth training, and slum clearance. "How can the $3 billion a year, present deficit, or the $8 billion a year, new deficit, if such projects carried out, be financed?" he asked.

Eleanor acknowledged that she had no ready answers. But she, like Harold Ickes, was determined to continue fighting for liberal reform. At a Youth Congress dinner in February, when a Republican speaker attacked the NYA and CCC as "ineffective and wasteful," she sprang to their defense. She agreed that the programs were not "fundamental" solutions to jobs for young people, but rather "stop-gap measures" that nonetheless provided an opportunity for a united country to address its larger economic problems. She emphasized the importance of cooperative advance rather than carping about the limits of New Deal reforms. A journalist in the audience described her remarks as inspiring, and as "one of the finest short speeches ever made in our times." Eleanor believed that the survival of American democracy depended on an enduring national commitment to a just society with a minimum of unemployment and racial injustice. Franklin didn't dispute her vision, but his "deference to what is" separated him from her "spirited impatience with what ought to be." She appreciated that he had "done much for many people" and urged him to "just go on thinking of others & not of yourself & I think an undreamed of future may lie ahead for the masses of people not only here but everywhere."

Developments in the Spanish Civil War and Central Europe, meanwhile, had commanded Roosevelt's attention. His ideas about ways to preserve Spain's republican government had come up short, and even worse, his policy had actually abetted Spain's Fascists in their war against the republican government. In January, as Franco's armies, aided by German and Italian forces, threatened the government's survival, Roosevelt said in his State of the Union speech, "The mere fact that we rightly decline to intervene with arms to prevent acts of aggression does not mean that we must act as if there is no aggression at all. . . . We can and should avoid any action, or any lack of action, which will encourage, assist or build up an aggressor." America's neutrality laws were in effect proving to be an aid to aggressors and a detriment to its victims.

Eleanor Roosevelt had lobbied Franklin to face this reality. She was "furious over her husband's policy" and protested repeatedly against ongoing trade with Germany and Italy, which helped them supply Spanish Fascists. But he had defended his actions by invoking "political realities," especially the Catholic vote. "This annoyed me very much," she admitted, ". . . by trying to convince me that our course was correct. Though he knew I thought we were doing the wrong thing, he was simply trying to salve his own conscience. . . . It was one of the many times I felt akin to a hair shirt." Yet Franklin didn't cut off her protests, and instead welcomed them as a convenient way of hearing liberal opinion in the debate over foreign affairs. As Blanche Wiesen Cook explains, "FDR appreciated that ER's work benefited him in countless ways. He relied upon her ability to get out and meet the people, and he trusted her to introduce controversies and her own convictions, not only to test the political climate but to move public opinion."

By the beginning of 1939, with Spain's republican government on the verge of collapse, Roosevelt began to voice his regrets over his policy. At a cabinet meeting on January 29, he said that the embargo on arms shipments to Spain to support the loyalists "had been a grave mistake." He acknowledged that he had unwisely followed the guidance of the State Department and Congress in denying Madrid access to U.S. matériel. He pledged "never [to] do such a thing again, but," as Ickes observed, "I am afraid that will not help us much." The neutrality policy had in effect meant aligning America with Franco and the destruction of Spanish democracy. "The President said that the policy we should have adopted was to forbid the transportation of munitions of war in American bottoms. . . . Loyalist Spain would still have been able to come to us for what she needed to fight for her life against Franco — to fight for her life and for the lives of some of the rest of us as well, as events will very likely prove," Ickes wrote in his diary with great foresight. Roosevelt considered revoking the arms embargo either by executive order or by congressional action, but was dissuaded from doing so by arguments that he lacked the legal standing to do so, and by opposition from congressional isolationists and Catholic prelates, who favored a Franco government over one supported by Communists. In February, after Madrid fell to the Fascists and the British and French, eager to discourage Spanish support of Berlin and Rome in a potential European war, recognized Franco's government, Roosevelt followed their lead.

Just as discouraging was Hitler's renewed assault in February and March on Czechoslovakia. He had viewed the Munich agreement, which limited his acquisition to the Sudetenland, as a defeat for his plans of reclaiming German territory across all of East Central Europe for *Lebensraum* ("living space"). As early as October 1938, he had directed his Wehrmacht to prepare for the seizure of all of Czechoslovakia. Because the economic and strategic advantages of taking over the Czech state outweighed whatever concerns the Nazis had that their aggression might trigger a larger war, Hitler plunged ahead. On March 15, after he had forced Emil Hacha, the Czech president, into passively accepting German control of Prague and the rest of his nation, Hitler told some of his associates, "I will go down as the greatest German in history." The Czech occupation gave the lie to Hitler's promise at Munich that the Sudentenland had been "his last territorial demand."

The British and the French were now forced to acknowledge that their policy of appeasement had failed. On March 17, in a speech in the north of England, Chamberlain asked: "Is this the last attack upon a small state or is it to be followed by others? Is this, in fact, a step in the direction of an attempt to dominate the world by force?" The French made it clear that they endorsed Chamberlain's policy shift, and both governments, anticipating Hitler's next move, declared their intention to fight should he move against Poland.

Hitler's aggression also shattered Roosevelt's conviction that he could help intimidate or at least discourage him from further actions that might lead to a continental war. Bullitt in Paris and Kennedy in London had advised the president that his remarks about America's Rhine frontier had been praised as a "body blow for peace." Winston Churchill sent word that "the very best thing the United States could do was to keep on beating the drum and talking back to the dictators. The one thing that might make them hesitate in plunging the world into war was the fear that the United States would soon be in it in a big way." But

Czechoslovakia's demise destroyed "any illusions [in Washington] that the German Napoleonic machine will not extend itself almost indefinitely." Roosevelt told his ambassador in Athens: "Hitler and Mussolini are still on the war-path," and wrote a peace advocate: "Never in my life have I seen things moving in the world with more cross currents or with greater velocity." He had been confident about the future, he added, but using a horse racing metaphor, declared, "Today, I have stopped being a mental bookmaker because so many horses are scratched . . . We are not even certain that the trainers, jockeys and spectators may not end up in a 'free-for-all' fight in which the grandstand will be burned down and most of the spectators, horses, trainers, and jockeys go to the hospital or the cemetery. What a day we have to live in!"

When a reporter asked him, "What do you think of the foreign situation?" he replied: "Well, I am not happy." Another journalist wanted to know if there was "any basis whatever for reports coming from Europe that you have suggested to certain nations of Europe a general boycott of Germany?" Still concerned not to provoke isolationist protests, he answered, "That is not so; nothing in it." In fact, when he retaliated against German subsidies of exports to the United States with countervailing duties, Morgenthau recorded, "The President is tickled to death he has a weapon and he's tickled to death to use it." When he sought to bar Berlin from seizing Czech bank deposits in the United States, he remarked to Morgenthau, "I am a bit of a devil." He also wanted to ban the export of arms and munitions to Germany, but he and Morgenthau were told that any such action would be illegal.

On March 31, after Hitler marched troops into Memel, a Balkan port that had been transferred from Germany to Lithuania after World War I, and Chamberlain announced Britain's commitment to defend Poland against German demands for the return of Danzig and what was known as the Polish corridor to the Baltic Sea, Roosevelt told his press conference, strictly off the record, that all the world was now concerned about Hitler's broken promise at Munich not to seek additional former German territories. His latest actions, Roosevelt said, meant the subjugation of millions of Slavs, Hungarians, and Romanians. It could mean the eventual subjugation of all the small states of Europe, which had created a "general fear of an effort to attain world dominance." Germany was now on notice that, should it invade any other nation, it would result in war. The president repeated: The world was "being put on notice as to where the responsibility will lie if there is war."

In press conferences on April 8 and April 11, he warned that acts of aggression by dictator-led nations with barter systems would reduce U.S. trade and shipping and jeopardize the country's national security by expansion into Latin America. He enthusiastically endorsed a *Washington Post* editorial that had argued that "nothing less than the show of preponderant force will stop them [the dictators], for force is the only thing they understand." The editors cautioned Berlin and Rome that American power should not be unheeded in their diplomatic calculations.

In a Pan American Day speech on April 14, 1939, Roosevelt celebrated the cooperative spirit of the American nations and declared himself confident that the New World could rescue the Old World from another disastrous war. "Do we really have to assume that nations can find no better methods of realizing their destinies than those which were used by the Huns and Vandals fifteen hundred years ago?" he asked. "We have an interest, wider than that of the mere defense of our sea-ringed continent. We know now that the development of the next generation will so narrow the oceans separating us from the Old World, that our customs and our actions are necessarily involved with hers, whether we like it or not." In a blunt warning to isolationists, he declared, "within a scant few years air fleets will cross the ocean as easily as today they cross the closed European seas." Peaceful relations among the American republics should be a "light opening on dark waters," showing "the path to peace."

Roosevelt also sent Hitler and Mussolini direct messages pressing the case for peaceful dealings in international relations. Peoples everywhere were living "in constant fear of a new war," he told Hitler. Such a conflict would inflict grievous losses on all nations, but their leaders had the where-withal to prevent "the disaster that impends." The world "is moving toward the moment when this situation must end in catastrophe. . . . Are you willing to give assurance that your armed forces will not attack or invade the territory or posses-sions of the following independent nations?" He then listed thirty-one countries in Europe and across the Middle East and asked that such guarantees be given for at least ten years. Agree-ing to this pledge would open the way to beneficial political and economic discussions. Specifically,

Roosevelt proposed an international conference to reduce "the crushing burden of armament" and to facilitate international commerce that would advance prosperity everywhere.

In addressing Hitler as a rational statesman open to negotiation, Roosevelt was largely aiming his message at the American public rather than the Nazi leadership. He had listened closely to the assessments of his ambassadors in Berlin, Paris, and London: Dodd considered Hitler a throwback to primitive medieval rapaciousness and simply not open to reason, while Bullitt in France and Kennedy in England believed that he could be drawn into a Western alliance against the Soviet Communist menace. Siding with Dodd, Roosevelt also shared Henry Wallace's conviction that "the two madmen respect force and force alone." Appealing to them for peace would be like "delivering a sermon to a mad dog."

The odds of receiving a positive response from Hitler were one in five, Roosevelt acknowledged to Morgenthau. "What may come of my effort I do not know," he told Mackenzie King. "I am none too hopeful but my conscience is clear." He added, "If we are turned down, the issue becomes clearer and public opinion in your country and mine will be helped." He felt as if he had inherited the challenge Woodrow Wilson had taken on earlier in the century of making the world safe for democracy.

Like Churchill in Britain, who had feared that appeasement and pacifism would lead only to disaster, Roosevelt faced an even greater challenge in combating isolationism in the United States. If a war occurred, Americans had no objection to selling foodstuffs and war materials to

Britain and France. They were also sympathetic to a boycott of subsidized German goods and favored the countervailing duties Washington had put on German imports. They had no desire to see cuts imposed on Army and Navy budgets, and 60 percent of Americans approved of Roosevelt's message to Hitler. However, 69 percent disapproved of loans to England and France to buy war supplies from the United States, and 84 percent opposed sending the Army and Navy to help the democracies in the event of war.

Signaling his contempt for the American president, Hitler did not reply to Roosevelt's message for two weeks. Hitler believed that someone leading a country with so little military power did not deserve respectful treatment, remarking, "He who does not possess power loses the right to life." Because Roosevelt's message had stirred considerable discussion around the world, however, Hitler felt compelled to answer him. He did not do so with a message from one head of state to another, however, but with a two-hour-and-twenty-minute-long speech before the Reichstag in which he dismissed Roosevelt's concerns as groundless and absurd. He mocked the call for a conference from a nation that had rejected membership in the League of Nations. To derisive laughter from his Nazi audience, he made his way through the names of each nation Roosevelt wanted him to agree not to attack. Hitler insisted that inquiries he had made as to their supposed fear of Germany had resulted in denials and bewilderment that Roosevelt had included them in his appeal. He announced his readiness to give guarantees to any nation that wished it, including America. Hitler viewed the United States as nothing more than a "mongrel society" populated by Jews, blacks, and inferior Slavs. It "could not possibly construct a sound economy, create an indigenous culture or operate a successful political system."

Ian Kershaw, Hitler's most thorough biographer, believes that his unopposed steps toward rearmament and seizures of Austria and Czechoslovakia had greatly increased his domestic appeal and his own grandiosity: "His self-belief had by this time been magnified into full-blown megalomania." In private, he ecstatically "compared himself with Napoleon, Bismarck, and other great historical figures."

Hitler's public response to Roosevelt may have been an effective act of vaudeville for his domestic audience, but it only deepened Roosevelt's determination to meet the Nazi threat. Among the isolationists, however, it stiffened resolve to combat what they viewed as a reckless provocation that could lead to a war Roosevelt believed essential for him to assume dictatorial power. California senator Hiram Johnson, a leader of the isolationist bloc, predicted that despite Roosevelt's forceful stance, there would be no war. "Roosevelt wants to fight for any little thing," Johnson said. "He wants . . . to knock down two dictators in Europe, so that one may be fairly implanted in America." The *Christian Century* belittled the president's message as taking a "stand before the Axis dictators like some frontier sheriff at the head of a posse."

Roosevelt could have dismissed warnings of his dictatorial ambitions as paranoid nonsense or politically motivated, but his critics were not wrong in believing that he wished to prepare the United States for a significant role in a European

535

war. They would have found evidence of his intentions in a secret note he sent to his naval aide, instructing him to ask the chief of naval operations whether it was possible to have "two 8,000 ton light cruisers carry four 11[-inch] guns plus as many 5[-inch] dual purpose guns as possible? . . . Such a ship would have a good chance of standing up against the German pocket battleship type. . . . An 8,000 ton light cruiser, mounting only ten 6[-inch] guns, provides too light an armament for this tonnage."

Yet Roosevelt saw little likelihood that the United States would take any direct part in fighting he expected to erupt before the end of the year. Instead, he wanted to help the European democracies by revising the neutrality law so that America could supply the British and French with as many modern weapons as possible. At a press conference in March, as Hitler moved to seize Czechoslovakia, Roosevelt responded emphatically to what was doubtless a planted question: "Has the neutrality legislation contributed to the cause of peace? No, It has not. We [the democracies] might have been stronger if we had not had it." Ten days later, after Nazi troops had completed the takeover of the Czech state, a reporter asked, in what was surely another White House–inspired query: "Do we need legislation on neutrality at this session?" Roosevelt predictably responded, "Yes," agreeing that "the developments of the last few days in Europe demonstrated the need."

Roosevelt now told Texas senator Tom Connally, "If Germany invades a country and declares war, we'll be on the side of Hitler by invoking the [Neutrality] act. If we could get rid of the arms embargo, it wouldn't be so bad." On March 20,

Senator Key Pittman, the chairman of the Foreign Relations Committee, responding to White House pressure, proposed revising the existing neutrality statute to put trade with belligerents on a cash-and-carry basis. The measure was a sop to all those who feared a repetition of what they believed had drawn the United States into World War I. If belligerents were forced to pay cash for arms, there would be no threat of defaults on loans, which bankers allegedly used to promote a greater receptivity to entering the war; nor would there be unpaid war debts, as remained from the earlier conflict. Further, if the democracies were forced to transport the munitions in their own ships, it would prevent submarine attacks on U.S. vessels and the loss of American lives that had gone so far to draw us into the Great War. Cash-and-carry was a transparent attempt to give Britain and France, which controlled the Atlantic, military aid. On further consideration, however, Roosevelt realized that this policy would put China at a disadvantage in its conflict with Japan. He asked Pittman to consider repealing the neutrality law "in toto without any substitute."

Roosevelt told Italy's ambassador to the United States that the neutrality law would be revised, that Germany would lose a European war, and that Italy could preserve the peace and prevent German domination of the continent by siding with the democracies. But he was either too optimistic or too willing to stretch the truth in order to head off Mussolini's support of Berlin. Privately, he doubted that he could influence Mussolini's behavior. "I hope and pray, every day, that the influence of Mussolini will be definitely against war," Roosevelt wrote his ambassador in

Rome. "But on the other hand, I am worried by the fact that both Germany and Italy are maintaining such an enormous number of men under arms and continuing to spend such vast sums. . . . If Germany visualizes a peaceful working out of the political and economic problems, common sense would require the starting of conversations as soon as possible in order to avoid an even worse financial situation." Roosevelt understood that the Italian dictator had little incentive to heed the advice of a leader of a distant country determined to isolate itself from overseas affairs.

At the end of March, Pittman advised the president that "repeal of the Neutrality Act was politically impossible." As distressing to Roosevelt was the fact that even revision of the law came up against fierce resistance from isolationists on Pittman's committee. In April, Roosevelt summoned senators and representatives to the White House to lobby them to reconsider revision. He pled his case for cash-and-carry as serving the peace by intimidating Hitler, and should war occur, it would serve the national interest by helping the democracies win the conflict. Hull took up the argument with legislators as well, warning them that they were "making the mistake of their lives" in assuming that a European war would be merely "another goddamn piddling dispute over a boundary line." It would in fact be nothing less a struggle against "barbarism" that threatened not only to engulf Europe but also to endanger the United States. Opposition to repeal of this "wretched little bobtail, sawed off domestic statute" was "just plain chuckle-headed." Hull's down-home rhetoric, however, left them unmoved. They refused to believe that a war was imminent, and even if it were, they declined to see that a Nazi-Fascist victory would have dire consequences for the United States. The failed peacemaking after World War I had convinced them that the United States could have little effect on Europe's predilection for regional conflicts.

Facing an unresponsive Senate, Roosevelt turned to House leaders to argue for the neutrality revision. In a meeting with them on May 19, he warned that a German-Italian victory in a war would threaten to surround the United States with hostile states in the hemisphere and draw Japan into an alliance with the Fascists, who would "try another quick war with us." Roosevelt urged the House to act as a demonstration of solidarity with the democracies before the British monarchs visited the United States on June 12, But the House was no more inclined to make international commitments than the Senate.

The royal visit was intended to make it clear to Hitler that America would stand with Britain in any possible war with Germany. But symbols without power left Hitler unmoved. Even a neutrality revision would not have had a meaningful impact on his determination to recapture German lands from Poland and thus risk a war with Britain and France. Whatever its potential as a supplier of arms, the United States was a non-factor in Hitler's push for living space and European domination. He could not imagine a distant America, with its isolationist, antimilitary outlook, as being of the slightest consequence in his struggle against the apocalyptic forces of Bolshevism and Judaism.

Roosevelt's hosting the royals was aimed as much, if not more, at public opinion in the United

States as it was at the dictators abroad. He agreed with the British ambassador that the king and queen should "pay a formal visit to me at the Capital," but this should not be "the principal part of the plan." Roosevelt urged that emphasis be placed upon a trip to Hyde Park, where "the simplicity and naturalness of such a visit would produce a most excellent effect." It would be "the essential democracy of yourself and the Queen [that] makes the greatest appeal of all," he wrote King George. Roosevelt also proposed possible stops in Chicago and New York, where the royal couple could make an appearance at an "institution of cultural importance," and an outing by yacht on the Potomac to see George Washington's Mount Vernon. The latter would symbolize the ultimate reconciliation between Great Britain and the United States — the British monarch paying homage to the architect of America's rebellion against British rule. Roosevelt ended his letter to the king by writing, "I need not tell you how happy I am that Great Britain and the United States have been able to cooperate so effectively in the prevention of war — even though we cannot say that we are 'out of the woods' yet."

The visit from June 7 to June 11 fulfilled all Roosevelt's expectations, especially the royals' stay at Hyde Park, where church services and a picnic with hot dogs, ham, and chicken salad struck exactly the right chords with popular opinion. No detail had escaped Roosevelt's notice, and in his subsequent recounting of the occasion, he described the king as "grand!" with "an American sense of humor" and "an extraordinary knowledge of this country. . . . He was completely natural and put all the 'royalness' aside when in private."

Descriptions in the press of tripping waiters and broken dishes added to the common touch that made the occasion something all Americans could identify with. The press also reported that the president and king had stayed up until 1:30 in the morning talking about "everything under the sun," when Roosevelt, tapping the king's knee, said, "Young man, it's time for you to go to bed." The visit also paid off handsomely in generating public sympathy for a soon to be embattled Britain.

Yet the more substantive alterations to the neutrality law that Roosevelt hoped might help shape events abroad remained beyond his control. Bullitt told him that German foreign minister Joachim von Ribbentrop used the American refusal to eliminate its arms embargo as a reason for Hitler to fight Britain and France. Although Representative Solomon Bloom, the chairman of the House Foreign Affairs Committee, informed Roosevelt that he could achieve neutrality reform, he was overly optimistic: The conviction among Republicans and half the Democrats in the House that Roosevelt was eager "to line us up with Britain and France in war" spelled defeat for a Bloom proposal for repeal of the arms embargo by a 159 to 157 vote. Roosevelt responded by telling a congresswoman that the House vote "has caused dismay in democratic peaceful circles. The anti-war nations believe that a definite stimulus has been given to Hitler by the vote of the House, and that if war breaks out in Europe, because of further seeking of territory by Hitler and Mussolini, an important part of the responsibility will rest on last night's action. . . . I honestly believe that the vote last night was stimulus to war and that if the result had been different it would have been a definite encouragement to peace."

Vice President Garner and Ickes now urged Roosevelt to simply ignore the neutrality law as an unconstitutional restriction on executive power. Ickes wanted Roosevelt "to announce that his was the duty and obligation to conduct foreign affairs and that he proposed to do so without any assistance from Congress." In response, Roosevelt asked the attorney general, "If we fail to get any Neutrality Bill, how far do you think I can go in ignoring the existing act — even though I did sign it?" Because he believed that the House would consider impeachment if he acted without regard for the existing neutrality law, Roosevelt went back to Key Pittman's Senate committee for action on a cash-and-carry revision. He accepted Pittman's quid pro quo of a higher price on domestic silver, but even that didn't ensure a favorable vote by the Foreign Relations Committee. Roosevelt was so frustrated, he told Morgenthau, that "I will bet you an old hat . . . that . . . when he [Hitler] . . . finds out what has happened, there will be great rejoicing in the Italian and German camps. I think we ought to introduce a bill for statues of [Senators Warren] Austin, Vandenberg, Lodge and Taft . . . to be erected in Berlin and put swastikas on them."

Roosevelt now asked Senate leaders to meet with him at the White House, where he could make a final appeal for neutrality reform. On July 18, accompanied by Garner and Hull, he pressed Democrats Barkley and Pittman and Republicans Charles McNary, the Chamber's minority leader, and Foreign Relations Committee members Austin and Borah to understand that war was coming and revision was essential to preserve the peace. Borah dismissed the president's argument as speculation, insisting that Germany wasn't ready to fight and that Hull's sources confirming Roosevelt's forecast were faulty, adding that he had more reliable informants than those in the State Department. Hull, "on the verge of an explosion" following Borah's comment, was "outraged at the brusque manner in which" Borah disputed his "mass of facts" disproving Borah's "theory that there will be no war." As for Roosevelt, he conceded that he had "fired my last shot." "Well, Captain," Garner replied, "we may as well face the facts. You haven't got the votes and that's all there is to it." A desultory Roosevelt told a press conference, "I have practically no power to make an American effort to prevent . . . a war from breaking out."

The isolationists mystified Roosevelt. He could understand a progressive senator like Thomas D. Schall of Minnesota, who displayed his ignorance of foreign affairs in his declaration on the Senate floor, "To hell with Europe and the rest of those nations!" He could even comprehend why someone like Senator Homer T. Bone of Washington wanted to steer clear of "the poisonous European mess," which he thought could infect American democracy. "I believe in being kind to people who have the smallpox, such as Mussolini and Hitler," Bone said, "but not in going inside their houses."

Roosevelt was hard-pressed, however, to fathom the fervent parochialism of progressive senators like Borah and Hiram Johnson. Borah, who had voted for numerous New Deal initiatives and supported official relations with the Soviet Union, dumbfounded Roosevelt by declaring his regard for Hitler as someone who spoke for the German people in aiming to revise the Versailles settlement, and by remarking, when World War II finally did break out in September 1939, "Lord, if I could only have talked to Hitler — all this might have been averted." Borah's words "ran like a prayer," the journalist who heard him make the comment reported. As for Hiram Johnson, his impeccable credentials as a TR progressive Republican clashed with his adamant refusal to see anything but disaster in any U.S. involvement in Europe's affairs, especially another one of its wars. TR, after all, was a devoted internationalist who thought the world could only profit from U.S. engagement abroad. For Johnson, however, being drawn into foreign conflicts meant jeopardizing American democracy. "The first casualty when war comes is truth," he is alleged to have said.

If the Senate isolationists were not enough to frustrate Roosevelt, he also had to deal with a report from Ickes about Kennedy in London. Kennedy, Ickes said, "was privately telling [the pro-Nazi] Cliveden set that the Jews were running the United States and that the President would fall in 1940. . . . Carried away by his pro-Franco sentiments, Mr. Kennedy, an ardent Catholic, who wrongly believes that in this way he is serving the interests of his church, goes so far as to insinuate that the Democratic policy of the United States is a Jewish production." Concerned not to lose the Catholic vote in 1940, Roosevelt nonetheless left Kennedy in his post in London.

An opinion survey about neutrality revision conducted in the summer of 1939 showed a 50-50 split in American opinion. Under the banner of "America First," Charles Lindbergh, the most popular man in America, held in even higher regard than Roosevelt, was firmly against U.S. involvement in another European war. Lindbergh had accepted decorations from Hitler, which incensed American liberals, but it did little to diminish his public standing and gave considerable weight to his outspoken support of accommodation with the Nazis as a deterrent to Communist expansion. Roosevelt had met with him at the White House in April 1939, ostensibly to learn more about German air power, but also as a political gesture that could disarm public antagonism to overt differences between him and so popular a hero.

With the New Deal stalled and a belief among mainstream economists that the United States had a "mature economy" with little prospect of significant future growth, Roosevelt could not imagine campaigning for a third term on a domestic agenda. The only justification he saw to run again was in the event of a war, which he expected to begin in the fall or before the end of the year. But a Gallup poll at the end of July showed a split of 40 to 38 percent against his running for another term, with 22 percent undecided.

In August, the war that Roosevelt and the State Department feared grew even more likely with Nazi pressure on Poland to give up the corridor to the Baltic and Danzig and the consummation of a Nazi-Soviet nonaggression pact. In April, the Soviet Union had proposed a mutual nonaggression treaty between Moscow, London, and Paris that ensured military support should any of them come under attack by an aggressor. With the British reluctant to commit themselves to a Soviet alliance, Stalin turned to Berlin. Churchill said later that a Soviet tie would have threatened Hitler with a two-front war, which "he had so deeply condemned. . . . It was a pity not to have placed him in this awkward position." The Nazi-Soviet agreement on August 23 seemed to make a war inevitable. "Everybody agrees that war is unthinkable," a prominent British journalist observed, "but the gulf between the British and Hitlerian viewpoints is so wide that it really seems all but unavoidable."

Although Hitler rationalized the agreement with Moscow as "a pact with Satan to cast out the Devil," he was frantic in the run-up to unleashing the attack that would begin the war. As witnessed by the British ambassador and a Swedish observer, he seemed like a madman, spouting diatribes against all his presumed enemies. In their presence he worked himself into "a nervous frenzy, marching up and down the room, his eyes staring, his voice at one moment indistinct, hurling out facts and figures about the strength of the German armed forces, the next moment shouting as if addressing a party meeting, threatening to annihilate his enemies, giving . . . the impression of someone 'completely abnormal.' " One German general who listened to Hitler's rationale for war remarked, "Its bragging and brash tone was downright repulsive. One had the feeling that here a man spoke who had lost all feeling of responsibility and any clear conception of what a victorious war signified." Mindful that he would be accused of starting an unnecessary conflict, Hitler declared, "The victor will not be asked afterwards whether he told the truth or not. When starting and waging a war it is not right that matters, but victory. . . . The stronger man is right."

Roosevelt, for his part, had tried to discourage Moscow from allying itself with Berlin. On August 4, he had warned the Russians that they could not trust Hitler, for after he had defeated the French, he would likely turn against them. A Soviet alliance with Britain and France, however, would deter Hitler and would "have a decidedly stabilizing effect in the interest of world peace." But Stalin was less interested in peace than in enabling a German war with the West that could discourage Hitler from attacking the Soviet Union. Roosevelt also sent messages to Italy's king Victor Emmanuel, Hitler, and Poland's president Ignacy Mościcki urging negotiations to avert war. "These messages will have about the same effect as a valentine sent to somebody's mother-in-law out of season," Adolf Berle in the State Department said. Joe Kennedy wanted Roosevelt to pressure Warsaw into making concessions to Hitler that would prevent a conflict, which the president dismissed as nothing more than fostering another Munich. Berle sarcastically condemned the suggestion as effectively asking the Poles to commit suicide. Such a proposal, Berle said, would have to begin: "In view of the fact that your suicide is required, kindly oblige."

Between August 12 and August 24, Roosevelt had tried temporarily to escape the pressures of the looming international crisis by taking a vacation cruise along the East Coast to Maine and Nova Scotia. It was not just the European situation that worried him; continuing Japanese aggression in China also agitated him. In the first half of 1939, the Japanese took control of foreign settlements in China, which they saw as aiding Chiang Kai-shek's Nationalist government. Because Britain seemed more vulnerable or less able to resist Japanese pressure than the United States, Tokyo assaulted British civilians in Tientsin, blockading their compound and humiliating the residents by forcing them to disrobe when leaving or entering it. Especially angered by the "indiscriminate bombing" of Chungking, the Nationalist capital, Roosevelt instructed Hull to protest against these actions. He also directed the State Department to inform Tokyo that the United States was giving the required six-month notice that it was withdrawing from its 1911 trade treaty with Japan. Yet Roosevelt was reluctant to be too antagonistic lest it persuade the Japanese to consummate an alliance they were discussing with Italy and Germany.

J. Pierrepont Moffat, the assistant secretary of state for Western European Affairs, remarked that he had "the feeling of sitting in a house where somebody is dying upstairs. There is relatively little to do and yet the suspense continues unabated." For Berle, Europe's descent into another great power conflict gave him "a horrible feeling of seeing . . . a civilization dying even before its actual death." After German armies crossed into Poland on September 1 and the Luftwaffe began bombing Warsaw, killing thousands of civilians, and Chamberlain issued a war declaration before Parliament on September 3, Joe Kennedy, fearful that America would eventually be drawn into the fighting, with risks to his two oldest sons, declared: "It's the end of the world, the end of everything."

With the outbreak of war, Roosevelt took to the radio to assure Americans that he would keep the country out of the fighting. "This nation will remain a neutral nation," he said, "but I cannot ask that every American remain neutral in thought as well. Even a neutral has a right to take account of facts." He did not want any American "to close his mind or his conscience"; he hoped the majority would not give up its antipathy for Nazi aggression. However, mindful of the country's opposition to belligerency, he ended with an "assurance and reassurance that every effort of your Government will be directed toward that end. As long as it remains within my power to prevent, there will be no blackout of peace in the United States."

With an eye on the following year's election, Roosevelt also urged potential voters to understand that he remained their best hope for leading the country through this period of tumultuous events abroad. When he received word that war had broken out, he made it clear that "the machinery of democratic government moved swiftly and moved efficiently." He had "a strange feeling of familiarity — a feeling that I had been through it all before." He reminded people of how he had dealt with the outbreak of World War I as assistant secretary of the Navy. "It was *not* strange to me," he said, "but more like picking up again an interrupted routine. . . . History does in fact repeat."

CHAPTER 12
FAUX NEUTRAL

That Europe was again at war left people across the continent bewildered and horrified. Whether in France or Britain or Italy or in any of Europe's smaller countries, the shared feeling was one of incomprehension that governments could be so reckless as to repeat the bloodletting of the Great War, which had led to such mayhem only twenty years before. In Spain, where a million people had already perished in the three-year-long civil conflict, Francisco Franco, the country's newly anointed Fascist leader, understood that despite German and Italian contributions to his victory, participation in the war would be overwhelmingly unpopular.

Even in Germany, where sentiment strongly favored reversing the penalties imposed by the Versailles Treaty, people were sullen and depressed at the prospect of a major conflict with Britain and France. William Shirer, a U.S. correspondent in Berlin, saw "anxiety, fears [and] worries" on the faces of the populace. "Everybody against the war," he wrote. "How can a country go into a major war with a population so dead against it?" But the public had little or no say in Hitler's decisions. He had consolidated his power, and dissent or opposition of any kind invited personal disaster, if not death. Still, his successfully having reoccupied the Rhineland and seized Austria and Czechoslovakia without bloodshed made him a hero to millions of Germans. Even Germany's most ardent antiwar opponents could not ignore the possibility that with a Polish victory Hitler would recoup the losses of Versailles. If he could reach a quick settlement with Britain and France, which he said he wanted, his popularity in Germany would reach unprecedented heights.

In the United States, the antiwar feeling remained as strong as ever. However hateful Hitler's behavior and regime were to almost all Americans, they did not see him or Nazi Germany as a genuine threat to the homeland. Although most people hoped that Germany would be defeated in the emerging conflict with Britain and France, they shared the belief of Charles Lindbergh, whose expertise as an aviator helped shape public opinion, that German air power was simply not capable of reaching the United States. Moreover, if America did become involved, it would mean the rise of a national security state like those in Europe, with government agencies limiting customary freedoms. Millions of Americans feared belligerency as threatening traditions of individualism that had set the nation apart from the Old World with its militarism and restrictions on free expression.

However eager Roosevelt was to help the British and the French with war supplies, he understood the limits of what he could do. But even becoming a nonbelligerent supplier was a challenge that required the most delicate political handling. On the eve of the war, only 50 percent of Americans favored changing the neutrality law. Once the war began, however, sentiment quickly shifted in favor of a cash-and-carry policy, and the likelihood that exports of war supplies would spur a sluggish U.S. economy was not lost on businesses and ordinary citizens.

A week after the war began, Roosevelt was confident that he could get the votes in the House and the Senate for neutrality reform. But he feared a filibuster in the latter that could block legislation. Isolationists, led by Borah, who had never traveled outside of the United States, launched a radio campaign to prevent revision. On September 1, Herbert Hoover told the nation, "We Must Keep Out"; on September 15, Charles Lindbergh urged Americans to "Look to Our Own Defense"; and on September 17, Martin Dies chimed in with warnings that if democracy was to be preserved in the United States, it had to eliminate foreign "-isms" from its midst instead of plunging into a foreign war.

Roosevelt now had to carefully orchestrate congressional action on neutrality. On September 20, he convened a bipartisan conference in his Oval Office, where he made the case for cash-and-carry to keep the country at peace. When one of the conferees said he favored this revision because it would aid the democracies, Roosevelt exclaimed, "I am darned glad you said something I couldn't say and that is without question the overwhelming sentiment in this country is in favor of France and England winning the war." It was surprising that Roosevelt acknowledged his true intentions, for if his comment were leaked to the press, it would have triggered a furor among isolationists who were already convinced that the president's principal goal was to influence the outcome of the war rather than keep the United States out of the fighting.

On September 21, after he called Congress into special session, Roosevelt spoke in person to a packed House and a larger audience on the radio. He repeated what he had said on September 3 about there being no blackout of peace in America. But the route to a peaceful world, he asserted, was through revision of the neutrality law and arms sales to the democracies fighting fascism. Entirely mindful of how strong the national sentiment against taking part in the conflict was, Roosevelt declared that the entire nation was in the peace bloc. We "must exert every possible effort to avoid being drawn into the war," he insisted and added that "by the repeal of the embargo the United States will more probably remain at peace than if the law remains as it stands today." In short, cash-and-carry would insulate Americans from conditions that could draw them into the conflict, as they had in 1917. If anything, the neutrality law, with the arms embargo, had helped precipitate the fighting. It was a poor idea, he said, and he regretted having signed it into law. A prompt revision of the existing statute was the best defense against belligerency by helping the democracies defeat the Fascist states that were all too ready to commit additional acts of aggression that could eventually force America to fight.

At the same time, concerned about the number of displaced persons who would become refugees from the fighting — "refugees of various Christian faiths, as well as Jewish refugees coming not from one country but from many countries" — Roosevelt directed Cordell Hull, who had a Jewish wife, to consider ways to rescue them from their plight. Fearful that any proposal favoring Jews would stir anti-Semitism, which was already intense in the United States, especially across the South and the Midwest, Roosevelt said privately that he wanted to put "the refugee problem on a broad religious basis, thereby making it possible to gain the kind of worldwide [and American] support that a mere Jewish relief set up would not evoke." Because he believed that many of those displaced by the war would be Polish Catholics, he hoped to involve the Vatican in such a humanitarian effort. On Christmas Eve of that year he appointed an ambassador to the Holy See through whom discussions could occur.

But Roosevelt's focus remained on neutrality revision, as his greatest concern — though he would not acknowledge it publicly — was to help ensure a British-French victory over the Nazis. According to reports reaching him from London and Paris, this meant their receiving U.S. arms shipments as promptly as possible. Kennedy informed him that British officials thought it would be "a sheer disaster" if cash-and-carry failed. The French premier told Bullitt that a successful offensive against Germany depended on American supplies. Bullitt predicted that the key factor that would determine an Allied victory or defeat would be American arms. And should the Allies lose, the United States would have to fight Hitler in the Americas.

When Lord Tweedsmuir, the governor-general of Canada, proposed to "slip down inconspicuously" to Hyde Park at the end of September, Roosevelt and Hull counseled him to wait until they had won the neutrality fight. Roosevelt wrote

Tweedsmuir: "I am almost literally walking on eggs, and having delivered my message to congress, and having good prospects of the bill going through, I am at the moment saying nothing, seeing nothing and hearing nothing." He told Frank Knox, the progressive Republican publisher of the *Chicago Daily News,* "Have you noticed that, as you suggested . . . I have been trying to kill all war talk? I have treated the report of the War Resources Committee [which was examining what would be required in case of war] as just an ordinary instance of normal preparedness work and they will go home in two weeks with my blessing."

In all his public statements and actions, he aimed to hide any suggestion that he was more concerned with helping defeat Hitler than with keeping the country out of the war. He told Morgenthau that he was "considering leasing hangars and bases for seaplanes in Bermuda and elsewhere in the British West Indies," but wanted it kept quiet lest it arouse domestic opposition. He had "used more weasel words in the last two weeks than in the last seven years," he complained to Morgenthau. But "he saw no alternative until after the Congress amended the Neutrality Act." In the meantime, he relied on others to make the case for reform. When Bishop Sheil of Chicago gave a radio speech urging Catholics "to rally behind F.D.R. in the neutrality law controversy," Roosevelt saw it as a godsend in disarming Irish and Italian Catholic opposition.

Roosevelt enlisted Alf Landon, former secretary of state Henry Stimson, and a host of university presidents and prominent faculty members to counter the isolationists with talks and writings that encouraged the public to support the president's initiative. When Charles Edison, the acting secretary of the Navy, asked Roosevelt to put a list of Navy appointments before the Senate, the president replied: "No appointments of any kind can be sent to the Senate until after the Neutrality Bill has been acted on." When the *New York Times* reported that Roosevelt had made a truce proposal to Hitler, Franklin wrote Marvin McIntyre, his press secretary, "If you believe this morning's papers you will expect me to be in Berlin talking peace with Hitler next Monday morning. Fortunately you agree with me about what one reads in the papers."

Berlin had begun issuing stories saying that Hitler was ready for mediation "now that he had gained his objectives in Poland." It put pressure on Roosevelt to mediate an end to the conflict, as it wanted — temporarily at least — to settle tensions with Britain and France as a prelude to striking at Russia. London and Paris perceived such a settlement as resulting in nothing more than a lull in the fighting during which Hitler could consolidate his gains in Eastern Europe before striking at them again.

Roosevelt wanted no part of helping Berlin achieve its aims, as he feared that a British and French defeat would likely lead to "the complete collapse of everything we hope and live for." In London, however, Kennedy was eager for a settlement, predicting that if Germany lost, it would mean its "going Communist in the Russian manner." Roosevelt by then had little interest in anything Kennedy advised, as he was well aware that Kennedy had been doing "some pretty loud and inappropriate talking about" him with remarks that were "vulgar and coarse and highly critical." When Ickes told the president that Chamberlain was considering putting Kennedy in his cabinet, Roosevelt "threw back his head and laughed." But Roosevelt did not see him as a laughing matter. Roosevelt told Morgenthau that "Joe Kennedy . . . has been an appeaser and always will be an appeaser. If Germany or Italy made a good peace offer tomorrow, Joe would start working on the King and his friend, the Queen, and from there on down to get everybody to accept it . . . He's just a pain in the neck to me." He said to Jim Farley that Kennedy's recommendation for peace talks with Germany was the "silliest message to me I have ever received" and dismissed Kennedy's appeal as "frantic." Roosevelt was more diplomatic in his direct response to Kennedy, writing him, "I do not think people in England should worry about Germany going Communist. . . . They might blow up and have chaos for a while but the German upbringing for centuries . . . would not, in my judgment, permit the Russian form of brutality for any length of time."

At the same time, though, Roosevelt launched a correspondence with the sixty-five-year-old Winston Churchill, the newly installed first lord of the admiralty. He understood that he and Churchill, who had been a Roosevelt counterpart during World War I, shared a common view about Hitler and the Nazis. "What I want you and the Prime Minister to know is that I shall at all times welcome it, if you keep me in touch personally with anything you want me to know about," Roosevelt wrote him. Their communications had to be kept strictly secret lest isolationists in the United States attack the president for secretly exchanging views with a British cabinet member who would have liked nothing more than to involve the United States in the war. When Kennedy learned that Roosevelt had taken Churchill into his confidence, he privately railed against Churchill, whom he called "an actor and a politician," and whom he thought would be willing "to blow up the American Embassy and say it was the Germans if it would get the U.S. in."

In his campaign for cash-and-carry, Roosevelt was careful to avoid any suggestion that he was supporting the cause not only to bring America into the war but also to create a favorable climate of opinion for him to run again in 1940. In October, when the journalist Ernest K. Lindley published an article in the *Washington Post* suggesting that Roosevelt's pro-British, pro-French, anti-German bias would draw the United States into the conflict, the president made a lengthy reply through Steve Early declaring that Lindley's column was "definitely pure invention. (I am being polite.) Ernest's failure to investigate is rather pathetic, as is his knowledge of history." In fact, Roosevelt did have a pro-British, pro-French bias, but not because of family ties or early life experience, as Lindley alleged, but because he favored their democratic political systems and despised Hitler's Nazi regime. But in the antiwar climate of 1939, it was politically essential that Roosevelt deny Lindley's assertions. When Henry Wallace announced publicly that "the war made a third term for F.D.R. a necessity," Roosevelt believed that "the worst thing that could happen to the move to repeal the embargo was to entangle it with presidential politics." In response, Steve Early told the press, "It would have been kind and polite of the speaker to have consulted the victim before he spoke." The White House thought that Early's statement "wiped out all the damage that Wallace had done" or at least they hoped so.

Roosevelt worked studiously to keep all political controversy to a minimum during the period in which he advocated neutrality revision. He took pains to mollify his sharpest critics or at least not get into public arguments with them. In October, when the neutrality question was being hotly debated in Congress and General Robert E. Wood, the chief executive of Sears Roebuck, predicted that the United States would become involved in the fighting, Roosevelt chided him privately, writing, "You are forming opinions on hearsay nonsense and are not reading the record. If you are a 'doubting Thomas' you had better run down to Washington, run in to see me and let me in person quiet your troubled mind!" He sent Joe Kennedy a placating letter, playing to his bias for free enterprise, in which he recounted a joke Ambassador Josephus Daniels in Mexico had told him: "Suppose you had two cows. The Socialist would take one and let you keep one. The Nazi would let you keep both cows but would take all the milk. The Communist would take both cows." As for Republican representative Hamilton Fish from Roosevelt's New York congressional district, he said nothing publicly about misrepresentations of White House policies Fish made during a trip to England and France, but privately complained, "I wish this great Pooh-bah would go back to Harvard and play tackle on the football team. He is qualified for that job."

As the fight over neutrality unfolded in Congress, Roosevelt tried to keep a low profile, but because he believed he couldn't disappear from public view entirely, continued to hold his regular biweekly press conferences. Leaving it to Garner and allies in Congress to manage the neutrality battle, he was tired and did not relish taking part in a tough political fight. At fifty-seven, nearing the end of seven years in the White House, he was grayer, a bit heavier, and less energetic than before. When he addressed Congress on September 21, a reporter described him as looking "tired and worn." Although he would never acknowledge to anyone that he was slowing down, he faced current events and the future with greater trepidation than when he took office in 1933 or began his second term in 1937. The setbacks of the past two years had raised self-doubts about his enduring mastery of politics and a divided public.

By contrast, no one in the administration had weathered the political crosscurrents more successfully than Eleanor Roosevelt. She had become "a rather welcome part of the national life," a popular magazine asserted. "Women especially feel this way. But even men betray relatively small masculine impatience with the work and opinions of a very articulate lady. . . . Even among those extremely anti-Roosevelt citizens who would regard a third term as a national disaster, there is a generous minority . . . who want Mrs. Roosevelt to remain in the public eye." Another national publication lauded her for keeping up the good fight. "She never lets the President or his administrators think that all is well, that there is time to rest from advancing their liberal objectives. . . . No matter how deeply absorbed he may become in international affairs, she will keep him from forgetting the New Deal."

For the moment, however, domestic reform had become a secondary concern to a White House trying to combat Nazi gains. Roosevelt briefly considered asking for full repeal of the Neutrality law, followed by executive orders for cash-and-carry, but realized that the congressional fight that would be sure to follow would become about him rather than defeating Hitler. He accordingly supported replacing the arms embargo with cash-and-carry. To his surprise, the Senate proved to be an easier sell than the House, though opponents demonstrated at the Capitol and protested that the president was in the pockets of "Merchants of Death" and taken into camp by British propaganda. "One might have thought the President had asked permission to sell the United States to England," an ardent interventionist complained. When the rector prayed for England's victory over its enemies at a church service during the royals' visit to Hyde Park, newspapers and House isolationists seized upon it as evidence of Roosevelt's un-neutrality, which he dismissed as "grasping at straws."

By the middle of October, Garner had informed Roosevelt that they could win the Senate but was less certain about the result in the House. On October 26, the day before the Senate was scheduled to vote, Roosevelt, taking nothing for granted, delivered a radio address. In a time when Nazi gains seemed to eclipse representative government, he made the case for liberal democracy, saying "I am reminded of four definitions: A Radical is a man with both feet firmly planted — in the air. A conservative is a man with two perfectly good legs who, however, has never learned to walk forward. A Reactionary is a somnambulist walking

561

backwards. A Liberal is a man who uses his legs and hands at the behest — at the command — of his head." The metaphors involving legs and walking from someone as immobilized as Roosevelt were as much an expression of how he felt about his work as president as his view of public affairs: While he might not be able to walk himself, every action he took represented a step forward, or so he liked to think.

At the close of his speech, he left his listeners with a scathing observation about the outcry against neutrality reform: "In and out of Congress we have heard orators and commentators and others beating their breasts and proclaiming against sending the boys of American mothers to fight on the battlefields of Europe. I do not hesitate to label that as one of the worst fakes in current history. It is a deliberate setting up of an imaginary bogeyman. The simple truth is that no person in any responsible place in the national administration in Washington . . . has ever suggested in any shape, manner or form the remotest possibility of sending the boys . . . to fight on the battlefields of Europe." In the fall of 1939, Roosevelt had no intention of sending ground forces anywhere abroad. He understood that majority opinion would not support such a commitment. He could, however, imagine U.S. naval and air forces joining the battle against Germany and Japan, but certainly not then, and not if Britain and France could defeat them.

On October 27, the Senate made America's industrial might a factor in the conflict with a positive 63 to 30 vote for cash-and-carry. The following week, after a sharp debate in the House, where isolationists mounted a last-ditch stand, a

62-vote margin gave Roosevelt the legislative victory he hoped could shape the course of the war.

With cash-and-carry secure, he moved quickly to assist the democracies. As the war threatened to engulf Belgium and Holland, he wrote King Leopold and Queen Wilhelmina offering to shelter their children in the United States. "I want you to know," he cabled both of them, "I want to help in any personal way which lies in my power." More substantively, he used a "subterfuge" to begin rushing supplies to Britain and France. Because the revised neutrality law still forbade U.S. transports to use Atlantic shipping lanes that had been designated war zones, Roosevelt wanted American-owned ships under Panamanian registry to take up the assignment. His decision came under fire from William Allen White, the Kansas editor who had led a committee promoting neutrality reform, who complained about the "registration trick" the president was using to put American ships in jeopardy. But Roosevelt defended the sale of a " 'laid-up' ship, for which there is no American use" as legal as the sale of "Kansas wheat or California airplanes." He cautioned White: "Do you really honestly believe everything you read in the 'tarnation' newspapers?" But White could identify a ruse when he saw one.

The difficulty in getting supplies to the combatants was due as much to the British and French indecisiveness as it was to the restrictions imposed on Roosevelt by the neutrality law. "The only trouble," he wrote Bullitt in Paris on November 23, "is that the dear British and French Governments are failing, as usual, to be definite between themselves and to be definite to me. They shifted back and forth a dozen times on their . . . purchase methods and finally got everyone so disgusted that we had to tell them what to do." He wanted representatives from the two nations to affirm "what they want and when they want it." Although a purchasing mission would be established in December to clarify their requests, London and Paris were reluctant to spend precious reserves on arms they believed they could produce themselves over the course of the three years they expected the war to last.

The rush of events abroad soon began to frustrate Roosevelt and raise doubts in his own mind about his ability to influence the outcome of the conflict. First, on November 8, within days of the congressional action, he considered giving a national speech describing the "fallacies" in isolationist thinking. "Geography, distance and speed of transportation" no longer gave the United States the security it previously enjoyed. He warned that a war would not only place a huge tax burden on the country but would also play havoc with American commerce, which would find itself competing with "government-controlled and government-subsidized trade, arising out of every part of a dictator-dominated Europe and a dictator-dominated system of colonies in almost every part of the world." In the end, the likelihood that the speech would trigger shrill predictions of administration plans to take the country into the war persuaded him to shelve the speech. Only the harsh realities of, and not words of caution about, national security seemed likely to change intransigent minds.

Roosevelt hoped at least to enlist all the American Republics in a plan to create a neutral zone in the western Atlantic and Caribbean that would bar German submarines from preying on British shipping in these waters. At a Pan American conference in Panama in late September, the Republics issued a declaration forbidding belligerent actions in an area 300 to 1,000 miles off the Atlantic coast south of Canada. But U.S. naval chiefs argued that patrolling so large an area was impossible, and during the first three months of fighting, incidents in the zone bore out their judgment. Between September and December the German heavy cruiser *Graf Spee,* the prize of the fleet, freely roamed the South Atlantic sinking nine Allied ships before being attacked by three British cruisers. In a spectacular battle off the coast of Uruguay that gave Roosevelt some small satisfaction, the British inflicted enough damage on the German vessel to force its scuttling. When Hans Langsdorff, the German commander, committed suicide in Buenos Aires, where he had been given sanctuary, his note pledging his fidelity to "the cause and the future of the nation and of my Fuhrer" underscored for Roosevelt that the democracies were fighting a fanatical dictatorship that valued conformity to ruthlessness over traditional freedoms practiced in Britain, France, and the United States.

Roosevelt also hoped to promote hemisphere solidarity with American loans and credits to guarantee economic stability across Latin America and guard against German economic penetration of the southern Republics. But resistance from Congress and U.S. financial institutions to providing risky investments to unreliable borrowers killed the plan. This only heightened White House fears of Nazi influence in Latin America, with particular concern about control of the Panama Canal, which it considered critical to deterring Japanese aggression in Asia, and more directly, Nazi threats to U.S. national security.

On November 30 the Soviet Union invaded Finland. Having established control over the Baltic states of Estonia, Latvia, and Lithuania in September and October and pressured Finland to yield territorial concessions that would serve Soviet security, Moscow had ignored pleas from Roosevelt to act with restraint. "The Soviet Union," he said privately, "is run by a dictatorship as absolute as any other dictatorship in the world. . . . It has invaded a neighbor so infinitesimally small that it could do no conceivable possible harm to [it]." He was horrified by the possibility of a combined German-Russian expansion that, as Adolph Berle told him, would "have two men [Hitler and Stalin] able to rule from Manchuria to the Rhine, much as Genghis Khan once ruled and nothing to stop the combined Russian-German force at any point, with the possible exception of the Himalayan Mountains north of India." From his post in the State Department, Berle warned the president: "The rest of my life . . . will be spent trying to defend various parts of this world from economic, military and propaganda attempts to establish domination over it."

If Roosevelt had concluded that the war and the dangers it posed to the United States compelled him to run again, the sense of powerlessness he felt following neutrality reform made him question the wisdom of seeking a third term. On November 19, he presided at a cornerstone-laying ceremony in Hyde Park, where a Franklin Roosevelt presidential library was being built. The "peaceful countryside" evoked thoughts of his childhood, climbing old oak trees, picking ripe sickle pears, eating sun-warmed strawberries, sailing "toy boats in the surface water formed by melting snow," and retiring from the tumultuous events abroad that shadowed the world. Instead of the burdens of office another White House term were certain to bring, he could retreat into the calm of writing his memoirs.

But in the face of the perils he saw that fall, he could not imagine turning away from the field of political combat. Two broad considerations shaped his thinking and plans for the coming year, before the electorate would decide whether to break tradition and reelect him yet again. First, he aimed to do everything he could within the domestic and international constraints on him to defeat the dictators menacing free peoples everywhere. And second, he aimed to do all in his power to convince potential voters to extend his presidency for another four years. Throughout the fall, Gallup polls showed up to 65 percent approval for him and 57 percent expecting him to run for a third term. But the challenges before him promised to test the wisdom and effectiveness of even the most astute politician. It seemed certain to be as arduous a test of his physical and emotional strength as anything he had confronted since his polio. As Richard Moe believes, Roosevelt's decision to run again was "more the result of duty than of desire; as much as he enjoyed being president . . . more important was his supreme confidence in his own capacity to lead the country facing a dire emergency. Humility was not a factor here; it seldom was with FDR."

By the middle of December, with the Soviet attack on Finland and Hitler's war machine preparing an assault on Western Europe, Roosevelt complained to Bill White that the "world situation seems to be getting progressively worse. . . . No human being . . . has the slightest idea how this war is going to come out." He thought the fighting would either lead to "greater chaos or to the kind of truce which could last only a very short period." He worried about Soviet expansion and the possibility that Norway, Sweden, Romania, and Bulgaria were in its sights. Worse yet was the possibility of a German-Russian alliance gaining control of "Asia Minor, Persia, Africa and the various British, French, Dutch, Belgian, etc. colonies." Such an outcome, he told White, would imperil "your civilization and mine." The greatest challenge he faced, he also told White, was "to get the American people to think of conceivable consequences without scaring the American people into thinking that they are going to be dragged into this war." Or, expressed in another way, how could he prepare the country for war while convincing it that he was tirelessly working to keep it out of the fighting?

Part of the answer was a secret exchange he had had with the internationally famous scientist Albert Einstein, who had immigrated to the United States to escape Nazi Germany and had become a fellow at Princeton's Institute of Advanced Studies. In October, Alexander Sachs, an economist at Lehman Brothers and friend of both the president and Einstein, agreed to carry a letter from Einstein to the White House alerting Roosevelt to the possibility of building a super bomb and advising him that German scientists might already be working toward that end. After Sachs, who was eager to ensure that Roosevelt would not give cursory attention to Einstein's warning, read the letter to the president in the Oval Office, Roosevelt said, "Alex, what you are after is to see that the Nazis don't blow us up." Roosevelt then passed the letter to an aide with the direction, "This requires action." Five months later, when it was confirmed that the Germans were indeed developing a bomb, he instructed aides to give U.S. efforts greater urgency.

The winter of 1939–40 saw a pause in the fighting after Hitler quickly conquered Poland, creating doubts that the war would continue or hopes that the Allies and Germany would see the folly of continued battle and would make some kind of lasting peace. In Britain, the conflict during this period was called the "Bore War"; in France the *"Drôle de guerre"* or strange war; in Germany, the *"Sitzkrieg"* or sitting war; and in the United States, it was dismissed as the "phony war." The *Denver Post* declared, "The smallest domestic problem is now more important to the American people than the most momentous European crisis." According to Gallup polls, 59 percent of Americans believed that even if the fighting resumed, the Allies would be victorious. While 79 percent of a survey endorsed Roosevelt's plan to increase defense spending, a comparable number remained determined to stay out of the war, even if Britain and France appeared to be losing. And if Hitler seemed ready to make peace, 75 percent of Americans favored an Allied effort to end the conflict.

On December 29, Roosevelt wrote Frank Knox, whom he was planning to make secretary of the Navy, "Your suggestion that the country as a whole does not yet have any deep sense of world crisis must I fear be admitted by me." To counter American parochialism, he used his seventh State of the Union speech, which he delivered five days later before Congress, to argue that isolationism was an outdated concept. He cautioned that there was "a vast difference between keeping out of war and pretending that this war is none of our business." As a consequence, he called for greater defense spending, the only budget increase in his message. In addition, he proposed that the United States "be a potent and active factor in seeking the reestablishment of peace." Few things, he said, would better serve the national well-being than "the kind of peace that will lighten the troubles of the world. For it [has] become clearer and clearer that the future world will be a shabby and dangerous place to live in . . . if it is ruled by force in the hands of a few. . . . I hope," he concluded, "that we will have fewer American ostriches in our midst. It is not good for the ultimate health of ostriches to bury their heads in the sand." He urged Americans to appreciate the importance of U.S. leadership in the maintenance of world peace and he called for a unity that justified democracy's "existence as the best instrument of government yet devised by mankind."

His message was a prelude to launching a peace mission — less because he perceived there was a real chance for a negotiated settlement than because he hoped to delay a German spring offensive that could lead to an Anglo-French defeat. The longer it took before full-scale fighting occurred in the West, the better prepared the Allies would be to defend themselves and possibly even win the war, or so Roosevelt believed. He privately acknowledged that he had a "one in a thousand" chance of arranging a lasting settlement and that he would need the combined powers of "the Holy Ghost and [boxer] Jack Dempsey" to succeed.

With his eye on the 1940 election, domestic politics played a large part in his proposing peace talks. On Christmas day, he published a letter to Pope Pius XII declaring American interest in promoting world peace. In January and February, he invited neutral nations to discuss arms control and international trade at a world conference, and he announced that Undersecretary of State Sumner Welles would go to Europe to advise him and Hull on current conditions. Warned by Chamberlain and Hull that any public acknowledgement of inviting Berlin to the peace table would undermine Anglo-French determination to fight the war, and fearful that news of U.S. mediation would provoke new isolationist complaints that Roosevelt's meddling would pull the country into the war, he insisted that the Welles trip be presented as only a fact-finding mission. At the same time, he thought that this initiative would encourage views of him as an indispensable world statesman.

Roosevelt's decision to ask Welles to represent him rested on the conviction that sending Hull, the country's top diplomat, would stir greater isolationist concern. It also demonstrated Roosevelt's limited regard for Hull, who continued to impress him as too cautious and unimaginative. In addition, he did not want to raise Hull's political profile for a 1940 presidential campaign. As for the State Department professionals, Roosevelt simply didn't trust them, regarding them as conservative opponents of his new domestic order and too indifferent to the fate of the democracies, or too willing to see Berlin win the war. When the State Department suggested that he remove a reference in a speech to "American citizens, many of them in high places, who unwittingly in most cases are aiding and abetting" the work of Nazi agents, by which he meant the ultra isolationists, an irritated Roosevelt "snorted and said forcefully: 'Leave it in — in fact I'm very much tempted to say many of them in high places — *including* the State Department.'" He viewed the department's professionals as "too apt to use 'weasel words'" that masked their sympathies for Hitler's anticommunist regime.

In assessing foreign affairs, Roosevelt was more inclined to rely on the reports of men outside the Foreign Service — like Dodd in Berlin and Claude Bowers in Madrid, whose principal loyalty was to him rather than to the State Department. Ickes reinforced the president's antagonism to the Foreign Service, suggesting that too many in the department were career men who felt "no obligation to follow Administration policy." Ickes also criticized the department as "undemocratic in outlook and . . . shot through with fascism," as well as clearly anti-Semitic and sympathetic to Chamberlain's appeasement policy. He saw Hull's group as architects of the arms embargo that had undermined Spain's democracy and encouraged Hitler's aggression. In 1940, Ickes accused it of being "not without responsibility, serious responsibility at that, for the dreadful situation in which the world today finds itself."

Roosevelt shared Ickes's judgment, complaining that the department was full of "deadwood" and was unwilling to implement his policies. On reading a State Department letter, he dismissed it as a typical example of their empty rhetoric, observing, "It says nothing at all." He viewed the department's professionals as effete, striped-pants dandies, "old maids" and "stuffed shirts" on whom he could not rely to follow orders or convey his thinking. Fearing that state officials would give greater emphasis to their own views than to his, he directed that especially sensitive cables be sent through Navy channels rather than State Department lines. As he said to a friend: "You should go through the experience of trying to get any changes in the thinking, policy and action of the career diplomats and then you'd know what a real problem was."

On February 9, Roosevelt announced Welles's mission to the press, explaining that he would visit Italy, France, Germany, and Great Britain and that he was instructed solely to gather information on European conditions. He was given no authority to make proposals or commitments but merely to listen and learn. Unconvinced that fact-finding was the sole purpose of the trip, reporters asked if Welles would offer information to the European governments on American views regarding a peace settlement. Roosevelt dismissed the question as speculation wholly without foundation, adding, "It might be a good thing to get somebody to see all of the conditions in all of the countries so that one mind would be able to cover the situation instead of having four separate minds reporting on separate things." Eager not to create any sense of urgency about the visit, Roosevelt gave no date as to when Welles would leave or how long he would be away. Pressed further for details on the purpose of the mission, Roosevelt said, "I have not got any idea . . . on whom he will talk to and what he will say and what they will say to him. Now that is the whole thing."

In fact Welles did not leave the United States until February 17, traveling for eight days across the Atlantic on an Italian liner. Since Italy was not a belligerent and all sides were eager to court her — Germany to bring her into the fighting, and the Allies and Roosevelt to convince Mussolini to remain out of it — crossing on an Italian ship was the safest mode of transportation, and stopping first in Naples and Rome was an effective way to court the Duce.

Because the U.S. press insisted on characterizing the mission as an administration "peace offensive," Roosevelt sought to underscore his detachment from the conflict and his calm view of Welles's mission by going off on a two-week fishing vacation and visit to the Panama Canal on a U.S. Navy cruiser. As he wrote Daisy at the start of the voyage, "We have all been laughing at the complete ignorance and gullibility of the Press. They 'fell for' the visit to the Andaman Islands (Indian Ocean) Celebes (No. Pacific) & South Hebrides (Antarctic) and, believe it or not, the Cherable Isles," a Roosevelt invention. His deception on this trip also included some surgery performed aboard ship to remove a mole or possibly cancerous melanoma above his left eye. In photographs taken afterward the dark spot that had been above his eye was now a small scar. He wanted no hint that he had a health issue that would make him seem incapable of dealing with current problems or affect a run for a third term.

Welles's arrival in Italy on February 25 began

the first act of twenty-three days of political theater. The American press closely followed his every move, while Italian government officials greeted him with considerable fanfare. But the controlled Italian press featured little coverage of his visit, and citizens who ate silently in Rome's outdoor cafes sat under signs forbidding any discussion of politics. Welles's conversations with Foreign Minister Galeazzo Ciano, Mussolini's son-in-law, and with Mussolini himself were exercises in deceptive diplomacy. Ciano, who gave Welles indications of his contempt for German diplomats, whom he denounced as "presumptuous vulgarians," showed himself open to Welles's assertions about the benefits to Italy of closer relations with the United States and neutrality in the war. Although only thirty-six at the time and an unqualified mouthpiece for Mussolini, Ciano, who spoke excellent English, impressed Welles as charming, "intelligent and frank."

Welles's audience with the Duce at his palace in Rome's Palazzo Venezia was also more of a theatrical occasion than a substantive exchange affecting international affairs. Meeting in a huge cavernous room with a balcony from which Mussolini gave his legendary harangues to agitated crowds, the two men made every outward effort to strike congenial chords. To underscore his receptivity to the Roosevelt-Welles plea for peaceful relations, Mussolini made his appearance in civilian garb rather than his customary ostentatious uniform. Handed a letter from the president urging a meeting between them in the near future, Mussolini expressed pleasure at Roosevelt's expression of regard. Yet Welles did not judge Mussolini to be a trustworthy proponent of better relations between their two countries. He later described the Duce as a ponderous, out-of-shape, fifty-six-year-old braggart who "moved with elephantine motion." Welles recorded that the meeting was "friendly and cordial" enough, but Mussolini made it clear that his notion of an enduring peace was based upon the satisfaction of German and Italian claims to territorial and economic conditions respectful of their standing as great powers. The Duce's affability and an Italian press campaign that praised the benefits of the conversations masked Mussolini's true intentions of playing a part in the war that would elevate Italy to a more prominent role in world affairs.

From Rome, Welles proceeded to Berlin, where a wintery cold snap matched the icy reception he received from Foreign Minister Joachim von Ribbentrop and Hitler himself. Every Nazi official was programmed to convey the same message to Roosevelt's envoy: The war was Britain's fault; the Allies aimed to annihilate Germany, yet Germany would win the war; and the United States had nothing to fear from a German victory. Czechoslovakia and Poland did not come up in the conversations, nor was the persecution of Germany's and now Poland's Jews discussed. Hitler's interpreter reported, "The conversations played out like a series of gramophone records."

The forty-four-year-old Ribbentrop was a businessman who had traveled in the United States as a wine salesman and spent two years in London (from 1936 to 1938) as Hitler's ambassador. He spoke excellent English but insisted on conversing with Welles through an interpreter, an all too clear indication that Ribbentrop would concede nothing to an American peace initiative.

He had a palpable hatred of the British, who had ridiculed him during his time in London as an inept diplomat, notable for such faux pas as "saluting the King with the 'Hitler greeting.' "

During a two-hour meeting with Welles, which began "glacially and without the semblance of a smile or a word of greeting," he sat in a chair with his eyes closed, pronouncing on American slights against Hitler's regime and Germany's desire for a Monroe Doctrine across Central Europe. Welles's response that strained relations with the United States were principally the result of Nazi treatment of minorities and "unfair trade practices" and that the Monroe Doctrine was not used to seize control of other countries or inhibit trade evoked no response from Ribbentrop. Welles later described him to Roosevelt as a brute with "a completely closed mind" and "a very stupid mind. The man," Welles added, "is saturated with hate for England, and to the exclusion of any other dominating mental influence . . . He was guilty of a hundred inaccuracies in his presentation of German policy during recent years. I have rarely seen a man I disliked more." Astonished that a great nation would have someone like Ribbentrop responsible for its foreign affairs, Welles told the American journalist Drew Pearson that Ribbentrop was "one of the weirdest individuals in history."

But Ribbentrop was never more than a tool of Hitler's own designs. The Führer was the architect of all German policy — whether attacking other nations or persecuting the Jews. As early as 1934, when Hitler purged dissenting elements from his government with transparent disregard for law and humanity, American ambassador William E.

Dodd concluded that there was nothing to be gained by conversations with him. "I certainly would not ask to see any man who has committed a score of murders," Dodd noted in a diary. Hitler "is such a horror to me," he told the British ambassador. "I cannot endure his presence." Although Hitler made an effort to be reasonable in his discussion with Welles and presented himself as "dignified both in speech and movement," it was playacting on his part. During their hour and a half together, Welles heard nothing different from what Ribbentrop had already told him.

Successive meetings with Rudolph Hess and Hermann Göring only echoed what Hitler had already told him about Germany's determination to defeat Anglo-French plans to destroy the Reich. Hess impressed Welles as a man of "a very low order of intelligence." Göring, who received Welles in an "incredibly ugly" building, disgusted him with his girth and corpulence. By contrast, Welles found momentary respite with Hjalmar Schacht, the former head of the Reichsbank, who seemed to speak some sense. He gave Welles false hope that Germany's generals were plotting Hitler's overthrow, and personally denounced Hitler as the "greatest liar of all time" and "a genius but an abnormal, a criminal genius."

The remainder of the trip — London, Paris, and then back to Rome — was, for Welles, a matter of going through the motions. "I am fearful of the international situation," Roosevelt wrote the chairman of the Federal Reserve as Welles left Berlin. "Confidentially, the news from Welles' visit in Berlin does not make me any happier." Welles's discussions in Paris and London left him with the impression that only a miracle by which Hitler would give up his gains in Czechoslovakia and Poland and would agree to conditions ensuring disarmament and Anglo-French security could provide a stable peace. Essentially, it would mean the toppling of the Nazi regime, which realists in the French and British governments understood could only result from Hitler's defeat in battle.

Welles received a mixed reception in Paris, as his positive assessments of Mussolini as someone who could help broker an end to the war were not welcomed by the French government. Nor was Welles's demeanor especially pleasing to them. The joke began to make the rounds that a new cocktail had been invented in Welles's honor at the bar of the Hotel Crillon, a favorite American hangout: "Its sole ingredient was ice water." Nonetheless, most French officials valued his private expressions of contempt for Hitler and the Nazis and took for granted that the United States would do nothing to pressure the democracies into premature peace talks.

Between March 10 and March 14, Welles consulted in London with British officials. Chamberlain, who had regained public approval with a show of defiance toward Germany, assured Welles that Britain was determined to defeat Hitler, while Foreign Secretary Lord Halifax and especially Winston Churchill at the admiralty underscored British convictions that any attempt to deal with Hitler would only lead to another political dead end, as it had at Munich. The British were hard-pressed to see the value of Welles's mission since only additional warfare, and not unproductive talks, could lead to the sort of lasting peace Roosevelt and Welles envisioned. Robert Vansittart, a leading figure in Britain's Foreign Office and an unqualified opponent of appeasement, was scathing about what he viewed as the pointlessness of Welles's undertaking. He described Welles as "naive, glib and facile" and nothing less than "an international danger." He dismissed his mission as committing a "crime towards common sense and humanity" by wanting "us to make peace with Hitler."

Mindful of the resistance to any peace proposal that would appear to open a new round of appeasement, Roosevelt issued a statement on March 16 stating that "he could not condone Hitler's military conquests, and that the United States sought peace based on moral values, not military conquest." On March 29, as Welles returned from Europe, Roosevelt read a statement at his press conference thanking him for his service and reiterating that Welles had made no peace proposals nor received any. To make certain that the press and the public had no illusions about the results of the mission, Roosevelt added that there was "scant immediate prospect for the establishment of any just, stable and lasting peace in Europe." He was "afraid" that that was all he could offer.

On April 9, Roosevelt's pessimism became political reality when Nazi armies invaded Denmark and Norway and threatened to strike at Belgium and the Netherlands. Roosevelt thought this new round of German aggression might be the impetus that would finally convince Americans that they could not escape the consequences of the fighting. "I certainly do not rejoice in my prophecies" the previous summer of a dangerous European war, when he was disparaged as a "calamity-howler," he wrote Britain's King George

VI on May 1. "But at least it has given me [the] opportunity to bring home the seriousness of the world situation to the type of American who has hitherto believed, in much too large numbers, that no matter what happened there will be little effect on this country." A week later, he told his representative in Brussels that while he was "much depressed and much occupied with world affairs," he hoped that "the good people in this country will wake up to the world situation. They are already beginning to but still have a long way to go." Shortly after, when Harvard professor Roger Merriman wrote to complain about the "peace at any price kids" on the country's college campuses, Roosevelt was gratified that Merriman considered them "shrimps publicly and privately. Most of them [he hoped] will eventually get in line if things should become worse."

While Germany's lightning-fast conquest of Denmark and Norway demoralized Roosevelt, it also energized him: He was "hitting on all cylinders about seventeen hours a day," he told his daughter on June 1. He was distressed that he had not "been able to get away to Hyde Park for weeks and weeks" but found some relief in "running down the river for one night of sleep on [the] U.S.S. Potomac." But in the face of the alarming news of Hitler's Scandinavian conquests and concern that the Low Countries were about to suffer the same fate, Roosevelt drew upon his native resiliency and inveterate optimism, which had done so much to see him through his polio almost twenty years earlier, He wrote Joe Kennedy in London, who saw nothing but disaster ahead, "These are bad days for all of us who remember always that when real world forces come into conflict, the final result is never as dark as we mortals guess it [is] in very difficult days."

He found some comic relief in a note Lela Stiles, a White House secretary, sent him around this time about "the various ways people address you in their letters: To our dear President — the greatest man in the world; kind friend of the people; humanitarian friend of the people; Our revered President, the most godlike ruler in the history of civilization; Our Darling Ruler; Your most Noble Majesty; Franklin Dillinger Roosevelt; Your Highness; Sublime Prince of the Royal Secret; Dear Buddy; My Pal!"

At the end of March, he had lobbied New York's governor Herbert Lehman to accept standing as the state's favorite son candidate at the Democratic Party's summer convention. It was in fact a ploy to bar Jim Farley, whom Roosevelt viewed as a competitor for the presidential nomination, from controlling New York's delegation. Although Roosevelt told Illinois' Democratic governor Henry Horner that he dismissed suggestions that only his candidacy could ensure another Democratic president in 1941, he also decried the possibility of a reversion to conservative control of government by those who "put property ahead of human beings," which, he predicted, would place the nation once again into "a bad situation." Nor did he want to see a bipartisan Roosevelt–Wendell Willkie ticket, as some were suggesting. Never offering a definitive promise that he would not run again, he left the possibility open that he would accept the nomination.

On May 9, Hitler launched his feared assault on Belgium and the Netherlands and France. For Roosevelt, the rush of events now was almost overwhelming: How could he aid the Allies? What was the best way to build U.S. military strength? How should he convince the public that isolationism was no answer to ensuring the national security? How would he manage an unprecedented presidential campaign that would provoke attacks on him for harboring dictatorial ambitions?

His greatest immediate challenge was to prevent German acquisition of Dutch and Belgian assets in the United States. On May 10 he called Morgenthau at 12:15 a.m. and again at 2 a.m. to plan a freeze on exchange controls and signed an order to that effect at 7:55 a.m. At the same time, he had the "jitters" over a potential German conquest of Greenland and Iceland, both Danish possessions, with the threat this would pose to North America. He hoped that British and Canadian naval forces could prevent gains in the North Atlantic, though he opposed having them seize control of either Danish territory for fear that it would give the Japanese an excuse to seize the Dutch East Indies following the Netherlands' defeat. He also feared German seizure of the island of Fernando Noronha, a Brazilian possession in the South Atlantic that could become a German air and sea base and pose a menace to hemisphere shipping lanes and the Panama Canal. He alerted his chief of naval operations to consider either occupying the Brazilian island or preparing to bomb the airfield should Germany seize it.

As the Nazis overwhelmed the Belgian and Dutch armies in a week, Roosevelt struggled with anxieties about America's military vulnerabilities. Although the United States population of 130 million was almost twice the size of Germany's, Hitler had an army of over 6 million men, compared to U.S. armed forces of half a million, the eighteenth largest army in the world. (Belgium, Holland, Portugal, and Switzerland, none of which had populations exceeding 9 million people, were among those with larger armies than the United States.) Moreover, the Germans were armed with the most up-to-date tanks, artillery, and air power. Their aircraft had decimated the city center of Rotterdam and threatened to devastate other Dutch cities unless they surrendered.

In the spring and summer of 1940, nothing underscored the disparity in U.S. and German military capacity more than the woefully inadequate maneuvers of U.S. Army divisions in Louisiana and upstate New York. Infantry men, short of rifles, took part in military exercises armed with broomsticks and stovepipes to simulate antitank weapons; milk trucks, rolling into fields with "TANK" written on pieces of cardboard attached to their windshields, stood in for Hitler's mobile units, which had made such short work of Polish, Dutch, and Belgian forces. No combat planes were available to battle imagined Luftwaffe fighters attacking the skeleton American ground troops. "Against Europe's total war," *Time* magazine reported, "the U.S. Army looked like a few nice boys with BB guns."

To his frustration, Roosevelt found himself with War and Navy secretaries he considered inadequate. He was eager to replace War Secretary Harry Woodring, a Kansas isolationist who had resisted Roosevelt's plan to aid France and Britain by selling them scarce arms. Roosevelt, who had a constitutional reluctance to firing anyone, waited until the crisis in Europe reached a new intensity in the spring before replacing Navy Secretary Charles Edison with sixty-six-year-old Republican Frank Knox, the *Chicago Daily News* editor and Republican vice-presidential candidate in 1936, and Woodring with seventy-three-year-old Henry Stimson, Herbert Hoover's former secretary of state. Knox and Stimson were much more committed to aiding the democracies, and their credentials as conservative icons with close Republican Party affiliations gave the administration bipartisan credibility, promoting national unity. The announcement of these appointments three days before the Republican convention in Philadelphia provided Roosevelt and the Democrats with political benefits that they could carry into the fall campaign.

On May 10, after having been awake half the previous night, Roosevelt held a press conference. As he waited for the largest gathering of reporters ever to attend such a meeting, he seemed uncharacteristically nervous. No one in the crowded room could miss the fact that this was a historic moment, and they waited for Roosevelt's remarks with great anticipation. Mindful that a display of self-confidence in a moment of crisis was essential to the national well-being, the president carried off the occasion with reassuring composure. When he was asked, "Would you care to say . . . what . . . the chances are that we can stay out?" Roosevelt replied: "Don't, for heaven's sake, say . . . that we may get in." He declared himself in full sympathy with the Netherlands' Queen Wilhelmina's statement protesting Germany's attack as an "unprecedented violation of good faith and all that is decent in relations between cultured states," but he refused to go any further than condemning

German aggression for fear of isolationist complaints.

That same day, Winston Churchill replaced Chamberlain, who had lost public confidence in his leadership, as British prime minister. In a speech to Parliament, he famously declared, "I have nothing to offer but blood, toil, tears and sweat." Calling himself "Former Naval Person," Churchill quickly cabled the president: "The enemy have a marked preponderance in the air," but "the battle on the land has only just begun." Although the "small countries are simply smashed up, one by one, like matchwood," and the French seemed all too vulnerable, Churchill declared Britain ready to "continue the war alone and we are not afraid of that." He warned, however, of "a completely subjugated, Nazified Europe established with astonishing swiftness," and predicted that "the voice and force of the United States may count for nothing if they are withheld too long." He urged America to "help us with everything short of actually engaging armed forces." Specifically, he asked "the loan of forty or fifty of your older destroyers" and "several hundred of the latest types of aircraft." He also hoped that the United States could keep the "Japanese dog quiet in the Pacific," and offered Singapore as a base for its operations.

Roosevelt's initial response, however, was not encouraging. He could not transfer the destroyers without congressional approval and "our own defense requirements" in the hemisphere and the Pacific also made this unlikely. The best he could offer was the fullest possible effort to sell Britain aircraft.

In a series of three speeches delivered over the

following three weeks, Roosevelt made clear where America stood vis-à-vis German aggression and how determined he was to build the country's defenses against any attempt by Hitler to extend his conquests to the Americas. On May 10, in an address before a Pan American Congress meeting in Washington, he denounced "conquest and war." Recent attacks, he said, posed a "challenge to the continuance of the type of civilization to which all of us in the three Americas have been accustomed for so many generations." In words principally aimed at America's isolationists, he warned that advances in transportation had greatly shrunk the globe, and though the United States shared an affinity for pacifism with other American states, he warned the aggressor nations that, should it be necessary, all the Americas would "act together to protect and defend . . . our American freedom and our civilization."

On May 16, in a speech before a joint session of Congress, he faced an audience of 531 congressmen and senators — 526 men, only 5 women, and a single African American. Although many of them were devoted isolationists and distrusted the president's intentions, they received him with deafening applause that bespoke the mutually recognized need for unity in a time of crisis. With Holland defeated, Belgium on the verge of surrender, and France's armies retreating under the weight of Germany's blitzkrieg tactics, Americans felt the country or at least democracy was facing a clear and present danger. Sensing the receptivity of Congress to a call to arms or at least to the marshaling of America's productive capacity, Roosevelt quoted Churchill's warning about the importance of quick action if the country's voice and force were to count. In graphic detail, he recounted the transformation of modern warfare such that enemy air forces that could strike the Americas in a matter of hours from bases in the Atlantic and the Caribbean. He asked Congress for $900 million for defense and stressed that these expenditures were earmarked for the defense of American freedoms and did not represent a prelude to engagement in the war.

On May 26, in a Sunday evening Fireside Chat, Roosevelt spoke as British and French forces desperately began an evacuation from Dunkirk in northern France, six miles from the Belgian border. The two-to-four-hour journey across the English Channel of between 39 and 87 nautical miles ran a gauntlet of air and sea attacks from German planes and mines. Millions tuned in to hear the president despair of the fact that so many in the United States had closed their eyes to the harsh realities of Nazi victories, which were now shattering illusions that we were insulated from their horrors. But those victories were generating fears that we could not stand up to the challenge they threatened. "I did not share those illusions. I do not share these fears," Roosevelt declared. "Today we are (now) more realistic. But let us not be calamity-howlers and discount our strength. Let us be done with both fears and illusions. . . . Let us calmly consider . . . what we must do." He then recounted all the advances that had been and were being made in building the country's military strength. He ended by emphasizing current dangers from Nazi agents known as Fifth Columnists and implicitly from isolationists, whose dissenting influence was undermining the nation's unity and its ability to meet the historic challenge before it.

Roosevelt's Fireside Chat was largely a response to political opponents who were warning that he wasn't just building the country's defenses; he was aiming to take the country into the war. In charging that Roosevelt was eager to bring about U.S. belligerency, the isolationists had the wind at their backs. While large majorities continued to favor preparedness and material aid to Britain and France, between 93 and 96 percent opposed declaring war on Germany and sending American forces abroad to fight. Isolationists complained that in raising alarms about Fifth Columnists and German plans to strike at the Americas, Roosevelt was operating "with diabolical cleverness." At the forefront of the effort to prevent Roosevelt from taking the country into the war was Charles Lindbergh, who denounced the president for encouraging false concern that Hitler had targeted Latin America and the United States. Privately, Roosevelt described Lindbergh as "a Nazi" who was parroting propaganda that Josef Goebbels, Hitler's minister of information, could have written. Roosevelt's allies in the House and Senate took to the airwaves to attack Lindbergh, comparing him to Fifth Columnists who had helped defeat Norway and Denmark. While the debate did little to change many minds about entering the war or aiding Britain and France, it generated renewed political support for Roosevelt. In polls between the middle of May and the beginning of June, 57 percent of Americans said they were amenable to giving the president a third term.

On June 4, as some 220,000 British troops and another 120,000 French infantry, transported by vessels of every kind — "yachts and trawlers, gunboats and destroyers, motorboats and life-boats" — streamed across the Channel to Dover, in a speech before Parliament, a defiant declaration of determination to never surrender, Churchill praised the evacuation as "a miracle of deliverance." But he counseled against illusions: "Wars are not won by evacuations," he said. The Allies had suffered "a colossal military disaster," but it was not the final act in the current titanic struggle. He promised that "We shall not flag or fail. We shall go on to the end. We shall fight in France, we shall fight in the seas and oceans . . . We shall defend our island, whatever the cost may be, we shall fight on the beaches, we shall fight on the landing grounds, we shall fight in the fields and in the streets, we shall fight in the hills; we shall never surrender, and even if, which I do not for a moment believe, this Island or a large part of it were subjugated and starving, then our Empire beyond the seas, armed and guarded by the British Fleet, would carry on the struggle, until, in God's good time, the New World, with all its power and might, steps forth to the rescue and liberation of the old."

The forty-nine-year-old Charles de Gaulle, a tank general who was determined to preserve France's honor by supporting an exile government based in London and France's African colonies, perceived at once the brilliance of Churchill's oratory and his ability "to rouse the heavy dough of the English as well as to impress the minds of foreigners. . . . From one end of the drama to the other," de Gaulle observed, Churchill was "the great champion of a great enterprise and the great artist of a great history."

Churchill's oratory resonated with Roosevelt as

well, confirming his decision to have the United States do all it could to help Britain replace the rifles, machine guns, and field guns abandoned in the scramble of the evacuation from Dunkirk, even though that would mean leaving American forces with a bare minimum of arms. "It was a supreme act of faith and leadership," Churchill wrote later, "for the United States to deprive themselves of this very considerable mass of arms for the sake of a country which many deemed already beaten."

On June 7, Roosevelt wrote Lewis Douglas, his former budget director, who had urged him to provide prompt help to the Allies, replying, "Very many planes are on the way to the Allies, deliveries to this Government being put off. . . . The more effective immediately usable material we can get to the other side will mean the destruction of an equivalent amount of German materiel — thereby aiding American defense in the long run. So you see I am doing everything possible — though I am not talking very much about it because a certain element of the Press . . . would undoubtedly pervert it, attack it and confuse the public mind."

It wasn't only the isolationist press that was on the attack, but even some of Roosevelt's own subordinates raised questions about the wisdom of donating supplies needed by America's armed forces. At a cabinet meeting on June 9, Navy Secretary Edison, who would hold office for only another ten days, resisted obeying Roosevelt's order, as the Navy's judge advocate general had ruled that the transaction was illegal. An "impatient" Roosevelt dismissed the "sea lawyer" as misinformed and told Edison to send him away on vacation, as well as anyone else in the Navy Department who objected. Ickes watched as "Edison kept repeating over and over again his original statement until an exasperated Roosevelt told him to 'forget it and do what I told you to do.' "

Nothing angered Roosevelt more, however, than Mussolini's decision on June 10 to declare war on Britain and France "to collect his share of the loot of civilization," as Churchill characterized it. Although Roosevelt had made strenuous efforts in late May to discourage Mussolini from allying himself with Hitler in the conflict, the Duce had rejected his advice and dismissed his warnings about America's aligning itself with the Allies as of no concern to Italy. As a consequence, on June 10, Roosevelt used a commencement address at the University of Virginia as a platform from which to speak to all Americans. In a searing condemnation of Mussolini's decision to enter the war, he said: "On this tenth day of June, nineteen hundred and forty, the hand that held the dagger has struck it into the back of its neighbor." He then promised every effort to extend to "the opponents of force the material resources of this nation" and the development of the "equipment and training equal to the task of any emergency and every defense." Although Roosevelt's speech heartened Churchill and French premier Paul Reynaud, they urged him to go further than commit U.S. war materiel and publicly promise to bring America into the war. Roosevelt responded that this was out of the question and instead stressed that should France surrender, it was essential that its fleet not come under German-Italian control. "Naval power in world affairs still carries the lessons of history," he cabled Reynaud.

France's capitulation in the next twelve days turned Roosevelt's anger against a country that, despite having the largest army in the world, had given up the fight. Newsreels of German troops marching down the Champs-Élysées, German flags with swastikas flying over French government buildings and atop the Eiffel Tower, and photos of a jubilant Hitler accepting France's surrender in the same railway car in the Compiègne Forest where Germany had surrendered in 1918, ending World War I, stunned Americans. Although de Gaulle declared that a government in exile would continue the struggle under the banner of the Free French, the refusal of French naval commanders to move the fleet from North Africa to Britain or to French possessions in the Americas incensed and worried both Churchill and Roosevelt. If the fleet came under German control through an arrangement with France's collaborationist Vichy regime, it would be an added blow to British and U.S. national security. Despite a written commitment in the capitulation agreement that Germany would not seize the ships, British distrust of the German pledge persuaded Churchill to attack the French fleet on July 3, killing nearly 1,300 French sailors and destroying several of the ships. Although it embittered many in France against Britain, the assault underscored British determination to maintain the fight at whatever cost and heartened Roosevelt. It was a tiny ray of hope in a very dispiriting time.

CHAPTER 13
"SAFE ON THIRD"

The defeat of the French exhilarated Hitler, frustrated Mussolini, and shocked Roosevelt. On June 28 the Führer flew to Paris, a city he had never before visited, to underscore his triumph by receiving a VIP tour of its landmark sites. He landed at 5:30 in the morning, accompanied by Albert Speer, his favorite architect. Over the course of three hours, he visited L'Opéra, which dazzled him; drove up the Champs-Élysées; passed under the Arc de Triomphe; viewed the Eiffel Tower; stopped at Napoleon's Tomb; looked at the church of Sacré-Coeur; and stood where millions of tourists had preceded him overlooking the city atop Montmartre. His competitiveness moved him to tell Speer: "When we're finished with Berlin, Paris will only be a shadow. Why should we destroy it?" Obsessed with destroying any and all competitors, his paranoia gave ground to a rare expression of generosity, and he was momentarily the benign conqueror who would preserve a historic treasure. Besides, if he had ordered the city's destruction, after the French had withdrawn their forces and declared Paris an open city, it would have deepened the hostility of world opinion toward him for acts of barbarism that had already taken thousands of innocent lives and devastated treasured sites across Western Europe.

When he returned to Berlin on July 6, he received a tumultuous welcome. Partly fueled by the belief that he would reach a settlement with the British that would end the war, but mostly by the sense of pride in German superiority as Europe's — and indeed the world's — greatest power, which had expunged the shame of defeat in World War I, crowds cheered themselves hoarse shouting Hitler's name as he soaked up the adulation from the balcony of the Reich Chancellery. His conviction that he deserved recognition as a world-renowned historical figure found full expression in the worshipful reception of Germany's masses.

A disconsolate Mussolini, whose "hopes of getting his hands on part of the French Fleet" the German leader had dispelled, was forced into a subsidiary position in his alliance with Berlin. Hitler wanted no indication that he had needed any help from the Italians in inflicting the humiliating defeat on France's vaunted armies. Mussolini was nowhere to be seen when Hitler took his triumphal tour of Paris. As Ian Kershaw writes, "Hitler was determined that the embarrassed and disappointed Mussolini, now forced to swallow his role as junior partner, should not participate in the armistice negotiations with the French."

Meanwhile, Roosevelt took no comfort in the knowledge that he had been more prescient than the isolationists about world affairs. He identified with Churchill, who had been a lonely voice warning about appeasement and Hitler's ruthless ambitions until his sensible realism elevated him to prime minister in May. At the end of June, as the reality of the French collapse and Britain's uncertain prospects set in, Roosevelt struggled to ensure that American resupply of Britain's depleted armaments proceeded rapidly and that his renomination for an unprecedented third term succeeded.

On June 21, as France was about to capitulate, Roosevelt decided to spend the weekend in Hyde Park. His only companions were Harry Hopkins, now secretary of commerce, and presidential secretary Missy LeHand. In 1940, when it became clear to Daisy that Franklin was not about to retire and that they would not live together at "Top Cottage" on his Hyde Park estate, she temporarily took some distance from him, making Roosevelt's reliance on Hopkins and LeHand all the more essential to get him through the day.

The forty-nine-year-old Hopkins was the president's closest companion. He had been a central figure in the administration since day one and had become even more important to Roosevelt after Louis Howe's death in 1936. In 1937, Hopkins had undergone surgery for cancer that left him with only a quarter of his stomach and a reduced ability to absorb nutrients. He returned to the Mayo Clinic in 1939 for additional treatment and became a permanent resident at the White House in May 1940, where he was an all-purpose aide to Roosevelt. His gaunt, almost cadaver-like appearance belied a fighting spirit that defied doctors' predictions of an early death. His infirmity deepened his bond to Roosevelt, who identified with Hopkins's determination in spite of his disability to sustain a public career. Hopkins's buoyant, irreverent personality was an elixir to Roosevelt, lightening his evenings with humor and engaging dinner talk.

When asked by a rival for the White House who viewed Hopkins as a political liability why he kept Hopkins so close to him, Roosevelt replied: "I can understand that you wonder why I need that half-man around me. But — someday you may be sitting here where I am now as President of the United States. And when you are, you'll be looking at that door over there and knowing that everybody who walks through it wants something out of you. You'll learn what a lonely job this is, and you'll discover the need for somebody like Harry Hopkins who asks for nothing except to serve you."

Roosevelt also treasured the forty-one-year-old Missy LeHand, who, like Hopkins, gave him her all. She was an essential workmate whose lively personality brought levity, enjoyment, and moments of relaxation that eased the pressures on a president besieged by seminal international troubles and domestic political crosscurrents. Le-Hand, the offspring of an Irish working-class family who had gone to secretarial school, had been Roosevelt's secretary since 1921 when he was struggling to recover from polio. Like Daisy Suckley, she adored him and devoted herself to his every need. She traveled with him to Hyde Park and Warm Springs and not only instinctively read his moods but also was able to answer most of his correspondence, saving him countless hours of dealing with nonessential matters.

But Missy, who was physically attractive at five foot seven with blue eyes and black hair, and charmed people with her genial demeanor, had a vulnerable personality. Described by one observer as "cheerful and vigorous," with "wit and laughter that flew around in her presence," she also harbored inner feelings of distress at being considered by Roosevelt more of an employee than an equal with the man she adored. Shunning a private life with various men who courted her, she devoted herself to Franklin, taking pains to accommodate his every need. "She loved Franklin," historian Doris Goodwin writes, ". . . Her whole existence was wrapped up in him." But she was never more than a kind of surrogate wife, however much her "great tact . . . charm and ease" made her an ideal companion. In 1927, when she thought the pattern of her life with him was being disrupted, she suffered a nervous collapse. And though she recovered in six months, and remained a devoted acolyte who could speak frankly to "F.D.," as she alone called him, she lived in fear of losing her place in his life, and, like Daisy, despaired at his running for a third term.

In June 1941, she suffered another collapse. Unlike Hopkins, she had become demanding, asking Roosevelt, "Why don't you respond to me, acknowledge me more, give me what I give you?" Her ability to entertain and relax him had largely disappeared, and she had become an irritant. In fact, bouts of insomnia now plagued her, and the opiates she had been taking to ease her through the night left her weary and on edge. She suffered a series of strokes and had to be hospitalized. She lost movement in an arm and a leg and slurred her words. Roosevelt visited her several times in the hospital, where he felt helpless to stem her episodes of uncontrolled crying. Outwardly, he detached himself from her suffering, which angered some in his circle. Harold Ickes confided to his diary, "Missy, who has been desperately ill for several weeks, might pass out of his life and he would miss her. The same might be true as to Harry, but I doubt whether he would miss either of them greatly or for a long period." Yet, as Goodwin points out, Roosevelt's exterior passivity hid a deep concern for both of them: In Missy's case, he took steps to see that she received the best possible care, and paid her medical bills, which she could not cover. When efforts at rehabilitation made it clear that, at the age of forty-three, she would be disabled for the rest of her life, Roosevelt instructed his attorney to change his will so that half his estate would go to Missy, who had "served me so well for so long and asked so little in return."

During Roosevelt's June 1940 weekend in Hyde Park, the Republican nominating convention met in Philadelphia. Roosevelt's silence about a possible third term convinced them that he was planning another run. Moreover, with 79 percent of a poll supporting his handling of the war crisis, 92 percent of Democrats favoring his candidacy, 57 percent of the public disposed to give him a third term, and 71 percent of the public enthusiastic about his choice of Stimson and Knox as War and Navy secretaries, the Republicans were desperate to find a candidate who might shake public faith in the president. Offered a choice between New York City district attorney Thomas Dewey, Michigan senator Arthur Vandenberg, Ohio senator Robert Taft, and prominent corporate lawyer Wendell Willkie, a former Democrat and internationalist, Republican voters had given Dewey a 52 percent lead over the other three in a May Gallup poll.

Neither Taft nor Vandenberg had much chance of becoming president. The fifty-year-old Taft, the son of President William Howard Taft, as regular a Republican and conventional midwestern isolationist as anyone in the party, was simply too orthodox to convince the Republican faithful, let alone the larger American electorate, that he could see the country successfully through such tumultuous times. "There is a good deal more danger of the infiltration of totalitarian ideas from the New Deal circles in Washington," he was quoted as saying, "than there ever will be from the activities of the . . . Nazis." He came across as "cold, aloof, and backward-looking," and his "reserved demeanor," Richard Moe writes, "coupled with his owllike appearance and air of supreme confidence did not play well on the campaign trail." The fifty-six-year-old Vandenberg, who had been in the Senate since 1928 and echoed Taft's views on foreign policy, was likewise a too-familiar and unexciting candidate without Roosevelt's appeal as a savvy and quick-witted politician who could hold his own against the world's most prominent leaders. When Vandenberg tested his popularity in Wisconsin and Nebraska primaries in April, he lost by wide margins to Dewey.

By contrast, the thirty-eight-year-old Dewey was an exciting new face on the national scene. As New York City's district attorney, he had gained widespread fame as a prosecutor of organized crime and mafia mobsters like Lucky Luciano and Dutch Schultz. His crusade against corruption made him the subject of Hollywood films and a radio series, *Gangbuster,* and *Life* magazine dubbed him the "Number One Glamour Boy of the GOP." But in the 1940 nomination contest his youth and personality worked against him. On a personal level he was unlikeable and alienated people with his vindictiveness and cockiness. He was seen "as devoid of charm as a rivet or a lump of stone" and as "one of the least seductive personalities in public life." Nor was he especially engaging as a public speaker. The Republican Party leaders saw him as an inadequate challenger to the popular sitting president.

Although only 18 percent of Republican voters favored him in a poll three weeks before the party's convention, and Republican isolationists objected to his outspoken public support of Roosevelt's aid to Britain, the only Republican candidate who seemed capable of competing with Roosevelt was the Indiana-born New York utility counsel, forty-eight-year-old Wendell Willkie. Unlike Dewey, Taft, and Vandenberg, Willkie had a winning personality that was evident in public appearances and endeared him to audiences everywhere. In the months before the convention, *Fortune, Life* and *Time* (under publisher Henry Luce), the *Saturday Evening Post,* and other national publications touted Willkie as a modern Republican who as president could serve all Americans and support the fight against Hitler without drawing the country into the war. William Allen White, who led the Committee to Defend America by Aiding the Allies, defended Willkie against party isolationists by declaring that the Republicans would not even carry Maine and Vermont if they stuck with their peace-at-any-price response to the fighting.

In a calculated effort to wrest the nomination from front-runner Dewey, Willkie's backers packed the convention galleries with supporters who effectively dominated the proceedings with shouts of "We want Willkie." At the same time, millions of telegrams and letters from Willkie supporters inundated the delegates. A poll of Republicans on the eve of the convention giving Dewey a 47 percent to 29 percent advantage, and a first ballot gaining Willkie only 105 votes of the 501 needed for nomination served to energize his supporters rather than discourage them. Despite the blistering 100-degree heat in Philadelphia's convention hall, which lacked air-conditioning, when Willkie's name was put in nomination his supporters paraded the aisles with unmatched enthusiasm. Willkie's delegate count jumped to 171 on a second ballot, while Dewey's fell from 360 to 338 and Taft's increased from 189 to 203. After a dinner break, Willkie gained 88 votes on a third ballot and commanded second place with 259 delegates. The fourth ballot all but ended Dewey's hopes when he fell into third place, and Willkie rose to 429 ballots on the fifth roll call. After midnight the Michigan delegation fell into line behind Willkie amid continuing shouts of "We want Willkie!" and the convention defied the party's old guard by nominating him. The former Democrat and product of the Eastern establishment made his fringe position in the party's hierarchy clear when he declared in an acceptance speech, "So, you Republicans, I call you to join, help me. The cause is great, we must win." Neither Republicans nor Democrats were clear on precisely what his policies in domestic or foreign affairs would be if he became president.

Roosevelt was of two minds about how to proceed in light of Willkie's victory. On one hand, he judged Willkie to be a formidable obstacle. At a press conference on the morning after Willkie's nomination, Roosevelt apologized to the reporters for being late, explaining that someone had turned the power off on the elevator. "I hope it is not a connotation of what happened in Philadelphia last night," he joked, evoking laughter from members of the press pool, who understood that he viewed a Willkie administration as all too likely to shut down government programs.

The jocular remark was also a kick-off to Roosevelt's campaign for what he understood would be his most difficult run for the White House. As always, he kept his intentions largely hidden. But his remarks and actions suggest that he regarded Willkie as a distinct threat to his New Deal gains and perceived no one among the Democrats who could be as effective as himself in defeating him. Willkie would be "a very formidable candidate," Ickes predicted, and would be "distinctly dangerous" to liberal reform. "With him in the White House," Ickes feared, "the monied interests would be in full control and we could expect an American brand of fascism as soon as he could set it up." Roosevelt agreed with him, at least as far as his popular appeal, telling the columnist Walter Winchell that Willkie's "sincerity comes through with terrific impact. The people believe every word he says. We are going to have a heck of a fight on our hands with him."

After a conversation with Roosevelt the day after the Republican convention, Ickes left "firmly convinced that he has every intention to run. In fact, he all but clearly said so." Roosevelt wanted to postpone the Democratic convention, which was scheduled for July, until September, explaining, "Anything that I may say after the convention

603

will be regarded as coming from a candidate and so subject to discount, whereas anything that I may say before the convention will be coming from the President." He also made the outlines of his anti-Willkie campaign clear to Ickes: He planned "to tie Willkie in with the idea of the 'corporate state' . . . corporate entrenched wealth against the great mass of the people." Roosevelt and Ickes agreed that Willkie was a smooth but "unscrupulous . . . corporation man."

Roosevelt failed to delay the convention, but a conversation Ickes had with the president on July 11, four days before the Democrats met in Chicago, only strengthened Ickes's impression that Roosevelt intended to run again. But he refused to say who would represent him at the meeting or how he would be nominated. Roosevelt believed it essential that he not be seen as actively campaigning, as any such effort would tar him as a power-hungry dictator with no regard for the two-term tradition. In a telegram Ickes sent from Chicago, he urged Roosevelt to exert leadership by declaring his willingness to run. Were he not to do so, Ickes warned, forces of reaction might take control and nominate someone "that will assure the election of Willkie, and Willkie means fascism and appeasement." Roosevelt ignored his advice, because he understood that he was the convention's choice, as was made evident when a fifty-three-minute demonstration on the second day imitated the Willkie chorus with shouts of "We want Roosevelt!" Behind the scenes, Harry Hopkins organized support, including shouts for Roosevelt by Chicago's superintendent of sewers over a microphone from the basement of the hall, which gave lie to the illusion of a spontaneous draft of the president.

The next day's voting resulted in Roosevelt's receiving a first-ballot nomination with 962 delegates, against 138 dissenters split among three other candidates, including Farley with 72 votes, Garner with 61, and Hull with only five. None of the three ever had a serious chance of getting the nomination, but they were stalking horses, especially Hull, whom Roosevelt had encouraged right up to the convention. They provided Roosevelt political cover by suggesting that he was not really running and received the nomination only by popular demand.

Roosevelt insisted on making Henry Wallace his running mate. He was eager to rid himself of Garner, whom he had come to regard as too conservative and disloyal. Although as secretary of agriculture, Wallace had been a staunch supporter of all New Deal programs, the choice angered Democratic loyalists. Wallace was a former Republican, and they believed several long-serving party men were more deserving. When open dissent threatened Wallace's selection, Roosevelt became convinced that conservative opponents were behind the vocal opposition and threatened not to run if the convention defied him. For Roosevelt, Wallace represented the party's commitment to his eight-year campaign to bring the country into the twentieth century, but the dissent became so palpable that Roosevelt persuaded Eleanor to fly to Chicago to make the case for Wallace in a public address. Commanding the respect of the great majority of Democrats, who now saw her as the greatest first lady in the country's history, she spoke before the delegates with a plea for national unity in a time of national peril. After eight arduous years, she said, the terrible burdens of office entitled the president to choose a vice president who he believed would be best able to assist him. Convention tensions dissolved in response to Eleanor's compelling appeal. Wallace was nominated on the first ballot.

Within minutes of the Wallace vote, Roosevelt spoke to the delegates via a radio hookup. Although it was by now the middle of the night, he wanted to move quickly to calm the tensions that had divided the party. He spoke feelingly to the delegates of his eagerness to retire to Hyde Park, but like so many others in the country who were making personal sacrifices in defense of the national interest, he felt compelled to do his duty and aid the cause of freedom against authoritarian aggression, averring, "My conscience will not let me turn my back upon a call to service." Because the European crisis demanded his fullest possible attention, he explained that he would not run a traditional campaign, but largely remain in Washington. He ended with an elegant appeal for Americans to recognize that they "face one of the great choices of history . . . Government by the people versus dictatorship . . . freedom versus slavery. . . . It is the continuance of civilization as we know it versus the ultimate destruction of all that we hold dear."

Privately, he told Progressive Republican senator George Norris that he had accepted the nomination as a way to stymie the Democratic Party's establishnment. "I was, frankly, amazed by the terrific drive which was put on by the old-line conservatives to make so many things adverse to liberalism occur." He described them as "the Hater's Club — . . . fellows like [Senator Burton K.] Wheeler, [Senator Pat] McCarran and [Senator Millard] Tydings and [Senator Carter] Glass and [Representative] John J. O'Connor and some of the wild Irishmen from Boston." He believed that his nomination represented "a great victory" over these reactionaries, who wanted to put "the Democratic party back where it was 1920, 1924 and 1928." The nomination of Wallace was a triumph over what he hoped would be the last stand of the troglodytes, while recognizing that their opposition would "cost the ticket a great many votes this autumn."

Despite the eloquence of his heartfelt speech, his actions and those of his supporters at the convention produced a bitter aftermath. A group of prominent journalists criticized his performance as substituting "tricks for morals, smartness for passion, cunning for a soul." His tactics in getting Wallace nominated were "an insult to . . . the American tradition of democracy." Willkie's backers chimed in with complaints that "the greatest democracy treated the world to one of the shoddiest and most hypocritical spectacles in its history." Roosevelt was the great manipulator who had relied on "the voice from the sewer" to work his will.

But the war crisis quickly eclipsed any ill will that Roosevelt's behavior had provoked. In a Gallup poll, 59 percent said they opposed a constitutional amendment barring a third term and 53 percent favored Roosevelt's reelection; a like number wanted the administration to give England more aid, and 87 percent supported "immediate possession of the English, French, and Dutch territories" near the Panama Canal. Because national security had become the public's greatest concern, and he had promised not to run a traditional campaign, which customarily began on Labor Day, Roosevelt could focus the six weeks following his nomination on two major defense measures: the transfer of World War I warships to Britain and the passage of a draft law expanding the U.S. Army.

On July 31, with German air and sea attacks reducing Britain's destroyer force by almost half, Churchill cabled the president about the urgency of sending fifty or sixty reconditioned American destroyers to meet the threat of a German invasion and defend its merchant shipping fleet. "Mr. President, with great respect," Churchill wrote, "I must tell you that in the long history of the world, this is the thing to do now . . . I know you will do all in your power but I feel entitled and bound to put the gravity and urgency of the position before you." At a meeting on August 2, Roosevelt and the cabinet agreed in principle to provide this aid, on the condition that the British fleet come to the Americas if the Germans should succeed in invading the British Isles. The cabinet also wanted London to agree to give U.S. forces access to all of Britain's Caribbean and Atlantic Coast bases.

Roosevelt, however, saw major political liabilities in trying to arrange the transfer. He did not believe that Congress would consent to any measures that would appear to reduce the country's defensive capacity, and if he acted on his own, it would likely raise cries of "dictator" and jeopardize his reelection. Admiral Harold Stark, chief of naval operations, had declared the destroyers essential to American defense, and isolationists warned that any transfer of warships would turn the United States from a neutral into a nonbelligerent and edge the country toward involvement in the war. This was exactly what Churchill hoped would occur, though he believed that Hitler's reluctance to draw America into the fighting would persuade him to hold his hand.

Despite the potential political fallout, Roosevelt shared Churchill's conviction that history would judge a British deal as being in the interest of America's national security. By now advocates of assisting Britain and even of entering the war were mounting a compelling campaign to provide crucial aid to a besieged ally. The Battle of Britain, which was now fully engaged, stirred great compassion in Americans when they read reports of German air assaults on London and other cities, with forced evacuations of children and massive civilian casualties. Now, 63 percent of respondents favored bringing British women and children to the United States until the war was over. By September, 52 percent of Americans thought it more important to help Britain win the war than to stay out of the fighting — a stunning shift in sentiment. When Wendell Willkie privately agreed not to make the warship transfer an issue in the campaign, it largely eliminated the political constraints on executive action.

On September 3, persuaded by prominent lawyers outside and within the administration that he had the power to act, Roosevelt sent a message to Congress informing them of a destroyer-for-bases exchange with Britain. He described it as "the most important action in the reinforcement of our national defense that has been taken since the Louisiana Purchase." In August, when he initially outlined the details of the deal, he had consistently emphasized the value of obtaining seven strategically important bases in return for the transfer of what he called old tin cans or "ships which are on their last legs." "I do hope you will not oppose the deal," he wrote Senator David I. Walsh, the chairman of the Naval Affairs Committee, "which, from the point of view of the United States, I regard as being the finest thing for the nation that has been done in your lifetime and mine. I am absolutely certain that this particular deal will not get us into war." At a press conference on August 16, he stressed that the key benefit of the transfer was "the acquisition of the bases — that is the main point — for the protection of this Hemisphere, and I think that is all there is to say." An isolationist senator conceded Roosevelt's point: "You can't attack a deal like that," he said. "If you jump on the destroyer transfer, you're jumping on the acquisition of defense bases in the Western Hemisphere. . . . Roosevelt outsmarted all of us when he tied up the two deals."

Roosevelt now also pressed his case for an unprecedented peacetime draft of young men for a year's Army service. Again, public opinion was warmly supportive. August polls showed between 66 and 71 percent of the country favoring a draft of men between the ages of twenty and thirty-one. An even greater number, 85 percent, supported calling up National Guardsmen for a year of additional training. Meanwhile, the election was a dead heat — unless Britain was defeated in the meantime and the U.S. had to fight Germany — then Roosevelt opened up a 16 point advantage, 58 percent to 42 percent. German victories had frightened Americans, who increasingly wanted more planes, tanks, ships, and guns for national defense. Nearly half the country thought Hitler would invade the United States if he was successful in defeating Britain. In September, after Roosevelt had announced the destroyer-bases exchange, Gallup showed him with an eleven-point lead over Willkie, 55 percent to 44 percent. Roosevelt seemed likely to win 38 states to Willkie's 10, with Roosevelt commanding 51 percent in three states and between 69 percent and 98 percent across the old Confederacy. Rather than an impediment to his popularity, the war was giving him a significant advantage over Willkie.

Still, Roosevelt didn't trust the steadfastness of the public's support for the defense buildup, and doubted the reliability of the polls, as he perceived the flood of letters and telegrams he had been sent opposing a draft as more representative of public sentiment. In early June 1940, when advocates of a draft managed to present a bill in Congress, he himself had been less enthusiastic about expanding U.S. ground forces than marshaling support and funding for air and naval power. From the very start of his presidency he had been reluctant to add to the national deficit by spending tax dollars on an Army that he believed Americans would strongly oppose sending abroad. His clash with MacArthur in the spring of 1933 over the Army's budget had demonstrated his preference for the Navy and a potential air arm, which he judged would serve the principal forces in any future war. In 1940, he was still more inclined to invest in domestic projects that would provide work to the more than eight million unemployed — 14 percent of the workforce — and to pay for ships and planes that could become a first line of defense for Britain and France against Hitler's forces. After telling a press conference in June that he liked a *New York Times* editorial supporting a system of universal military training, he retreated from the endorsement by saying that he "should not have spoken so fast. I did not intend to imply that there should be compulsory military training for every boy in the country."

But with Italy's entrance into the war and the fall of France, Roosevelt became a convert to a draft, backing a selective service bill introduced in the House at the end of June. Isolationist-pacifist opposition to the legislation stirred fierce debate in Congress and in the country as a whole about whether such a law would mean the militarization of the United States, as in Germany and Italy, and become the prelude to involvement in the war, or would serve as a prudent measure of defense.

Fearing the impact on his candidacy, Roosevelt then gave only tepid support to the bill, until Willkie effectively made it a nonissue in the election by publicly giving unequivocal backing to a law he asserted was essential to the national security. On August 23, after observing inadequate Army maneuvers in upstate New York, Roosevelt followed with his own unqualified support. In remarks at a press conference and a confidential letter to a small-town Illinois newspaper editor, Roosevelt explained that the maneuvers demonstrated that Hitler's well-trained armed forces could defeat this U.S Army in "a day or two." Voluntary enlistments, which the editor favored, were, Roosevelt explained, "far short of the essential numbers we require. There are some occasions in the national history where leaders have to move for the preservation of American liberties and not just drift with what may or may not be a political doubt of the moment." Although the bill limited service to one year and forbade the dispatch of draftees to locales outside the Western Hemisphere, its passage in mid-September represented a significant step forward in national defense.

Through September and October Roosevelt's principal focus was on ensuring his reelection. And while he decried the "drift" of momentary political currents that seemed to change voters' minds overnight, he was highly sensitive to lending his support to any unpopular political issue. Few subjects were then more charged than lax immigration policies, which allowed existing quotas to be exceeded and permitted political refugees into the United States who might compete for scarce jobs in a still-depressed economy. Moreover, since many of the displaced migrants seeking asylum were Jews fleeing Nazi expansion across Europe, resistance to providing a haven in the United States also stirred up anti-Semitism from not only residents of the Deep South and West but also from competing urban ethnic groups like the Irish and Italians. Many of the latter were already angry with Roosevelt for his UVA speech attacking Mussolini.

As for the Irish, no one seemed more capable of turning them against the president than Joe Kennedy. His continuing presence in the London Embassy rested more on Roosevelt's sensitivity to the political fallout from dismissing him than on any value he placed on Kennedy's judgment on Britain and the outcome of the war. By the fall of 1940, Roosevelt had grown weary of Kennedy's pessimism about British prospects in the war and his advice that they reach some kind of accommodation with Hitler. Roosevelt feared that removing Kennedy from his post would drive him into Willkie's camp and, more important, agitate Irish opposition in Boston and Massachusetts, where Roosevelt held a narrow two-point lead in a straw poll.

When Kennedy asked to return home in October 1940, it triggered fears in the White House that the ambassador would not only endorse Willkie but also report that Roosevelt had made secret agreements with Churchill to enter the war. To head off both possibilities, Roosevelt invited Kennedy to the White House for dinner on his arrival in Washington, where he not only flattered him but also promised to support him for president in four years, and also to help his oldest son, Joe, Jr., win the governorship of Massachusetts in 1942. That was sufficient to persuade Kennedy to agree to Roosevelt's request to endorse his reelection in a radio talk a week before the vote. In fact, Roosevelt had no more intention of backing Kennedy for the presidency than he had of making peace proposals to Hitler, for he regarded Kennedy as a self-indulgent millionaire who saw "the future of a small capitalist class as safer under Hitler than Churchill."

Roosevelt also took steps to keep Breckinridge Long, the assistant secretary of state assigned to handle special war problems, including visas, from making trouble over lax rules admitting refugees to the United States. Long was a wealthy Southern conservative with roots in North Carolina, Kentucky, and Missouri, and became acquainted with Roosevelt when both served in Wilson's administration. A major contributor to Roosevelt's 1932 campaign, Long won appointment as his ambassador to Italy, where he served from 1933 to 1936. In January 1940, Long became an assistant secretary of state with the power to oppose relaxed immigration policies, which he claimed risked the infiltration of Nazi agents. He was especially opposed to allowing Jews to enter the country, and urged all U.S. counsels to do everything in their power "to put every obstacle in the way and to . . . resort to various administrative devices which would postpone and postpone and postpone the granting of the visas."

For all Roosevelt's concern for finding safe havens for persecuted Jews, he would not take issue with Long's resistance to lowering barriers to refugees. When eighty Portuguese Jews arrived in Norfolk, Virginia, in September 1940, for example, Long resisted pressure from Mrs. Roosevelt to grant them access to the United States. The dispute made its way to the president, who again declined to become involved in a politically sensitive controversy so soon before the election, and left the matter entirely to Long, who "remonstrated violently" against bending the rules. It opened Roosevelt to later criticism that he had showed little, if any, moral courage in challenging public opinion on providing haven for a persecuted people.

The larger issues of war and peace in the campaign gave Roosevelt a clear electoral advantage, as Willkie seemed unlikely to defeat an incumbent better schooled in world affairs than he. In any case, Willkie seemed to be a mere pale image of Roosevelt, a Democrat who had converted to the Republican Party but continued to support much of the president's New Deal as well as his foreign defense policies, including all-out aid to Great Britain. In September and early October, Gallup polls showed Roosevelt with decisive leads over Willkie — 56 percent to 44 percent in one survey. Polls also showed that 68 percent of the country thought Roosevelt would be reelected. With the Royal Air Force's effective defense of the home isles against the German air assault persuading Americans that Britain would not succumb to Nazi aggression, 83 percent said they saw no need for the United States to enter the war. That finding echoed sentiment in Britain, where 80 percent of the population said it would be impossible for Germany to win the war by its air attack on their homeland. Still, it was ultimately the war that persuaded voters to support Roosevelt for a third term. If there were no war in Europe today, respondents were asked, whom would you vote for? In that poll, Willkie came out on top, 53 percent to 47 percent.

As the campaigns moved toward the election on November 5, Willkie saw the need to separate himself from Roosevelt's policy of aiding Britain without getting drawn into the war. The campaign then became a contest about who could best achieve these two possibly contradictory goals. For Willkie, whose campaign seemed to be gaining no traction until he began warning that Roosevelt was planning to enter the war, the formula was to frighten Americans into believing that a third Roosevelt term would see the boys on troop transports with some of them returning home in body bags. Roosevelt, for his part, sent William J. Donovan, a prominent New York attorney and decorated World War I veteran, on a presidential mission to England to report back on Britain's likely survival and ultimate triumph, in order to counter Joe Kennedy's pessimism about its ability to win the war.

In the closing weeks of the contest, however, with polls tightening and 59 percent of a survey indicating that Americans believed the country would eventually enter the war, Roosevelt felt compelled to aggressively refute a number of Willkie's charges against him, including accusations that he had made "secret understandings" to join the fighting. In addition, Willkie's campaign managers considered releasing material about Henry Wallace's affinity for mysticism as another tactic for putting the president on the defensive, but fears that the Democrats would retaliate by reporting a Willkie extramarital affair kept the scandal mongering to a minimum. The Roosevelt campaign was more concerned about voter disaffection in the Midwest, where isolationism was strongest and Roosevelt refused to make personal appearances. He felt compelled to stay within twelve hours of Washington by train and ruled out flying because it "would take a whole squadron of planes to move me." He was in any case convinced that he could reach nationwide audiences by means of the radio.

In October, pressed by local and state Democratic Party leaders worried about a Willkie surge over the war issue, Roosevelt gave five speeches principally aimed at convincing voters that he would avoid belligerency while helping Britain win the war. On October 23, in a nighttime appearance in Philadelphia that excited listeners across the nation, he attacked the "deliberate falsifications" leveled against him by his opponents: Assertions that he had "telephoned

Mussolini and Hitler to sell Czechoslovakia down the river; or to state that the unfortunate unemployed of the nation are going to be driven into concentration camps; or that the social security funds . . . will not be in existence when the workers of today apply for them; or that the election of the present Government means the end of American democracy." He dismissed these inexcusable falsehoods as nothing other than stirring up fear. "I will not pretend that I find this an unpleasant duty," he said with evident pleasure. "I am an old campaigner, and I love a good fight." "The worst bombshell of fear," he added, was the assertion that he had entered into secret agreements to take the country into the war, which he branded as a "fantastic misstatement." He ended by promising: "We will not participate in foreign wars and we will not send our army, naval or air forces to fight in foreign lands outside of the Americas except in case of attack."

Five days later, after touring New York City's five boroughs, where he received tumultuous receptions, he spoke to a capacity house at Madison Square Garden. He reminded the audience that he remained on constant call, reporting that he had been in touch with the State Department throughout the day about the outbreak of fighting between Italy and Greece. But the main task of the evening was again to respond to the falsification of facts by Republican opponents. He also discussed the fact that while some Republican business leaders were helping him build national defenses, a number of Republicans in Congress had played politics with the country's security needs, voting against them in 1937 and 1938 and now complaining loudly that the administration was failing to ensure the country's defense. And who were these hypocrites, he said in what he described as a "perfectly beautiful rhythm," Martin, Barton and Fish: congressmen Joe Martin, Bruce Barton, and Hamilton Fish. When Roosevelt repeated what Sam Rosenman called the "euphonious and rhythmic sequence," the audience gleefully joined in chanting "Martin, Barton and Fish." The chant carried over into the remainder of Roosevelt's public appearances, ridiculing the transparent Republican change in position to serve Willkie's campaign. Worse yet, Roosevelt said, it was a reprisal of the policies that had brought down France and made England so vulnerable before Churchill became prime minister.

On October 30, Roosevelt spoke in Boston after a daylong train ride from Washington with stops along the way in Hartford and New Haven, Connecticut, and Springfield and Worcester, Massachusetts, where he spoke to Democratic audiences at a defense plant and an arsenal and from the back of the train.

At Boston Garden, where he gave an hour-long address after having dinner at his son Jimmy's home, he once again lambasted the Republicans in what was by now familiar campaign rhetoric. But what made this speech memorable was his decision to refute Republican charges decisively and issue a blanket assurance that he would not take the country into war. Gone was the qualification that he would only do so if America was attacked by a foreign power.

Willkie understood that such a promise could be a game changer, acknowledging privately, "That hypocritical son-of-a-bitch. This is going to beat me." Even Eleanor took issue with such an absolute promise, writing in a column, "No one can honestly promise you today peace at home and abroad. All any human being can do is to promise that he will do his utmost to prevent the country from being involved in war." Roosevelt later confessed to his son James, "I knew we were going to war. I had to delay until there was no way out of it. I knew we were woefully unprepared. . . . But I couldn't come out and say a war was coming, because the people would have panicked and turned from me. I had to educate the people to the inevitable, gradually step by step . . . So you play the game the way it has been played over the years, and you play to win." Since the Republicans were clearly not hesitant to disregard the truth, he had no qualms about overstating the case for himself, as he had every confidence that he could better serve the national well-being than Willkie. The unspoken issue in the campaign was Roosevelt's health. Turning fifty-nine in January, when he would begin a third term, he had a medical history, as well as being a heavy smoker, that might have raised questions about his ability to serve another four years in so stressful a job without the risk of disabling illnesses, especially a stroke or a heart attack.

On Saturday, November 2, as a train carried Roosevelt toward Cleveland, where he was scheduled to deliver his last nationwide campaign speech that night, he gave brief remarks at Batavia, Buffalo, Rochester, and Dunkirk, New York, and at Erie, Pennsylvania, where he inspected airplane plants. At noon, he met with his speechwriters, including Robert Sherwood, for lunch. Sherwood found him "gray and worn and sagging. I was shocked at his appearance and thought," Sherwood recalled, " 'this is too much punishment to expect any man to take.' I almost hoped he would lose the election for it seemed that flesh and blood could not survive another six months — let alone four years — in this terrible job." Yet Roosevelt's storytelling during lunch seemed to revive him: "The grayness of his face gave way to healthy color, the circles vanished under his eyes, the sagging jowls seemed to tighten up into muscles about his jawbone. By the end of a brief, light lunch he was in wonderful shape and was demanding, 'Now! What have you three cut-throats been doing to my speech?' " When he arrived in Cleveland, he gave what Sherwood thought was the most animated, best speech of the campaign. It struck powerful chords with voters by reminding them that they were not only "characters in this living book of democracy" but "also its authors. It falls upon us now to say whether the chapters that are to come will tell a story of retreat or a story of continued advance. I believe that the American people will say: 'Forward!' "

On November 5, at Hyde Park, where he had gone to vote and track the election returns, as he had in all his past elections, he sat in his family dining room, surrounded by telephones and radios tuned to different stations, with coat off and tie loosened. Tally sheets and pencils for him to record the returns coming in from around the country sat before him on the dining room table. No one assumed that the president would sweep the country as he had in 1936. This had been a hard-fought contest in which Lindbergh and Labor leader John L. Lewis had come out against

Roosevelt. Ickes spoke for many in the president's camp when he recorded in a diary on election day: "I desperately want the President to win. I am horribly afraid of Willkie. I believe him to be unscrupulous, unfair, reckless to the point of daring, and greedy for power. If he should be elected, I would honestly fear for the future of my country."

As the first returns came in, Roosevelt broke into a heavy sweat and ordered Mike Reilly, his Secret Service agent, to shut the door and let no one in. He seemed to have lost his nerve, or so Reilly believed, as the possibility of losing the election had apparently badly shaken him. In fact, a more persuasive argument is that the profuse sweating was a reaction to severe pain caused by one of three possible factors: an atypical vasovagal syncope; cardiac angina; or a transient ischemic attack — possibly triggered by his perception of facing a devastating defeat in the election, but more likely it was another episode of what his White House physician Ross McIntire had described earlier in 1940 as "a very slight heart attack," and what Sherwood had seen on the train. It was a prelude to what would afflict him in 1944, when high blood pressure and congestive heart failure periodically sapped his strength and caused him to suffer temporary blackouts. In the words of a physician who was consulted for this book, "Based on the president's history of tobacco use, high blood pressure, and eventual death from stroke, it is not unlikely that by 1940 he already suffered from significant atherosclerotic cardiovascular disease."

For the moment, however, Roosevelt was able to recover within an hour and revel in the victory that became clear over the course of the evening. At midnight, he went out on the lawn of his Hyde Park mansion to greet his neighbors, who had assembled in a traditional torchlight parade, as they had after every one of his electoral victories. "We seem to have averted a putsch, Joe," he told Joe Lash, an Eleanor protegé, who spent the evening with the family observing the historic events.

Although the full results wouldn't be known until the middle of the night, there was already enough information to indicate that Roosevelt was "Safe on Third," as a sign held up to Roosevelt's great amusement declared. To be sure, his five-million-popular-vote advantage over Willkie — 27,244,160 to 22,305,198 — was well below the eleven million votes by which he had drubbed Landon in 1936. Moreover, his margin of 55.7 to 44.8 percent made it the closest election since Wilson's victory in 1916. But he had won almost five million more votes than he had in 1932, and the 449 electoral votes from 38 states dwarfed Willkie's ten-state count of 82 electoral ballots. Almost as gratifying, the Democrats increased their majority in the House by five seats, for a total of 267 against 162. The Democrats lost three Senate seats, but they still had a 66 to 28 edge, with one seat held by a Wisconsin Progressive. The improving economy, spurred by industrial mobilization, played a significant role in his victory, but it was ultimately the war that had made an unprecedented third term possible. A majority of voters preferred the experienced president to a novice who had never served in an elected office and was too much of a blank slate to be dependable in a world crisis.

However pleased Roosevelt was by his victory,

he could not avoid confronting the pressures that the next four years were bound to bring. Although Britain now seemed capable of surviving Hitler's air assault, and a successful attack in the fall on Italian warships in the Mediterranean combined with effective Greek resistance to Mussolini's armies sparked hopes of a British victory, no one could judge conclusively how long Britain might be able to hold out against Hitler's powerful land armies. While Hitler had indefinitely postponed a cross-Channel attack, long-term optimism in Britain was in short supply. Hitler's record of conquests made a British triumph seem at best a distant dream. Meanwhile, the air assault on Britain continued to inflict destruction across the isles. On November 14, for example, German bombers devastated Coventry in the Midlands, killing over 800 people and destroying three quarters of the city's industrial plants, which had been contributing greatly to British rearmament.

When fifty-eight-year-old British ambassador Lord Lothian returned to the United States on November 23 after a visit to London to confer with Churchill, he told the reporters who greeted him, "Well, boys, Britain is broke. It's your money we want." At a press conference three days later, a reporter asked the president if the ambassador presented any specific requests for additional help. "Nothing was mentioned in that regard at all," Roosevelt disingenuously replied, "not one single thing — ships or sealing wax or anything else." The reporters laughed, but Roosevelt's humor masked ongoing discussions of how to get around the cash restriction in the cash-and-carry law. He had told Lothian that Britain would have to liquidate its holdings in the Western Hemisphere before asking for financial assistance, but he did not regard this as the last word on how to continue helping Britain arm itself. A note from Churchill congratulating him on his reelection deepened Roosevelt's perception of what was at stake in the conflict. "We are now entering a somber phase of what must evidently be a protracted and broadening war," Churchill wrote him. ". . . Things are afoot which will be remembered as long as the English language is spoken in any quarter of the globe." He avowed his "sure faith that the lights by which we steer will bring us all safely to anchor." Despite Churchill's assurances, Roosevelt still feared that without additional U.S. help, Britain might lose the war.

For the moment, he had no answer for Churchill's indirect plea for U.S. participation in the fighting. He was determined not to allow any interruption in the flow of matériel, and so on December 1, he "authorized the placing of a sizeable number of British orders for military supplies." Under pressure from Morgenthau and the British, he backed away from his suggestion to Lothian that the British convert their Western Hemisphere possessions into cash. He was still without a plan that could eliminate the "cash" side of the neutrality law.

Roosevelt desperately needed a vacation, or some sort of break from past and current pressures, as he would have put it, to recharge his batteries. As always, he sought rejuvenation in a sea voyage. On December 3 he fled Washington for a ten-day holiday in the Caribbean on the cruiser *Tuscaloosa,* accompanied by Pa Watson, Roosevelt's military aide and appointments secretary, and Ross McIntire, the White House physician.

The only policy aide aboard was Harry Hopkins, who had resigned as secretary of commerce but was still living at the White House. Hopkins remained so weak from his recent illness that he could not reel in a twenty-pound fish. Asked by reporters where he was going on the trip, Roosevelt said, "It's perfectly vague where I go," and joked that he would sail for Christmas Island to buy Christmas cards and Easter Island to buy Easter eggs. In fact, he justified the trip by explaining that he would inspect recently acquired bases.

On December 7, Roosevelt received an almost four-thousand-word letter from Churchill, over which he and Lothian had labored and which Churchill considered "one of the most important I ever wrote." It reached Roosevelt by seaplane and engaged the president's attention for the several days remaining on the cruise. He read and reread the missive while sitting alone in a deck chair, during which, Hopkins recalled, he was "plunged in intense thought, and brooded silently." Churchill's letter was a tour d'horizon of Britain's current and future war prospects. While he said that the danger of a swift defeat by an overwhelming blow had greatly receded, "a long gradually, maturing danger" had replaced it. The "mortal danger is the steady and increasing diminution of sea tonnage." It was in shipping and the power to transport goods across the ocean "that in 1941 the crunch of the whole war will be found." But this was only a part of the challenge; as important was the "industrial energy of the [Great] Republic" to give Britain the wherewithal to withstand the Nazi air and sea assault. Finally, and most essential, was the matter of finance:

America's stripping Britain of all its saleable assets "would not be in the moral or economic interests of either of our countries," Churchill said. He left it to Roosevelt to figure out how to serve their common purpose.

Roosevelt's ruminations had led him to what Sherwood described as a political "masterpiece," and Frances Perkins called a "flash of almost clairvoyant knowledge." After returning home "tanned and exuberant and jaunty," he revealed his plan to the press at a news conference on December 17. He began by asserting that the best defense of the United States was the survival of the British Empire. According to prevalent thinking, Britain needed financial support to outlast Germany. Because, Roosevelt argued, no major war had ever been won or lost because of finances, any discussions about repealing laws prohibiting loans or simply giving Britain gifts of armaments with no financial obligations were ultimately "banal." He dismissed all such considerations as pedestrian thinking. "Now, what I am trying to do is to eliminate the dollar sign, and that is something brand new . . . get rid of the silly, foolish old dollar sign." Instead, his plan was to lend or lease the arms. "Let me give you an illustration," he said:

Suppose my neighbor's home catches fire, and I have got a length of hose four or five hundred feet away; but, by Heaven, if he can take my hose and connect it up with his hydrant, I may help him to put out his fire. Now, what do I do? I don't say to him before that operation, 'Neighbor, my garden hose cost me $15; you have got to pay me $15 for it.' . . . I don't want $15 — I want my garden hose back after the fire is over. . . . If it goes through the fire all right, intact, without any damage to it, he gives it back to me . . . But suppose it gets smashed up . . . I say to him 'I was glad to lend you that hose; I see I can't use it anymore; it's all smashed up.' . . . He says, 'All right I will replace it.' . . . It is a gentlemen's agreement to pay in kind.

Roosevelt proposed the lend and lease plan for many types of war materiel for Britain. The reporters asked if this would take America into the war, or if Lend-Lease would require congressional legislation. No, Roosevelt declared on the United States becoming a belligerent, and, yes, Congress would have to enact the plan.

For all Roosevelt's cleverness in describing a program of aid that did away with formal financial arrangements, and making it clear that bankers, who were so despised by New Dealers, would have no say in the arrangement, his proposal intensified isolationist fears of a backdoor to war. "Look," Senator Robert Taft declared, "lending war equipment is a good deal like lending chewing gum. You don't want it back." Another concern was that if Britain didn't have the means to finance the purchase of arms now, where would it get the funds to pay for the replacements later? The America First Committee, an organization that began at Yale and attracted college undergraduates across the country, warned that Lend-Lease was an irreversible step toward war, as it would effectively make America Britain's ally and eventually force a confrontation with Berlin. The public was deeply divided: In December, 88 percent said they would vote against entering the war, but 60 percent said it was worth risking involvement in the fighting to help Britain win.

Anticipating a tough fight ahead in Congress over Lend-Lease, Roosevelt took to the airwaves for a Fireside Chat on December 29. He had not used this forum since the previous May, and his talk drew a large national audience. Because he knew that his key message was to reassure Americans that he was not proposing involvement in the war, he began by declaring: "This is not a fireside chat on war. It is a talk on national security." His duty, he explained, was "to keep you now, and your children later, and your grandchildren much later out of a last-ditch war for the preservation of American independence."

He reminded listeners how in the first of his Fireside Talks he had helped see the country through the banking crisis of 1932–33. He hoped that Americans would face this new emergency with the same "courage and realism." He did not understate the threat posed by the Axis alliance of Germany, Italy, and Japan codified in a September 1940 agreement. They were on a mission to exercise world control and subject all free peoples, including the United States, to their dictates. If Great Britain should be defeated, Americans would be forced to live at the point of a gun, entering upon "a new and terrible era in which the whole world, our Hemisphere included, would be run by threats of brute force." No nation could achieve peace with the Nazis without total submission, he warned, as the world was facing "an unholy alliance . . . to dominate and enslave the human race." The surest path to peace was through helping the nations currently fighting these aggressors. "We must be the great arsenal of democracy," he said. "For us this is an emergency as serious as war itself. We must apply ourselves to our task with the same resolution, the same sense of urgency, the same spirit of patriotism and sacrifice as we would show were we at war." The phrase "arsenal of democracy," which was originally used by French economist Jean Monnet, caught the public's imagination and helped advance the resupply of Britain.

In his preoccupation with British survival, Roosevelt had said relatively little in public about Japan. He wanted, as Churchill had urged, to keep "the Japanese dog quiet in the Pacific," and he hoped that the presence of naval forces in Pearl Harbor could serve as a deterrent to Tokyo. His inclusion of Japan in his speech as one of the nations seeking world control, and his mention of China as serving as a "great defense" against Japan and the presence of the American fleet in the Pacific, therefore marked a departure. Ever since the war had erupted in Europe in September 1939, he had struggled with how to contain Japan without provoking a Pacific conflict that would divert the United States and Britain from addressing the German threat. His cabinet had become a battleground of proposals for how to deal with Tokyo — with Ickes, Morgenthau, and Stimson urging economic embargoes on scrap metals and high-grade aviation fuel, to deprive Japan's military of key products and impede its three-year-old war in China, and Hull's State Department cautioning against economic measures that could impel Tokyo toward seizure of French- and Dutch-controlled resource-rich areas in Southeast Asia.

In July 1940, Ickes complained that Hull and

his State Department subordinates were appeasers, and that any consideration of Hull as a presidential candidate was a terrible idea. "He would make a rotten president," Ickes told Roosevelt. Ickes found it difficult to understand "how the President can put up with the State Department." As for Hull, Ickes complained "the fellow can't think straight and he is totally lacking in imagination. . . . If we had embargoed scrap and petroleum products two or three years ago, Japan would not be in the position that it is, and our position, relative to Japan, as well as that of England, would be infinitely stronger."

In July 1940, Roosevelt took a middle ground, agreeing to increased oil shipments to Japan from the Dutch East Indies as a way to restrain it from a seizure of the vulnerable Dutch colony. At the same time, however, after Japanese forces had occupied part of French Indochina, and Tokyo signed its tripartite agreement with Germany and Italy, he consented to a full embargo on all iron and steel scrap exports to Japan. But he refused to include oil in the embargo and directed Morgenthau to stop pressing him on the matter. With his Navy chiefs warning that the Pacific fleet was unprepared for offensive operations and General Marshall also cautioning against provoking Tokyo into a war, Roosevelt decided it was wiser to exercise restraint and not incite Japanese aggression, while at the same time displaying sufficient indications of resolve to make Tokyo understand that if pressed too hard, the United States would turn its superior military power against Japan.

As 1940 came to an end, those closest to Roosevelt wondered if he had the stamina to bear the burdens of a world that now seemed to be in perpetual crisis. The physical toll that the demands of the presidency had taken on him was all too evident. As he prepared to take the oath of office again, his consideration for his physical well-being paled alongside the larger obligations that demanded his continued service — not just to the nation but to the very principles the country represented.

The poet Archibald MacLeish expressed Roosevelt's feelings articulately when he wrote him: "In the face of our danger which confronts our time, no individual retains or can hope to retain the rights of personal choice which free men can enjoy in times of peace. He has a first obligation to serve in defense of our institutions of freedom — a first obligation to serve his country in whatever capacity his country finds him useful — which must override all personal preferences." Harold Laski, the British political theorist and Labor Party leader, asked Supreme Court associate justice Felix Frankfurter to tell Roosevelt that "Fascism is so literally the enemy of mankind that there is no price that you can pay for its destruction that is too high."

CHAPTER 14
THE PATH TO WAR

Fresh from his election and Caribbean cruise, Roosevelt entered the New Year with his public image as positive as ever, the press describing him as buoyant and optimistic. Still, no one could deny that eight years in office had aged him, or that his appearance suggested that he might be suffering from health problems brought on by immobility, age, and the unrelenting pressures of his job. Though it provided a relaxing outlet, his cigarette smoking was also contributing to his decline. His personal physician, who claimed to examine him twice a week, described his physical condition as "the best in many years." Dr. McIntire reported that the president enjoyed a perfect weight, swam regularly in the White House pool, drank a nightly cocktail, and awoke each morning after a good night's sleep. "We are looking ahead to the next four years without any apprehension," he declared.

But if the president was indeed as healthy as asserted, why would McIntire even have mentioned "apprehension?" Privately, he had been concerned about Roosevelt. Before he left on his Caribbean cruise he had looked especially tired and exhausted, and hypertension had been evident in his health exams as early as 1937. The trip had done him a world of good, McIntire believed, but there was every reason to believe that additional strains could bring a further decline in his health. The *New York Times* was dubious about the state of Roosevelt's health, observing: "The President does not always reveal his true feelings" But reluctant to undermine public confidence, the *Times* took McIntire's assessment of the president's health at face value. As with his disability, which the press had largely opted not to discuss during the previous eight years, the *Times* avoided expressing concerns about his capacity to get through another term. For Roosevelt, concealing the strains crowding in on him was nothing more than an acceptance that he shared with so many other Americans of the harsh realities besetting their lives. It was Roosevelt's way of saying, *I have no right to complain when so many of my countrymen are living with even greater burdens than my own — not to mention what people in Britain, who were under daily attack, were living through.*

On returning to Washington, Roosevelt's first order of business was to win congressional approval for a Lend-Lease law. British ambassador Lord Lothian thought that American public opinion stood in the way and reported to London that the country was "saturated with illusions . . . that we have vast resources available that we have not disclosed . . . and that we ought to empty this vast hypothetical barrel before we ask for assistance."

At a White House cabinet meeting on January 17, three days before the end of Garner's vice presidency, he said that the British had sufficient funds to finance additional war supplies. Agriculture Secretary Claude Wickard echoed Garner's complaint, "saying the same thing over and over and over again. When he and the vice president both sounded off at the same time, it was like a boiler factory," in Ickes's words. The argument left Ickes "depressed and anxious. We know what is involved for us in this situation, and yet we are as ungenerous and selfish and mean as we can be." In a survey, 55 percent favored changing the Johnson Debt Default Act, which prohibited loans to World War I debtor nations. Because 68 percent of a survey believed that America's future safety depended on a British victory and 85 percent expected England to lose the war if the United States stopped supplying her, Roosevelt believed that Congress would pass his measure.

On January 6, his State of the Union address was a rallying cry to save the American way of life through aid to Britain. Roosevelt appeared energized and determined — a leader on a mission to save not only the United States but also its global values. The energy he exuded and the words he spoke were meant to rally the country to take the next step in the role he had defined for it in the war, declaring, "at no previous time has American security been as seriously threatened from without as it is today." He recalled the history of past threats to the nation to demonstrate that the current danger was unprecedented. "The need of the moment is that our actions and our policy should be devoted primarily — almost exclusively — to meeting this foreign peril." He repeated earlier assertions about the need to help Hitler's adversaries if we were to keep war away from our shores. And he briefly made a case for Lend-Lease.

But the principal thrust of his speech was an appeal to the country's highest ideals, and an affirmation of his commitment to what he called the Four Freedoms: freedom of speech, freedom of religion, freedom from want, and freedom from fear, or the elimination of national acts of aggression against peace-loving countries everywhere in the world. In brief, nothing less was at stake in the war than the American way of life, and Churchill's Britain was defending it. "You have raised the standard of the moral order and the peoples of the world will respond," Felix Frankfurter told him in response to his speech. As compelling to most Americans was the prospect of helping the British win the war without shedding American blood.

At the beginning of January, Roosevelt decided to send Harry Hopkins to London. Aside from Eleanor, no public figure was seen as representing the president more faithfully than Hopkins. The journalist Marquis Childs said that if Roosevelt had directed Hopkins to jump off the Washington Monument to serve the national welfare, Hopkins would take the plunge, and whether he did it with or without a parachute depended on what Roosevelt thought best for the nation. Hopkins's health remained precarious, but the president was confident that he could weather the trip and bolster British determination to outlast the Nazis.

Although Roosevelt now enjoyed regular cabled exchanges with Churchill, he saw the need for a more direct link. For the moment, neither nation had an ambassador in its respective capital. In December, the fifty-eight-year-old Lord Lothian, who had been a highly effective advocate for Britain's interests since his appointment at the start of the war in September 1939, had died suddenly. Churchill sent word that Lord Halifax, the foreign secretary, would replace Lothian, but it would take time before the White House would see Halifax to be as trustworthy as Lothian. In addition, no one had replaced Joe Kennedy in London since his retirement from the Embassy in November 1940 after being quoted in the *Boston Globe* that democracy was finished in Britain. Kennedy, who was seen as a "defeatist" in England, had also fostered doubts in London about America's reliability in combating Hitler. While Churchill had praised Roosevelt's arsenal of democracy speech for having "heartened and fortified" the British for the uncertain days ahead, it did not allay their concerns about how he would make the promised program of aid effective.

Hopkins left for London on January 7, taking a safe route to Portugal by Pan Am Clipper, arriving in England two days later aboard a British airliner. When Brendan Bracken, Churchill's private secretary, met Hopkins at the plane, he found him "still sitting [in his seat] looking sick and shrunken and too tired to unfasten his seat belt." Taking a train to London, which was in the midst of a German air raid, he was too weak to dine with Churchill at 10 Downing Street, eating instead in his room at Claridge's hotel.

Accompanying Hopkins to London was fifty-eight-year-old William J. Donovan, a World War I hero who had been awarded a Medal of Honor. Roosevelt had sent him to gather information on Britain's current capacity to withstand Germany's assault and to report on its needs. Donovan had been urging the president to establish an intelligence-gathering agency, which resulted in the creation of the Coordinator of Information

(COI), which in 1942 would become the Office of Strategic Services (OSS), the predecessor to the Central Intelligence Agency (CIA).

Hopkins took heart, as did Roosevelt, from the success of British forces in North Africa, where the Italians were being routed. "If I may debase a golden phrase," Anthony Eden, Churchill's new foreign secretary, wrote Roosevelt, "never has so much been surrendered by so many to so few." (Eden's reference was to Churchill's praise of the Royal Air Force : "Never was so much owed by so many to so few.") The capture of some forty thousand Italian troops, including a Catholic bishop and three nuns, was the basis for the joke that there would be a sale on Italian rifles — never been fired and only dropped once.

Hopkins's London trip brought cheer to Churchill and his War Cabinet. Herschel V. Johnson, the U.S. chargé d'affaires in London, was "heartened by the sincerity and intensity of Harry Hopkins's determination to gain firsthand knowledge of Britain's needs and of finding a way to fill them. . . . He made me feel that the first real assurance of hope had at last come — and he acted on the British like a galvanic needle."

No one perceived the advantages of Hopkins's visit more fully than Churchill, who lunched with him in the basement of 10 Downing Street the day after Hopkins arrived. "A rotund — smiling — red faced, gentleman appeared — extended a fat but none the less convincing hand and wished me welcome to England," Hopkins reported. He told him that Roosevelt was anxious to see him, and Churchill echoed the wish for a meeting — "the sooner the better." When Hopkins described his mission, Churchill promised to provide every bit of information that clarified "the urgent necessity of the exact material assistance Britain requires to win the war." After five days in Britain, Hopkins wrote Roosevelt "the people here are amazing from Churchill down and if courage alone can win — the result will be inevitable. But they need our help desperately and I am sure you will permit nothing to stand in the way. . . . This island needs our help now Mr. President with everything we can give them."

As for Churchill, Hopkins impressed him as "a soul that flamed out of a frail and failing body. He was a crumbling lighthouse from which shone the beams that led great fleets to harbor." During their first three-hour meeting, Churchill perceived Hopkins's "personal dynamism and the outstanding importance of his mission." Hopkins had assured him: "The President is determined that we shall win the war together. Make no mistake about it. . . . At all costs and by all means he will carry you through, no matter what happens to him — there is nothing he will not do so far as he has human power." Although no promises were made regarding America's entrance into the conflict, Hopkins made it clear that Roosevelt was committed to defeating Hitler and the Nazis. It was also a tacit acknowledgement that the president was risking his health for the sake of the cause. For Churchill, Hopkins's assurances were welcome at a most difficult time when "many local worries imposed themselves upon us. . . . There he [Hopkins] sat," Churchill recalled, "slim, frail, ill, but absolutely glowing with refined comprehension of the cause. It was to be the defeat, ruin, and slaughter of Hitler, to the exclusion of all other purposes, loyalties or aims. In the history of the United States few brighter flames have burned." One evening, near the end of Hopkins's visit, he shared what he would tell the president of their meetings by quoting the Bible: " 'Whither thou goest, I will go and where thou lodgest, I will lodge, thy people shall be my people, and thy God my God!' " concluding, "Even to the End." Overcome with emotion, Churchill wept.

When Hopkins returned to Washington after six weeks in Britain, the push for congressional action on Lend-Lease was in full swing. Because the policy was essentially "a giveaway program," Roosevelt dressed it up in language that hid this reality. Stimson understood that it was "a clever scheme" and as such would be more acceptable than repealing the Johnson Act as a prelude to extending Britain large loans. Unlike the deception that underlay the president's Court-packing plan, which angered many Americans and failed to get the approval of Congress, Lend-Lease had substantial popular appeal. As Roosevelt told Morgenthau, "We don't want to fool the public, we want to do this thing right out and out."

Introduced in the House with the symbolically arresting title "H.R. 1776," the law gave the president "blanket permission as to how much and to whom to distribute war goods." It also satisfied Roosevelt's direction to be vague about how countries "whose defense is related to the defense of the United States" would repay American largess. Although the British had estimated they would need fifteen billion dollars, Roosevelt wanted the initial authorized amount to be limited to five or six billion. After the bill was introduced, the isolationists, led by Senator Burton K. Wheeler of Montana, mounted a caustic opposition.

Wheeler scathingly declared that "the Lend-Lease give program is the New Deal's triple A foreign policy; it will plow under every fourth American boy." Roosevelt denounced the comment "as the most untruthful, as the most dastardly unpatriotic thing . . . that has been said in public life in my generation." The bill was also criticized as a "power grab" by Roosevelt and was described as nothing less than "an act of war."

To combat the isolationists, Roosevelt encouraged public officials to go to England, where they could witness firsthand the courageous battle against German air forces and the deaths of innocent civilians. No one served Roosevelt's purposes better in conveying the conditions of wartime London than thirty-two-year-old CBS broadcast journalist Edward R. Murrow. Stationed in the city in the summer and fall of 1940, he described the rain of bombs, the people running to take cover in underground stations converted to air raid shelters, and the devastation caused by the raids. Wendell Willkie also helped make Roosevelt's case for supporting the British. Encouraged by Stimson to visit London, Willkie agreed to see the president before crossing the Atlantic. Understanding how helpful his trip would be in boosting British morale and winning passage of the Lend-Lease Bill, Roosevelt gave him a letter of introduction to Churchill, assuring him that Willkie "is being a true help in keeping politics out of things." Roosevelt added a verse from Longfellow that he thought "applies to you people as it does to us":

"Sail on, O Ship of State!
Sail on, O Union Strong and great!

Humanity with all its fears,
With all the hopes of future years,
Is hanging breathless on thy fate!"

To dispel fears that Lend-Lease would lead to American belligerency, Roosevelt urged Churchill to state his conviction that Britain would win the war without U.S. armies coming to the rescue. In a speech on February 9, Churchill explained how the current war was unlike World War I, when two million American troops landed in Europe. "We do not need the gallant armies which are forming throughout the American Union. We do not need them this year, or next year, or any year that I can foresee." He then read the Longfellow verse Roosevelt had sent and added: "What is the answer that I shall give in your name to this great man. . . . Here is the answer I will give to Mr. Roosevelt. Put your confidence in us. . . . We shall not fail or falter. . . . Give us the tools and we will finish the job."

Although Roosevelt believed he had safe majorities in both Houses for Lend-Lease, he could not rule out a Senate filibuster. When the House passed the bill 260 to 165 on February 8, the scene of action shifted to the Senate, where Willkie testified before a committee on the day he returned from England. Looking tired and rumpled from the journey and the six-hour time change, he predicted that Republican opposition to the bill would permanently sink the party. Willkie angered the isolationists, who reminded him that he had predicted involvement in the war by April 1941 if Roosevelt won a third term. Willkie good-naturedly declared it "a bit of campaign oratory," which brought forth "goodhearted laughter" from the crowded hearing room. Roosevelt acknowledged later that without Willkie's help, Lend-Lease could not have passed.

Joe Kennedy's testimony also fell short of what the isolationists hoped would be a decisive blow to the bill. In November, Franklin had told Eleanor, "I never want to see that son of a bitch again as long as I live. Take his resignation and get him out of here." But because Roosevelt knew what he testified could jeopardize the bill, he invited Kennedy to the White House, where he sweet-talked him into agreeing to tell the Senate committee that Lend-Lease would help keep the United States out of war. When a large majority enacted the measure on March 11, Roosevelt was grateful for Willkie's support and delighted that he had cajoled Joe, whom angry isolationists denounced for "blowing hot and blowing cold at the same time — trying to carry water on both shoulders." Roosevelt immediately asked Congress to appropriate seven billion dollars to further help arm Britain.

But the president did not consider the passage of Lend-Lease to be an end in itself, as he believed that an essential next step was a united country embracing and implementing the aid program. When a rash of strikes that slowed the production of planes and other weapons threatened to block the transfer of arms to Britain, a prominent columnist declared, "Labor is working itself into a role of irresponsible obstruction to war production." In response to a reporter's question about whether he was concerned about "the labor situation as affecting the defense projects," Roosevelt denied the existence of a problem, but administration plans to create the Defense Labor Board and discussions about taking over plants where it seemed impossible to get settlements refuted his disavowal. But with one in twelve workers going out on strike, the problem soon became too large to ignore.

On March 19, Roosevelt fled Washington for another badly needed rest on a ten-day fishing trip in the Caribbean. On March 29, he used Jackson Day as an occasion to speak to the country from the yacht *Potomac* in the Fort Lauderdale, Florida, harbor. The trip, he explained, had not only given him a chance to reduce the daily pressures confronting him at the White House but also to think things through. Now that he had won his third term, he was remarkably candid about the strains of being president, and admitted that fifteen-hour days compelled him to take "short trips on salt water," where he could reduce his workload to two or three hours a day. More important, he used his speech to tell Americans that Jackson offered enduring lessons for their own time — in particular, "his devotion to his country above adherence to party" or to any sort of partisanship or self-interest. His ability to do so distinguished America from the dictatorships currently attacking democracies. "In our country," Roosevelt said, "disagreements among us are expressed in the polling place. In the dictatorships, disagreements are suppressed in the concentration camp." In brief, although rival parties might fight hard in election contests, when faced with external threats, the nation was one America. Eleanor Roosevelt reinforced his message with a "My Day" column in which she described a visit to the Tuskegee Institute in Greensboro, North Carolina, where she observed the training of

African American pilots and had the pleasure of a brief flight with the head instructor.

The next two months brought growing unease about Britain's ability to win the war. Churchill cabled that "the sinkings are bad and the strain is increasing at sea," in reference to Lend-Lease supplies being shipped to Britain being jeopardized by German sea and air attacks, which were taking a heavy toll on British transports. "I cannot conceal from you that rate of loss due to inadequate escorts is terribly costly," Churchill confided, in the hope that Roosevelt would promise to fill the gap. In addition, German troops had joined the fighting in the Balkans and North Africa to stem the tide of defeats suffered by Mussolini's forces. Roosevelt, however, resisted ordering U.S. destroyers to convoy supplies to Britain, fearing it would bring America into the war, and without a stable national consensus, would undermine and possibly defeat any war effort.

Still, he had no illusions about the seriousness of the military threats. On April 1, he told Josephus Daniels in Mexico that a meeting with Mexican president Manuel Camacho in Mexican waters would have to wait until "the Balkan problems quiet down and the shipping problem becomes at least no worse." In March, Roosevelt had directed U.S. forces to occupy Greenland to keep it out of German hands and facilitate the shipment of aircraft to Britain. On April 10, after Churchill had announced the "Battle of the Atlantic" to underscore the imperative to combat Nazi sea attacks, Roosevelt secretly agreed to "patrols" — not escorts. If word did leak out about the use of American naval forces to aid

Britain, Roosevelt planned to defend his decision as a defensive action rather than a step toward belligerency. Still, he did not wish to mislead the public on what was at stake. Consequently, he signed off on a speech Secretary of the Navy Knox gave to a group of publishers, in which he asserted that "We cannot allow our goods to be sunk in the Atlantic — we shall be beaten if they are. We must make good our promise to give aid to Britain."

Confronting the Nazi attack in the Atlantic, however, could not halt their gains in the Balkans, North Africa, or the Mediterranean. On April 17, German forces overcame resistance in Yugoslavia and a week later celebrated the conquest of Greece. Meanwhile, under the direction of General Erwin Rommel, the *Afrika Korps* regained much of the ground that the Italians had lost in Libya. Roosevelt encouraged Churchill by advising that "supplies . . . are to be rushed to the Middle East at the earliest possible moment. . . . Should the Mediterranean prove in the last analysis to be an impossible battleground I do not feel that such fact alone would mean the defeat of our mutual interests. I say this because I believe the outcome of this struggle is going to be decided in the Atlantic and unless Hitler can win there he cannot win anywhere in the world." Knox's and Roosevelt's language spoke volumes about the administration's view of the war as an American conflict that the nation could not afford to lose.

The United States' actions "assured" Churchill that "no temporary reverses, however heavy, can shake your resolution to support us until we gain the final victory." And in a sentence he crossed out before cabling the message, he added: "Naturally I am (depressed) concerned by your message in spite of all the kindness and comradeship it conveys." But Churchill then was direct in his appeal: "Mr. President, I am sure that you will not misunderstand me if I speak to you exactly what is in my mind. The one decisive counterweight I can see to balance the growing pessimism . . . would be if the United States were immediately to range herself with us as a belligerent power."

Roosevelt did not reply for a week after he declared his conviction that the war ultimately would be decided in the Atlantic. He said nothing in response to Churchill's suggestion that the United States enter the war. In fact, he was quite ill and confined to bed. He was suffering from bleeding hemorrhoids, which had reduced his hemoglobin to 4.5 g/100ml, producing severe anemia, which was treated with two blood transfusions and injections of ferrous sulfate. While he recovered, he remained cloistered in the White House, largely cut off from almost everyone. When Sherwood got in to see him on May 10, Roosevelt impressed him as being in "fine shape. . . . What is really the matter with him?" he asked Missy Le-Hand. She replied: "What he's suffering from most of all is a case of sheer exasperation." But his physical health was a source of continuing anxiety. "Constant worry about C[ertain]P[erson]," Daisy wrote him. And though her brother, who visited Franklin, reported him "looking well," she fretted that her brother wasn't seeing "beneath the surface."

Distressing information about Sumner Welles was also troubling him. In September 1940, during a train ride back to Washington from a funeral in Alabama for House Speaker William Bankhead,

Welles drank himself into a stupor and propositioned three black porters. When Bill Bullitt, who resented Welles's closeness to the president and appointment as undersecretary of state, a job Bullitt coveted, learned of the episode, he began spreading rumors about Welles's homosexuality. In the spring, he brought the information to Roosevelt, who had known about the incident since January, when FBI director J. Edgar Hoover gave him a report on it. Although Bullitt cautioned Roosevelt that Welles was vulnerable to criminal charges and blackmail and jeopardized public support of the administration, Roosevelt dismissed Bullitt's warnings. He explained that no criminal charges were to be filed, that no newspaper would write about the matter, and that Hoover had assigned an agent to travel with Welles to ensure that no such episode occurred again. Bullitt's hectoring angered Roosevelt, who had strong regard for Welles as both a friend and a diplomat. After ending the meeting with Bullitt, an exhausted Roosevelt canceled his remaining appointments and returned to the presidential quarters to lie down.

As well as British setbacks, public irresolution in the United States was disturbing Roosevelt. While his public standing had risen to 73 percent, the country remained ambivalent about how to respond to the war. Americans wanted Britain to defeat Germany and even expressed a willingness to have the United States become a belligerent if it appeared certain that Britain would lose. But a large majority wanted to stay out of the fighting, and most Americans continued to believe that Britain could win without our direct involvement. As for assisting Britain with naval escorts of ships transporting goods across the Atlantic, the country was sharply divided. "So confused and so volatile was public opinion in the spring of 1941," Goodwin writes, "that Roosevelt was like a man staring into a fog." In addition, labor troubles continued to dog him. The "strike situation," Ickes reported, "is very serious indeed." The seizure of plants producing defense goods was a constant topic in the administration. John L. Lewis, whom Ickes called an "appeaser," was suspected of engineering strikes as a way to "sabotage our preparedness program."

With Roosevelt sidelined by illness during the first part of May, Ickes, Stimson, and Knox privately expressed concern about the "comatose state of the nation" and "the President's lack of leadership." Ickes grumbled that Roosevelt had gone "into a state of innocuous desuetude." Had he known how "inactive and uninspiring" the president would be, he acknowledged, "I would not have supported him for a third term." On May 23, when Roosevelt held his first cabinet meeting in three weeks, he looked tired, and Ickes wondered "if he is going to have the physical stamina to lead us during these next critical years." Ickes believed that "many people are beginning to have doubts upon this." The three cabinet members urged the president to transfer some of the fleet at Pearl Harbor in Hawaii to the Atlantic to combat the Nazi sea and air campaign. But an April Soviet-Japanese neutrality agreement had heightened Roosevelt's fears of Tokyo's aggression in Southeast Asia and made him reluctant to reduce the main U.S. deterrent to Japanese expansion. But Ickes, Stimson, and Knox judged Berlin to be the greater menace and hoped a fortified U.S.

naval presence in the Atlantic might bring America into the war. "The German line is closing in," Ickes said, "the British are falling back, although fighting desperately, and we are still talking." When they pleaded with Roosevelt to "do something," he replied, "I am not willing to fire the first shot." According to Ickes, he seemed to be "waiting for the Germans to create an incident."

Morgenthau had also come to the conclusion that Roosevelt had to take the United States into the war to save England and preserve national security, but he understood the president's reluctance to enter the conflict without some form of provocation. He and Hopkins agreed that where this issue was concerned, Roosevelt was wiser to follow public opinion than to lead it, as a national commitment to fight would result in a more effective effort than a directive from above to expend blood and treasure. Morgenthau believed it would be more prudent to take precautionary measures like declaring a state of national emergency and the creation of a civil defense agency to protect the homeland and mobilize the country's resources. Roosevelt shared Morgenthau's conviction about taking such steps prior to any declaration of war. "I am waiting to be pushed into this situation," he told Morgenthau.

On May 20, Roosevelt established an Office of Civil Defense (OCD) with New York mayor Fiorello La Guardia as its director. The fifty-eight-year-old La Guardia, who had served six terms in Congress and been a progressive mayor of New York since 1934 as well as a staunch supporter of New Deal programs, had been lobbying Roosevelt for several months to set up a national agency to protect U.S. cities from the sort of devastating air attacks inflicted on London during 1940. Edward R. Murrow's graphic reports from England had done much to foster public receptivity to civil defense preparations. In choosing the indefatigable La Guardia to head the agency, Roosevelt believed that he would not only ready New York and other cities for air attacks but also encourage Americans to accept the likelihood that they would have to enter the war.

The OCD became part of the Office of Emergency Planning (OEP), which was an executive bureau under presidential control. La Guardia was instructed to plan the defense of the entire home front, and especially a response to air raids like those in London. He was also assigned responsibility for national morale and a public relations campaign to counter isolationist propaganda from Lindbergh, certain senators, and newspaper publishers denouncing Lend-Lease and other administration actions. Ickes, however, thought tying morale to civil defense was a mistake, as it would require a separate and substantial effort that would be more than he could handle in managing the physical and emotional disturbances air attacks would bring. "After all," Ickes said, "Fiorello is not God and he has to eat and sleep like other human beings." Establishing an Office of Civilian Defense was Roosevelt's way of signaling that war was on the way and the country needed to prepare itself, but he stopped short of creating an office of war propaganda, such as had existed during 1917–18, which would have been too overt a step that would have sparked an isolationist response dividing the country and making it less ready to fight.

On May 27, in his ninth year as president, Roosevelt gave only his seventeenth Fireside Chat. At 10:30 in the evening in an oppressively warm White House East Room before representatives of Latin American countries, whose presence signaled Roosevelt's desire to bring war dangers home to all the Americas, the president announced that he was declaring an unlimited national emergency. "The pressing problems that confront us are military and naval problems," he said, that could not be wished away by unrealistic attachments to false assumptions. They were facing a Nazi-provoked "world war for world domination." Every step he had taken since the war began in 1939, he asserted, had been in the service of national security. There should be no illusions that the Americas were beyond the reach of German aggression. "The war is approaching the brink of the Western Hemisphere itself," he declared. "It is coming very close to home." Only the "magnificent" resistance of Britain and China had spared the Americas from the perils of Axis control.

But the battle of the Atlantic, which was the key to American security, was still very much in progress, and the United States could not afford to play a passive role. "Anyone with an Atlas (and) anyone with a reasonable knowledge of the sudden striking force of modern war knows that it is stupid to wait until a probable enemy has gained a foothold from which to attack," he said. He now came to the principal point of his talk: "We have, accordingly, extended our patrol in north and south Atlantic waters. . . . It is well known that the strength of the Atlantic Fleet has been greatly increased during the past year, and that it is constantly being built up. . . . We must be willing to fight" if necessary to keep the Nazis from gaining a foothold in the Americas. In the meantime, it was "imperative" to ensure the delivery of Lend-Lease supplies to Britain. After describing the function of the Office of Civil Defense, he asked: "Shall we now . . . hesitate to take every single measure necessary to maintain our liberties? Our people and our Government will not hesitate to meet that challenge." He ended by declaring an unlimited national emergency that "requires the strengthening of our defense to the extreme limit of our national power and authority."

The forty-five-minute speech, which may have reached the country's largest radio audience ever, was all but a declaration of war. While 56 percent of Americans favored a national referendum before sending American troops to fight abroad, 55 percent supported using naval forces to ensure the delivery of supplies to Britain, and 77 percent endorsed the president's determination to help the United Kingdom. The response to his speech could hardly have been more positive. Of the thousand telegrams that arrived at the White House that night, 95 percent were supportive. The president's approval rating with the mass public rose from 73 to 76 percent. "We are uplifted and fortified by your memorable declaration," Churchill commented. "The way you spoke was quite perfect," Daisy wrote him. But she "realized . . . how *alone* you stood, speaking to the world — and what it must have meant to you — you, at one time a small boy lying in the grass over a woodchuck hole." In the days following his speech, Roosevelt marveled at the extent of public approval, speeded the delivery of bombers to England, and increased preparations to defend

Portugal's Azore and Cape Verde Islands against Nazi occupation.

But the president's caution after his speech perplexed his inner circle of advisers when he refused to ask for repeal of the neutrality act or to make a commitment to convoying. It became clear that he was not going to lead the country into war — at least not in the spring of 1941. When he told his cabinet that patrolling represented "a step forward," Stimson replied, "Well, I hope you will keep on walking, Mr. President. Keep on walking." Ickes complained that "to declare a total emergency without acts to follow it up means little." Despite Roosevelt's forceful promises to "do everything necessary to defend our own land as well as the other Americas," Ickes observed, ". . . we really are in the same *status quo*."

However eager he may have been to take the country into the war, Roosevelt continued to feel that doing so would be a mistake or a step beyond what the public was ready to support. He saw the country moving "slowly" toward a more resolute response to the fighting, but accepted the judgment of a Morgenthau aide who said: "It would appear to be preferable to have the people push the President into danger than to have them pulled into it by him." He told Churchill that the United States was "frozen in uninformed indecision" with a "fairly large element" of the population "confused by details" and blind to "the simple facts." A poll in late May prepared for the White House showed only 51 percent of the public ready to go to war if Britain seemed to be losing. A British Foreign Office survey concluded that Americans remained eager to stay out of the war and refused to accept that Britain faced a critical situation.

Roosevelt was also discouraged from pressing the case for war by the counsel of his joint chiefs, including Marshall, who did not think the military could be ready for combat until March 1942. "As you know," Stimson told him, "Marshall and I have been troubled by the fear lest we be prematurely dragged into two major operations in the Atlantic . . . with an insufficiency of Atlantic Naval and shipping strength and an insufficient demonstrated superiority of American sea power to hold politics steady in South America." A report from an American Army officer in London, meanwhile, warned against viewing involvement in the war as "a piecemeal affair." Engagement, he said, would mean "throwing everything available at once, military, naval, air, economic, moral — including the kitchen stove, and following this up with everything else as soon as it can be got to working." Roosevelt did not believe Americans were ready for so great a commitment to "total war."

On June 11, when news reached Washington that a German submarine had sunk an unarmed American freighter, the *Robin Moor,* on May 21 in the South Atlantic, a nonwar zone, and set the crew adrift with limited rations, Roosevelt declined to consider it as an incitement. Believing that isolationists would blame the incident on White House provocations of Berlin and condemn any move toward war as an arbitrary presidential action, Roosevelt did not notify Congress of the incident until June 20, nine days after he had learned about it. Although he condemned Germany's "total disregard for the most elementary principles of international law," calling it "outrageous and indefensible," he resisted pressure from Hopkins and others to step up naval action in the Atlantic against hostile forces. Using words like "terrorism," "piracy," and "lawlessness" and describing it as an attempt at intimidation in Germany's campaign to control the Atlantic, Roosevelt echoed the language of his "unlimited emergency" speech, but his rhetoric again did not promise any decisive action. Ickes, who was on the verge of breaking with him over his restraint, privately complained that he "did not have the nerve" to stand up to the Nazi menace. But Roosevelt's reading of the domestic mood and the lack of preparation of the armed services persuaded him that the time was still not favorable for a bold move into war.

Roosevelt's decision not to respond militarily to the freighter's sinking also rested on intelligence that Germany was about to attack Russia. On June 14, Churchill cabled him, "From every source at my disposal . . . it looks as if a vast German onslaught on the Russian frontier is imminent. . . . Should this new war break out we shall of course give all encouragement and any help we can spare to the Russians, following the principle that Hitler is the foe we have to beat. I do not expect any class political reactions here and trust that a German-Russian conflict will not cause you any embarrassment," by which he meant that he hoped anti-Communists in the United States wouldn't stand in the way of helping Russia. In fact, they proved to be an immediate source of opposition. "Are we going to fight to make Europe safe for Communism?" isolationists asked. If we joined the war now, would we be fighting to save democracy? Herbert Hoover wondered. Senator

Harry Truman of Missouri called down a curse on both their houses: Nazis and Communists killing one another was a godsend, though he certainly most wanted to see Hitler's defeat. Catholics as a group were particularly opposed to rescuing godless communism, or so Roosevelt believed.

America's military leaders also opposed sending scarce Lend-Lease equipment to Russia. Influenced by Moscow's unimpressive military performance in the 1939–40 winter war against Finland and by Hitler's quick victory over France, Roosevelt's advisers did not think that Russian resistance could last more than a few of months, if that, and feared that Lend-Lease supplies would then fall into German hands. It would be better, they argued, to use the period of German engagement in Russia to expand U.S. efforts in the Atlantic and send all Lend-Lease weapons to Britain. Germany's rapid advances after its June 22 invasion, with the capture of thousands of Soviet troops, reinforced predictions of a quick Russian defeat.

Advocates of aiding Russia were not without voices in the administration. A Churchill radio talk in which he embraced Russia as an ally and warned that Hitler's attack was "a prelude to an attempted invasion of the British Isles. . . . and the subjugation of the Western Hemisphere" stiffened the resolve of Americans ready to support the cause. Churchill's remark to his private secretary that "If Hitler invaded Hell, I would at least make a favorable reference to the Devil in the House of Commons" became additional encouragement to U.S. interventionists.

Hull and Ickes were disposed toward aiding the

Soviets, and argued that if a good conservative like Churchill could urge all-out aid to Moscow, Americans should be no less prepared to help. Ickes initially complained that Roosevelt was likely to be equivocal about how to respond, waiting to see how public opinion would trend. But to his surprise and satisfaction, on June 24, two days after the German attack, the president told a press conference, "Of course we are going to give all the aid that we possibly can to Russia. We have not yet received any specific list of things." The only qualifier he put on his promise was that aid would take a while to reach the fighting front. Still, he was hedging his bets by refusing to state that the defense of Russia was vital to America's defense. If Russia fell in two or three months, as most military leaders believed, Felix Frankfurter told Roosevelt that the president "would never forgive himself if he gave help on an inadequate scale to the Russian people in throwing back the common Nazi enemy — help that would be timid, tiny, tentative, and tardy." Frankfurter also said that Russian history and literature had taught him "that Russian patriotism — fierce, implacable, avenging — always became a shield and sword against the invader." Roosevelt replied that, "he wished other advisers could state the reasons for the faith within them so clearly." Recalling Napoleon's invasion, which also began on June 22, Roosevelt also hoped that Russian resistance could extend the conflict into November, when winter, Russia's greatest ally, would arrive.

Joseph E. Davies also urged Hopkins and Roosevelt to view the Soviets as capable of standing up to the Nazi assault and predicted that, "the resistance of the Red Army would amaze and surprise the world." The sixty-four-year-old Davies, a wealthy corporate lawyer who had served in the Wilson administration as the first chairman of the Federal Trade Commission and as Roosevelt's ambassador to the Soviet Union from 1936 to 1938, was an uncritical supporter of Stalin's Russia. He had accepted Stalin's explanations of the 1937 purge trials against Soviet military chiefs as gospel, and he advised Roosevelt to join Churchill in aiding Moscow lest Stalin make peace with Hitler and join the war against the democracies. To his surprise, Roosevelt also found backing for helping Russia in public opinion, which rested on a perception of the Russians as another victim of German aggression. Ten days after the German attack, 72 percent of a Gallup poll, including 65 percent of Catholics, said they hoped that Russia would win the war. Like Roosevelt, a majority of Americans judged Nazism to be a far greater menace to the United States than communism; they could imagine a German attack on the United States, but not a Soviet one.

In the first weeks of the fighting, the Germans ran roughshod over the Russian defenders. But by the middle of July, it was becoming clear that however great their losses in men and territory, the Soviets were not about to capitulate. In July, while only 93 of the original 164 Soviet divisions seemed capable of combat, it was double the original German estimate of Soviet fighting strength. "The enemy had been 'decisively weakened,' " the German high command declared, "but by no means 'finally smashed.' " Since the "Soviet reserves of manpower were now seen to be inexhaustible," the conflict was almost certain to last into winter. By August, the German chief of staff acknowledged that "the whole situation makes it increasingly plain that we have underestimated the Russian colossus."

The constant sense of crisis was taking a further toll on Roosevelt's appearance and health. "I hope the Dr. is still being strict with you," Daisy wrote him in June. And when she saw him at Hyde Park on the July 4 weekend, where he "did not look quite as spry" as Daisy wished, she urged him to remember "that you are going to be needed *more & more* with every passing month. *And still* more when the period of reconstruction comes!" She shared his frustration at the isolationists, whom he chided in his Fourth of July address for believing that the United States could "survive as a happy and fertile oasis of liberty surrounded by a cruel desert of dictatorship." Daisy wished he could ease his burdens by moving more decisively to enter the war but told him, "I understand perfectly why you don't. One would like to put a snowplow on the road, & shovel all the objectors, et al, to one side!"

On July 11, less than three weeks after the German invasion of Russia and before it became clear that the Soviets would hold out until winter and beyond, Roosevelt and Hopkins, who was heading the Lend-Lease operation, held a lengthy nighttime discussion about how to balance aid to Britain and Russia and whether Churchill would be receptive to a meeting with the president somewhere at sea. Using a map of the Atlantic torn from a copy of *National Geographic* magazine, Roosevelt outlined a zone to establish a U.S. naval presence that would relieve British naval forces to escort supply ships on the "Murmansk run" to Russia. Hopkins, who had established a trusting relationship with Churchill, was dispatched to London, where he could discuss these issues, but still without making any commitments to involve the United States in the fighting. Roosevelt believed that Churchill would be all too willing to leak any such agreement to the American public, undermining any effort to lead the country into the war.

For twelve days Hopkins conferred with Churchill about the Atlantic battlefront, combat plans for the Middle East, and aid to both Britain and Russia. Although he made no overt pledge of U.S. participation in the fighting, he made clear that Roosevelt wished to do everything in his power to defeat Hitler. On his last night in Britain, he gave a radio talk in which he assured British listeners "that big things were on the way; that substantial help was coming under Lend Lease." He then said, "The President is at one with your Prime Minister in his determination to break the ruthless power of that sinful psychopath in Berlin. . . . People of England, people of the British Commonwealth of Nations — you are not fighting alone." It created the impression, helped by British propaganda, that an inevitable clash of American arms with German naval forces in the Atlantic would bring the United States into the war.

Because the administration had so little information about Soviet supply needs and the state of the war on the Russian front, Hopkins proposed that he travel to Moscow to confer with Stalin. Roosevelt promptly replied that he and Welles "highly approve Moscow trip" and instructed Hopkins to inform Stalin that he had come to Moscow to learn how the United States could meet Russia's "most urgent requirements." Although "he was dog-tired" and acknowledged that he had "a touch of 'grippe,' " Hopkins prepared for the trip with Churchill's blessing. When he asked Churchill if he had any message for Stalin, the prime minister replied: "Tell him, tell him that Britain has but one ambition today, but one desire — to crush Hitler. Tell him that he can depend on us."

Taking off from Scotland on July 27 in bad weather on a seaplane, Hopkins braved the conditions of combat flying sitting in the rear gunner's position through much of the twenty-one-hour trip, snatching a few hours sleep on a canvas stretcher. Ignoring the personal discomfort and arctic cold, he landed in Archangel, where American embassy officials and Russian military personnel greeted him. After an elaborate four-hour dinner with his Russian hosts, Hopkins took a four-hour flight to Moscow. He marveled at the vast stretches of forest, which he believed would impede a Nazi conquest. In Moscow, he was able to get a night's sleep and took a tour of the city the following day before heading to the Kremlin for an evening meeting with Stalin. Two three-hour conversations with Stalin over the next two days gave Hopkins a chance to take the measure of the Soviet leader, whom he described as "an austere, rugged, determined figure in boots that shone like mirrors, stout baggy trousers, and snug-fitting blouse. He wore no ornaments, military or civilian. He's built close to the ground, like a football coach's dream of a tackle. He's about five feet six, about a hundred and ninety pounds. His hands are huge, as hard as his mind. His voice is harsh," possibly as a result of his chain smoking. Hopkins had no doubt that he was an absolute dictator whose subordinates lived in "awful fear" of him.

Stalin hid from Hopkins the terrible losses in men and equipment his forces were suffering, and showed no signs of the depression that had silenced him for eleven days after his failure to heed warnings from several sources that the Nazis were about to attack. He put on a confident face, predicting that his armies would withstand the German onslaught. At the same time, however, he spoke with a sense of urgency about the need for a variety of military supplies to help overcome the enemy. He acknowledged that Britain and Russia alone could not defeat Hitler's powerful military machine, and that a path to victory necessitated that the United States "come to grips with Hitler on some battlefield." He even went so far as to make the astonishing proposal that America send an army commanded by its own generals to fight on the Russian front. He also predicted that America's entrance into the war would demoralize and possibly even lead to a quick surrender by the Germans.

Whether Hopkins saw through Stalin's reasonable geniality to the ruthless brutality that had marked his years of rule was not a topic either Hopkins or Roosevelt was inclined to dwell on. When the military attaché at the U.S. embassy urged Hopkins not to trust anything Stalin said and advised him to demand specific information about the state of Soviet capacity to meet the Nazi offensive before making commitments to send Lend-Lease supplies, Hopkins replied, "I don't care to discuss the subject further." Hopkins saw himself as in Moscow to offer help, not to inflame Soviet suspicions about American motives.

At a cabinet meeting on August 1, having been informed by Hopkins by cable about Stalin's determination to combat Hitler and his supply needs, Roosevelt raised hell with the State and War departments about their failure to get munitions on their way to Russia. Ickes described it as "one of the most complete dressing downs that I have witnessed." Roosevelt complained that after five weeks of fighting nothing had "started forward" and suspected that their "run-around" reflected their anti-communist bias or their conviction that the Soviets were doomed to defeat. The tie up was in the Lend-Lease agency. The next day, he wrote a Lend-Lease administrator: "Please get out the list and please, with my full authority use a heavy hand — act as a burr under the saddle and get things moving. . . . Step on it!" Morgenthau, who was trying to facilitate the president's directive, said, "They have just got to get this stuff and get it fast. . . . because this is the time to get Hitler. We will never have a better chance."

Hopkins's return to Scotland was an even rougher flight. Though he was "desperately ill" and despite terrible turbulence from powerful headwinds, he made it back in time to join Churchill on the battleship *Prince of Wales* for the Atlantic crossing and a Churchill-Roosevelt summit off Newfoundland. On the ship Hopkins "was given blood transfusions and sedated by the ship's doctors. He slept for the next eighteen hours." As Churchill began his journey, he cabled the president, "Hopkins returned dead beat from Russia but is lively again now. We shall get him in fine trim on voyage. We are just off. It is 27 years ago today that the Huns began their last war. We all must make good job of it this time. Twice ought to be enough. Look forward so much to our meeting."

On August 3, Roosevelt left Washington by train for New London, Connecticut, where he was to board the yacht *Potomac* for a ten-day fishing holiday, or so the press was informed. It was actually a cover story for the president's voyage on the USS cruiser *Augustus* to his meeting with Churchill in Placentia Bay off Newfoundland in Canadian waters. Public knowledge of the president's fatigue after so many years in office, and of his distress over Missy LeHand's immobilizing illness, rendered the need for a holiday plausible. The cloak-and-dagger evasion of the prying eyes of the media and the prospect of meeting and conferring with Churchill buoyed Roosevelt, and a lookalike posted on the deck of the *Potomac* as he departed on the *Augustus* especially delighted him. "Even at my ripe old age I feel a thrill in making a getaway — especially from the American press," he wrote Daisy, the one person with whom he felt free to share his secret journey. Roosevelt had hidden the true nature of the trip even from Eleanor and his mother. He justified the outing to Sara by explaining that he was "feeling really well and the progress of the war is more conducive to my peace of mind."

For his part Churchill also enjoyed the subterfuge. He was about to meet the man he believed held the key to British success in the war, and they were engaged in history-making events on a world stage. "Am looking forward enormously to our talks, which may be of service to the future," Churchill had written him in July. On his trip across the Atlantic, Churchill had tried to size up the president from details he garnered from Hopkins. "You'd have thought Winston was being carried up into the heavens to meet God!" Hopkins later told friends. Hopkins worried that the two prima donnas would not get along and would step on each other's lines. But even these outsize personalities understood that the very survival of democracy was at stake, and that it was essential to contain their egos. At the first meeting in London with Hopkins, Churchill had already demonstrated his regard for Roosevelt, praising him as the soul of "resistance to aggression and oppression and . . . [the] undoubted champion of justice and of freedom, and of the victims of wrongdoing wherever they may dwell." As head of state, Roosevelt also outranked Churchill, who was only head of government. It was the sort of detail that mattered to the conservative Churchill.

All the overt details of the meeting, which famously became known later as the Atlantic Conference, bespoke cooperation and collaboration between Britain and the United States. On Saturday morning, August 9, Churchill came aboard the *Augustus,* where he approached the president, who was standing on the ship's upper deck with his son Elliott, on whose arm he leaned for support. While a British ensemble on the *Prince of Wales* serenaded both ships' complements with strains of "Stars and Stripes Forever," the Americans welcomed the prime minister with the familiar "God Save the King." "At last we have gotten together," a smiling president declared. An equally buoyant Churchill responded, "Yes, we have," and handed Roosevelt a letter of greeting from the king. Joined by Hopkins, the two leaders went off to lunch, where they could engage in un-monitored discussion reflecting their respective goals for the meeting. "He is a tremendously vital person," Roosevelt later wrote Daisy about Churchill. ". . . I like him — & lunching alone broke the ice both ways."

While overt cordiality was the principal public impression conveyed by the two men, each had a grand design he hoped to advance. Churchill's highest priorities were cementing arrangements for aid from the Americans and drawing them ever closer to involvement in the war. For Roosevelt, a joint declaration on war aims that would quiet isolationist rumblings about secret agreements to involve the United States in the conflict to rescue Britain's Empire was essential to the management of America's divisive politics. He wanted a state-ment explicitly denying any commitments other than what Congress had authorized under the Lend-Lease law. He wanted it made clear that he and the prime minister "had discussed certain principles relating to the civilization of the world and had agreed on a statement of them." Churchill cabled his War Cabinet that the president attached great "importance to the Joint Declaration, which he believes will affect the whole movement of United States opinion."

A presentation by Churchill on current condi-tions at the fighting fronts to the respective staffs after an evening dinner on the *Augustus* served the optics. "I held the official dinner, 16 of us — very grand — in my cabin," Roosevelt told Daisy. "Then I asked him [Churchill] to sum up the war," which was followed by briefings from the British military chiefs. Churchill performed up to expectations, chewing on a cigar, "slashing the air

667

with his hands," reporting on the battles in North Africa, across the Middle East and the Mediterranean, in the Atlantic, and in Russia, about whose capacity to withstand the Nazi assault he expressed doubts. Despite his reservations, he and Roosevelt agreed to aid the Russians as fully as possible and to discuss Russia's long-term needs at a meeting with Stalin. Churchill above all emphasized Britain's resiliency in fighting Hitler, and the importance of U.S. intervention to achieve victory. He later reported to his War Cabinet that Roosevelt had promised to "wage war but not declare it," while becoming "more and more provocative." For the moment, the president believed that a request to Congress for a declaration of war — in 1941 it would have been inconceivable to fight without such approval — would only result in a demoralizing three-month debate. Churchill thought that Roosevelt expected an "incident" in the Atlantic, like the sinking of the *Lusitania* before U.S. involvement in World War I, would eventually bring America into the fighting.

Roosevelt hoped that when news of the shipboard meeting was made public, followed by a joint declaration of principles, it would encourage Americans to join Britain in fighting Germany. In fact, the conference ultimately had more of an impact on him personally than it did on popular feeling in the United States in deepening a commitment to destroy Hitler's Reich. Aside from the conversations about supplying Britain and Russia and what contributions U.S. naval forces could make in the battle of the Atlantic, nothing resonated so powerfully with Roosevelt and Churchill as a Sunday morning religious service on the quarterdeck of the *Prince of Wales.*

Ferried to the British ship by an American destroyer, the president was hoisted on board and walked the length of the vessel to a place alongside Churchill. Three hundred American sailors and Marines along with the British crew watched as the president, displaying "great courage and strength of character," propelled his lifeless legs across the ship's deck. British and American chaplains read the prayers, and everyone onboard, including the prime minister and president, joined in singing three hymns chosen by Churchill. It was "a deeply moving expression of the unity of faith of our two peoples," Churchill recalled, "and none who took part in it will forget the spectacle presented that sunlit morning . . . the symbolism of the Union Jack and the Stars and Stripes draped side by side on the pulpit . . . and the close packed ranks of British and American sailors, completely intermingled, sharing the same books and joining fervently together in the prayers and hymns familiar to both. . . . Every word seemed to stir the heart. It was a great hour to live. Nearly half those who sang were soon to die." Roosevelt told Daisy, "I so wish you could have been at the Church service . . . how easy it is really to do big things if you can get an hour off!"

Roosevelt's top priority was formulating a declaration of shared principles that he hoped would make war more palatable to Americans. The final document they agreed to release at the end of the conference required some spirited negotiations. Roosevelt wanted it to avoid revealing the existence of any future commitments they made, but Churchill convinced him that doing so would give comfort to Hitler and "would be a source of profound discouragement to the neutrals and the vanquished." Roosevelt agreed to empha-size providing aid to the democracies instead. Understanding that the president would be greatly distressed at the failure to issue a joint statement, Churchill signed off on an eight-part declaration they dubbed "The Atlantic Charter." In brief, it was an updated statement of the ideals Woodrow Wilson had proposed at the end of World War I: self-determination, democratically elected govern-ments, free speech, free trade among nations, freedom of the seas, reduced armaments, "the final destruction of the Nazi tyranny," and a last-ing peace facilitated by collective security. While it seemed calculated to strike resonant chords with most Americans, it also promised to agitate isolationists, who were bound to view it not only as a declaration of war on Germany but as a com-mitment to join a postwar community of nations in preserving the peace.

As Roosevelt returned to Washington, he wrote Daisy, "So end these four days that I feel have contributed to things we hold dear." While com-ing back produced "a bit of a let-down!" he acknowledged that "the afterthoughts are good & we hope the country will approve." But the initial reception of the two leaders' summit angered him: "The radio talks & talks of the conference & the commentators are mostly very silly or very menda-cious! Why can't they stick to the facts?" he rhetorically asked Daisy. As he prepared to get on a train to Washington, he complained: "I fear that 50 news hawks will meet us. That part will be harder than the conference itself."

During a press conference on the *Potomac* on August 16 and then in Washington on August 19, he tried to persuade the press to put a positive face on his meeting with Churchill. He recounted how all the officers and enlisted men who attended the religious gathering on the *Prince of Wales* "felt that it was one of the great historic services. I know I did." But Roosevelt's attempt to share the spirit of that occasion fell flat. "Are we any closer to entering the war?" the reporters wanted to know. "No!" Roosevelt emphatically replied. He emphasized how much his discussions with Churchill clarified the horrors of a world under Nazi control, and described a parallel between Lincoln's observation in 1862 and the present that "This country hadn't yet waked up to the fact that they had a war to win." He chided the press to distinguish between the larger issues facing the country and the "tawdry accompaniment of cheap journalism." He quoted a letter from Felix Frankfurter, who had written him: "Somewhere in the Atlantic you *did* make history for the world. And like all truly great historic events, it wasn't what was said or done that defined the scope of the achievement. It's always the forces — the impalpable, the spiritual forces, the hopes, the purposes, the dreams and the endeavors — that are released that matter. . . . You two in that ocean, freed from all the tawdry accompaniments of cheap journalism . . . give meaning to the conflict between civilization and arrogant brute challenge." Frankfurter ended with an expression of hope that the meeting would "kindle actions toward . . . ridding the world of this [Nazi] horror."

While the conference and the Atlantic Charter did not diminish Roosevelt's popularity, which stood at 73 percent in August, they simply hardened familiar battle lines: interventionists applauded the president's initiative with Churchill in defining the larger stakes at risk in the war, and isolationists cautioned against likely secret commitments that would lead to American engagement. Still 74 percent of Americans opposed taking part in the conflict, and the antiwar sentiment had found solid support in Congress, where an argument over extending the one-year draft had sharply divided senators and representatives. It reflected the mood in the country, where only 50 percent of a poll said that the troops should serve for another eighteen months and 45 percent said they should be released. As significant, 50 percent in another poll opposed changing the draft law to let the men serve outside the Western Hemisphere, while only 27 percent approved. The troops themselves had grown restive, going so far as to threaten to desert in October when their terms of service were up. Reporters described a piece of graffiti that appeared on barracks' latrine walls: "OHIO," Over the Hill in October. When the extension passed in the Senate with only 45 members voting yes and 25 absenting themselves, and then by a one-vote margin in the House, 203 to 202, Roosevelt told the press, "A lot of people . . . haven't waked up to the danger, a great many people."

A host of problems awaited Roosevelt upon his return to Washington — above all, how to expedite the delivery of supplies to Britain and Russia and unify American opinion behind the use of American air and naval power against the Axis. The vote in Congress on extending draftees' service made him more cautious than ever about rushing into war. He did not believe that Congress always reflected popular opinion, but he knew he couldn't ignore it if he was to avoid domestic struggles over the sacrifice of blood and treasure, however eager Americans might be to see Hitler defeated. At the same time, his public declarations of determination to keep the country at peace had strained relations with Churchill. On August 29, the prime minister wrote Hopkins that the president's antiwar pronouncements had caused "a wave of depression in England. If 1942 opens with Russia knocked out and Britain left alone again, all kinds of dangers may arise." Hopkins advised Roosevelt that if the British concluded that America would not get into the war, "the British appeasers might have some influence on Churchill."

To counter Churchill's disappointment, Roosevelt declared in a Labor Day speech that the United States was making every effort to produce unprecedented amounts of war matériel. "Why are we determined to devote our entire industrial effort to the prosecution of a war which has not yet actually touched our own shores?" he asked. Because, he answered, "I know that I speak the conscience and determination of the American people when I say that we shall do everything in our power to crush Hitler and his Nazi forces."

A further test of Roosevelt's political skill and the national will came quickly on September 4, when a German U-boat attacked the American destroyer *Greer* patrolling waters off of Iceland, where U.S. troops had taken up stations to ensure against a German occupation. "At last," historian James MacGregor Burns wrote, "Roosevelt had his incident. [But] it was not much of an incident" and was no different from the earlier sinking of the *Robin Moor*. The attack had in fact been a consequence of the destroyer's tracking of the U-boat for a British patrol plane.

With Churchill warning that the Soviets "might be thinking of separate terms," Roosevelt instructed Stimson and Knox to give all possible aid to Russia. He also told Churchill of his plan to give a radio address in response to the *Greer* attack that would "make perfectly clear the action we intend to take in the Atlantic."

The death on September 7 of his mother, who passed away at the estate in Hyde Park two weeks before her eighty-seventh birthday, delayed Franklin's address until September 11. Wearing a black mourning armband, he carried on with characteristic statesmanship, keeping his personal loss separate from the needs of the nation. But his mother's passing had deeply distressed him. When he spent part of an afternoon sorting through her closets and drawers with the help of his secretary Grace Tully, he dissolved in tears when he found a box in which she had stored his childhood clothes and gifts he had given her. His stoic performance also masked the continuing decline in his health, which registered in higher blood pressure readings and the evident strain witnessed by those closest to him. "What 'headaches' you are having," Daisy soon wrote him. "I wish I could help — you know I do, with thoughts and understanding." Mindful of the pain of his loss, Eleanor reached out to console him, showing him more affection than at any other time her children could recall.

In his Fireside Chat on September 11, Roosevelt falsely asserted that the *Greer* had been the target of an unprovoked U-boat attack. Despite "what any obstructionist American organization may prefer to believe," he said, the assault had come "without warning and with deliberate design to sink her." It was an act of "piracy" and "international lawlessness" by what he called "rattlesnakes of the Atlantic." It was one of a series of attacks on American ships aimed at ending freedom of the seas, and was part of a larger plot to take control of the Western Hemisphere. "For Hitler's advance guards — not only his avowed agents but also his dupes among us — have sought to [establish] bridgeheads in the New World." While the United States did not seek to engage in a shooting war with Hitler, the time had come for "active defense." Axis ships would now enter our defensive waters "at their own peril." In short, the American Navy was now ordered to convoy supplies to Britain and to shoot on sight German submarines and warships of any kind that threatened American and other friendly ships.

If Roosevelt's version of the attack and his warning of the threats of Nazi subversion aimed to strengthen public determination to confront Hitler's Germany, it also gave implicit justification to secret countermeasures that he had already undertaken. Because the Nazis had no regard for traditional civil liberties, Roosevelt believed that he had to meet this threat with every resource at his command. In 1940, he had directed the Federal Bureau of Investigation (FBI) to use wiretaps, mail surveillance, and the infiltration of organizations suspected of espionage and other Fifth Column activities. The FBI was also instructed to gather information on "the attitude of Congressional groups [critical] toward the President's international relations or foreign policy." With a national emergency facing the country, he had no qualms about dispensing with traditional strictures against executive overreach.

In July 1941, Roosevelt had established the office of the Coordinator of Information (COI), headed by the fifty-eight-year-old Donovan, the highly decorated World War I hero and prominent New York attorney who had traveled to Britain, the Balkans, and the Middle East in 1940–41 to assess conditions and recommend actions to the president. The COI was a counterpart to the British Security Coordination (BSC), an information-gathering agency in the United States headed by forty-four-year-old William Stephenson, a British spy-master, who operated under the codename of Intrepid. Part of his mission was to promote anti-Nazi sentiment in the United States and help bring America into the war. Both the COI and BSC were charged with "planning covert activities against the Axis throughout the world."

With the draft law renewed and the production of ships, planes, and tanks reaching new levels under what the administration dubbed a "victory program," Roosevelt, along with Harry Hopkins, as well as millionaire businessman W. Averell Harriman, whom Roosevelt had sent to London and Moscow to coordinate plans for aiding Britain and Russia, believed it was now time to send U.S. air and naval forces into combat. While there was little question that a majority of Americans now believed it more important to defeat Hitler than to avoid involvement in the war, a Gallup poll conducted in early November revealed that 63 percent opposed a congressional declaration of war on Germany; 69 percent of Americans were still confident that England would win the war.

Given public opinion, Roosevelt believed that

incremental steps toward involving America were a wiser course. In October, he asked Congress to revise the neutrality law to allow the arming of all U.S. ships. Public opinion was highly supportive of enabling American transports to defend themselves, but when asked if the vessels should be permitted to carry war materials to Britain, there was a clear division: 46 percent said yes, and 40 percent said no. A conversation with congressional leaders convinced Roosevelt that "it would be disastrous" to neutrality revision "if one of our transport proceeding to or from Britain . . . were to be sunk, when manned by U.S. Navy officers and men." However, in October, when a U-boat torpedoed the USS destroyer *Kearney,* public approval for allowing U.S. merchant ships to carry Lend-Lease supplies to Britain jumped to 61 percent.

Roosevelt took to the airwaves again on Navy Day, October 27, to underscore what was at stake in the growing tensions with Hitler's Germany. He recounted the killing of eleven sailors aboard the *Kearney* and hoped to alarm Americans by revealing that he had come into possession of a secret document "made in Germany by Hitler's government." It was alleged to contain Nazi plans to seize the republics of Central and South America and turn them into vassal states. The plan included an assault on the United States and a program "to abolish all existing religions." Although no such German document actually existed, or was even the product of British machinations, Roosevelt's claims about them met with Churchill's approval, which he expressed in a cable: "Deeply moved by your wonderful speech." The *Kearney* attack and Roosevelt's speech, however, were still not sufficient to end the congressional debate on neutrality revision. If anything, they deepened the divide rather than provided support for the neutrality revision, as did another more decisive attack in the Atlantic on October 31: the sinking of the USS destroyer *Reuben James,* with the loss of 115 lives. The law was finally passed in November, when the Senate approved the bill by 3 votes and the House by an 18-vote margin.

When the America First chairman challenged him to ask Congress for a declaration of war, however, Roosevelt refused, convinced, as were the isolationists, that he would suffer a "certain and disastrous defeat." Ickes, like other interventionists, thought his caution at this juncture a terrible mistake. "The President is going to wait," he wrote, "God knows for how long or for what." But Roosevelt judged isolationist sentiment to be "more strident . . . and aggressive" than ever and felt "relatively powerless to combat it." He still believed that only a more overt and substantial attack would unify the nation into agreeing to war.

To Roosevelt's surprise, the decisive blow would come in the Pacific. Since 1939, he had tried to avoid a war with Japan, which could distract Britain and the United States from defeating Hitler. He had largely turned discussions with Tokyo over to Hull and had resisted pressure from Stimson, Ickes, and Morgenthau to threaten the Japanese with sanctions in response to their aggression in China and their ties to the Axis. On July 1, 1941, he had told Ickes that "the Japs are having a real drag-down and knock-out fight among themselves and have been for the past week trying to decide which way they are going to jump — attack Russia, attack the South Seas (thus throw in their lot definitely with Germany), or whether they will sit on the fence or be more friendly with us. No one knows what the decision will be but, as you know, it is terribly important for the control of the Atlantic for us to help keep the peace in the Pacific. I simply have not got enough Navy to go round — and every little episode in the Pacific means fewer ships in the Atlantic."

Roosevelt's cabinet hawks did not believe that sanctions would lead to a larger conflict but were convinced that a hard line would inhibit Japanese aggression. Moreover, they saw public opinion on their side. In July 1939, a slight majority of Americans favored an embargo on "all shipments of war materials" to Japan. The following month, when Roosevelt canceled the 1911 Trade Treaty with Tokyo, 81 percent of Americans approved. By January 75 percent opposed the sale of any arms or commodities to Tokyo and by October, the number had reached 90 percent. Early in the New Year, the country was divided over whether to risk war with Japan by opposing its possible seizure of the Dutch East Indies and Singapore, where it could obtain embargoed resources. After the Japanese expanded into Indochina in July, however, 70 percent of a survey favored opposition to additional Japanese conquests, even at the risk of war.

At the end of July 1941, when Tokyo occupied French Indochina with 40,000 troops, Roosevelt felt compelled to embargo high-octane aviation fuel to Japan but declined to close off all oil shipments, explaining that he didn't want "to draw the noose tight. He thought that it might be better to slip the noose around Japan's neck and give it a jerk now and then." Still convinced that it would do more to constrain Japan than provoke it, Ickes favored "a complete job as quickly as possible." The most Roosevelt would agree to was to warn Japanese ambassador Kichisaburo Nomura against Japan's seizure of Dutch East Indies oil wells and to urge withdrawal from Indochina. He promised that the United States would then help neutralize the region, turning it into a kind of Switzerland. He described it to Churchill as an "effort to avoid Japanese expansion to South Pacific," but like Roosevelt's cabinet hawks, Churchill thought it an insufficient gesture. Consequently, at the Atlantic Conference, Churchill, who feared Britain might also be left to fight Japan alone, pressed Roosevelt to join him in strongly warning Tokyo against additional aggression. Still concerned to buy time before a conflict erupted in the Pacific, Roosevelt resisted Churchill's pressure.

On August 17, Roosevelt embraced a Japanese proposal for a possible rapprochement. Prime Minister Fumimaro Konoye suggested a conference with the president in Hawaii, which Roosevelt interpreted as signaling a Japanese plan to strike at Russia rather than expanding to the south and risking war with the United States and Britain. He told Nomura that he would consider a meeting in Juneau, Alaska, in mid-October if Japan would "suspend its expansionist activities." He had little expectation of a positive response, but conversations at least served the purpose of delaying a conflict while he strengthened America's Pacific defenses, including sending new B-17 heavy bombers to the Philippines.

680

The stalling tactics, however, seemed to come to naught in mid-October, when Japanese general Eiki Tojo replaced Konoye as premier. His ascension convinced Roosevelt that Tokyo now was preparing to fight the United States. Churchill counseled: "The stronger the action of the United States towards Japan, the greater the chance of preserving peace." On November 5, Churchill added that the policy of "gaining time . . . has been brilliantly successful so far. But our joint embargo is forcing the Japanese to decisions for peace or war." Churchill urged issuing warnings to Tokyo against attacks that could close the Burma Road, a supply route for China, and predicted that Japan seemed "more likely to drift into war than to plunge in."

But Roosevelt remained resistant to any provocation that might trigger an attack. When Hopkins remarked that it was a shame that America could not strike the first blow, Roosevelt exclaimed, "No, we can't do that. We are a democracy and a peaceful people." In late November, discussions with Tokyo about a modus vivendi gave some slight hope that a war might be avoided or further delayed. But as Roosevelt confided to Churchill, "I am not very hopeful and we must all be prepared for real trouble, possibly soon." The public shared the president's concern. Between November 27 and December 1, when the Gallup Poll asked a cross section of Americans whether the United States would be at war with Japan in the near future, 52 percent said yes and only 27 percent said no. Always mindful of the need for an unqualified consensus, Roosevelt hoped that if war did come, U.S. opinion would unequivocally hold Tokyo responsible. Because a majority of opinion continued to "hope that war might be avoided," Roosevelt remained doubtful about commanding national support for either a Pacific or an Atlantic war.

On December 7, the Japanese ended Roosevelt's dilemma when they bombed Pearl Harbor. His declaration of war the following day famously characterized the surprise assault as "a date which will live in infamy." Isolationists, however, clung to their belief in America's insularity from a foreign attack by arguing that Roosevelt had engineered Pearl Harbor as a back door to the European war. There is no doubt that the attack relieved Roosevelt of a terrible burden of decision. "I think the boss must have a great load off his mind," Frank Knox told Frances Perkins. "I thought the load on his mind was just going to kill him, going to break him down."

Even granting Roosevelt's talent for dramatic gestures it is undeniable that the Japanese offensive, which took more than 2,400 American lives and destroyed a substantial part of the country's Pacific fleet and air forces, genuinely shocked and appalled him, and he was sickened by photos of slain U.S. servicemen and burning ships. At a meeting with congressional leaders, Texas senator Tom Connally voiced everyone's incredulity as he "shouted, banging the desk with his fist, his face purple" with rage: "How did it happen that our warships were caught like lame ducks in Pearl Harbor?" When Roosevelt spoke to his cabinet, he "could hardly bring himself to describe the devastation." According to Perkins, he was "having actual physical difficulty in getting out the words that put him on record as knowing that the Navy was caught unawares. . . . [He] was having a dreadful time just accepting the idea." As the shock of the extent of the tragedy set in, a mood of "solemnity and anger" descended on Roosevelt and the cabinet. The president was shaken and gray with anxiety and fatigue. The Navy, *his* Navy, for which he had special affection, had been struck a grievous blow. Although the three aircraft carriers stationed at Pearl were at sea on maneuvers and escaped the destruction suffered by the ships, including eight battleships, in the harbor, Roosevelt would hardly have left so much of the fleet vulnerable to attack if he knew a raid was coming.

Proponents of the theory of Roosevelt's duplicity in fostering the surprise attack to force America into the war use as evidence the existence of Operation Magic: the U.S. ability to read Japanese cables that pointed to an attack on Pearl Harbor. But as Roberta Wohlstetter, the most astute analyst of the surprise attack, argued in 1962, indications of a Pearl Harbor strike were buried in a body of "noise" that also suggested the Japanese were contemplating attacks on Russia, Hong Kong, Singapore, the Philippines, the East Indies, and Indochina. Moreover, Hawaii seemed the least likely place for Japan to strike. When the news arrived on December 7, Harry Hopkins exclaimed, "Surely, the Japanese would not attack Honolulu!" while Navy Secretary Knox said, "My God! This can't be true, this must mean the Philippines." Where American chiefs saw the U.S. fleet at Pearl Harbor as a deterrent to Japanese aggression, Tokyo considered it an inviting target. In addition, U.S. naval intelligence had erroneously estimated that Japanese planes would need to be at least 300 miles from Hawaii to be capable of launching an attack, a distance at which they would surely be detected, and that their torpedoes could not be effective in the shallow depths of Pearl Harbor. U.S. analysts were not aware of the fact that the engines on the carrier planes and the torpedoes had been altered to give the aircraft a 500-mile range and the torpedoes the capacity to be effective against the warships anchored in shallow waters.

When Churchill received the news, he could hardly contain his pleasure — not at the losses suffered by the Americans, of course, but at the prospect of now having so formidable an ally. While Lend-Lease and the Atlantic patrols had been a godsend, the full weight of 130 million Americans, bolstered by their vast industrial capacity and fighting force, gave Churchill "the greatest joy. The United States was in the war, up to its neck and in to the death. So we had won after all. . . . England would live; Britain would live; the Commonwealth of Nations and the Empire would live. . . . Many disasters, immeasurable cost and tribulation lay ahead, but there was no more doubt about the end. . . . Being saturated and satiated with emotion and sensation, I went to bed and slept the sleep of the saved and the thankful."

Before Churchill could take full satisfaction from the Pacific fighting, however, he had to see formal declarations of war between Germany and Italy and the United States. Although Roosevelt had every expectation of joining Britain and Russia in fighting Hitler and Mussolini, he remained reluctant to make the first move. He believed that initiating U.S. participation in the European conflict would be met with isolationist insistence that he had facilitated the Japanese attack as an incentive to take part in the wider war. To his relief, Magic intercepts revealed that Hitler would formalize what he suspected was already the case — namely, a declaration of war against the United States on December 11. "A great power doesn't let itself have war declared on it, it declares war itself," Ribbentrop said, echoing Hitler. Convinced that an isolationist America would lack the will to fight and confident that it would mean a decline in U.S. ability to supply Britain while it fought in the Pacific, Hitler issued a scathing attack on Roosevelt as a tool of American Jews. "We can't lose the war," Hitler declared. "We now have an ally which has never been conquered in 3,000 years."

But Japan's Admiral Isoroku Yamamoto, who had planned the Pearl Harbor attack, did not have Hitler's confidence. Mindful of America's vast "industrial might and matchless resources" from years spent living in the United States as a student and a diplomat, he did not believe that Japan could fight a successful naval war with the Americans or ultimately defeat them in a long, drawn-out conflict. Only an early decisive blow might succeed, and without that, he shared Churchill's conviction that "silly people . . . might discount the force of the United States." But they ignored the fact that America was like "a gigantic boiler. Once the fire is lighted under it, there is no limit to the power it can generate."

CHAPTER 15
SETBACKS AND LOSSES:
"WE MIGHT LOSE THIS WAR"

For the second time in a generation, nations across the globe now found themselves engaged in what their governments described as a life-and-death struggle. Across Europe, the Americas, and Asia, productive energies were devoted to the building and deployment of arms and armies. Each side saw itself taking part in a titanic struggle for survival. No one doubted that a loss would mean the end of the defeated party's way of life. Either democracy in the United States and Western Europe and communism in Russia, or Nazism, fascism, and Japanese militarism would shape the future. Few, if any, could imagine a peaceful compromise. This was a total war, and leaders on both sides warned to expect nothing less than annihilation should they fail to achieve victory. After the Atlantic Conference, Roosevelt had described the stakes in the conflict as America's traditional freedoms; two days after Pearl Harbor, he told the country that it was "fighting for its existence and future life." Tojo's government cautioned the Japanese of the threat of extermination by white America; Stalin urged sacrifices to save not communism but mother Russia; Hitler predicted that losing the war would mean the destruction of Germany at the hands of the Jews, who he claimed had caused both world wars. Such apocalyptic warnings motivated every belligerent to fight to the death.

All sides characterized their opponents as less than human and unworthy of mercy. The Germans and the Japanese were foremost in using racial inferiority as a rationale for killing and subjugating their enemies, whether from Britain, the United States, Russia, China, the Philippines, or the East Indies. They were opponents of the civilized standards the Nazis and Tokyo claimed to represent. Hitler described America as "a decayed country. . . . Everything about the behavior of American society reveals that it's half Judaised, and the other half negrified. How can one expect a state like that to hold together . . . ?" Japanese propaganda warned their forces against surrendering to U.S. Marines, who were merciless, as demonstrated by Japanese claims that membership in the Corps rested on a requirement to kill their parents.

American contempt for the Japanese, or the "Japs," as they were universally known in America during the war, was reflected in characterizations of them as "yellow rats" or "vermin" who were "uncommonly treacherous and savage." If they were indeed human, they were in a state of arrested development, best thought of as "monkey men." Their 1937 "Rape of Nanking," in which thousands of Chinese were brutalized and killed, and their deviousness in pretending to negotiate with American diplomats while launching the attack on Pearl Harbor, illustrated their total disregard for any sort of civilized standard. Fighting Japan quickly became a crusade, "a holy war" to preserve enlightened Western standards against a barbaric people who engaged in subhuman behavior.

No group or collective was at greater risk in the war from racial stereotyping and hatred than Europe's 8.8 million Jews. Hitler's Nuremberg laws discriminated against them in ways that made it difficult for them to remain productive members of the economy. *Kristallnacht,* the nationwide attack on Jewish establishments, and Nazi propaganda blaming Jews for everything from defeat in the First World War to the victory of Bolshevism in Russia, made clear the plight of Germany's Jews, which extended to Jews across Europe as Hitler's armies conquered Poland, Denmark, Norway, Belgium, Holland, France, and parts of Soviet Russia. Anyone who took Hitler's anti-Semitic rhetoric seriously could not doubt his determination to rid Europe of its Jews. More than once he publicly declared that "the war can only end either with the extermination of the Aryan peoples or the disappearance of Jewry from Europe." On December 12, the day after he had declared war on the United States, Hitler "prophesied that, if they [the Jews] brought about another world war, they would experience their annihilation. . . . The world war is there. The annihilation must be the necessary consequence."

In the fall of 1940, a German Jewish physician who had been sent to a concentration camp in France managed to get a written description of its conditions to someone in the United States, who then passed it along to Eleanor Roosevelt. "Thirteen thousand refugees were living 'like criminals behind barbed wire in dark, cold, wet unhealthy barracks without beds, table or chair,' " he reported and, recounting how people were rapidly dying, declared, "For us here there only exists one solution, the quick emigration from Europe. All our appeals in that respect have been in vain so far. If the United States continues to work so slowly the number of dead here is going to increase in a most deplorable manner."

Eleanor passed the letter along to Franklin, who never replied. When Eleanor told him that the pleas for access to America were turned aside by Breckinridge Long, she described him as "a fascist." "You must not say that," Franklin told her. "But he is," she insisted. She had little hope of persuading Franklin to press Congress for changes in immigration limits, as he was then in the midst of his third-term campaign, the battle to win congressional approval for Lend-Lease, and the struggle to win passage of neutrality revision, and was unwilling to fight what he believed would be a losing political cause. In any case, he shared concerns that Long had put before him about Nazi saboteurs and Fifth Columnists lurking among the potential migrants.

In January 1942, in a conference at Wannsee, a Berlin suburb, the Nazis committed themselves to an extermination program against Jews everywhere, the "Final Solution of the Jewish question," as they called it. Although Reinhard Heydrich and Adolf Eichmann, Nazi functionaries, would be the principal implementers of the agenda, the architect of the plan was Hitler himself. "Complicity" in the program, Kershaw writes, "was massive, from the Wehrmacht leadership and captains of industry down to Party hacks, bureaucratic minions, and ordinary Germans hoping for their own material advantage through the persecution." But while "Hitler's role . . . had often been indirect, rather than overt" and "consisted of authorizing rather than directing . . . there can be no doubt about it: Hitler's role had been decisive and indispensable in the road to the Final Solution." The Nazi commitment to exterminating the Jewish people was a goal as powerful as any among Hitler's war aims. Once the Nazis began implementing what would later become known as the Holocaust, the chances of escape for Jews from Europe to a safe haven in the United States were almost nonexistent. Had immigration laws been relaxed before 1941, certainly more could have found their way to America.

While the Nazis were plotting the extermination of European Jewry, Roosevelt was primarily focused on determining how best to fight the war. The public was so angry at Japan for the surprise attack and so eager to retaliate that a Pacific-first campaign would have won almost universal support. But Roosevelt, who had a keen understanding of international power, believed that the quickest way to win the war with the smallest sacrifice in blood and treasure would be to defeat Hitler and Mussolini before turning the full power of the United States and Britain against Japan. With the isolationist press clamoring for an all-out effort against the Japanese, Roosevelt told the country in a Fireside Chat on December 9, "We expect to eliminate the danger from Japan, but it would serve us ill if we accomplished that and found that the rest of the world was dominated by Hitler and Mussolini." Because he knew that Churchill would support his grand strategy, Roosevelt was eager to confer with him and use the prime minister's popular appeal in the United States to promote an Atlantic-first or Europe-first strategy.

Although he was worried about the peril Churchill might face in crossing the ocean, Roosevelt invited him to Washington. When the prime minister informed his War Cabinet of his intention to travel to America, one member wondered if it might not unsettle U.S. opinion, because isolationists might complain that he was pushing the president into global commitments. Churchill replied, "Oh! That is the way we talked to her while we were wooing her; now that she is in the harem, we talk to her quite differently!" Although Hopkins warned against setting an agenda that would appear to cede war strategy to the British, Churchill cabled Roosevelt that he "hoped to reach agreement" on a "joint strategy" that included the "redistribution of forces" and the creation of "joint machinery for implementing" the strategy.

Roosevelt and Churchill appeared together at a press conference on December 23, the day after the prime minister arrived at the White House. Churchill understood perfectly what his presence was meant to achieve. Wearing a polka-dot bowtie that lightened the moment, and standing on a chair when reporters in the back of the room asked him to make himself more visible, Churchill came across as deferential to the crush of reporters who applauded and cheered as he praised the productive power of the United States and predicted victory. By opening himself to reporters' questions, Churchill disarmed some of the hostility voiced by isolationists.

Harry Hopkins made certain to circulate an anecdote that not only humanized Churchill but was also aimed to refute suggestions of any devious intent to use the United States for self-serving British purposes. Hopkins recounted that as Roosevelt entered the guest room in the White House where Churchill had just emerged from one of his daily baths "stark naked and gleaming pink, . . . Roosevelt started to apologize and made as if to leave, but Churchill protested it was quite all right. 'The Prime Minister of Great Britain,' he said, 'has nothing to conceal from the President of the United States.'" When Hopkins asked Churchill if the story was true, the prime minister replied that it was "nonsense — that he never received the President without at least a bath towel wrapped around him." With great amusement Churchill added, "I could not possibly have made such a statement as that. The President himself would have been well aware that it was not strictly true." Churchill understood that his presence in America would involve not only discussions about strategy and marshaling of resources to defeat Hitler and ultimately the Japanese but also strengthening his stature in U.S. political and public opinion. On Christmas Eve, he joined the president in speaking to Americans from the White House. Although he was far from his country and his family, he said, "I cannot truthfully say that I feel far from home." "Common cause" with Americans in the service of "the same ideals" gave him a "sense of unity and fraternal association." On December 26, he addressed a joint congressional session where he was received with "the utmost kindness." He gained the immediate appreciation of his audience when he declared, "I cannot help reflecting that if my father had been American and my mother British, instead of the other way round, I might have got here on my own." The loudest applause greeted his rhetorical question about the outrage committed by the Japanese: "What sort of people do they think we are? Is it possible that they do not realize that we shall never cease to persevere against them until they have been taught a lesson which they and the world will never forget?"

The announcement that the combined chiefs of staff would be stationed in Washington rather than London gave additional assurance to congressional skeptics that America, not Britain, would shape war strategy, or at least that the United States would not become the instrument of British designs. The arrangement was partly intended to refute isolationist assertions that "the British wish to fight to the last American."

On December 30, Churchill addressed the Canadian parliament, where he cited the memorable warning of France's defeated generals that within three weeks of their surrender, England would suffer the same fate and "have her neck wrung like a chicken." Churchill added with much pleasure and applause from the parliamentarians, "Some chicken! Some neck!"

The meetings between Roosevelt and Churchill and their staffs lasted until January 14. The public appearance of unqualified unity hid considerable behind-the-scenes disputes about how to organize and implement a winning strategy. To function at his best in these crucial talks, Churchill insisted on maintaining his accustomed habits: late-night work sessions, two-hour afternoon naps, chain-smoking cigars, and having access to an abundance of liquor — sherry before breakfast, scotch and soda before lunch, wine at dinner, brandy before going to bed. His imbibing astonished and disturbed Eleanor, who was a long-standing opponent of drink. When she complained to Franklin about all this drinking and warned him not to join Churchill in consuming so much alcohol, Franklin cruelly remarked, reminding her of her father's alcoholism, that "she needn't worry because it wasn't his side of the family that had a drinking problem."

In his eagerness to promote unity at home and abroad in the war against the Axis, Roosevelt seized upon a suggestion by Hull that the president and prime minister issue a Declaration of the United Nations in the struggle to "defend life, liberty, independence and religious freedom . . . against savage and brutal forces seeking to subjugate the world." News about Nazi atrocities against innocent civilians in Yugoslavia and other occupied countries animated Roosevelt's insistence on a statement that would have global resonance. Concerned not to agitate isolationists by calling it an "Allied declaration" or mentioning "Associated Powers," which would remind Americans of how Wilson described joint American and British involvement in World War I, Roosevelt and Churchill agreed on the term "United Nations." "Yes," Churchill exclaimed, pointing to a line from Lord Byron's *Childe Harold's Pilgrimage:* "Here, where the sword united nations drew." Because they wanted the declaration to be seen as "a demonstration that the war was being waged for freedom of small nations as well as great," they agreed to invite all the countries fighting Hitler to affix their signatures. And since they did not wish to suggest that Moscow was about to fight the Japanese, they ended the declaration by asking other nations to join "the struggle for victory over

Hitlerism."

Roosevelt then convinced Churchill to include India, a prize British colony, in the document, and the Soviets to include religious freedom, which was notoriously absent in Communist Russia. To disarm Stalin's antireligious bias, Roosevelt explained that the statement could be interpreted to mean the right to have no religion or to be an atheist with no belief in God. Impressed with Roosevelt's powers of persuasion, Churchill told him that he would "recommend him for the position of Archbishop of Canterbury if he should lose the next presidential election." After they released the Declaration on January 1, Roosevelt told Churchill, "Winston we forgot Zog! [Albania's king]. We must get him to sign our little document."

While he and Churchill conferred on war strategy, Roosevelt never lost sight of the need to inspire public commitment to sacrifice for the war effort. In his January 6 State of the Union message, he urged the country to take the long view rather than fix its attention on recent short-term defeats — the losses at Pearl Harbor, the Philippines, Wake Island, and Guam, where the Japanese had overwhelmed thinly defended outposts. "We may suffer further setbacks," he declared with an eye on potential British reverses in Burma, at Singapore, and across the southwest Pacific. "We must face the fact of a hard war, a long war, a bloody war, a costly war," he cautioned but struck an optimistic note with predictions of overwhelming superiority in the production of planes, ships, tanks, and arms of every kind. And he assured Americans of the ultimate uncompromising victory of "the champions of tolerance and decency and freedom and faith."

Nowhere were symbolic gains more important than across Asia. Japanese advances had heightened public fears of bombardment and even an invasion of the West Coast of the United States, which triggered domestic pressure, supported by Chinese demands, for primary military action in the Pacific and across East Asia. But Roosevelt continued to share Churchill's conviction that a Nazi defeat was the primary goal, and that America's initial major campaign should target North Africa against General Erwin Rommel's *Afrika Korps* rather than a cross-Channel attack, for which, despite pleas from Stalin for opening a second front in Europe, the United States and Britain were unprepared. Roosevelt's dilemma was how to persuade the public that stopping Hitler was for now the top priority. For the moment, he had to resort to rhetorical pronouncements that promised that Allied cooperation would eventually be victorious over Japan, and persuaded Churchill to create a combined American, British, Dutch, and Australian (ABDA) command for the southwest Pacific under British general Archibald Wavell. To heighten Chinese president Chiang Kai-shek's sense of importance and guarantee his commitment to continue fighting in a conflict that kept a million Japanese troops tied up in China, Roosevelt swayed Churchill to make Chiang the Supreme Commander of the United Powers in China, Thailand, and Indochina. Roosevelt then appointed General Joseph W. Stilwell to head American forces in the China, Burma, India (CBI) theater of operations and to be Chiang's chief of staff.

Stilwell recognized that his new position and Chiang's title were largely symbolic gestures intended to boost both American and Chinese morale. At a meeting with Roosevelt in February, as Stilwell was about to leave for his command, the president directed him to tell Chiang that Hitler was not our only enemy. "The real strategy," Roosevelt added, "is to fight them all." Stilwell, who was known as "Vinegar Joe" for his caustic personality and antagonism to Roosevelt's New Deal, privately dismissed the president's rhetoric as "just a lot of wind." Unimpressed by Roosevelt's "pleasant — frothy" manner, he asked him if he had a message for Chiang. "He very obviously had not," Stilwell recorded in a diary, after "hunting around for something world-shaking to say. Finally, he had it — 'Tell him we are in this thing for keeps, and we intend to keep at it until China gets back all her lost territory.'"

Because Roosevelt understood how powerful China's appeal was in the United States, he urged Stilwell to encourage Madame Chiang Kai-shek, a shrewd, effective politician with a fine command of English and ability to influence press and public opinion, not to accept lecture invitations in the United States. Roosevelt's desire to keep China engaged in fighting was in large part based on his fear of the possibility of a Chinese collapse. "If China goes under," he said to his son Elliott, "how many divisions of Japanese troops do you think will be freed — to do what? Take Australia, take India. . . . Move straight on to the Middle East."

Churchill, who believed that "American opinion overestimated the contribution which China could make to the general war," did not share Roosevelt's concern about keeping up public pressure to help the Chinese defeat Japan. He was not unmindful of Roosevelt's public relations problems on this issue, but he considered them distinctly secondary to decisions on how best to fight the war, which did not include rescuing China as a high priority. He did understand, however, that a Chinese defeat would also demoralize British opinion and he was anything but indifferent to sentiments in his own country. When he returned from Washington in January, he found "an embarrassed, unhappy, baffled public opinion . . . swelling and mounting about me on every side." To counter the "airily detached criticism of the newspapers" as well as the constant complaints of some "twenty or thirty able Members of Parliament," Churchill demanded a vote of confidence to sustain his personal control and direction of war policy. After a three-day debate, he won an overwhelming endorsement, 464 to 1. Roosevelt cabled his congratulations, thanked him for a wire offering birthday wishes, and whimsically declared, "It is fun to be in same decade with you." As for Churchill's one dissenting vote, Roosevelt remarked: "We also had one vote in opposition" on the war declaration against Japan. (It was registered by pacifist and suffragette Jeannette Rankin of Montana, the first woman elected to Congress in 1916, and again in 1940, and the only member of Congress to vote against participation in both World Wars.)

After Tokyo conquered the Philippines in February, Roosevelt ordered General Douglas MacArthur to leave the Islands for Australia, where he was to take command of all U.S. forces and prepare an offensive against Japan. Arriving in Australia after an arduous journey by PT boat and plane, MacArthur received a hero's welcome, which Roosevelt underscored by awarding him a

Congressional Medal of Honor, the highest military tribute. MacArthur, never one to overlook a chance to polish his public image, and eager to dispel any mood of defeatism, announced that in response to the president's order "to break through the Japanese lines and proceed from Corregidor to Australia," he had come "through and I shall return." His promise produced a surge of optimism in the United States. Eager for a war hero, the press celebrated the general as "MacArthur the Magnificent," with a syndicated columnist comparing him to Alexander the Great and Napoleon.

But these were grim times for Americans, whose traditional insularity from world affairs discouraged convictions that the United States could fight and win a global war. Roosevelt saw "apathy" in the country, but he thought "the real trouble is not in the people or the leaders, but in a gang which unfortunately survives — mostly made up of those who were isolationists before December seventh and who are actuated today by various motives in their effort to instill disunity in the country. Some are publishers like Bertie McCormick and the Pattersons and the Roy Howard papers. The hearts of these people are not in unity and some of them still want a negotiated peace. Some of them are columnists or radio commentators who are actuated by the same motives. Some of them are politically minded and seek election gains. Some of them are antiracial and antireligious like the K.K.K. crowd and some are extreme nationalists like the wild Irish." He agreed with liberal commentator Elmer Davis's assessment that "some people want the United States to win so long as England loses. Some people want the United States to win so long as Russia loses. And some people want the United States to win so long as Roosevelt loses."

But the president was too shrewd a politician to give critics he saw undermining the war effort the satisfaction of a public outburst. Instead, he railed against them in private and used sarcastic humor to refute them. When Morris Ernst, a prominent liberal lawyer, told Roosevelt that as columnist Walter Winchell's representative in a suit against newspaper publisher Eleanor (Cissy) Patterson he intended to "examine Cissy down to her undies," Roosevelt replied that he wished not to be present: "I have a weak stomach." When conservative banker Fred I. Kent wrote to say that the Philippines, Dutch East Indies, and Singapore could have all been saved if strikes by unions had not slowed war production, Roosevelt responded that he sounded "like Alice in Wonderland," and told him "something [even] more fantastic": If the country had not lost sixty million man-days as a result of the scourge of the "common cold," the Japanese would have never attacked Pearl Harbor, and "we could undoubtedly have had enough planes, and guns and tanks to overrun Europe, Africa and the whole of Asia. Take good care of yourself. Don't go on strike and for god's sake don't catch a common cold." Against the advice of his cabinet, but to the amusement of journalists, he shared this response at a press conference.

Despite his contempt for critics, Roosevelt understood, as J. P. Morgan chairman Russell Leffingwell advised, that he needed "to rouse people from apathy and passiveness." At the same time, however, he was concerned not to become a redundancy. As he told one supporter who urged him to speak out, "From now on, for the duration of the war, there are going to be periods of hysteria, misinformation, volcanic eruptions, etc., and if I start the practice of going on the air to answer each one, the value of my going on the air will soon disappear. . . . For the sake of not becoming a platitude to the public, I ought not to appear oftener than once every five or six weeks."

On February 23, Washington's birthday, he felt compelled to address the setbacks in Asia with a radio talk to stiffen public resolve. He candidly acknowledged the harsh details of the current struggle, but also predicted an inevitable upturn in the country's military fortunes. He reminded his audience of Washington's travails at Valley Forge and the counsels of defeatism that he faced. As it had in the War of Independence, he expected America to prevail again. But Americans needed to understand that this was a vastly different war from the one Washington fought, for it was a global contest, which meant that U.S. forces had to meet their enemies in distant, unfamiliar places with the most modern weapons that were just now being produced by American factories. Isolationists who wanted the American eagle to behave like an ostrich or a turtle afraid to stick its head out were offering a prescription for defeat. The American eagle would be "flying high and striking hard," Roosevelt assured his audience. And the United States would do so by outbuilding and overwhelming Japan. He ended by recalling Tom Paine's brave words during the Revolutionary War: " 'Tyranny, like hell, is not easily conquered; yet we have this consolation with us, that the harder the sacrifice, the more glorious the triumph.' So spoke Americans in the year 1776. So speak

Americans today!"

When reporters at a press conference asked if he thought professional sports competitions should continue in wartime, he made a case for the importance of relaxation and diversion from the burdens of everyday pressures. In so doing he was speaking as much for himself as for others involved in war work. Were it not for his trips to Hyde Park, where he could find some release from the daily pressure of war business, Eleanor said, she did not see how he could get through this third term. Unable to escape Washington on cruises in the Caribbean or even on his yacht, the *Potomac,* where he might be vulnerable to enemy attacks, he began taking regular respites at his New York home. "The one essential in war time," he told Eleanor, "is complete lack of any distraction on the very occasional weekend I can get away from Washington." During these retreats, he dressed in casual, comfortable clothes, drove his hand-controlled Ford, inspected trees he had planted on the estate, and enjoyed early morning bird-watching. He relished "every minute" of listening to a "bird chorus at dawn. . . . In that far-off silent place, with myriads of birds waking up, it was quite impossible to think much of the horrors of war." It was as much the company of guests at Hyde Park as the pleasures of the countryside that revived him. Surrounded by Hopkins, Dr. McIntire, secretaries Bill Hassett and Grace Tulley, military aide Pa Watson, and his loving cousin Daisy, he was able to relax and fill the gap left by his mother's passing.

When Eleanor showed up, he found it more difficult "to stay away from the terrible problems of the day." She usually arrived with the people Roo-

702

sevelt called "uplifters" or "splendid people" who were "trying to do good and improve the world," but they limited his freedom to "relax and really rest." By contrast, he most appreciated casual banter, gossip about Washington notables, stamp collecting, card games in the evening, and the affection of aides and family, especially Daisy, who had become a paid member of his presidential library being built at Hyde Park. Ever mindful of his public image and concerned not to be seen as a part-time president, Roosevelt instructed everyone involved with his travels to keep them a secret. He was also concerned that these frequent excursions might also raise questions about his health and stamina, which were declining or at least less robust than in the immediate past. In fact, by his ninth year in the White House, he was feeling the strains of a presidency initially burdened with difficult choices about widespread suffering in the Depression, and now with life and death decisions in the war: He needed not only to identify a strategy that could defeat the Axis without terrible losses of American lives but also to maintain a hold on the public while he guarded against immobilizing health problems.

In maintaining public commitment to the war effort, Roosevelt recognized that there was no substitute for direct action against the Axis, especially Japan. Because it was the Japanese who were making all the gains in the first three months of the fighting and Americans were eager for some form of retaliation, Roosevelt agreed to a relocation of 120,000 Japanese Americans, 70 percent of whom were American citizens, concentrated on the West Coast. There was no evidence that any of them were spies who jeopardized the country's security, and Roosevelt was well aware that moving so large a group to camps in the mountain states and arid deserts of the West constituted what the American Civil Liberties Union later called a gross violation of civil rights. He tried to give himself plausible deniability in the matter or to let subordinates initiate and manage the incarceration, instructing them to be as reasonable as possible. He also found some justification for his abuse of Japanese civil liberties by recalling that during the Civil War, President Lincoln had declared martial law and suspended habeas corpus. In times of war, national security had to take priority over adherence to domestic freedoms.

It is difficult to capture the fear and anxiety that engulfed the Pacific coast in response to news of Japanese victories, as Hong Kong, Manila, and Singapore had all fallen by the end of January 1942. The surprise attack on Pearl Harbor had inflamed suspicions of all Japanese as untrustworthy. Fears of Fifth Columnists who had been instrumental in Nazi victories added to concerns about Asian subversives. Long-standing racial antagonism to a group that had outstripped many Caucasians only reinforced impulses to punish Japanese Americans for Japan's military aggression.

Opposition to so radical an action as internment was limited and inconsequential. Attorney General Francis Biddle resisted measures against the Japanese, which reminded him of anti-German actions taken during World War I: assaults on German-Americans, the suspension of German language classes in high schools, and renaming sauerkraut "liberty cabbage." But by 1941, there were far too many German-Americans and Italian-

Americans to consider segregating them in isolated camps, and they did not bear the sort of racial stigma that America's Asian populations did. "We're charged with wanting to get rid of the Japs for selfish reasons," a California business leader declared. "We might as well be honest. We do. It's a question of whether the white man lives on the Pacific Coast or the brown man." In addition to the racial animus that distinguished Japanese Americans from the Germans and Italians, the latter had become well assimilated and had ties to Roosevelt's New Deal, which had cultivated the support of European ethnics by bringing prominent members of these groups into the government.

When Roosevelt signed the executive order relocating the Japanese, Biddle called it "ill-advised, unnecessary, and unnecessarily cruel." Roosevelt silenced him by saying: "[T]his must be a military decision." Warnings from the military of possible espionage and sabotage convinced Roosevelt not to place civil liberties above national security. "I do not think he [FDR] was much concerned with the gravity or implications of this step," Biddle wrote later. ". . . What must be done to defend the country must be done. . . . The military might be wrong. But they were fighting the war. Public opinion was on their side, so that there was no question of any substantial opposition, which might tend toward the disunity that at all costs he must avoid." However, FBI investigations demonstrated there was little actual basis for significant concern, as no identifiable spies or traitors were uncovered among the Japanese Americans.

The roundup and incarceration of the Japanese

frightened African Americans, who saw it as racially motivated. Given the barriers they themselves faced to equal treatment, especially across the South, it was understandable that they discounted Roosevelt's warnings in his State of the Union Address "against racial discrimination in any of its ugly forms." They understood that Nazi Germany under Hitler fostered racism and brutal intolerance, and they had little expectation that segregationists across the old Confederacy would be supportive of any sort of racial accommodation. Although both the first lady and Ickes had consistently spoken out for equal treatment under the law, Ickes, who thought the incarceration of the Japanese "both stupid and cruel," made no protest to Roosevelt. For African Americans, the relocation was a disturbing development that shook their confidence in an administration they had repeatedly helped vote into office.

But Roosevelt's focus was on fighting the war, and he was now preoccupied with holding the Allied coalition together and urging the Russians and British to take the brunt of the battlefield losses while the United States prepared to transport men and equipment across the oceans to move beyond defensive actions in the Pacific. In January, as Churchill headed back to Britain from Washington, he and Roosevelt had attempted to sort out "the control of raw materials and supplies, and their distribution." The competition for war material was no small matter, as the acquisition of precious munitions could dictate the extent of battlefield activities. Among the many other issues that concerned Roosevelt were control of ABDA forces; the use of fighter squadrons that made up the American Volunteer Group in China;

bringing "French North Africa into the war"; reaching a master Lend-Lease agreement with Britain without exacerbating differences over trade practices, particularly imperial preference; setting up "an adequate air transport scheme . . . between India and China" to ensure the delivery of supplies to Chiang's armies; deterring the Vichy government from collaboration with the Axis; and the surrender of Singapore to a smaller Japanese force on February 15, a defeat Churchill described as "the greatest disaster to British arms" in history. Roosevelt cabled Churchill: "No matter how serious our setbacks have been, and I do not for a moment underrate them, we must constantly look forward to the next moves that need to be made to hit the enemy." The prime minister in turn acknowledged: "I do not like these days of personal stress and I have found it difficult to keep my eye on the ball. . . . Democracy has to prove that it can provide a granite foundation for war against tyranny."

At the end of February, against the backdrop of these daunting events, Roosevelt fled Washington again for Hyde Park, where, Daisy recorded, "he tries to stay away from the terrible problems of the day during the short hours he can spare for the Library & his books & collections." He urged Daisy to come to dinner with the "rather pathetic" explanation that "I shall be lonely." As they returned to Washington on March 4, he began "to think of his harassing schedule for the day." When he reached his Oval Office desk, where Harry Hopkins and other aides brought him the latest news, Daisy could see the " 'relaxation' vanish, & concentrated intenseness take its place." She found him "looking worried," and when she saw

707

him again the following day, he said that "he will have several bad days 'catching up' on top of bad news from the Far East." At dinner, Daisy thought that he "wants to relax — looks tired — tries several lighter subjects of conversation, which, however, are invariably turned to some 'problem' by the others."

The trips to Hyde Park continued to be a godsend. As he told Churchill in March, "I know you will keep up your optimism and your grand driving force, but I know you will not mind if I tell you that you ought to take a leaf out of my notebook. Once a month I go to Hyde Park for four days, crawl into a hole and pull the hole in after me. I am called on the telephone only if something of really great importance occurs. I wish you would try it, and I wish you would lay a few bricks or paint another picture." Churchill's wife, Clementine, shared Roosevelt's concern about Winston's morale. As she told Hopkins: "He is carrying a very heavy load and I can't bear his dear round face not to look cheerful and cherubic in the mornings, as up to now it has always done. What with Singapore and India . . . we are indeed walking through the Valley of Humiliation."

As spring arrived in Washington, Roosevelt struggled not only to boost public morale but also to keep differences with Churchill, Stalin, and Chiang from impeding the war effort. The Japanese advances deepened concerns about the possible loss of India. Mindful of Churchill's sensitivity and resistance to outside advice regarding anything relating to the British Empire, Roosevelt approached the issue of India with circumspection. Informed by Harriman in London of Roosevelt's urgency about getting India to mount a steadfast defense against the Japanese, Churchill told the president that he was considering a declaration of dominion status for India after the war with the right to secede, but feared throwing it "into chaos on the eve of invasion." The Muslims, who made up "the main Army elements," would perceive any change in status as turning them into a minority population under Hindu command. Churchill warned that any general announcement on Indian independence "would be disastrous." Roosevelt tried to prod Churchill with a suggestion that he set up "a temporary Indian government, headed by different castes, occupations, religions and geographies — . . . a temporary Dominion Government" that would remain in place until after the war. But he ended his cable by saying, "For the love of Heaven don't bring me into this, though I do want to be of help. It is, strictly speaking, none of my business, except insofar as it is a part and parcel of the successful fight that you and I are making."

Churchill dismissed the president's recommendation as "superficial' and "an act of madness." But Roosevelt pressed his case, telling Churchill that universal sentiment in the United States held that Britain's troubles with India stemmed from its refusal to grant it "the right of self-government." Roosevelt's assertion "made Churchill furious," and provoked "a string of cuss words . . . for two hours in the middle of the night." No suggestions during the war were "so wrathfully received," Hopkins said, "as those relating to the solution of the Indian problem." One Churchill associate told Hopkins "that India was one subject on which Winston would never move a yard." After regaining his composure, he cabled

Roosevelt: "You know the weight which I attach to everything you say to me, but I did not feel I could take responsibility for the defence of India if everything had again to be thrown into the melting-pot at this critical juncture. . . . Anything like a serious difference between you and me would break my heart, and would surely deeply injure both our countries at the height of this terrible struggle." As Hopkins observed this debate, he concluded "that the subcontinent of India was one area where the minds of Roosevelt and Churchill would never meet." Roosevelt dropped the subject, and Churchill stuck to his policy of not discussing Indian independence during the war.

Eager to show Churchill that he had no desire to promote dissolution of the British Empire as a war aim, Roosevelt took an entirely different approach to Burma, where the Japanese were overwhelming the British, and Burmese independence leaders were negotiating with Tokyo for their country's freedom. In April, as British forces retreated before the Japanese invasion, Roosevelt sent Churchill a copy of a journalist's letter reporting on Burma's negotiations for independence. He added a sympathetic note and belittled Burmese prime minister U Saw, whom the British had put in prison for dealing with the Japanese. "I have never liked Burma or the Burmese!" he wrote Churchill. "And you people must have had a terrible time with them for the last fifty years. Thank the Lord you have HE-SAW, WE-SAW, YOU-SAW under lock and key. I wish you could put the whole bunch of them into a frying pan with a wall around it and let them stew in their own juice."

Roosevelt's war worries extended to sustaining the relationship with Stalin and the Soviets.

Memories of the Nazi-Soviet Pact raised apprehensions of a new Russian accommodation with Hitler that would free the bulk of German forces on the eastern front to threaten British and American prospects of winning the war. Mindful of the Anglo-American dependence on Russian cooperation, Stalin pressed Churchill and Roosevelt to make political concessions that would serve postwar Soviet territorial ambitions and more immediately, military commitments that could relieve the pressure on his front. When British foreign secretary Anthony Eden visited Moscow in December 1941, Stalin had asked for a secret treaty conceding the Soviet Union's June 1941 boundaries, which would grant it control of the Baltic States — Estonia, Latvia, and Lithuania — parts of Finland and Romania, and the eastern provinces of Poland seized in 1939. During their discussions in January, Churchill and Roosevelt had agreed that accepting Stalin's demands would violate the principles of the Atlantic Charter and would risk fierce domestic opposition and Allied unity.

As they struggled with battlefield setbacks in February and March, Churchill pressed Roosevelt to reverse course on refusing the Soviet demands. On March 7, he cabled, "The increasing gravity of the war has led me to feel that the principles of the Atlantic Charter ought not to be construed so as to deny Russia the frontiers she occupied when Germany attacked her." Churchill wanted "a free hand to sign the treaty which Stalin desires. . . . Everything portends an immense renewal of the German invasion of Russia in the spring and there is very little we can do to help the only country that is heavily engaged with the German armies."

Roosevelt remained opposed to any such agreement, as he did not believe that Stalin would actually "quit the war" over territorial matters and was confident that promises of opening a second front in Western Europe would quiet his demands. On March 11, he told Morgenthau that Stalin did not trust Churchill but that America had kept its promises to him and therefore enjoyed good standing. He acknowledged that "nothing would be worse than to have the Russians collapse" but asked Soviet ambassador Litvinov to tell Stalin that any territorial arrangements agreed to now would have a terribly negative impact in the United States and would undermine cooperation between the two nations. He also promised to favor "legitimate security" for Russia after the war.

When Roosevelt wrote Churchill on March 18, he summarized the obstacles facing both of them: "I have been thinking a lot about your troubles during the past month. We might as well admit the difficult military side of the problems. . . . Next in order is that delightful god, which we worship in common, called 'The Freedom of the Press.' . . . We are both menaced by the so-called interpretive comment by a handful or two of gentlemen who cannot get politics out of their heads in the worst crisis." He complained that they "persistently magnify relatively unimportant domestic matters." These "survivors of isolationism" wanted him to do "the turtle act" and only defend the homeland, when he was already formulating plans for a "joint attack in Europe." In the meantime, he expected a response from Stalin and told Churchill with brutal frankness that he thought he could "personally handle Stalin better than either your Foreign Office or my State Department. Stalin hates the guts of all your top people. He thinks he likes me better, and I hope he will continue to do so."

The compelling questions Roosevelt faced in dealing with the Russians were how to keep the Soviets fighting and keeping the bulk of the German armies occupied, and how best to bring U.S. troops into action against Germany in a way that would help relieve the pressure on the Russian front while giving the American forces experience in combat. Roosevelt agreed with Churchill that an early offensive in North Africa, where British troops remained engaged with Hitler's *Afrika Korps,* would benefit both the United States and Britain, but it would only confirm Stalin's suspicions that his allies were content to leave Russia responsible for conducting the bulk of the land war against the Nazis.

Because U.S. military chiefs, led by Stimson and George Marshall, believed that an invasion of western Europe was essential in defeating Hitler, Roosevelt agreed to the plan to open a second front. He had the greatest respect for the sixty-one-year-old Marshall, who in a forty-year Army career had come up through the ranks. Marshall had demonstrated independence from political crosscurrents and excellent judgment about military affairs, which had won Roosevelt's admiration. Marshall made a point of never laughing at the president's jokes or allowing himself to be charmed by him, nor was he on a first-name basis with him. Roosevelt, for his part, always felt compelled to address Marshall by his title or surname. When he wanted to overcome Churchill's resistance to a cross-Channel assault that the prime minister feared might fail, it was Marshall, along with Hopkins, whom Roosevelt sent to London to convince him about the plan. On April 1, he told Churchill that his two advisers would present "the salient points" of his "vital" proposal, which he hoped Churchill would support and Stalin would "greet with enthusiasm."

Churchill acknowledged that "all now depends upon the vast Russo-German struggle." He was ready to welcome Hopkins and Marshall, and the sooner their arrival, the better. Roosevelt responded: "What Harry and Geo. Marshall will tell you about have my heart and *mind* in it. Your people and mine demand the establishment of a front to draw off pressure on the Russians, and these people are wise enough to see that the Russians are killing more Germans and destroying more equipment than you and I put together." When Churchill approved of Roosevelt's plan, Roosevelt wrote Stalin on April 11, expressing regret that distance kept them apart but the hope they might spend a few days together in the summer "near our common border off Alaska." In the meantime, he wished to discuss "a very important military proposal involving the utilization of our armed forces in a manner to relieve your critical western front. This objective carries great weight with me." He asked Stalin to send his foreign minister Vyacheslav Molotov to Washington for consultations and added: "The American people are thrilled by the magnificent fighting of your armed forces and we want to help you in the destruction of Hitler's armies and material more than we are doing now."

With Churchill's agreeing to establishing a second front and Stalin promising to send Molotov to Washington by the end of May, Roosevelt saw the Allies turning a corner in the conflict. On April 18, led by Jimmy Doolittle, sixteen B-25 bombers launched from the aircraft carrier USS *Hornet,* 650 miles from Japan and outside the range of Japanese fighter planes, bombed Tokyo and a few other cities. Fifteen of the bombers flew on to China, and one reached Russia. Seventy-one of the eighty airmen survived. One died in a crash landing. The other eight were captured in China: The Japanese executed three of them for attacking civilian targets. For the Japanese, who had been ruthless in killing Chinese civilians, it was an act of unqualified hypocrisy. The five other captured airmen died in captivity. Although the Doolittle raid caused little damage, it humiliated Japan's military leaders, who had promised to protect the homeland from assault. Its success buoyed Americans and especially pleased Roosevelt, who had endorsed the mission. He told Churchill: "While our mutual difficulties are many I am frank to say that I feel better about the war than at any time in the past two years." When reporters asked him how the planes had reached Tokyo, since heavy bombers were not known to fly off aircraft carriers, Roosevelt, to everyone's amusement, declared: "They came from a secret base at Shangri-La," the mythical paradise described in James Hilton's popular novel of the 1930s, *Lost Horizon.*

The decision to open a second front and the Doolittle raid were no more than temporary boosts in an otherwise gloomy season. Demoralizing setbacks overshadowed promising gains and served as constant reminders of how much loss and suffering remained to be endured in the war.

In April, U.S. and Filipino forces on the Bataan peninsula, plagued by hunger, thirst, and disease, had surrendered. On May 6, holdouts in Corregidor also capitulated. American general Jonathan Wainwright cabled Roosevelt: "Please say to the nation that my troops and I have accomplished all that is humanly possible and that we have upheld the best traditions of the United States and its Army. . . . With profound regret and with continued pride in my gallant troops I go to meet the Japanese commander." In Washington, General Dwight Eisenhower, deputy chief of war plans, lamented Wainwright's plight, while MacArthur "got such glory as the public could find." He was an undeserving "hero." And troops on the front line deplored his failed leadership, cynically singing:

"Dugout Doug's not timid, he's just cautious, not afraid;
He's protecting carefully the stars that Franklin made.
Four-star generals are as rare as good food on Bataan;
And his troops go starving on.

A division commander complained, "A foul trick of deception has been played on a large group of Americans by a commander in chief and small staff who are now eating steak and eggs in Australia. God damn them!"

The surrenders at Bataan and Corregidor brought new, unforeseen miseries at the hands of the Japanese, aided by Korean troops used for guard duty. The "Bataan Death March," as it would later be known, cost the lives of 600 out of

10,000 American captives and 10,000 out of 60,000 Filipino prisoners. Contemptuous of the capitulating troops, the Japanese beat and bayoneted them along the 80-mile march to prison camps, where many more of them perished. Although declaring themselves architects of an Asian co-prosperity sphere and Asia for Asians, the Japanese military became masters of sadism toward POWs — whether British and American or Chinese and Filipinos. Their abuse of prisoners and subject populations rivaled the horrors perpetrated by Nazi SS guards in concentration camps.

The surrender of U.S. forces in the Philippines coincided with a standoff in a battle on the Coral Sea. The body of water between Australia, New Guinea, and the Solomon Islands was the site of a clash between American and Japanese aircraft carriers from May 4 to May 8. Alerted by deciphering coded Japanese naval plans to capture Port Moresby in New Guinea and Tulagi in the Solomons, two U.S. carrier groups surprised the Japanese invaders, and in an exchange of aircraft attacks, each side lost the use of two carriers. It was the first naval battle in history where ships never came within sight of each other. Although the Japanese captured Tulagi, they withdrew without taking Port Moresby. If Roosevelt could not claim the battle as an out-and-out victory, he could cite it as the first success in blocking the Japanese advance across the South Pacific. Moreover, what was not evident at the time, but would shortly become of consequence, was the fact that the Japanese lost ninety-three of their skilled aircrews and were unable to replace them quickly enough to make a difference in the next major sea battle, at Midway Island in June.

Whatever comfort Americans took from holding the line in the Coral Sea, they could not deny the Japanese success in the Pacific. Roosevelt saw himself in a constant struggle to boost not only domestic morale regarding its victories, but also that of Chiang Kai-shek's government and of the Chinese people. On May 28, he gave his twenty-first Fireside Chat, in which he confronted the painful losses in the Pacific: "The Malayan Peninsula and Singapore are in the hands of the enemy;" he said, "The Netherland East Indies are almost entirely occupied. . . . Many other islands are in the possession of the Japanese." But encouraged by the results in the Coral Sea, he added, "There is good reason to believe that their southward advance has been checked. . . . And we are determined that the territory that has been lost will be regained." In the meantime, however, he acknowledged that "the news in Burma tonight is not good." He anticipated the loss of the Burma Road, "but I want to say to the gallant people of China that no matter what advances the Japanese may make, ways will be found to deliver airplanes and munitions of war to the armies of Generalissimo Chiang Kai-shek." Moreover, Roosevelt heartened his audiences by reporting that the Japanese were paying "a heavy toll in warships, in transports, in planes, and in men. They are feeling the effects of those losses."

What Roosevelt did not discuss was the dispirited outlook of Stilwell, whose forces retreated in the face of the Japanese advance in Burma. After reaching China in March, Stilwell found nothing to raise hopes of effective Chinese resistance to the Japanese. Chiang was "cordial and welcoming" but gave no evidence of a determination to risk the sacrifice of his armies in the battle for Burma. Hollington Tong, Chiang's information minister, impressed Stilwell as "oily and false," an architect of public relations dispatches announcing fictitious Chinese triumphs. In Chungking, Stilwell conferred with Chiang Kai-shek, Madame Chiang, and China's minister of war, who gave him "double talk and tea." Stilwell had plans for an offensive in Burma, followed by an air and ground assault on Japanese forces in China. But he was up against a corrupt government and army, whose commanders had little regard for their troops, who died in great numbers from battlefield wounds and unsanitary conditions. "The one thing we have plenty of in China," one Chinese officer said, "is men." Burma became a breeding ground of mistrust among American, British, and Chinese forces. As an American major told Stilwell, the Burma campaign had "no plan, no reconnaissance, no security, no intelligence, no prisoners."

Above all, the battle for Burma led to a divide between Chiang and Stilwell. "I have to tell CKS with a straight face that his subordinates are not carrying out his orders, when in all probability they are doing just what he tells them," Stilwell said. In April, Chiang promised to compel his officers to follow Stilwell's commands. With American newspapers also publishing false accounts of Chinese victories in Burma, Stilwell said, "What a sucker I'll look like if the Japs run me out of Burma." In the meantime, the U.S. press was turning Stilwell into a miracle worker who was leading the Chinese to victory. For Roosevelt, Stilwell — or at least the press accounts about him

719

— was something of a boon. Whatever their reality, the journalistic accounts of his exploits were raising hope in both the United States and China. In truth, neither the British nor the Chinese believed they could win in Burma and were writing it off as a lost cause. At the end of May, after an arduous forced march out of Burma into India, Stilwell told a press conference in New Delhi the truth: "I claim we got a hell of a beating. We got run out of Burma and it is humiliating as hell. I think we ought to find out what caused it, go back and retake it."

Although Stilwell's resolve did not resonate in the United States the way MacArthur's "I shall return" had, it provided a note of hope that echoed Roosevelt's promises of better days ahead. When Chiang, who was now in conflict with Stilwell over Chinese timidity in using its troops in Burma, complained to Roosevelt about being treated as a fifth wheel compared to Britain and Russia, Roosevelt tried to soothe him with assurances that no question regarding his "illustrious country" would be acted upon without the full collaboration of his "distinguished representative" in Washington. But his guarantee was essentially rhetoric. As Roosevelt told John Winant, his ambassador in London, a Pacific Council in Washington "serves primarily to disseminate information as to the progress of operations in the Pacific — and secondly, to give me a chance to keep everybody happy by telling stories and doing most of the talking!" But Chiang wasn't fooled and warned Roosevelt that, without greater direct support, Chinese resistance might collapse. In June, he pressed Roosevelt for U.S. troops and planes to reopen the Burma Road and to increase supplies being flown over the Himalayas. In response, Roosevelt urged him to consider the larger war picture. The fall of the Libyan port of Tobruk on the Mediterranean to Rommel's forces threatened the loss of the Middle East, the isolation of India and China, and defeat across the entire Far East.

Throughout the spring, troubles with Chiang were a secondary concern given Roosevelt's focus on sustaining Soviet opposition to German forces in Russia. A spring offensive that threatened Leningrad in the north and Rostov and Stalingrad in the south raised fears that the Germans would seize the oil fields of the Caucasus and capture all of European Russia. In addition, German U-boats were sinking Allied merchant ships in the North Atlantic at a prodigious rate — two-and one-half times the capacity to replace them — and greatly impeding the flow of supplies to Russia along the route to Murmansk and Archangel. On April 26, Roosevelt had cabled Churchill that he was "greatly disturbed" by the supply problem, which would have "political repercussions." He felt that "the losses which we may have to undergo may well be worth the risk. . . . Any word reaching Stalin at this time that our supplies were stopping for any reason would have a most unfortunate effect."

It was against this backdrop that Roosevelt asked Stalin to send Molotov to Washington. Eager to advance British and American commitments to open a second front in 1942 that could draw off forty German divisions from the fighting in Russia, Stalin agreed. The fifty-two-year-old Molotov was notable for his unsmiling countenance and rigid, formal interactions. Apprehensive of his hosts, who themselves harbored unfriendly feelings toward a signatory of the Nazi-Soviet pact, or so he believed, Molotov carried a pistol and black bread and sausage in his suitcase lest he be confronted with unpalatable Western food. He arrived first in London on May 22 after a risky flight over Germanheld areas of Norway with a large contingent of stiff-backed aides who could not hide their "inveterate suspicion" of all foreigners. After pressing the case for postwar territorial advantages, Molotov gave in to British insistence that they sign a twenty-year peace pact without territorial commitments, which could have provoked political problems in Britain and the United States as well as with exile governments protective of their homelands. Molotov was much more concerned, in any case, to extract an agreement to a second front. Though Churchill expressed every wish to relieve hard-pressed Soviet armies, he was equivocal about the ability of his and U.S. forces to mount a cross-Channel assault in 1942.

Churchill's reluctance to pledge a second front left Molotov all the more eager to see Roosevelt, who had initiated discussions of the proposed assault. He arrived in Washington on May 29 and went directly to the White House, where he stayed for four days. Fully informed by Churchill of what he had told Molotov about a western front, Roosevelt was nevertheless all the more determined to boost his hopes for an invasion — however much the reality of what the Allies might be able to accomplish contradicted what he promised Molotov. Roosevelt had told Daisy that he had heard that this "visiting fireman . . . is *not* very pleasant and *never smiles.*" Roosevelt found Molotov as expected, and slowed by cumbersome translations, realized that it would be impossible to establish the kind of human contact that usually disarmed unfriendly adversaries. On the second day of talks, when Molotov gave a gloomy description of the current struggle to contain Hitler's armies, warned of a possible Soviet collapse, and pressed Roosevelt for an answer on a second front, Roosevelt asked Marshall, who attending the meeting, if America could give the foreign minister definite assurances of a cross-Channel attack. Marshall told Molotov what he wanted to hear, and Roosevelt asked Molotov to inform Stalin that the campaign would be launched by August or September. Roosevelt even agreed to let Molotov publish a communiqué forecasting a second front in 1942.

Roosevelt was anything but certain that he could persuade Churchill and muster the U.S. resources for such an assault, but his immediate concern was to give the Soviets enough hope to keep them fighting. If they seemed near actual collapse, he was even prepared to consider some sort of "sacrificial landing" that might further sustain them. He cabled Churchill: "I am especially anxious that he [Molotov] carry back some real results of his mission and that he will give a favorable account to Stalin. I am inclined to think that at present all the Russians are a bit down in the mouth. *But the important thing is that we may be and probably are faced with real trouble on the Russian front and must make our plans to meet it.*"

Few factors animated Roosevelt's determination to defeat Hitler more than reports of Nazi atrocities. At the beginning of June, Reinhard Heydrich, Hitler's deputy administrator of Czechoslovakia, was assassinated by Czech commandos trained in

Britain. In response, Hitler ordered the destruction of Lidice, a village near Prague, where the assailants were allegedly hidden. All the men in the village were killed and most of the rest of the population were sent to concentration camps, where they perished. On June 10, the Nazis openly announced the destruction of Lidice as retaliation for Heydrich's killing and as a warning to others who took up arms against the Nazi occupation. When Yugoslavia's king Peter asked for Roosevelt's help in combating "cruelties and persecutions by the Nazis," the president proposed to Hull that they issue "a public warning to the Bulgarian and Hungarian Governments" collaborating with the Nazis. He also directed William Donovan, who had become the director of the Office of Strategic Services (OSS), to see the Yugoslav minister about helping "eighty Yugoslavian airmen and saboteurs."

Roosevelt's commitment to a second front and worries that he might give in to pressures to fight Japan first so concerned Churchill that he returned to Washington for another series of talks, including a discussion about the potential for an atomic bomb. The latter was so closely guarded a secret that Churchill wanted only to discuss it in person. Roosevelt shared Churchill's eagerness for another meeting, and the prime minister arrived at Hyde Park on June 19. Invited to lunch with the president and Churchill, Daisy thought that "F.D.R.'s manner was easy and intimate — His face humorous or very serious, according to the subject of conversation, and entirely *natural.* Not a trace of having to guard his words or expressions, just the opposite of his manner at a press conference, when he is an actor on the stage —

and a player on an instrument, at the same time." Daisy's teenage niece, Margaret Hambley, who was also present, described Churchill as "about 5'7" and quite fat about the waist . . . He has a very pink face, whitish-red thin hair, and very piercing pale blue eyes. He looks just like his pictures and his nose has a very strange shape — it looks as if it were chiseled. He doesn't have nearly as much social charm and personality as the President, but he is very quiet and asks leading questions." She especially enjoyed his observation that "a woman was as old as she looked; a man was as old as he felt; and a boy was as old as he was treated."

The hard business of how to bring U.S. forces into action against the Germans in 1942 dominated the conversations over the next three days. Churchill and his chiefs were dead set against a cross-Channel assault in 1942, and since the bulk of the troops for such an attack would be British, they were bound to have their way. The alternative, which Roosevelt found most appealing, was an amphibious invasion of North Africa. The clinching argument for carrying out this plan was news on June 21 that Rommel's numerically smaller force had overwhelmed the British garrison at Tobruk. Churchill regarded it as a disgrace that would compel him to face another vote of confidence in Parliament; Roosevelt judged that it demonstrated that the Germans were "better trained and better generaled." He also feared the loss of Egypt and control of "everything across from the Atlantic to the Pacific" by the Germans and the Japanese. When Churchill raised the question of cooperation in the construction of an atomic bomb, which British scientists had also been working on, Roosevelt was happy to agree.

Churchill's fears of American focus shifting to the Pacific rested on a victory of U.S. naval forces at Midway, 1,100 miles from Pearl Harbor. The Doolittle raid on Japan's home islands had persuaded admiral Yamamoto to alter his plans and strike at Midway Island, from where he thought the raid had originated. He reasoned that such an attack would draw the U.S. fleet into a decisive battle that would eliminate any threat to Japan's homeland and open the way to winning the war.

But his assault, carried out on June 4 and June 5, proved to be a disaster. Intercepts of Japanese coded messages had alerted American forces to the attack, and Admiral Chester Nimitz deployed aircraft carriers and island-based planes to combat the Japanese fleet. On June 6, Roosevelt told Churchill that "the business in the Pacific is going well and I am sure we are inflicting some very severe losses on the Jap fleet. The outcome, however, is still indecisive but we should know more before the day is over. I am sure our aircraft are giving a very good account of themselves." As the fog of war lifted, it became clear that the Japanese had suffered a major defeat: "Four carriers and the most experienced pilots had been lost, a heavy cruiser sunk, and another damaged — against one carrier and a destroyer lost by the United States." The Japanese also lost 330 planes compared to 150 for the United States. Fortunately for Roosevelt and the U.S. military, Midway "was an ill-conceived, sloppily executed operation."

Although the full implications of the battle were not yet entirely clear, it was evident to Roosevelt

726

that the tide of the Pacific war might be turning. It certainly seemed that way to Churchill, who on June 13 cabled Roosevelt "heartiest congratulations on the grand American victories in the Pacific which have very decidedly altered the balance of the Naval war." Considerable fighting and losses lay ahead, and the outcome in the main theater of operations against the Germans in Russia remained far from certain. But by June, with the full industrial might of the United States coming online, a glimmer of hope emerged from the gloom that had shadowed the half year after Pearl Harbor.

CHAPTER 16
THE END OF THE BEGINNING

While the naval victory in the Pacific was a most welcome reversal of fortune against the Japanese, it promised nothing in the war against Hitler. Churchill's visit had not clarified the way forward. Stimson and Marshall were unyielding in their conviction that only a cross-Channel assault that relieved the Russian front, defeated Hitler's armies, and brought an end to Nazi rule in Germany would guarantee a victory. Churchill had no quarrel with their strategy, but believed timing was critical. "No responsible British military authority has so far been able to make a plan for September 1942 which had any chance of success," he told the president. Moreover, he feared that a premature assault would likely end "in disaster" and "would decisively injure the prospect of well organized large scale action in 1943."

Yet Churchill did not think that they could "afford to stand idle in the Atlantic theatre during the whole of 1942." He was mindful of pressure from Douglas MacArthur and U.S. naval chiefs to focus on the Pacific front. When Texas congressman Lyndon B. Johnson, temporarily commissioned a lieutenant commander in the Navy, traveled to Australia to tour the fighting front for the president and joined a perilous bombing mission against Japanese forces in New Guinea, MacArthur awarded him a Silver Star in return for promising to press Roosevelt for a stronger commitment to the Pacific fighting. It was soon described as the most talked-about and least deserved medal in U.S. military history. The invasion of Europe would have to wait until 1943.

Losses on the northern route to Murmansk in northwest Russia on the Barents Sea added to the urgency of helping the Russians. When only a quarter of a convoy's supplies made it to the Soviet port at the beginning of July, Churchill informed Stalin that they would have to suspend shipments along this corridor. They would try to make up for the deficit by increasing the rail traffic through Persia, but it was impossible to close the gap fully. Churchill implored Stalin, addressing him as "my comrade and friend," to understand that "there is nothing that is useful and sensible that we and the Americans will not do to help you in your grand struggle. The president and I are ceaselessly searching for means to overcome the extraordinary difficulties which geography, salt water and the enemy's air power interpose." But Stalin, whose own forces were making such great sacrifices, had little sympathy for British efforts to limit their losses.

For Roosevelt, dealings with the Soviet dictator illustrated Churchill's observation that the only thing worse than having allies is not having them. Stalin opposed a project to deploy three divisions of Polish troops to the Middle East, fearing that it would undermine his goal of preventing postwar Polish independence. Churchill's insistence that a

Polish army would be to their "common advantage" did not overcome Stalin's reluctance to support a potential anti-Soviet force. Roosevelt did not want to press the Soviets on issues like better relations with Poland's exile government in London or the treatment of Polish Jews in the Soviet Union, including Jewish Socialist Workers leaders Victor Alter and Henryk Ehrlich, who were arrested by the NKVD, the Soviet Secret Police, as German agents and disappeared in the Soviet penal system, where they were executed. Moreover, in the summer of 1942, Stalin, suspicious of Western intentions, delayed for months granting permission for U.S. military personnel to fly desperately needed planes to Soviet airfields in Siberia. Even Roosevelt's warnings that he had "tangible evidence" of Japanese preparations "to conduct operations against the Maritime Provinces of the Soviet Union" did not sway him.

With Rommel following his victory at Tobruk by an invasion of Egypt, and the Germans seizing Sevastopol and then Voronezh in south central Russia, a frustrated Roosevelt spent several days in Hyde Park and during the first week of July at a new presidential retreat in Maryland's Catoctin National Forest 75 miles from Washington. The compound included a cottage with guest rooms and other houses for overnight members of the president's party and soon became a frequent hideaway, which Roosevelt described as his Shangri-La. His trips there and to Hyde Park were kept secret — allegedly to thwart potential enemy attempts on his life, but also as a guard against suspicions of his declining health or capacity to deal with daunting wartime challenges.

At the Maryland retreat, he took comfort from

both the bucolic vistas and the companionship of adoring women. He freely admitted that he loved to be surrounded by attractive women who were openly flirtatious with and affectionate toward him. "Nothing is more pleasing to the eye than a good-looking lady, nothing more refreshing to the spirit than the company of one, nothing more flattering to the ego than the affection of one," he said. Daisy, of course, was chief among them, but he also had a special relationship with Crown Princess Martha of Norway. She and her husband and two young children had become temporary exiles in the United States in 1940 after the Nazi conquest. Attractive, vivacious, and full of youthful charm, she endeared herself to the president, especially with her adroit ways of making him feel as if he was the center of the universe.

His affectionate relations with Daisy and Princess Martha formed a sharp contrast to what had become an increasingly tense relationship with Eleanor. Although she had become a liberal mainstay of his administration, drawing the support of millions of women and minorities, she had also become something of a rival. In June 1942, Odell Waller, a young black Virginia sharecropper who had killed his white landlord in an act of self-defense, was convicted of murder by an all-white jury and sentenced to die in the electric chair. A written appeal from Waller to Eleanor to urge the governor to grant him clemency, coupled with an outpouring of protest from African Americans citing the case as a classic example of Southern racism, moved her to ask Franklin to press the governor to commute the sentence. Roosevelt agreed to her request and passed the letter he sent the governor along to Eleanor with a plea for recognition for having done "good." Eleanor acknowledged his letter as "grand," but was frustrated by his refusal to follow it up with additional pressure. She became angry with Harry Hopkins, who was acting as a buffer for the president, when he refused to plead her case with Franklin for a last-minute intercession with the governor. It led to a very unpleasant argument that depressed Eleanor and added to the burdens besetting the president.

Although most newspapers and commentators agreed that domestic political conflicts should be suspended in wartime, the clash of beliefs about the role of government remained as robust as ever. Roosevelt saw no reason to let Republicans take advantage of his focus on the war and at the end of July began trying to influence the 1942 congressional elections and the 1944 presidential race. He wrote Tony Biddle, the offspring of a wealthy Philadelphia family and ambassador to Norway, who had taken up residence in London: "A lot of good people in Pennsylvania are anxious to have you . . . come home to make one or two speeches in behalf of the ticket in Pennsylvania this fall — in September, if possible." At the same time, he enthusiastically favored a trip for Wendell Willkie that would take him to the Middle East, Russia, and China. Not only could he serve as a good will ambassador or "special representative of the President," but his excursion would also deter him from mounting another presidential campaign that could jeopardize a possible Roosevelt fourth term. When the *New York Herald Tribune* criticized Roosevelt for ignoring war work to spend "a lot of time on the New York political situation," he complained that he had "the skin of a rhinoceros," but felt compelled to correct the paper's "false statement."

His impatience with political opponents boiled over at the beginning of September when he spoke to the International Student Assembly in a radio talk addressed at young people around the globe. He urged them to stand fast against the Axis nations, who would deprive them of a better future. But he could not resist slamming the "handful of men and women, in the United States and elsewhere, who mock and sneer at the Four Freedoms and the Atlantic Charter. . . . They play petty politics in a world crisis. They fiddle with many sour notes while civilization burns."

On the trip back to Washington from one of his retreats in July, he impressed Daisy as "funny & relaxed." He enjoyed teasing her and had "a wonderful time seeing me act my part of prim spinster!" As soon as he arrived at the White House, however, he told Daisy that he was "going to have an awful day . . . I am going over to my office & will spend the day blowing up various people." But ever the optimist, he also told her that "underneath" things were "not as bad . . . as they look." He found some comic relief in a letter Eleanor forwarded to him from a well-meaning correspondent suggesting that America drop bee, hornet, and wasp hives on enemy lines, which would force the Germans to retreat "in utter confusion." Roosevelt remarked that this fellow had "bees in his bonnet."

In July, he sent George Marshall, Harry Hopkins, and Admiral Ernest J. King, chief of naval operations, to London to organize invasion plans. Above all, he wanted "a quick agreement with the British that would enable U.S. ground forces to confront the Germans sometime in 1942," preferably in October, but by November at latest. He hoped the assault could take place before the November elections, but he did not press the point with his military ambassadors.

Because Churchill remained adamantly opposed to a landing in France that fall, the group finally settled on an incursion into French North Africa, codenamed TORCH. Churchill cabled Roosevelt on July 27 of their decision and the imperative for secrecy. Marshall was a reluctant supporter, but Roosevelt was "very happy in the result" of the decision to launch an offensive that could not only defeat Rommel but convince Stalin of Anglo-American determination to destroy Hitler. "I cannot help feeling that the past week represented a turning point in the whole war," he told Churchill. "He is not as despondent about the war as he was, some time ago," Roosevelt told Daisy, yet his countenance betrayed his anxieties. "The P. has heavy worries about the world just now," Daisy recorded in August, "& when in repose, his face is over serious & drawn. His moments of relaxation are few."

No Allied leader, however, faced more immediate wartime challenges than Stalin. At the end of July, the effort to combat the German offensive was costing the Soviets thousands of lives. That it took greater courage to retreat than to advance was accepted wisdom for Soviet troops, who were under orders from Communist apparatchiks pressing them to mount offensives against superior German forces. The news that the British were temporarily suspending convoys and could not reveal the "time and place" of an invasion incensed Stalin. What are the Allies contributing to the war effort? Stalin sarcastically asked. The Soviets were giving blood, the British time, and the Americans money.

Roosevelt, who sympathized with Stalin's complaint, urged Churchill to handle him "with great care. We have got always to bear in mind the personality of our ally and the very difficult and dangerous situation that confronts him. No one can be expected to approach the war from a world point of view whose country has been invaded. I think we should try to put ourselves in his place." Without identifying where the assault would occur, he wanted Churchill to assure Stalin that they had "determined upon a course of action in 1942." He then wrote Stalin directly, informing him of Wendell Willkie's visit to the Middle East and Moscow in September, which he described as a way to convince Muslim countries to join in resistance to the Nazis, who would endanger "their greatest hopes for the future." He described Willkie as "heart and soul with my Administration in our foreign policy of opposition to Nazism and *real friendship with your government.*" He also expected the visit to "be of real benefit to both of our countries if he can get a firsthand impression of the splendid unity of Russia and the great defense you are conducting." Willkie's trip to Moscow was a gesture partly intended to boost Soviet morale in the interim before U.S. troops directly struck at Hitler's forces in Africa.

Difficulties with Chiang Kai-shek compounded worries about Stalin's faith in Anglo-American support. At the close of July, Roosevelt received an "urgent" and "strictly confidential" message from Chiang, lobbying him to pressure Churchill into granting India its independence, which

Chiang saw as a symbol of emerging independence for all Asia, including China. Roosevelt instantly sent the message to Churchill, who urged Roosevelt to do his "best to dissuade Chiang Kai-shek from his completely misinformed activities." Roosevelt counseled Chiang against any action that would undermine current arrangements in India. But, as Roosevelt told Churchill, it was important to give Chiang the impression that his requests received "friendly consideration. I fear that if I did not do so he would be more inclined to take action on his own initiative, which I know you will agree might be very dangerous at the moment."

On August 12. Churchill flew to Moscow, accompanied by Averell Harriman, for a three-day conference. Since he would be delivering Stalin the news about a peripheral invasion of North Africa rather than a cross-Channel attack in 1942, Churchill felt as if he was "carrying a large lump of ice to the North Pole." But determined to convince the Russian leader of the Allies' commitment to break Hitler's power, Churchill plunged into four hours of talks immediately after his arrival. The first two hours of their exchange "were bleak and somber." As soon as he began describing plans for "the ruthless bombing of Germany" and TORCH, Stalin "became intensely interested." An amused Harriman watched a rapport develop between the two leaders as they animatedly foresaw the destruction of "most of Germany's important industrial centers." Stalin also warmly endorsed the North African invasion, saying, "May God prosper this undertaking." The description of the invasion, Churchill advised the president, "seemed a great relief" to the Russians. "All ended cordially," he added, believing that he could now convince Stalin "of our ardent desire . . . to get into battle heavily and speedily."

But by the following day their conversations had become unpleasantly hostile. The group argued for two hours, "during which [Stalin] said many disagreeable things, especially about our being too much afraid of fighting the Germans . . . ; that we had broken our promises about 'Sledgehammer' [the invasion of France]; that we had failed in delivering the supplies promised to Russia and only sent remnants after we had taken all we needed for ourselves." When Churchill refuted Stalin's contentions, protesting that "there was no ring of comradeship in his attitude," he predicted with great animation that they could win the war if "we did not fall apart." Stalin, Churchill reported, exclaimed that "he liked the tone of my utterance."

Stalin then launched into a description of powerful trench mortars that he offered to share and then asked, probing to see if Churchill would reveal anything about Anglo-American research on atomic explosives, if Churchill would agree to share this most closely guarded secret. Although the Americans and British were nowhere near completing the atomic project, Churchill's failure to mention this research, which the Soviets were well aware was in progress, confirmed Stalin's distrust of his allies. Churchill suspected that Stalin's sudden shift in attitude may have been prompted by his Politburo associates' pressing him to take a harder line with the prime minister, but he came away convinced that "in his heart, so far as he has one, Stalin knows we are right." Most important, Churchill saw no indication of a Soviet surrender and believed that Stalin was confident of victory.

On August 18, three days after Churchill departed Moscow, Roosevelt cabled Stalin about a "toehold in the Southwest Pacific" gained by the invasion of the Solomon Islands. He expected to press the advantage they had established but emphasized, "I know *very well* that our real enemy is Germany and that our force and power must be brought against Hitler at the earliest possible moment. You can be sure that this will be done, *just as soon as it is humanly possible to put together the transportation. The United States understands that Russia is bearing the brunt of the fighting and the losses this year. We are filled with admiration of your magnificent resistance. Believe me when I tell you that we are coming as strongly and as quickly as we possibly can.*"

Just as he sought to rally the Soviets with encouraging news, he did the same on the home front to inspire determination to make the sacrifices and meet the demands of the war. On September 7, in a Labor Day speech, he related the heroic self-sacrifice of a naval aviator who gave up his life in the battle of the Coral Sea to destroy a Japanese ship. The selflessness of this pilot was meant to serve as an inspiration to all Americans who were now being asked to hold down inflation on food, which was running at an economically destructive 3 percent a month, and to pay taxes to meet the costs of fighting the war. "Battles are not won by soldiers or sailors who think first of their own personal safety," Roosevelt said. "And wars are not won by people who are concerned primarily with their own comfort, their own convenience, their own pocketbooks. . . . All of us here at home are being tested — for our fortitude, for our selfless devotion to our country and to our cause."

In appealing for "fortitude" and "selfless devotion," Roosevelt was implicitly describing his own personal commitments to bearing presidential burdens. When Morgenthau listened to him describe the struggles the Russians faced in fighting Hitlerism, he was impressed with the president's ability to "state these facts coolly and calmly whether we win or lose the war, and to me it is most encouraging that he really seems to face these issues, and that he is not kidding himself one minute about the war. That, to me, seems to be the correct attitude for a commander-in-chief."

Roosevelt's speech was partly a response to the appalling fact that great numbers of Americans had "no clear ideas of what the war is about." "To win this war," the anthropologist Margaret Mead declared, "we need the impassioned effort of every individual in the country. . . . The government must mobilize people not just to carry out orders but to participate in a great action and to assume responsibility. . . . We gotta feel we have victories in us." The Office of Civilian Defense (OCD) promoted civilian commitment to the war effort with rationing, scrap drives, and blackouts, all of which served to remind Americans across the country that they were fighting a war in which everyone had a part to play.

Although Roosevelt believed that his Fireside Chats remained an effective weapon in mobilizing public support against the isolationists, who remained anti-British, anti-Russian, and anti-Roosevelt, he knew that personal appearances were also a valuable means of informing Americans about war aims and of stimulating national unity. To this end, on September 17, he embarked on a two-week cross-country trip to visit the factories producing planes, ships, tanks, and other weapons. The journey, which he made in a ten-car train, also gave him a feeling of actively promoting the war effort. His presence was not only a way of thanking the troops and workers devoted to the fight for U.S. freedom and security but also a way to heighten his own sense of direct participation in the struggle. The chance to escape the daily grind of Washington politics and to relax with those closest to him shaped his commitment to the excursion as well. He was "keyed up and rather excited over getting away on this trip," Daisy thought. He was also "afraid . . . that something might happen to keep him from going."

He was much relieved when his entourage boarded the train at 10:00 in the evening. Eleanor accompanied him as far as Chicago, but Franklin's old friend and former law partner Harry Hooker, Daisy, and Laura Delano, his flamboyant fifty-seven-year-old cousin, accompanied him throughout the tour. He greatly enjoyed their company, telling them, "You're the only people I know that I don't have to entertain." As compelling for him, they were delightful companions: Both the women were "charming, witty, intelligent, and full of fun." He also loved their affinity for dogs, including Fala, a sixteen-month-old Scottish Terrier that Daisy had given him as a gift in August 1940 and had become the president's constant companion.

The trip was kept a secret, or at least hidden from the mass public, until he returned to Washington. He wanted to avoid the usual hullabaloo that the press and local politicians would raise if they had advance notice of his arrival in the cities he planned to pass through along the way. There were to be "no publicity, no parades, no speeches," he told advisers and the three reporters and eight photographers, who covered the journey and who were sworn to silence until it ended. Roosevelt also wanted to avoid any claims that he was on a 1942 campaign tour, while still expanding Democratic support in the coming elections.

For Franklin and Eleanor, it was a deeply satisfying trip. At each stop he would appear at defense plants and military bases on short notice in an open car, where startled workers and troops clapped, cheered, and waved with "broad smiles on their faces" and exclaimed, "Geez, it's the President!" Franklin took special satisfaction in seeing the most advanced tanks roll off the assembly lines in Detroit's former auto factories. He visited cartridge manufacturing plants in Minnesota, the Great Lakes Naval Training station outside of Chicago, and a turbine factory in Milwaukee. When Daisy walked Fala at a station stop outside Bismarck, North Dakota, a little girl was startled when she read his dog tag: "Fala, The White House, Washington, D.C." They proceeded to a naval training station in Idaho, an Army base in Tacoma, a Navy Yard in Bremerton, Washington, and the Boeing aircraft plant in Seattle.

At Henry Kaiser's shipyard in Portland, Oregon, he joked with the assembly line workers, "You know, I'm not supposed to be here today. I hope you will keep it a secret." The California leg of the trip included appearances at bustling shipyards and aircraft factories; a naval hospital in San Diego, where wounded seamen were excited to meet the president; and the Marine Corps base at Camp Pendleton, where trainees were preparing to ship out to fight the Japanese in the Solomon Islands. Heading east across the southern tier of the United States, the Roosevelt party stopped in Uvalde, Texas, where he visited former vice president John Nance Garner, who patted the president on the head and said, "God bless you, Boss." The train then crossed the state, stopping at some of the airfields that were training Army Air Force men being sent to England to fly bombing raids against German targets. At the navy yard in New Orleans, "a relaxed & cheerful" president visited the Higgins boat plant, which produced the craft that would become the principal vehicle for transporting men and equipment in amphibious assaults. Roosevelt remarked on how he had to battle to free Higgins from its normal production to build these innovative vehicles.

By the end of the trip Roosevelt had traveled nearly nine thousand miles over a two-week period and was able to witness firsthand the facilities that gave meaning to his promise to make America "the arsenal of democracy." The country's factories were producing 10,000 tanks a month, ten times the German output, while Boeing was manufacturing 12,677 B-17 bombers, the aptly named "Flying Fortress" and mainstay of the air campaign against Hitler's Germany and ultimately Japan's home islands. The Kaiser shipyards were breaking every record for production and won Roosevelt's praise for "wonderful work," as did their head, Henry Kaiser, whom he called a "dynamo." As important, in the nine months after Pearl Harbor, the armed services swelled nearly fourfold from 1.6 million to 5.4 million. It was a fighting force that neither Germany nor Japan nor Italy could hope to match in determination and equipment. "The whole thing is an extraordinary achievement," Daisy noted.

At the same time that Roosevelt marveled at the country's productive genius, Eleanor found much to celebrate in the emergence of women and African Americans as vital contributors to the country's factories and armed services. The prejudice against them did not disappear, especially across the South, where segregation remained a fixed part of blacks' daily life. But to Eleanor's delight, Franklin publicly acknowledged the "large proportion of women employed doing skilled manual labor running machines." In the coming year, he expected the number of women working in the country's war plants to equal the number of men, and he condemned the bias that barred women and blacks from essential war work, insisting, "We can no longer afford to indulge such prejudices or practices." Rosie the Riveter, the topic of a popular song, became a national icon who was lauded as "the woman behind the man behind the gun." At the height of the war as many as 20 million women formed a part of the work force, and 350,000 served in the armed forces.

While Roosevelt could privately boast that "American reserves and American planes and tank production are at least up to all reasonable schedules," he felt compelled to acknowledge that "the controlling factor is to get these reserves and munitions to the scene of actual fighting." With the Burma Road still under Japanese control, for example, flying supplies into China over the Himalayas was a daunting challenge that cost American lives and planes and undercut promises of building a robust Chinese fighting force. The perilous northern convoy route to Murmansk as well remained an imperfect way to supply Russia's armies.

Despite these obstacles, his cross-country trip deepened Roosevelt's belief in the country's wherewithal to win the war. He mentioned to his companions several times that "this was the most restful & satisfactory [trip] he had ever taken." On October 1, the day after he returned, he announced to the press that he had seen "an amazing example of what can be done with proper organization, with the right spirit of carrying it through, and proper planning." He recounted the many defense facilities and training camps he had visited in the eleven states to which the group had traveled. He brimmed with praise for the women workers handling all sorts of technical jobs and for the spirit of commitment to build the most advanced weapons coming out of the factories and shipyards. He declared himself entirely satisfied with the 94 or 95 percent output of what had been projected would be the total for the year. He praised the popular determination to hold down inflation and emphasized the apolitical nature of his trip. Yes, he had seen the governors of the eleven states they had passed through, but no senators or congressmen running for office or local or state candidates.

While he could not have been more emphatic about his detachment from the coming November elections, he couldn't resist throwing a barb at the "doubting Thomases" in Congress and the press who argued that the defense plants wouldn't be able to achieve half of what they had actually accomplished. He described how the spirit of unity and support flourished everywhere except in Washington, D.C. He ended his press conference with a political attack on members of Congress, the press, and the administration who were undermining the war effort by self-serving pronouncements. That his eye was in fact firmly focused on the November elections was made evident by his correspondence with Churchill, in which he stressed the importance of making the North African invasion appear to be an American offensive, which he hoped would generate fresh and timely enthusiasm for his party.

Compounding these problems, his press conferences gave evidence of something that neither he nor the journalists remarked on. He responded to almost all the reporters' questions by asking them to repeat themselves. Almost sixty-one in the fall of 1942, Roosevelt seemed to have experienced a loss of audio capacity. His physical health was declining, though it was not yet evident to the journalists who usually saw him twice a week. And even if it had been, they would have been reluctant to report any physical decline. He was the country's most important leader in the midst of a world war that threatened America's future, and no one wanted to undermine public morale by suggesting that health problems imperiled the president's ability to lead.

In a Columbus Day, October 12, Fireside Chat to the nation, Roosevelt lauded the "unbeatable spirit" he found across the country, praised the men and women who were producing the sinews of war, decried the prejudice that barred African Americans, women, and the elderly from making a valued contribution to the war effort, counseled against the influence of "typewriter strategists" and Axis propaganda, called for an expansion of the draft to eighteen-year-olds, warned that acts of criminal savagery by Nazi leaders would be punished in time, and urged the importance of not just fighting the war but also preserving the postwar peace. "It is useless to fight a war unless it stays won," he said.

In celebrating the work of blacks and women and denouncing the bias that limited their contributions to the war effort, Roosevelt's rhetoric outran the actualities of knocking down barriers to their participation in the conflict. This was especially the case for a significant number of blacks in the military. While there were black Army units and black air squadrons, the War Department and joint chiefs refused to integrate black and white troops and rejected suggestions that black officers lead black troops. The Navy was especially resistant to any sort of combat role for African Americans and was content to have them serve as mess men, working as cooks and servants for officers. A Navy study concluded that "the enlistment of Negroes (other than as mess attendants) leads to disruptive and undermining conditions." Roosevelt pressed the Navy to change its policy, but it insisted that any sort of integration would undermine "teamwork and discipline." In response, Roosevelt asserted that the one-tenth of American citizens who happened to be black deserved a chance to serve their country. In light of the heroics of Dorie Miller, a black mess man on a battleship at Pearl Harbor who won a Navy Cross for carrying his wounded captain to safety and manning a machine gun to shoot down a Japanese plane, the Navy was forced into accepting a larger role for African Americans, but only on the condition that they remain segregated from whites.

Domestic divisions were only a small part of Roosevelt's agenda in the summer and fall of 1942. On August 7, U.S. forces landed on Guadalcanal in the Solomon Islands, where they expected to achieve a quick victory over Japanese troops. Instead, in naval combat U.S. and Australian forces suffered a severe defeat: Four cruisers and two destroyers were sunk and another cruiser was damaged. The battle for Guadalcanal took on special significance when, five days after the Marines landed, twenty of them on patrol were "ambushed, shot, and bayoneted" by Japanese troops pretending to surrender. The incident became infamous as an example of Japanese deceit on the battlefield and was used to justify atrocities against surrendering Japanese soldiers. The struggle to control the island, a tropical rain forest that bred disabling illnesses among the troops, was centered on control of an air base the Marines had named Henderson Field. The battle would last for six months until February 1943 and demonstrated to Roosevelt just how difficult defeating Japan would be.

When he returned from his inspection tour, he faced hard decisions about Germany and Russia. He was eager to send U.S. forces into combat in North Africa as soon as possible while helping the Russians withstand the Nazis' summer offensive. Questions of when and where to land troops dominated the cable traffic between Washington and London. Roosevelt was convinced that the Vichy French would be much less inclined to oppose an American invasion in French territory than one led by the British, and the prime minister did not object to having the United States take on "the whole burden, political and military, of the landings." But Churchill wondered if the United States would "have enough American trained and equipped forces to do this all by themselves," since the plan now was to land at Casablanca in Morocco and Oran and Algiers in Algeria. With the burden of decision on the offensive now entirely in Roosevelt's hands, Churchill told him in mid-September, "In the whole of TORCH, military and political, I consider myself your Lieutenant." However great this responsibility, Roosevelt believed it essential for the public to see U.S. troops engaged in the fighting, which he hoped would have a significant impact in fostering a national sense of participation in the war.

While Churchill and Roosevelt moved ahead on invasion plans, new problems erupted over the convoys to Murmansk when German planes and ships operating from Norway imperiled the supply vessels and their escorts. Churchill wanted to plan an assault on German forces there, code-named JUPITER, to drive them back from the Norwegian coast or at a minimum compel them to weaken their eastern front by transferring men and supplies to northwestern Europe.

On September 15, as Roosevelt was preparing for his cross-country inspection tour, Churchill gave him the bad news that it seemed "almost impossible to fit in another convoy before TORCH." Should they decide against attempting one, Churchill asked the president to help him with Stalin, who seemed certain to complain loudly about a British refusal to risk additional losses when the Russians were then engaged in defending Stalingrad. Roosevelt promised to "do everything I can with Stalin." At the same time, his commitment to TORCH prevented him from sending more aircraft to fight the Japanese in the Solomon Islands or from supporting expanded air raids from Britain on Germany. The demands of TORCH also meant they would not be able to send another convoy to Russia until January. In the midst of his trip, Roosevelt insisted that they not pile up new issues with Stalin by telling him about delayed shipments until absolutely necessary. He had every hope that a successful assault on North Africa and the defeat of German forces there would help ease their difficulties with Moscow, especially since his chiefs had advised him that TORCH would delay a cross-Channel attack until 1944. Disagreements with Churchill, who favored peripheral assaults, such as the strike on Norway, also loomed over an invasion of France — whether it came in 1943 or after.

While Roosevelt's highest priority was to ensure the success of TORCH, sustaining the Russian front was never far behind. He told Churchill it "is today our greatest reliance and we simply must find a direct manner in which to help them other than our diminishing supplies." He considered it essential to take all possible risks to do so rather than "endanger our whole relations with Russia at this time." He was especially disturbed by a telegram from Stalin at the beginning of October describing the deterioration of the defense of Stalingrad and the dangers it posed to Russia's whole southern front. Whatever they wrote Stalin, Roosevelt cautioned Churchill, it was essential to phrase their messages so "as to leave a good taste in his mouth."

Wendell Willkie had eased some of the tensions with the Soviet leader by his visit to Moscow in September, having given a sympathetic hearing to

Stalin's "complaints about insufficient deliveries of aircraft." Moreover, Willkie had flattered him with compliments about his popularity among his people. Why, he was being so democratic, Willkie observed, that he might open the way to elections that could cost him his job. According to Willkie's account, Stalin laughed heartily at his guest's joke.

By October 8, though TORCH was still a month away and there was little evidence of a reduction in German forces on the eastern front to meet a threatened assault in the west, Churchill convinced Roosevelt to tell Stalin "the blunt truth" about the delayed convoys. He thought they could soften the blow somewhat by informing him of their plans to put an air force in the Caucusus and of their expectations that the combination of TORCH, a British offensive in Egypt against Rommel's armies, shipments of additional fighter aircraft to Russia, and the dispatch of single supply ships rather than convoys would bring some relief to Stalin's southern front. When the British chiefs wrote Churchill that "the Russian army is, to-day, the only force capable of defeating the German army" and that it was "the war in Russia which is most rapidly sapping Germany's strength," Churchill told them, "I hope Stalin will not see this." But that was an assessment that Roosevelt subscribed to as well, convinced that encouraging words could make a difference, he told Stalin, "Everyone in America is thrilled by the gallant defense of Stalingrad and we are confident that it will succeed."

As they moved into the second half of October, Roosevelt was optimistic about the prospects for TORCH, though the continuing fight for Guadalcanal also troubled him. He worried that "the large concentration of Japanese forces may drive us out," and told Churchill: "Every day we are killing a number of Jap ships and planes, but there is no use blinking the fact that we are greatly outnumbered," or that the demands of TORCH were reducing the number of men and amount of matériel going to the Pacific. Still, because he understood how essential it was to boost U.S. morale and gain the initiative by defeating the Japanese on Guadalcanal, he ordered that "every possible weapon" be sent there. In response, U.S air, land, and naval units flowed to the Pacific in greater abundance than Roosevelt had actually wanted. By the close of the year, nine of the seventeen divisions and nineteen of the thirty-six air groups sent overseas were fighting the Japanese.

At the same period in October, with his eye on the coming congressional elections, he sent Eleanor on a good will trip to England. Because she was one of the most public symbols of his administration's liberal partisanship, he wanted her out of the country as a sign that, as commander in chief, he was keeping out of politics. Moreover, in the days directly before the election, he urged Churchill to keep her "official business to a minimum." He had been promoting an apolitical message from the first day of the war. "I would say it is about time," he told a pre-election press conference, "for a large number of people — several of whom are in this room — to forget politics. . . . We read altogether too much politics in our papers. . . . They [the people] haven't waked up to the fact that this is a war. Politics is out. Same is true in Congress." In this, he had Willkie's cooperation. The titular head of the

Republican Party had made his nonpartisanship clear when he left the country on his world tour during the 1942 political season. Roosevelt was determined not to repeat Woodrow Wilson's mistake in 1918 by calling for a Democratic Party victory to maintain control of Congress. He hoped that his stratagem of a nonpolitical approach to the elections and his suspension of overtly political activism would ensure his continuing and possibly even expanded control of the House and the Senate.

Even if Roosevelt had wanted to intervene in the elections, pressing war business kept him preoccupied and on edge. The fighting in Guadalcanal, in which he advised Churchill that U.S. forces were "hard-pressed"; his conviction that production of escort vessels, merchant ships, and especially fighter planes was falling short of what was needed for the following year; and anxiety that Stalin might be considering a negotiated settlement with Hitler all worried him. Stalin's silence in response to Churchill's messages about providing planes for the southern front and asking for Russian assistance on the convoy route left Churchill "perplexed."

Roosevelt was no less concerned, but his inveterate optimism gave him the wherewithal to see beyond the dark moments demoralizing so many others. On October 27, he cabled Churchill, "I am not unduly disturbed about our respective responses or lack of responses from Moscow. I have decided they do not use speech for the same purposes that we do. . . . I feel very sure the Russians are going to hold this Winter and that we should proceed vigorously with our plans both to supply them and to set up an air force to fight with them. *I want us to be able to say to Mr. Stalin that we have carried out our obligations one hundred percent.*"

When the polls closed on November 3, the outcome was typical of a midterm election. After ten years of Democratic governance, the electorate was receptive to granting Republicans greater power. Helped by a low turnout — only half the number of people who had voted in 1940 went to the polls — Republicans made significant gains: Their House delegation increased by 44 seats, only 13 short of a majority, while their Senate contingent grew by 9 seats. Though Democrats continued to hold a 59 to 37 seat advantage in the upper house, they no longer had the lopsided majority of the previous decade. With the North African offensive four days away, the battle for Guadalcanal still at issue and even in some doubt, families frustrated by wartime rationing of gasoline, meat, coffee, and other foodstuffs, and unions irritated by wage controls, the electorate was in no mood to rally behind Roosevelt.

Three days after the vote, he put the best possible face on the outcome. When asked at a press conference, "How do you account for the election results?" he replied with a grin and a wave of his cigarette holder: "I know very little about this election." Would the Republican gains make any difference in his attitude? a reporter inquired, trying to draw him out. "I assume," he blithely answered, that "the new Congress would be as much in favor of winning the war as the Chief Executive himself." His secretary William Hassett "found the President in high spirits." He just seemed to be glad that the election was over and showed "not a trace of the post election gloom which, according

753

to his enemies, should encircle him." He told Ambassador John Winant in London, "I hope the country will forget politics for two years. That, however, is an almost impossible miracle." As someone who was consistently aware of his impact on public opinion, he never lost sight of politics.

For all his optimism and refusal to be overtly political in domestic affairs, Roosevelt was enough of a realist to see that he confronted great obstacles in adjourning politics or, more important, winning the war.

In the run-up to the North African invasion, he clashed with Churchill over how to calm Spanish and Portuguese concerns about British threats to their African possessions. Roosevelt wanted them to understand the invasion as being strictly "under American command," while Churchill thought that candor about British participation was the best way to "remove any suspicions about the object of our concentrations at Gibraltar."

Roosevelt believed that keeping the United States in the forefront was even more essential in assuring the French that "the allies seek no territory and have no intention of interfering with friendly French authorities in Africa." In November 1940, he had appointed Admiral William D. Leahy ambassador to Vichy France. It was a calculated attempt to have a prominent U.S. military leader persuade Marshal Henri Pétain, France's eighty-four-year-old World War I hero and Vichy chief of state, to resist German pressure to join the Axis side in the war. Roosevelt particularly hoped that diplomatic relations with Pétain's government could dissuade it from resisting the North African invasion. Roosevelt's "Vichy gamble," as some called it, opened a conflict in

Washington between the Board of Economic Warfare, under the aegis of Vice President Henry Wallace and Milo Perkins, an associate from the Agriculture Department, and Hull's State Department, who battled over providing supplies to the Vichy French in North Africa, which State favored as a way to head off opposition to an invasion and the board saw as aiding the Axis. The dispute reached the White House, where Roosevelt sided with Hull.

Tensions also arose with Charles de Gaulle, who led Free French resistance to Vichy and the German occupation. Roosevelt took pains to ensure that de Gaulle was kept in the dark about the November attack, as he was certain any sign of collaboration with de Gaulle would signal Free French involvement in the North African campaign and trigger a militant Vichy response. De Gaulle was already at odds with the U.S. decision to maintain diplomatic relations with Vichy, which he viewed as a betrayal of France's future. Although Churchill gave de Gaulle sanctuary in London and recognized his Free French authority, he accepted Roosevelt's judgment about denying him a part in the invasion or recognizing him as the legitimate head of North Africa's French colonies. During a visit to London in July, when Marshall and King refused to share any information with de Gaulle about U.S. plans, he walked out of the meeting in a huff. By now de Gaulle had come to suspect that the Allies were planning a North African assault, which only deepened his hostility to Roosevelt and Washington's Vichy accommodation and marked the beginning of a feud that would continue throughout the war. For Roosevelt, de Gaulle represented a France that had failed to mount a defense against the Germans and was unworthy of a central role in the war councils or discussions shaping Europe's future. For his part, de Gaulle regarded the president as an opportunist who was dismissive of France's history and potential contribution to a Nazi defeat.

Problems with Spain, meanwhile, continued to simmer in the weeks before the launch of TORCH. When the U.S. ambassador reported Spanish threats to enter the war on Germany's side if the United Nations invaded North Africa, Roosevelt passed the report along to Churchill. American interference in a matter Churchill considered under British control angered him. Fortunately, tensions between the Allies evaporated after the invasion on November 8 made it clear that Francisco Franco's warnings were no more than an empty threat.

The differences over Spain underscored Churchill's concern at Britain's growing dependence on the United States — not only for the wherewithal to fight the war but also for Britain's future role in world politics. However much he appreciated the vital U.S. support, Churchill understood that the war was draining Britain of its resources, undermining its empire, and consigning it to a greatly diminished influence on the world stage. On October 31, in a cable to the president, Churchill lamented the approach of "our last remaining reserves of manpower" and Britain's "deteriorating maritime strength." "All our labour and capacity is engaged in the war effort," he told Roosevelt. ". . . We have lost enormously in ships used in the common interest, and we trust to you to give us a fair and just assignment of your new vast construction to sail under our own flag." He cited

Britain's dependence on U.S. food stores, explaining that "our stocks are running down with dangerous rapidity." In his closing, which was as much an expression of distress as a statement of support for the invasion, he wrote: "I pray that this great American enterprise, in which I am your lieutenant and in which we have the honour to play an important part, may be crowned by the success it deserves."

Roosevelt was not insensitive to the price Britain was paying in both power and influence. He could not miss Churchill's irony in describing himself as the president's lieutenant and in his mentioning "the honour to play an important part" in the invasion, when in fact British naval and infantry forces were slated to make a significant contribution to the offensive. His dispatching Eleanor on a four-week visit to Britain was intended not only to distance her from the congressional elections but also to demonstrate American regard for Churchill and the British people. "I confide my Missus to the care of you and Mrs. Churchill. I know our better halves will hit it off beautifully," he wrote the prime minister on October 19, two days before Eleanor made the somewhat perilous flight to England. Feted by the king and queen and housed at Buckingham Palace, Eleanor endeared herself to the English and received unanimous praise for her courage in facing the danger from German attacks in England. The fifty-eight-year-old Eleanor was a whirlwind of activity: On November 1, Churchill reported that "Mrs. Roosevelt has been winning golden opinions here from all for her kindness and her unfailing interest in everything we are doing. . . . We are most grateful for her visit and for all the encouragement it is giving to our women workers. I did my best to advise a reduction of her programme . . . but I have not met with success, and Mrs. Roosevelt proceeds indefatigably." She visited Dover and Canterbury, which were in range of German artillery and bombers. (The day after she left Canterbury it suffered a heavy daylight raid.) Roosevelt glowed with satisfaction over the "almost unanimously favorable press" she received in the United States and hoped it would pay dividends in the upcoming congressional voting. More important, her visit underscored Roosevelt's genuine regard for Churchill and all the British were doing in the war.

During 1942, no ally was more consistently irritating or troubling than Chiang. The loss of Burma and his unwillingness to follow Stilwell's advice on how to mount an offensive against the Japanese tested Roosevelt's patience. The differences between Chiang and Stilwell were so sharp, General Claire Chennault, the head of the American Volunteer Air Group in China, reported, that Chiang would have had Stilwell shot if he were a Chinese general. Stilwell complained that Chiang "made it impossible for me to do anything," and secretly called him "the Peanut," deriding him as a "stupid, gutless" wonder with no interest in anything beyond his own power and grandiosity. During the spring, Chiang had complained to Roosevelt about China's peripheral role in joint staff conferences and supply decisions, protesting that "China is treated not as an equal like Britain and Russia, but as a ward." In response to a Japanese offensive in southern China in May, Chiang had threatened "an undeclared peace involving cessation of hostilities." He wanted to know if and when U.S. aid would arrive, declared that China's faltering war effort was at its "most crucial stage," and warned that a collapse might be imminent. Given his other wartime commitments, Roosevelt had little to offer beyond reassurances of future supply deliveries and a role for a great-power China in postwar world affairs. But Roosevelt's promises impressed Chiang as little more than rhetoric. Stilwell wired: "The Generalissimo wants a yes or no answer whether the Allies consider this Theater necessary and will support it." Chiang again cautioned that the Chinese fighting front would collapse unless three American divisions were sent to India to recapture the Burma Road. In response the United States assigned five hundred combat planes to fight the Japanese in China and began shipping five thousand tons of supplies a month over the Himalayas. Roosevelt did not reply directly to Chiang's demands but urged him to understand that the United States was "doing absolutely all in our power to help China win this war."

Stilwell, who found himself in the middle of this dispute between the two leaders, especially resented the pressure being placed on him from the Generalissimo and Madame Chiang "to be a Chinese, a stooge that plugs the U.S. for anything and everything they want." They tried to win him over by arranging his promotion to full general, but Stilwell knew better, noting in a diary, "The hell they are." Given Stilwell's resistance to act as a lobbyist for China's demands, Chiang pressed Roosevelt to make Stilwell totally subordinate to him and to transfer his control over Lend-Lease supplies entirely to him.

Counseled by Marshall and limited by the

demands the fighting in the Middle East, the Pacific, and the coming African offensive made on U.S. resources, Roosevelt continued to resist the pressure from China. Mindful of how starved the CBI theater would remain, Stilwell remarked wryly, "Peanut and I are on a raft, with one sandwich between us, and the rescue ship is heading away from the scene." He was all too aware that "the Chiang Kai-shek regime is playing the USA for a sucker, . . . that it is looking for an Allied victory without making any further effort on its part to secure it; and that it expects to have piled up at the end of the war a supply of munitions that will allow it to perpetuate itself indefinitely." Chiang's strategy was guided by the old Chinese adage: Let the barbarians fight the barbarians. He expected the Americans to take responsibility for defeating the Japanese while he prepared to battle his old domestic enemy, Mao Tse-tung's Communists. Although Roosevelt saw no way to meet Chiang's demands, he believed it essential to keep him engaged in the war. A Chinese collapse would not only free several Japanese divisions to join the fighting in the Pacific but also demoralize Americans who considered China their best ally — a nation that, unlike Britain, had no colonial history, and, unlike Russia, had a government allegedly aspiring to imitate that of the United States. When Roosevelt briefly considered removing Stilwell, observing, "I cannot help feeling that the whole situation depends largely on the problem of personalities rather than on strategic plans," Marshall dissuaded him, arguing that Stilwell was "a troop leader rather than a negotiator or supply man who would only serve to promote harmony in Chungking."

In the fall of 1942, all the battlefield uncertainties across Asia, the Pacific, the Middle East, and Russia, combined with domestic divisions, led Roosevelt to wonder why he had fought so hard to win a third term. As the congressional elections had demonstrated, national divisions remained as sharp as ever. Unlike Britain, China, and Russia, where lives were being lost on battlefields and home fronts alike, Americans were insulated from the terrors of air raids destroying their cities, but they worried that they might suffer the same fate as London and Berlin. Nonetheless, the politics of postwar arrangements were very much the topic of current debate. Vice President Henry Wallace weighed in with a speech promising a "people's peace" that would mark the dawn of "the century of the common man." Reluctant to see another round of idealistic preachments calling for an end to realpolitik and the initiation of universalism under collective security, conservatives called Wallace's idealism "globaloney." Adolf Berle in the State Department mocked Wallace's world vision as needing "gods to run it. I don't know how it is with you," he told an English official, "but here in Washington there is quite a bottle-neck in archangels."

Although Roosevelt hardly wanted a divisive domestic argument over postwar international politics, he took some satisfaction in noting that for the first time in their history, Americans felt compelled to think about distant regions of the world. He wrote Joseph Alsop, his cousin and a prominent columnist, who was heading to China to join General Claire Chennault's Flying Tigers, "What a privilege it is to be alive in this particular day and age! Until now almost every practical philosophy and ideal has been confined to national thinking or perhaps regional planning. I wonder what your classmates at school would have thought of you if you had announced that you would be part and parcel of American military operations in Africa, Asia and Polynesia. If I had suggested that at Groton in 1900 they would have put me down as more unorthodox than I actually was." Yet Roosevelt knew that such isolationist thinking still flourished, and so he sent word to Clark Eichelberger, the head of the League of Nations Association, who wished to revive discussions about creating an international organization, advising him, "for heaven's sake [don't] do anything specific at this time." He told Harry Hopkins that he "was determined not to go to the Senate with any treaty before the end of the war," which he feared would undermine the consensus he believed essential to the war effort.

At the same time, however, he was quietly pondering how to organize the postwar world in order to keep the peace for more than twenty years — the time that had passed between the two world wars. In a conversation with Grace Tully and Sam Rosenman in mid-November, he proposed that the League of Nations change its name to "The United Nations Association" and that world peace become the responsibility of four key nations or "four policemen" — Britain, China, Russia, and the United States. He also suggested that Eichelberger put out a trial balloon of these ideas "without associating him with them." He then told Jan Smuts, the president of South Africa, that he was eager to discuss with him "plans now for the victorious peace which will surely come," including a system of trusteeships he intended to propose for former colonies that were not yet ready for self-governance. At the end of November, in what Daisy described as a "momentous" conversation during a visit to Hyde Park, Roosevelt expressed his determination to meet with Churchill and Stalin in order to begin discussing postwar plans: He hoped they would agree to his notion of a group of four international powers who would use their authority and power to prevent acts of aggression, promote universal disarmament for everyone but the four peacekeepers, and endorse ultimate self-determination for former colonies. He saw his plan as a combination of Wilson's idealism and hardheaded realism.

During the first week of November, however, Roosevelt had been focused on the imminent commencement of TORCH. The campaign represented the first great U.S. offensive against Hitler's armies, and he was desperately concerned to see it succeed. On Friday, November 6, on the eve of the invasion, he led a procession to Shangri-La with Harry Hopkins, Grace Tully, Daisy, and military aides. Although Daisy was given no details about the attack, Roosevelt offered broad hints that something serious was about to take place and said that they might have to return to Washington suddenly — no doubt concerned that a faltering assault might require his presence in the White House Map Room, where he could closely monitor developments. He was especially concerned that U-boats might sink some of the six hundred ships carrying the 90,000 troops and weapons staging the attack; that the Atlantic seas off Morocco and Oran, which could produce fifteen-foot waves, might imperil the landing; and that German and French resistance might repel the invaders.

General Dwight D. Eisenhower, the fifty-two-year-old U.S. officer commanding the operation from a tunnel under the Rock of Gibraltar, shared the president's anxiety. A significant amount of chaos had attended the preparation for the landing of the untested troops, who were thrown into combat with much hope and no battlefield experience. Eisenhower himself, who was an up-through-the-ranks career officer, had had no previous testing in battle. Burdened with every conceivable modern warfare tool in their knapsacks that U.S. factories could produce, some of the troops drowned in the struggle to get ashore from the landing craft. But the bulk of the invaders reached the beaches unopposed. When Roosevelt took a call from the War Department with the first reports of the attack, his hand shook as he lifted the receiver to his ear. His relief was evident as he put down the phone and exclaimed, "Thank God. Thank God. We have landed in North Africa. Casualties are below expectations. We are striking back."

Despite some Vichy French resistance, the Anglo-American forces captured Oran, Algiers, and Casablanca within three days. "I am happy today," he wrote Josephus Daniels, ". . . for three months I have been taking it on the chin in regard to the Second front and that is now over." A simultaneous British victory at El Alamein in Egypt with the capture of 36,000 German troops, Rommel in retreat, and the emergence of Lieutenant General Bernard Montgomery as a celebrated British war hero sparked fresh optimism. Churchill caught the spirit of renewed hope when he said, "Now, this is not the end. It is not even the beginning of the end. But it is, perhaps, the end of the beginning."

Along with the success, however, the invasion triggered new controversies and tensions. Determined as ever to discourage Vichy forces from opposing the Allies, Roosevelt sanctioned an agreement with Admiral Jean Darlan, the Vichy commander in chief. Darlan was fortuitously present in Algiers on the day of the attack, visiting a gravely ill son, and so was in a position to halt his troops' resistance. Eager to respond to a German occupation of Vichy France in retaliation for limited French opposition to the invasion, and a commitment to grant him political control across French North Africa, Darlan agreed to cooperate with the Allies.

The arrangement provoked a firestorm of anger and opposition in both Britain and the United States. Describing it as "a sordid nullification of the principles for which the United Nations were supposed to be fighting," critics warned against a compromise peace with Germany and Japan that would leave fascists in power. Because Roosevelt continued to see de Gaulle as a divisive influence and because General Henri Giraud, the Frenchman Roosevelt had identified as an alternative future leader to de Gaulle and Darlan, was proving to be difficult to manage, Roosevelt tried to fend off detractors by declaring, "We are opposed to Frenchmen who support Hitler and the Axis. . . . The future French Government will be established not by any individual in metropolitan France or overseas, but by the French people themselves after they have been set free by the victory of the United Nations." In the meantime, he publicly rationalized the collaboration with

Darlan by quoting an old Balkan proverb: "My children, you are permitted in time of great danger to walk with the Devil until you have crossed the bridge." He also told the public that it was "only a temporary expedient justified solely by the stress of battle."

Churchill warned Roosevelt that the Darlan pact might be doing "serious political injury . . . to our cause . . . by the feeling that we are ready to make terms with local Quislings." (Vidkun Quisling was Norway's Nazi collaborator.) Churchill also advised Roosevelt that "His Majesty's Government are under quite definite and solemn obligations to De Gaulle and his movement. We must see they have a fair deal. It seems to me that you and I ought to avoid at all costs the creation of rival French Émigré Governments each favored by one of us. We must try to fuse all anti-German French forces together, and make a United Government." De Gaulle haughtily declared, "The U.S. can pay traitors but not with the honor of France. What remains of the honor of France will stay intact in my hands." The *Nation* magazine condemned Roosevelt for embracing a "prostitute." The deal drove Henry Morgenthau into a depression, and he told Roosevelt that it was "something that afflicts my soul." Stimson accepted that the arrangement with Darlan had provided "enormous benefits," but had dishonored the administration.

Sam Rosenman recalled that Roosevelt "showed more resentment and more impatience with his critics throughout this period than at any other time I know about. . . . At times he bitterly read aloud what some columnist had written about them, and expressed his resentment." He was painfully distressed at being accused of cozying up to Fascists and Nazis, whom he despised. He lost his temper when two de Gaulle supporters complained about the Darlan deal, shouting at them: "Of course I'm dealing with Darlan since Darlan's giving me Algiers! Tomorrow I'd deal with [Vichy Premier Pierre] Laval, if Laval were to offer me Paris!" Since the arrangement reduced combat, saved lives, and forced the repeal of some Vichy laws discriminating against Jews, Roosevelt could not understand the outcry against his policy. Churchill summed up the problem by telling Roosevelt: "Not only have our enemies been thus encouraged, but our friends have been correspondingly confused and cast down."

Over the next six weeks, the controversy subsided as the Allies advanced across North Africa; Vichy broke relations with the United States; Stalin endorsed the deal, saying defeating Germany made arrangements with "even the Devil himself and his grandma" justifiable; and, on Christmas Eve, a young French monarchist shot and killed Darlan. But the alliance would cast a shadow of suspicion over Roosevelt's intentions and leave deep wounds that would affect his future dealings with the French.

Pressured by Hitler, Pétain summoned more than 300,000 German and Italian troops to defend Tunisia as U.S. forces pushed east from Morocco and Algeria and British forces led by Montgomery and buoyed by their victory at El Alamein advanced on Tunisia from Libya to the west. The initial tank battles with the superior Nazi panzers demonstrated that the Germans might now be on the defensive but that they remained a formidable enemy. Although Eisenhower saw U.S. operations as in violation of "every recognized principle of war," he would use them as object lessons for all future tank battles. From these early skirmishes, Eisenhower and his subordinates took instruction on what would bring them victory in Africa in the opening months of 1943.

CHAPTER 17
"HIGH PROMISE
OF BETTER THINGS"

By December 1942, Roosevelt believed that the Allies had "turned the corner" in the fighting "even though killing and suffering must continue for some time to come." Not the least of these horrors was the Nazi extermination campaign against Europe's Jews. By the end of 1942, Roosevelt and other Allied leaders knew that the Nazis had set up concentration camps across Poland at Bełżec, Sobibór, Auschwitz, and Treblinka for the purpose of killing Jews. In October, he had issued a warning that war criminals would pay for their crimes at the end of the fighting. At the same time, however, he reflected public sentiment in explaining that it would be Germany's leaders and not its people who would face punishment. He feared that any talk of "mass reprisals" would only stiffen the resolve of enemy populations to continue fighting. In the run-up to the November elections, he was also reluctant to say anything that might antagonize German American or Italian American voters.

After the elections, Roosevelt tried to persuade the new Congress to ease restrictions on immigrants and imports coming into the United States. But House and Senate leaders told him that Congress feared he would use any such change "to open the doors to indiscriminate immigration." Although war production had spurred an economic boom, fear of a postwar collapse was used as an argument against any relaxation of immigration restrictions. Hostility to Jewish refugees by ethnics of every stripe strengthened the determination to keep barriers in place.

Although he had received mounting evidence in the fall of 1942 of Nazi atrocities, Roosevelt resisted meeting with American Jewish leaders, who he feared would press him to take up an issue that would deepen antagonism to him in Congress and stir opposition in the State Department. With the exception of Sumner Welles, department officials refused to acknowledge the existence of an extermination program. While American newspapers printed stories about allegations of mass killings, they resisted making them front-page stories. After Eleanor attended a day of mourning ceremony in New York on December 2 and the press carried additional accounts of mass killings, the president finally agreed to meet with a Jewish delegation on December 8. Although he condemned Hitler as "an insane man" and his associates as psychopaths and agreed to issue another statement condemning their atrocities, he told the delegation that it would harm the war effort to condemn all German people, and predicted that the Germans themselves would rise up against Hitler and the Nazis as they began to lose the war. It was a prophecy based more on hope and eagerness to rationalize his incapacity to halt the killings than on any realistic estimate of effective opposition to the Nazi regime.

While Roosevelt gave the delegation a sympathetic hearing, he saw nothing he could do to stop or even limit the Jewish catastrophe: Current military circumstances and public sentiment in the United States were bars to action. He took some satisfaction in appointing New York governor Herbert H. Lehman as the State Department's Relief and Rehabilitation administrator, and looked forward to the day when "some of those Goddamned Fascists" in Germany and Italy will be "begging for their subsistence from a Jew." But he continued to say nothing to Congress and the American people that might have spurred some kind of rescue effort.

Although Roosevelt had publicly distanced himself from the recent political contests for control of Congress, the Republican gains had frustrated and angered him. He saw them as an assault on New Deal reforms and was eager to mount a defense of liberal advances. Doing so would have to wait until the fighting ended, but he found it irresistible "to speak of jobs and further security for the postwar period. This is contrary to nearly all political advice I receive," he told Canadian prime minister Mackenzie King. "Nevertheless it is bound to be an issue and we might as well get on the right side of it now."

War critics especially irritated him. When Pennsylvania Republican senator James Davis criticized him for miscalculating the military's need for gasoline in the African invasion, Roosevelt sarcastically invited people who attacked his military supply policies "to tell me, or the Military and Naval Staffs how this can be done." When Clare Boothe Luce, the wife of *Time* and *Life* publisher Henry Luce and a freshman congresswoman from Connecticut, took issue with the president's "soft" war policies, Roosevelt tried to enlist a Democratic congressman to enter a satirical poem in the *Congressional Record* written by Howard Dietz, a well-known librettist.

"O Lovely Luce — O Comely Clare!
Do you remember — way back there —
Holding your lacquered nails aloft,
'The war we fight,' you said, 'is soft.'
Remember this: that words are ghosts.
And when it's mealtime, never stoop
To see the letters in the soup.
The ghosts may form like homing birds.
'My God,' you'll cry, 'I ate my words!' "

No congressman was willing to take on the Luces or to counter the recent Republican gains with praise for Roosevelt. But with Gallup polls showing 70 percent approval of his performance as president and 73 percent of Democrats favorable to a fourth-term run in 1944, Roosevelt decided to use his January 7 State of the Union Address to make the case himself for his presidency and war policies.

He acknowledged that "the coming year will be filled with violent conflict — yet with high promise of better things." He praised the American heroes fighting in the Pacific, the courage of the Russians defending their homeland, and "the successful defense of the Near East" by the British in Egypt and Libya. The success in North Africa was opening the way to attack what Churchill called "the under-belly of the Axis." In the air, the Germans were losing two planes for every one the Allies lost, while the Japanese were suffering a four-to-one deficit. On the sea lanes in the Atlantic and the Pacific as well, the Allies were gaining the advantage. "Yes," the president declared with the same optimism that had buoyed the country in the Depression, "the Nazis and the fascists have asked for it — and they are going to get it." On the home front, Americans were showing their eagerness to get on with the job by exceeding production goals. But he could not let pass the "guesswork and even malicious falsification of fact" leveled at his administration, which he said "creates doubts and fears, and weakens our total effort." No one should doubt that "the arsenal of democracy is making good," he declared. He acknowledged that "inconveniences and disturbances — and even hardships" had accompanied the country's miracle of production. "The sharp pinch of total war" was painful, but he had every expectation that it would not deter Americans from the job at hand. Yes, Washington might be a "madhouse — but only in the sense that it is the capital City of a nation which is fighting mad." Above all, he stressed that it was essential not to "get bogged down in argument over methods and details" with adversaries at home or Allies abroad. It was essential that Americans find common ground on which to establish permanent employment at home and a lasting peace. The men and women returning from the war deserved assurance against "bogus prosperity" or being relegated to the "slums" or put on the "dole," he said. He expected the new Congress to join him in achieving freedom from want and freedom from fear. But the assembled members of the House and Senate showed no enthusiasm for his message. "Silence greeted [his] reference to postwar social welfare," a British observer noted. By contrast, remarks about America's Allies did evoke a response: "sparse applause" greeted his mention of Britain with "louder applause [for] the words on Russia, and the mention of China brought thunderous applause."

Like his remarks on postwar domestic reform, his observations about postwar international affairs received a respectful but undemonstrative hearing. He hoped that Congress would agree that, unlike after the previous war, America could not again revert to isolationism or "climb back into an American hole and pull the hole in after" us. Although it was evident that Congress intended to have its say about postwar arrangements, Roosevelt had the wind at his back in calling for internationalism. Polls showed that two-thirds of all Americans favored universal military training to keep America safe as well as participation in a world organization to prevent another war.

Roosevelt's upbeat public message and confidence about what Americans could achieve at home and abroad underplayed his own uncertainties. When Daisy saw him after the speech, he asked, "Did you think that speech was alright? Did you like it?" She thought he was acting "almost like a small boy" who needed reassurance.

War planning was a particular concern. During November and December, as Soviet forces fought a titanic battle against the Germans at Stalingrad, Roosevelt struggled to determine where U.S. and British troops could strike most effectively against the Nazis after North Africa. Would they be able to cross the Channel in 1943? To reach an agreement on strategic plans, he told Churchill at the end of November, "I feel very strongly that we have got to sit down at the table with the Russians." "Only at a meeting between principals will real results be achieved," Churchill agreed and hoped they could meet in January, as "[by] that time Africa should be cleared and the great battle in south Russia decided." He was too sanguine about Africa, as it would not be until May that Rommel's forces surrendered in Tunisia, while the Germans capitulated in Stalingrad on February 2.

Coordination between the Allies proved to be a challenge. Stalin welcomed the idea of a meeting, but explained that "front business" made it impossible for him to leave the Soviet Union. He also rejected a proposal from Roosevelt that they delay meeting until March, insisting that it was essential for him to remain near his troops. His constant presence in Moscow was in fact less of an issue than his conviction that the president and Churchill would use the meeting as an occasion to delay opening the second front in France. He was so suspicious of Allied aims that he refused to allow American air bases on Soviet soil.

Churchill and Roosevelt ultimately decided to meet without Stalin to confer in Casablanca, Morocco, beginning in mid-January. Mindful of Stalin's mistrust, Roosevelt rejected Churchill's suggestion that General Marshall travel to London before joining them in Africa, which seemed likely only to intensify Stalin's concern that U.S. and British chiefs were aiming to let Soviet forces bear the brunt of the fighting as a prelude to overturning Communist rule in Russia. Roosevelt also wanted no foreign affairs officials present at their meeting lest it raise Soviet suspicions that his Allies were discussing postwar plans behind his back. "It is the only thing to do," Churchill agreed. Because both leaders loved a bit of intrigue, they agreed on the need for code names to keep their conference site and presence secret. Roosevelt cabled Churchill that he and Hopkins would assume the aliases of Don Quixote and Sancho Panza. Apprehensive that the Roosevelt-Hopkins presence in Casablanca might then be characterized as "quixotic," Churchill teased the president: "However did you think of such an impenetrable disguise?" He proposed instead that they be called "Admiral Q and Mr. P. (NB). We must mind our P's and Q's." Churchill was no more resourceful than Roosevelt in hiding his identity: He traveled to the conference in a blue R.A.F. uniform under the alias "Air Commodore Frankland." "Any fool can see that is an air commodore disguised as the Prime Minister," one of his chiefs joked.

Roosevelt welcomed the trip as not only a chance to plan strategy but as an opportunity to make history by becoming the first president to fly to a conference and to be the first since Lincoln to visit frontline troops. He believed the meeting to be so important that he sent Daisy a record of the trip. On January 9, he began a two-day train ride to Miami. Keeping the shades drawn to hide his presence, he complained of feeling isolated. On the night of January 10, he slept on the train, but had to get up at 4:30 to board a Pan Am Clipper at 5 a.m.: "You know how I 'hate to get up in the morning,' " he wrote her. The plane crew "had a fit" when they learned that they were flying the president to Trinidad in the Caribbean, so concerned were they for his safety, a concern that Daisy shared: "It is a long trip, with definite risks. But one *can't* and *mustn't* think of that." Harry Hopkins, who accompanied Roosevelt, believed it was "dangerous to ride in airplanes" and was so worried about the potential perils facing them that he brought along "an unusual certificate" that named him as a "member of the party of the President of the United States"; listed his age, height, weight, and hair and eye color; and included the president's signature. He hoped it would help identify his remains in the event of a disaster.

An initial eleven-hour flight from Miami at 9,000 feet with some turbulence was exhausting. "I hate flying as the hrs of rising are uncivilized," he wrote Eleanor. He was relieved to land in Trinidad and spend the night at a U.S. naval base. One of his companions on the trip, the sixty-eight-year-old admiral Willliam D. Leahy, who had been Roosevelt's chief of staff since July after serving as ambassador to Vichy, was ill with the flu and a temperature. "This is not civilized," Roosevelt repeated, when they arose at 4:00 the next morning. Leahy was too ill to continue with them, and Roosevelt wrote Daisy: "I shall miss him as he is such an old friend & a wise counselor."

They took off at 5:30 a.m. on January 12 and flew above the clouds for hours — "thrill at first but I am bored to death with them," he recorded. Lunch, a nap, and "the Amazon below," he told Daisy. "I have no desire to show you this part of the world. But if we are exiled by postwar isolationists," he joked, "we may have to try our luck in So. America." At 3:00 p.m. they landed at Belém, the capital of the state of Pará in Brazil, where they spent two and a half hours in the officers' club at a U.S. air base. They took off again at 5:30 for the 2,400-mile flight to Africa. After "a good long night's sleep," they landed in Bathurst in British Gambia, where Roosevelt was transported the short distance to the USS *Memphis,* a cruiser docked in Port Alfred, which he described as an "awful, pestiferous hole." After dinner and a night's rest, at 7 a.m. they drove 22 miles to an American-built airport past "crowds of semi-dressed natives" displaying "great poverty and emaciation." It made him "glad the U.S. is not a great Colonial power."

Taking off at 8:45 a.m. in a C54 transport, they flew north along the coast, passing over Dakar in West Africa and then turned inland to fly over the Sahara Desert — "not flat at all & not as light as I had thought — more a brown yellow with lots of rocks and wind erosion." Five hours of this scenery at an altitude of 6,000 feet was more than enough. The snow-topped Atlas Mountains were a welcome change, though climbing to 10,000 feet to fly over a pass forced him to try "a few whiffs of oxygen." North of the mountains they came in sight of the ancient city of Marrakesh, where they would go "if Casablanca is bombed." They reached Casablanca "at last" at 4 p.m. on January 14. The sight of the ocean; of his son Elliott, who was serving in the Army Air Corps and met them at the airport; and of a "delightful villa" outside of Casablanca, where Churchill, who was staying nearby, joined him for dinner, contributed to a feeling of well-being. His absence from Washington, which now seemed on "the other side of the world," was creating "a wonderful mind set."

The next six days featured exhausting rounds of conferences with Churchill, which tested Roosevelt's endurance. Morning, luncheon, afternoon, and evening talks, with only an hour out for a nap, kept Roosevelt up until 2 a.m. when he could finally snatch seven hours of sleep. The fact that they got "on very well" and that Franklin, Jr., who was serving as a junior naval officer, showed up for a long weekend reduced the strain of so many meetings and consequential decisions.

The conference principally involved establishing future military plans to defeat Germany and then conquer Japan. The British were firmly fixed on using the success in Africa to strike next against Sicily and then Italy as a prelude to a cross-Channel attack in 1944. The American contingent, led by Marshall, preferred an assault on France in 1943, though Admiral Ernest King, American chief of naval operations, favored focusing on expanded operations in the Pacific to hasten the conquest of Japan. Because Roosevelt doubted that they had the capacity to carry off a successful cross-Channel invasion in 1943, he supported Churchill's Mediterranean strategy. By January 18, the British, who had prepared themselves for the meeting with charts and arguments to refute Marshall's concerns that striking at Sicily and Italy would risk delaying a 1944 invasion of France, carried the day.

The final plan emerging from the discussions called for a five-part strategy: overcoming the U-boat menace in the Atlantic; assisting Russia to the fullest, as "a paying investment," in Roosevelt's words; launching an assault on Sicily, as a prelude to Italy's defeat; conducting unrelenting air raids on Germany, combined with preparations for the assault on German forces in France in 1944; and continuing offensive operations against Japan in the Pacific and China, but without details of how the latter could be accomplished. The British were resistant to making any commitments that would divert resources from Europe. Hopes of a campaign to recapture Burma had fallen victim to British reluctance and Chiang Kai-shek's refusal to risk his armies, which he wished to keep in reserve for a future civil war against the Communists. As Marshall described it, Chiang's attitude was "let the other fellow do it." Stilwell was even more negative: China's military "is generally in desperate condition, underfed, unpaid, untrained, neglected, and rotten with corruption. We can pull them out of this cesspool," he declared, "but continued concessions have made the Generalissimo believe he has only to insist and we will yield."

Difficulties with Chiang, however, paled alongside the more immediate ones involving Charles de Gaulle and the French. A fierce political struggle between Vichyites and Gaullists was besetting Dwight Eisenhower, who commanded U.S troops in North Africa. A contest had also arisen between General Henri Giraud and de Gaulle for control of the anti-Vichy forces in French North Africa. From Roosevelt's perspective, France was a nation of defeatists who, given a chance to cooperate with the Allies fighting Hitler, entered instead into a fratricidal conflict. Giraud agreed to come to Casablanca, but de Gaulle resisted pressure to cooperate. "Today I asked W.S.C. who paid De Gaulle's salary," Franklin wrote Daisy on January 20 "— W.S.C. beamed — good idea — no come — no pay!" When de Gaulle did finally show up from London on January 22, he was as difficult as ever. He upbraided Giraud for submitting to American directives, complained to Churchill about subjecting him to American commands on French territory, and dismissed Roosevelt's plan for a Giraud–de Gaulle government of North Africa as "adequate at the quite respectable level of an American sergeant."

A meeting between Roosevelt and de Gaulle did little to relieve tensions. Roosevelt saw him as "cold, austere, rigid, and unresponsive," complaining that he refused to "go to war" and was nothing but a "headache." His arrogance led Roosevelt to describe him as a combination of Joan of Arc and First World War premiere Georges Clemenceau. De Gaulle reciprocated the animosity: "Behind his patrician mask of courtesy," de Gaulle said, "Roosevelt regarded me without benevolence." He was convinced that Roosevelt intended to dictate the peace and "that the states that had been overrun should be subject to his judgment, and that France in particular should recognize him as its savior and arbiter." Because de Gaulle understood that a "clash would lead to nothing and that, for the sake of the future, we each had much to gain by getting along together," he submitted to Roosevelt's urging to give at least the appearance of cooperation with Giraud, effectively agreeing with the president's observation that "in human affairs, the public must be offered a drama." Even if there was only "a theoretical agreement," Roosevelt told him, it "would produce the dramatic effect we need." De Gaulle assented to a show of unity by shaking hands with Giraud before press photographers.

"Do you know that you have caused us more difficulties than all our other European allies put together?" British foreign secretary Anthony Eden later good-humoredly asked de Gaulle. "I don't doubt it" de Gaulle smilingly replied. Justifying his recalcitrance by explaining, after all, "France is a great power." When de Gaulle later wrote about events in Casablanca, he dismissed the conversations as "comedy."

Roosevelt's more worrisome problem was Stalin's response to the news that a cross-Channel attack would not be attempted until 1944. On January 25, when he and Churchill wrote Stalin from Marrakech about their plans for the first nine months of 1943, they avoided the mention of a second front. They described their hopes that the combination of what they were able to accomplish and "your power offensive," which was on the verge of eliminating the German forces at Stalingrad, "may well bring Germany to her knees in 1943." They emphasized their "desire . . . to divert strong German land and air forces from the Russian front and to send to Russia the maximum flow of supplies." The letter outlined their plans "to launch large scale amphibious operations in the Mediterranean" and to "prepare themselves to re-enter the continent of Europe as soon as practicable." Because the message left Stalin uncertain about whether they would strike across the Channel that year, five days later he asked for more "information on the concrete operations planned . . . and on the scheduled time of their realization." In their joint response on February 9, Roosevelt and Churchill expressed their hope of a cross-Channel assault in August or September, but they hedged their commitment with the qualification that "the timing of this attack must of course be dependent upon the condition of German defensive possibilities across the Channel." Because they knew that the likelihood of an invasion was small, if even that, they wished to give Stalin some guarantee that they were not leaving Russia alone responsible for defeating Hitler or intending to reach a settlement with a weakened Germany that barred a Russian advance into Central Europe. An announcement by Roosevelt at a press conference in Casablanca on January 24 of a commitment to unconditional surrender aimed to assure Stalin of their good intentions. Although Roosevelt delivered that message as if it were a spontaneous declaration on his part, he and Churchill had been exchanging views on the wisdom of making such a pronouncement. Roosevelt hoped that unconditional surrender could avert the post-1918 conditions that enabled an unoccupied Germany to rearm and bring on another conflict. Since Churchill did not want to apply the doctrine to Italy, which both the president and his War Cabinet favored, he pretended that Roosevelt's comments on unconditional surrender surprised him. For his part, Roosevelt saw advantages in appearing to be the principal architect of such a doctrine. For one, it could refute criticisms of the Darlan deal as a prelude to a compromise peace with the Axis. At the same time, an apparently extemporaneous rather than an ironclad commitment by him and Churchill to a total victory over the Axis countries might discourage heightened determination in Germany, Italy, and Japan to fight the war to the death. It seemed better to leave some hope among Axis peoples that the war might end short of total destruction of their homelands.

Over the next six days, before returning to Washington on January 31, Roosevelt pursued an exhausting schedule, visiting Gambia again on the way home. "I am not impressed by what I have seen of the Colonial Gov. of Gambia," he told Daisy. "I think I picked up sleeping sickness or Gambia fever or some kindred bug in that hell-hole of yours called Bathurst," he wrote Churchill. "A bit of bronchial trouble and a slight fever" partly shaped his negative view of West Africa. Hopkins and Churchill were worried about his health: Hopkins believed he was plagued by "a bad cough" and thought that he looked "very worn." Churchill, who may have felt guilty about straining him with late-night meetings, expressed surprise that he seemed "not at all fatigued." But years of living with his physical disability had made him stoic about his health, and despite his weariness, he took the opportunity to meet with the presidents of Liberia and Brazil on the trip home.

"All his party have been feeling miserable since they got back," Daisy recorded on the Roosevelt contingent's return to Washington. But the president "just hasn't let himself give in until he got here. Then, he 'let go' & feels exhausted." He struggled through February to recover, confiding to Daisy that he remained worn out. "He looked it," she said. It made her "feel terrible — I've never heard a word of complaint from him, but it seemed to slip out unintentionally, & spoke volumes." Frances Watson, Roosevelt's appointments secretary, told Daisy, "He is the loneliest man in the world. . . . He has no real 'home-life' in which to relax, & recoup his strength & his peace of mind. If he wasn't such a wonderful character, he would sink under it." At the end of February, he spent four days in bed, and "still feels miserable," Daisy noted. He ran a temperature of 102 and was prescribed "4 doses of a sulpha drug." On February 27, she observed, "The P. doesn't look well, but is improving." He had diminished stamina and told Churchill and Daisy that he felt "like a rag." He was "no good after 2 P.M." He said he supposed it was " 'old age.' . . . There is a pinched look in his face," Daisy observed, "and his hand sometimes shakes."

He was grateful for Daisy's loving attention. "When I gave him his aspirin, he suddenly said: 'Do you know that I have never had anyone just sit around and take care of me like this before.' He meant that, outside of trained nurses, which men hate to have hanging around, he is just given his medicine or takes it himself. Everyone else has been too busy to sit with him, doing nothing." His affection for Daisy and hers for him was palpable.

On his return from Casablanca, news of a German surrender at Stalingrad brightened hopes for Allied victory in the war, though this was soon followed by the report of American defeat in a tank battle at Kasserine Pass in Tunisia, shattering hopes of a quick end to the fighting in North Africa. Yet the setback had little impact on American confidence about the ultimate outcome of the war. Politics as usual in the capital suggested that few now doubted the likelihood of Allied victory.

In a Washington's Birthday speech on February 23, Roosevelt put war planning aside to chide his critics. He compared the carping of Republicans and conservative Southern Democrats to the fainthearted patriots complaining about Washington's leadership during the Revolution. His remarks only fueled the political acrimony. An anti–New Deal Democrat was quoted as saying,

"On Lincoln's birthday he thought he was Lincoln. Today he thought he was Washington. What will he say on Christmas Day?" The question of a fourth term was already being discussed in the news, with the Patterson-McCormick conservative press issuing "violent attacks" on the president, and Jim Farley and Mississippi congressman John Rankin taking the lead against him among Democrats. Polls showing that 51 percent favored a fourth term if the war was still on, and convictions among Democrats that they could not hold the White House without him "fully resolved [Roosevelt] to stand again," or so a report from the British embassy concluded. The likelihood of another FDR campaign was moving Farley "to fight bitterly" against the president's running again.

Few things burdened Roosevelt more during these February weeks, however, than the presence in the United States and at the White House of Madame Chiang Kai-shek. She had arrived in November to an adoring reception. Having spent ten years in America from the age of ten to nineteen, and attended Wellesley College in Massachusetts from 1913 to 1917, she spoke an American-accented English and was masterful in reading and exploiting the national mood. She traveled the country, speaking before twenty thousand people at Madison Square Garden in New York and thirty thousand at Los Angeles's Hollywood Bowl. National radio broadcasts persuaded some Americans to favor a China-first strategy over the fighting in Europe or the Pacific. On February 18, she addressed a joint session of a dazzled Congress, receiving a four-minute standing ovation and bringing tears to the eyes of some of the "captivated" politicians. "Goddam it," one congressman declared, "I never saw anything like it." The press fawned over her as well, echoing the comment of Carl Sandburg, poet and noted Lincoln biographer, "What she wants, she wants for the family of man over the entire earth." In 1943, *Time* magazine gave her the cover for the third time.

While Eleanor Roosevelt called her "a very sweet person," others in the administration, including the president, saw her as imperious and dictatorial. Her abrupt manner with servants offended them; she demanded deference and accommodation to her every whim, clapping her hands for attention and service like some royal potentate. When Daisy watched Madame Chiang with Roosevelt, she saw her as "all smiles . . . always acting — [but] F.D.R. does too. You never get beneath the charming manner" of either of them.

She deferred to no one, including the president, even embarrassing him at a press conference. When he answered a reporter's question about how soon supplies would reach China by saying, "just as fast as the good Lord will let us," she added, "I understand you have a saying in your country, Mr. President, that the Lord helps those who help themselves." Reporters detected a reddening of the silent president's neck. At a White House dinner, when he asked her what her government would do about a labor leader threatening a strike in wartime, she ran a finger across her throat. Roosevelt laughed and called out to Eleanor sitting across the table, "Did you see that?" He later asked Eleanor in private, "Well, how about your gentle and sweet character?" Morgenthau told his staff, "The President . . . is just crazy to get her out of the country." His desire to see her gone was less because he disliked her, or because he thought she could manipulate a change in grand strategy, than because he feared she would reveal her true self and undermine public favor for postwar collaboration with China and U.S. internationalism.

By March 1943, Americans were increasingly focused on the postwar world. Although the fighting was far from over, confidence in America's capacity not only to win the war but also to establish postwar conditions was reflected in a great deal of newspaper coverage of the discussion of what was to be done after the conflict ended. By the beginning of April, Roosevelt impressed Daisy as "relaxed & peaceful, & talked mostly about his hopes for future peace. He has it all worked out in his mind already. . . . He thinks the country will be powerful enough to *force* the others — if necessary. After all, we haven't gone into this war to have the whole thing start up again." He hoped that Germany might "crack" by July 1944 and that he could then give up any thoughts of attempting to remain in office and instead become the chairman of a peace organization. He believed, as a Gallup poll demonstrated, that if the war were over, he would have limited support for a fourth term. Besides, his declining health made him eager for a less demanding job, and he assumed that heading a peace institution would be a popular, noncontroversial position.

The arrival in Washington of British foreign secretary Anthony Eden on March 12 for eighteen days and a proposal by four U.S. senators to create a United Nations organization stimulated "a burst of speculation and discussion on postwar questions." Encouraged by Sumner Welles, the leading voice in the State Department for a Wilsonian settlement, and thirty-eight-year-old Minnesota Republican senator Joseph Ball, the press devoted daily attention to the question of how the United States should organize the peace. Roosevelt and Hull believed it premature for the Senate to debate such questions, which could provoke a sharp political conflict. Although Roosevelt was well disposed toward Eden, who he said was "the nicest type of Englishman, very clever," their conversations made it clear that future international relations would remain a source of contention. They agreed on a major role for Russia in postwar Europe, conceding that Moscow would control the Baltic States, but they differed over French influence, and could not concur on the role of China in overseeing postwar peace in East Asia. Eden could not conceive of China as one of the world's four great powers, and Roosevelt had to acknowledge that it was more of "a potential world Power" than a nation ready to manage East Asian affairs. In this period, when Churchill spoke publicly about postwar relations, he omitted any mention of China. "It is quite untrue to say that China is a world power equal to Britain, the U.S., or Russia," he privately declared. Like Churchill, Eden regarded China as an unstable nation and had little tolerance for the notion of its "running up and down the Pacific."

Roosevelt was not unrealistic about the limits of China's capacity to control international relations. But he believed that a country with four hundred million people and a leader like Chiang, who had weathered the formidable problems of governing it, would inevitably play a significant part in global politics. After all, the president told Marshall, it was not as if they were dealing with someone as inconsequential as the sultan of Morocco. Roosevelt understood that the great majority of Americans wanted a large role for China in postwar affairs, a judgment that was reinforced by the public reception of *One World,* an overnight best seller published by Wendell Willkie in April 1943. Willkie's report on his worldwide tour for the president echoed Woodrow Wilson's hopes for a revolution in international diplomacy that would mark the end to war. In the flush of the United States' emerging dominance — or what *Time* publisher Henry Luce called the advent of "the American Century" — Americans believed that they possessed the wisdom and power to shape the future of global relations.

Willkie captured the public mood when he declared that inside of every foreigner was an American waiting to emerge. "There are now, during the war," he asserted, "common purposes in the minds of men living as far apart as the citizens of Great Britain and the Free Commonwealth of Nations, the Americans, the Russians, and the Chinese." Luce echoed Willkie's outlook when he asserted that the Russians were "one hell of a people . . . [who] to a remarkable degree . . . look like Americans, dress like Americans, and think like Americans."

> While the America First Committee had once
>   asked the country:
> "Over there there's mud and shedding of blood,
> And Tongues confusing and strange,
> So why lend a hand to an alien band
> Whose dreams we can never change?"

790

Its citizens now indulged in dreams that they could institute universal reforms. Whatever skepticism Roosevelt had about casting aside traditional instruments of great power politics — and it was considerable — he believed it essential to seize upon this resurgent idealism.

But even the victory at Stalingrad; progress in Tunisia, with the prospect of German defeat there by May; and gains in the Atlantic as a result of British capacity to read coded messages revealing the whereabouts of U-boats and air and surface forces combating them did not promise a quick end to the war in Europe. Germany was still in control of France, and its millions of troops in Russia, including thirty-six new divisions dispatched there in March 1943, continued to pose a grave threat to the Soviet Union. In East Asia the Japanese remained dominant in China and across vast stretches of the South Pacific.

Cables from Stalin to Churchill and Roosevelt in March and April pressing the case for a prompt opening of a second front in western Europe and complaining about reduced supply shipments to Russia made Roosevelt mindful of how much remained to be done before any serious discussions about postwar arrangements could take place. Churchill worried that "in April, May and June, not a single American or British soldier will be killing a single German or Italian soldier while the Russians are chasing 185 divisions around." Churchill affirmed the need to back Stalin with "every conceivable means."

Roosevelt accordingly proposed a personal meeting with Stalin, which he described in a letter of May 5 to him as "an informal and completely simple visit for a few days" without "the difficulties of large Staff conferences or the red tape of diplomatic conversations." He hoped they could do so during the coming summer near Alaska on the off chance that there would be a complete German "crack-up" by the winter, for should this occur, they needed to "be prepared for the many next steps" facing them. He did not want Churchill to be present, and he hoped they could "talk very informally and get what we call 'a meeting of the minds.' " He saw no need for "official agreements or declarations." Since Roosevelt wished to assure Stalin of American goodwill and shared opposition to imperialism and a common interest in a postwar world without empires, he believed that Churchill's absence would best serve their mutual outlook. Since there would be no second front in western Europe in 1943, this was Roosevelt's way of discouraging a negotiated Nazi-Soviet settlement and keeping Stalin tied to the Allies.

In April, before he sent his invitation to Stalin, Roosevelt made plans for another inspection tour across the United States and a visit to Mexico to solidify relations. Convinced, as he told Churchill, that "it takes about a month of occasional let-ups to get back your full strength," he proposed a fifteen-day train trip through the South and the Midwest. On April 10 he told his former running mate Jim Cox that he was fed up with the "pettiness" of Washington politics. "Sometimes I get awfully discouraged when I see what is going on on the Hill. The truth . . . is that neither we nor the Republicans have fighting leadership up there. However, however, however — I still believe in representative democracy!" When he read *New Yorker* writer E. B. White's short piece, "The

792

Meaning of Democracy," Roosevelt roared with laughter and declared: "I love it!" White wrote: "It is the line that forms on the right . . . It is the hole in the stuffed shirt . . . it is the dent in the high hat. Democracy is the recurrent suspicion that more than half of the people are right more than half of the time. It is the feeling of privacy in the voting booths . . . the feeling of vitality everywhere. Democracy is a letter to the editor. It is an idea which hasn't been disproved yet."

On April 13, Roosevelt, who "looked very tired," boarded the specially equipped presidential train with Daisy; cousin Laura Delano; Fala and Laura's dog, a nine-year-old Irish setter named Sister; and the White House retinue of Dr. McIntire, Steve Early, Grace Tully, and former law partner Basil O'Connor. During the first week they visited training camps in South Carolina, Georgia, and Texas, and an air base in Alabama, where Roosevelt watched a small representative group of the 4.3 million men and handful of women (members of the Women's Army Auxiliary Corps) preparing for overseas assignments. Artillery trainees, infantry inductees, and paratroopers showed off their combat skills to the commander in chief. The Marine commandant at Parris Island, South Carolina, said that the president's presence had "a tremendous effect on the morale" of the troops. On April 16, the group stopped in Warm Springs, Georgia, where the president greeted one hundred or so mostly wheelchair-bound patients, who were thrilled to see him. On April 17 and April 18, they traveled to Arkansas and Oklahoma, where an Army base had been constructed on former farmland. The following day they arrived in Fort Worth, Texas, for a visit to the family of Elliott Roosevelt, who was still posted in North Africa with his Air Force unit.

On April 20, Franklin and Eleanor, who had joined the party the previous day for three days, crossed into Mexico for a meeting with President Avila Camacho in Monterrey. After dinner with the Mexican president and first lady, the Roosevelts returned to Texas to spend a relaxing day at Elliott's ranch outside of Fort Worth. On April 22, Eleanor flew to Phoenix and the West Coast, while the president traveled to Colorado and Fort Riley, Kansas, for an Easter Sunday service. The trip ended on April 28 with him feeling exhilaration at the impressive state of the armed forces he had reviewed. In the less than three years since the enactment of the draft, isolationist America with its bare-bones military now had a formidable fighting force. As for Roosevelt himself, he "looked fresher" and "his spirits were higher."

As he moved through the South, Roosevelt gave a wide berth to facilities housing black troops. In response to pressure from Eleanor, the Army had reined in some of the overt instances of segregation in Southern Army bases, eliminating separation of the races in all recreational base facilities. Eleanor's greatest triumph, however, came in response to a request from the director of the Tuskegee Air Field, where the 99th Pursuit Squadron, a group of 1,000 black combat pilots, was located. The Army's failure to deploy them out of a reluctance to trust the combat skills of African Americans incensed Eleanor, who said, "What a lot we must do to make our war a real victory for democracy." On April 15, the 99th was deployed to Africa, where it compiled an exceptional record of success and beyond. In more than

1,500 combat missions in North Africa, Italy, and Germany, the squadron destroyed 261 enemy aircraft. A hundred citations for its achievements included the distinction of being the only U.S. air arm "that never lost a single bomber" in combat. As Doris Kearns Goodwin wrote, "Blacks could fly in combat with the best of the pilots of any nation."

Concerned by a warning from Harold Ickes that the ten internment camps in the West's interior mountains and deserts to which Japanese Americans had been moved were becoming a breeding ground for hostility toward the government and the country, Roosevelt asked Eleanor to visit one of them in Arizona. Her report confirmed Ickes's concern that confining so many thousands of citizens whose only offense was their race violated American concepts of fairness and justice. As a consequence, Roosevelt and the War Department agreed to let all draft-age U.S.-born citizens enlist in the Army and allow overage citizens with work assignments to leave the camps. By the end of 1943, nearly one-third of the Japanese-American detainees had been released. The Nisei volunteers and draftees compiled an extraordinary combat record, fighting their way up the Italian peninsula, participating in the taking of Rome, and liberating the Nazi concentration camp at Dachau in 1945. Over 9,000 of the 14,000 men who served in the 442nd infantry regiment, the principal Japanese American unit, received Purple Hearts. Another twenty-one members of the regiment received Congressional Medals of Honor, making it the most decorated unit in U.S. military history. An additional 6,000 Japanese Americans served in the Military Intelligence Service, working as translators and interrogators of Japanese prisoners of war.

In April, Roosevelt exchanged cables with Churchill about the strategy following the invasion and conquest of Sicily, which was expected in July. The British leader believed that "the mere capture [of the island] will be an altogether inadequate result for the campaign of 1943," and while Roosevelt perceived "two or three good alternatives" to post-Sicily fighting, he wanted to wait until their staffs came up with proposals before they made a final decision. In the meantime, Roosevelt said that the recent successful air raids on Germany encouraged him to "give them an ever increasing dose." At the same time, testy exchanges with Churchill over who would have the primary authority over the postwar administration of Sicily and Italy underscored for Roosevelt why he would prefer a retirement in which he led an international peace organization.

His discussions with Churchill about postwar Italy, however, were as nothing compared with the emerging strife between Stalin and the Polish exile government in London. The Poles wanted Stalin to concede the return of Polish territory after the war, which he adamantly refused to do. Even more explosive was the discovery of the mass graves containing the bodies of thousands of Polish nationals in Poland's Katyn Forest. The Germans claimed that the Soviets were responsible for the massacre, and Moscow in turn accused the Germans. When the London Poles called for a Red Cross investigation, Stalin broke relations with them. Roosevelt told Stalin, "I have several million Poles in the United States, incidentally, a large proportion of them being in the Army and

Navy. Knowledge by them of a complete break between you and [Polish premier Władysław] Sikorski, in view of the fact that they are all bitter against the Nazis, would not help the present situation." Roosevelt's appeal fell on deaf ears, as did Churchill's: "We owe it to our armies . . . to maintain good conditions behind the fronts. I and my colleagues look steadily to the ever closer cooperation and understanding of the USSR, the USA and the British Commonwealth and Empire. . . . What other hope can there be than this for the tortured world?" Stalin remained unmoved. The controversy was another instance of future strife that Roosevelt saw as likely to trouble him should he win another term.

In the meantime, however, the prime minister worried that they might squander the victory in North Africa by failing to strike quickly against a vulnerable Italy. He feared that Roosevelt and his generals would resist moving north by arguing for all-out preparations to cross the Channel later that year or in early 1944. He saw these as "fateful questions, which could only be answered by a personal conference with the President." He proposed to Roosevelt that they meet in Washington beginning on May 11, and Roosevelt agreed "most heartily that we have some important business to settle at once; the sooner the better."

In the twelve days before Churchill reached Washington, Roosevelt found himself beset by both domestic and foreign problems. At home, a coal miners' strike led him to order Ickes to take over all the country's coal mines and have the Army operate them. On May 2, as he was preparing to go on the radio to explain the necessity of his action, his nemesis John L. Lewis announced a settlement that forestalled the seizure. At the same time, the collapse of German resistance in Tunis at the beginning of May revived questions of who would administer France's North African territories. De Gaulle openly took issue with U.S. assumptions that Anglo-American forces had that authority. As Churchill sailed to the United States (his doctors insisted that a recent bout of pneumonia precluded air travel), Roosevelt wrote to the prime minister complaining of de Gaulle's aggravating behavior: "His course and attitude is well nigh intolerable. . . . De Gaulle may be an honest fellow but he has the messianic complex." He seemed to believe that the French people were "strongly behind him." Roosevelt described himself as "more and more disturbed by the continued machinations of De Gaulle." Moreover, he wanted Churchill to agree that when they get "into France itself we will have to regard it as a military occupation run by British and American generals." He thought this situation might have to continue for a year, until "a new form of government" emerged.

After a week's crossing on the *Queen Mary,* which also carried five thousand German prisoners of war for incarceration in the United States, Churchill arrived in New York at Staten Island. Traveling to Washington by train, where Roosevelt insisted he stay at the White House, he began two weeks of conversations with Roosevelt about future strategy. Not a day passed without some mention by Roosevelt of de Gaulle's troubling behavior. It convinced Churchill that his differences with the president on how to treat de Gaulle might lead to an estrangement between their two governments. As a consequence, Churchill briefly considered breaking with de Gaulle, "this most difficult man," but "time and patience afforded tolerable solutions."

There were, in any case, more pressing matters to deal with than de Gaulle. Churchill had come to Washington to receive assurances that an invasion of Italy would follow the conquest of Sicily. At a White House meeting on May 12 with the leading British and American military chiefs, Roosevelt declared, "The keynote of our plans at the present time should be an intention to employ every resource of men and munitions against the enemy. Nothing that could be brought to bear should be allowed to stand idle." It was Roosevelt's acknowledgement of the wisdom of striking against Italy rather than simply shepherding resources for the 1944 cross-Channel attack. Churchill underscored the president's assertion by arguing that the "great prize" in the Mediterranean was "to get Italy out of the war. . . . The collapse of Italy would cause a chill of loneliness over the German people, and might be the beginning of their doom." It would eliminate twenty-five Italian divisions occupying the Balkans and might compel the Germans to divert forces in Russia to Greece and Yugoslavia, and "In no other way could relief be given to the Russian front on so large a scale this year." The president then echoed Churchill's case for keeping the more than twenty divisions in the Mediterranean active in the fighting, while making it clear that this strategy could not become a diversion from the ultimate attack on the Germans in France in the spring of 1944.

Roosevelt did fear, however, that the fall of Italy might also free German troops to fight elsewhere.

Churchill countered that it would be a grave error to allow Allied troops to remain idle until the attack on France in 1944. It would also agitate the Russians and fan their suspicions of Anglo-American intentions.

Having made their positions clear, Churchill and Roosevelt left it to their staffs to wrestle with strategic particulars while they departed for a three-day weekend at the president's Maryland retreat. Accompanied by Eleanor, their daughter Anna, Harry Hopkins, and Lord Beaverbrook, Britain's most well-known newspaper publisher and Churchill's minister of airplane construction, Roosevelt and Churchill put their larger-than-life personalities on full display, especially Churchill. On the car ride to Maryland, he recited poetry, described the battle of Gettysburg, and illustrated a prodigious command of the American Civil War. At dinner, he captured Anna's attention by picking his teeth, sniffing snuff, sneezing with the power of a foghorn, and telling amusing stories. Not to be outdone by the prime minister, Roosevelt and Beaverbrook regaled the dinner party with tales of their own.

When they returned to Washington, Churchill addressed Congress on May 19. He celebrated the results in North Africa, where they had killed and captured 950,000 enemy troops and destroyed nearly 8,000 aircraft, 2,550 tanks, and 2,400,000 tons of shipping. He expressed gratitude that "the military intuition of Corporal Hitler. . . . The same insensate obstinacy" that had doomed the Germans at Stalingrad had now "brought this new catastrophe upon our enemies in Tunisia." He begged Congress to do everything in its power so that the current "favorable position . . . against Japan and against Hitler and Mussolini in Europe shall not be let slip." His remarks were well received and pleased the president.

Because they were determined to reach a consensus on continuing action against the Axis, "an almost complete agreement was reached about invading Sicily, though nothing definitive was said about Italy." As for China, only long-term plans were considered, though Roosevelt urged more concrete designs, because he worried about a collapse without them and suggested mounting an air campaign against Japan from China. The final report on military strategy included a renewed commitment to unconditional surrender of the Axis powers, and the full use of Anglo-American resources, with Russia, if possible, to defeat Japan. In addition, Roosevelt and Churchill agreed to reverse a breakdown in cooperation on nuclear research and reinstate the full exchange of information on "tube alloys," the British code name for the atomic bomb.

Churchill's reliance on the president as a congenial partner also led him to raise the issue of the 1944 election. He told Roosevelt "I simply can't go on without you," and that he needed him to stay in place until at least the close of the fighting. Roosevelt reciprocated Churchill's regard, but given the hours the prime minister kept and the pace he set, his company could become exhausting. After Churchill left, Roosevelt fled to Hyde Park, where he "slept ten hours a day for three days straight until he recovered from Churchill's visit." Bill Hassett, the president's secretary, described Churchill as "a trying guest — drinks like a fish, smokes like a chimney, irregular routine, works nights, sleeps days, turns the clock upside down."

As the conference ended, the two leaders prepared a summary of their decisions to send to Stalin. It emphasized their determination to control the submarine menace and to "employ every practicable means to support Russia." They described their commitment to increase the air offensive against the Axis and to eliminate Italy from the war, but with the understanding that it would not distract from the buildup for the cross-Channel assault in the spring of 1944. The message evoked a bitter complaint from Stalin about the contradictions in their promises to begin the assault on France by August or at latest by September of the current year. The Soviet Union remained alone in combating Hitler's forces, which, Stalin warned "may result in grave consequences for the future progress of the war."

In response, Roosevelt notified him of increased shipments of fighter planes and bombers to Russia during the rest of the year. For his part Churchill argued that there would be no point in sacrificing 100,000 men in a disastrous cross-Channel attack that led "only to useless massacre." He hoped that they could achieve the defeat of Italy that year, and by "doing so we shall draw far more Germans off your front than by any other means." He also predicted "a massive return" from the Allied air offensive, which was already "ruining a large part of the cities and munitions centers of Germany." He ended with an appeal for a meeting to take place soon at which Stalin would receive "a most hearty welcome from your British and American comrades." Roosevelt then added a message stating that he was "in full accord with what the Prime Minister telegraphed you. I assure you that we are really doing everything that is possible at this time."

Stalin was anything but appeased by the messages from the president and prime minister. He answered them on June 24 with a scathing condemnation of their failure to follow through on their promises for a second front. He reminded them of their commitment to a full-scale invasion in 1943 that "would force Germany to its knees." The victories in North Africa, in the Atlantic against the U-boats, and in the air across Europe during the previous six months had improved conditions for a cross-Channel assault and made the decision to delay until 1944 even more difficult to understand. "The Soviet Government cannot reconcile itself with such ignoring of the fundamental interests of the Soviet Union in the war against the common enemy," Stalin wrote. It was not simply a matter of disappointment but the "preservation" of Soviet "confidence in the Allies."

At the beginning of July, when the Soviets defeated a German offensive at Kursk in western central Russia in the largest tank battle in history, Roosevelt was quick to congratulate Stalin on the victory and repeated his eagerness for a face-to-face meeting, which he described as "of great importance to you and me." While Roosevelt labored to keep relations with Stalin on even keel, he also had to deal with domestic strife that roiled the war effort. On June 2, the coal miners, led by John L. Lewis, walked out in protest against a War Labor Board refusal to approve a two-dollar-a-day increase in wages. Doris Kearns Goodwin describes the strike, which idled 500,000, as "devastating," as it slowed "the production of guns and tanks . . . and reached deep into the national economy." The walkout provoked outrage among U.S. troops and citizens alike. They denounced Lewis and the miners as "traitors" and called for a ban on all strikes during the war. In response, Congress passed the Smith-Connally Act, restraining labor actions in government-run plants. Roosevelt was furious at Lewis and told his budget director that he "would be glad to resign as President if Lewis committed suicide." Faced with such pressure, Lewis ordered the miners back to work. Roosevelt then decided to veto the Smith-Connally bill, arguing that it went too far in penalizing labor. But Congress disagreed and overrode it.

Roosevelt also had to respond to domestic race riots. In June, a conflict arose pitting whites against blacks in a Mobile, Alabama, shipyard, where segregationists who could not abide working alongside African Americas sent eleven blacks to the hospital and persuaded the company to have the races work in separate facilities. An outbreak of rioting in Detroit on June 20 overshadowed even the Mobile clash. Whites resented the arrival of black workers from the South who took the opportunity of filling war production jobs and competing for housing in a city with a swelling population, and their resentment exploded in physical attacks that provoked black retaliation. Federal troops quelled the rioting, which lasted two days and took twenty-five black and nine white lives and injured over a thousand residents. Ever reluctant to find himself at cross-purposes with Southern congressmen and senators, Roosevelt let the racial discord play out without a pronouncement on the evils of discrimination or the demoralizing demonstration that America, like its war opponents, had biases that led to lawless violence. His silence was a blow to the war effort, which rested on the idea that America was fundamentally different from nations that practiced brutal discrimination.

CHAPTER 18
"DR. WIN THE WAR"

On July 7, after an overnight train ride from Hyde Park, where he had spent the holiday weekend, Roosevelt returned to the White House, which, after ten years of living there, he called his "back yard." That afternoon, he met with Admiral Leahy, General Marshall, and General Giraud, who the president hoped could eclipse de Gaulle. Giraud impressed Daisy, who joined them for afternoon tea, as "charming" and "a real gentleman of the old school." Roosevelt spoke with him in French, even telling a joke. But Giraud proved to be no match for de Gaulle, who was dominating the emergence of a French authority in North Africa. In mid-June Roosevelt had told Churchill that he was "fed up with De Gaulle. . . . The last few days indicate that there is no possibility of our working with De Gaulle." Roosevelt thought he was "a very dangerous threat" to the war effort but confessed that he did "not know how to deal with" a man who was "out for himself, & wants to be the next ruler of France — in whatever capacity may be expedient when the time comes."

As Milton Viorst noted, de Gaulle's behavior was especially offensive to Roosevelt's sense of propriety. De Gaulle knew that his arrogance and independence irritated Roosevelt no end and reciprocated his contempt in response to the president's reluctance to remember that France was a great nation. But it was France's failure to have fought, the way Britain did, that especially irked Roosevelt and angered him about de Gaulle's insistence that he be treated as the leader of a great power.

Leahy and Daisy, who had spent the weekend with the president at Hyde Park, worried that the burdens of office, including the difficulties with de Gaulle, were wearing him down. They confided to each other that the president still looked tired from his trip to Casablanca, and they agreed that plane travel especially exhausted him. But they saw no way to deter him from making overseas air trips. In contrast with Wilson, who had limited freedom to influence his counterparts at Versailles in 1919, Roosevelt saw himself in an advantageous position in any meeting he might have with Churchill and/or Stalin. The emergence of U.S. productive might and his own talent for personal persuasion, which had carried him through three elections and continued to be reflected in high public approval, convinced him that his successful interactions with his allies were essential in fighting the war and assuring a stable postwar peace.

But his weariness wasn't simply the result of arduous travels abroad. It was also the product of the constant demands on his social skills. Louise Hopkins, Harry's new wife, for example, who lived in the White House, impressed Roosevelt as "not very bright" and full of tiring conversation that wore on him. He had developed the habit of forcing "himself to keep up the outward appearance of energy and force — It must be very exhaust-

807

ing," Daisy thought. He enjoyed a bit of solitude or those occasional moments he spent alone with Daisy, confiding in her that "it was the greatest possible rest to be able to just be as he felt & not have to talk & be the host."

The constant turmoil in domestic affairs continued to test his resilience. Isaiah Berlin, the head of an operation called the Special Survey Section in the British embassy, reported that labor and race strife, in conjunction with the lull in military advances, had temporarily generated "universal dissatisfaction" by the public with the administration and moved "the troubled home front into the centre of attention. . . . Anti-Roosevelt columnists are playing it for all they are worth, and [columnist Walter] Lippmann . . . has addressed severe words to the President on his lack of clear guidance to the nation and failure to bring facts home to the public." In response, Churchill wrote Roosevelt: "I have been so much distressed and angered to see the way you are being harried. Knowing what war burdens are, I greatly admire the splendid calm and buoyancy with which you bear them amidst so much clatter."

Although Anglo-American forces successfully invaded Sicily on July 10, despite gale winds that blew paratroopers off their target, and Italy's king Victor Emmanuel III forced Mussolini's resignation, the gratifying war news was not enough to quiet divisions at home. The greater the prospects for victory, the more critics felt free to complain about the administration's shortcomings. Roosevelt wrote to Churchill describing the "unfortunate feeling in this country that victory is in sight." At a press conference on July 27, when he announced that the following night he would hold a

808

Fireside Chat regarding the war, a reporter asked: "Abroad or at home?" Roosevelt dismissed the suggestion that the two could be separated. There is only one front, he said: Everything we do at home influences what happens abroad; the two are indelibly linked.

In his radio address, Roosevelt celebrated Allied victories on the Russian front, in the Pacific, and in Europe. "The first crack in the Axis has come," he declared. "The criminal, corrupt Fascist regime in Italy is going to pieces." He predicted that Mussolini and "his fascist gang will be brought to book, and punished for their crimes against humanity. No criminal will be allowed to escape by the expedient of 'resignation.' " Mindful of Soviet disappointment in the absence of a second front, Roosevelt stressed his continuing determination to compel unconditional surrender. Also eager to remind Hitler and the Nazis of the price they would pay for their atrocities, and if possible, to deter them from committing additional crimes, he declared, "We will have no truck with Fascism in any way, in any shape or manner. We will permit no vestige of Fascism to remain." No one will forget that "in every country conquered by the Nazis and the Fascists or the Japanese militarists, the people have been reduced to the status of slaves or chattels. It is our determination to restore these conquered peoples to the dignity of human beings."

Roosevelt also sought to refute assertions he was "playing party politics at home," and that his administration was "failing miserably on the home front." He dismissed this as "a false slogan easy to state but untrue in essential facts." He insisted that America was performing brilliantly, producing the sinews of war that promised the ultimate victory. In addition, he concluded, "while concentrating on military victory, we are not neglecting the planning of the things to come," including "the return to civilian life of our gallant men and women in the armed services. They must not be demobilized into an environment of inflation and unemployment, to a place on the bread line or a corner selling apples. We must, this time, have plans ready — instead of waiting to do a hasty, inefficient, and ill-considered job at the last moment." He called on "Congress to do its duty in this regard."

While Roosevelt used a Fireside Chat to quiet and control the home front, he laid plans for future overseas offensives. He saw face-to-face discussions with Churchill and Stalin as essential to wise war plans. Although travel to distant places seemed more than likely to strain his physical stamina, which was growing less robust, he was uncomfortable with plans devised through written communications. Now, more than ever, with the war moving toward ultimate victory, he had supreme confidence in his judgment and ability to dominate his allies. And so he was eager to meet with Stalin as well as Churchill. He did not think he could entirely disarm Stalin's suspicions of his former western adversaries, but he thought he could make meaningful progress in persuading him that he and Churchill shared his determination to destroy Hitler's regime and genuinely wanted a cooperative postwar relationship.

Stalin remained reluctant to meet before the end of the year at earliest. But a "man to man" talk with Stalin, Roosevelt told Daisy, might enable him "to establish a constructive relationship," though it might also "result in a complete stalemate." Daisy came away from the conversation thinking: "How much F.D.R. has on his shoulders! It is always more & more, with the passing months, instead of less & less, as he deserves as he gets older." On August 8, Stalin advised Roosevelt that he could not "go on a long journey" to meet him at any time that summer or fall. He offered congratulations on "the outstanding successes in Sicily," which had brought the "collapse of Mussolini and his gang." But he was still not convinced that the Allies would commit themselves to a cross-Channel attack, and the failure of a British-Canadian assault on the French port of Dieppe in April 1942 only increased his uncertainty about Anglo-American resolve to cross the Channel.

With Soviet victories at Kursk and soon after, the city of Orel, 225 miles southwest of Moscow, Stalin had more leverage than ever to implicitly threaten to make a negotiated settlement with Hitler. He gave no hint of doing so, but as long as the Allies delayed an invasion of western Europe, the possibility remained all too worrisome. But because he did not wish to rule out entirely a meeting with Roosevelt, he finally suggested a conference at some indefinite time in Astrakan in southern Russia on the banks of the Volga or in the port of Archangel in the northwest. If these sites were too inconvenient for the president, Stalin proposed a meeting of representatives instead. Roosevelt admitted to Daisy that he wasn't eager for a long, arduous trip to see Stalin, as she recalled: "He doesn't *want* to go, but he has to put every possible effort into going because he thinks it will help in planning the future of the world."

In the meantime, he worked to coordinate plans with Churchill, feeling compelled to blandish him a bit. When Roosevelt issued a public statement on the eve of the Sicily invasion lauding American forces and urging the Italian people to abandon Mussolini and the Fascists as Hitler's tools, he failed to mention the British contribution to the effort. An irritated Churchill, unhappy about having become the junior partner in the Anglo-American alliance, warned Roosevelt that while he had no objection to the president's appealing to the Italians for prompt capitulation, "in all the frankness of our friendship, untoward reactions might grow among the British people and their forces that their contribution had not received equal or sufficient recognition."

With Stalin still noncommittal about a date for a conference, Roosevelt suggested to Churchill that they confer in Quebec. Churchill was most eager for another meeting and suggested coming over to the States in mid-August before proceeding to Canada. He was especially eager to "settle the larger issues" about the invasion and ultimate governance of an occupied Italy. Churchill feared that the U.S. chiefs would convince the president to forgo an Italian campaign in order not to delay the cross-Channel attack. "I trust we can keep all important options in this theatre open until we meet," Churchill cabled him. The collapse of Mussolini's government before the end of July provoked an Anglo-American debate about recognizing a new authority in Italy. Roosevelt wanted assurances that any new government would be recognized by Americans as a genuine representative of the people. He believed that U.S. involvement in postwar international affairs depended on the conviction that democratic values or self-determination would inform discussions and actions everywhere. Churchill was more concerned with Italian stability, which he believed would best be served by a monarchial regime.

During the first week of August, Roosevelt went freshwater fishing on the north shore of Lake Huron in Canada. After arriving in Canada, the prime minister came to Hyde Park for two nights on August 13, and had a picnic lunch the following day with Harry Hopkins, who was under almost constant attack in the conservative press and "looked sick — white, blue around the eyes, with red spots on his cheek bones." The assault on his character was so ugly that he considered a libel suit, which the president talked him out of. Eleanor Roosevelt, her friends Nancy Cook and Marion Dickerman, Sam Rosenman, Daisy, Churchill's daughter Mary, and other Roosevelt kin were also in attendance. They ate traditional American fare — hot dogs, hamburgers, corn pudding, and watermelon. Neither Cook nor Dickerman knew who Daisy was. It was evidence, Geoffrey Ward writes, "of how secretive FDR could be and of how wide was the gulf between the intimate worlds of the two Roosevelts."

Daisy recorded her impressions of the guests, but particularly Churchill. She noted the "special little ice-pail for his scotch." She described him as "a strange looking little man. Fat & round, his clothes bunched up on him. Practically no hair on his head, he wore a 10-gallon hat. He talks as though he had terrible adenoids — sometimes says very little, then talks quite a lot — His

813

humorous twinkle is infectious. . . . In a pair of shorts, he looked exactly like a kewpie [doll]. He made a good dive in [the swimming pool], soon came out, wrapped a large wool blanket around himself & sat down to talk to F.D.R. . . ." She found that Churchill was "difficult in conversation when he doesn't want to talk, perfectly delightful and witty when he wants to be. He makes no effort just to 'talk' with the person next to him, but is very responsive *if* interested." She was keenly aware of the nature of the relationship between the two larger-than-life leaders. She had "the impression that Churchill *adores* the P., loves him as a man, looks up to him, defers to him, leans on him." His regard for the president convinced her that the prime minister had "real greatness" in him. In the bosom of so many friends deferring to him, "the P. was relaxed and seemingly cheerful in the midst of the deepest problems."

In Daisy's presence, "the P. & the P.M. talked rather casually," but they also focused on some of the grave difficulties besetting them. As a prelude to their more formal meetings in Quebec beginning on August 17, they discussed the Katyn massacres in Poland and the "hopes and horrors" of the Nazi occupation and rivalries in the Balkans. The details of atrocities, Churchill said, were enough to make "one's blood boil." Although it would not serve the war effort to publish their suspicions of Soviet responsibility for the Polish killings, Churchill's report to the president raised doubts about their ability to remain close allies with Stalin's brutal, imperious regime. For the time being, however, they saw no choice but to cooperate with the Russians. As Churchill rode a train back to Canada for their meeting in Quebec, he wrote Roosevelt that he was "pretty sure that we ought to make a renewed final offer to U.J. [Uncle Joe] to go to meet him at Fairbanks [Alaska] . . . as soon as this Military Conference is over. If he accepts it will be a very great advantage; if not, we shall be on very strong ground," as to their eagerness for cooperation. On August 18, they sent Stalin a joint cable from Quebec, emphasizing the importance of a tripartite meeting. But if he still could not commit himself to a time and place, they suggested the alternative of a prompt conference of foreign office chiefs.

The following day, before Stalin could respond to their latest invitation, they sent him a detailed cable about a possible Italian surrender and occupation. When a garbled version of the cable left Stalin confused about the terms of surrender, he responded angrily that he was being treated as "a passive third observer. I have to tell you that it is impossible to tolerate such a situation any longer." He demanded the creation of a tripartite commission based in Sicily to enforce unconditional surrender on all their enemies. When Churchill read Stalin's reply, he exclaimed, "Stalin is an unnatural man. There will be grave troubles." Roosevelt later told Daisy that Stalin's message was "rude — stupidly rude" and that Stalin's reluctance to meet signaled a possible intention to make a separate peace with Hitler, acknowledging, "It is what I have feared right along." The recall of Russia's ambassadors in London and Washington added to fears that Stalin might be planning a negotiated exit from the war. In the following week, however, after he received the full details of the Italian surrender talks, Stalin sent a more conciliatory cable, endorsing the Allies' action as "entirely" in line with "the aim of unconditional surrender of Italy." To avoid future confusion, however, he agreed that, "the time has fully come for the establishment of a military-political commission of representatives of the three countries."

Stalin's threatening tone could not help but foster a conviction during the Quebec talks that a firm commitment to a cross-Channel assault was now more essential than ever. Churchill, who had been the most skeptical, conceded that they should commit themselves to a May 1, 1944, date or as close to then as possible. He took comfort from the understanding that they would mount the greatest assault in terms of men and equipment ever undertaken. Because Churchill now seemed so solidly in favor of the invasion of France, Roosevelt accepted his recommendation that they follow the conquest of Sicily with an attack on Italy at the beginning of September. As he had before the Sicilian campaign, Churchill argued that it would be a grave error to wait eight months before launching anther major offensive, especially since it seemed realistic to believe that they could take advantage of Mussolini's collapse and Italian reluctance to continue fighting. That supposition, however, underestimated the intensity of German determination to oppose an Allied conquest of Hitler's fascist partner.

Churchill and Roosevelt also made a secret pact regarding "tube alloys," or the creation of an atomic bomb. On August 19, two days into their weeklong meeting, they committed to sharing their results of current research on atomic power, but not to include the Soviet Union in their efforts toward such a powerful weapon. The five-part agreement included commitments not to use the potential weapon against each other or against a third party without mutual consent. It also pledged nondisclosure of information about the weapon without shared agreement. Finally, because of U.S. production burdens in manufacturing the atomic bomb, they agreed to American postwar industrial or commercial advantages with respect to it. They ended by providing for the establishment of a policy committee to oversee future work on the weapon.

Although Churchill and Roosevelt were aware that Soviet informants had told Moscow about Anglo-American research on an atomic bomb, they knew that if they relayed to Stalin the current state of its development, he would insist on equal access to any bomb-building capability. Russia's likely responsibility for the Katyn Forest massacres, concern about postwar Soviet expansionist ambitions in Europe, and the suspicions aroused about Stalin's possible interest in a separate peace with Hitler left Churchill and Roosevelt unwilling to treat Russia as a reliable future ally.

The Roosevelt administration's doubts about the Soviets were by now an open secret. In August, the columnist Drew Pearson had railed against the State Department, led by Cordell Hull and supported by subordinates Adolf Berle, James Dunn, and Breckinridge Long, for its anti-Russian sentiments. Hull denounced the assertions as "monstrous and diabolic falsehoods." In a press conference on August 31, Roosevelt himself condemned Pearson's undermining of Allied unity, stating, "The whole statement from beginning to end was a lie" and calling Pearson "a chronic liar in his columns." But Pearson's claims stung not just because they threatened to destabilize relations with Moscow but also because they were true.

More disturbing was the fact that the Quebec meeting had failed to advance any responses to the growing evidence that the Nazis were systematically murdering Europe's Jews in concentration camps. In April, a Bermuda conference, principally including British and U.S. representatives, had deadlocked over ways to rescue Europe's Jews from Hitler's extermination program. In July, Roosevelt had proposed to Churchill that they share the cost and responsibility for relocating an estimated five or six thousand Jewish refugees in Spain to temporary camps in North Africa. "At the earliest possible moment," he hoped they could find a more permanent place for their settlement. Concerned about a hostile Arab reaction to the presence of Jewish refugees in North Africa and specifically "a limited number" in Palestine, while Roosevelt wanted a quick and uncontroversial solution to the problem, that seemed out of reach, for every proposal was wrought with innumerable controversies; the only answer to the dilemma was the quickest possible defeat of the Nazis. In August 1943, Eleanor described Jewish suffering in Europe as unparalleled and called upon the world to protest Nazi crimes, but added "I do not know what we can do to save the Jews in Europe and to find them homes." She echoed Franklin's conviction that the best solution was "rescue through military victory." That summer, when Jan Karski, a member of the Polish underground, told Roosevelt that "without Allied intervention, Polish Jewry would cease to exist," the president replied: "Tell your people we shall win the war."

Roosevelt returned to Hyde Park on August 26, and although Daisy thought he looked "well, but tired," he was in fact suffering a variety of life-threatening ailments. He described his general condition to Daisy as feeling "so sleepy his brain wouldn't work." He fell asleep twice when trying to write a message to Congress, he told her, and she suspected a serious decline in his health, confiding to a diary: "He just is *too* tired *too* often. I can't help worrying about him." She thought that the constant barrage of domestic criticism of the president's leadership was "more wearing on F.D.R. than the *real big* problems of the war & the future peace — the 'little foxes' that gnaw at the roots of the vine." In fact, at almost sixty-two, Roosevelt was beset by severe hypertension, an enlarged heart, and "acute bronchitis, which was responsible for a persistent cough," and showed evidence of "chronic obstructive pulmonary disease." Dr. Jerrold M. Post, who studied Roosevelt's heath records, believes that his complaint about the imperfect functioning of his thinking was " 'sub-acute chronic diffuse hypoxia of the brain' — chronic insufficient oxygenation of the brain. This is a very reasonable explanation for the drowsiness, problems in concentrating, and episodes of semi-stupor that affected Roosevelt during his last two years of life."

In September, however, after he had returned from Canada and Churchill came to Washington for more conversations and several public appearances, including the receipt of an honorary degree from Harvard, those closest to Roosevelt "remarked on how well the P. looked — we all agreed that it was extraordinary," Daisy noted. "It seems as though the trials & difficulties of the office of President . . . acts as a stimulant to the P. They may take the place of the exercise which he can't have like other people." It was, however, wishful thinking, for while the challenges of being president in wartime may well have energized him, the increasing deterioration of his health was a reality that no external conditions could contain.

By contrast with the president, whose growing health problems were not yet fully evident in September 1943, Harry Hopkins was transparently exhausted and ill. Since 1935, after Hopkins had much of his stomach removed because of a cancer, "blood transfusions, intravenous feedings, and injections of vitamins and iron" had saved his life, but he continued to suffer from bouts of diarrhea, insufficient stomach acids to assure digestion, "vitamin B-12 deficiency, pernicious anemia, and liver disease." He took so many medicines he thought of himself as a walking drugstore.

When he returned from Quebec, he was in terrible shape and had to be hospitalized again — this time for three weeks. Although his doctors prescribed three months of total rest, he refused to stay sidelined. "All those boys at the front are fighting & getting hurt & dying," he said. "I have a job to do here & I'm going to do it." His plan to move from the White House to Georgetown also troubled Roosevelt, who anticipated that it would mean that he would be less able to rely on Hopkins for daily support. The president regarded it as "a form of abandonment, which left him more alone than ever." It was Harry's talent to cut through a disagreement to capture the essential point that especially appealed to Roosevelt. "When a group of men are arguing and haggling over the details of some problem and perhaps talking at cross purposes," Roosevelt said, Harry, "in one sentence, will put his finger on the point of the argument and clarify the whole thing." Churchill called him "Lord Root of the matter." However much distance opened between Roosevelt and Hopkins, they shared a determination not to let their physical maladies deter them from the work of winning the war and preserving the New Deal. Given the length and general success of their service, neither of them could accept that healthier successors could do their jobs as well as they could.

There was no question in Roosevelt's mind about the obligations of a leader in wartime. Like soldiers on a battlefield, they were obliged to risk their lives for a larger good. In conversation with royal visitors from Austria, Greece, and Yugoslavia, he urged them to join their respective armies. "Go into the Army;" he said, "go to the front with the soldiers; if you get killed, it's just too bad, but you will have done the right thing."

One of those conflicts was a long-simmering battle between Cordell Hull and Sumner Welles, whose loathing was so mutual that, as Roosevelt told Daisy, they wanted "to kill each other." His own preference for Welles over Hull irked the secretary no end. He constantly complained in private about Welles's frequent visits to the White House and denigrated him as "my fairy" and "the polecat in the next room." Hull had his eye on Welles's job, and with the help of William Bullitt, spread stories about Welles's homosexual proclivities and warned Roosevelt that Welles's presence in the administration was a ticking time bomb. Roosevelt had limited regard for Hull: Privately he complained that Hull was too thin-skinned about criticism, which he should have taken in stride, as the president himself did. But ever mindful of Hull's Senate connections, which could prove invaluable for future treaty approvals, Roosevelt gave him priority over Welles. He urged Hull to accommodate himself to Welles's presence, but Hull could not tolerate so strong a competitor as a colleague. In fact, because Hull was in poor health and often absent from Washington recuperating from physical maladies, he needed Welles to run the department. Still, he could not reconcile himself to the president's greater reliance on Welles for advice and the execution of foreign policy.

The conflict between Hull and Welles came to a head during the summer of 1943. When Ralph Brewster, Maine's Republican senator and a staunch foe of the New Deal, learned of Welles's sexual activities from Bullitt and Hull, he threatened to expose the administration's coddling of a national security threat unless Welles resigned. Warned that Welles's continued presence in the government could jeopardize the Democrats' hold on the White House in 1944, Roosevelt, who was considering running for a fourth term, accepted Welles's decision to resign. He was having a hard time "keeping the old boy sweet," Roosevelt told Vice President Henry Wallace, and he needed to keep Hull as secretary "for the general welfare of the country."

The loss of Welles had resulted in what Roosevelt described as a "dreadful day" and left him "very tired & keyed up." He was not only pained at having to let Welles go, but his departure left a yawning gap in the State Department's utility as an instrument of Roosevelt's foreign policy. Soon after, when Bullitt asked Roosevelt to support his election as mayor of Philadelphia, he vented his anger over the Welles incident, telling him: "If I were the angel Gabriel and you and Sumner Welles came before me seeking admission into the gates of Heaven, do you know what I would say? 'Bill Bullitt, you have defamed the name of a man who toiled for his fellow man, and you can go to hell.' And that's what I tell you to do now!" After Bullitt left his office, Roosevelt's secretary Dorothy Brady said, the president "was raving, raving!" The president ordered Philadelphia's Democratic bosses, "Cut his throat!" and Bullitt lost the election by a wide margin.

At the beginning of October, Roosevelt complained to Churchill that "the newspapers here, beginning with the Hearst, McCormick crowd, had a field day over General Marshall's duties. . . . It seems to me that if we are to be forced into making public statements about our military commands we will find ourselves with the newspapers running the war." Because he was reluctant to let Marshall leave Washington, as he relied on him heavily for military counsel, Roosevelt wanted to give command of the cross-Channel attack to Eisenhower. But he was determined not to let conservative press publishers undermine his leadership by forcing him into a premature or unwanted appointment. In addition, he complained to Churchill about a press leak reporting differences with Stalin over the venue for an October foreign ministers conference. The story was the product of "a dangerous leak somewhere. . . . Don't you think perhaps it would be beneficial to us both if this leak could be run down and so avoid another one in the future when there is more at stake?" he asked Churchill.

After a successful landing in Italy at the beginning of September, Allied forces had come up against stiff German resistance. Churchill was eager to expand the fighting to the Eastern Mediterranean, but American military chiefs, supported by Roosevelt, regarded this as a potential "suction pump" that would divert forces from an increasingly difficult Italian campaign and disrupt arrangements for the attack on France. As it became clear that the Germans intended to maintain "a full-scale defense of Italy," discussions about the Eastern Mediterranean were soon abandoned.

But Churchill's doubts about crossing the Channel remained, as he believed that "present plans for 1944 seem open to very grave defects." He worried that the division of American and British forces between Italy and France would leave one of the fronts vulnerable to a massed German counterattack. "It is arguable," he advised Roosevelt, "that neither the forces building up in Italy nor those available for a May OVERLORD [code name for the French invasion] are strong enough for the tasks set them." He also feared "a startling comeback for Hitler" if they became too rigid about their decision to cross the Channel. "My dear friend," Churchill added, "this is much the greatest thing we have ever attempted, and I am not satisfied that we have yet taken the measures necessary to give it the best chance of success." He judged the ongoing Italian campaign to be a great aid to the Russians by forcing Hitler to divert "powerful forces to this theatre." The Allies had "to win the battle in Italy, no matter what effect is produced on subsequent operations." He also requested an early conference with Roosevelt before they met Stalin in Tehran, which is where the Russian leader finally agreed to meet in December.

In late October Roosevelt became ill and joked with Churchill that "It is a nuisenza to have the influenza." But it was no joking matter: He ached all over and had a fever of over 104. Ten days later, on October 30, he was still feeling "miserable and very tired, but he can't give in to it." He had begun drinking coffee in the morning to pep him up, but it left him shaky and with trembling hands. He dreaded the thought of flying over the Atlas Mountains to Tehran and worried that Hopkins, who was determined to go with him, would also suffer the ill effects of so arduous a journey. But Roosevelt considered the meeting as of "paramount importance" and believed he had to go, "regardless of the cost to him" or Harry.

Roosevelt agreed that they should meet in November but asked Stalin to consider coming to Egypt, which would be an easier, more convenient journey for him. Since he had agreed to send Hull to a foreign ministers conference in Moscow, he hoped that Stalin would be more flexible about where he and Churchill convened with him. At the Moscow conference, however, when Stalin went along with an Anglo-American pronouncement on the need for a postwar international peacekeeping organization, sent word of his readiness to join the war against Japan after Germany's defeat, but refused to meet anywhere but in Iran, Roosevelt conceded to his insistence on the Big

Three gathering in Tehran.

Dr. McIntire recommended that the president travel by sea as a restorative health measure. But McIntire surely knew that at best a sea voyage would be a small palliative. He could not have been unaware of the fact that Roosevelt's health was in serious decline, but he consistently hid the truth from the press and public about the president's medical condition. To McIntire and millions of Americans Roosevelt had become indispensable, though the physician was clearly doing the president's bidding in revealing nothing about the true state of his health. As Roosevelt understood, as soon as the war ended, Americans would be more than ready to see him retire. He told Daisy, "*If* the war is over next year, it will be impossible to elect a liberal president." He had every hope that the war *would* end in 1944 and that he could devote himself in retirement to international peace.

In the meantime, he saw a meeting with Stalin, however far he had to travel and whatever the risks to his health and person, as essential if they were to bring the wars in Europe and Asia to the swiftest possible conclusion and begin arranging a more stable, peaceful postwar world. "I still think it vital that we see him [Stalin]," Roosevelt cabled Churchill on October 29. "I too am most anxious that you and I get away from this dispatch method of talking."

When Hull saw Roosevelt just before he left for his Middle East meetings, he observed that the president "was looking forward to his meeting with Stalin with the enthusiasm of a boy." On November 13, Roosevelt was carried aboard the *Iowa,* a new battleship, for a seven-day crossing to

Oran in Algeria, from where they were scheduled to fly to Tunis and then on to Cairo for the beginning of a conference with Chiang Kai-shek on November 22. A near disaster had marked the sea crossing: An accompanying U.S. destroyer had inadvertently fired a torpedo that barely missed the *Iowa* while it was in the midst of an antiaircraft drill. "All is in the hands of God," Roosevelt wrote Daisy from on board the battleship.

Aside from the torpedo incident, which gave Roosevelt the excitement of facing combat, the sea crossing was a very pleasant one. "Everything is very comfortable and I have with me lots of work and detective stories and we brought a dozen good movies. . . . It is a relief to have no newspapers! I am going to start a one page paper," he wrote Eleanor. "It will pay and print only news that really has some relative importance!" His son Elliott met him at the pier in Oran when the ship docked. "The sea voyage had done Father good," Elliott noted. "He looked fit; and he was filled with excited anticipation of the days ahead."

A night flight to Cairo brought Roosevelt to the banks of the Nile at dawn, where he could glimpse the pyramids and the Sphinx. "Man's desire to be remembered is colossal," he said to Mike Reilly, his Secret Service agent, speaking as much about himself as surely as about the ancient Egyptians. After getting settled in a villa "way out of town, I've visited the pyramids and been fortified by the Sphinx," he also told Eleanor. "I'll give free transportation to any Senator or Congressman who will go over and look at her for a long, long time," he wryly declared. On November 20, the party, including Churchill and his daughter Sarah, celebrated Thanksgiving with dinner at Roosevelt's residence, where he presided over the gathering while he carved two huge turkeys. "For a couple of hours we cast care aside," Churchill recalled. To Roosevelt's great amusement, the guests danced to music played on a gramophone. With Sara the only woman present and in much demand, Churchill danced with presidential aide Pa Watson. Roosevelt "roared with laughter." "I had never seen the President more gay," Churchill recalled.

Eleanor and their daughter Anna had been annoyed with him for his refusal to let them join the trip. Women are not permitted on naval warships; nor would they be welcome at the conference, he informed them. But when both Sarah Churchill and Madame Chiang Kai-shek showed up in Cairo, Eleanor and Anna were furious. "I've been amused that Madame Chiang and Sarah Churchill were in the party," Eleanor wrote Franklin. "I wish you had let me fly out. I'm sure I would have enjoyed Madame Chiang more than you did," she added. She felt she could have handled Chiang better than Franklin, "I think the men (including FDR) are afraid of her," Eleanor told Anna, as Madame Chiang had the ability to make the most powerful of men "squirm."

Churchill had wanted British and American leaders to meet without a Soviet general present, as all he would do, Churchill complained, is lobby for a second front. But Roosevelt was convinced that Stalin would protest about being excluded. "It would be a terrible mistake if U.J. thought we had ganged up on him on military action," Roosevelt told Churchill. Also, Roosevelt and Marshall, who had accompanied him to Cairo, did not wish to give the British an opportunity to argue for any postponement of OVERLORD while they battled the Germans in Italy. The president and his chiefs saw the coming meeting in Tehran as the occasion to form a united front with the Russians against any diversion from the French campaign. During the Cairo conversations, Churchill affirmed his commitment to a cross-Channel attack but also confirmed American suspicions of his eagerness for a Balkans campaign by declaring that OVERLORD "should not be such a tyrant as to rule out every other activity in the Mediterranean."

With the Chiangs present in Cairo, however, Stalin declined to send a Soviet representative there lest it give the Japanese a pretext for declaring war on Russia. Roosevelt had conceived of a meeting with China more as a boost to their prestige and stature than as a forum at which to consider possible military agreements. To be sure, the discussions with Chiang Kai-shek, which included General Stilwell, involved hypothetical plans for reopening the Burma Road as a prelude to a large-scale assault on Japan's million-man army in China. But these talks were more symbolic than substantive, as China was a source of unremitting conflicts and insoluble problems. Stilwell was contemptuous of both Chiang and U.S. policy in China, as he had concluded America was locked into a no-win policy of backing a "rotten regime . . . a one-party government supported by a Gestapo and headed by an unbalanced man with little education." Stilwell was also angry with Roosevelt, as the general believed that he had "been ignored, slighted, blocked, delayed, double-crossed, lied to." While he was eager for a campaign to retake Burma, Stilwell felt that it was "absolutely impossible to do anything."

Churchill did not care very much if China collapsed. He was convinced that an island-hopping campaign across the Pacific would eventually bring Japan to defeat. While willing to give lip service to CBI military campaigns, Roosevelt shared his belief in combating Japan outside China. He accepted Stilwell's view of Chiang as "highly temperamental" and his regime as shot through with "corruption and inefficiency." This is not to say that Roosevelt discounted China's importance. On the contrary, he viewed China as a potentially powerful influence in postwar affairs. As a country with over 400 million people, it would eventually become a great power. Because he believed that Chiang was the only one who could hold China together, he wished to grant the Generalissimo the appearance of being a political equal. Consequently, in conversations with him in Cairo he encouraged illusions about military action that to Stilwell and Churchill seemed unrealizable. Churchill complained that the talks with Chiang were "lengthy, complicated and minor . . . [and] occupied first instead of last place at Cairo." Roosevelt was not sure Chiang could last. Maybe "we should look for some other man or group of men to carry on," he told Stilwell in Cairo. But regardless of whom he dealt with in China, his objective remained the same: to keep Japan's million troops in the country occupied in fighting there so that they would be unable to join the Pacific battles, and to foster the image of China as a great power in order to use it as a surrogate for U.S. designs in postwar Asia.

Stalin's reluctance to come to Cairo was partly a matter of his fear of flying, which he had never done before he traveled to Tehran. Fearful that domestic opponents might sabotage his plane, he switched aircraft at the last minute. For all his talk about visiting the front lines, he rarely left the Kremlin, where he was well guarded and safe from potential assassins.

From the moment he first met Roosevelt and Churchill on November 28 to the end of the talks on December 1, Stalin's competitiveness and reach for power were on full display. He convinced Roosevelt to stay at the Soviet embassy, where he asserted that the president would be safer from attack than he would be by driving the five miles from the American legation to the site of the meeting each day. Roosevelt's presence in the Soviet compound enabled the Russians to plant listening devices in his rooms, but mindful of Soviet spying, Roosevelt took care to reveal nothing damning and to indicate only genuine regard for Stalin. For his part, his decision to stay at the Soviet embassy was calculated to promote trust between them.

To Churchill's distress, he was too ill to join an initial dinner with Roosevelt and Stalin on November 27. Exhausted and with "his voice almost completely gone, . . . he had dinner in bed like a sulky little boy." At that first Roosevelt-Stalin meeting, Roosevelt "made it clear that he was eager to relieve the pressure on the Russian front by invading France." When Hopkins, who was a guest at the dinner and eager to restrain Churchill from arguing against a second front, informed Lord Moran, the prime minister's physician, of what Roosevelt had told Stalin, Moran concluded "that the President's attitude will encourage Stalin to take a stiff line in the conference." Churchill still believed that Stalin's fixation on the French assault rested to some degree on his desire to keep his Allies out of the Balkans, which he planned to make into an exclusive Soviet sphere of control.

When the three leaders assembled on the following day, they began with an exchange of conviviality. As diplomat George Kennan related the occasion, Churchill passed around a silver cigar case inscribed with "To Winston from his fellow Conservatives, 1925." Roosevelt responded by sharing his own silver cigarette case with the inscription: "To Franklin from his Harvard Classmates, 1904." Stalin, not to be outdone by his capitalist colleagues, offered them *his* silver cigarette case, which had found its way from Budapest with the inscription: "To Count Karoli: From his Friends at the Jockey Club, 1910." In Kennan's telling, Stalin was happy to demonstrate his appropriation of a valuable taken from a European nobleman.

Mindful of their history-making power, Churchill and Stalin began the first tripartite discussion with grandiose pronouncements. "In our hands," Churchill announced, "we have the future of mankind." Their meeting represented "the greatest concentration of world power that has ever been seen in the history of mankind." Stalin was equally majestic: "History has spoiled us," he said. "She's given us very great power and very great opportunities . . . Let us begin our work." Roosevelt, who as the only head of state presided over the conference, went directly to the tasks at hand: Although he described the U.S. strategy against Japan, he acknowledged that the most important topic of their discussions was how to strike most effectively at Hitler by drawing the greatest weight off the Soviet forces.

Churchill did not dispute Roosevelt's assertion and declared that "North or North-West France [was] the place for Anglo-American forces to attack, though it was of course true that the Germans there would resist desperately." He followed this cautionary note with the admonition that while they prepared for the invasion over the course of the next six months, they needed to find a use for the forces available to them in the Mediterranean. He asked: Should they move northeast toward the Danube, or should they invade the south of France? Stalin, who remained intent on dominating the Balkans, offered that no doubt, striking at southern France was the wisest strategy. He also promised to join the fighting against Japan once Germany was defeated. Unwilling to raise overtly a divisive political issue, Churchill nonetheless remarked on potential tensions confronting them: "Although we were all great friends," he said, "it would be idle for us to delude ourselves that we saw eye to eye on all matters. Time and patience were necessary" if they were going to follow the war with a stable peace. Privately, Stalin had anticipated Churchill's hint at their differences, saying, "I dislike and distrust the English. They are skillful and stubborn opponents. . . . If England is still ruling the world it is due to the stupidity of other countries, which let themselves be bluffed."

As all three of them understood, were it not for Hitler, they would be more openly suspicious of one another's intentions. Their opposing points of view, however, could not be entirely suppressed. After dinner on the evening of November 28, as they sat in a circle drinking coffee and smoking cigars, Churchill remarked: "I believe that God is on our side. At least I have done my best to make Him a faithful ally." Stalin could not resist a rejoinder: "And the devil is on my side," he said with a taunting grin. "Because, of course, everyone knows that the devil is a Communist — and God, no doubt, is a good Conservative."

That evening, Roosevelt was showing the effects of his declining health. He said little and looked as if he was going to faint. "Great drops of sweat began to bead on his face." We can only speculate that he was suffering another angina attack. After coffee, he excused himself and went to bed, and Churchill and Stalin continued their discussion. When Stalin expressed his fears of a postwar German resurgence that could lead to yet another conflict, Churchill suggested that they might be able to ensure a fifty-year peace by controlling German aviation and rearmament. Friendship between their two countries and the United States would be essential to keeping Germany in check. They then turned to Poland, and Stalin asked if Churchill and Eden, who was also present, thought that Russia intended "to swallow Poland up." They answered the question by agreeing that what Poland might lose in the east could be balanced by gains to the west.

On the second day Churchill invited Roosevelt to meet with him privately, but the president declined, saying that it would irritate Stalin. That afternoon, the three discussed coming military operations. Churchill emphasized the need to keep pressure on Germany by fresh assaults in Italy and the Mediterranean, while Stalin, backed by Roosevelt, pressed the case for OVERLORD. He argued that anything other than the attack on

France would be a pointless "diversion," and Roosevelt predicted that limited actions in the Mediterranean could grow into larger operations and delay the French campaign. Stalin pressed Churchill to state whether he genuinely believed in OVERLORD, and asked Roosevelt who the invasion commander would be, insisting that the attack not occur without one man's taking charge. When nothing seemed to be resolved at the close of this discussion, Stalin offered an olive branch by inviting everyone to dine at the Soviet embassy.

Tensions between Churchill and Stalin erupted that evening when Stalin proposed that after the war, fifty thousand of Hitler's principal officers be shot. Churchill declared it an act of barbarism that his Parliament and people would never accept. When Elliott Roosevelt, who had accompanied his father to the conference, stated his conviction that the U.S. Army would back Stalin's proposal, an enraged Churchill left the room. Stalin and Molotov followed him to assure him that they were only joking. Although Churchill returned to the dinner, he believed that given half a chance, Stalin would follow through on his idea. Afterward, at the British embassy, he vented his anger and frustration, seeing nothing but disaster ahead — another bloody war and "impending catastrophe" with an end to civilization and a "desolate" Europe.

The next morning, November 30, anxious to put aside residual tensions, Churchill arranged to see Stalin alone. He again made the case for further action in the Mediterranean, but Stalin remained adamant about a May 1944 deadline for OVERLORD. He warned that if the operation were to be further delayed, it would encourage sentiments in Russia of ending the war. His countrymen "were war-weary" and expected the Allies to honor their commitments. At their afternoon meeting, Roosevelt promised to name a commander within the next three or four days, and they agreed to issue a communiqué announcing "complete agreement as to the scope and timing of the operations which will be undertaken from the east, west and south." They also agreed to conceal the timing and point of attack of the French campaign with what Churchill called "a bodyguard of lies." That evening, at a sixty-ninth-birthday dinner for the prime minister, the conviviality was palpable, with endless toasts from the three leaders. "I drink to the proletarian masses," Churchill exclaimed. "I drink to the Conservative Party," Stalin responded. When Churchill added, "England is getting pinker," meaning more like red Russia, Stalin noted, "It is a sign of good health."

During the last day of the conference, December 1, the discussions focused on postwar affairs. Roosevelt had already convinced Stalin to accept a postwar peacekeeping organization that was a worldwide body rather than a group of regional organizations directly concerned with local areas. U.S. opinion, the president said, would oppose regional arrangements as being too much like great power politics with spheres of control. They agreed to leave the details of how such a body be organized until later in the war. Roosevelt also urged consideration of a system of trusteeships to govern former colonies: One of the victors would take responsibility for a former colony for twenty or twenty-five years. It was Roosevelt's way of putting an idealistic face on U.S. postwar diplomacy by turning Asian and African colonies into U.S. naval and air bases while those peoples moved toward self-government. He also agreed to Soviet control over the Baltic States of Estonia, Latvia, and Lithuania, but on the condition that they enjoy a right to self-determination. He then joked with Stalin that he had no intention of going to war with the Soviet Union over the fate of these countries. Roosevelt was effectively informing Stalin that while American public opinion would object to arbitrary Russian control of other nations, he personally accepted spheres of control as a great-power reality that the United States would have to live with.

France and Poland were other subjects of potential discord that they hoped to avoid. Stalin declared "the entire French ruling class . . . rotten to the core and . . . now actively helping our enemies." Roosevelt enthusiastically agreed to stripping the French of their empire and turning their former colonies, like Indochina and Senegal, into trusteeships. As for Poland, he resisted any public expression of whatever resolution they reached, explaining that he needed the Polish vote in the 1944 election, thus privately acknowledging his plans to run for a fourth term. He did, however, endorse proposals to cede Polish territory in the east to the Soviets in return for Polish acquisition of German territory in the west. They also agreed on the need for permanent restraints on Germany and Japan, including the dismemberment of the German state so that it could not pose a renewed threat to Russia.

Roosevelt left Tehran confident that he had improved relations with Stalin and increased the prospects for postwar stability, but in meetings in

Cairo afterward with Churchill and British military leaders, he expressed doubts about Stalin's keeping his promise to join the fighting against Japan once Germany surrendered. When Churchill argued that Soviet engagement in the Far East conflict would make an invasion of Burma superfluous, Roosevelt responded: "Suppose Marshal Stalin was unable to be as good as his word; we might find that we had forfeited Chinese support without obtaining commensurate help from the Russians." He described keeping "the Russians cozy with us" as a "ticklish" business. After his return to the United States on December 16, he informed the cabinet that it was a "nip and tuck" issue whether the Russians would come into the war against Japan. He was likewise not certain that Stalin would take his side in support of a world peacekeeping body, as opposed to the regional organizations that Churchill favored. "I'll have to work on both of them," he told a Democratic senator.

Roosevelt's concerns were, in fact, fully justified, for Stalin considered his allies as untrustworthy and all too ready to serve their own interests at Russia's expense. In 1944, in a famous conversation with Milovan Djilas, the Yugoslav Communist leader, Stalin, his paranoia on full display, castigated Churchill and Roosevelt as treacherous. He did not misread them in assuming that their primary consideration was their own goals, but he could not imagine that anyone could be, like him, less than ruthless in pursuit of them. "Churchill is the kind of man who will pick your pocket for a kopeck if you don't watch him," he said. "Yes, pick your pocket for a kopeck! By God, pick your pocket of a kopeck. Roosevelt is not like that. He dips in his hand only for bigger coins. But Churchill? Churchill — will do it for a ko-peck."

At a press conference on December 17, Roosevelt lauded the Tehran talks as establishing a basis for international understanding that could spare future generations the horrors of another world war. When asked to describe his personal impressions of Stalin, he said that the meeting confirmed his highest expectations. The same was true of his assessment of Chiang Kai-shek, and their mutual rapport bode well for future relations, as did the congressional repeal of the Chinese Exclusion Act of 1884. When questioned whether he found Stalin to be "dour," Roosevelt replied that he thought Stalin was like him — "a realist." Anyone who knew anything about Stalin's and Chiang's merciless suppression of domestic opponents and their indifference to democracy was aware that Roosevelt's characterization of the two leaders overstated their virtues. Roosevelt's description of himself as a realist reflected his conviction that he had no power to reform the regimes in Russia and China, both of which were nonetheless essential to winning the war with the least possible loss of men and material well-being. In addition, he believed that any truthful account of these Allies would not only undermine co-operation in conducting the war but also weaken public resolve in the United States to participate actively in postwar international affairs.

On Christmas Eve, Roosevelt spoke to Americans about his meetings in the Middle East, and his image making was on full display. "At Cairo and Tehran," he reported, "we devoted ourselves not only to military matters, we devoted ourselves also to consideration of the future — to plans for the kind of world which alone can justify all the sacrifices of this war." He described his meetings with the "unconquerable" Stalin and Chiang as deepening his regard for them and convincing him that they shared the same objectives in the war and for the postwar world. Singling out Chiang as "a man of great vision and great courage," he stated that he had every confidence that together they would not only defeat Japan but also put in place a peacekeeping system that would ensure tranquility for "many generations to come." Likewise, he and Stalin reached agreement on future policies to defeat Germany and establish a "durable peace." He saw no "insoluble differences" with Russia. "I got along fine with Marshal Stalin," he asserted. ". . . He is truly representative of the heart and soul of Russia; and I believe that we are going to get along very well with him and the Russian people — very well indeed." He ended with the announcement that General Dwight Eisenhower would head a future combined attack in Europe and warned Americans against assuming a quick end to the fighting that would allow them to revert to isolationism.

On December 28, when he held a follow-up press conference, a reporter asked what he meant when he told another journalist that he no longer liked the term "New Deal." Did his focus on postwar world politics signal an end to domestic reform? Roosevelt explained that the collapse of the economy in 1932 required "Dr. New Deal," an internist, to attend to the nation's ills. After Pearl Harbor, the new affliction facing the country required a different specialist, "Dr. Win the War. This certainly did not mean that the remedies of

Dr. New Deal should now be cast aside. "It seems pretty clear," he said, "that we must plan for . . . an expanded economy, which will result in more security, more employment, more recreation, in education, in more health, in better housing for all our citizens, so that the conditions of 1932 and the beginning of 1933 won't come back again." But all this would take place only after Dr. Win the War had used his skills to lead the country successfully through the fighting. So did this pronouncement "add up to a fourth-term declaration?" a reporter asked. "Oh, we are not talking about things like that now," Roosevelt evasively replied. But it was clear that he was not ruling out the possibility.

As he welcomed in the New Year at the White House with Eleanor, their daughter Anna, several grandchildren, and Daisy, he struggled with yet another cold or flu. Did he have the physical stamina to seek another term? As long as the war continued, he could not imagine retiring to Hyde Park. It would be too much like a ship's captain abandoning his crew to make their way through a perilous storm. Besides, as he told Daisy, when it came to the question of a fourth term, Churchill had said, "I simply can't go on without you." And then there was so much unfinished other business: When he returned from Tehran, he told Felix Frankfurter, "I realized on the trip what a dreadful lack of civilization is shown in the countries I visited — but on returning" his encountering striking coal miners and railroad workers and complaints about secret postwar agreements with Churchill and Stalin made him "not wholly certain of the degree of civilization in *terra Americana.*" The key issue, he told Edward Stettinius,

Jr., his new undersecretary of state, was not whether the United States could make the world safe for democracy, as Woodrow Wilson hoped, but whether democracy could make the world safe from another war.

CHAPTER 19
THE "GOOD SOLDIER"

Roosevelt began the New Year "coughing & sneezing & feeling like a boiled owl." He was plagued by a fever, constant fatigue, and severe headaches. Despite his health problems, he was "so accustomed to playing his part on all occasions" that he carried on his usual daily routine without complaint, but his physical ailments had become a constant strain on his capacity to perform his presidential duties. His daughter Anna, who now lived at the White House with her children, tried to alleviate the stress placed on him: "I found myself trying to take over little chores that I felt would relieve Father of some of the pressure under which he was constantly working," she recalled. He was pleased to have her companionship and help. He hated eating alone or being left on his own and complained about Eleanor's neglect. When Daisy suggested that "Mrs. R." accompany him on afternoon drives, he said, "I would have to make an appointment a week ahead!" But he was determined not to allow his physical condition to interfere with his presidential performance. So many American soldiers and sailors were perishing in the war that he viewed himself as a member of the armed services who had to put aside personal considerations for the sake of the national well-being.

The first demand upon him in 1944 was a January 11 State of the Union message. While the actual work of drafting the speech fell on White House aides, he had to judge the political consequences of what he said and how best to mobilize the country in support of what he believed was needed in the war and at home. Congress was badly divided, with Republicans and Southern Democrats alike lining up against the administration; they were particularly critical of anything suggesting long-term bonds with Communist Russia and of new proposals for domestic reform. Harold Ickes, ever the voice of the administration's liberal activism, took to the radio to denounce the "four [conservative] lords of the press — Hearst, McCormick and the two Pattersons." In the twelfth year of his presidency, Roosevelt still enjoyed an iconic status, but the war gave him a hold on the public that only deepened the animus of his foes, who longed for the day they would see him leave the White House.

He was mindful of the antagonism that his continuing presence in power generated, and he accepted the challenge of trying to promote a new round of national approval. He saw his speech as a fresh test of his ability to excite public enthusiasm and support. Too ill to appear before Congress, he had worked on the address with Sam Rosenman and Robert Sherwood while lying in bed, and then delivered it as a Fireside Chat.

He began by warning against assumptions that the country could revert to "ostrich isolationism" at the close of the fighting. He also dismissed "suspicions" that he had entered into secret treaties in his talks at Cairo and Tehran. Such rumors, he said, came from "self-seeking partisans," from "selfish pressure groups who seek to feather their nests while young Americans are dying" and labored under "the delusion that the time is past when we must make prodigious sacrifices — that the war is already won." In fact, because 58 percent of Americans believed that the war would end in 1944, the thrust of much of Roosevelt's message was addressed to what they should expect at home when the fighting stopped. He asked Congress to enact a tax bill that would "reduce the cost of the war to our sons and daughters" and rein in war profits. He urged plans for not only establishing "a lasting peace," but also addressing the painful fact that a part of the nation remained "ill-fed, ill-clothed, ill-housed, and insecure." He asked everyone to understand that "necessitous men are not free men," and that the national well-being demanded an "economic bill of rights," which, like the original Bill of Rights, would now guarantee a decent standard of living for every American.

In raising these concerns, Roosevelt was speaking to public anxieties about postwar domestic affairs, which were reflected in the results of a recent Gallup poll. If you could attend a White House press conference, Gallup asked, what question would you like to ask the president? The most frequent responses included: How will we avoid a depression after the war? Will there be jobs for all of us? Will soldiers be able to find work? In focusing on domestic economic fears, Roosevelt was also looking ahead to the 1944 presidential election. He knew that his party favored his reelection to a fourth term: In polls, 82 percent of Democratic men and 88 percent of Democratic women said they wanted Roosevelt to run again. Another survey indicated that the Democrats remained the favored party in the presidential race, especially if the war continued. If the war was still going on, 55 percent of voters said they preferred Roosevelt, but if it ended, only 42 percent of the electorate was ready to give him a fourth term. Roosevelt's support declined to 51 percent if the war seemed likely to be over in a few weeks or a few months after the election.

There were also underlying doubts about allowing anyone to hold the presidency for more than eight years. When asked if they favored an amendment to the Constitution barring future officeholders from more than two terms, 57 percent of a survey endorsed the idea. Roosevelt's difficulties with Congress at the beginning of 1944 only intensified reservations about long-standing presidencies. In January, Roosevelt pressed Congress to pass three major bills he believed essential. First, he wanted a law compelling national service, giving the government power to direct labor to work in vital war production industries. But Republicans and Southern Democrats rejected the proposal as an expansion of executive control that would undermine free enterprise and individual liberties.

Likewise, Congress sharply amended a Roosevelt measure that would facilitate GI voting rights, ensuring that the 11 million members of the armed services would have the ability to cast a ballot in the November election even though they were abroad or absent from their home state and locale. Opponents argued it would effectively transfer control over voting from states to the federal government and facilitate the possibility of Negro voters' avoiding Southern poll taxes and literacy tests, which inhibited their use of the ballot. Denounced as a measure sponsored by "kikes" and "Communists," the amended law would have actually given the vote to only 85,000 of the 11 million servicemen. Critics also accused the bill of being a ploy to facilitate Roosevelt's reelection. "Why, God damn him," one senator fulminated. He says, "We're letting the soldiers down. The rest of us have boys who go into the Army and navy as privates and ordinary seamen and dig latrines and swab decks and his scamps go in as lieutenant colonels and majors and lieutenants. . . . Letting the soldiers down! Why, that son of a bitch." Unwilling to disenfranchise the small number of GIs singled out in the amended bill, Roosevelt allowed it to become law without his signature.

Finally, when Roosevelt asked Congress to approve a tax law that would generate $10.5 billion in revenue, and it responded with one producing less than $2 billion, including a host of benefits for the affluent, Roosevelt vetoed it. In his State of the Union message, he complained that what Congress had proposed was "not a tax bill but a tax relief bill providing relief not for the needy but for the greedy." Many congressmen, including the sixty-six-year-old Senate majority leader Alben Barkley, a long-standing ally, were incensed at his refusal to accept their decision, as well as at his dismissal of their judgment and suggestion that they were in the pockets of the most affluent. Barkley resigned his leadership post in protest and was promptly voted back in by his Democratic Senate colleagues. In turn, they overrode the president's veto, making the bill "the first revenue act in history to become law over a veto." Roosevelt's defeat reminded some observers of his overreach on Court packing and demonstrated his waning influence with Congress. Although he appeared to be unbothered by its opposition, in fact the defeat frustrated and angered him and added to the strains on his health.

At the same time, new difficulties had arisen in the war. The Allies had scored victories over U-boats in the Atlantic, aided by British code breaking; made inroads against Japanese strongholds in the Marshall and Gilbert Islands; and isolated other Japanese garrisons, preventing them from being resupplied. They had also been successful in the air war over Germany, where long-range fighters gave B-17 and B-24 bombers protection against the Luftwaffe, which had extracted a heavy price on U.S. air forces. This enabled the Allies to target German factories and cities, including Berlin, which suffered attacks that promised to cost Germany the war.

By January 1944, however, the offensive in Italy, having encountered fierce resistance from German divisions, had come to a halt south of Rome. To reinvigorate the campaign, Churchill proposed using fifty-six landing ship tanks (LSTs) that had been slated for OVERLORD to transport two divisions behind the German lines at Anzio, twenty miles from Rome. Roosevelt worried that the transfer of these ships might delay the attack on France and agitate Stalin, who would view this as a broken promise. When Churchill promised that it would not interfere with the attack on France, Roosevelt agreed to the plan. Although the initial landing on January 22 succeeded, a failure to move forward quickly from the beachheads enabled the Germans to stall any advance. Similarly, when U.S. bombers leveled Monte Cassino, a monastery 80 miles from Rome at the center of the 100-mile Gustav Line, which the Germans had established across Italy and where its forces holding the high ground had halted the U.S. offensive, the Germans converted the rubble into another defensive obstacle. By February, the Italian campaign had become a costly stalemate and given pause to U.S. and British military planners about what they might face in France.

In January and February, Roosevelt faced pressure to take action on the extermination of Jews in concentration camps. Aware that they were losing the war, the Nazis had stepped up their efforts to destroy European Jewry. In December, mindful of the relentless pace of Nazi atrocities, Treasury Department officials around Morgenthau, none of whom was Jewish, agreed to challenge the State Department over its resistance to finding ways to help rescue Jews from the Nazi death camps. The Department had, for example, shown no inclination to pressure the British Foreign Office into helping transport Jews from Nazi-occupied countries to Palestine. On December 20, Morgenthau spoke to Breckinridge Long about State Department inaction, telling him, "Well, Breck . . . the impression is . . . that you, particularly, are anti-Semitic." Long, joined by Hull, blamed foreign indifference for the passivity regarding Nazi crimes. But Treasury officials were unwilling to accept this explanation and wrote a report titled, "To the Secretary on the Acquiescence of this Government in the Murder of the Jews." Pointing to the State Department's culpability, the report warned that unless there was a shift in policy, the United States would share responsibility for the failure to counter the extermination program.

When Morgenthau brought the report to the president's attention and informed him that it might generate "a nasty political scandal," Roosevelt, mindful of potential negative consequences in the 1944 vote, especially in New York, where Tom Dewey, New York's governor, was a likely opponent and Jewish voters could influence the outcome, he agreed to establish a War Refugee Board. Roosevelt also feared that a negative image of the State Department could jeopardize postwar plans for a major role in international affairs. He wanted Hull's Department to be regarded not as ineffective in promoting humane values but as advancing international harmony and progress toward a better world. Richard Breitman and Allan Lichtman believe that, aside from any domestic political considerations and concerns about resurgent isolationism, Roosevelt also recognized the limits of his existing rescue-through-victory policy and had come "to realize that at least some Jews could be rescued during the war." Finally, creating the War Refugee Board was a statement offering the world yet another striking contrast with the Nazis, one of a benevolent America at war with cruel regimes in Germany and Japan, and informing the peoples in those and occupied countries as well that the United States favored enlightened arrangements in postwar affairs.

At the end of February, Churchill apologized to him for differences arising between them over postwar economic questions, saying, "I am deeply grieved that all these troubles should arise at a time when you have so many worries to contend with." At the beginning of March, Roosevelt had a tooth pulled and was "feverish & generally miserable." When his secretary Grace Tully saw him "occasionally nodding over his mail or dozing during dictation," she became alarmed. Likewise, his daughter Anna, who had become concerned about his repeated head colds, fevers, and constant weariness-inducing daytime naps, insisted that Dr. McIntire, who had resisted suggestions that the president needed additional medical attention, reluctantly arranged a full examination at the Bethesda Naval Hospital.

Roosevelt was unhappy that he had to submit to a health assessment. "I am very angry with myself," he wrote Churchill on March 20. "The old attack of grippe having hung on and on, leaving me with an intermittent temperature, Ross [McIntire] decided about a week ago that it is necessary for me to take a complete rest of about two or three weeks in a suitable climate which I am definitely planning to do at the end of this month. *I see no way out and I am furious.*" He spent the weekend of March 25–26 at Hyde Park, where he napped and sat in the sun. He told Daisy, as he had Churchill, that "he was furious at himself — I've never done such a thing in my life before — Robert Louis Stevenson in the last stages of consumption," he said. Any hint that he was too incapacitated to perform his duties defied his determination to see the war through to the end and lead the country into an active part in postwar peace arrangements.

On March 27, despite his reluctance to acknowledge his health issues, he entered Bethesda Naval Hospital. The president's condition alarmed Dr. Howard G. Bruenn, a cardiologist, who conducted his examination and found a sixty-two-year-old man in severely declining health, with symptoms of "significantly elevated blood pressure of 186/108"; "classic signs of long-standing hypertension"; an enlarged heart; congestive heart failure; an ashen countenance and blue lips, "evidence of inadequate oxygenation deriving from cardiac insufficiency" as well as pulmonary disease; acute bronchitis, causing a persistent cough; and severe anemia.

Did Bruenn inform the president of his findings? Or more to the point, did McIntire, to whom Bruenn reported his assessment, reveal the results to Roosevelt or the family? We don't know exactly what McIntire told the president, but he did downplay the results to the family, assuring them that Roosevelt's condition was nothing more than what might be expected in a man in his early sixties. He described the exam to the press as "satisfactory," giving no hint of a severe illness that suggested retirement. "McIntire was lying — not only to the world but to the President himself," two scholars studying the president's health concluded. It is clear from what Franklin confided in Daisy that he was aware that he had some kind of heart problem and that the doctors "were not telling him the whole truth & that he was evidently more sick than they said!" They were apparently putting the best possible face on how Roosevelt could manage his health, advising him that a "low fat diet, digitalis, weight reduction," limited working hours, and sedated sleep would substantially help his condition. But it also seems more than likely that Roosevelt simply did not wish to hear any diagnosis that would prevent him from performing his duties, regardless of the personal cost.

On April 1, a week before Roosevelt departed for a month's rest at Bernard Baruch's estate in South Carolina, Churchill wired him: "May I express the earnest hope that you will be accessible to my personal telegrams and that full arrangements will be made for their speedy transmission to you. I shall be sending a lot of stuff unless you tell me not to, which would be disastrous." Roosevelt assured him that they would remain fully in touch and that messages would be delayed no more than ten minutes from when they would normally reach him in Washington. To ease the burdens of work during his stay in South Carolina, Admiral Leahy, Roosevelt's chief of staff, who accompanied him on the retreat, apparently drafted most of the president's replies to Churchill's messages.

As Churchill had predicted, there was indeed "a lot of stuff" that had to be dealt with, and the leaders exchanged nearly fifty cables during Roosevelt's four weeks away from Washington. They argued over the allocation of LSTs to British operations in the Pacific, aimed at recapturing territories lost to the Japanese; they differed over a conciliatory meeting with de Gaulle in Washington; they agreed to a shared message to Stalin, asking assurances of a Soviet offensive coordinated with the cross-Channel attack; they went back and forth over whether there were "compelling military reasons" preceding the launch of OVERLORD for censorship of all diplomatic communications from London; they discussed the need for ground rules about postwar economic collaboration; they agreed to the resumption of an offensive in Italy; they differed over which political side to support in Greece after the Germans were expelled; Churchill urged him to give "personal consideration" to Spain's trade relations with Germany; they considered issues arising in Anglo-American-Canadian relations; they explored ways to unite contending anti-Nazi groups in Yugoslavia; and they discussed unsettled questions about invading southern France and the wisdom of conducting air attacks that killed French civilians preparatory to crossing the Channel.

During the month in South Carolina, Howard Bruenn, who accompanied Roosevelt to monitor his health status, took daily readings of the president's blood pressure, usually twice each day. Although the warm weather and relaxed environment made him feel better — he was less weary and less prone to the pulmonary symptoms that had plagued him — his blood pressure remained distressingly elevated, evidence of irreversible hypertension. The readings ran as high as 236/126, but more commonly between 200–220 over 102–120. Daisy came to visit him and found him "under his tan" looking "thin & drawn & not a bit well." He suffered a gallstone attack and told Daisy, "I am really feeling 'no good' — don't want to do anything & want to sleep all the time."

When he returned to Washington in early May, his blood pressure averaged 196/112 in the mornings and 194/96 in the evenings. To control the hypertension, the doctors counseled him to follow a work schedule of two office hours in the morning with "preferably no irritation," early and late afternoon rests lying down for one hour, and another two office hours with as little stress as possible. He was also advised to give up swimming for the time being. Evening work was ruled out, and ten hours of sleep at night was prescribed. A bland diet excluding "pastry, pie, and rich desserts" made his White House meals, which had never satisfied him much under the watchful eye of Henrietta Nesbitt, the chief housekeeper, even less appealing. His doctors were recommending the impossible: How could a president confronting daily life and death decisions in the war and domestic foes eager to see an end to his presidency in 1944 not struggle with personal agitation?

His daughter Anna and Daisy, who watched over him on his return to Washington, discussed the difficulty in keeping him to the "routine" prescribed by his doctors. He insisted that he " 'kept the rules' pretty well" and was feeling "all right," and while it was evident to them that the time away from the White House had brought some improvement in his health, he was still "not right yet." When Daisy saw him at Hyde Park on May 22, he looked "worried and tired and his color is not good." He managed temporarily to "cast off his heavy responsibilities," including worries about the French campaign, which was scheduled to be launched within the next two weeks. His anxiety regarding it was so intense that he confided the most closely guarded secrets of the attack to Daisy, whom he trusted and used as a sounding board. In that respect she served as a substitute for Eleanor, who seemed to make him tense when she ate dinner with him and shifted the conversation away from the teasing and "nonsense" that diverted him to serious subjects she insisted they consider. As the date of the invasion approached, he seemed "very tired . . . talking rather excitedly . . . [while] pushing himself" to focus on the war. When the Allies entered Rome on June 4, it gave him a huge boost, but his days at the White House during early June exhausted him and seemed to increase the danger of his getting "sick again."

Also preying on him were questions about the upcoming presidential election. On May 22, during a visit to Hyde Park, when Daisy asked him whom he would choose as his running mate, he said: "I haven't even decided if I will run myself." "What is going to decide you?" Daisy asked. "You are practically nominated already." She reflected the fact that 90 percent of Democrats wanted Roosevelt to run again, and 79 percent of all voters believed he would attempt a fourth term. He replied that it depended on "the way I feel in a couple of months. If I know I am not going to be able to carry on for another four years, it wouldn't be fair to the American people to run for another term." When Daisy asked, "Who else is there?" Roosevelt said that he had a candidate in mind, but told her, "don't breathe it to a soul." His choice was the shipbuilder Henry J. Kaiser. It is difficult to believe, however, that he was serious about a Kaiser candidacy, although he must have been considering a possible replacement if a health crisis eliminated him. He felt compelled to keep his options open until the eve of the Democratic convention.

While he refused to confirm that he was running again, he was also coy about the choice of a running mate. He encouraged several potential candidates for the vice presidency to think that he favored them. He gave Henry Wallace, his sitting vice president; James Byrnes, who headed the Office of War Mobilization and was known as the "Assistant President"; Supreme Court justice William O. Douglas, a committed New Dealer; and Missouri senator Harry S. Truman, another reliable Roosevelt supporter, reason to think about joining him on the ticket. But as with his candidacy, he was determined to hold off making a decision until the last possible moment, since circumstances might change.

Anyone reading his correspondence with Churchill during these spring days would be hard-pressed to conclude that he was preparing to stand aside. He was focused on postwar affairs in Europe, and a primary concern was who would govern a liberated France. De Gaulle, who headed the French Committee of National Liberation (FCNL) headquartered in Algiers, had the strongest claim on leadership. But Roosevelt still didn't trust him and believed he had little regard for democratic procedures and would not hesitate to seize power. Nonetheless, he could not ignore de Gaulle's standing as France's unyielding Axis opponent. De Gaulle had arranged for two French divisions to join the fighting in Italy, where the 74,000-man force was making an impressive contribution to the campaign. Churchill, who also had reservations about de Gaulle but saw him as essential to the success of OVERLORD, lobbied Roosevelt to invite him to Washington.

While Roosevelt was willing to see him, he refused to extend an invitation. De Gaulle was neither the head of a government or state, which was a point of protocol that the president could have ignored, but by declining to do so he was making de Gaulle understand that he was beholden to the United States, and specifically to

857

Roosevelt himself, for the essential help of liberating France. He insisted that de Gaulle take the initiative in requesting an invitation, but made it clear that he did not wish to hear from him until he returned from South Carolina in May, which would bring them closer to the launch of the French campaign and afford de Gaulle less of a chance to lobby for a larger role in the invasion. Roosevelt was receptive to including a French armored division in the campaign, but only after the invasion had secured a foothold in France. He also opposed the release of any details as to the timing or composition of the Anglo-American forces launching the attack, as both he and Churchill believed that de Gaulle's FCNL was infiltrated by Vichy agents all too ready to reveal invasion secrets to Berlin.

Because Eisenhower was eager for an agreement with de Gaulle to incorporate the two hundred thousand members of the French Resistance into invasion plans, Roosevelt agreed to have de Gaulle visit him in Washington after June 6, the date of the assault. De Gaulle arrived in London on June 4, two days before OVERLORD began. He refused to broadcast a speech prepared by Eisenhower's headquarters, preferring his own address, which urged the French "to obey the instructions of their government." He was not allowed to declare his FCNL as the governing body to which French citizens should turn, which incensed him. When Churchill urged de Gaulle to go to Washington, where Roosevelt would recognize his authority, de Gaulle asked: "Why do you seem to think that I need to submit my candidacy for the authority in France to Roosevelt? The French government exists. I have nothing to ask, in this sphere, of the United States of America nor of Great Britain." When he read a statement Eisenhower planned to address to the French nation, de Gaulle complained that "he appeared to be taking control of our country even though he was merely an Allied general entitled to command troops but not in the least qualified to intervene in the country's government." Roosevelt cabled Churchill, "Good luck in your talks with prima donna. . . . Please for the love of Heaven do not tell De Gaulle that I am sending him 'a friendly message to come over to see me.' " Yet he remained ready to receive de Gaulle if he asked.

At the same time that Roosevelt tried to ensure a postwar transition to democratic government in France, he sought to guard against any form of American occupation of Europe that would draw the United States into postwar continental politics. He saw nothing but trouble from involvement in the inevitable jousting among political factions likely to battle for political control in France. He believed that any attempt by U.S. authorities to dictate the outcome of French politics was likely to stir isolationist sentiment and undermine any U.S. commitment to long-term overseas peacekeeping. While de Gaulle certainly read Roosevelt's hostility to him correctly, he misread the president's postwar intentions regarding France, except for the revival of democratic elections to decide who would govern the country. "Self-determination really means absence of coercion," Roosevelt had told Churchill.

Roosevelt took a compelling lesson from tensions that had erupted between Churchill and the Soviets over postwar governance in Romania. In May, a secret British mission to the Romanian government, which Moscow had agreed to but London had forgotten to inform Soviet authorities about when it was actually taking place, had brought protest against British intrigues aimed at limiting Soviet influence in the Balkans. Churchill told Soviet foreign minister Molotov that he was "astounded at" believing "that we have any evil interest in Romania to the detriment of your operations and of the common cause." Privately, Churchill told his War Cabinet that "he could not continue to correspond with M. Molotov whose attitude led him to despair of the possibility of maintaining good relations with Russia." Churchill also saw "Communist intrigues in Italy, Yugoslavia and Greece" and anticipated a "showdown" with them over their self-serving reach for control in southern and southeastern Europe. "I must say," he complained, "their attitude becomes more difficult every day."

Roosevelt, meanwhile, had asked Churchill to agree to instruct the combined chiefs of staff to assign U.S. occupation forces to the Netherlands and northwest Germany. "It will be assumed in this plan," he told Churchill, "that France, Austria, and the Balkans will not be included in an American zone of responsibility." When Churchill took issue with Roosevelt's intentions, the president responded, "I am absolutely unwilling to police France and possibly Italy and the Balkans as well. . . . I hope you will realize that I am in such a position that I cannot go along with the British General Staff plan," which called for American forces to occupy areas that Roosevelt feared would dissolve into "political chaos" after the war and would mean "long-term involvement in Europe." His reasons for opposing any occupation other than northwest Germany, he advised Churchill, "are political. . . . Over here," he explained, "new political situations crop up every day but so far, by constant attention, I am keeping my head above water."

Aside from what these cables revealed about Roosevelt's expectations about managing foreign affairs in a fourth term, they did offer evidence of his optimism about success in the invasion and subsequent fighting in western Europe. Nonetheless, he and Churchill faced OVERLORD with understandable apprehensions. Foul weather initially threatened to put the cross-Channel attack on hold, but a window of good conditions on June 6 gave Eisenhower the chance to proceed. When he asked de Gaulle his opinion, the French general urged him not to delay: "Atmospheric dangers seem to me less than the disadvantages of a delay of several weeks, which would prolong the moral tension of the executants and compromise secrecy." So, on June 6, D-Day, the greatest armada of forces in history transported by some seven thousand craft left England for the Normandy coast, where six divisions — three American, two British, and one Canadian — consisting of 132,000 troops came ashore. Stalin cabled Churchill and Roosevelt to congratulate them on having "succeeded in realizing with honor the grandiose plan of the forcing of the channel. History will record this deed as an achievement of the highest order." Churchill, who visited Normandy a week after the invasion began, told Roosevelt that what he saw could only be described as "stupendous."

Although preceded by massive aerial and naval bombardments, three airborne divisions of 23,000 seizing inland positions, and deceptions, including a fictitious Fourth Army of twelve divisions that fooled the Germans into thinking the principal landing would come at the Pas de Calais, the landing forces suffered many losses. Thousands of invading troops, especially at Omaha beach, a U.S. landing site, encountered coastal defense guns and "multiple lines of massive obstacles," including minefields. When a second wave of troops came ashore, they witnessed the carnage of the attack, with floating corpses and wrecked vehicles strewn across the beaches. By the end of June, more than 850,000 Allied soldiers had landed in France, supported by 150,000 armored vehicles and massive amounts of supplies to back them. Fifty-nine German divisions in France posed a formidable defense, but the great superiority of Allied air power, which disrupted the movement of troops and armored vehicles to the front, put the Germans at a serious disadvantage. Although an aerial assault on Britain by unmanned rockets ("buzz bombs") launched from the Belgian and French coasts cost the British some 20,000 casualties, effective countermeasures and the limited success of the attack did nothing to slow the Allied advances in France.

Continuing impressive gains in the Atlantic war against German U-boats complemented the forward movement in France. The resumption of "northern convoys" to Russia to support a developing offensive in the East against weakened German armies retreating before a Soviet advance gave unqualified hope that Hitler's day of reckoning was now only months away. "How I wish I could be with you to see our war machine in operation!" Roosevelt cabled Churchill on June 6.

But his continuing struggle with health issues, the start of the 1944 election, with the Democratic convention scheduled to meet in Chicago in July, and a visit from de Gaulle also scheduled for July precluded any trip to Britain.

Not the least of the considerations persuading Roosevelt to remain in Washington was the passage of a major piece of social legislation he signed into law on June 22. The Servicemen's Readjustment Act, popularly known as the GI Bill of Rights, provided financial incentives for returning soldiers to complete their education, enabled them to obtain a low-cost mortgage or low-interest loan to start a business, and guaranteed them one year of unemployment insurance if they could not find a job. It applied to any soldier who had been on active duty for at least four months and countered any fears that returning troops would face a new economic collapse that would deprive them of a chance to earn a decent living. It was a return to the New Deal ethos that affirmed that young Americans should be guaranteed hope for a better future, which a well-thought-out government program could provide.

Also deterring Roosevelt from a trip to London was a commitment he had made to travel to the Pacific. The trip was partly intended to quiet rumors that he was too ill to handle presidential responsibilities. Letters from worried concerned supporters throughout the country urging him to consider retiring reflected the general public concern about his health. His evident physical decline — he looked "thin & pale, and old" — convinced Anna Roosevelt that should her father run again, the Republicans would make an issue of his health. He himself was not convinced that he could master his condition, and so viewed the Pacific visit as a test of his resilience before he committed himself to another campaign.

Most of all, though, he hoped to address the sense of neglect experienced by almost half the country's fighting forces, who had been eclipsed by the public's focus on the war against Germany. While the Navy, Army, and Marines had been effectively making their way across the Pacific in costly island campaigns, the defeat of Japan seemed almost to have been postponed. A plan for setting up air bases in eastern China from which attacks could be launched against Japan's home islands had come to naught, as had a proposed Burma campaign to reopen a vital supply line to China. Roosevelt had sent Eleanor on a tour of the South Pacific in the summer of 1943 with stops in seventeen islands as well as Australia and New Zealand, where she visited U.S. troop bases and hospitals filled with wounded and permanently disabled men. Admiral William (Bull) Halsey, who initially dismissed her visit as nothing but a "nuisance," came to regard it as a terrific morale booster. Everywhere she went she conveyed genuine concern for the men and their personal sacrifices. Her visits were anything but perfunctory, Halsey said: She "went into every ward, stopped at every bed, and spoke to every patient. . . . Could she take a message home for him?" When Halsey saw her off at the end of her tour, he told her that "she alone had accomplished more good than any other person, or any group of civilians, who had passed through my area."

The president's visit was also calculated to counter fears that Anglo-American-Chinese differences over how best to defeat Japan had left the

Pacific war adrift. After the Cairo and Tehran meetings, the preference shown for General Claire Chennault's air campaign from China against Japan's home islands had incensed Stilwell, who wanted backing for a Burma assault, led by Chinese troops under his command. In 1943–44, when Chennault received the lion's share of supplies flown over the Himalayas, Stilwell complained that the meager resources allotted to his Chinese forces left them "trying to manure a ten-acre field with sparrow shit." Stilwell had little other than contempt for Chiang and privately decried Washington's naïveté in dealing with him. He called Chiang's government "a one-man joke. The KMT is his tool. Madame is his front. The silly U.S. propaganda is his lever. We are his suckers." In May 1944 the public became aware of China's plight when *Time* and *Life* journalist Theodore White described Chiang's Nationalist Party as a "corrupt political clique that combines some of the worst features of Tammany Hall and the Spanish Inquisition." He predicted the possible loss of control of the country to Mao Tse-tung's Communists.

At the same time, British policies aimed at reclaiming their Asian possessions provoked American complaints that the South East Asian Command (SEAC) stood for "Save England's Asiatic Colonies." U.S. journals warned against Churchill's unyielding devotion to the British Empire and asserted that "the British are subordinating military strategy to the political aim of reconstituting her colonial empire." Stalin's promise at Tehran to take part in the Pacific war after Germany's defeat persuaded the British to contest U.S. combat plans involving China with the argument that Russia's entrance into the conflict made a China campaign superfluous. The wait for a German collapse as a prelude to Soviet engagement in the Pacific made the fight against Japan seem all the more a secondary priority.

Although an assault on Saipan in the Mariana Islands occurred nine days after D-Day, lasted thirty days, and promised to position American air forces only 1,200 miles from Japan, and thus within striking distance for new B-29 heavy bombers, the invasion and arduous struggle against 32,000 Japanese troops there had little of the resonance of the fighting in France. The battle of the Philippine Sea, in which three Japanese aircraft carriers and over four hundred planes were destroyed (in what came to be known as the "Great Marianas Turkey Shoot") did not capture public imagination in the United States the way the setbacks for Hitler's forces in France and Russia did.

In the aftermath of D-Day, Roosevelt had grown concerned about Soviet expansion into the Balkans. When Stalin advised on June 9 that his "general offensive" would not begin until the end of June and would only become an all-out effort in July, Roosevelt told Churchill, "The plans of U.J. promise well even if the beginning is a little later than we hoped for, but it may be for the best in the long run," suggesting his worries about Soviet armies occupying so much territory to its west. In a cable Roosevelt sent Churchill on June 10, he refused to give his blessing, as Churchill had asked, to a British-Soviet agreement designating Romania and Greece as Soviet and British spheres of influence, respectively. Roosevelt shared the Wilsonian conviction that areas of control were sources of conflict and potential incentives to war. Although pressed by Churchill to consent to a three-month trial of the British-Soviet arrangement, Roosevelt reiterated that he wanted no part of any "post war spheres of influence."

Meanwhile, he also had an unpleasant argument with Churchill over choosing between an assault on the south of France and expanding gains in Italy into a Balkan campaign; struggled to appease Polish-American voters who supported the Polish exile government in London resisting Soviet pressure for territorial concessions without antagonizing Moscow; and anguished over how to deal with "prima donna" de Gaulle and the fate of postwar France. The closer the Allies came to victory in Europe, the more their differences over postwar arrangements and spheres came into the open.

On June 14, Churchill told Roosevelt that "the Chiefs of Staff are searching about for the best solution of problems as between the Mediterranean and OVERLORD." But Churchill had already made up his mind: He wished to switch the planned attack on southern France (ANVIL) with the movement of forces into Yugoslavia and Greece, with the ultimate goal the capture of Vienna. Because the campaign in northern France was moving less rapidly than hoped, Eisenhower, supported by Roosevelt, who also did not wish to provoke Soviet concerns about British forces in the Balkans, insisted that the assault on southern France was essential to the success of OVERLORD. Roosevelt told Churchill that he was unequivocally opposed to an advance from northern Italy to the northeast. Churchill responded by sending Roosevelt "a very full argument" for the Balkans offensive, "earnestly beg[ging]" him "to examine this matter in detail for yourself."

"History will never forgive us if we lose precious time and lives in indecision and debate," he wrote Churchill. "Let us go ahead with our plan. Finally, for purely political considerations over here I would never survive even a slight setback in OVERLORD if it were known that fairly large forces had been diverted to the Balkans."

Roosevelt's resistance incensed Churchill. "The whole campaign in Italy is being ruined, and ruined for what?" he asked. He argued that a drive up the Rhone valley, led by ten "many quite unproved" divisions, many of them "French almost entirely black," could do only negligible damage. He was willing to resign over this matter, he asserted, but feared it "would do great injury to the fighting troops." He added: "There is nothing I will not do to end this deadlock except become responsible for an absolutely perverse strategy." He offered to come to Washington at once and reiterated his conviction that they would be abandoning opportunities in the Mediterranean for inconsequential gains in OVERLORD, telling Roosevelt, "I think I have a right to some consideration from you, my friend, at a time when our joint ventures have dazzled the world with success." Convinced finally by his own chiefs to accept Roosevelt's decision, he nonetheless complained to the president that they were making "the first major strategic and political error for which we two have to be responsible." They then exchanged expressions of regard for each other that eased the strains provoked by the sharp divergence of their strategic views.

At the same time, Roosevelt wrestled with his Polish problem. He considered Polish-American voters as crucial to winning a fourth term, and so tried to avoid saying or doing anything about Soviet-Polish differences that would antagonize these voters. He had resisted meeting with Polish prime minister Stanisław Mikołajczyk with explanations that he did not want to become involved in a remote border dispute of little interest to Americans. But under pressure from Polish-Americans to weigh in on Poland's right to self-determination, he agreed to a Washington visit in June by Mikołajczyk. While Roosevelt showed him every courtesy, he took pains to avoid openly endorsing Polish opposition to Soviet demands. He then assured Stalin that he had no interest in inserting himself "into the merits of the differences which exist between the Soviet Government and the Polish-Government-in-exile. . . . I am in no way trying to press my personal views upon you in a matter which is of special concern to you and your country." The effort to satisfy both Polish-American voters and Soviet interests demonstrated Roosevelt's concern with pleasing his ally and assuring himself of crucial bloc votes in an upcoming campaign.

Less cordiality, or less tactfulness, marked the exchanges between Roosevelt and de Gaulle during the latter's five-day visit to Washington between July 6 and July 10. Both men began on their best behavior: A seventeen-gun salute greeted de Gaulle's arrival at the Washington National airport; de Gaulle responded with remarks in English; and Roosevelt welcomed him to the White House in French. But fundamental differences soon clouded their exchanges. De Gaulle's principal goal was to restore France's honor in the war and reestablish its standing as a major European and world power. For Roosevelt, France's defeat by the Nazis meant its demise as a leading European democracy. He viewed it as a perpetually divided country and feared that de Gaulle's emergence at its head would likely provoke civil strife that would discourage American hopes for a stable postwar Europe and willingness to participate in world affairs. In addition, Roosevelt expected the restoration of France's colonial empire to trigger international conflicts that would further undermine the possibility of a tranquil world order. Roosevelt also wanted the United States to take the place of France in Senegal, West Africa, and Indochina, where he hoped to install air and naval bases as part of twenty-year trusteeships imposed on these former colonies that would allow the United States to become the peacekeeper in both regions. By using the benign term "trustee" he hoped to mask the assertion of American military power in Africa and Asia.

De Gaulle had arrived in Washington with powerful indications of support for his claims on French leadership: Following the invasion, the Czech, Polish, Belgian, Yugoslav, and Norwegian governments-in-exile recognized the FCNL as France's ruling authority. On a June visit to Normandy, when local citizens greeted him with shows of enthusiasm, de Gaulle declared that the French people were showing "to whom they entrusted the duty of leading them." During their conversations, Roosevelt did not dwell on "immediate issues," but "permitted" de Gaulle "to glimpse the political objectives he wished to achieve through victory." Roosevelt described his "Four Policemen" vision of postwar affairs: "A parliament of the allied nations would give a democratic appearance to the authority of the 'big four.' " He also made clear his intention to install "American forces on bases distributed throughout the world and of which certain ones would be located in French territory."

De Gaulle later characterized Roosevelt as possessing a "will to power cloaked . . . in idealism," and described him in his memoirs as an "artist" and a "seducer." He advised Roosevelt that he needed to consider the restoration of French greatness as essential to the preservation of ancient values. In response, Roosevelt reminded de Gaulle of the divisions that had brought down France and believed would challenge her in the future. De Gaulle refrained from reminding him that U.S. isolationism had contributed to France's collapse before Hitler's onslaught. On one matter, however, they were in full agreement: France could "count only on herself." Roosevelt replied: "It is true that to serve France no one can replace the French people."

De Gaulle gained what he sought from the talks: Roosevelt agreed to recognize the FCNL as the "temporary *de facto* authority for civil administration in France." But this did not put to rest all the two nations' mutual suspicions and antagonisms. At a dinner hosted by Secretary of State Hull, de Gaulle and Hull sat "stiffly in informal silence, the American drooping a little, the Frenchman solemnly and forbiddingly erect, all six feet of him, balancing a chip like an epaulette on each martial shoulder." To break the ice with the unsmiling, aloof de Gaulle, Congressman Solomon Bloom, chairman of the House Foreign Affairs Committee, offered him a trick cigar that disappeared up

Bloom's sleeve when de Gaulle reached for it. "Now you see it, General, now you don't," Bloom teased. De Gaulle was not amused: "What does the American statesman wish?" an annoyed de Gaulle asked an aide. The transcript of a Roosevelt letter to a congressman that secretly came into de Gaulle's hands described him as "very touchy in matters concerning the honor of France. But I suspect that he is essentially an egoist." De Gaulle dryly commented: "I was never to know if Franklin Roosevelt thought that in affairs concerning France Charles de Gaulle was an egoist for France or for himself."

Partly to push news of de Gaulle's visit off the front pages the day after he left Washington, Roosevelt captured the headlines on July 11 by announcing at a press conference that he would accept his party's nomination if it were offered to him. Only the day before, Dr. Frank Leahy, one of the physicians who had examined him, wrote a secret memo describing the perilous state of the president's health: He "did not believe that, if Mr. Roosevelt were elected President again, he had the physical capacity to complete another term. . . . He would again have heart failure and be unable to complete it." He saw it as the result of "high blood pressure he has had for a long time." With no knowledge of the president's dire condition, however, 90 percent of Democrats in a Gallup survey said they favored Roosevelt's nomination, and 71 percent of voters said they expected him to win a fourth term.

In private, Roosevelt complained of being "tired and listless." At times, he looked "fine, other times . . . thin, & pale, and old." McIntire told him he could serve another term if he cut his workload in half. Because he had lost so much weight that his shirts and suits "hung on him like a bat," McIntire also urged him to buy new clothes. In a letter to the Democratic Party's chairman, Roosevelt wrote, "All that is within me cries to go back to my home on the Hudson River." But the stakes in the war and peacemaking were too great for him to shirk his duty. "As a good soldier . . . I will accept and serve in the office, if I am so ordered by the Commander in Chief of us all — the sovereign people of the United States."

CHAPTER 20
WINNING THE WAR, PLANNING THE PEACE

By July 1944, with Hitler's hopes of driving the Allies back into the sea or mounting an effective counterattack failing, Roosevelt and most Americans believed the war would come to an end that year. The progress of Soviet armies into the Baltic States and Poland against weakened German forces, and devastating day and night air raids on German cities, only strengthened this conviction. News of an attempt on Hitler's life by German military chiefs eager to end the war before Germany fell under Soviet control, and of the resignation of the Japanese cabinet, including Premier Hideki Tojo, was received in the United States with "evident relish" and "greatly strengthened" a "spreading belief that the war both in Europe and the Pacific is moving swiftly to a climax."

Although Hitler survived the attack and inflicted awful retribution on its perpetrators (several of the conspirators were executed "by slow hanging with a noose of piano wire from a meat hook"), the assassination plot had signaled the erosion of his power and the ultimate collapse of his regime. Still, in Britain and the United States, there was little doubt that Nazi fanaticism and Hitler's tightened control after the failed attempt on his life would compel the Allies to fight their way across Europe to Berlin. Even if the coup had succeeded and Hitler's successors had offered a negotiated peace, there was no chance that Churchill, Roosevelt, or Stalin would have agreed to anything but an unconditional surrender. The ruthlessness of the Nazis had convinced Allied leaders that there could be no substitute for an occupation of Germany and a recasting of its government if Europe was to avoid future wars.

Indications that the war would not actually end until early in 1945 did not discourage Roosevelt from mounting a campaign for another term. Opponents railed against the prospect of any president's serving twelve, let alone sixteen years, with so much power over the public and Congress. But progress in the war, with difficult campaigns still in the offing against formidable German and Japanese units, encouraged convictions that it would be a mistake to replace so experienced a leader with an untested one, or to make a major change in an administration that had proven itself to be so effective in combating the Axis. Moreover, millions of Americans believed that Roosevelt was the best leader to manage the postwar peace and the transition to a flourishing domestic economy.

Republican leaders chose to use the president's waning health as the best issue with which to challenge him in the campaign. In an acceptance address for the Republican nomination, Thomas E. Dewey exploited the issue of Roosevelt's potential incapacity, citing his evident weight loss and apparent diminished energy and describing him and his closest advisers as "tired old men." Harold Ickes urged the president to hit back promptly before the argument impressed itself on voters. The way to do so, Ickes said, was to remind Americans of what "we 'tired old men' have done, with particular emphasis on what has been accomplished in connection with the war. . . . A partial catalogue of accomplishments during this administration of 'tired old men' would put Mr. Dewey's issue right back in his snug little lap with the detonating power of one of the German robot airplanes."

Unknown to the public, Roosevelt's son Jimmy witnessed him struggle with an angina attack while preparing to leave a train he had taken to San Diego, where he would board a ship to Hawaii for a conference with Pacific commanders. The president turned ghostly pale with "an agonized look" on his face and told his son, "I don't know if I can make it. I have horrible pains." He insisted on lying flat on the floor of the train car until the pain passed, but forbade Jimmy from calling his doctor. He was prone "for perhaps ten minutes. . . . His eyes closed, his face drawn, his powerful torso occasionally convulsed as the waves of pain stabbed him." When the pain stopped, he stood up with Jimmy's help and proceeded to his car to watch military maneuvers on the beach without giving any indication of the episode. But he still felt the aftereffects of the attack. He wrote Eleanor the next day, "Jimmy and I had a grand view of the landing operation at Camp Pendleton, and then I got the collywobbles and stayed in the train in the p.m."

On July 20, he received word that the Democratic convention had nominated him to run for another term. That night, he spoke to the convention on the radio from his train in San Diego. He outlined what he hoped to accomplish in the next four years: An end to the war; the creation of a worldwide peacekeeping organization; and a domestic economy that could assure all Americans a decent standard of living. He reminded the country of why it did not want to repeat the aftermath of World War I, with its breadlines and retreat into old-fashioned isolationism, which he said was becoming "extinct." He also explained that he would not run a traditional campaign, as he considered it an inappropriate use of precious time that should be devoted to war work. He promised, however, to issue periodic reports, "especially to correct any misrepresentations." No one could dispute his priorities, but his tactic also served his need to avoid the rigors of an exhausting coast-to-coast campaign.

His words may well have inspired voters to recall why they had voted for him and his party in the previous three elections, but a photo of him giving his speech that appeared in newspapers everywhere the following day showed "a thin, slack-jawed" president who looked anything but capable of taking on the burdens of another term. Sam Rosenman saw "a tragic-looking figure; the face appeared to be very emaciated because of the downward angle and open mouth; it looked weary, sick, discouraged, and exhausted."

A dispute over the selection of his running mate, and an argument among his Pacific admirals and generals about combat strategy, added to strains on his health. For days before the convention, he considered candidates for the vice presidency, keeping in mind that his choice would be responsible for difficult end-of-war decisions and peacetime priorities should he not be able to serve out his term. Doubtful about his ability to do so, party bosses viewed the selection of a vice-presidential candidate as an especially significant matter.

Roosevelt preferred sitting vice president Henry Wallace. But Wallace had established a reputation as an unconventional advocate of liberal causes and had particularly put off conservative Southern Democrats, who feared his sympathy for Negro rights and one-world "globalony." Southerners were eager to nominate South Carolina's Jimmy Byrnes, whose broad-ranging experience as a senator, Supreme Court associate justice, and, most recently, war mobilization czar seemed to make him a fine successor to Roosevelt. But a party split between Byrnes and Wallace supporters troubled the president, who thought the party already too divided between North and South. He feared that a convention fight could "kill our chances for reelection this fall and if it does it will prolong the war and knock into a cocked hat all the plans we've been making for the future." As an alternative to Wallace, the idea of Associate Supreme Court Justice William O. Douglas, a staunch liberal who would continue the fight for New Deal programs, appealed to Roosevelt. But he injected himself into the contest by encouraging all the candidates to believe that he favored each of them.

In the end, he chose Senator Harry S. Truman of Missouri — in part because Democratic bosses were more enthusiastic about the sixty-year-old Truman than more controversial alternatives, but also because he was regarded as a thoroughly reliable party man and Roosevelt supporter. A World War I veteran with a reputation as a successful opponent of war profiteering, which had earned him the cover of *Time,* he was an ideal uncontro-versial choice for the number-two job. When the convention nominated him on the second ballot after a floor fight between Wallace and Truman backers, newspaper columnists dubbed Truman "the Second Missouri Compromise."

With the Democratic Party nominations settled, Roosevelt boarded a Navy cruiser on the evening of July 21 for a five-day voyage to Hawaii. He welcomed the opportunity for a "sustained rest. . . . He read a great deal, slept late in the morning, took a nap in the afternoon," and watched movies each evening. After arriving in Pearl Harbor, he spent part of his days touring training camps, where troops were being prepared for combat. He took special satisfaction from visits to hospitals, where he met wounded soldiers, Marines, and sailors, especially those who had lost limbs in the fighting. He had a Secret Service agent propel him down the aisle of a ward in his wheelchair as an unspoken message to these men that their disabilities need not diminish their postwar lives. "I never saw Roosevelt with tears in his eyes; that day as he was wheeled out of the hospital he was close to them," Sam Rosenman recalled.

The ostensible reason for the trip was confer-ences with Admiral Nimitz and General Mac-Arthur about Pacific strategy. MacArthur, how-ever, did not see the need for such discussions, and dismissed Roosevelt's visit as little more than "a political picture-taking junket." MacArthur thought that Roosevelt wanted photos of himself with two of his military chiefs to use as surefire vote-getters and resented the summons to Hawaii to see "Mr. Big." Privately, he complained about being compelled to leave his frontline field troops, many of whom, in fact, were skeptical of his self-image as a frontline commander. They pilloried him as "Dugout Doug," and some Marines composed a ditty critical of his self-serving posturing to the tune of "The Battle Hymn of the Republic":

> Mine eyes have seen MacArthur with a Bible on
>   his knee.
> He is pounding out communiqués for guys like
>   you and me.
> And while possibly a rumor now,
> Some day 'twill be a fact
> That the Lord will hear a deep voice say,
> "Move over, God, it's Mac."

When Roosevelt's ship docked in Pearl Harbor, a large, enthusiastic crowd and all the local military officials had gathered to greet him. The only conspicuous absence was MacArthur, who appeared soon after in a siren-screaming military car and boarded the ship with waves to cheering onlookers. Roosevelt ribbed him about arriving clad in a leather jacket, but MacArthur explained that he had just come from Australia and a high-altitude flight, where it was "pretty cold." Roosevelt was well aware that MacArthur had applauded a Republican Nebraska congressman who had denounced the New Deal as endangering the American way of life and had described Roosevelt as establishing a monarchy that "would destroy the rights of the common people." When MacArthur's sentiments became public knowledge, it killed his chances of becoming the Republican nominee, which was his ambition.

Not surprisingly, MacArthur, who was so mindful of his own public image, read everything Roosevelt did as animated by political considerations in an election year. He was not off the mark. When he asked Roosevelt "what he thought of Dewey's chances in November, the president said he had been too busy to think of politics." MacArthur couldn't contain a laugh, and Roosevelt began laughing as well. "If the war against Germany ends before the election," Roosevelt finally said, "I won't be reelected." Then added: "I'll beat that son of a bitch [Dewey] in Albany if it's the last thing I do." But MacArthur doubted that Roosevelt would live to see the war's end, for the president's ashen, gray appearance told him that Roosevelt was a dying man. As he told his personal physician: "Doc, the mark of death is on him! In six months he'll be in his grave." But MacArthur had to admit that their meeting in Honolulu was a political masterstroke by Roosevelt. Newspaper coverage of the conference evoked "grudging admiration" from Republicans about "the President's skill as a political opportunist." His presence in Hawaii refuted charges that he had neglected the Pacific fighting and encouraged convictions that he had not allowed "personal feelings" of antipathy toward MacArthur, an obvious rival for the White House, to get in the way of war policies.

Roosevelt also scored political points in the alleged debate between MacArthur and naval chiefs over recapturing the Philippines or striking at Formosa as a prelude to using air bases in China for the air war against Japan. MacArthur had seized the public's imagination with assertions about America's moral obligation to free loyal

881

Filipinos from Japanese oppression, and his cry of "back to the Philippines," which was a variation on his earlier promise to that nation, "I shall return," after being ordered to abandon it. MacArthur asserted that he privately warned Roosevelt that he would lose many votes in November if he failed to keep the promise of freeing the Philippines from Japanese control. MacArthur was so forceful in his remarks to Roosevelt that the president asked his doctor to give him an aspirin before he went to bed. "In fact, give me another aspirin to take in the morning. In all my life nobody has ever talked to me the way MacArthur did." That may have been true, but MacArthur's argument won the day, especially as Japanese forces on the Chinese mainland seized the bases that were to be instrumental in the air war against Tokyo after occupying Formosa.

After what Roosevelt described to Eleanor as a "hectic 3 days with very good results," he arrived in the Aleutians on August 3. From there he sailed to Alaska and then to the navy yard at Bremerton, Washington, where on August 12, he spoke to the country about his trip and the future security of the West Coast and the Pacific. Standing on the deck of his ship at a podium with a "brisk wind" blowing and the ship rocking, he struggled to keep his composure. Over the previous six months he had lost thirty pounds — the result of cardiac cachexia, a condition associated with congestive heart failure. His steel braces, which he had put on for the first time in months, were of limited use in keeping him erect. He clung to the lectern to maintain his balance and spoke in a halting voice. A few minutes into his speech, he suffered sharp chest pains that spread to his shoulders and lasted for half an hour. As in 1940, he began "sweating profusely." This time, however, he informed Dr. Howard Bruenn, the cardiologist who had examined him in March and accompanied him on the trip, of the incident. After an examination, Bruenn concluded that he had suffered an angina attack.

During the voyage to Hawaii, Roosevelt had received news that Missy LeHand had passed away after her long illness. The stress of his long journey, combined with the tension generated by MacArthur's hectoring and Missy's death, further undermined his health. Did he have thoughts of abandoning the upcoming campaign? If so, he never let anyone know that he was considering retirement. On the contrary, he dismissed any suggestions of stepping aside as jeopardizing his domestic and foreign plans. In July, before he left for Hawaii, he had asked Wendell Willkie, who had been defeated by Dewey and conservatives at the Republican convention for a second presidential campaign, whether he would consider joining him in establishing a liberal party that would expel Southerners from Democratic ranks and force them into a conservative party. "We ought to have two real parties," Roosevelt told Sam Rosenman, "one liberal and the other conservative. As it is now, each party is split by dissenters." Willkie was keen to work with Roosevelt on this proposal, but he thought they should wait until after the election.

When he told MacArthur that he was too busy to think of politics, Roosevelt was only half joking. As he sailed to Hawaii, he had been pressed by Churchill about when they and Stalin could expect to meet again to discuss postwar plans.

Churchill believed it should be no later than the last ten days in August. Mindful of Roosevelt's delicate health, the prime minister offered to meet almost anywhere Roosevelt preferred, including "Quebec if that is easiest for you." Roosevelt promptly consented to another meeting and unsuccessfully tried to persuade Stalin to join them, but proposed that the conference not occur until September. Because of "domestic problems," which "are unfortunately difficult for three months to come," by which he meant the election, Roosevelt suggested that they meet in Bermuda. But when Churchill reported that unpleasant weather conditions were likely to greet them there in early September, they agreed to convene again in Quebec on September 10 or September 11.

Churchill's sense of urgency was a response to war-ending campaigns in Europe and Japan, and his growing fears of Soviet expansion into eastern and southeastern Europe. In August, he was preoccupied with the danger of a Communist takeover in Athens as German forces left Greece. At the same time, he noted anxiously Soviet resistance to helping the Polish underground in Warsaw, which had been urged to rebel against the German occupation by the Soviets in order to facilitate the capture of Warsaw. He also hoped that Stalin would reach a compromise with Polish exile leaders in London through Mikołajczyk, who was in Moscow for talks. In mid-August, Churchill flew to Italy, where he met with Josip Broz Tito, the Yugoslav partisan chief, in an attempt to dissuade him from setting up a Communist government in Belgrade after the Germans abandoned the city and the country.

Churchill faced nothing but frustration on all three issues. Stalin had no interest in supporting the Polish underground, which he believed would set up an independent Poland. His armies stopped their advance toward Warsaw on the banks of the Vistula, and he rejected Allied requests to allow British or U.S. planes to land on Soviet airfields after delivering supplies to the underground. Despite the fact that the Soviets had instigated the Warsaw uprising, Stalin condemned it as "reckless" and dissociated his government from "the Warsaw adventure" as a prelude to installing a pro-Soviet Communist government in Poland. In addition, Churchill was stymied in trying to counter Communist insurgencies in Greece and Yugoslavia with monarchial regimes. In an audience with Pope Pius XII at the Vatican, the topic that "bulked the largest . . . was the danger of Communism."

Roosevelt shared some of Churchill's concerns. A report on Nazi atrocities in response to the Warsaw uprising horrified Roosevelt, who called them "appalling" and "inhuman." But he acknowledged the "practical impossibility of our providing supplies to the Warsaw Poles." Roosevelt also shared the concern of his joint chiefs that if they tried to force the issue with Stalin, as Churchill then suggested, they would jeopardize prospects of using Siberian air bases for raids against Japan. "I do not consider it advantageous to the long range general war prospect for me to join with you" in pressing the case with "Uncle Joe," he wrote Churchill. He also considered Churchill to be too wedded to long-standing anti-Communist views. In August and September, as they exchanged messages about Russian refusal to aid the Polish underground, Eleanor reminded Franklin that Stalin seemed "slow to forget" Churchill's anti-Communism, which the Kremlin associated with the Warsaw fighters. In Stalin's calculations, if the Nazis destroyed the Polish rebels, it would open the way to a Communist regime in Warsaw once the Germans were driven out of Poland. While Roosevelt endorsed Churchill's plans for sending British forces into Greece to head off a Communist takeover there, he did so reluctantly, probably more to avoid any pressure to have the United States take a role in an occupation, and out of a disinclination to see Communists control the seat of ancient democracy in Greece. As for Poland, he believed that the Soviet military presence across Eastern Europe put it under Moscow's control.

Roosevelt continued to battle health problems that limited any impulse he might have had to argue with Churchill. When Daisy saw him on August 21 after he returned from the West Coast, she detected "a sort of pallor and a strained look about the mouth which you see in sick people." He complained that he was "*tired,* most of the time," and thought it essential "to save his energy to appear a few times in public before election." When she saw him again eight days later he looked "awfully tired." He had lost another 2.5 pounds during his trip to Hawaii and his doctors were trying to restore his weight with high-calorie snacks between meals. Yet he seemed "in good spirits," with "much joking & teasing" at dinner. When Daisy saw him again on September 4 in Hyde Park, he was too tired to do any work and complained of "feeling 'low' and 'logy' . . . and didn't know what was the matter with him." Two days later, she noticed that, "his back is not so straight as it was — he is tired, and sitting upright is an effort." At lunch, he was "too tired to eat & 'picked at' his plate." On September 10, he again complained to Daisy that he "had had four awful days and was really tired."

In September, a team of five doctors, including Bruenn, who conducted physical examinations over a two-week period, declared his "general condition satisfactory." While they acknowledged that the "Patient [is] under weight" and seemed unable to regain lost pounds, that his "cardiovascular system shows moderate arteriosclerosis," and that "only small annoyances [can] cause rise[s] in systolic pressure," he was "responding well" to the regimen of rest and diet they had prescribed. They found that his "blood pressure averages had lowered," though a reading of 226/118 on D-Day was "life-threateningly high." But there were "no cardiac symptoms at any time," which "sounds good in character." Although he hated the dietary restrictions they had imposed — no "fried, greasy food" or "highly seasoned foods" or "pastry, pie and rich desserts" or use of salt in cooking — he seemed "more relaxed and at ease." Bruenn admitted later that Roosevelt's condition was "critical but not desperate." And so, given the issues that seemed much larger to Roosevelt than any one man's life, including his own, he saw good reason to run again and aim to introduce transformative initiatives that his reelection could possibly bring to frution.

Yet the state of his health did not impede his determination to fulfill his presidential duties. Between August 18 and September 8, for example, he held four lengthy press conferences. These appearances seemed to energize him. Although he had difficulty hearing some of the reporters' questions, he engaged in the combination of serious discussion and amused banter that had characterized his exchanges with the press since 1933. Reflecting on the capture of Paris on August 26, he declared "the recent favorable developments on the world's battlefronts has emphasized the need to speed up preparations for the eventual reconversion of the nation's productive energies to peaceful pursuits." He discussed the "return to a peacetime economy"; preparations for the employment of returning troops; and the establishment of a United Nations Organization to do a better job of peacekeeping than that of the failed League. He was coy about his campaigning in the coming election, but criticized Republican nominee Tom Dewey and announced his intention to speak to a gathering of the International Teamsters Union in Washington on September 23.

Churchill, who had been ill with pneumonia and planned to travel by ship to Canada for their meeting beginning on September 11, cabled Roosevelt on September 1 that he looked forward "to making good plans with you for the future in these days of glory," acknowledging that the invasion of southern France that had begun on August 15 was a great success and that Germany's defeat was now only a matter of time. Roosevelt counseled Churchill against traveling if it would put his health in jeopardy: "The armies keep rolling along and a few weeks delay on our part will not slow them up."

But Churchill was eager to meet as soon as possible, telling his wife that this visit would be "the most necessary one that I have ever made since the very beginning, as it is there that various differences that exist . . . must be brought to a decision." During his Atlantic crossing, Churchill was in a dejected mood. He did not believe that the German resistance would collapse before 1945, as their "stand on the frontier of the native soil should not be underrated." He feared Soviet advance into the Balkans. He worried that the Russians might occupy Belgrade, Budapest, and even Vienna, describing the "political effect upon Central and Southern Europe" of such a development as "formidable in the last degree." During a staff conference on shipboard three days before reaching Canada, he "looked old, unwell and depressed."

Nonetheless, the conference began as planned on September 11. They met in Quebec's historic Citadel fortress, where they were also housed. Churchill was distressed at how "very frail" Roosevelt appeared to be. With the Americans hopeful that the war in Europe would end by Christmas, the discussions focused on postwar political arrangements. Although Churchill had his doubts about a quick end to the fighting, he acknowledged that "everything they had touched had turned to gold." With the election less than two months away, Roosevelt did not want to create the impression that political considerations were eclipsing military planning at the meeting. He was especially concerned to head off speculation that he was making secret agreements with Churchill that would agitate isolationists in the United States and Stalin and his cohorts in the Kremlin. Keeping Great Britain powerful enough to help police the world, but particularly Europe, was at the forefront of Roosevelt's planning. When

Treasury Secretary Morgenthau had returned to Washington from a London visit in August, he told the president that Churchill described Britain as bankrupt. Morgenthau accepted the reality of Britain's plight and favored what he called Lend-Lease II. "Britain made this fight for democracy. Now we have got to help her. . . . We have to put her back on her feet" for the sake of "a permanent world peace," he said.

Greatly troubled by prospects of a bankrupt ally, Roosevelt kept returning to the subject of Britain's financial problems during his discussion with Churchill. He shared Morgenthau's wish to assist it financially but in the midst of the election campaign, he was reluctant to sign on to anything that might be seen as allowing Britain to take advantage of the United States and enabling it to preserve its empire. At Quebec, the British made it clear that they needed aid if they were to maintain civilian morale while they rebuilt their damaged cities and began restoring their depleted economy. "One of the most important things I have to discuss with you is Stage II," Churchill told Roosevelt at the conference on September 12. Mindful of how sympathetic Morgenthau was to Britain's needs, he hoped the president would include him in their conversation. Roosevelt agreed and invited Morgenthau to join them in Quebec after Churchill requested his presence.

On September 14, the third day of the conference, after Churchill had told Roosevelt that a continuation of Lend-Lease was "of extreme and vital importance . . . for reasons that are only too painfully apparent," they agreed on a plan of support. When Roosevelt delayed signing the agreement, however, an emotional Churchill burst out:

"What do you want me to do? Get on my hind legs and beg like Fala?" As he watched Roosevelt finally put his signature to the document, Churchill had "tears in his eyes." He told the president "how grateful he was, thanked him most effusively, and said that this was something they were doing for both countries," meaning that a resilient Britain was essential as a barrier to what Churchill described as "the rapid encroachment of the Russians into the Balkans and the consequent dangerous spread of Russian influence in this area."

Roosevelt himself was apprehensive about Soviet expansion. During a meeting at the conference with Archduke Otto of Austria, he stated his interest in keeping "the Communist[s] out of Hungary and Austria. . . . It is evident," the archduke recorded, "that the relationship between R. and the Russians is strained." While Roosevelt was playing to the archduke's bias in hopes of using him to help arrange a Hungarian surrender that would end their alliance with Germany, he genuinely supported Churchill's eagerness to get British forces into Austria ahead of the Soviets.

Roosevelt had been especially alarmed by exchanges he had had with Stalin about the membership of a postwar peacekeeping organization. When discussions about the creation of this body were held at the Dumbarton Oaks estate in Washington at the end of August between the United States, Great Britain, and the Soviet Union (with China excluded because of Soviet objections that it could prematurely force them into the war against Japan), Andrei Gromyko, the Soviet ambassador to the United States, announced Stalin's demand that all sixteen of their

Soviet republics be included as member states. Roosevelt sent word to Gromyko that "we could never accept this proposal," as the Senate and the larger public would never agree to such a plan. Roosevelt later wrote Stalin to advise him that even raising this as a Soviet condition for entry into the world body "would very definitely imperil the whole project." He asked for assurances that this issue not be raised again before the organization came into being but encouraged Stalin to believe that the matter could be considered once the United Nations, as Roosevelt hoped to call it, was functioning. "I attach exceptional importance" to the proposal, Stalin replied, and argued that Ukraine and Byelorussia, two of the republics, were more populous and significant than some of the smaller states that would be included as U.N. members.

Even more troubling was Soviet insistence that any one of the four permanent members — Britain, China, the United States, and the USSR — of the proposed organization's Security Council, or decision-making body, could exercise veto power. "The British and ourselves," Roosevelt wrote Stalin, "both feel strongly that parties to a dispute should not vote in the decisions of the Council even if one of the parties is a permanent member." Roosevelt once again cited U.S. public opinion as a bar to any such arrangement, explaining that it would violate an American tradition of never allowing a party to a disagreement to vote in his own case. It would also be viewed as permitting the Great Powers to place themselves above the law, and the U.S. Senate would then reject American participation in a world body, as it had in 1919–20. While Stalin hoped that they could find common ground to resolve their differences, he cited Soviet concerns with "certain absurd prejudices which *often* hinder an actually objective attitude toward the USSR." He warned against what "the lack of unanimity among the leading powers may bring about."

South African prime minister Jan Christian Smuts, a confidant of Churchill's, urged him against alienating Russia as threatening hopes of a peaceful world. Unanimity seemed essential for a benign future, and he counseled against "a clash . . . at all costs." He did not think that "the future of world peace and security should be sacrificed on this issue." In any case, veto power would enable the United States and Great Britain to deter Russia from provoking "crises disapproved" of by them. Roosevelt agreed with Smuts "as to the necessity of having the U.S.S.R. as a fully accepted and equal member of the great powers formed for the purpose of preventing international war." Echoing what he believed had worked best in American politics, he added, "It should be possible to accomplish this by adjusting our differences through compromise by all the parties concerned *and this ought to tide things over for a few years until the child learns to toddle.*"

Roosevelt hoped he could soften Soviet doubts about Anglo-American intentions by ensuring that Germany did not threaten another war in the foreseeable future. At the first plenary session of the Quebec conference on September 13, Roosevelt criticized the outlook among some groups in Britain and the United States that Germany "could be rejuvenated by a kindly attitude of approach to them." At dinner that evening, Morgenthau spoke up for Germany's deindustrialization.

He had warned Roosevelt against "a soft policy" that would be limited to reparation payments, predicting that it would enable Germany to rearm and fight another war within ten years. Roosevelt had warmly endorsed Morgenthau's view, telling him, "We have got to be tough with Germany, and I mean the German people not just the Nazis. We either have to castrate the German people or you have got to treat them in such manner so they can't just go on reproducing people who want to continue the way they have in the past." After two world wars and the atrocities the Germans had committed against their neighbors and Europe's Jewish population, Roosevelt expressed popular sentiment in Britain, Russia, and the United States that Germany was incorrigibly aggressive and inhumane. Morgenthau proposed to convert it into "an agricultural population of small land-owners," a pastoral society divided into several small states.

At the end of August, when Secretary of War Henry Stimson showed the president a "Handbook of Military Government" drawn up in the War Department, Roosevelt dismissed it as "pretty bad." He complained that it suggested bringing Germany back "as quickly as possible to their pre-war estate." Instead, he wanted "every person in Germany" to "realize that this time Germany is a defeated nation." He wanted no reiteration of the post-1918 experience, when the Nazis asserted that the Weimar government had stabbed the Army in the back and unnecessarily surrendered. This time he wanted everyone in Germany to understand that they were "a defeated nation, collectively and individually." This was to "be so impressed upon them that they will hesitate to start any new war." It needed to be "driven home to them that the whole nation has been engaged in a lawless conspiracy against the decencies of modern civilization." A transformation of the German economy along the lines Morgenthau had suggested also appealed to Roosevelt as a way to support Britain. It would reduce, if not eliminate, German economic competition, and it could lessen Soviet suspicions that London and Washington intended to rebuild German power as a bulwark against Moscow's might.

Initially, Morgenthau's plan horrified Churchill. He shared American eagerness to disarm Germany, but, as he told Morgenthau, "we ought not to prevent her living decently. There are bonds between the working classes of all countries, and the English people will not stand for the policy you are advocating. . . . You cannot indict a whole nation." Churchill went on to unleash "the full flood of his rhetoric, sarcasm and violence," warning that what Morgenthau proposed would be like "chaining himself to a dead German." But the prime minister was ultimately willing to accept the Roosevelt-Morgenthau vision of Germany's future as a way to speed Britain's economic recovery; he also hoped it would facilitate American commitments to Lend-Lease II. When Foreign Secretary Anthony Eden objected to the Morgenthau Plan, Churchill replied: "The future of my people is at stake, and when I have to choose between my people and the German people, I am going to choose my people."

The issue of Germany's deindustrialization quickly became too controversial to be feasible. Russian demands for reparations from German industry reduced the appeal of Morgenthau's proposal, and when newspaper reports of it were tied to stiffening German resistance on the western front, Roosevelt published a statement that postwar planning for Germany remained unsettled and advised Hull that he opposed turning Germany into "a wholly agricultural nation." He repeated his disapproval of the idea to Stimson and explained that, "he had no idea how he could have initialed" such an agreement.

For Roosevelt, Quebec proved to be a testing ground of sorts. He seemed so "frail" that one of Churchill's military chiefs thought him "hardly to be taking in what was going on." Clementine Churchill, the prime minister's wife, who attended the conference, worried that Roosevelt "does not — indeed cannot (partly because of his health and partly because of his make-up) function round the clock . . . I should not think that his mind was pinpointed on the war for more than four hours a day, which is not really enough when one is a supreme war lord." One night during the conference he and Churchill had watched a Hollywood film biography about President Wilson, which "included a poignant portrayal of the ailing Wilson's decline and death. Afterward, Dr. Bruenn found the president's blood pressure dangerously elevated." When he returned from Quebec on September 17, he told Daisy that he "wanted to *sleep* all the time." When she saw him back in Hyde Park, she wondered if he could "get through four more years. . . . I am really frightened at his condition. He seems to be slowly failing."

For all his health problems, Roosevelt had a reserve of strength or ability to recover from a physical downturn that kept him focused on what he saw as the principal problems confronting him and the country. One of his primary aims was keeping the Allies working together productively. At Quebec Churchill had declared his intention "to have a showdown with the bear pretty soon," meaning before Russian-sponsored Communist parties gained control in Greece or France. And though he and Roosevelt were scathing about de Gaulle, Churchill said "that he would rather have a de Gaulle France than a Communist France."

Roosevelt sought to ease Churchill's fears of Communist expansion by giving Britain and the United States a future military advantage over Russia's larger land armies. After the conference, he and Churchill conferred at Hyde Park, where they focused on the development of the atomic bomb. They were confident that this device, which scientists told them would have at least three times the explosive power of what 2,600 planes could drop on enemy targets, would be operational by the summer of 1945. Because Roosevelt knew that the Soviets were aware of Anglo-American work on a nuclear weapon, he had encouraged Niels Bohr, a fifty-eight-year-old Danish Nobel scientist who had come to the United States as a consultant on atomic research and to lobby the president for international control of it, to believe that he shared his desire for such an arrangement. It was Roosevelt's way of signaling Moscow in the name of good relations that he ultimately would share atomic secrets with them, but not immediately. He wanted Stalin to understand that he was as capable of power politics as the Russian leader was.

At Hyde Park, he and Churchill signed an aide-mémoire that proposed limiting atomic secrets to Britain and the United States. The agreement included a proviso calling for the monitoring of Bohr's activities, with "steps" to "be taken to ensure that he is responsible for no leakage of information, particularly to the Russians." Roosevelt apparently hoped that a British-American monopoly on atomic power could allow them "to control the peace of the world."

Whatever his fears of Russian expansionism, Churchill was as mindful as Roosevelt of the importance of accommodations with Stalin. He told the Soviet leader that he and Roosevelt shared "an intense conviction that on the agreement of our three nations . . . stand the hopes of the world." When he returned to London, he told the Parliament that Russia had rendered "measureless services . . . to the common cause, through long years of suffering, by tearing out the life of the German military monster . . . [The] future of the whole world and certainly the future of Europe, perhaps for several generations, depends upon the cordial, trustful and comprehending association of the British Empire, the United States, and Soviet Russia, and no pains must be spared and no patience grudged which are necessary to bring that supreme hope to fruition." To that end, he proposed to fly to Moscow for talks with Stalin: "first, to clinch his coming in against Japan and, secondly, to try to effect a friendly settlement with Poland," though he also intended to discuss Greece and Yugoslavia. Roosevelt told Churchill that he regretted that he could not meet with him and Stalin until after the November election, but wished him "every success in your visit to U.J." His only counsel was to recognize that "Stalin is at the present time sensitive about any doubt as to his intention to help us in the Orient," and he encouraged Churchill to "find some means of reaching an agreement between the three great powers" on establishing the United Nations. "This is not a hope but a 'must' for all three of us," Roosevelt added. "Failure now is unthinkable."

It was unthinkable not only because it would undermine postwar peacekeeping, but also because it could play havoc with his chances for reelection. He wanted Churchill to postpone discussion of the contentious veto issue until he could participate in another summit meeting. "There is after all no immediate urgency about this question," he cabled Churchill, "which is so directly related to public opinion in the United States and Great Britain and in all the United Nations." Churchill agreed to delay any conversation with Stalin about Security Council voting until "we are all three together."

In the meantime, Roosevelt focused his attention on the election. A not-so-secret "whispering campaign" had alleged that he was too ill to continue as president. His "lost weight, thinning hair, and heavily furrowed face all too plainly showed the toll taken by crowded years" and fueled trepidation about his capacity to serve another four years. As his White House physician Ross McIntire said later, his appearance gave rise to gossip that he had "suffered a paralytic stroke, that he was being treated for cancer of the prostate, that he was the victim of a mental breakdown, and, favorite whisper of all, that his heart had played out." None of this was true, but his hypertension, enlarged heart, and gaunt appearance gave credence to some of these rumors. When a reporter asked him if he had read "the ominous reports about your health," he bristled, replying, "Don't get me commenting . . . because I might say things that I will be sorry for." He dismissed the promoters of these rumors by stating, "I know more about their health than they know about mine." As for his own condition, he asserted: "I think it's pretty good health." In fact, he was too unhealthy to engage in an exhausting campaign trip and principally relied on radio to reach voters and demonstrate his resilience as a combative candidate.

On September 23, before a sympathetic audience of labor union members at the Hotel Statler in Washington, D.C., Roosevelt launched his campaign with a masterful speech ridiculing Republican critics (though he never mentioned Dewey) with humor that amused and reassured voters of his mental acuity. "These Republican leaders have not been content with attacks on me, or my wife, or on my sons," he said with a zest and sparkle that not only captivated those present but his radio audience as well. "No, not content with that they now include my little dog, Fala. Well, of course, I don't resent attacks and my family doesn't resent attacks, but Fala does resent them. You know Fala is Scotch, and being a Scottie, as soon as he learned that the Republican fiction writers *in Congress and out* had concocted a story that I had left him behind on an Aleutian island and had sent a destroyer back to find him — at a cost of two or three or eight or twenty million dollars — his Scotch soul was furious. He has not been the same dog since. I am accustomed to hearing malicious falsehood about myself — such as that old worm-eaten chestnut that I have represented myself as indispensable. But I think I have a right to resent, to object to libelous statements about my dog." Sam Rosenman considered this Roosevelt's best speech.

In his talk he reminded listeners of all the New Deal reforms that had been achieved despite Republican opposition. But he scored his most telling political points by emphasizing the tasks ahead — ending the war and winning the peace. The speech convinced many voters who had been skeptical that he had the fortitude to take on the challenges of the next four years. Having led the country through the war, it seemed reasonable and even essential to have him administer the peace. Before he spoke, he thought there was "an excellent chance" that Dewey, who he thought was "making a very good campaign," would win. This speech, however, marked a shift in the campaign, even though there were still six weeks before the election, and he needed to make additional appearances to sustain the momentum it achieved.

A strenuous effort, however, remained out of the question. He complained that he was suffering from "sleeping sickness" or that he was constantly exhausted. He fretted over the demands on him to campaign, including having to answer a lot of "stupid questions" at a press conference and seeing "uninteresting people" for the sake of the election.

In October, with Churchill promising to keep him closely apprised of his conversations with Stalin, and Averell Harriman, his ambassador to Moscow, also informing him about the talks, Roosevelt judged the Churchill-Stalin meeting to be the first order of business. With the campaign against Germany in the west stalled at the end of September by stiff resistance to allowing the Allies to cross the Rhine, Russian operations in the east seemed more essential than ever. Because "the questions which you will discuss" are of "real interest to the United States," Roosevelt cautioned Churchill against committing him to anything. He suggested that Churchill's meeting with Stalin be considered "a useful prelude" to a tripartite conference after the election. He then told Stalin that he regarded the talks with Churchill "as preliminary to a meeting of the three of us." He wanted Harriman to emphasize to both the British and Russians that he viewed the Moscow meeting as "nothing more than a preliminary exploration" of matters that greatly interested him and would in no way limit his "freedom of action."

Sensitive to Roosevelt's insistence on not pledging the United States to postwar political obligations of any kind, Churchill and Stalin cabled him after their first meeting that they were engaged in "an informal discussion" with "a preliminary view of the situation as it affects us." In a follow-up message, Churchill assured him that "we shall handle everything so as not to commit you." Churchill omitted to inform him, however, of the bargain he struck with Stalin at their first meeting on October 10. "It was better to express these things in diplomatic terms," Churchill explained to Stalin, "and not to use the phrase 'dividing into spheres,' because the Americans might be shocked." In fact, Churchill and Stalin signed on to what Churchill called a "naughty document" agreeing to 90 percent Soviet predominance in Romania, 90 percent British dominance in Greece, and a fifty-fifty split in Yugoslavia. Churchill wrote these ratios on a piece of paper and pushed it across the table to Stalin, who endorsed it with a large tick from a blue pencil and passed it back to Churchill. "Might it not be thought rather cynical if it seemed we had disposed of these issues, so fateful to millions of people, in such an offhand manner?" Churchill asked and suggested, "Let us burn the paper." "No," Stalin replied. "You keep it."

Although it became clear in the course of the talks that Stalin would settle for nothing less than a pro-Communist regime in Warsaw, Churchill pressed him to understand that having initially gone to war in response to German aggression against it, an independent Poland was for Britain a moral issue. To underscore the moral aspect of Poland's fate, Churchill cited the Pope's desire for Polish independence. Stalin, unmoved, asked, "How many divisions does the Pope have?" When Pius XII was told of Stalin's remark, he rejoined, "You may tell my son Joseph that he will meet my divisions in Heaven."

Although Churchill and Stalin reached an agreement on Poland's postwar borders, extending Moscow's western frontier at Poland's expense and compensating Poland with German territory to its west, Churchill assured Roosevelt that "you are not committed in any way by what I have said and done." In any case, Churchill added, any final decisions would be left to a "peace conference, which alone can give a final and legal validity to all territorial changes." He also assured Roosevelt "that no indiscretion will occur from the Russian side." Stalin stressed repeatedly during the talks his "earnest desire for your return at the election." As for the Balkans, Churchill believed it essential to "get a common mind . . . so that we may prevent civil war breaking out in several countries when probably you and I would be in sympathy with one side and U.J. with the other." But he also reiterated to Roosevelt that nothing was being "settled except preliminary agreements . . . subject to further discussion and melting down with you." Churchill thought that the percentage agreements for Greece and Yugoslavia were "the best that are possible," and he did not believe that they could deter the Soviets from "ascendancy in Rumania and Bulgaria," given their strategic access to the Black Sea.

With Roosevelt in an uncertain election battle, Churchill and Stalin wished to support him in any way possible. The Gallup polls were worrisome: A majority of voters said they thought Roosevelt would win, but the surveys of how people would actually vote suggested a contest too close to call. But convictions that Roosevelt would end the war more quickly than Dewey gave the president an important edge. "Although I hear most encouraging accounts from various quarters about United States politics," Churchill wrote him in October, "I feel the suspense probably far more than you do or more than I should if my own affairs were concerned in this zone." Stalin wrote with the agreeable observation that his meetings with Churchill were "extremely useful for the mutual ascertaining of views" on questions about Germany, Poland, the Balkan states, and "further military policy."

In September and October, Churchill told the president that they needed to reach agreement on the postwar handling of major war criminals. Were they to be tried in a court of law, or should they be summarily executed? Churchill believed that publishing a list of the names of the war's key perpetrators would enable the German people to separate themselves from these wrongdoers, who would then have less of a chance of convincing the mass of the populace "to fight to the last man, die in the last ditch" because they shared the fate of the Nazi leadership. During his October meeting with Stalin, the Soviet leader advocated for war crime trials. Without them, he said, there could be no death penalties, but only lifelong confinements. It was better to convince the world of Nazi criminality with hearings justifying their executions. Although 76 percent of Americans believed that the Nazis had "murdered many people in concentration camps," and 88 percent wanted Japanese leaders subjected to severe punishments, such as "torture them to a slow and awful death," "get rid of every one of them," or "kill them like rats," Roosevelt wanted to leave decisions on how to deal with Axis atrocities to a postelection meeting with Churchill and Stalin.

Roosevelt certainly had no intention of showing either Nazi or Japanese leaders mercy. At a press conference earlier in the year, he had stated his determination to bring them to justice: "In most of Europe and in parts of Asia the systematic torture and murder of civilians — men, women, and children — by the Nazis and the Japanese continues unabated," he told reporters on March 24. "In one of the blackest crimes of all history — begun by the Nazis in the day of peace and multiplied by them a hundred times in time of war — the wholesale systematic murder of the Jews of Europe goes on unabated every hour." He mentioned the current Nazi effort to destroy Hungary's 750,000 Jews, who until the German occupation on March 19 had "survived a decade of Hitler's fury" but were now threatened with annihilation. "It is therefore fitting," he asserted, "that we should again proclaim determination that none who participate in these acts of savagery shall go unpunished. . . . All who knowingly take part in the deportation of Jews to their death in Poland, or Norwegians and French to their death in Germany, are equally guilty with the executioner himself." He promised to "persevere . . . in [the] rescue of [the] victims of brutality of the Nazis and the Japs."

He was unwilling, however, to agree to a Nazi proposal that he exchange 10,000 trucks, which would be used for nonwar purposes, for 100,000 Hungarian Jews. Such a trade would have both jeopardized Soviet-American relations and undermined Roosevelt's commitment to unconditional surrender. It seemed certain to inflame Soviet suspicions that the democracies were contemplating making peace with Hitler in order to facilitate his ability to continue fighting Russia. The shadow of Munich also hung over any contemplation of whether the Nazis could be relied upon to keep to their end of any bargain. Providing them with trucks or any other equipment seemed certain to be of use to their war effort.

Nor was anyone in the administration inclined to consent to suggestions that U.S. air forces bomb the railway lines into Auschwitz-Birkenau in Poland, or the death camp itself. While U.S. bombers based in Italy were in striking distance of the lines and the camp, the War Department and in particular John J. McCloy, its assistant secretary, rejected such measures as likely to have little impact on preventing the transport of Jews to their deaths; in fact, such raids seemed certain to kill many of them inadvertently. Advocates of the air attacks argued that destroying the gas chambers and crematoria would at least temporarily put them out of commission. But there was no assurance that they would be successful in destroying the killing facilities, and U.S. military authorities refused to sanction such a raid on the grounds that their task was to strike only strategic targets. Although McCloy later asserted that Roosevelt himself had vetoed any proposal to attack the death camp, there is no evidence that he was ever consulted on the matter, and as a rule, he was not involved in selecting bombing targets. As historians Richard Breitman and Allan Lichtman assert, even if Auschwitz had been neutralized, the Nazis were so intent on the elimination of Europe's remaining Jews that they would have found other means to carry out the Holocaust. As it was, in the closing months of the war, they killed an additional 98,000 Hungarian Jews and as many as 250,000 from other countries.

A more concerted effort to rescue Hitler's victims could have saved some of them, but certainly not many. Once the war began, bringing them out of harm's way was not a simple matter. The Nazi obsession with the destruction of European Jewry effectively precluded anything the Allies could have said or done to rescue them. The fastest, fullest way to put an end to Hitler's horrors was through Nazi defeat, and that could not have come quickly enough to save six million Jewish victims of Nazi madness.

Roosevelt's dilemmas in the fall of 1944 extended to the Asian theater and tensions over how to guarantee China's stability and advance its effectiveness in fighting the Japanese. When Chiang Kai-shek asked for a billion-dollar loan, Morgenthau complained that the Chinese "are just a bunch of crooks and I won't go up [on the Hill] and ask for one nickel." General Marshall judged China to be of no military value and believed that the Allies could defeat Japan by destroying its navy and bombing it with planes launched from aircraft carriers and from adjacent islands. In the spring, deteriorating economic conditions, combined with the ongoing struggle with Chinese Communist forces concentrated in the northern part of the nation, foretold a likely Nationalist collapse. In June, Roosevelt unsuccessfully pressured Chiang to settle with Mao Tse-tung for the sake of the war effort. In July, the president, who had always taken a deferential approach toward Chiang, felt compelled to confront him with harsh realities. He warned in a cable that Nationalist ineffectiveness against the Japanese threatened to bring a "disastrous setback" that would up-end all they had been battling to achieve in the fight against Japan. He asked that General Stilwell be given full command of all forces in China, including the power to arrange an alliance with the Communists.

Although Chiang agreed in principle to Roosevelt's demands, he was anything but ready to implement them. In August, Roosevelt sent Patrick J. Hurley to China as his personal representative to move the discussion forward. An Oklahoma oil businessman who had served as Herbert Hoover's secretary of war and enjoyed a reputation as a keen conciliator, Hurley knew next to nothing about China. (When he wrote a note to Chiang thanking him for a courtesy, he addressed him as "Mr. Shek.") Yet he served Roosevelt's political purposes by being a conservative Republican supporting a coalition with China's Communists. Chiang's continued resistance, however, moved Stilwell to explode in a diary: "the crazy little bastard . . . will sabotage the whole Goddamn project — men, money, material, time and sweat that we have put on it for two and a half years. . . . He will not listen to reason." Roosevelt dispatched a cable to Chiang warning again that "you are faced in the near future with the disaster I have feared." Despite American advances across the Pacific, it would be too little to save "China unless you act now and vigorously." After conversations with Roosevelt at Quebec in September, Churchill concluded that "the American illusion about China is being dispelled. The Soong family oligarchy regime is . . . very likely nearing its end."

Stilwell, whose hatred of Chiang had only grown with time, savored the opportunity to deliver Roosevelt's tough message to the "Peanut." After he presented the cable on September 18 and watched Chiang read it in translation, Stilwell recorded, "The harpoon hit the little bugger right in the solar plexus, and went right through him. It was a clean hit, but beyond turning green and losing the power of speech, he did not bat an eye." Having "played the avenging angel," Stilwell sent his wife a snarky poem:

For all my weary battles,
For all my hours of woe,
At last I've had my innings
And laid the Peanut low.

909

I know I've still to suffer,
And run a weary race,
But oh! The blessed pleasure!
I've wrecked the Peanut's face.

In fact, the one to suffer was Stilwell. Chiang complained to Roosevelt that the general had become an obstacle to good relations and progress in the war and urged his removal, promising to allow another U.S. general to be placed in command. The president felt compelled to comply, in part because Chiang was head of state and Roosevelt did not wish to treat him as the chief of a subordinate colony under U.S. command, in part to have a more compliant Chiang. But Stilwell knew it was wishful thinking and predicted that Chiang would not "prosecute the war" but would block or eliminate anyone who pressed him to take action. He expected the United States to achieve the defeat of Japan without Chinese assistance. Roosevelt took Stilwell out of China and wanted him to command forces in Burma, but Chiang would not agree to that either, so Stilwell returned to the United States. Having concluded that the ground war in China was hopeless, Roosevelt now withdrew his request for a U.S. commander of all Chinese armies. It was clear that the war against Japan would have to be won by sea and air forces and by the likelihood of Russian troops entering the fighting after Germany's collapse.

In October, when Bernard Baruch told him: "You have just one object at the present, the war & the following peace," Roosevelt responded that "it was difficult to concentrate on that double object with everyone insisting on his doing so many other things, such as speeches & appearances in the campaign." Roosevelt believed that Dewey, who was attacking the New Deal as Communist inspired, was conducting the meanest campaign in history. He understood that he could make additional radio speeches, but they would not have as much impact as a personal appearance demonstrating his physical capacity to serve another term. Consequently, on October 21, in spite of a rainstorm, or because of it, Roosevelt rode for four hours in an open car around four of New York City's five boroughs, stopping at the Brooklyn Navy Yard; Ebbets Field, home of the Brooklyn Dodgers; then heading across the Triborough Bridge to Queens; then to the Bronx campus of Hunter College; and finally back to Manhattan for an evening speech at the Waldorf Astoria Hotel before the Foreign Policy Association. "I was delighted to see the proofs of your robust vigor in New York," Churchill wrote. "I cannot believe that four hours in an open car and pouring rain with a temperature of 40 and clothes wet through conform to those limits of prudence which you would be so ready to prescribe if it were my case." But Roosevelt knew that it was an effective response to reports of his waning health.

On November 6, he ended his campaign with a tour of the Hudson River Valley, as he had in all previous elections. That night he gave a national radio address from his Hyde Park home, celebrating American dedication to free elections. In the closing weeks of the campaign, he had shown himself impervious to inclement weather and to have a hearty capacity to withstand the rigors of another four years as president. Though he won 3.6 million more popular votes than Dewey, 52.8

percent of the total, and bested him by four to one in the electoral column, it was the closest of his four elections. Nonetheless, he had been elected for an unprecedented fourth time. Churchill cabled him: "I always said that a great people could be trusted to stand by the pilot who weathered the storm. It is an indescribable relief to me that our comradeship will continue and will help to bring the world out of misery." "We should now be permitted to continue our work together," Roosevelt responded, "until this worldwide agony is ended and a better future ensured."

CHAPTER 21
LAST FULL MEASURE

His victory at the polls freed Roosevelt to retreat to Hyde Park and Warm Springs for badly needed rest. It also enabled him to begin to exchange messages with Churchill and Stalin to discuss the specifics of their planned meeting about the establishment of occupation zones in Germany, a strategy for forcing Japan's surrender, and the reconstruction of Russia and other devastated countries.

Yet Roosevelt wasn't quite ready to put the election behind him. On November 10, at the first postelection cabinet meeting, he said he felt "like the old man Dante wrote about, who had gone to Hell four times." He cabled Churchill, "I finally got angry toward the end of the campaign and replied to the worst type of opposition I have ever met." That "little man [Dewey] made me pretty mad," he told his son Jimmy. He was more direct with his secretary Bill Hassett, remarking after Dewey conceded defeat, "I still think he is a son of a bitch." Sidney Hillman, CIO labor chief, who had come under attack from Dewey as a front man for the Communists, and in Republican campaign rhetoric as the "biggest political boss in America" running Roosevelt's campaign, received a laudatory note from the president. "I send you no condolences for the licks you took in the campaign," Roosevelt wrote him. "You and I and Fala have seen what happened to the people who gave them." When an old friend asked what color socks he preferred she knit him for the inauguration, he replied: "I would suggest either black or blue because that is a little bit the way I felt after going through THE DIRTIEST CAMPAIGN IN ALL HISTORY." The satisfaction of his triumph came not just from defeating his mendacious critics, as he saw them, but from the support of people at the bottom of the economic pyramid who had demonstrated their trust in him. A black woman from Pittsburgh wrote him: "When God put you in the White House, He shore did no that you were the right Man for the poor people. . . . You are the man for us."

In the closing days of the campaign, the competition and drive to win had been a stimulant: "He was in splendid form," Daisy noted, "cheerful and full-of-the-devil. The campaign seems to have done him more good than harm." Even a week after the election, he was still buoyant, but by November 22 familiar health problems had resurfaced: He was tired and felt poorly, with aches and pains around his midriff and no appetite. He was worried about an additional loss of ten pounds. His color continued to be a troubling gray, and he seemed to have aged ten years in the last twelve months.

Yet work still functioned like an elixir that fixed his attention and kept him on track from day to day. For all his health distractions, he had developed a clear idea of what should be done to end the fighting and secure the peace. He wanted

Churchill to join him in a statement that would "help break down German morale." He proposed a message that assured Germans that the Allies had no desire "to devastate Germany or eliminate the German people." Their objective was, rather, the elimination of Nazi control. Churchill convinced him, however, that any such declaration would be viewed in Germany as a confession of weakness or uncertainty about an early victory and at the same time would raise Russian concerns about Allied commitment to unconditional surrender. Churchill doubted that the Germans worried about either American or British occupying forces but were only fearful of the Soviets.

For the second Big Three meeting Stalin wanted Roosevelt and Churchill to come to a port on the Soviet Black Sea. Roosevelt wanted no part of that and hoped he could persuade Stalin to agree to a site somewhere in the Mediterranean — preferably in a Greek or Turkish seaport. He feared that sanitary conditions in the Black Sea region threatened everyone's health, and a location in the Mediterranean would make for an easier sea voyage. Churchill shared the president's reluctance, agreeing that the Black Sea was "out of the question," and suggested Jerusalem, Haifa, Beirut, Alexandria, or Malta as an alternative. The president believed that Stalin would refuse to come to Jerusalem, Egypt, or Malta, and so he proposed they not meet until after his inauguration on January 20 at a port on the Adriatic, or Rome or Sicily, sometime in late January or early February.

Stalin was content to postpone their convening, for the longer they waited, the deeper into Germany Soviet forces would be, and the stronger

Russia's postwar position in Europe. In November and December, with Russian armies heading for Berlin and Anglo-American forces halted by a German offensive west of the Rhine, Stalin saw himself at an increasing advantage in dictating postwar control of the Balkans and all of Eastern Europe.

As for a meeting place, Stalin remained determined to confer in a Soviet Black Sea port. He justified his insistence on Yalta in the Crimea as essential to his own health, or so he claimed his doctors had advised him. An isolated city that had been subjected to total destruction by the Nazis, Yalta was described by Churchill as "The Riviera of Hades." Stalin's motivation for this choice was not his health but rather his fear of western assassins, which kept him from traveling outside the Soviet Union. At the Yalta Conference, which was held in February, he brought with him an astonishing array of bodyguards. In addition to 620 men acting as personal shields, there would be "two circles of guards by day, three circles by night, and guard dogs. Five districts spanning twenty kilometers had been 'purged of suspicious elements' — 74,000 people had been checked and 835 arrested." It also seems plausible that his insistence that Churchill and Roosevelt, who he must have known was in declining health, come to Yalta was a statement of his ascendant power against the backdrop of Soviet battlefield victories. Believing it essential to confer with Stalin if a path was to be found to a stable postwar peace, and convinced that Soviet losses in the fighting gave them a compelling claim on where to meet, Roosevelt, despite the strain on his frail health, gave in to Stalin's demand.

During the Thanksgiving and Christmas holidays, Roosevelt found some relief in retreats to Hyde Park and Warm Springs, but the pressures of dealing with diplomatic issues crowded his days. Despite his expectations about America's greater role in postwar Asian affairs than in European ones, the latter of which he expected Britain and Russia to manage, Roosevelt could not imagine a total U.S. retreat from the Continent. An American occupation zone in Germany, for example, would provide a base for American forces in Europe for the indefinite future. In addition, when Churchill pressed the case for a larger French role in the occupation of Germany and the reconstruction of western Europe, Roosevelt objected, calculating that Britain's inability to entirely fill the vacuum left by the absence of the French power would allow room for greater American influence. On November 14, as Churchill visited Paris to confer with de Gaulle, Roosevelt chided him: "Don't turn up in French clothes."

When Roosevelt cautioned that the United States would have to remove the bulk of its armed forces from Europe within months of an Allied victory, Churchill remained insistent on including the French in postwar diplomacy, as well as refusing to concede a quick U.S. withdrawal from Europe. On his return from France, he advised Roosevelt that nothing would be decided without his agreement because the United States had "by far the largest forces in France." He also wanted Roosevelt to equip eight French divisions to ensure both French domestic stability and that there was "a French army to take on the main task of holding down Germany." He also warned

Roosevelt against weakening de Gaulle's control in France lest it facilitate Communist influence, adding, "I hope you will not consider that I am putting on French clothes when I say this." Although Roosevelt remained determined to take U.S. troops out of Europe as quickly as possible, he stubbornly took issue with treating France as an equal power and refused to provide equipment for the French army. "How will it be possible to hold down western Germany beyond the present Russian occupation line?" Churchill replied. "We certainly could not undertake the task without your aid and that of the French. All therefore would rapidly disintegrate as it did last time. I hope, however, that my fears are groundless. I put my faith in you."

Nothing, however, quite challenged the goodwill developed through the wartime alliance as discussions about future civil aviation routes. A conference in Chicago in the winter of 1944–45 put surprising strains on the Roosevelt-Churchill friendship. British eagerness to claim a significant share of postwar air routes revived long-standing suspicions of its desire for imperial control and threatened to provoke public repercussions seriously affecting "many other things," including congressional readiness to continue Lend-Lease aid to the United Kingdom, or so Roosevelt notified Churchill, telling him Americans "will wonder about the chances of our two countries, let alone others, working together to keep the peace if we cannot even get together on an aviation agreement." Churchill replied that Roosevelt's message had caused him "much anxiety" and he agreed that it was "a grave matter in which not only governments but parliaments and peoples may become deeply agitated, with consequences which cannot fail to be disastrous both to the prosecution of the war and to the prevention of future wars." Yet Churchill hoped that "the American people under your re-acclaimed leadership will not give themselves over to vainglorious ambitions, and that justice and fair-play will be the lights that guide them." Roosevelt expressed the hope that they would resolve their differences in a spirit of cooperation serving both sides.

Conflicts also continued with Stalin over the United Nations National Security Council and the question of Poland's future independence. Roosevelt finally felt compelled to give in to Stalin's demand that each of the four permanent Security Council members have a veto over a dispute involving one of them. He feared that an unbridgeable dispute over setting up a world organization would only provide support to American isolationists and jeopardize U.S. participation in what was to be the League's successor.

In December, Stalin's condemnation of Poland's exile government in London and announcement of his determination to put the Soviet-backed Lublin Poles in power angered and frustrated Roosevelt. On December 16, he wrote Stalin, "I feel it is of the highest importance that until the three of us can get together and thoroughly discuss this troublesome question there be no action . . . which would render our discussions more difficult. . . . Because of the great political implications, which such a step would entail, you would find it possible to refrain from recognizing the Lublin Committee as a government of Poland before we meet. . . . I know that Prime Minister Churchill shares my views."

But Stalin, who saw a pro-Soviet government in Poland as essential to Russia's security, was unyielding. He responded that the London exiles were the enemies of Russia, allied to Hitler's Germany. By contrast, he argued, the Lublin Poles were true representatives of the Polish people and supporters of the common struggle against the Nazis. Not persuaded that the Lublin group was anything but a creature of Soviet interests, Roosevelt told Stalin that he was "disturbed and deeply disappointed" by his reply, and reproved the Russian leader for his failure to "realize how extremely unfortunate and even serious it would be at this period in the war in its effect on world opinion and enemy morale if your Government should formally recognize one Government of Poland while the majority of the other United Nations, including the United States and Great Britain, continue to recognize and to maintain diplomatic relations with the Polish Government in London. I must tell you with a frankness equal to your own that I see no prospect of this Government's following suit." He also disputed the assertion that the Lublin group represented the Polish people, adding that the Polish question was so "difficult and dangerous" that it might well open a serious breach among the Allies. Stalin, however, still refused to back down, on the unconvincing grounds that the Presidium of the Supreme Soviet of the USSR had already extended recognition to the Lublin Poles. "It is interesting to see that 'the Presidium of the Supreme Soviet of the USSR' has now been brought up into the line," Churchill sarcastically observed.

Roosevelt's worries about postwar relations extended to the fate of the European Jews who survived Hitler's extermination campaign. When Congress considered passing a resolution pressing Britain to abandon its resistance to Jewish migration to Palestine, Roosevelt wrote Senator Robert Wagner of New York, a principal sponsor of the motion: "There are about half a million Jews there. Perhaps another million want to go. They are of all shades — good, bad and indifferent. On the other side of the picture there are approximately seventy million Mohammedans who want to cut their throats the day they land. The one thing I want to avoid is a massacre or a situation that cannot be resolved by talking things over. Anything said or done over here just now would add fuel to the flames and I hope that at this juncture no branch of the Government will act. Everybody knows what American hopes are. If we talk about them too much we will hurt fulfillment." Roosevelt planned to meet with Saudi Arabia's king Ibn Saud on his way back from Yalta and hoped he could persuade him to adopt a humane approach to Jewish resettlement.

Roosevelt's views on this matter, which guaranteed that no congressional action would be taken on Jewish resettlement, was of a piece with his reluctance to press the case with Congress to relax barriers to allow Europe's displaced Jews to immigrate to the United States. Such rescue initiatives were likely to incite anti-Semitism among Americans, which he believed was all too prevalent. He also feared that it, too, would rekindle isolationist sentiment.

On December 6, Churchill cabled the president about "the serious and disappointing war situation which faces us at the close of this year. . . . We have definitely failed to achieve the strategic

921

object, which we gave to our armies five weeks ago. We have not yet reached the Rhine." The Allied advance through Germany was proving to be a great challenge, and Churchill was especially troubled by the continuing presence of twenty-six German divisions in Italy, which, should they retreat to Germany, would be "a powerful reinforcement to the German homeland." Because of "the obstinacy of the German resistance on all fronts," five British divisions had not been transferred to Asia to fight in Burma. Only in the Pacific were Allied forces "not in a temporary state of frustration." Still, Churchill's anxiety about the "elimination of China as a combatant" was "increased by the destruction of all hopes of an early meeting between the three of us and the indefinite postponement of another meeting of you and me with our staffs."

As Churchill wrote this to Roosevelt, political divisions in Italy, Greece, and Belgium, and the threat of Communist takeovers there also disturbed him. A published State Department communiqué criticizing Britain's interference in these countries' political futures especially angered him. He told Roosevelt that he "was much astonished at the acerbity of the State Department's communiqué" and declared himself "much hurt" by this "public rebuke." An American order not to provide supplies to British forces in Greece enraged the prime minister, who wrote, "It grieves me very much to see signs of our drifting apart at the time when unity becomes even more important as danger recedes and faction arises."

Roosevelt tried to calm Churchill while holding firm to American requirements for a postwar role in overseas affairs. He wrote him, "I deplore any offense which the press release on Italy may have given you personally or any implication of my lack of understanding of your responsibility for your country." He hoped that Churchill would recognize that "while military operations continue, Italy is an area of combined Anglo-American responsibility," and they needed to act in ways that presented a public face that masked any friction between them. He also cautioned Churchill against signing "a possible tripartite Anglo-French-Soviet pact," not only because it would raise France's international profile but also because he was dubious about "the effect of such an arrangement on the question of an international security organization to which, as you know, I attach the very highest importance. I fear that a tripartite pact might be interpreted by public opinion here as a competitor to a future world organization."

Roosevelt then urged Churchill against being too disappointed in the current "war situation as you are . . . because six months ago I was not as optimistic as you were." Yet he hoped Churchill would accept that "our current broad strategy is developing according to plan. . . . Our ground and air forces are day by day chewing up the enemy's dwindling manpower and resources." Although he was unwilling to predict when they would see a "decisive break in our favor," he had every confidence that they were "inflicting losses in excess of the enemy's capability to form new units." And while he was "not at all happy about" the Far Eastern situation, he believed that Japanese losses greatly exceeded "ours and they, too, cannot keep this up." And then, referring to a natural catastrophe that had stricken Japan, he added, "Even the Almighty is helping. This magnificent earthquake and tidal wave is proof."

Finally, he tried to minimize differences with Churchill over Greece. "I have been as deeply concerned as you have yourself in regard to the tragic difficulties you have encountered in Greece. . . . I regard my role in this matter as that of a loyal friend and ally. . . . I am constantly guided by the fact that nothing in any way shake the unity and association between our two countries in the great task to which we have set our hands." He expressed his hope that Churchill could find a way to calm the Greek political scene by promising democratic elections in the not too distant future.

Their shared outlook on Poland, however, gave them renewed grounds for postwar cooperation. "Knowing that we have in mind the same basic objectives in regard to Poland, I want to be sure to coordinate with you any steps which I may contemplate in this matter," Churchill cabled him in December. Like Roosevelt, the prime minister did not consider the Lublin group to be representative of majority Polish opinion, and he endorsed Roosevelt's pressure on Stalin to withhold recognition of it as doing "nothing but good." At the same time, when Roosevelt sympathized with Churchill's management of his Greek problem, Churchill responded, "We seem to be getting into step on both these tangled questions."

As Roosevelt struggled to manage these issues, his health continued to deteriorate. He and those closest to him now feared he might actually be dying. Dr. Bruenn, Roosevelt's cardiologist, "begged Eleanor time and again not to upset her husband" with complaints about State Department appointments of anti-Communist conservatives and advocating for liberal causes. Cabinet members also besieged Roosevelt with demands for attention and their own agendas.

While he had periods of appearing to be his old self, telling stories and charming dinner guests, Daisy and Lucy Mercer Rutherford, who had come back into his life as a friend who shared moments of relaxation with him, worried terribly about his condition and feared he could not last out another term. Roosevelt "himself said it was a 'cardiac' condition and that his muscles are 'deteriorating' and that they [the doctors] don't know why." In December, Daisy recorded in her diary, "The more I see the Pres. the more convinced I am that the *only way he can live* is by having shorter sessions, and repeated rests in between. . . . I am entirely convinced that he cannot keep up the present rate — he will kill himself if he tries." His lowest blood pressure measurement was now 190/98, and when Woodrow Wilson's widow visited him at the White House, she told Frances Perkins that the president's appearance frightened her, as "he looks exactly as my husband looked when he went into his decline."

But Roosevelt was determined to persevere. He fretted over his children's dysfunctional marriages, enjoyed his thirteen grandchildren, who he insisted attend his inauguration, and worried about the country's future economic health. Above all, he was determined to see an end to the war and to forge an enduring peace, or at a minimum a peace that lasted twenty-five or thirty years. His frame of reference was the recent past: Only twenty years had separated the two world wars. His would be a masterful legacy if he succeeded in working in concert with Churchill, Stalin, and Chiang — or even better, a coalition government in China, which seemed a more likely path to a stable Chinese regime — to relieve the world of more bloodshed.

On January 6, Roosevelt gave his twelfth State of the Union address. It was, as he himself said, at fifteen pages and over eight thousand words, "unconscionably long." Because his braces no longer fit him and his health precluded him from standing for over an hour to deliver the speech, he returned to the tradition of sending it to Congress in writing. But eager to put his plans for the future before a larger audience, he presented a shortened version of it over the radio.

His desire to obscure his physical condition by avoiding a personal appearance before Congress was not just an act of vanity by someone who could not bear to think of himself as less than robust. He had spent over twenty years resolved to assure himself and the world that he was not a disabled man whose paralysis limited his reach for extraordinary achievements. He understood that the image of him as in decline would compromise his ability as a leader. His health had by now become so uncertain that he felt a sense of urgency about putting his reform proposals before the country and the world and about promoting public support for U.S. leadership of the postwar world. He told Harold Laski in England, "Our goal is . . . identical for the long range objectives but there are so many new problems arising that I still must remember that the war is yet to be won." He believed that at the upcoming meeting with Churchill and Stalin, he "could put things on a somewhat higher level than they have been for the past two or three months."

In his message, he said that because winning the war was the country's highest priority, it needed to be mindful of "the wedge that the Germans . . . are continually attempting to drive between ourselves and our allies." Rumors of dissent among them were "evil and baseless" and meant to "weaken our faith in our allies" and "to sabotage our war effort. . . . It was right militarily as well as morally to reject the arguments of those shortsighted people who would have had us throw Britain and Russia to the Nazi wolves. . . . In the future we must never forget the lesson that we have learned — that we must have friends who will work with us in peace as they have fought at our side in war." He emphasized the "perfect co-operation and perfect harmony" that existed between Britain and the United States, which of course was not the case, but he wanted Americans to remember that a common danger had united them and now "a common hope" should inform their goal of a peaceful future. He stressed not only that America's enemies had to be compelled to accept an unconditional surrender, but that "the many specific and immediate problems of adjustment connected with" postwar affairs not "delay the establishment of permanent machinery for the maintenance of peace. . . . The aroused conscience of humanity will not permit failure in this supreme endeavor."

He ended his talk by reminding Congress and the country of his commitment to the administration's economic bill of rights, assuring everyone a decent living and the greatest human benefit of all — an enduring peace. The subtext of his message was: Let us not return to our post-1918 behavior, when our isolationism facilitated the rise of fascism, Nazism, and Japanese militarism and helped open the way to World War II. The world has experienced too much suffering for America to turn away now from taking a central part in peacekeeping.

Two weeks later he delivered his inaugural address. Wartime conditions dictated a brief, austere ceremony, but it was Roosevelt's compromised health that necessitated the shortest speech in inaugural history: a five-minute address from the White House south porch, rather than from the Capitol steps, to a notably small audience. Pale and drawn, with trembling hands and a weak voice that his listeners strained to hear, Roosevelt nonetheless believed that the force of his words would resonate around the globe. He said that the war had been a test of the country's resolve. "If we meet that test — successfully and honorably — we shall perform a service of historic importance which men and women and children will honor throughout all time." The objective now was "a just and honorable peace, a durable peace," which would be achieved by recognizing that "we cannot live alone. . . . We must live as men not ostriches, not as dogs in the manger." As he retreated from the arctic cold of a January day into the White House to host a luncheon for two thousand guests, he suffered another angina attack. A half-full tumbler of whiskey, which he drank in one swallow, gave him the wherewithal to make a brief appearance before his admiring guests.

Roosevelt was determined to make one of the first priorities of his new term a Big Three meeting, as he believed it critical to reach an understanding with Stalin. He had few concerns about Churchill's ideas and interests, as he understood that the United Kingdom would no longer stand in the front rank of the world's powers. That mantle had passed to Russia and the United States. As he told Edward Stettinius, the secretary of state who had replaced an ill Cordell Hull in November, Moscow "had the power in Eastern Europe" and would now become the premier force on the Continent. When he met with a bipartisan group of senators in January, Roosevelt rebutted protests against British and Russian actions that promised to reestablish spheres of influence following the war, arguing that they were a reality that the United States lacked the ability to abolish. "The idea kept coming up," he explained, "because the occupying forces had the power in the areas where their arms were present and each knew that the other could not force things to an issue." He stated that the Russians had the hegemony in Eastern Europe, "that it was obviously impossible to have a break with them and that, therefore, the only practicable course was to use what influence we had to ameliorate the situation." Similarly, when Arthur Bliss Lane, a former U.S. Ambassador to Poland, urged him to press Russia to ensure Polish independence, Roosevelt asked: "Do you want me to go to war with Russia?"

Because he did not discount the ultimate significance of military strength in shaping the postwar world, he remained determined to delay in telling Stalin about the atomic bomb. He was certainly aware that well-meaning spies in the Manhattan Project had informed Moscow about U.S. work on developing a super weapon but agreed with Secretary of War Henry Stimson's belief that it was "essential not to take them [the Russians] into our confidence until we were sure to get a real quid pro quo from our frankness."

In gauging the public mood on postwar internationalism, he had become a devoted follower of "scientific" opinion polls, relying on data from Hadley Cantril, a Princeton professor of psychology and director of its Office of Public Opinion Research. The reports Roosevelt received in December and January suggested volatility to domestic sentiments about foreign affairs that made him eager to encourage views of the coming tripartite conference as an exchange of mutual goodwill.

At the end of December, eager to ensure Stalin's presence, Roosevelt had told Churchill that he was willing to meet in the Crimea at Yalta, "which appears to be the best place available in the Black Sea." He intended to leave America very soon after his inauguration and planned to sail to Malta, from where he could fly to the Crimea without straining his health by "reaching any high altitude." Stalin and Churchill promptly concurred, and Churchill promised to "be waiting on the quay" when he reached Malta, adding a bit of doggerel to Roosevelt's amusement: "No more let us falter! From Malta to Yalta! Let nobody alter!" He also suggested that they use the code name ARGONAUT, a reference to the band of heroes in Greek myth who searched for the Golden Fleece on the shores of the Black Sea in the ship *Argo.* Roosevelt welcomed the suggestion and playfully acknowledged to Churchill: "You and I are direct descendants," implying that they were also on a perilous journey reaching for an elusive prize — lasting peace.

While they did not alter, they did falter. Churchill was, in fact, still not pleased at the prospect of having to go to Yalta. He told Harry Hopkins, who had come to London in January, that "if we had spent ten years on research, we could not have found a worse place in the world." At the age of seventy, he struggled with depression and occasional bouts of pneumonia, and said he would bring "an adequate supply" of whiskey to combat the threat of typhus and kill the "lice, which thrive in those parts."

Churchill was less annoyed about the locale of the meeting, however, than by Roosevelt's refusal to stop in Britain on his trip east for a private conference beforehand. Nor would he agree to preliminary talks in Malta, which he feared would persuade Stalin that his western allies were scheming to present a united front or making plans to oppose him. Mindful of Churchill's eagerness for an alliance with the United States against Soviet power, and of Stalin's suspicions of that coalition, Roosevelt's advisers joked that the Russian leader would be sending a cable declaring, "I said Yalta, not Malta." At Malta, Roosevelt did have lunch and dinner with Churchill but shunned any conversation about the issues on the Yalta agenda and showed no inclination to coordinate their plans. Foreign Secretary Anthony Eden complained that it was "impossible even to get near business" and worried to Hopkins "that we were getting into a decisive conference and had so far neither agreed what we would discuss nor how to handle matters with a Bear who would certainly know his mind."

Churchill told his wife that he feared "increasingly that new struggles may arise out of those we are successfully ending." He asked Roosevelt how long he expected the conference to last, stressing, "This may well be a fateful conference, coming at a moment when the great allies are so divided and the shadow of the war lengthens out before us. At the present time I think the end of this war may well prove to be more disappointing than was the last." Although Churchill felt the meeting should last as long as needed to address the many issues before them, Roosevelt believed it should not extend beyond five or six days.

Roosevelt's reluctance to commit himself to a lengthy meeting partly rested on his lack of stamina to sustain discussions over the course of many days. At Malta, his physical condition greatly disturbed his British colleagues. When a Churchill secretary, who had last seen the president in October in Hyde Park, encountered him, his lost weight, "dark circles under his eyes," and obvious frailty gave her the impression that "he is hardly in this world at all." Sir Alexander Cadogan, British permanent undersecretary for foreign affairs, observed, "The President looked old and thin and drawn; he had a cape or shawl over his shoulders and appeared shrunken; he sat looking straight ahead with his mouth open, as if he were not taking things in. Everyone was shocked by his appearance and gabbled about it afterwards." At lunch and dinner with Churchill and his daughter Sarah, however, he managed to muster the familiar charm and humor, so much so that the prime minister wrote his wife that "my friend has arrived in the best of health and spirits."

The final leg of the trip took place on February 3: a seven-hour flight from Malta to Crimea, followed by a close to six-hour car ride to Yalta along eighty miles of "bumpy, slushy roads." At the Saki airfield, where Roosevelt landed, Churchill watched as the president was carried from his plane to a jeep. Churchill saw him as "a tragic figure. You have only to look at the photographs," he recorded later. "He could not get out of the open motor car, and I walked at his side as he inspected the guard." Sarah Churchill thought that Averell Harriman, Roosevelt's ambassador to Moscow, "must be mad to make his poor President endure that endless and very boring drive." But the trip, along roads revealing the systematic destruction the Germans had inflicted on everything in sight, including Yalta, which was "ground to rubble," incensed the president. He told Stalin that what he had seen had made him "more bloodthirsty in regard to the Germans than he had been a year ago."

Roosevelt's companions included his thirty-eight-year-old daughter, Anna; Harry Hopkins, who was ill and weak and lay collapsed on a cot on his flight from Italy to Yalta; Admiral Leahy; "Pa" Watson; General George Marshall; Admiral Ernest King, Stettinius and Harriman; Dr. McIntire and Dr. Bruenn; as well as two political intimates, Jimmy Byrnes, the current director of war mobilization, and Bronx Democratic boss Ed Flynn. Leahy, Watson, Marshall, and King were present as military experts; Stettinius and Harriman were the delegation's foreign affairs counselors; and Byrnes and Flynn provided the sort of companionship that Roosevelt enjoyed. He also liked having Byrnes along as an adviser on economic affairs, and Flynn as a Catholic who would be attentive to matters that might affect the

Church in Soviet-occupied Europe.

Roosevelt was housed in the fifty-room Livadia palace, the czars' summer residence, four miles outside of the city and 150 feet above sea level with a commanding view of the mountains and sea to the east and the north. The gardens and parks surrounding the palace, which held many rare and attractive plants and trees, appealed to Roosevelt's fascination with flora. In his opening remarks at the conference Roosevelt expressed his "deep appreciation for the hospitality and splendid arrangements made by Marshal Stalin . . . for their comfort and convenience." Churchill was housed in a villa some twenty-five minutes' drive away.

The palaces housing the Big Three were "the only buildings left intact" or were the only buildings restored by the Soviets for the conference, as every other house in the city was "a roofless shell." Under Stalin's directive, the Soviets had made heroic efforts to improve the facilities housing the president and prime minister. But an " 'acute shortage of bathrooms and no shortage of bedbugs, which showed a total disregard for rank by biting ministers, butlers, generals, and privates," corroborated concerns about the suitability of Yalta as a meeting site. Its primitive conditions also confirmed impressions of Soviet Russia and its state-run system as hopelessly backward. Alexander Cadogan had nothing but contempt for his hosts: "We tell the Russians everything and play square with them," he said. "They are the most stinking creepy set of Jews I've ever come across." The Soviets reciprocated with their own private expressions of distrust: They suspected their Allies of using the conference as an opportunity to plant agents in the Soviet Union, who would spy on them and foster "provocations and other anti-Soviet manifestations."

The prewar years of hostility between Russia and the West, and the long-standing expressions of anti-Communism in Britain and America, including Republican attacks on Roosevelt as a tool of the Soviets, cast a shadow over the proceedings. Stalin and Molotov, his foreign minister, remained convinced that at heart the British and Americans were anti-Soviet imperialists intent on defeating Communism. The presence alone of the new secretary of state, Stettinius, who had been a corporate executive at General Motors and U.S. Steel, was sufficient to reinforce Stalin's misgivings. In June 1944, Stalin had told Milovan Djilas, the head of the Yugoslav Communist Party, "Perhaps you think that just because we are the allies of the English we have forgotten who they are and who Churchill is. They find nothing sweeter than to trick their allies." He dismissed their rhetoric lauding democracy as a cover for their "criminal intentions."

With Soviet forces less than fifty miles from Berlin and Anglo-American divisions preparing an offensive to cross the Rhine only in March, military actions were the first topic of the conference's opening session on the evening of February 4. "We had the world at our feet," Churchill later recalled. "Twenty-five million men marching at our orders by land and sea. We seemed to be friends."

Out of deference to Roosevelt's disability and the state of his health, Stalin agreed to hold the meetings in the grand ballroom of the Livadia palace. Moreover, he insisted that Roosevelt chair the plenary sessions of the talks. Roosevelt was pleased to take the chair, which was close to a large fireplace and the most comfortable seat in the room. Churchill and Stalin sat facing him at a round table. Roosevelt hoped to use his chairmanship to guide discussion topics, but each leader had a different agenda. For Roosevelt, it was essential to secure Stalin's promise to join the war in the East. His chiefs believed it might take another eighteen months of fighting to defeat Japan, at a cost of thousands of American lives, especially if the Russians did not engage the alleged millionman Japanese army in Manchuria. Roosevelt also sought to win commitments from Stalin and Churchill on Poland and the United Nations. Both issues could play havoc with global postwar relations if public opinion believed that the powers were reverting to traditional sphere-of-influence diplomacy instead of an updated Wilsonian universalism. For Churchill, the conference was an opportunity to advance European security against the revival of German power, which meant Anglo-French dominance of the Continent. Stalin was primarily focused on postwar Soviet security, which he interpreted as a disarmed Germany and a Poland under Russian domination. He was receptive to joining the war against Japan in return for Soviet territorial gains in Asia.

Roosevelt's first goal was to create the closest possible rapport with Stalin. From the president's vantage point, Churchill was already beholden to the United States, but with his commanding military position in Europe, especially across Poland, Stalin was effectively an obstacle to be overcome. When Stalin visited him at Livadia an hour before the initial plenary session, Roosevelt sympathetically expressed his revulsion at the German destruction of so much in the Crimea, and declared his eagerness to support Stalin's Tehran proposal to execute German officers. He also proposed Soviet annexation of German territories and declared reparations to Moscow small compensation for the damage that had been inflicted on the USSR. He further tried to ingratiate himself with Stalin by describing his disagreements with Churchill over strategy on the western front and by criticizing the British as "a peculiar people" who "wished to have their cake and eat it too." He complained about Churchill's pressure on him to restore French power, but voiced his support for a French zone of occupation in Germany. Stalin undoubtedly registered Roosevelt's approach as a less than subtle way of limiting Russia's control of postwar Germany.

If Roosevelt's tactics did not deceive Stalin, he nonetheless had genuine regard for a man who had overcome so much to become a world leader. After their meeting, he said of Roosevelt: "Why did nature have to punish him so? Is he any worse than other people?" Andrei Gromyko was amazed at Stalin's compassion for Roosevelt, as the Russian leader, who was so harsh toward so many, "rarely bestowed his sympathy on anyone from another social system."

At the first plenary session, Roosevelt intentionally arrived ahead of his counterparts, eager to complete the awkward business of being transferred from his wheelchair to his conference seat before the others entered the room or before the cameras began photographing the delegations. But once the talks were under way he said little, sat with his mouth open, and seemed to be "woollier than ever." Churchill attempted to fill the apparent gap, but his theatrical pronouncements had little impact on Stalin, who sat stolidly listening to Churchill's remarks. His calculated "hooded calm" belied the authority that the positions of his several armies gave him and the Soviets. Their advance into Germany had made him a hero with Americans. *Time* magazine honored Stalin with a cover that made him appear to be a benign grandfather. Roosevelt's lack of involvement at this point rested as much on the nature of the initial discussions as on his health, as the focus on military affairs meant that most of the comments from the U.S. side came from General Marshall.

That evening at 8:30 Roosevelt hosted a dinner party for thirteen guests. The general goodwill of the opening plenary meeting did not carry over into the dinner conversation. Stalin refused to toast the British king's health and took exception to Roosevelt's calling him "Uncle Joe," the president's attempt to ease the tensions that developed over Stalin's snub of the Crown. Secretary Byrnes countered by asking: "After all, you do not mind talking about Uncle Sam, so why should Uncle Joe be so bad?" Stalin, who was no more eager to encourage conflict among the Allies than Roosevelt, was pacified. He was genuinely grateful to Churchill for having resisted Hitler when Britain was left to fight alone. Stalin toasted Churchill's courage and especially praised his support of Russia immediately following the Nazi invasion in 1941. Churchill twitted his two colleagues by declaring that he was "the only one dependent from day to day upon the vote of a representative elected on a universal suffrage. They were both dictators." The three then clashed on the postwar status of the small powers. Stalin was adamant about not allowing countries like Albania to dictate to the three victors or play more than a subordinate role in postwar Europe. Roosevelt agreed that small countries should be excluded from postwar arrangements, but Churchill declared, "The eagle should permit the small birds to sing and care not wherefore they sang."

The next day's meeting, which convened at 4 p.m., launched political discussions, which seemed certain to be more contentious than those regarding military planning. Although it was not Roosevelt's highest priority, in deference to Stalin he proposed that they discuss the postwar breakup of Germany. Churchill, who feared the total destruction of German economic production would only give rise to a new round of European instability, as it had after 1918, advised against any hasty action. It was "much too complicated to settle here in five or six days," he said, but would "need prolonged consideration by a special committee." Stalin took exception to Churchill's suggestion, and Roosevelt, sensitive to Soviet qualms, counseled against public discussions of Germany's future as likely to result in "a hundred different plans" and ultimately, immobility. He urged instead that the three foreign secretaries produce a plan of German dismemberment within thirty days. Reluctant to appear an obstructionist, Churchill agreed, which enabled him to press the case for a French zone of occupation. Roosevelt gave Churchill tacit support for a French part in policing Germany, since he doubted that the United States would be able to stay in France for more than two years. At the same time, he sided with Stalin in opposing a French membership in a control commission. The best Churchill could achieve here was agreement to discuss the issue at a later time.

Over the next six days, the Big Three wrestled with the problems of the United Nations, Poland, a declaration on Liberated Europe, and Russian participation in the Asian war.

For Roosevelt, the creation of a United Nations Organization was crucial in overcoming residual isolationist sentiment in America. But fearful of a world body that would be hostile to Communist Russia, Stalin continued to hold firm for sixteen Soviet votes in a General Assembly and veto power in a Security Council with four permanent members — America, Britain, China, and Russia. It was reflected in Stalin's refusal to grant equal status to the small states promised membership in the new world body. (Public unease about great power dominance was captured wryly by the British cartoonist David Low, who depicted a group of children, representing the small states, begging Roosevelt, Stalin, and Churchill to take them into a "Security News Theatre" with the proviso, "No look-in for little ones unless accompanied by grown-ups.") While Stalin was ultimately successful in obtaining the Security Council veto, he agreed to reduce Assembly membership to Russia and only two other Soviet republics. The British, who would have assembly support from Commonwealth countries — Australia, Canada, India, New Zealand, and South Africa — supported this compromise. Apprehending that the agreement would provoke outcries of unfairness to the United States, Roosevelt won agreement from Churchill and Stalin for two additional American votes.

Stalin was not, however, as accommodating on

Poland. When they began discussing its future, Churchill wired his War Cabinet, "We are having a hard time here. Poland will be very difficult." Poland had a particular significance for each of the Big Three. Roosevelt broached the subject at the opening of the third session by stating, "I come here from a great distance and therefore have the advantage of a more distant point of view of the problem." He cited domestic pressures from the six or seven million Poles in the United States who insisted on a settlement ensuring Polish security and independence. To Stalin, this was nothing but American parochialism. For Roosevelt, however, it represented a larger problem: A great power arrangement that dismissed Poland's interests would stir up latent isolationist sentiment and complaints that Europe was resuming its characteristic imperial behavior, from which the United States should remain detached. He affirmed that he was prepared to support territorial adjustments in eastern Poland that benefited Soviet security but also alterations to boundaries in the west that would compensate the Poles with German territory. But the greater challenge was to demonstrate that the Poles were allowed self-determination — a freely elected government that represented the Polish people rather than the imposition of a foreign power primarily focused on its interests. Specifically, Roosevelt opposed installing the Lublin Poles, Stalin's Communist minions, as a representative government in Warsaw. He avoided pointing out their affiliation with Moscow, but he did assert that they represented only "a small portion of the Polish people."

Churchill echoed Roosevelt's concern. Like the president, he was amenable to supporting changes in Poland's borders, but he explained that he "was much more interested in sovereignty and independence of Poland than in the frontier line. . . . Britain had gone to war to protect Poland against German aggression." In so doing it had risked its own survival, so that the issue now was effectively one of honor: His government would never consent to a solution that did not leave Poland a free and independent state. He also felt compelled to put himself on record as believing that the Lublin group represented no more than one-third of the Polish people and would thus not be elected in a free national vote.

After a ten-minute break, during which Stalin gathered his thoughts, he declared Poland a matter of not only Soviet honor but also its security. Poland was the corridor through which adversaries had repeatedly attacked Russia, including Germany, twice in the last thirty years. For Russia, this was a question of "life and death." Border issues needed to be settled not by British and French statesmen, as in the past, but by Russians dedicated to the survival of their country. As for the Polish government, Stalin disputed the Churchill-Roosevelt view of the Lublin Poles, whom he characterized as "good" and much more likely to secure the Red Army's rear than the London Poles, who threatened to provoke a Polish civil war. Mocking his critics and chiding Churchill and Roosevelt, he declared, "They all say I am a dictator but I have enough democratic feeling not to set up a Polish government without Poles." Because unlike the Russians, neither the British nor Americans had representatives in Poland to dispute Stalin's claims about the Lublin Poles' popularity, Stalin could describe himself as the real democrat.

It was an astonishing bit of cynicism that, reinforced by his armed might, inhibited Churchill and Roosevelt from disputing. Roosevelt had in fact confronted this aspect of the Polish dilemma as early as 1943. When a British visitor raised the question of coming conflicts with Moscow over Poland, Roosevelt told him of a conversation he had had with the Polish ambassador to the United States, whom he mimicked. The president described himself as "sick and tired of these people" (the Poles) and related how he asked the ambassador: "Do you expect us and Great Britain to declare war on Joe Stalin if they cross your previous frontier?" Given Russia's growing military strength, he said, "We would just have no say in the matter at all." His attitude was a reflection of Great Power realities and was even more relevant in 1945 following additional Russian battlefield gains.

Poland remained a source of contention for the rest of the conference, raised repeatedly in the subsequent plenary sessions as well as in meetings between the three foreign secretaries. Pressed by Churchill, who feared that the conference would be regarded as a failure if they could not reach agreement on Poland, and repeated by Roosevelt in a letter to Stalin, urging him that they needed to show the American people a united front on Poland, they finally issued a joint statement supporting free elections in which all of Poland's political factions would take part. When Roosevelt insisted that elections had to be "beyond question, like Caesar's wife. . . . They say she was pure." Stalin replied, "They said that about her but she had her sins."

To give greater substance to their pronounce-ment on Polish freedom, Roosevelt persuaded Churchill and Stalin to sign a "Declaration on Liberated Europe," promising the right of self-determination to countries formerly under Nazi control through free and unfettered elections. Poland was to be the first test of the Declaration, Roosevelt explained, but when Leahy saw the final report on Poland, he told Roosevelt, "This is so elastic that the Russians can stretch it all the way from Yalta to Washington without ever technically breaking it." "I know, Bill, I know it," Roosevelt replied. "But it's the best I can do for Poland at this time." Shortly after returning to Washington, he saw Adolf Berle, an assistant secretary of state and a staunch anti-Soviet voice in the administra-tion. When Berle expressed distrust of what the Soviets promised, Roosevelt threw his arms up and said with regard to a speech he had given to Congress on the conference agreements: "Adolf, I didn't say the result was good. I said it was the best I could do."

However sympathetic Roosevelt was to the cause of democratic governments for Poland and all the other European states the Nazis had conquered and occupied, he remained unwilling to risk a break with Stalin and the Soviets before Germa-ny's surrender and Russia's joining the Pacific war. Any such difficulties would put not just the new world organization at risk but also U.S. involvements abroad. For Americans at the time, isolationism was a tradition stretching back to the eighteenth century, and it required a revolution in thinking for the population to abandon an ideal that they had, up until now, seen as precious to their national security.

On the afternoon of February 8, before the fifth session of the conference began, Roosevelt held a private meeting with Stalin. He informed him that a recent U.S. victory in the Philippines opened the way to an invasion of Japan's home islands, but he hoped to avoid this course of action, as he feared it would cost the United States many lives to conquer Japan's four-million-man army. He hoped, but was uncertain, that bombing attacks could make an invasion unnecessary, and reasserted his conviction that Soviet forces could make a decisive difference in speeding an end to the Pacific war. Stalin made it clear that as a price of Soviet involvement, he expected the transfer of the southern half of Sakhalin Island and the Kuriles to the Soviet Union, which would give them Asian naval bases. He also emphasized his desire to have the use of the warm-water port at Darien on the Kwangtung peninsula and of the Manchurian railway lines. He put a democratic face on his demands by explaining that his people would find it difficult to accept joining the war against Japan without these concessions. Roosevelt saw no problem in granting the island properties to the Soviets and expected Chiang Kai-shek to be amenable to establishing international commissions sanctioning Soviet use of the port and the rail lines. He explained that he had no intention of informing Chiang about these secret arrangements at the present as anything told to the Chinese leader would become "known to the whole world within twenty-four hours." Since Stalin readily agreed to encourage a coalition government that would help preserve Chiang's rule, Roosevelt believed that Chiang would readily accept the deal.

As the conference drew to a close, Stalin, who had a sense of triumph about Russia's emerging position in postwar Europe and around the globe, was in a good humor. At the closing dinner, to which he had invited Lavrenti Beria, his head of secret police, Roosevelt asked Stalin, "Who is that with the pince-nez opposite Ambassador Gromyko?" "Ah, that one," Stalin replied. "That's our [Heinrich] Himmler [Hitler's Gestapo chief]. That's Beria." When British ambassador Sir Archibald Clark Kerr, who was quite drunk, stood and toasted Beria, Churchill reprimanded Kerr with a wave of the hand.

Stalin was elated at having won some form of reparations from the Germans and with the agreements over Poland. But the Polish settlement quickly became a source of controversy, with charges of the president's incapacity to pose a strong defense to Stalin's aggressive stance. Roosevelt was, in fact, a dying man in February 1945, as Churchill's physician Lord Moran recorded in a diary at the time: Roosevelt "has all the symptoms of hardening of the arteries of the brain in an advanced stage, so that I give him only a few months to live."

But did his physical state actually have an effect on his dealings with Stalin at Yalta, as critics later asserted? The most judicious assessments by those who witnessed his dealings at the conference thought not: They agreed that "on all the central issues — the United Nations, Germany, Poland, Eastern Europe, and the Far East — Roosevelt largely followed through on earlier plans, and gained most of what he wished: the world body, the division of Germany into four zones, the pronouncement on Polish autonomy, and the

Declaration on Liberated Europe." These arrangements promised to sustain U.S. presence abroad and promote useful diplomatic accommodation with the USSR. "Similarly, Soviet involvement in the Pacific war seemed certain to save American lives" and to preserve Chiang's Nationalist regime. That so much of what Roosevelt hoped to achieve ultimately fell short of realization was not the result of his debilitated health but rather the realities of Soviet power.

On February 10, the last scheduled plenary session, Stalin urged Roosevelt to hold one final meeting to finish the business of the conference. Roosevelt, who was planning to stop in the Middle East to confer with Arab leaders about Jewish migration to Palestine, replied that "he had three kings waiting for him in the Near East, including Ibn Saud" of Saudi Arabia. "The Jewish problem was a very difficult one," Stalin remarked. Mindful of the Soviet leader's abusive treatment of minorities in Russia, Roosevelt said that he was a Zionist and asked Stalin if he was one. Stalin replied that "He was one in principle but he recognized the difficulty."

As Roosevelt departed Yalta on February 12, he wrote Eleanor, "We have wound up the conference — successfully I think and this is just a line to tell you that we are off for the Suez Canal and then home. . . . I am a bit exhausted but really all right." The worldwide response to the results of the summit was exhilaration at what was described as "a landmark in history," surpassing "most of the high hopes placed on this fateful meeting." Roosevelt himself told Eleanor, "Look at the communiqué from the Crimea, the path it charts. . . . It's been a global war, and we've already started making it a global peace." Hopkins said later, "We really believe in our hearts that this was the dawn of the new day we had all been praying for."

In Egypt Roosevelt boarded the cruiser USS *Quincy,* anchored in the Great Bitter Lake, part of the Suez Canal. He dressed in a long black cape to give him a royal air commensurate with that of the three Middle Eastern monarchs — Farouk of Egypt, Haile Selassie of Ethiopia, and Ibn Saud of Saudi Arabia — and discussed economic and territorial matters of concern to each of them. When he raised the issue of Palestine with Saud, making the case for Jewish migration to the British possession and emphasizing that so small a number of Jews would present no threat to the populous Arab countries, he met with great resistance. He told Eleanor that "his one complete failure" on the trip was with Ibn Saud, but added that he had had "a fantastic week" meeting with these leaders. He acknowledged that he was still quite tired and hoped to get more sleep on his way home.

While he had to prepare a report to Congress and the country on Yalta, he hoped that the nine-day sea voyage back to the United States would provide a period of relaxation and rest that might improve his health and restore some of his energy. But unexpected events made that impossible. Harry Hopkins had intended to cross the Atlantic with him to help draft his speech, bit was so ill that he decided to fly home, angering Roosevelt, who felt abandoned. When sixty-one-year-old Pa Watson, Roosevelt's appointments secretary, who was a year younger than him, suffered a cerebral hemorrhage and died on February 20 during the crossing, it deepened Roosevelt's sense of loss and greatly disheartened him — no doubt reminding him of his own mortality.

On March 1, two days after he returned to Washington, he appeared before a joint congressional session to make the case for the resolutions of the conference. The senators and congressmen crowding the House chamber greeted him with a standing ovation. He began his speech by explaining, "I hope that you will pardon me for this unusual posture of sitting down during the presentation of what I want to say, but I know that you will realize that it makes it a lot easier for me not to have to carry about ten pounds of steel around on the bottom of my legs; and also because of the fact that I have just completed a fourteen-thousand-mile trip." It was the only time in his twelve years as president that he ever made public reference to his disability. What he didn't mention was that his loss of over thirty pounds in the past year, dropping from a weight of 188 to 150, and the discomfort of his leg braces made standing an agony. While delivering his address, he spoke haltingly, slurred some of his words, and stumbled over the text. His right hand trembled so badly that he had to awkwardly turn the pages of his text with his left hand.

But what he related to his audience registered as forcefully as his weakened condition. He stressed that the outcome of the meeting, which he said had resulted in agreements promoting lasting peace, now depended on whether Congress and the country would support it. He asserted that shared commitments on how to end the war, control postwar Germany, establish a world peacekeeping organization, and assure autonomy for Poland were landmark achievements. "Never before have the major Allies been more closely united," he proclaimed "— not only in their war aims but also in their peace aims — . . . so that the ideal of lasting peace will become a reality." He elaborated on each of these goals, which would commence with Germany's unconditional surrender and a meeting in San Francisco on April 25 to establish a new international security organization. But the main point of his speech was to persuade a majority of Americans as well as their representatives that "responsibility for political conditions thousands of miles away can no longer be avoided by this great Nation." In short, America must now assume its role as a permanent member of the world community opposing aggression and promoting an international rule of law. It was a landmark achievement that, like the New Deal, made Roosevelt feel as if he had indeed been the prophet of a new order.

He concluded his address by affirming that the Crimean conference represented "a turning point in history — I hope in our history and in the history of the world." If America were to shun international collaboration in the future, it would share responsibility for the occurrence of another world war. The attempt at Yalta to establish common ground for world peace, he said, "ought to spell the end of the system of unilateral action, the exclusive alliances, the spheres of influence, the balances of power, and all the other expedients that have been tried for centuries — and have always failed." The speech was ultimately a compelling appeal for a new world arrangement, one in which the United States would take a leading part.

As Roosevelt suffered a decline of his health over the next six weeks, events undermined his hopes for a new era in international relations, as disagreements soon arose about all three key Yalta agreements. In March, when the ranking German SS officer in Italy began negotiations of surrender in Switzerland with Allen Dulles, the head of OSS operations there, the Soviets demanded to take part in the process. But convictions by American and British officers that the Soviets would make "embarrassing demands" that would extend the discussions from four hours to four months led them to refuse to include Russian military representatives in the talks. It angered Stalin and only confirmed his long-held fears that the Allies would come to terms over something less than an unconditional surrender that would favor them over the Soviets. On March 24, Roosevelt sent him an appeasing cable, assuring him that no skullduggery was involved in the exploratory contacts. Stalin was not convinced and responded that the Germans were using these talks as an opportunity to shift divisions to the eastern front and create "grounds for mistrust" between the Allies.

On March 31, Roosevelt replied in turn that these exchanges were creating "an atmosphere of regrettable apprehension." Surrender discussions quickly collapsed, and no German divisions were being transferred to the East. But Stalin refused to yield, insisting that he had been misinformed about negotiations, and that not only had they taken place but they also included an agreement with the Germans exchanging easier peace terms for allowing the advance of Anglo-American forces to the East in order to limit the Soviet occupation of Germany. Roosevelt expressed "astonishment" at Stalin's accusations and protested that his misinformation must have come from German sources, which aimed "to create dissension between us." He expressed "bitter resentment toward your informers . . . for such vile misrepresentations." Stalin denied that his informants were misleading him, describing them as "very honest and modest people who carry out their duties accurately."

Stalin responded to these imagined offenses by deciding to send Ambassador Gromyko instead of Foreign Minister Molotov to the U.N.'s inaugural conference in San Francisco. On March 24, when Gromyko informed the State Department that he would head the Russian delegation, Roosevelt promptly cabled Stalin reminding him that most of the participating countries would send their foreign ministers to the meeting and that Molotov's "absence will be construed all over the world as a lack of comparable interest on the part of the Soviet Government in the great objectives of this conference." Stalin, unmoved, told Roosevelt that Molotov was obliged to attend a meeting of the Supreme Soviet and that Gromyko would be a worthy substitute. Roosevelt then chided him for not appreciating the importance of public opinion in U.S. foreign policy. Stalin's refusal to send Molotov to San Francisco "made me wonder," he wrote the Russian leader, "whether you give full weight to this factor." For Roosevelt, the founding of the United Nations actually had more symbolic than substantive importance. He did not know if it could function as a genuine peacekeeping body, but he understood that a majority of Americans believed it could do so, and their conviction made all the difference in convincing them to abandon their isolationism.

Where their disputes about surrender negotiations and the San Francisco meeting were largely kept private, their public disagreements regarding Poland bred antagonism toward Moscow. In mid-March, Roosevelt complained that "Poland seems to be acting up again — or, more accurately, the Russian Foreign office." He was annoyed that the Soviets were also insisting on sending representatives of the Lublin government to represent Poland in San Francisco. The question of the government of Poland had become a concern earlier in the month when Churchill cabled him: "There are many stories put about of wholesale deportations by the Russians and of liquidations by the Lublin Poles of elements they do not like." Churchill foresaw a grave turnabout in British public opinion once it was realized that Moscow was installing a totalitarian regime in Poland. Churchill urged Roosevelt to challenge Stalin directly on his apparent failure to honor the Yalta Declaration on Liberated Europe.

While Roosevelt was in full agreement with Churchill about supporting democratic arrangements for Poland, he had been reluctant to press the case too forcefully with Stalin himself for fear that it would affect postwar Soviet-American cooperation. By the end of March, however, Roosevelt believed it essential that he confront him on the matter: "I cannot conceal from you the concern with which I view the development of events of mutual interest since our fruitful meeting at Yalta." The decisions they reached there had been received with enthusiasm around the world, and "We have no right to let them be disappointed." Americans viewed events in Poland as revealing the Yalta agreement to be "a fraud" (a term Roosevelt softened in his final draft to "having failed"). He ended by saying, "I wish I could convey to you how important it is for the successful development of our program of international collaboration that this Polish question be settled fairly and speedily."

On April 5, Churchill urged Roosevelt to join him in making "a firm and blunt stand" to make clear that "there is a point beyond which we will not tolerate insult." It was "the best chance of saving the future. If they are ever convinced that we are afraid of them and can be bullied into submission, then indeed I should despair of our future relations with them and much else." Roosevelt agreed: "We must not permit anybody to entertain a false impression that we are afraid. Our Armies will in a few days be in a position that will permit us to become 'tougher' than has heretofore appeared advantageous to the war effort."

Nonetheless, Roosevelt remained reluctant to force a crisis with Stalin. When Stalin told Churchill that "neither I nor Molotov had any intention of 'blackening' anyone," that he was opposed to "any possibility of sowing discord between us," and offered assurances that "I had and have no intention of offending anyone," Roosevelt took his message at face value. On April 11 he wrote Stalin: "The Bern [Switzerland] incident . . . appears to have faded into the past without having accomplished any useful purpose. There must not, in any event, be mutual mistrust and minor misunderstandings of this character should not rise in the future. I feel sure that when our armies make contact in Germany and join in a fully coordinated offensive the Nazi armies will disintegrate." To Churchill, he wrote, "I would minimize the general Soviet problem as much as possible because these problems, in one form or another, seem to arise every day and most of them straighten out as in the case of the Bern meeting. We must be firm, however, and our course thus far is correct."

During this period of strain with Moscow, Roosevelt's health was swiftly declining and he struggled to keep abreast of events. By now Leahy was drafting most of Roosevelt's correspondence, which he then signed off on. But on March 30, William D. Hassett, Roosevelt's secretary, recorded in a diary: "He [the President] is slipping away and no earthly power can keep him here . . . To all the staff, to the family and with the Boss himself I have maintained the bluff, but I am convinced that there is no help for him." On March 24, Roosevelt agreed to spend a few days in Hyde Park, where Daisy saw him. "The President looks terribly badly," she recorded, "— so tired that every word seems to be an effort. He just can't stand this strain indefinitely." She was relieved to know that he planned a trip to Warm Springs for a rest.

When he got on the train for Georgia on March 29, he "looked completely exhausted." And though he seemed "really ill — thin & worn," he was "joking & laughing & carrying on the conversation as usual." Daisy urged Dr. Bruenn to press him to rest more and take care of himself if he were to realize his "one really great wish . . . to get this international organization for peace." Despite Roosevelt's effort to put the best possible face on his condition, Daisy found him "depressed, both physically and mentally." He himself expressed doubts about how much longer he could carry the burdens of office, telling her "that he thinks he can retire by next year, after he gets the peace organization well started." In the meantime, he wanted the postmaster general to issue a three-cent stamp with the engraving: "April 25, 1945: Towards United Nations." It would tell "[the] country what the San Francisco Conference is all about!"

During his stay in Warm Springs he seemed to have become aware of the seriousness of his condition. At times, in Daisy's words, he "relapsed into babyhood." At night, before going to sleep, he would "put on his little act of helplessness" so that Daisy would feed him like a baby. "He lay on his back, & began to pull the covers up to his chin — shivering & saying he felt so cold. A moment before he had been sitting up reading a detective story, so I knew it was another 'act' to get himself fed. On paper it sounds too silly for words and it is silly — but he's very funny and laughs at himself."

On April 12 he awoke and complained of a slight headache. Dr. Bruenn massaged his neck, which seemed to provide some relief. At one in the afternoon, while he sat in a chair accompanied by Daisy, Laura Delano, another cousin, Lucy Mercer Rutherford, and the portrait artist Elizabeth Shoumatoff, who was making sketches for a painting, he put his left hand behind his head and said, "I have a terrific pain in the back of my head" and then, slumping in his chair, fell into unconsciousness. With the help of the president's butler and another aide, they carried him into his bedroom. Dr. Bruenn arrived within fifteen minutes and began trying unsuccessfully to resuscitate him. At 3:35 p.m., with Bruenn and another physician summoned from Atlanta in attendance, they pronounced him dead.

When Eleanor received a call in Washington informing her that Franklin had fainted, she feared the worst, and when Press Secretary Steve Early called her away from a charitable event she was attending in the afternoon, she knew that "something dreadful had happened." At the White House, Early and Dr. McIntire told her, "The President had slipped away. She was silent for a minute and then said: 'I am more sorry for the people of this country and of the world than I am for ourselves.' " When Vice President Harry Truman, summoned from a pre-dinner drink on Capitol Hill with House Speaker Sam Rayburn, arrived at the White House, she put her arm on his shoulder and said: "Harry, the President is dead." After a few moments, as he recovered from the shock of realizing that he was now the president, he asked: "Is there anything I can do for you?" She replied: "Is there anything *we* can do for you? For you are the one in trouble now." It spoke volumes about the decency of both of them.

When the news reached Churchill, he said: "I felt as if I had been struck a physical blow. My relations with this shining personality had played a large part in the long, terrible years we had worked together. Now they had come to an end, and I was overpowered by a sense of deep and irreparable loss." Churchill once again recalled the moment when he first met President Roosevelt. He said it was like uncorking your first bottle of champagne.

Ambassador Averell Harriman brought the news to Stalin in the early morning of April 13. The

Soviet dictator stood holding Harriman's hand for nearly thirty seconds before asking him about the circumstances of the president's death. He wanted to know if Roosevelt had been poisoned.

Senator Robert Taft of Ohio, a tough-minded Republican critic, reflected the sense of loss that now engulfed the nation when he observed: "The President's death removed the greatest figure of our time . . . and shocks the world to which his words and actions were more important than those of any other man." And the *New York Times,* no uncritical voice of Roosevelt and his administration, declared in a rare display of sentiment: "Men will thank God on their knees a hundred years from now, that Franklin D. Roosevelt was in the White House."

The president's remains were transported by train from Warm Springs to Washington, where his body lay in state at the White House, and then on to Hyde Park for final burial in the garden of his library. In the outpouring of national mourning thousands of people stood along the railway tracks and crowded stations to catch a glimpse of the funeral train. Anna, his beloved daughter, sat up all night as the train traveled from Washington to Hyde Park and "watched the people who had come to see the train pass by. There were little children, fathers, grandparents." He was the people's president, and their silent tribute to his passing was the greatest accolade that could be given to him.

EPILOGUE

Seventy-two years after Franklin Roosevelt passed away in the thirteenth year of his presidency, his reputation as a great president is secure. In 1940, Robert Jackson, Roosevelt's attorney general, said: "FDR had wrought great changes, culminating . . . in fundamental governmental powers that never existed before: the ability 'to govern the powerful, [and] protect the weak.' " Samuel Rosenman, Roosevelt's White House counsel and speechwriter, observed that Roosevelt "left a mark upon the post-war world which has not been erased, and never will be. He was not only a pre-war President, and later a war President; he was also, in a very real and practical sense, a post-war President."

His hold on the public and historians, as well, as one of the country's three greatest presidents is based in significant part on his courage and power to inspire Americans during such perilous times as the 1930s and 1940s. The amazing story of a man so severely handicapped by polio who overcame his disability to take on the arduous tasks of running for president four times and mobilizing the country to struggle through the Depression and war is a saga that has become the stuff of legend. That legend is on a par with those of Washington and Lincoln, who, respectively, launched what Churchill later called the Great Republic and saved it from disunion. All three inspired their countrymen to lay down their lives and expend national treasure in the service of the nation. All three had their flaws, which their critics did not hesitate to enumerate. Acknowledging their own limitations and understanding that they governed not by some divine right but by the will of the people, they left legacies that permanently resonate through American history.

Roosevelt's thirteen successors in the presidency — six Democrats and now seven Republicans — have displayed various degrees of competence and at times even brilliance, but none has had what one journalist called Roosevelt's "touch of genius." Like his most effective immediate predecessors, TR and Wilson, Roosevelt had an uncanny sense of the country's shifting national mood and a talent for articulating it in the most perilous of times — depression and war. Even with the Twenty-Second Amendment to the Constitution's barring anyone from serving more than two terms, it is inconceivable that any of his successors could have won four.

Without the outbreak of the war, it is more than likely that Roosevelt would have been in office for the conventional eight years. But even accounting for the war, commanding sufficient public support to win four presidential elections, especially in light of the forceful complaints about the administration's honesty and policies, was a most impressive political feat. In 1939, the seventh year of the New Deal, unemployment still stood at ten million workers. When Eleanor Roosevelt toured the states that fall, she "was disheartened to see, first-hand, how economically depressed parts of the country remained. The New Deal had achieved much in housing, employment and hope, but . . . its failure and limitations were [also] apparent."

Roosevelt's New Deal reforms — Social Security, the Tennessee Valley Authority, the Securities and Exchange Commission, the Federal Deposit Insurance Corporation, unemployment insurance, the National Labor Relations Board, the legitimization of labor unions, the Rural Electrification Administration, the many dams and other conservation projects, and the Fair Labor Standards Act, which provided for minimum wages and maximum hours, to cite just some of the most memorable domestic programs — were giant steps in humanizing the American industrial system. No economist disputes the argument that it was not the New Deal that ended the Depression, but rather the industrial mobilization required for the war that restored the economy and ended national unemployment. But in the long pull of history, the creation of a welfare state ensuring a minimal standard of living for all Americans endures more meaningfully than any episodic shift in the economy. Even in its failure to decisively end the Depression, however, the Roosevelt administration taught us that Keynesian prescriptions for deficit spending have served to avert another economic collapse.

Roosevelt's New Deal not only aimed to restore prosperity, but also to bring all the country's citizens into the mainstream of its governance. Under Roosevelt, a new inclusiveness replaced the social tensions of the 1920s between modernists and fundamentalists, and the antagonism toward recently arrived immigrants, which deepened with the National Origins Act of 1924 and its limits on immigration. In the 1930s and 1940s, the millions of immigrants from Ireland and southern and Eastern Europe who arrived in America between 1870 and 1920 no longer felt like residents in an alien land. Roosevelt's administration was notable for its appointment of representatives of the Irish, Italians, Slavs, Catholics, and Jews, who gave their various ethnic and religious groups a new sense of national belonging. When Roosevelt named Joseph Kennedy the ambassador to Great Britain in 1938, for example, it was a signal event in his determination to secure the support of all recent Americans for his New Deal coalition and for the advancement of national unity.

In foreign affairs as well, Roosevelt presided over an enduring national transformation. He had felt compelled to endorse isolationist convictions by signing the neutrality statutes of the 1930s, as his assumption that any foreign policy action that threatened to cost the country blood and resources had to rest on a stable national consensus. Even with the outbreak of war in 1939, his gradual efforts to advance a realistic assessment of the country's national security interests required a careful management of domestic opposition to expanded U.S. participation in international affairs. During World War II, mindful of the need for widespread support for a large international role for the United States after the conflict, Roosevelt encouraged hopes that the wartime allies — Britain, China, Soviet Russia, and the United States — would cooperate in assuring the postwar peace, including the fulfillment of Woodrow Wilson's dream of collective security through a global organization, the United Nations. His private doubts about prospects for Soviet cooperation and a great power role for China were reflected in his determination to delay the revelation of the atom bomb to Stalin and his fears of civil strife between Chiang Kai-shek's Nationalists and Mao Tse-tung's Communists following Japan's defeat.

It was inevitable that a president who won four elections would become the subject of retrospective criticism. No president, however long he has held office, has escaped the judgment of history. The challenges facing every occupant of the White House have been met with complaints and disputes about their performance in response to them. As the Dutch historian Pieter Geyl said, "History is argument without end." Roosevelt's effectiveness as our longest-serving president has never shielded him from controversy — in and out of office. The enduring economic dislocations at home and the disastrous conflicts abroad invited recriminations about Roosevelt's management of both domestic and foreign affairs.

Although efforts to repeal or alter his landmark achievements like TVA and Social Security have fallen short and there are no longer significant attempts to do away with these reforms, the rise of the welfare state continues to be a central controversy in American politics. Every presidential election brings renewed disputes about the virtues of federal programs tracing from the New Deal through Harry Truman's Fair Deal, John Kennedy's New Frontier, Lyndon Johnson's War on Poverty and Great Society, and more recently Barack Obama's Affordable Care Act.

While calls for reducing and eliminating federal

programs are a constant refrain in the country's political discourse, even Ronald Reagan, the most popular of our post-Roosevelt conservative presidents, failed to eliminate such welfare programs as food stamps and agencies like the Department of Education. Other conservatives, like Dwight Eisenhower and Richard Nixon, added to Roosevelt's legacy by introducing the departments of Health, Education, and Welfare and Environmental Protection. Roosevelt would have been the first to acknowledge that social engineering was and is an inexact enterprise. But in the more complex world of the twentieth and twenty-first centuries, states and their localities alone cannot ensure the well-being of the many Americans who depend on government assistance to deal with the uncertainties of economic life and aging. Despite the enduring debate over the proper place of government in people's lives, the Roosevelt legacy guarantees that federal authority will continue to play some significant part in offsetting the perils facing all of America's citizens.

The fierce debates of the 1930s over America's role in the world have likewise continued to be a divisive issue in the decades since. However, once popular assertions about the causes of Pearl Harbor, Roosevelt's deceit in bringing the country into the war, and his unrealistic view of Stalin and the Soviets, especially at Yalta, where his health problems allegedly left him vulnerable to Moscow and supposedly compelled him to concede Eastern Europe to its control, have largely faded away with America's victory in the Cold War. Likewise, critiques that Roosevelt's policies resulted in Communist control of China have also subsided since the rapprochement with Beijing. George

Kennan, the most thoughtful of our twentieth-century diplomats, believed that postwar Communist advances in Europe and Asia were the price we paid for Soviet efforts in vanquishing the Nazi war machine and for our wartime dependence on Chiang Kai-shek's corrupt and unpopular regime. These issues no longer shadow Roosevelt's reputation as a great leader, and certainly not among serious historians.

But criticism persists about a number of Roosevelt's policies at home and abroad: his failure to support antilynching laws for fear of losing Southern congressional support for his New Deal programs; his internment of 120,000 Americans of Japanese ancestry; and the Roosevelt administration's timid response to Hitler's persecution of Germany's and all of Europe's Jews.

Roosevelt rationalized his alliance with Southern segregationists by citing the movement of Negro voters to the Democrats, whose New Deal programs benefited millions of them. Still, his presidency is not notable for the advancement of civil rights, which would have to wait until the judicial and congressional actions of the 1950s and 1960s, and especially the leadership of Lyndon B. Johnson. During the 1930s and 1940s, when blacks trying to exercise their constitutional right to the ballot box were beaten or even lynched, Roosevelt remained silent, and his Justice Department effectively went through the motions of conducting investigations without producing meaningful results. Although Eleanor Roosevelt pressured him to promote equality for black Americans, he remained "as mum as the Sphinx." However, under pressure from Eleanor, who told him that black exclusion from the armed services and defense jobs was "very bad politically besides being intrinsically wrong," and from other advocates of black rights on the eve of the 1940 election, Roosevelt announced his determination to integrate the military "to ensure that Negroes are given fair treatment on a non-discriminatory basis." It was a small step forward in the long fight to end racial discrimination and fulfill the Constitution's commitment to American democracy.

Roosevelt's placement of Japanese Americans in what he himself called "concentration camps" was characterized after the war by the American Civil Liberties Union as the greatest breach of civil liberties in American history. Mindful of the anger of Americans in the wake of the Pearl Harbor attack, Roosevelt set aside his reservations about this violation of the Constitution. Allowing Japanese Americans to volunteer for military service, where they served with great distinction in the battles to defeat German forces in Italy, could not redress the balance in the abuse of their rights. Recent proposals to round up American Muslims have recalled the injustice visited on Americans of Japanese descent decades ago and Roosevelt's expediency in the matter.

No issue in Roosevelt's legacy remains as contested as his response to the Holocaust: Hitler's annihilation of six million Jews. As Blanche Wiesen Cook wrote in the third volume of her splendid Eleanor Roosevelt biography, "Debates over FDR's 'indifference' to the Jewish slaughter will surely continue. Those who argue that FDR did 'everything possible' are contradicted by ER's assertion that nobody did all they could have. . . . 'We let our consciences realize too late the need of standing up against something that we knew was wrong.' " In 2003, when Cook asked Arthur Schlesinger, Jr., Roosevelt biographer and John Kennedy White House adviser, "How can you argue that FDR did everything 'possible' to rescue and save the perishing?" Schlesinger responded by pointing to the realities of American politics of the era, in which anti-Semitism was prevalent. "Look at the numbers," he said. "Thirty percent of the U.S. population was German-American; the Democratic Party was Irish, Italian, and Southern. There was no congressional support to save the Jews, no movement to save them, and intense division among Jewish leaders — many of whom remained silent throughout. Silence. Denial. Complicity."

While Schlesinger makes a compelling case for Roosevelt's reluctance to risk political capital in what appeared to be an unwinnable battle, the moral question of his failure to do everything possible in the face of such an unprecedented and heinous crime cannot be brushed aside with a justification of the realities of political circumstances. If bombing the railway lines into Auschwitz, as many have suggested, might not have stopped the slaughter, it would at least be remembered as a genuine attempt to achieve a worthy end.

Roosevelt's caution in dealing with crosscurrents regarding allowing greater numbers of Hitler's persecuted peoples into the United States also raises questions about his political courage when faced with a potentially unpopular policy. When he put Breckinridge Long in charge of issuing visas to desperate victims of Nazi persecution, he tacitly closed off avenues of escape for many who perished in Hitler's concentration camps.

Under the National Origins Act, Long's resistance to facilitating the legal migration to America of roughly 125,000 additional victims of Hitler's madness remains an ugly mark on Roosevelt's presidency. Only after Henry Morgenthau confronted him in the 1944 election with the political consequences of keeping Long at his post — the potential loss of Jewish votes in New York and defeat in a state crucial to his reelection — did Roosevelt remove him and agree to set up the War Refugee Board, which rescued some Jews in Romania, France, and Hungary.

Yet even with these failings, Roosevelt's stature as one of the country's greatest and most respected leaders cannot be denied. He offered the best judgment of his own achievements in comments he made in his 1936 acceptance address at the Democratic convention. "Governments can err, Presidents do make mistakes, but the immortal Dante tells us that divine justice weighs the sins of the cold-blooded and the sins of the warm-hearted in different scales. Better the occasional faults of a Government that lives in a spirit of charity than the consistent omissions of a Government frozen in the ice of its own indifference."

It remains a guidepost, as Roosevelt himself does, for every administration and every president who takes up the responsibility of leading our democratic Republic.

ACKNOWLEDGMENTS

The inspiration for this book came from Rick Kot and Wendy Wolf at Viking, who suggested me when Susan Petersen Kennedy, then-President of the Penguin Group, proposed that a historian take a fresh look at Franklin Roosevelt's life and times in a single volume. Stuart Proffitt at Penguin Random House UK also signed on to the idea. I am grateful to all of them for asking me to write the book. Rick Kot has been especially involved every step of the way. His line-by-line editing of the manuscript has made this a more readable and considered study of Roosevelt the man and his extraordinary contributions to America's domestic and foreign affairs.

The book largely rests on the extraordinary publication of first-rate edited and written works about Franklin Roosevelt. The earlier studies on, and compilations of, FDR records that proved most helpful to me are by Conrad Black, John Morton Blum, Alan Brinkley, James MacGregor Burns, Kenneth S. Davis, Frank Freidel, Saul Friedlander, Martin Gilbert, Doris Kearns Goodwin, Harold L. Ickes, Fred L. Israel, David M. Kennedy, Warren Kimball, Ian Kershaw, William E. Leuchtenburg, Elliott Roosevelt, Samuel I.

Rosenman, Arthur M. Schlesinger, Jr. and Geoffrey C. Ward, as well as Joseph P. Lash and Blanche Wiesen Cook on Eleanor Roosevelt.

Several people read parts of or the entire manuscript. First and foremost was Rick Kot. Dick Moe, the prize-winning director of the National Trust for Historic Preservation for sixteen years and an expert on FDR and his presidency, favored me with a close reading of the manuscript that made a significant difference in the accuracy of what I wrote. Geri Dallek gave the book a thorough reading and once again constantly reminded me of the need to engage a general audience with arresting details and pen portraits that bring the main characters of the Roosevelt era to life. Peter Kovler, the principal advocate and supporter of building the FDR memorial park, encouraged my decision to remind people of Roosevelt's impressive achievements. He also read part of the manuscript and offered helpful suggestions. I am also indebted to Kai Bird, who read the opening chapters, and John W. Wright, my agent, for wise counsel. As usual, he provided the friendship and support that has served all my projects over the last twenty-five years. I am also once again indebted to Dr. Jeffrey Kelman, who counseled me on the medical issues shaping Roosevelt's battle with polio and especially heart disease in the last five years of his life.

I am grateful to the talented production team at Viking/Penguin for their close work publishing the book, particularly Diego Núñez, who skillfully worked on the endnotes and oversaw the work of turning the manuscript into a printed book; Christina Caruccio, whose copyediting saved me from numerous errors; and Alison Klooster, who worked so hard to promote the book.

NOTES

Prologue: Everything to Fear

"you may need": For the quotes, see Leuchtenburg, *Hoover,* 144–6; *New York Times,* January 1, 1933; Kennan, *Kennan Diaries,* 83; Kennedy, 131; Levine, 208; Katznelson, 30–1; Davis, *New York Years,* 446; Schlesinger, *Crisis of the Old Order,* 4–5.

successful presidential term: Farley, *Behind the Ballots,* 208–9.

sense of desperation: Schlesinger, *Crisis of the Old Order,* 3, 155–7, 248–51; Amadeo, "US GDP by Year"; Kennedy, xiv, 65–9; Leuchtenburg, *Roosevelt,* 1–3, 18–19.

a failing economy: Rosenman, *Public Papers, 1933,* March 4, 1933; Schlesinger, *Crisis of the Old Order,* 244–6.

on the nation: Rosenman, *Public Papers, 1933,* March 4, 1933.

work and prosperity: Schlesinger, 252; Kennedy, 89.

indolence and quick-rich schemes: My analysis rests on Levine's penetrating discussion of popular culture at the start of the Depression, 209–21.

along with the economic crisis: The Dos Passos quote is in Hofstadter, *American Political Tradition,* xxxiii.

the country's "great cities": Hofstadter, *Age of Reform,* 174–84, 287–91, 295–9; Gusfield; Levine, 193–5, 199–200; Kennedy, 13–6.

darkest days of the Depression: Hofstadter, *Age of Reform,* 291–5; Levine, 196–9; Kennedy, 19–20.

"throughout the decade": Levine, 200–5.

"played in human affairs": Steel, 327.

"now of foreign affairs": Dingman; Kennedy, 93–4; Leuchtenburg, *Hoover,* 122–5.

a compelling argument: *New York Times,* January 7, 1933.

"more courage" than electoral systems: Steel, 279, 299–300.

"amiable boy scout": Posner, xiv–xv; Steel, 291–2.

Chapter 1: The Making of a Patrician

"believed to be so": Jay, 364.

America's other leaders: Ibid., 363.

study at Hyde Park: Davis, *Beckoning of Destiny,* chapter 1, esp. 27, 36–9, 76; Smith, *FDR,* 3–5, 10–16; Roosevelt, *Personal Letters,* II: 1224; Roosevelt, "History of the President's Estate," in the Franklin D. Roosevelt Library [FDRL]; Freedman, 655–6.

apparent to Franklin: Davis, *Beckoning of Destiny,* 46–9, 56–7, 70–4; Smith, *FDR,* 17–23; Roosevelt's Recollections, n.d., in the FDRL.

other boys his age: Davis, *Beckoning of Destiny,* chapter 2, and 73–8; Smith, *FDR,* 22–6; Roosevelt to the Robbinses, May 30, 1891, in Roosevelt, *Personal Letters,* I: 35. His father's "invincible sense": Davis, 16.

"too slight for success": Davis, *Beckoning of Destiny,* 117–9, 125, 128.

lacking "school spirit": Smith, *FDR,* 26–8; Davis, *Beckoning of Destiny,* 101–4, 109–11; Roosevelt to his parents, October 1, 1896, and May 15, 1897, in Roosevelt, *Personal Letters,* I. Also see 33, 42, 100 of that work.

people he wished to control: Roosevelt, *Personal Letters,* I: 130–1, 34.

"masters and boys alike": Ibid., 253–4, 34.

"whole school cheered": Ibid., 110, 226, 230, 379.

"perpetually growing larger": Peabody's quote is in Davis, 130.

ethnic political bosses: Smith, *FDR,* 28–9; Davis, *Beckoning of Destiny,* 129–30.

and constitutional government: Smith, *FDR,* 30; Roosevelt, *Personal Letters,* I: 423–5.

gloomy holiday season: Roosevelt, *Personal Letters,* I: 425–38; Davis, 143–7.

through the Norwegian fjords: Roosevelt, *Personal Letters,* I: 438–58.

ended his memorable visit: Ibid., 459–68, especially 467–8; Davis, *Beckoning of Destiny,* 149–53.

part of his life's work: Davis, *Beckoning of Destiny,* 150, 153; Roosevelt, *Personal Letters,* I: 434–6, 486–502.

most elite of the elite: Davis, *Beckoning of Destiny,* 152, 155–6; Schlesinger, *Crisis of the Old Order,* 322–3; Brands, 24.

place of rememberance: Davis, *Beckoning of Destiny,* 155–7.

friends and subordinates: Ibid., 157–64.

world under their command: The photos are in Roosevelt, *Personal Letters,* I, between 480 and 481.

"Mais elle n'est pas gaie": Lash, chapters 1–8, especially 33, 46, 74, 84, 86, 87.

like her late husband: Ibid., chapter 10, especially 84, 105, 107.

"be absolutely happy": Ibid., 105, 109.

"this golden loop": Ibid., 109–13, and 162 for James's quote; Smith, *FDR,* 47, 56.

notice of the assembled party: Lash, 136–41; Davis, *Beckoning of Destiny,* 191–3.

at least not yet: Roosevelt, *Personal Letters,* I: 73; Lash, 145–6; Davis, *Beckoning of Destiny,* 191, 194.

fostered by their kinsman: Roosevelt, *Personal Letters,* I: 4–85, especially 10–11 and 84 on TR; Lash, 147–51.

striking out against her: Lash, 152–66, especially 156–7, 161–4.

municipal court cases: Davis, *Beckoning of Destiny,* 208, 212; Roosevelt, *Personal Letters,* I: 136.

foresee in 1910: Davis, *Beckoning of Destiny,* 212–4; Roosevelt, *Personal Letters,* I: 139.

Chapter 2: The Making of a Politician

"express the private man": Schlesinger, *Crisis of the Old Order,* 331; on what Richard Hofstadter called the status politics of the progressive era, see Hofstadter, *Age of Reform,* 135–66.

"president of the United States": Davis, *Beckoning of Destiny,* 62–3, 220–1.

so well in the past: Roosevelt, *Personal Letters,* I: 151–5; Davis, *Beckoning of Destiny,* 221–3.

progressive statewide candidate: Roosevelt, *Personal Letters,* I: 153–8; Schlesinger, *Crisis of the Old Order,* 331–2; Davis, 239–42.

"split it wide open": Schlesinger, *Crisis of the Old Order,* 332; Davis, *Beckoning of Destiny,* 245–8; Freidel, *Rendezvous with Destiny,* 20.

onto the national scene: Roosevelt, *Personal Letters,* I: 158–9.

political change was succeeding: Ibid., 160–3; Schlesinger, *Crisis of the Old Order,* 333–4; Freidel, *Rendezvous with Destiny,* 18–9; Davis, *Beckoning of Destiny,* 248–57; Jay, *Oxford Dictionary of Political Quotations,* 370.

happy to pay lower rates: Perkins, 9–14; Schlesinger, *Crisis of the Old Order,* 334–9; Freidel, *Rendezvous with Destiny,* 19–21; Davis, *Beckoning of Destiny,* 257–66.

conduct its public affairs: Schlesinger, *Crisis of the Old Order,* 336–8.

"All my plans vague": Link, *Road to the White House,* chapters x–xiii, especially 413; Roosevelt, *Personal Letters,* I: 192; Davis, *Beckoning of Destiny,* 270–7.

acceptable to the progressives: Davis, *Beckoning of Destiny,* 277–82.

lined up behind him: Roosevelt, *Personal Letters,* I: 192–6.

"wishes to ride in front": Ibid., 197; for a superb portrait of Howe and Roosevelt's reelection campaign, see Davis, *Beckoning of Destiny,* 283–96, 301–5; Schlesinger, *Crisis of the Old Order,* 342–3.

"May history repeat itself": Roosevelt, *Per-*

sonal Letters, I: 199–200; Schlesinger, *Crisis of the Old Order,* 348; Freidel, *Rendezvous with Destiny,* 27; Link, *Progressive Era,* 81; Davis, *Beckoning of Destiny,* 321.

resign his office: Schlesinger, *Crisis of the Old Order,* 344–5; Davis, *Beckoning of Destiny,* 320–2.

"hated by everybody": Schlesinger, *Crisis of the Old Order,* 348; Davis, *Beckoning of Destiny,* 309–14.

preparing for a possible conflict: Link, *Road to the White House,* 84–7; Schlesinger, *Crisis of the Old Order,* 348–9; Davis, *Beckoning of Destiny,* 329–33.

rhetoric was not appreciated: Schlesinger, *Crisis of the Old Order,* 349; Link, *Progressive Era,* chapter 5; Davis, *Beckoning of Destiny,* 333–9.

"very sweet but very sad": Roosevelt, *Personal Letters,* I: 228–30, 232–3, 235–9, 243.

"handing out to a gullible public": Cooper, *Woodrow Wilson,* 263; Roosevelt, *Personal Letters,* I: 246, 248–9, 256–7.

Republicans in November: Link, *New Freedom,* 164–73; Davis, *Beckoning of Destiny,* 356–62.

new Navy Department entity: Roosevelt, *Personal Letters,* I: 269–72, 291–3; Davis, *Beckoning of Destiny,* 390–3, 406.

involvement in the war: Roosevelt, *Personal Letters,* I: 282–4, 288–9; Davis, *Beckoning of Destiny,* 414–5.

center of national events: Roosevelt, *Personal Letters,* I: 300–3, 338–9; Schlesinger, *Crisis of the Old Order,* 350; Brands, 76–7.

he said later: Schlesinger, *Crisis of the Old Order,* 351; Davis, *Beckoning of Destiny,* 430; Freidel,

Rendezvous with Destiny, 29.

commitment to self-determination: For discussions of the Wilson administration's foreign policy thinking and view of World War I in particular, see Osgood, *Ideals and Self-Interest,* and Hofstadter, *Age of Reform,* 270–80.

better off under American control: Link, *Progressive Era,* 99–103; Davis, *Beckoning of Destiny,* 435–42.

fighting was meant to restore: Link, *Road to the White House,* 281–2; Davis, *Beckoning of Destiny,* 449, 454–7.

Wilson told Daniels: Burns and Dunn, 151–3.

violence by vigilantes: Roosevelt, *Personal Letters,* I: 347–73; Davis, *Beckoning of Destiny,* 507–8, 512; Burns and Dunn, 154.

service than the smaller crafts: Roosevelt, *Personal Letters,* I: 351–2, 354, 362; Davis, *Beckoning of Destiny,* 466–7.

the end of the war: Roosevelt, *Personal Letters,* I: 355–6; Davis, *Beckoning of Destiny,* 469–76.

passed it along to Wilson: Roosevelt, *Personal Letters,* I: 374–441, especially 414, 416–7, 420–2; Davis, *Beckoning of Destiny,* 516–30.

other than Franklin's lover: Cook, *Eleanor Roosevelt: 1884–1933,* 217–32; Davis, *Beckoning of Destiny,* note on 493.

herself or her family: Cook, *Eleanor Roosevelt: 1884–1933,* 232–6.

an "ill-advised" initiative: Burns and Dunn, 156–7.

summer of 1920: Davis, *Beckoning of Destiny,* 614, 588–93, 603.

fighting fronts invaluable: Golway, 247–9.

vice-presidential standard-bearer: Hofstadter,

Age of Reform, 279–80, on progressive exhaustion; Davis, *Beckoning of Destiny,* 607–14.

"I am very grateful": Schlesinger, *Crisis of the Old Order,* 360–3; Davis, *Beckoning of Destiny,* 615–7; Freidel, *Rendezvous with Destiny,* 39; Burns and Dunn, 161.

how prophetic his words were: Schlesinger, *Crisis of the Old Order,* 364–6; Freidel, *Rendezvous with Destiny,* 39–40; Davis, *Beckoning of Destiny,* 617–26; Burns and Dunn, 161–2; Lash, chapter 24.

Chapter 3: Polio

another round of reform: Davis, *Beckoning of Destiny,* 626–7, 640.

American politics required: Richard Hofstadter used the atmosphere metaphor in a conversation with me in 1963.

into harbor on August 8: Davis, *Beckoning of Destiny,* 640–6; Tobin, 15–6, 27, 29, 32–3, 40–2.

had from past afflictions: Tobin, 40–9.

mistaken about this as well: Ibid., 50–1, 56–60.

"treatment in New York": Ibid., 61–78.

extent of Franklin's disability: Ibid., 83–6.

temporarily laid low: Davis, *Beckoning of Destiny,* 663–4.

require substantial practice: Ibid., 663–6, 668–9, 671–2; Tobin, 110–1, 341.

transform her future: Lash, 268, 271–2; Cook, *Eleanor Roosevelt, 1884–1933,* 309–11.

"weak character forever": Lash, 268, 273–6.

"watches or pajamas": Davis, *Beckoning of Destiny,* 629–30; Lash, 271.

capacity to lead the nation: Ansbacher and Ansbacher, *Individual Psychology of Alfred Adler;* Way, *Alfred Adler.*

the user's immobility: When the Franklin D. Roosevelt memorial in Washington, D.C., opened in 1998, it included a statue of him seated in the kitchen chair with the small wheels that gave no clear evidence of his disability. Protests from the disability community, however, persuaded the memorial commission to add a statue of Roosevelt in a recognizable wheelchair at the entrance to the site.

efforts to mask his disability: Smith, *FDR,* 193–7.

resume his labored walk: Ibid., 197–8, 200–1.

"pajamas, nighties, and bathing suits": Ibid., 204–7; Roosevelt, *Personal Letters,* I: 534–5. Also see Tobin's fascinating discussion of the inner life of those with disabilities, 116–21.

"could well be established here": Tobin, 199–203; Roosevelt, *Personal Letters,* I: 564–9; Smith, *FDR,* 215–6.

political and philanthropic talents: Smith, *FDR,* 216–9; Tobin, 205–7, 213–26.

wrath for sinful actions: Tobin, 241–2.

enjoyed normal mobility: Ibid., 158; Adler, *Understanding Human Nature,* 69, 191.

youthful, vibrant Franklin intact: Perkins is quoted in Tobin, 155; Roosevelt, *Personal Letters,* I: 530–1.

make the same sacrifice: Smith, *FDR,* 198–9.

"usual male environment": Cook, *Eleanor Roosevelt, 1884–1933,* 248–9, 256–7, 329; Lash, 277–8.

a run for office: Lash, 277–8, 281–3.

"And sit down": Ibid., 278–82; Cook, *Eleanor*

Roosevelt, 1884–1933, 338–42; Smith, *FDR*, 199–200; Davis, *Beckoning of Destiny*, 689–90.

association with progressive causes: Cook, *Eleanor Roosevelt, 1884–1933*, 342–6.

politically useful to the other: For the details and quotes, see Golway, 256–7; Davis, *Beckoning of Destiny*, 720–8, 735–6, 757–8; Tobin, 186–95; Burns and Dunn, 188–9.

promoting peace abroad: Cook, *Eleanor Roosevelt, 1884–1933*, 351–2; Lash, 287–8.

minimum of help: Davis, *Beckoning of Destiny*, 609, 625; Tobin, 229–33, 242; Smith, *FDR*, 220.

Democratic Party in 1928: Davis, *Beckoning of Destiny*, 773, 775–9, 801; Golway, 261–2.

"make you the fair-haired boy": Davis, *Beckoning of Destiny*, 800–3; Tobin, 217, 235–7, 247.

himself to the public good: The Smith quote is in Tobin, 257. The best brief life of Hoover is Leuchtenburg, *Hoover*. Also see Davis, *Beckoning of Destiny*, 824–6, 829–30.

"for me to walk in": Smith, *FDR*, 221–5; Tobin, 253–65; Davis, *Beckoning of Destiny*, 838–40, 842–53; Davis, *New York Years*, 29–30.

compelling public talks: Davis, *New York Years*, 29–30, 32–5.

profits at the public's expense: Ibid., 39–43; Smith, *FDR*, 226–7; Tobin, 270–4.

made Roosevelt the governor-elect: Davis, *New York Years*, 44–7; Smith, *FDR*, 227–8.

Chapter 4: "Chameleon on Plaid"

progressive Democratic administration: Smith, *FDR*, 229–30; Tobin, 275–6.

"I won't either," Franklin answered: Schlesinger, *Crisis of the Old Order,* 386–7; Smith, *FDR,* 230–2; Tobin, 276–9; Cook, *Eleanor Roosevelt, 1884–1933,* 362–80, especially 379 for her comment on Roosevelt's victory. For a definitive study of Moses, see Caro, *Power Broker,* 29: What Rosenman saw "very early: Roosevelt was going to be his own Governor and take full charge. Any thought anyone of us might have had that Smith was going to run things was almost immediately dispelled."

conversation with him: Schlesinger, *Crisis of the Old Order,* 387–8, 393; Smith, *FDR,* 230–3, 238; Davis, *New York Years,* 72–3; Perkins, 72; Rosenman, *Working with Roosevelt,* 39–40.

"session of a legislative body": Schlesinger, *Crisis of the Old Order,* 393; Tobin, 288.

government, not business: Schlesinger, *Crisis of the Old Order,* 389–91; Smith, *FDR,* 237–41; Davis, *New York Years,* 89–90.

Democratic nomination in 1932: Rosenman, *Working with Roosevelt,* 41–7; Schlesinger, *Crisis of the Old Order,* 390–5; Smith, *FDR,* 240–5; Tobin, 288. On Hoover's response to the crash, see Leuchtenburg, *Hoover,* chapter 7.

his own against polio: Rosenman, *Working with Roosevelt,* 48–53; Schlesinger, *Crisis of the Old Order,* 276–81; Smith, *FDR,* 249–51; Davis, *New York Years,* 236–43. For Hopkins's early life, see McJimsey.

"prefix charged with hate": Schlesinger, *Crisis of the Old Order,* 244–5; Tobin, 297; Leuchtenburg, *Hoover,* 126, 128–31.

"would defeat Mr. Hoover": Leuchtenburg, *Hoover,* 131–5, 138.

"report the facts": For the Will Rogers quotes,

see online: "Will Rogers Quotes — Brainy Quotes."

organized stop-Roosevelt movement: Smith, *FDR,* 258.

first lady in new directions: Schlesinger, *Crisis of the Old Order,* 282; Cook, *Eleanor Roosevelt, 1884–1933,* 378–80, 445–7; Smith, *FDR,* 270.

converted him to their position: Schlesinger, *Crisis of the Old Order,* 286–8.

winning two-thirds margin: Ibid., 284–5.

the vice-presidential nomination: Ibid., 285–6; also see "John Nance Garner" Google online.

"above all try something": Burns and Dunn, 230–2; Schlesinger, *Crisis of the Old Order,* 283–4.

" 'weave the two together' ": Schlesinger, *Crisis of the Old Order,* 426–8; Leuchtenburg, *Roosevelt,* 10, 33.

"have a little faith": Schlesinger, *Crisis of the Old Order,* 289; Burns and Dunn, 225–7.

"like to be President": Davis, *New York Years,* 252–3, 256, 295.

Paris for the peace talks: See Gelfand.

would help or hinder: Rosenman, *Working with Roosevelt,* 56–8; Hofstadter, *Anti-intellectualism,* 210–3.

"efficiency of great value": Davis, *New York Years,* 289; Schlesinger, *Crisis of the Old Order,* 398–400.

"contact with destiny itself": Davis, *New York Years,* 268–72; Tugwell, *Democratic Roosevelt,* 213.

"has told him," Moley observed: Moley, 10–11.

getting to the White House: Leuchtenburg, *Roo-*

sevelt, 32–4; Berle and Jacobs, xv–xx; Davis, *New York Years,* 276–89, for an excellent discussion on Berle.

Hoover would defeat him: Leuchtenburg, *Roosevelt,* 4–10; Burns, *Lion and the Fox,* 134–8; Smith, *FDR,* 263–75, is an excellent account of the nominating process. Freidel, on the kangaroo ticket, *Rendezvous with Destiny,* 73. Interview with McCormick: "Roosevelt's View of the Big Job," *New York Times Magazine,* September 11, 1932.

1930 film, *Chasing Rainbows:* See Burns and Dunn on Hoover's search for a song as a remedy, 209–10. On "Happy Days," see Smith, *FDR,* 268–9.

emblematic of the administration: Smith, *FDR,* 275–7; Burns and Dunn, 236–8; Winik, 23; Rosenman, *Public Papers, 1928–1932:* "I Pledge You — I Pledge Myself."

"stay alive until election day": Schlesinger, *Crisis of the Old Order,* 413, 416.

"Right here at home": Ibid., 256–65; Leuchtenburg, *Roosevelt,* 13–6; Burns and Dunn, 241; Davis, *New York Years,* 344–53; Tugwell, *Brain Trust,* 427–34.

"Mayor [Jimmy] Walker": Freidel, *Rendezvous with Destiny,* 74, 76.

for a European tour: Davis, *New York Years,* 353–5; Burns and Dunn, 238–9.

years in his political career: Schlesinger, *Crisis of the Old Order,* 423–39; Burns, *Lion and the Fox,* 141–4; Leuchtenburg, *Roosevelt,* 10–13; Davis, *New York Years,* 355–74; Smith, *FDR,* 279–82, 285–7.

"road ahead would be": Smith, *FDR,* 287–8; Leuchtenburg, *Hoover,* 141; Roosevelt, *This I*

Remember, 74–5.

himself as president: Dallek, *Roosevelt,* vii; Schlesinger, *Crisis of the Old Order,* 452; Tugwell, *Democratic Roosevelt,* 62, 27.

"greatest actors in America": Freidel, *Launching the New Deal,* 205; Steel, 301; Alter, 53, 65; the Welles anecdote is in Moe, 310.

preserve the country's political institutions: Schlesinger, *Crisis of the Old Order,* 440–55.

"in slow waltz time": Burns, *Lion and the Fox,* 146–7; Smith, *FDR,* 289–90.

struggle with the Great Depression: Moley, 139; Davis, *New York Years,* 427–37; Freidel, *Launching the New Deal,* 169–74.

Chapter 5: "Instrument of Their Wishes"

"situation that now confronts us": Lippmann is quoted in Steel, 300; Reed is quoted in Katznelson, 12; Landon in Schlesinger, *Coming of the New Deal,* 3. The Hearst anecdote, as well as the America Legion speech, is in Alter, 4–7.

"puffy and expressionless": Davis, *New Deal Years,* 19–26; Boller, 95–6.

"I take it": Rosenman, *Public Papers, 1933,* 11–16.

recovered from his paralysis: The cartoons can be found online under FDR's First Hundred days — FDRL. Just google what I cited. Hill's discussion of FDR's disability is in Smith, *FDR,* 301.

"all back on the 9th": Schlesinger, *Coming of the New Deal,* 4–8; Leuchtenburg, *Roosevelt,* 41–4.

applauded his performance: Smith, *FDR,* 309–

10; Roosevelt Press Conference, March 8, 1933, online under The American Presidency Project.

working to make them whole: Roosevelt's Fireside Chat, March 12, 1933, is available at the Miller Center, University of Virginia, online. Also see Alter, 263–6.

"was a God-sent man": Schlesinger, *Coming of the New Deal,* 12–3; Leuchtenburg, *Roosevelt,* 44–5; Alter, 268.

enact a New Deal agenda: Roosevelt Press Conference, March 15, 1933; Burns, *Lion and the Fox,* 167–8; Leuchtenburg, *Roosevelt,* 47–8; Smith, *FDR,* 317.

"made the New Deal possible": The quotes are in Hofstadter, *American Political Tradition,* 410, 413, 432; and Freidel, *Launching the New Deal,* 500. Again, the first press conference is online under the American Presidency Project.

one divided by factionalism: Burns, *Lion and the Fox,* 168–9; Leuchtenburg, *Roosevelt,* 48–52; Fireside Chat, March 12, 1933, online.

"people needed to hear": The cartoon is in Burns, *Lion and Fox,* 169; Bellow is quoted in Alter, 220–1.

"by an interior decorator": Moley, 369–70.

roots of American democracy: Leuchtenburg, *Roosevelt,* 48–52, 72–8; Kennedy, 142, 200–7, 213; Alter, 279–83.

"almost always meant never": Alter, 284; Kennedy, 205, 207–10; Katznelson, 141, 166–7; Burns and Dunn, 185; Dallek, *Unfinished Life,* 596, 600.

his cousin Theodore: Roosevelt Press Conference, March 22, 1933, online; Schlesinger, *Coming of the New Deal,* 337–41; Burns, *Lion* and the Fox, 169, 243–6; Leuchtenburg, *Roosevelt,* 174; Kennedy, 144; Alter, 291–9; Davis, *New Deal Years,* 383–4. The fullest account of Roosevelt's devotion to conservation is Brinkley, *Rightful Heritage.*

devil-may-care attitude: Perkins, 182–5; Sherwood, 1–2, 5–6; Schlesinger, *Coming of the New Deal,* 263–7.

"they eat every day": Sherwood, 52, 106.

fallen on hard times: Perkins, 186; Schlesinger, *Coming of the New Deal,* 268, 270–3; Faber; Cook, *Eleanor Roosevelt, 1933–1938,* 477–80, 483–4; the photograph is in Smith, *FDR,* after 332; Goodwin, 219–22; Kennedy, 161–2, 169, 171, 173–4; Ward, 20–21.

"Depression in this country": Schlesinger, *Coming of the New Deal,* 274–5; Leuchtenburg, *Roosevelt,* 120–4; Davis, *New Deal Years,* 306–14; Kennedy, 175–6.

"confused, two-headed experiment": Schlesinger, *Coming of the New Deal,* 94–9; Burns, *Lion and the Fox,* 180–1; Leuchtenburg, *Roosevelt,* 55–8; Freidel, *Rendezvous with Destiny,* 104–5; Kennedy, 151–3.

"helped preserve American unity": Schlesinger, *Coming of the New Deal,* chapters 6–10, especially 103–6, 175–76; Burns, *Lion and the Fox,* 191–3; Leuchtenburg, *Roosevelt,* 64–71; Davis, *New Deal Years,* 249–50, 252–3; Schwarz, 286–98; Kennedy, 177–89; Alter, 300–4; Perkins, 205–6.

"plans are carried out": Schlesinger, *Coming of the New Deal,* 320; Roosevelt, Fireside Chat, May 7, 1933, online.

signed the law on May 18: Schlesinger, *Coming*

of the New Deal, 319–27; Leuchtenburg, *Roosevelt,* 54–5; Burns, *Lion and the Fox,* 179; Burns and Dunn, 247–9, 261; Kennedy, 147–9.

"joint efforts to this end": Roosevelt, Fireside Chat, May 7, 1933.

isolate itself from conflicts abroad: Freidel, *Launching the New Deal,* 390–407; Dallek, *Roosevelt,* 36.

"forecasts are dangerous": Freidel, *Launching the New Deal,* 458–64, 498; Dallek, *Roosevelt,* 47.

leading New Deal critic: Dallek, *Roosevelt,* 39–42, 47–58; Freidel, *Launching the New Deal,* 490–4. Also see Schlesinger's superb analysis of Roosevelt's control of subordinates, *Coming of the New Deal:,* 527–32, 549.

take up arms against Germany: For criticism of Roosevelt, see Leuchtenburg, *Roosevelt,* 202–3; Kennedy, 155.

"met a painless Waterloo": Leuchtenburg, *Roosevelt,* 59–62; Schlesinger, *Crisis of the Old Order,* 14–15, 22.

Chapter 6: "Trustee of the Existing Social System"

"quality of the food": Davis, *New Deal Years,* 201–8, 212; Dallek, *Lone Star Rising,* 178–80; Williams, 639; Ickes, *Secret Diaries,* I: 249; Smith, *FDR,* 333–9.

suffering during the Depression: Lash, 355–6; Cook, *Eleanor Roosevelt, 1884–1933,* 498–9.

administration of affairs: Lash, 357–8, 382.

"great deal to me": Lash, 360–5, 373; Burns and Dunn, 265–70.

"don't think and don't know": Cook, *Eleanor*

Roosevelt, 1884–1933, 499–500; Lash, 366.

in the community center: Lash, chapter 37; Cook, *Eleanor Roosevelt: 1933–1938,* 130–2, on Arthurdale, see 132–44; Burns and Dunn, 271–6. See the negative references to Arthurdale in Ickes, *Secret Diaries,* volume I.

family was enough: Burns and Dunn, 266; Lash, 390–1.

"headed in the right direction": Roosevelt, Fireside Chat, October 22, 1933, online.

interests in western states: Leuchtenburg, *Roosevelt,* 72–3, 78–84; Davis, *New Deal Years,* 284–94, 297–8; Kennedy, 196–9. On the Great Plains and the dust bowl, see Worster.

ground to a halt: Schlesinger, *Coming of the New Deal,* 563–6; Leuchtenburg, *Roosevelt,* 86, 90–1, 93–5; Burns and Dunn, 283–4; Davis, 319–20.

"hearts of a united people": Roosevelt speech at Gettysburg, PA, May 30, 1934, online.

committed to the "extreme left": Davis, *New Deal Years,* 416.

stones to a better life: Schlesinger, *Coming of the New Deal,* 484–97; Burns, *Lion and the Fox,* 206–8; Davis, *New Deal Years,* 399–400, 415–6; Kennedy: the cartoon is between 332–3; Brands, 8–9, 336.

"deified some one man": Burns, *Lion and the Fox,* 210–2; Leuchtenburg, *Roosevelt,* 96–9; Davis, *New Deal Years,* 493–4; Kennedy, 234–9. Also see, online, Henry Morgenthau, Jr., Diary, December 20, 1934, for Long's comment to the Mayor, FDRL; Schlesinger, *Politics of Upheaval,* 42–68; Williams, 200, 626, 640, and 699–700; Brinkley, *Voices of Protest,* 57–

64, 171–3; and White, 165, 167–8, 171–2, 197–200.

minor role in American politics: Schlesinger, *Politics of Upheaval,* 15–28; Brinkley, *Voices of Protest,* 82–127, 133–4, especially 82–3, 93, 107.

"Abraham Lincoln and General Grant": Schlesinger, *Politics of Upheaval,* 29–35; Brinkley, *Voices of Protest,* 222–6; Kennedy, 224–5; Brands, 300–1.

get out of the Depression: Perkins, 124; Davis, *New Deal Years,* 402–4, 409, 423–8; Kennedy, 225–7; Brands, 301–2.

so trying an adversary: Sherwood, 9; Ickes, *Secret Diaries,* I: 144, 154–5, 207, 218, 222–4, 239–40; Schlesinger, *Coming of the New Deal,* 541–2.

"crowned by the people": Ickes, *Secret Diaries,* I: 127; Burns, *Lion and the Fox,* 198–205; Schlesinger, *Coming of the New Deal,* 503–7; Davis, *New Deal Years,* 421–2; Kennedy, 216–7; Smith, *FDR,* 349–50.

an act of patriotism: Dallek, *Roosevelt,* 38–9, 59–66, 78–81, 86–7; Ward, 10.

Lincoln in the making: Sherwood, 8–10.

"I do, I do!": Schlesinger, *Coming of the New Deal,* 583–4.

Chapter 7: Mastering Washington "Bedlam"

"my happiness," he told her: *New York Times,* February 27, 1935; Ward, ix–xvii, 9, 13–5, 17; Goodwin, 39.

barracudas and sharks: Burns, *Lion and the Fox,* 186–91; Schlesinger, *Politics of Upheaval,* 8.

lead the country into war: Roosevelt, State of

the Union, January 4, 1935, online. Leuchtenburg, *Roosevelt,* 142.

but world peace: Ickes, *Secret Diaries,* I: 284–5, 287; Roosevelt, *Personal Letters,* II: 449–52; Dallek, *Roosevelt,* 95–6.

dictated that he do nothing: Roosevelt, *Personal Letters,* II: 463–4, 472–6; Dallek, *Democrat and Diplomat,* 172–3.

"main performance starts": Leuchtenburg, *Roosevelt,* 124–5, 131–3; Perkins, chapter 23; Ward, 18; Roosevelt, *Personal Letters,* II: 466–8.

"give us all a headache": Farley, *Behind the Ballots,* 65, 155; Schlesinger, *Coming of the New Deal,* 575; Davis, *New Deal Years,* 467; Roosevelt, *Personal Letters,* II: 469–72.

uncertainties of industrial life: Schlesinger, *Coming of the New Deal,* 309–12; Leuchtenburg, *Roosevelt,* 124–5; Roosevelt, *Personal Letters,* II: 476.

"dangerous duodenal ulcer": Ward, 23; Ickes, *Secret Diaries,* I: 328–31, 340–1; McJimsey, 78–9, 83–6; Sherwood, 52–3, 68–70, 93; Davis, *New Deal Years,* 467–71; Leuchtenburg, *Roosevelt,* 125; Watkins, 394–401.

"any of these projects": Leuchtenburg, *Roosevelt,* 125–8; Sherwood, 59–60.

distributed to the NYA: Schlesinger, *Politics of Upheaval,* 351–2; Lash, 462, 467, 536–40, 544–5; Cook, *Eleanor Roosevelt: 1933–1938,* 268–72; Dallek, *Lone Star Rising,* 125–6.

"what we are talking": Dallek, *Lone Star Rising,* 123–43; Cook, *Eleanor Roosevelt: 1933–1938,* 154, 159–60, 278–9; Goodwin, 163.

threaten his reelection: Leuchtenburg, *Roo-*

sevelt, 129; Lash, 544–6.

"doing all the talking": Schlesinger, *Politics of Upheaval,* 211–4, 249–50; Ickes, *Secret Diaries,* I: 342, 346; Leuchtenburg, *Roosevelt,* 146.

"You can do it anyway": Schlesinger, *Politics of Upheaval,* 214–5; Leuchtenburg, *Roosevelt,* 143–5; White, 254; Shesol, 41.

"as usual a bedlam": Shesol, 71, 126–45; Roosevelt, press conference, May 31, 1935, online; Ickes, *Secret Diaries,* I: 371–2; Roosevelt, *Personal Letters,* II: 453, 480–1, 484, 486; Ward, 23, 25–6.

millions of Americans: Schlesinger, *Politics of Upheaval,* 379–83; Leuchtenburg, *Roosevelt,* 157–8, 167–9; Davis, *New Deal Years,* 490–2; Ward, 27, 37.

signature made it law: Kennedy, 296–8; Perkins, 239; Smith, *FDR,* 357–8.

David Lilienthal announced: Roosevelt, *Personal Letters,* II: 98, 483; Schlesinger, *Politics of Upheaval,* 302–14, 323–4, 376–9; Leuchtenburg, *Roosevelt,* 157; Davis, *New Deal Years,* 529–37; Smith, *FDR,* 237.

between privilege and poverty: Schlesinger, *Politics of Upheaval,* 325–34; Morgenthau Diaries, June 14, 1935, online FDRL; Message to Congress on Tax Revision, June 19, 1935, FDRL, online; Ickes, *Secret Diaries,* I: 384–5, 472; Kennedy, 275–8; Roosevelt, *Personal Letters,* II: 252, 492.

"very decidedly so": Kennedy, 277–8; Leuchtenburg, *Roosevelt,* 168; *Gallup,* 2.

entered another war: Ward, 27–8; *Gallup,* 3, 5.

"would not be understood": Dallek, *Roosevelt,* 101; Roosevelt, *Personal Letters,* II: 499–501.

new acts of aggression: Roosevelt, *Personal Letters,* II: 472–3, 530–1; Dallek, *Roosevelt,* 101–108; Kennedy, 393–5.

Chapter 8: Triumph of the New Order

"anything might happen": White, 239–42; Brinkley, *Voices of Protest,* 80–1, 243–4; Roosevelt, *Personal Letters,* II: 452–3.

irritant to the administration: White, 262–6; Roosevelt, press conferences, September 11 and September 13, 1935, FDRL, online; Ickes, *Secret Diaries,* I: 462.

"Your affec F": Goodwin, 36, 119–21; Steel, 316–7; Lash, 337–8, 343–4; Ward, 30, 32, 34–5, 37–49, 54, 420.

"President's personal popularity": Roosevelt, speeches, September 30, October 1, October 2, 1935, FDRL, online; Ickes, *Secret Diaries,* I: 446; Davis, *New Deal Years,* 580–2; Sherwood, 80.

was a model host: Sherwood, 78–9; Ickes, *Secret Diaries, I:* 446–61.

draw America into the conflict: Roosevelt, *Personal Letters,* II: 516, 525; Ickes, *Secret Diaries, I:* 465; Ward, 50; *Gallup,* 3, 12, 26.

came to naught: Sherwood, 79; Dallek, *Roosevelt,* 110–6.

just, equitable, democratic society: Farley, *Jim Farley's Story,* 55–6; Roosevelt, State of the Union, January 3, 1936, FDRL, online; Schlesinger, *Politics of Upheaval,* 502–4; Ward, 56.

"possible out from that statement": Roosevelt, *Personal Letters,* II: 544–5, 555–6, 560.

future attacks abroad: *Gallup,* 14; Dallek, *Roo-*

sevelt, 117–21.

"a week or two": C. H. Sherrill to LeHand, September 14, 1935, PSF, FDRL; Ward, 69; Roosevelt, *Personal Letters,* I: 571.

informed student of politics: Ward, 65, 69–70, 77, 82; Ickes, *Secret Diaries,* I: 515; Anne O'Hare McCormick, "Still 'A Little Left of Center,' " *New York Times Magazine,* June 21, 1936; Leuchtenburg, *Roosevelt,* 169–70; Ickes, *Secret Diaries,* I: 695, 699.

been able to prevent: Roosevelt, *Personal Letters,* I: 534, 574, 583; Cook, *Eleanor Roosevelt, 1933–1938,* 353–4.

"a judicial tyranny": Ickes, *Secret Diaries,* I: 372, 523–4, 530; Schlesinger, *Politics of Upheaval,* 470–4, 487–9, 500, 502, 504–5; Roosevelt, *Personal Letters,* I: 569; Shesol, 182–97.

overturn Court rulings: Roosevelt, *Personal Letters,* I: 548–9; Ickes, *Secret Diaries,* I: 495, 529; Leuchtenburg, *Supreme Court,* 89–96.

"charges and countercharges": Leuchtenburg, *Supreme Court,* 106; Roosevelt, Jackson Day address, January 8, 1936, FDRL, online.

"durable political realignment": Smith, *FDR,* 362–3; Ward, 53–4, 56–8, 70; Kennedy, 283.

ambassador to Great Britain: Roosevelt, *Personal Letters,* I: 546–7, 552, 560, 569, 573, 577, 585–8; Farley, *Jim Farley's Story,* 63; Cook, *Eleanor Roosevelt, 1933–1938,* 377–8.

"County and State taxes": Roosevelt, *Personal Letters,* I: 562, 566, 573, 595–6, 612–3, 615, 623.

as a victory: Davis, *New Deal Years,* 618–20.

recent presidential elections: Schlesinger, *Politics of Upheaval,* 550–61, 619–20, 626–30; Roosevelt, *Personal Letters,* I: 397–8, 602; *Gallup,* 29–30.

"meant political death": Schlesinger, *Politics of Upheaval,* 524–6.

region of the country: *Gallup,* 1–4, 12, 14–5.

the "big interests": Ibid., 15–6, 24; Davis, *New Deal Years,* 623–7; "Alf Landon," Wikipedia, online; McCoy; Ickes, *Secret Diaries,* I: 646, 648–9, 667–8; Schlesinger, *Politics of Upheaval,* 602.

next four years: Schlesinger, *Politics of Upheaval,* 574–85.

"for the world": Roosevelt, speech, June 27, 1936, FDRL, online.

ten-page single-spaced reply: Farley, *Jim Farley's Story,* 58–9; Roosevelt, *Personal Letters,* I: 601–4; Ickes, *Secret Diaries,* II: 635, 638–46; Cook, *Eleanor Roosevelt, 1933–1938,* 376–80.

"any touch of reality": *Gallup,* 32–6; Schlesinger, *Politics of Upheaval,* 601–3, 606–7, 611, 614–6, 623–5.

Daisy in November: Roosevelt, *Personal Letters,* I: 605–6, 610; on the FCC, see Dallek, *Lone Star Rising,* 248–9; Roosevelt, Fireside Chat, October 12, 1937, FDRL, online; Schlesinger, *Politics of Upheaval,* 500; Ward, 92.

"a great Phillipic": Roosevelt, *Personal Letters,* I: 611–2, 616–20; Leuchtenburg, *Roosevelt,* 190–1; Ickes, *Secret Diaries, II:* 613, 627, 654, 657.

influence events abroad: Ickes, *Secret Diaries,* II: 655–8, 661–3, 665; Roosevelt, Chautauqua Speech, August 14, 1936, online; Dallek, *Roosevelt,* 126–9.

becoming a dictator: *New York Times,* August, 26, August 27, 1936; Davis, *New Deal Years,* 634–45.

"pounding in the surf": The speeches are all online at the American Presidency Project; *New York Times,* November 1, 1936. Schlesinger, *Politics of Upheaval,* 638–9.

margin in the Senate: *Gallup,* 38–9; Ward, 88; *New York Times,* October 23, 1936; Schlesinger, *Politics of Upheaval,* 640.

meaning to the words: Leuchtenburg, *Roosevelt,* 184–96; Kennedy, 286.

Chapter 9: Second Term Curse

some degree of opposition: Roosevelt, *Personal Letters,* I: 624–27; Roosevelt to Daisy Suckley, November 21, 1936, in Ward, 88–9; Roosevelt to Senator George Norris, quoted in Morgan, 530; Ickes, *Secret Diaries,* I: 703; *Gallup,* 45; Roosevelt, inaugural, January 20, 1937, online.

King Neptune's Court: Dallek, *Roosevelt,* 122–3; Roosevelt, *Personal Letters,* I: 630–3.

"Wed. eve about 6:30": Dallek, *Roosevelt,* 132; Roosevelt, *Personal Letters,* I: 634–7; Ward, 88–95.

could be unguarded: Roosevelt, *Personal Letters,* I: 635–7; Cook, *Eleanor Roosevelt, 1933–1938,* 27, 40, 401–3; Davis, *New Deal Years,* 659–60.

"Fascism or Communism": "Carlos Saavedra Lamas," Wikipedia, online; Hull, *Memoirs,* I: 493–503; Ickes, *Secret Diaries,* II: 7; Roosevelt, *Personal Letters,* I: 638, 648–9, 652, 656; Dallek, *Roosevelt,* 132–5.

"stands for the Trinity": Roosevelt, *Personal*

Letters, I: 625, 651, 659–60, 653; Roosevelt, State of the Union, January 6, 1937 online; Roosevelt, message to Congress, February 5, 1937, online;]; Ickes, *Secret Diaries,* II: 65–6, 74–5; Davis, *Into the Storm,* 63; Simon, 319; Leuchtenburg, *Supreme Court,* 130, 132–7; Shesol, 265–73, 304, 309.

"make American democracy succeed": Roosevelt, address at the Democratic victory dinner, Washington, D.C., March 4, 1937, American Presidency Project, online; Ickes, *Secret Diaries,* II: 88–9; Roosevelt, Fireside Chat, March 9, 1937, online.

economic and social reforms: Ward, 95–6; Roosevelt, *Personal Letters,* I: 669–70, 711; Leuchtenburg, *Supreme Court,* 137–41, 145–6; Shesol, 274–7, 299–304.

work of the older men: Simon, 341; *Gallup,* 45, 47, 50–1, 53–5, 57–8, 62, 68–70, 73, 76, 80; Leuchtenburg, *American President,* 203; Roosevelt, *Personal Letters,* I, : 692–94, 710–1; Ickes, *Secret Diaries,* II: 183, 222–3; Ward, 101; Levine and Levine, *People and the President,* 173, 194; Leuchtenburg, *Supreme Court,* 142–56, and his excellent chapter 7 on which my discussion of Black is based; Shesol, 332, 337–8.

clung to the past: Leuchtenburg, *Supreme Court,* 156–62; Shesol, 312–3; Farley, *Behind the Ballots,* 95–6; Roosevelt, *Personal Letters,* I, : 619; Ward, 88; Ickes, *Secret Diaries,* II: 165–6.

Roosevelt might have added: Roosevelt, speech, April 13, 1943, American Presidency Project, online.

respond to Japanese belligerence: Dallek, *Roosevelt,* 126–7; Davis, *New Deal Years,* 596–8;

Gallup, 46–7, 49–50, 54, 68–72; Ward, 10.

"first Southern President": Dallek, *Lone Star Rising,* 159–61.

further threaten world peace: Dallek, *Roosevelt,* 127–8; Davis, *New Deal Years,* 665–7, 734.

"attention to fascist threats": Dallek, *Roosevelt,* 135–8, 144; Roosevelt, *Personal Letters,* I: 680–1, 699–703.

in the event of war: Roosevelt, *Personal Letters,* I: 695, 709–10.

"how anyone could stand it": Ickes, *Secret Diaries,* II: 182.

"locked in deadly embrace": *Gallup,* 48, 52, 55, 58, 63, 69; Roosevelt press conferences, June 8, June 11, June 15, June 22, June 29, FDRL, online ; Ickes, *Secret Diaries,* II: 92; the best discussion of the labor strife is in Kennedy, chapter 10, 288–322, from which several quotes are drawn. The number of strikes and strikers is in Freedman, 421.

out of the downturn: Farley, *Jim Farley's Story,* 106; Leuchtenburg, *Roosevelt,* 243–8; Brinkley, *End of Reform,* chapters 1–5 are helpful in assessing these events; Kennedy, 350–62; *Gallup,* 75, 78, 80.

"save railroad fares": Roosevelt, *Personal Letters,* I: 712–3.

"search for peace": Ickes, *Secret Diaries,* II: 213–4, 221–2; Roosevelt, Quarantine Speech, October 5, 1937, online.

"other half misstated": *Gallup,* 80; Levine, 11; Rosenman, *Working with Roosevelt,* 165–8; Roosevelt, *Personal Letters,* I: 716–9, 732–4; Dallek, *Roosevelt,* 148–54.

restrictions on labor unions: Brinkley, *End of Reform,* 86–8.

"more or less given up": Ickes, *Secret Diaries,* II: 255–60.

"much love. Devotedly, F": Biographical sketches of the Roosevelt children are available on Wikipedia, online ; Davis, *Into the Storm,* 159–62; Lash, chapter 42; Cook, *Eleanor Roosevelt, 1933–1938,* 447, 482; Roosevelt, *Personal Letters,* I: 730.

satisfaction in his private life: Ward, 43, 94–100, 105–7.

Chapter 10: The Worst of Times

American social relations: Leuchtenburg, *Roosevelt,* 252–3; *Gallup,* 83, 87, 89, 94–6, 99; Ward, 109–12, 119.

"make fitting response": Ickes, *Secret Diaries,* II: 286–8, 292; Ward, 119; Leuchtenburg, *American President,* 203–4; Roosevelt, State of the Union, January 3, 1938, online ; *Gallup,* 84–5.

feeling largely powerless: Leuchtenburg, *Roosevelt,* 256; Brinkley, *End of Reform,* 88–91; Kennedy, 350–1; *Roosevelt, Personal Letters, II:* 758–60, 766–7; *Gallup,* 95; Roosevelt to Speaker Bankhead, January 6, 1938, online ; Dallek, *Roosevelt,* 151, 154–5, 158–5.

comfortable citizens as well: Roosevelt, speech, March 23, 1938, online.

"dictator under that bill": Schulman, 46–52; Leuchtenburg, *Roosevelt,* 277–80; Davis, *Into the Storm,* 213–4, 220–3; Brinkley, *End of Reform,* 21–22; Ickes, *Secret Diaries,* II: 339, 356–60; Roosevelt, *Personal Letters,* I: 774; Farley,

Jim Farley's Story, 130.

Liberty League in 1936: Ickes, *Secret Diaries,* II: 360.

Morgenthau stayed on: Ickes, *Secret Diaries,* II: 362; Farley, *Jim Farley's Story,* 131–2; Brinkley, *End of Reform,* 94–101; Davis, *Into the Storm,* 218–29; Kennedy, 350–61.

demands for social justice: Roosevelt, message to Congress, and Fireside Chat, both April 14, 1938, online.

"will really recover": *Gallup,* 96, 99–101, 103, 105–6, 108; Levine, 231–2, 235.

"C.[ertain] P.[erson] will understand": Ward, 113–4, 116–7.

"as Roosevelt's revolution": Roosevelt, message to Congress, April 29, 1938, online; Leuchtenburg, *Roosevelt,* 257–60; Brinkley, *End of Reform,* 122–4.

"still loves Roosevelt": Cook, *Eleanor Roosevelt, 1933–1938,* 512–4; Schulman, 54–63.

"pretty soggy ground": Roosevelt, press conference, April 21, 1938, online; Schulman, 46–9; Ickes, *Secret Diaries,* II: 262, 342.

opponent brought down: Levine and Levine, *People and the President,* 247; Rosenman, *Working with Roosevelt,* 176; "J. Parnell Thomas," Wikipedia, online.

a good idea: Rosenman, *Working with Roosevelt,* 176; "Martin Dies," Wikipedia, online ; Schulman, 55; *Gallup,* 106, 109.

even opposing them: Roosevelt, Fireside Chat, June 24, 1938, online.

determination to oppose him: Levine and Levine, *People and the President,* 255–65.

"don't care who wins": McJimsey, 117–9; Roosevelt, *Personal Letters,* II: 745, 786, 799–802;

Ickes, *Secret Diaries,* II: 393–5; Ward, 114–5, 117–8; Dallek, *Roosevelt,* 167; Davis, *Into the Storm,* 275–6.

of whom Connally disapproved: Burns, *Lion and the Fox,* 360–2; Davis, *Into the Storm,* 260–5.

"15,000,000 years ago": Ward, 116–24; Roosevelt, *Personal Letters,* II: 799.

Wages and Hours Law: Burns, *Lion and the Fox,* 362–3; "Walter George," Wikipedia, online; Roosevelt, speech, August 11, 1938, online.

fifty cents a day: Burns, *Lion and the Fox,* 363; "Cotton Ed Smith," Wikipedia, online; "United States Senate Election in South Carolina, 1938," Wikipedia, online.

quote what he had said: Roosevelt, press conference, August 16, 1938, online.

Roosevelt said privately: Roosevelt, *Personal Letters,:* 805–6, 808–9; Davis, *Into the Storm,* 295; Burns, *Lion and the Fox,* 363–4.

troubled personal relations: Cook, *Eleanor Roosevelt, 1933–1938,* 410–1, 538–9; Davis, *Into the Storm,* 295, 299–300, 324, 328.

"going to stay in bed": Ward, 124–5.

abandoned to Hitler's demands: Davis, *Into the Storm,* 327; Kershaw, 61, and chapter 2.

"you will have war": Davis, *Into the Storm;* Dallek, *Roosevelt,* 161–6; Ward, 125–6.

protect the British Isles: Churchill's speech in the House of Commons, October 5, 1938, is online.

"require that we be prepared": Roosevelt, *Personal Letters,* II: 806–7, 816–7, 824–6; Roosevelt, speech, October 26, 1938, online.

that of democratic allies: Roosevelt, *Personal*

Letters, II: 827, 837–8; Dallek, *Roosevelt,* 171–3.

ordered it to be stopped: Roosevelt, *Personal Letters,* II: 843; Dallek, *Roosevelt,* 173–5.

in the coming year: The best description and analysis of *Kristallnacht* is in Kershaw, 130–43; Roosevelt, *Personal Letters,* II: 810–11; Roosevelt, press conference, November 15, 1938, online.

millions of Americans believed: Roosevelt, press conference, November 15, 1938; Dallek, *Roosevelt,* 167–8; Breitman et al., chapter 7; Breitman and Lichtman, chapter 6, especially 105, 108–9, 116, 122, for an excellent discussion of the refugee issue; Ickes, *Secret Diaries, II:* 342–3; Cook, *Eleanor Roosevelt, 1933–1938,* 556–62, 564–5, 574; *Gallup,* 121–2, 128–30.

confident of victories: Roosevelt, *Personal Letters,* II: 826–8, 835–6; Davis, *Into the Storm,* 362–4, 378–9; McJimsey, 120–4; Ickes, *Secret Diaries,* II: 526–8.

Chapter 11: Dangers Abroad, Uncertainties at Home

"operation is successfully over": Roosevelt, *Personal Letters,* II: 835, 845; Ward, 126–9.

61 to 39 percent: Richard Moe to author, September 15, 2016; *Gallup,* 130, 134–5, 138–9, 141, 147, 152.

"best of his career": Gilbert, *A Life,* 545; Roosevelt, State of the Union, January 4, 1939, online; Ickes, *Secret Diaries,* II: 547–8.

Good Neighbor policy: Roosevelt, *Personal Letters,* II: 849–50; Ickes, *Secret Diaries,* II: 351, 555–6, 595.

"do anything about it": Roosevelt, *Personal Letters,* II: 832, 847–8; *Gallup,* 128; Ickes, *Secret Diaries,* II: 528–9, 546–9.

"before any actual declaration": Roosevelt, press conference, January 4, 1939; Roosevelt, *Personal Letters,* II: 854, 858–60, 862–4, 879–80, 885–6; Blum, *Morgenthau Diaries, II:* 64–78; Ickes, *Secret Diaries,* II: 571–2; Dallek, *Roosevelt,* 174–5, 179, 181–2; Davis, *Into the Storm,* 417.

"not only here but everywhere": Dallek, *Roosevelt,* 182; Brinkley, *End of Reform,* 140–1; Lash, 469, 500, 511, 551–3; Ickes, *Secret Diaries,* II: 577; Roosevelt, *Personal Letters,* II: 866–71.

commanded Roosevelt's attention: *Gallup,* 134, 139–40, 145, 151.

Roosevelt followed their lead: Roosevelt, State of the Union, January 4, 1939, online; Roosevelt, *This I Remember,* 161–2; Cook, *Eleanor Roosevelt, 1933–1938,* 443–5, 452–6, 496; Ickes, *Secret Diaries,* II: 562, 566, 569–70; Dallek, *Roosevelt,* 177–80.

move against Poland: Kershaw, 163–80.

"to live in": Dallek, *Roosevelt,* 182–3; Roosevelt, *Personal Letters,* II: 865, 872–3.

"if there is war": Roosevelt, press conferences, March 21, March 31, 1939, online; Ickes, *Secret Diaries,* II: 597; Blum, *Morgenthau Diaries,* II: 82–84; Kershaw, 175–6.

advance prosperity everywhere: Roosevelt, press conferences, April 8, April 11, April 15, 1939; Roosevelt, Pan American Day speech, April 14, 1939; Roosevelt, message to Hitler, April 14, 1939. All online.

in the event of war: Dallek, *Roosevelt,* 186; Roosevelt, *Personal Letters,* II: 878–9; *Gallup,* 149–50, 152, 154.

"head of a posse": Dallek, *Roosevelt,* 186–7; Gerhard Weinberg, "Hitler's Image of the United States," *American Historical Review,* July 1964; Kershaw, 178, 187–9; Davis, *Into the Storm,* 439–40.

"armament for this tonnage": Roosevelt, *Personal Letters,* II: 881.

"Europe demonstrated the need": Roosevelt, press conferences, March 7 and March 17, 1939, online.

commitments than the Senate: Connally, 226; Roosevelt, *Personal Letters,* II: 873, 875–6, 891; Hull, *Memoirs,* I: 641–5; Dallek, *Roosevelt,* 182–4, 187–8.

soon to be embattled Britain: Roosevelt, *Personal Letters,:* II: 824–6, 881–5, 893; Davis, *Into the Storm,* 446–9; Ward, 130–3.

post in London: Roosevelt, *Personal Letters,* II: 898–902; Ickes, *Secret Diaries,* II: 637, 676; Israel, *Nevada's Key Pittman,* 166–7; Hull, *Memoirs,* I: 641–51; Roosevelt, press conference, July 21, 1939, online; Dallek, *Roosevelt,* 95, 187–92. "William Borah," "Hiram Johnson," Wikipedia, online.

22 percent undecided: *Gallup,* 170, 178; on Roosevelt and Lindbergh, see Olson; on the domestic economy, see Brinkley, *End of Reform,* 131–6.

"stronger man is right": Davis, *Into the Storm,* 441–3; Ulam, 270–9; Kershaw, 205–230.

"History does in fact repeat": Dallek, *Roosevelt,* 193–8; Davis, *Into the Storm,* 458–61;

Roosevelt, Fireside Chat, September 3, 1939, online; Roosevelt, *Personal Letters,* II: 903–4, 915–7.

Chapter 12: Faux Neutral

reach unprecedented heights: Kershaw, 221–30; Shirer, 152, 156.

business and ordinary citizens: *Gallup,* 152, 154, 160, 177, 180–4, 186–8.

discussions could occur: Roosevelt, *Personal Letters,* II: 918–9, 921–6, 930–2; the various speeches, including Borah's and Roosevelt's of September 21, 1939, are at "1939 Documents relating to World War II," online. On Borah, see Olson, 66; On Roosevelt's Oval Office meeting on September 20, see Moe, 68–9. For various discussions Roosevelt had about rescue at this time, see Breitman and Lichtman, chapter 6.

"get the U.S. in": Roosevelt, *Personal Letters,* II: 921–3, 925–6, 929–30, 932–6, 949–50; Ickes, *Secret Diaries,* II: 685, 712; Blum, *Morgenthau Diaries,* II: 37, 98, 102; Dallek, *Roosevelt,* 200–3, 207; Nasaw, 413–5; Kimball, *Churchill and Roosevelt,* I: 24.

they hoped so: Roosevelt, *Personal Letters,* II: 942–4, 947.

"qualified for that job": Ibid., 947–51.

"forgetting the New Deal": Dallek, *Roosevelt,* 201; Olson, 91; Goodwin, 19, 205.

course of the war: Roosevelt, *Personal Letters,* II: 955; Dallek, *Roosevelt,* 202–5; Olson, 90–3; Roosevelt, speech, October 26, 1939, online.

when he saw one: Roosevelt, *Personal Letters,* II: 952–4; also see Roosevelt, press conferences,

November 7, November 10, November 14, 1939.

expected the war to last: Roosevelt, *Personal Letters,* II: 959–61.

change intransigent minds: Roosevelt, speech, "Three Fallacies: 'Isolation,' " November 8, 1939, PSF: Neutrality, FDRL.

U.S. national security: Dallek, *Roosevelt,* 205–6; also see *"Graf Spee"* and "Hans Langsdorff," Wikipedia, online.

"establish domination over it": Roosevelt, *Personal Letters,* II: 961; Dallek, *Roosevelt,* 208–12.

writing his memoirs: Roosevelt, speech, November 19, 1939, online.

"seldom was with FDR": *Gallup,* 187–8, 191, 196; Moe, 120.

give U.S. efforts greater urgency: Roosevelt, *Personal Letters,* II: 967–8; Isaacson, 473–8.

end the conflict: *Gallup,* 201, 208, 211–2; Olson, 94.

"devised by mankind": Roosevelt, *Personal Letters,* II: 975–7; Roosevelt, State of the Union, January 3, 1940, online.

indispensable world statesman: Dallek, *Roosevelt,* 215–17.

"what a real problem was": Sherwood, 134–5; Rosenman, *Working with Roosevelt,* 9, 261–2; Ickes, *Secret Diaries,* III: 216–9; Fullilove, 11–2.

"that is the whole thing": Roosevelt, press conferences, February 9, 1940, online.

run for a third term: Roosevelt, *Personal Letters,* II: 996; Fullilove, 30–4; Ward, 134; Lawrence K. Altman, "For F.D.R. Sleuths, New Focus on an Old Spot," *New York Times,* January 4, 2010.

role in world affairs: Gellman, 176–8; and Fullilove's excellent account, 34–7, and notes 77 and 78 on 373–4.

"weirdest individuals in history": Kershaw, 23–4; Gellman, 179–81; Fullilove, 37–40.

"a criminal genius": Kershaw, 90–1, 369–79; Dallek, *Democrat and Diplomat,* 235–7; Gellman, 181–3; Fullilove, 40–4.

"make peace with Hitler": Roosevelt, *Personal Letters,* II: 1004; Gellman, 183–94; Fullilove, 47–56; Ickes, *Secret Diaries,* III: 216.

all he could offer: Gellman, 190; Roosevelt, press conference, March 29, 1940, online.

accept the nomination: Roosevelt, *Personal Letters,* II: 1011–2, 1014, 1018–21, 1024, 1026–8, 1035.

carry into the fall campaign: Roosevelt, *Personal Letters,* II: 975–7, 1016, 1041–2; Blum, *Morgenthau Diaries,* II: 136–7; Ickes, *Secret Diaries,* III: 179–81; Dallek, *Roosevelt,* 219; Leuchtenburg, *Roosevelt,* 306–7; Goodwin, 22–5, 48–53.

fear of isolationist complaints: Goodwin, 25–6; Roosevelt, press conference, May 10, 1940, online.

sell Britain aircraft: Kimball, *Churchill and Roosevelt,* I: 37–9.

challenge before it: Roosevelt, speeches, May 10, May 16, and May 26, 1940, online; Goodwin, 40–2.

a third term: *Gallup,* 220, 222, 226–7, 230; Olson, 98–105.

"artist of a great history": Churchill, speech, June 4, 1940, online; Goodwin, 61–4; de Gaulle, 57–8.

"confuse the public mind": Churchill, *Second*

World War, II: 122–3; Hull, *Memoirs,* I: 775; Roosevelt, *Personal Letters,* II: 1037–8.

he cabled Reynaud: Ickes, *Secret Diaries,* III: 202–3; Dallek, *Roosevelt,* 223; Roosevelt, speech, June 10, 1940, online; Kimball, *Churchill and Roosevelt,* I: 43–52.

very dispiriting time: Sherwood, 145–51; Goodwin, 69–70.

Chapter 13: "Safe on Third"

"negotiations with the French": Kershaw, 294–300; Goodwin, 72–3.

"except to serve you": Goodwin, 31–2; Roll, 4–5, 43–4, 49–51, 59; Sherwood, 2–3.

"so little in return": Smith, *FDR,* 205–7; Goodwin, 115–21, 241–6.

May Gallup poll: *Gallup,* 227–31.

popular sitting president: Gunther, 533; Olson, 170, 174; Moe, 148–51.

if he became president: Olson, 170–83; Moe, 143–69.

"unscrupulous . . . corporation man": Roosevelt, press conference, June 28, 1940, online; Ickes, *Secret Diaries,* III: 211–2, 220, 223, 227–8; Olson, 183.

nominated on the first ballot: Ickes, *Secret Diaries,* III: 238, 240, 249–50, 259–63; Sherwood, 176–9; Goodwin, 124–36.

work his will: Roosevelt, speech, July 19, 1940, online; Roosevelt, *Personal Letters,* II: 1046–8; Olson, 189–90.

hold his hand: *Gallup,* 232–4, 236–7; Kimball, *Churchill and Roosevelt,* I: 56–7; Ickes, *Secret Diaries,* III: 291–2; Churchill, *Second World War,* II: 346–7.

"tied up the two deals": *Gallup,* 243; Roosevelt, *Personal Letters,* II: 1056–8; Roosevelt, press conference, August 16, 1940, online; Roosevelt, message to Congress, September 3, 1940, online; Olson, 161–9, 190–3; Moe, 255–71.

advantage over Willkie: *Gallup,* 236–42; Ickes, *Secret Diaries,* III: 312–3.

step forward in national defense: Roosevelt, press conferences, June 7, June 18, August 23, 1940, online; Roosevelt, *Personal Letters,* II: 1058–60; Olson, 196–219.

"safer under Hitler than Churchill": Breitman and Lichtman, 21–2, 74, 76, 90–1, 93, 108–9, 122; Israel, *War Diary,* 141–2, 146–8; *Gallup,* 249; Beschloss, 213–20; Moe, 296–9.

haven for a persecuted people: Breitman and Lichtman, 164–8; Israel, *War Diary,* 130–1.

53 percent to 47 percent: *Gallup,* 244–5, 247–8.

win the war: Moe, 256, 272–88; Fullilove, chapter 2.

means of the radio: *Gallup,* 249, 252; Moe, 277–81; Roosevelt, *Personal Letters,* II: 1072–3.

"except in case of attack": Roosevelt speech, October 23, 1940, online; Sherwood, 186.

Churchill became prime minister: Roosevelt, speech October 28, 1940, online; Moe, 291–3.

well-being than Willkie: Roosevelt, schedule, October 30, 1940, online; Roosevelt, speech, October 30, 1940, online; Moe, 300–1.

"will say: 'Forward!' ": Sherwood, 195–6; Roosevelt, speech, November 2, 1940, online.

"atherosclerotic cardiovascular disease": Ickes, *Secret Diaries,* III: 361; Moe, 294–5, 301–2, 308–9; Smith, *Gatekeeper,* 220; Dr. Jeffrey Kelman, November 27, 2015, conversation with author.

dependable in a world crisis: Burns, *Lion and the Fox,* 451–5; Davis, *Into the Storm,* 622–5; Goodwin, 188–9; congressional results, online.

contributing greatly to British rearmament: Sherwood, 221–2; Burns, *Soldier of Freedom,* 9–18; Kershaw, 306–10, 327–36.

Britain might lose the war: Roosevelt, press conference, November 26, 1940, online; Dallek, *Roosevelt,* 252–3; Kimball, *Churchill and Roosevelt,* I: 81.

recently acquired bases: Kimball, *Churchill and Roosevelt,* I: 87–8; Ickes, *Secret Diaries,* III: 374–5; Roosevelt, press conferences, November 29, December 3, 1940, online; Sherwood, 222–3.

serve their common purpose: Churchill, *Second World War,* II: 475–83; Sherwood, 223–4.

enact the plan: Sherwood, 224–5; Goodwin, 193; Roosevelt, press conference, December 17, 1940, online.

resupply of Britain: "Lend-Lease," Wikipedia, online; Olson, 220–7; Roosevelt, Arsenal of Democracy speech, December 29, 1940, online; Freedman, 573–4.

"destruction that is too high": Ickes, *Secret Diaries:* 232, 322, 339; Dallek, *Roosevelt,* 236–43; Freedman, 529, 533–6, 550.

Chapter 14: The Path to War

were living through: Ickes, *Secret Diaries,* III: 392, 402; Burns, *Soldier of Freedom,* 36; Evans, 119–20; Goodwin, 202–3.

pass his measure: Blum, *Morgenthau Diaries,* II: 199; Ickes, *Secret Diaries,* III: 409–11; *Gallup,* 257.

shedding American blood: Roosevelt, *Personal Letters,* II: 1106; Roosevelt, State of the Union, January 6, 1941, online; Freedman, 577.

program of aid effective: Ickes, *Secret Diaries,* III: 386; Kimball, *Churchill and Roosevelt,* I: 112, 115–6, 120; Nasaw, 489–504.

only dropped once: Sherwood, 234–5; Churchill, *Second World War,* III: 5–6, 12; Kimball, *Churchill and Roosevelt,* I: 126; Roll, 49–51.

"everything we can give them": Sherwood, 235–43.

Overcome with emotion, Churchill wept: Churchill, *Second World War,* III: 19–21; Goodwin, 212–3.

"an act of war": Blum, *Morgenthau Diaries,* II: 212; Kimball, *Most Unsordid Act,* 124–6, 131–2, 136, 145, 152, 154–5.

"finish the job": Roosevelt, *Personal Letters,* II: 1108–9; Kimball, *Most Unsordid Act,* 156, 179; Goodwin, 213.

help arm Britain: Roosevelt, *Personal Letters,* I: 1107; Beschloss, 229; Burns, *Soldier of Freedom,* 43–9; Goodwin, 211–4; Nasaw, 511–21.

the head instructor: Roosevelt, press conferences, February 28, March 4, March 7, March 18, 1941; Roosevelt, speech March 29, 1941; Eleanor Roosevelt, "My Day," April 1, 1941, online; Goodwin, 225–31.

could not afford to lose: Kimball, *Churchill and Roosevelt,* I: 145, 149–53, 155–6, 165–6, 169–75; Roosevelt, *Personal Letters,* II: 1138, 1142–5, 1148–50.

"sabotage our preparedness program": Kimball, *Churchill and Roosevelt,* I: 181–2, 184–5; Howard G. Bruenn, "Clinical Notes on the Illness and Death of Franklin D. Roosevelt," *An-*

nals of Internal Medicine, April 1970; Sherwood, 293; Ward, 135; Bullitt, 512–6; Gellman, 235–46; Faderman, 14–6; *Gallup,* 274–7, 279–81; Goodwin, 235–6; Ickes, *Secret Diaries,* III: 472–3, 477, 489–92, 495, 522.

"create an incident": Ickes, *Secret Diaries,* III: 508–11, 520, 523, 527.

he told Morgenthau: Blum, *Morgenthau Diaries, II:* 253–4.

less ready to fight: Dallek, *Defenseless under the Night,* chapter 6; Ickes, *Secret Diaries,* III: 518–20; "Fiorello La Guardia," Wikipedia, online.

against Nazi occupation: Roosevelt, speech, May 27, 1941, online; Ickes, *Secret Diaries,* III: 526; Gallup, 274, 284–6; Sherwood, 298; Roosevelt, *Personal Letters,* II: 1161–2, 1165; Kimball, *Churchill and Roosevelt,* I: 198; Ward, 136; Goodwin, 238–9.

commitment to "total war": Roosevelt, press conference, May 28, 1941, online; Sherwood, 298–9, 302, 304; Ickes, *Secret Diaries,* III: 526–7; Blum, *Morgenthau Diaries,* II: 254; Kimball, *Churchill and Roosevelt,* I: 196–7; Dallek, *Roosevelt,* 264–7, 596–8.

bold move into war: Sherwood, 299; Ickes, *Secret Diaries,* III: 552; Kennedy, 494–5.

not a Soviet one: Kimball, *Churchill and Roosevelt,* I: 208, 211; Burns, *Soldier of Freedom,* 110–2; Goodwin, 254–7; Hull, *Memoirs,* II: 973; Ickes, *Secret Diaries,* III: 548–50; Freedman, 614–5; Sherwood, 306–8; Roll, 112–4; "Joseph E. Davies," Wikipedia, online; *Gallup,* 288–9.

"the Russian colossus": Kershaw, 390, 393–4, 399, 407–12.

"to one side": Roosevelt, speech, July 4, 1941, online; Ward, 137–8.

into the war: Sherwood, 308–17, 320, 322; McJimsey, 170–3; Roll, 116–21.

"to our meeting": Sherwood, 323–48; Roll, 122–36; Deutscher, 461–7; Taubman, 31–2, 41–2; Ickes, *Secret Diaries,* III: 592–3; Butler, 38–9; Blum, *Morgenthau Diaries,* II: 263–65; Kimball, *Churchill and Roosevelt,* I: 226.

the conservative Churchill: Ward, 140; Kaiser, 265–8; Kimball, *Churchill and Roosevelt,* I: 223; Goodwin, 262–3; Roll, 137–8; Sherwood, 350–1, 236–7.

bring America into the fighting: Dallek, *Roosevelt,* 281–2, 285; Burns, *Soldier of Freedom,* 126–7; Goodwin, 265–6; Kimball, *Churchill and Roosevelt,* I: 227–30; Ward, 141.

"get an hour off": Churchill, *Second World War,* III: 364–5; Ward, 141–2; Burns, *Soldier of Freedom,* 126; Goodwin, 266–7.

preserving the peace: Churchill, *Second World War,* III: 366–9, 373–5.

"this [Nazi] horror": Ward, 142–3; Roosevelt, press conferences, August 16, August 19, 1941, online; Freedman, 612–3.

"a great many people": *Gallup,* 291–2, 295; Burns, *Soldier of Freedom,* 120; Dallek, *Roosevelt,* 276–7; Goodwin, 267–9; Roosevelt, press conference, August 19, 1941, online.

"his Nazi forces": Kimball, *Churchill and Roosevelt,* I: 234–5; Dallek, *Roosevelt,* 286–7; Roosevelt, speech, September 1, 1941, online.

her children could recall: Kimball, *Churchill and Roosevelt,* I: 237–40; Burns, *Soldier of Freedom,* 139–40, 143; Goodwin, 270–5.

other friendly ships: Roosevelt, speech, September 11, 1941, online.

"throughout the world": Dallek, *Roosevelt,* 225–6, 289–90; Olson, 123–5, 337–40.

jumped to 61 percent: Kimball, *Churchill and Roosevelt,* I: 245–6; Gallup, 297, 299–302, 304, 311; Olson, 400; on Harriman, see Fullilove, chapter 5.

agreeing to war: Roosevelt, speech, October 27, 1941; Kimball, *Churchill and Roosevelt,* I: 264–5; Ickes, *Secret Diaries,* III: 650; Sherwood, 382–3.

at the risk of war: Ickes, *Secret Diaries,* III: 564–7; *Gallup,* 168, 177, 208, 246, 268–9, 296.

Roosevelt resisted Churchill's pressure: Ickes, *Secret Diaries,* III: 588; Kimball, *Churchill and Roosevelt,* I: 229, 231.

an Atlantic war: Kimball, *Churchill and Roosevelt,* I: 231, 250, 256–7, 266, 274–6; Sherwood, 426–7; *Gallup,* 311; Dallek, *Roosevelt,* 299–311.

knew a raid was coming: Burns, *Soldier of Freedom,* 161–7; Dallek *Roosevelt,* 311; Goodwin, 288–94.

anchored in shallow waters: Wohlstetter; Burns, *Soldier of Freedom,* 162. Also see Prange.

"power it can generate": Churchill, *Second World War,* III: 511–3; Dallek, *Roosevelt,* 312; Kershaw, 444–6; Asada Sadao, "The Japanese Navy and the United States," in Borg and Okamoto, 236–7, 254–5, 257.

Chapter 15: Setbacks and Losses: "We Might Lose This War"

way to America: Roosevelt, Fireside Chat, December 9, 1941, online; Hitler, 188; Dower, chapters 1–5; Kershaw, 487–95; Dawidowicz, 136–9; Friedlander, 339–43; Goodwin, 172–6.

"implementing" the strategy: Sherwood, 445; Roosevelt, Fireside Chat, December 9, 1941, online; Kimball, *Churchill and Roosevelt,* I: 283–6, 288–90.

"not strictly true": Roosevelt, press conference, December 23, 1941, online; Sherwood, 442–3; Goodwin, 303.

"Some chicken! Some neck!": Churchill, *Second World War,* III: 564–7, 571–2; Goodwin, 304–5, 307–10.

"a drinking problem": Goodwin, 302–3.

"sign our little document": Roosevelt, *Personal Letters,* II: 1259–60; Burns, *Soldier of Freedom,* 183–5; Dallek, *Roosevelt,* 318–20.

"freedom and faith": Roosevelt, State of the Union, January 6, 1942, online.

Alexander the Great and Napoleon: Burns, *Soldier of Freedom,* 181, 201–9; Tuchman, 231, 238, 249–50; Churchill, *Second World War,* IV: 53–4; Kimball, *Churchill and Roosevelt,* I: 336–7; Dallek, *Roosevelt,* 328–31; Nicholas, 22, 27.

"So speak Americans today!": Roosevelt, *Personal Letters,* II: 1294–5, 1298–1300; Roosevelt, Fireside Chat, February 23, 1942; Roosevelt, press conference, March 17, 1942, online.

immobilizing health problems: Roosevelt, press conference, March 10, 1942, online ;

Roosevelt, *Personal Letters,* II: 1283; Ward, 147–9, 157–8; Burns, *Soldier of Freedom,* 199–201.

helped vote into office: The best brief discussion of the Japanese American incarceration is in Kennedy, 748–60; Roosevelt, State of the Union, January 6, 1942, online; Ickes, *Secret Diaries,* February 1, March 1, 1942, online, FDRL; Dallek, *Roosevelt,* 334–5; Geraldine R. Kronmal, "Jewish Opinion and the Relocation of the Japanese," senior honors paper, UCLA, January 1965.

"war against tyranny": Burns, *Soldier of Freedom,* 216; Kimball, *Churchill and Roosevelt,* I: 326–37, 344–6, 351, 353–4, 356–8, 361–2.

" 'problem' by the others": Ward, 148–51.

"their own juice": McJimsey, 247–8; Churchill, *Second World War,* IV: 184–6, 190–1; Kimball, *Churchill and Roosevelt,* I: 374–5, 388–9, 395–6, 402–4, 422, 446–9, 456–7; Sherwood, 512, 531.

"continue to do so": Kimball, *Churchill and Roosevelt,* I: 394, 420–1; Dallek, *Roosevelt,* 337–8.

novel of the 1930s: Spector, 154–5; Kimball, *Churchill and Roosevelt,* I: 436–7, 440–1, 458, 465–6; Butler, 62–5; Roosevelt, press conference, April 21, 1942, online; Dallek, *Roosevelt,* 334; Kennedy, 535.

guards in concentration camps: Spector, 106–119, 134–9; Kennedy, 526–31.

Midway Island in June: Spector, 158–63; "Battle of the Coral Sea," Wikipedia, online.

"effects of those losses": Roosevelt, Fireside Chat, May 28, 1942, online.

"go back and retake it": Tuchman, chapters 10–11.

entire Far East: Roosevelt, *Personal Letters,* II: 1229–30; Dallek, *Roosevelt,* 354–6.

"most unfortunate effect": Collier, 289, 296–302; Kimball, *Churchill and Roosevelt,* I: 471–3, 494; Dallek, *Roosevelt,* 350.

cross-Channel assault in 1942: Churchill, *Second World War,* IV: 284–94; Kimball, *Churchill and Roosevelt,* I: 494–500.

"plans to meet it": Burns, *Soldier of Freedom,* 231–5; Ward, 159; Kimball, *Churchill and Roosevelt,* I: 503–4 .

"airmen and saboteurs": Friedlander, 349–50; Butler, 71; Roosevelt, *Personal Letters,* II: 1334–5.

happy to agree: Kimball, *Churchill and Roosevelt,* I: 508–10, 513–6; Ward, 160–1, 163–7; Burns, *Soldier of Freedom,* 235–6.

half year after Pearl Harbor: Kimball, *Churchill and Roosevelt,* I: 507–8, 510; Spector, 166–78; Kennedy, 535–43.

Chapter 16: The End of the Beginning

did not sway him: Kimball, *Churchill and Roosevelt,* I: 515, 520–1, 529–33; Butler, 71–5; Dallek, *Flawed Giant;* Roosevelt, *Personal Letters,* II: 1332, 1346–7.

"bees in his bonnet": Goodwin, 149–51, 351–5; Roosevelt, *Personal Letters,* II: 1336, 1340, 1343–5; Roosevelt, speech, September 3, 1942, online; Ward, 167–9.

"moments of relaxation are few": Kimball, *Churchill and Roosevelt,* I: 534, 541–4; Ward, 170–1.

Hitler's forces in Africa: Kimball, *Churchill and Roosevelt,* I: 544–6; Butler, 82–3; Roosevelt,

Personal Letters, II: 1341–2.

"dangerous at the moment": Kimball, *Churchill and Roosevelt,* I: 546–50, 556–7.

"attitude for a commander-in-chief": Roosevelt, speech, September 7, 1942, online; Blum, *Morgenthau Diaries,* III: 81, 82, 85.

part to play: Roosevelt, *Personal Letters,* II: 1349; Burns, *Soldier of Freedom,* 272; Dallek, *Defenseless Under the Night.*

served in the armed forces: Burns, *Soldier of Freedom,* 268–70; Goodwin, 360–73; Ward, 174–83.

supply Russia's armies: Roosevelt, *Personal Letters,* II: 1337–9.

enthusiasm for his party: Roosevelt, press conference, October 1, 1942, online; Kimball, *Churchill and Roosevelt,* I: 584–7, 594.

"stays won," he said: Roosevelt, Fireside Chat, October 12, 1942, online.

segregated from whites: Goodwin, 166–72, 328–30.

defeating Japan would be: Spector, 190–201, 208–14, 217–8; Dower, 64, 89–91; Kennedy, 547–61.

participation in the war: Kimball, *Churchill and Roosevelt,* I: 585–9, 594.

came in 1943 or after: Ibid., 595–8, 602, 608–14.

his guest's joke: Ibid., 616–9; Willkie.

"it will succeed": Kimball, *Churchill and Roosevelt,* I: 620–5, 628–30.

rally behind Roosevelt: Roosevelt, *Personal Letters,* II: 1355; Kimball, *Churchill and Roosevelt,* I: 633, 639; Dallek, *Roosevelt,* 354; Burns, *Soldier of Freedom,* 273–81; Goodwin, 384–5.

winning the war: Kimball, *Churchill and Roosevelt,* I: 636–9, 643; Roosevelt, press conference, November 6, 1942; Roosevelt, *Personal Letters,* II: 1359; Goodwin, 385–6.

an empty threat: Kimball, *Churchill and Roosevelt,* I: 640–2, 660–6; Roosevelt, *Personal Letters,* II: 1363–4, 1371; Dallek, *Roosevelt,* 251, 362–3.

"success it deserves": Kimball, *Churchill and Roosevelt,* I: 647–51.

doing in the war: Kimball, *Churchill and Roosevelt,* I: 654–6; Goodwin, 379–84.

"harmony in Chungking": Dallek, *Roosevelt,* 354–8.

idealism and hardheaded realism: Roosevelt, *Personal Letters,* II: 1361, 1366–7, 1371–2; Dallek, *Roosevelt,* 358–61; Ward, 186–8.

"end of the beginning": Ward, 183–6; Kimball, *Churchill and Roosevelt,* I: 659–60; Burns, *Soldier of Freedom,* 291–2; Dallek, *Roosevelt,* 362; Goodwin, 385–9.

"confused and cast down": Kimball, *Churchill and Roosevelt,* I: 667–9; Dallek, *Roosevelt,* 363–6; Burns, *Soldier of Freedom,* 292–8; Goodwin, 389–90.

opening months of 1943: Burns, *Soldier of Freedom,* 298; Kennedy, 583–4.

Chapter 17: "High Promise of Better Things"

some kind of rescue effort: *Gallup,* 337, 339, 356; Breitman and Lichtman, 201–10; Goodwin, 396–7; Nicholas, 123.

prevent another war: Roosevelt, *Personal Letters,* II: 1378, 1382, 1384–5, 1389–91; *Gallup,* 346, 358; Roosevelt, State of the Union, January 7, 1943, online ; Nicholas, 134–6; *Gallup,* 361.

Stalingrad on February 2: Ward, 193; Kimball, *Churchill and Roosevelt,* II: 38–43; Collier, 296–311.

one of his chiefs joked: Butler, 101–5; Kimball, *Churchill and Roosevelt,* II: 51, 53–7, 63, 66–7, 72–4, 77–8, 80–1, 85–6, 108–9; Dallek, *Roosevelt,* 368–9.

"a wonderful mind set": Sherwood, 668–9; Ward, 194, 196–8; Roosevelt, *Personal Letters,* II: 1393.

"we will yield": Sherwood, 670–5; Dallek, *Roosevelt,* 369–72, 384–7; Kennedy, 585–8.

conversations as "comedy": Ward, 199; Sherwood, 678–93; de Gaulle, 382–99, 418; Dallek, *Roosevelt,* 376–9.

destruction of their homelands: Butler, 112–4, 116–7; Dallek, *Roosevelt,* 373–6.

hers for him was palpable: Kimball, *Churchill and Roosevelt,* II: 126–7, 156; Sherwood, 695; Ward, 200–5.

China and U.S. internationalism: Nicholas, 154–6, 162–3; *Gallup,* 371; Blum, *Morgenthau Diaries,* III: 88, 104–6; Ward, 202–3; Sherwood, 660–1; Tuchman, 349–53; Lash, 675–81; Ward, 222; Dallek, *Roosevelt,* 387–8.

"up and down the Pacific": Ward, 207; Nicholas, 165–8; Kimball, *Churchill and Roosevelt,* II: 155–6, 178; *Gallup,* 371; Dallek, *Roosevelt,* 389–90.

this resurgent idealism: See Dallek, *Roosevelt,* 388; and Dallek, *American Style of Foreign Policy,* chapter 5.

tied to the Allies: Kennedy, 588–91; Dallek, *Roo-*

sevelt, 380; Butler, 121–2, 128–30.

"hasn't been disproved yet": Roosevelt, *Personal Letters,* II: 1413, 1421; Sherwood, 734–5.

"his spirits were higher": Ward, 208–21; Goodwin, 424–7.

Japanese prisoners of war: Goodwin, 421–4, 427–31; "Japanese American Service in World War II," Wikipedia, online.

win another term: Kimball, *Churchill and Roosevelt,* II: 183–90, 192–202; Butler, 122–7.

"new form of government" emerged: Churchill, *Second World War,* IV: 680–1; Kimball, *Churchill and Roosevelt,* II: 202, 206, 208–211; Sherwood, 727–8.

"afforded tolerable solutions": Churchill, *Second World War,* IV: 696.

tales of their own: Ibid., 686–90; Goodwin, 437–9.

"turns the clock upside down": Churchill, *Second World War,* IV: 694–6, 701–3; Sherwin, 71–85; Ward, 221; Goodwin, 439.

"possible at this time": Butler, 136–43.

"you and me": Ibid., 144–8.

practiced brutal discrimination: Goodwin, 440–7.

Chapter 18: "Dr. Win the War"

"be the host": Ward. 222–5, 241; Kimball, *Churchill and Roosevelt,* II: 254–5; Viorst.

"amidst so much clatter": Nicholas, 208–9; Kimball, *Churchill and Roosevelt,* II: 290–1.

the two are indelibly linked: Kimball, *Churchill and Roosevelt,* II: 327; Roosevelt, press conference, July 25, 1943, online; Burns, *Soldier of Freedom,* 381–3.

"its duty in this regard": Roosevelt, Fireside Chat, July 28, 1943, online.

"equal or sufficient recognition": Ward, 226–7; Butler, 150–1; Kimball, *Churchill and Roosevelt,* II: 300–1, 303–4.

served by a monarchial regime: Kimball, *Churchill and Roosevelt,* II: 323, 328, 333, 336–7, 345, 348–52, 354–5, 360.

foreign office chiefs: Ibid., 387–400, 421; Ward, 228–30, 232; Goodwin, 456–9; Butler, 151–2.

"representatives of the three countries": Butler, 152–7; Ward, 231.

Hitler's fascist partner: Burns, *Soldier of Freedom,* 390–4, 399.

reliable future ally: Sherwin, 85–9, 102–3; Sherwood, 748–49.

"we shall win the war": Roosevelt, press conference, August 31, 1943, online; Burns, *Soldier of Freedom,* 395–8; Breitman and Lichtman, chapter 11.

no external conditions could contain: Ward, 235; Post and Robbins, 27–9; Ward, 238, 249.

"have done the right thing": McJimsey, 18–9, 126–8, 295; Ward, 235, 239, 245–6; Goodwin, 459; Roll, 284–7.

by a wide margin: Ward, 240, 242, 244; Gellman, chapters 13–14; Faderman, 14–6.

he asked Churchill: Kimball, *Churchill and Roosevelt,* II: 489–91.

agreed to meet in December: Ibid., 497–9, 501–6, 516–7, 554–7, 562–3.

gathering in Tehran: Ibid., 561; Ward, 249–52; Butler, 161–3, 166–7, 169–84.

to international peace: Ward, 251.

"more gay," Churchill recalled: Kimball, *Chur-*

chill and Roosevelt, II: 568; Hull, *Memoirs,* II: 1313; Sherwood, 766–71; Roosevelt, *Personal Letters,* II: 1469–70; Churchill, *Second World War,* V: 290; Goodwin, 473–5.

powerful of men "squirm": Goodwin, 474.

"activity in the Mediterranean": Kimball, *Churchill and Roosevelt,* II: 594–8, 600–1; Sherwood, 775–6; Dallek, *Roosevelt,* 424–5.

U.S. designs in postwar Asia: Tuchman, chapters 15 and 16, especially 378–9, 401–2, 410; Dallek, *Roosevelt,* 426–30.

"a good Conservative": The Kennan anecdote was told at a World War II panel at an Organization of American Historians meeting in Denver in 1985. Stalin's comment on the English was in a televised BBC documentary on World War II: "Dividing the World." For the rest, see Gilbert, *Road to Victory,* chapter 34; and Montefiore, chapter 42.

a "desolate" Europe: Gilbert, *Road to Victory;* Montefiore, 467.

renewed threat to Russia: Dallek, *Roosevelt,* 430–8; Gilbert, *Road to Victory.*

"for a kopeck": Gilbert, *Road to Victory,* 594–601; Dallek, *Roosevelt,* 440; Bullock, 856.

postwar international affairs: Roosevelt, press conference, December 17, 1943, online.

revert to isolationism: Roosevelt, Fireside Chat, December 24, 1943, online.

safe from another war: Roosevelt, press conference, December 28, 1943, online; Ward, 264, 266, 421; Freedman, 709; Dallek, *Roosevelt,* 440–1.

national well-being: Ward, 264–6, 271–5, 277–8.

for every American: Burns, *Soldier of Freedom,* 421–2, 424; Roosevelt, State of the Union, January 11, 1944, online.

endorsed the idea: *Gallup,* 427, 433–4, 442.

strains on his health: Burns, *Soldier of Freedom,* 429–37; Goodwin, 484–8.

cost them the war: Kimball, *Churchill and Roosevelt,* II: 647, 728; Burns, *Soldier of Freedom,* 443–6; Goodwin, 488.

might face in France: Kimball, *Churchill and Roosevelt,* II: 632–3, 636, 656–8, 705, 711–2, 728–9, 757, 759.

arrangements in postwar affairs: Blum, *Morgenthau Diaries,* III: 207–23; Breitman and Lichtman, 232–7.

regardless of the personal cost: Ward, 284–90, 296; Kimball, *Churchill and Roosevelt,* II: 754–5, III: 59–60; Howard G. Bruenn, "Clinical Notes on the Illness and Death of President Franklin D. Roosevelt," *Annals of Internal Medicine,* April 1970; Post and Robins, 27–30; Lawrence K. Altman, "For F.D.R. Sleuths, New Focus on an Odd Spot," *New York Times,* January 4, 2010; also see "FDR's Health," online.

struggle with personal agitation: Kimball, *Churchill and Roosevelt,* III: 74, 77–8, 88–126; Ward, 294–5; the health records are available online at "FDR health."

circumstances might change: Ward, 298–303, 305, 308–9, 311–3, 315; *Gallup,* 445, 453–4.

if he asked: Kimball, *Churchill and Roosevelt,* III: 86–90, 102, 104, 108–9, 128–30, 135–8, 145–

52, 156–7, 167–8; de Gaulle, 554–9.

"keeping my head above water": Gilbert, *Road to Victory,* 753–5; Kimball, *Churchill and Roosevelt,* III: 146–7, 150, 159–61.

advances in France: de Gaulle, 558; Collier, 387–403; Kimball, *Churchill and Roosevelt,* III: 164–5, 183, 186.

program could provide: Kimball, *Churchill and Roosevelt,* III: 165–7; "G.I. Bill," Wikipedia, online.

France and Russia did: Burns, *Soldier of Freedom,* 498; Ward, 315, 317; Goodwin, 462–5; Tuchman, 369, 460; Spector, chapters 14 and 16.

"spheres of influence": Kimball, *Churchill and Roosevelt,* III: 153–4, 173, 177–82.

their strategic views: Ibid., III: 185–6, 197–9, 212–32.

votes in an upcoming campaign: Ibid., III: 208–10.

"for France or for himself": Viorst, 190–209; de Gaulle, 570–6; Dallek, *Roosevelt,* 458–62.

"people of the United States": *Gallup,* 454, 458; Roosevelt, press conference, July 11, 1944, online ; Lelyveld, 143–7; Black, 951, 967.

Chapter 20: Winning the War, Planning the Peace

avoid future wars: *Gallup,* 452; Collier, 394, 400–1, 405, 413–7; Nicholas, 389–90; on the coup, see Bullock, 833–41; *Kershaw,* chapters 14 and 15.

"sick, discouraged, and exhausted": *Gallup,* 453; Ickes to Roosevelt, July 3, 1944 ; "FDR Accepting the 1944 Democratic Nomination,"

July 20, 1944, Roosevelt's Health Records, online; Roosevelt and Schalett, 351–2; Roosevelt, *My Parents,* 279; Roosevelt, speech, July 20, 1944, online; Rosenman, *Working with Roosevelt,* 453; Goodwin, 529–30.

"Second Missouri Compromise": Rosenman, *Working with Roosevelt,* 438–51; Goodwin, 525–30; Black, 965–75.

Sam Rosenman recalled: Rosenman, *Working with Roosevelt,* 455–9.

after occupying Formosa: Ibid., 456–7; Nicholas, 401; Manchester, 355–72; Spector, 418–20.

after the election: Roosevelt, *Personal Letters:* 527; "FDR's Health, September 20–October 4, 1944," online; Rosenman, *Working with Roosevelt,* 461–70; Ward, 321; Goodwin, 537.

September 10 or September 11: Kimball, *Churchill and Roosevelt,* III: 248–51, 266–7, 270–2, 274.

"danger of Communism": Kimball, *Churchill and Roosevelt,* III: 269–70, 272–6, 278–85; Gilbert, *Road to Victory,* 881–3, 889–96, 901, 906–8, 911, 923–9.

under Moscow's control: Kimball, *Churchill and Roosevelt,* III: 288, 292–7, 309–13.

"was really tired": Ward, 321–2, 325–6.

bring to fruition: "FDR's Health: Examination Report Summary, September 20–October 4, 1944" ; and "Historical Perspectives," citing Ferrell, online ; "The Heart Disease Conundrum," *New York Times,* November 29, 2015.

Washington on September 23: Roosevelt, press conferences, August 18, August 25, August 29, and September 8, 1944, online.

"old, unwell and depressed": Kimball, *Churchill and Roosevelt,* III: 305–7; Gilbert, *Road to Victory,* 941–3, 949.

ahead of the Soviets: Gilbert, *Road to Victory,* 958–9, 961; Kimball, *Churchill and Roosevelt,* III: 315–6; Blum, *Morgenthau Diaries,* III: 308–16, 322; Dallek, *Roosevelt,* 469–70.

"learns to toddle": Butler, 254–8; Kimball, *Churchill and Roosevelt,* III: 334–6, 339.

such an agreement: Blum, *Morgenthau Diaries,* III: chapter 7, 375–83; Dallek, *Roosevelt,* 472–5, 477; Gilbert, *Road to Victory,* 961–2, 965.

"seems to be slowly failing": Gilbert, *Road to Victory,* 965, 969; Ward, 326, 329.

"peace of the world": Gilbert, *Road to Victory,* 963–5, 969–70; Dallek, *Roosevelt,* 470–1.

"Failure is now unthinkable": Gilbert, *Road to Victory,* 975–8; Kimball, *Churchill and Roosevelt,* III: 339–43.

"we are all three together": Kimball, *Churchill and Roosevelt,* III: 344–5.

a combative candidate: "FDR's Health," October 20, 1944, online; McIntire, 14–7; Roosevelt, press conference, October 17, 1944, online.

momentum it achieved: Roosevelt, "Fala" speech, September 23, 1944, online; Ward, 328.

sake of the election: Ward, 330, 332–3.

"my divisions in Heaven": Kimball, *Churchill and Roosevelt,* III: 339–40, 344, 350–2; Butler, 260–3; Gilbert, *Road to Victory,* 989–93; Dallek, *Roosevelt,* 479; "Voices from Russia," December 10, 2009, online.

access to the Black Sea: Kimball, *Churchill and*

Roosevelt, III: 353, 357–9.

"further military policy": *Gallup,* 458–60, 464–5, 470; Kimball, *Churchill and Roosevelt,* III: 359; Butler, 263–4.

Churchill and Stalin: Kimball, *Churchill and Roosevelt,* III: 329–30, 364; *Gallup,* 472, 477–8; On Roosevelt's concern about rescuing Jews as a politically unpopular and isolated cause, see Breitman and Lichtman, 263–4.

victims of Nazi madness: Roosevelt, press conference, March 24, 1944, online; Breitman and Lichtman, chapters 13 and 14; Black, 811–21.

after Germany's collapse: Tuchman, 491–504; Dallek, *Roosevelt,* 485–501.

"better future ensured": Rosenman, *Working with Roosevelt,* chapter 25; Sherwood, 828–9; Ward, 332; "FDR's Health" October 21 and November 6, 1944, describes his campaign schedule, online; Kimball, *Churchill and Roosevelt,* III: 367–8, 383, 385.

Chapter 21: Last Full Measure

"the man for us": Campbell and Herring, 167; Kimball, *Churchill and Roosevelt,* III: 389; Roosevelt, *Personal Letters,* II: 1553, 1557, 1563; Burns, *Soldier of Freedom,* 530–1. The two best books on Roosevelt's last days are Lelyveld and Woolner.

last twelve months: Ward, 340, 344–8.

gave in to Stalin's demand: Kimball, *Churchill and Roosevelt,* III: 377–81, 388–9, 395–6, 403–4, 408–9, 411; Montefiore, 479–80.

"put my faith in you": Kimball, *Churchill and Roosevelt,* III: 389–94, 398–9.

serving both sides: Ibid., III: 407, 419, 421, 424–5.

Churchill sarcastically observed: Butler, 274–5, 280–4; Kimball, *Churchill and Roosevelt,* III: 497.

rekindle isolationist sentiment: Roosevelt, *Personal Letters,* II: 1559–60, 1564–5.

"danger recedes and faction arises": Kimball, *Churchill and Roosevelt,* III: 434–9, 451.

not too distant future: Ibid., III: 443–5, 447–58.

"these tangled questions": Ibid., III: 462–5, 468, 487–8.

"went into his decline": Ward, 348, 353–5, 361–4, 366–7, 380; Goodwin, 562–5, 568–9, 570–3.

central part in peacekeeping: Roosevelt, *Personal Letters,* II: 1565–6; Roosevelt, State of the Union, January 6, 1945, online.

his admiring guests: Roosevelt, inaugural, January 20, 1945, online ; Goodwin, 572–3.

"from our frankness": Kimball, *Churchill and Roosevelt,* III: 481–2; Dallek, *Roosevelt,* 507–8.

mutual goodwill: Dallek, *Roosevelt,* 505–6.

elusive prize — lasting peace: Kimball, *Churchill and Roosevelt,* III: 469, 477–9, 481–2, 484, 486, 488, 491.

"health and spirits": Kimball, *Churchill and Roosevelt,* III: 489, 491, 494–6, 501–3, 507, 511; Gilbert, *Road to Victory,* 1158–9, 1167–9, 1171; Goodwin, 576; Plokhy, 29.

their "criminal intentions": *FRUS,* 549–52, 574; Dallek, *Roosevelt,* 508; Gilbert, *Road to Victory,* 1171–3; Goodwin, 576–7; Plokhy, 4–10, 36–9, 44–7, 50–1, 64–5.

"another social system": Dallek, *Roosevelt,* 508–9; Burns, *Soldier of Freedom,* 565–6; Goodwin, 580; Gilbert, *Road to Victory,* 1173–4; Plokhy, 72–5; Montefiore, 482.

from General Marshall: *FRUS,* 574–88; Plokhy, 76–8, 91.

"care not wherefore they sang": *FRUS,* 589–90; Gilbert, *Road to Victory,* 1175–6.

at a later time: *FRUS,* 611–19; Gilbert, *Road to Victory,* 1178–81.

two additional American votes: Burns, *Soldier of Freedom,* 567–8; Dallek, *Roosevelt,* 510–1; Gilbert, *Road to Victory,* 1187–8.

Russian battlefield gains: *FRUS,* 667–70; Gilbert, *Road to Victory,* 1183–6; Burns, *Soldier of Freedom,* 569–71; Dallek, *Roosevelt,* 436–7.

their national security: Dallek, *Roosevelt,* 514–9; Bullock, 869–70; Gilbert, *Road to Victory,* 1189–93, 1209; *FRUS,* 860–3; Burns, *Soldier of Freedom,* 580.

accept the deal: *FRUS,* 766–70.

realities of Soviet power: Montefiore, 482–3; Burns, *Soldier of Freedom,* 573–4; Dallek, *Roosevelt,* 519; Goodwin, 585.

his way home: *FRUS,* 924; Lash, 717; Roosevelt, *Personal Letters,* II: 1570; Burns, *Soldier of Freedom,* 578–9; Goodwin, 583–4.

his own mortality: Burns, *Soldier of Freedom,* 579; Goodwin, 583–4.

take a leading part: Roosevelt, speech, March 1, 1945, online; Burns, *Soldier of Freedom,* 581; Dallek, *Roosevelt,* 520; Steven Lomazow, M.D., "Deadly Secret," September 30, 2009, online.

abandon their isolationism: Butler, 302–8, 312–5.

"course thus far is correct": Roosevelt, *Personal Letters,* II: 1575; Kimball, *Churchill and Roosevelt,* III: 539, 548–51, 560–5, 567–9, 595–7, 613, 617, 620, 624–5; Butler, 310–21.

"is all about": William Hassett Diary, March 30, 1945, "FDR's Health," online; Ward, 400–4, 411.

pronounced him dead: "Dr. Howard Bruenn's Examination Report of FDR's Last Day," April 12, 1945, online; Ward, 408, 410–1, 416–9.

both of them: Lash, 720–1.

"in the White House": Goodwin, 605–6.

could be given to him: Goodwin, 615.

Epilogue

"were [also] apparent": Jackson is quoted in Cook, *Eleanor Roosevelt: 1939–1962,* 205; the quote about the state of the economy is on 141–2. The other quotes are in Leuchtenburg, *Shadow of FDR,* 3–4, 33.

commitment to American democracy: Cook, *Eleanor Roosevelt: 1939–1962,* 333–43.

Romania, France, and Hungary: Ibid., 313, 498–501.

BIBLIOGRAPHY

Adler, Alfred. *Understanding Human Nature.* New York: Fawcett Books, 1981.

Alter, Jonathan. *The Defining Moment: FDR's Hundred Days and the Triumph of Hope.* New York: Simon & Schuster, 2006.

Amadeo, Kimberly. "U.S. GDP by Year Compared to Recessions and Events: The Ups and Downs of the U.S. Economy Since 1929." *Balance,* April 19, 2017. https:// www.thebalance.com/ us-gdp-by-year-3305543.

Ansbacher, H. L., and R. R. Ansbacher, eds. *The Individual Psychology of Alfred Adler.* New York: Harper & Row, 1964.

Berle, Beatrice B., and Travis B. Jacobs, eds. *Navigating the Rapids, 1918–1971: From the Papers of Adolph A. Berle.* New York: Harcourt Brace Jovanovich, 1973.

Beschloss, Michael R. *Kennedy and Roosevelt: The Uneasy Alliance.* New York: Open Road Media, 2016.

Black, Conrad. *Franklin Delano Roosevelt: Champion of Freedom.* New York: Public Affairs, 2003.

Blum, John M. *From the Morgenthau Diaries, 1938–*

1945. 3 vols. Boston: Houghton Mifflin, 1959–1969.

Boller, Jr., Paul S. *Presidential Inaugurations.* Orlando, FL: Harcourt Books, 2001.

Borg, Dorothy, and Shumpei Okamoto, eds. *Pearl Harbor as History: Japanese-American Relations, 1931–1941.* New York: Columbia University Press, 1973.

Brands, H. W. *Traitor to His Class: The Privileged Life and Radical Presidency of Franklin Delano Roosevelt.* New York: Doubleday, 2008.

Breitman, Richard, et al., eds. *Refugees and Rescue: The Diaries and Papers of James G. McDonald.* Bloomington: Indiana University Press, *2009.*

Breitman, Richard, and Allan J. Lichtman. *FDR and the Jews.* Cambridge, MA: Harvard University Press, 2013.

Brinkley, Alan. *The End of Reform: New Deal Liberalism in Depression and War.* New York: Vintage Books, 1996.

———. *Voices of Protest: Huey Long, Father Coughlin and the Great Depression.* New York: Vintage Books, 1983.

Brinkley, Douglas. *Rightful Heritage: Franklin D. Roosevelt and the Land of America.* New York: Harper Collins, 2016.

Bullitt, Orville H., ed. *For the President: Personal & Secret: Correspondence Between Franklin D. Roosevelt and William C. Bullitt.* Boston: Houghton Mifflin Co., 1972.

Bullock, Alan. *Hitler and Stalin: Parallel Lives.* New York: Alfred A. Knopf, 1993.

Burns, James MacGregor. *Roosevelt: The Lion and the Fox.* New York: Harcourt, 1956.

————. *Roosevelt: Soldier of Freedom.* New York: Harcourt, 1973.

Burns, James MacGregor, and Susan Dunn. *The Three Roosevelts: Patrician Leaders Who Transformed America.* New York: Grove/Atlantic, 2001.

Butler, Susan, ed. *My Dear Mr. Stalin: The Complete Correspondence of Franklin D. Roosevelt and Joseph V. Stalin.* New Haven, CT: Yale University Press, 2005.

Campbell, Thomas M., and George C. Herring, eds. *The Diaries of Edward R. Stettinius, Jr., 1943–1946.* West Sussex, England: Littlehampton Book Services LTD, 1975.

Caro, Robert A. *The Power Broker: Robert Moses and the Fall of New York.* New York: Alfred A. Knopf, 1974.

Churchill, Winston S. *The Second World War.* 6 vols. New York: Houghton Mifflin Company, 1948–1953.

Collier, Basil. *The Second World War: A Military History.* New York: William Morrow, 1967.

Connally, Tom. My Name is Tom Connally: As Told to Alfred Steinberg. New York: Crowell, 1954.

Cook, Blanche Wiesen. *Eleanor Roosevelt: 1884–1933.* New York: Viking Penguin, 1992.

————. *Eleanor Roosevelt: The Defining Years, 1933–1938.* New York: Viking Penguin, 1999.

————. *Eleanor Roosevelt: The War Years and After, 1939–1962.* New York: Viking Penguin, 2016.

Cooper, John Milton Jr. *Woodrow Wilson: A Biography.* New York: Alfred A. Knopf, 2009.

Dallek, Matthew J. *Defenseless Under the Night: FDR and the Origins of Homeland Security.* New

York: Oxford University Press, 2016.

Dallek, Robert. *Democrat and Diplomat: The Life of William E. Dodd.* New York: Oxford University Press, 1968.

———. *Franklin D. Roosevelt and American Foreign Policy, 1932–1945.* New York: Oxford University Press, 1979.

———. *The American Style of Foreign Policy: Cultural Politics and Foreign Affairs.* New York: Alfred A. Knopf, 1984.

———. *Flawed Giant: Lyndon Johnson and His Times, 1961–1973.* New York: Oxford University Press, 1998.

———. *Lone Star Rising: Lyndon Johnson and His Times, 1908–1960.* New York: Oxford University Press, 1991.

———. *An Unfinished Life: John F. Kennedy, 1917–1963.* Boston: Little, Brown and Co., 2003.

Davis, Kenneth S. *FDR: The Beckoning of Destiny, 1882–1928.* New York: Random House, 1972.

———. *FDR: Into the Storm: 1937–1940.* New York: Random House, 1993.

———. *FDR: The New York Years, 1928–1933.* New York: Random House, 1994.

———. *FDR: The New Deal Years, 1933–1937.* New York: Random House, 1986.

Dawidowicz, Lucy S. *The War Against the Jews, 1939–1945.* London: Weidenfeld and Nicolson, 1975.

De Gaulle, Charles. *The Complete War Memoirs of Charles de Gaulle, 1940–1946.* New York: Simon & Schuster, 1964.

Deutscher, Isaac. *Stalin: A Political Biography.* New York: Oxford University Press, 1967.

Dingman, Roger. *Power in the Pacific: The Origins*

of Naval Arms Limitation, 1914–1922. Chicago: University of Chicago Press, 1976.

Dower, John W. War Without Mercy: Race and Power in the Pacific War. New York: Pantheon, 1986.

Evans, Hugh E. The Hidden Campaign: FDR's Health and the 1944 Campaign. New York: Routledge, 2015.

Faber, Doris. The Life of Lorena Hickok: E.R.'s Friend. New York: W. Morrow, 1980.

Faderman, Lillian. The Gay Revolution: The Story of the Struggle. New York: Simon & Schuster, 2016.

Farley, James A. Behind the Ballots: The Personal History of a Politician. New York: Harcourt, Brace, 1938.

————. Jim Farley's Story: The Roosevelt Years. New York: McGraw Hill, 1948.

Ferrell, Robert. The Dying President: Franklin D. Roosevelt, 1944–1945. Columbia: University of Missouri Press, 1998.

Foreign Relations of the United States [FRUS]: The Conferences at Malta and Yalta, 1945. Washington: U.S. Government Printing Office, 1955.

Freedman, Max, ed. Roosevelt & Frankfurter: Their Correspondence, 1928–1945. Boston: Little, Brown & Co., 1967.

Freidel, Frank. Franklin D. Roosevelt: Launching the New Deal. Boston: Little, Brown, 1973.

————. Franklin D. Roosevelt: A Rendezvous with Destiny. Boston: Little, Brown and Company, 1990.

Friedlander, Saul. Nazi Germany and the Jews, 1939–1945: The Years of Extermination. New York: Harper Perennial, 2008.

Fullilove, Michael. *Rendezvous with Destiny: How Franklin D. Roosevelt and Five Extraordinary Men Took America into the War and into the World.* New York: Penguin Books, 2014.

Gallup, George H. *The Gallup Poll: Public Opinion 1935–1948.* New York: Random House, 1972.

Gelfand, Lawrence E. *The Inquiry: American Preparations for Peace, 1917–1919.* Ames: University of Iowa Press, 1963.

Gellman, Irwin F. *Secret Affairs: FDR, Cordell Hull, and Sumner Welles.* Baltimore: Johns Hopkins University Press, 1995.

Gilbert, Martin. *Churchill: A Life.* London: Heinemann, 1991.

———. *Winston S. Churchill: Road to Victory, 1941–1945.* Boston: Houghton Mifflin, 1986.

Golway, Terry. *Machine Made: Tammany Hall and the Creation of Modern American Politics.* New York: Liveright, 2014.

Goodwin, Doris Kearns. *No Ordinary Time: Franklin and Eleanor Roosevelt: The Home Front in World War II.* New York: Simon & Schuster, 1994.

Gunther, John. *Inside USA.* New York: Harper, 1947.

Gusfield, Joseph. *Symbolic Crusade: Status Politics and the American Temperance Movement.* Urbana: University of Illinois Press, 1963.

Hitler, Adolf. *Hitler's Table Talk: 1941–1944, His Private Conversations.* New York: Oxford University Press, 1988.

Hofstadter, Richard. *The Age of Reform: From Bryan to FDR.* New York: Alfred A. Knopf, 1956.

———. *Anti-intellectualism In American Life.* New

York: Alfred A. Knopf, 1963.

————. *The American Political Tradition and the Men Who Made It.* New York: Vintage Books, 1974.

Hull, Cordell. *Memoirs.* 2 vols. New York: The Macmillan Co., 1948.

Ickes, Harold L. *Secret Diaries of Harold L. Ickes, 1933–1941.* 3 vols. New York: Simon & Schuster, 1953–54.

Isaacson, Walter. *Einstein: His Life and Universe.* New York: Simon and Schuster, 2007.

Israel, Fred L. *Nevada's Key Pittman.* Lincoln: University of Nebraska Press, 1963.

————, ed. *The War Diary of Breckinridge Long.* Lincoln: University of Nebraska Press, 1966.

Jay, Anthony, ed. *The Oxford Dictionary of Political Quotations.* New York: Oxford University Press, 1990.

Kaiser, David. *No End Save Victory: How FDR Led the Nation into War.* New York: Basic Books, 2014.

Katznelson, Ira. *Fear Itself: The New Deal and the Origins of Our Time.* New York: Liveright Publishing Company, 2013.

Kennan, George F. *The Kennan Diaries.* Edited by Frank Castigliola. New York: W.W. Norton, 2014.

Kennedy, David M. *Freedom From Fear: The American People in Depression and War, 1929–1945.* New York: Oxford University Press, 1999.

Kershaw, Ian. *Hitler: Nemesis, 1936–1945.* New York: W. W. Norton, 2000.

Kimball, Warren F. *The Most Unsordid Act: Lend-Lease, 1939–1941.* Baltimore: Johns Hopkins University Press, 1969.

————, ed. *Churchill and Roosevelt: Complete Correspondence.* 3 vols. Princeton, NJ: Princeton University Press, 1984.

Lash, Joseph P. *Eleanor and Franklin: The Story of Their Relationship.* New York: W.W. Norton & Company, 1971.

Lelyveld, Joseph. *His Final Battle: The Last Months of Franklin Roosevelt.* New York: Alfred A. Knopf, 2016.

Leuchtenburg, William E. *The American President: From Teddy Roosevelt to Bill Clinton.* New York: Oxford University Press, 2015.

————. *Franklin D. Roosevelt and the New Deal, 1932–1940.* New York: Harper & Row, 1963.

————. *Herbert Hoover.* New York: Times Books, 2009.

————. *In the Shadow of FDR: From Harry Truman to Ronald Reagan.* Ithaca, NY: Cornell University Press, 1993.

————. *The Supreme Court Reborn: The Constitutional Revolution in the Age of Roosevelt.* New York: Oxford University Press, 1995.

Levine, Lawrence W. *The Unpredictable Past: Explorations in American Cultural History.* New York: Oxford University Press, 1993.

Levine, Lawrence W., and Cornelia Levine. *The Fireside Conversations: America Responds to FDR during the Great Depression.* Berkeley: University of California Press, 2010.

————. *The People and the President: America's Conversation with FDR.* Boston: Beacon Press, 2002.

Link, Arthur S. *Wilson: The Road to the White House.* Princeton, NJ: Princeton University Press, 1947.

————. *Wilson: The New Freedom.* Princeton, NJ: Princeton University Press, 1956.

————. *Woodrow Wilson and the Progressive Era, 1910–1917.* New York: Harper & Row, 1963.

Manchester, William. *American Caesar: Douglas MacArthur, 1880–1964.* New York: Little Brown & Co., 1978.

McCoy, Donald R. *Landon of Kansas.* Lincoln: University of Nebraska Press, 1966.

McIntire, Ross T. *Surgeon General of the Navy, White House Physician.* New York: G. P. Putnam's Sons, 1946.

McJimsey, George T. *Harry Hopkins: Ally of the Poor and Defender of Democracy.* Cambridge, MA: Harvard University Press, 1987.

Moe, Richard. *Roosevelt's Second Act: The Election of 1940 and the Politics of War.* New York: Oxford University Press, 2013.

Moley, Raymond A. *After Seven Years.* New York: Harper and Brothers, 1939.

Montefiore, Simon Sebag. *Stalin: The Court of the Red Tsar.* London: Weidenfeld and Nicolson, 2003.

Morgan, Ted. *FDR: A Biography.* London: Grafton Books, 1985.

Nasaw, David. *The Patriarch: The Remarkable Life and Turbulent Times of Joseph P. Kennedy.* New York: Penguin Press, 2013.

Nicholas, H. G. *Washington Dispatches, 1941–1945.* London: Littlehampton Book Services, 1981.

Olson, Lynne. *Those Angry Days: Roosevelt, Lindbergh and America's Fight Over World War II, 1939–1941.* New York: Random House, 2013.

Osgood, Robert E. *Ideals and Self-Interest in American Foreign Relations.* Chicago: University of Chicago Press, 1953.

Perkins, Frances. *The Roosevelt I Knew.* New York: Viking, 1946.

Plokhy, S. M. *Yalta: The Price of Peace.* New York: Penguin Books, 2011.

Posner, Richard A. *The Essential Holmes: Selections from the Letters, Speeches, Judicial Opinions, & Other Writings of Oliver Wendell Holmes, Jr.* Chicago: University of Chicago Press, 1997.

Post, Jerrold M., and Robert S. Robins. *When Illness Strikes the Leader.* New Haven, CT: Yale University Press, 1995.

Prange, Gordon W. *At Dawn We Slept: The Untold Story of Pearl Harbor.* New York: Penguin Press, 1982.

Roll, David L. *The Hopkins Touch: Harry Hopkins and the Forging of the Alliance to Defeat Hitler.* New York: Oxford University Press, 2013.

Roosevelt, Eleanor. *This I Remember.* New York: Harper and Brothers, 1949.

Roosevelt, Elliott, ed. *F.D.R.: His Personal Letters.* 2 vols. New York: Duell, Sloan and Pearce, 1947, 1950.

Roosevelt, James, and Sidney Shalett. *Affectionately, FDR: A Son's Story of a Lonely Man.* New York: Harcourt, Brace, 1959.

———. *My Parents: A Differing View.* New York: Playboy Press, 1976.

Rosenman, Samuel I., ed. *The Public Papers and Addresses of Franklin D. Roosevelt, 1928–1945.* 13 volumes. New York: Random House and Harper and Brothers, 1938–1950.

———. *Working With Roosevelt.* New York: Harper and Brothers, 1952.

Schlesinger, Arthur M., Jr. *The Age of Roosevelt: The Crisis of the Old Order, 1919–1933.* Boston: Houghton Mifflin Company, 1957.

———. *The Age of Roosevelt: The Coming of the New Deal.* Boston: Houghton Mifflin Company, 1959.

———. *The Age of Roosevelt: The Politics of Upheaval.* Boston: Houghton Mifflin Company, 1959.

Schulman, Bruce. *From Cotton Belt to Sunbelt: Federal Policy, Economic Development, and the Transformation of the South, 1938–1980.* New York: Oxford University Press, 1991.

Schwarz, Jordan A. *The Speculator: Bernard M. Baruch in Washington, 1917–1965.* Chapel Hill: University of North Carolina Press, 1981.

Sherwin, Martin J. *A World Destroyed: The Atomic Bomb and the Grand Alliance.* New York: Random House, 1975.

Sherwood, Robert E. *Roosevelt and Hopkins: An Intimate History.* New York: Harper & Brothers, 1948.

Shesol, Jeff. *Supreme Power: Franklin Roosevelt vs. the Supreme Court.* New York: W. W. Norton, 2010.

Shirer, William L. *Berlin Diary: The Journal of a Foreign Correspondent, 1934–1941.* New York: A. A. Knopf, 1941.

Simon, James F. *FDR and Chief Justice Hughes: The President, the Supreme Court, and the Epic Battle Over the New Deal.* New York: Simon and Schuster, 2012.

Smith, Jean Edward. *FDR.* New York: Random House, 2007.

Smith, Kathryn. *The Gatekeeper: Missy LeHand, FDR, and the Untold Story of the Partnership that Defined a Presidency.* New York: Touchstone, 2016.

Spector, Ronald H. *Eagle Against the Sun: The American War with Japan.* New York: Free Press, 1984.

Steel, Ronald. *Walter Lippmann and the American Century.* Boston: Little, Brown, 1980.

Taubman, William. *Stalin: Stalin's American Policy: From Entente to Détente to Cold War.* New York: W. W. Norton & Co., 1982.

Tobin, James. *The Man He Became: How FDR Defied Polio to Win the Presidency.* New York: Simon & Schuster, 2013.

Tuchman, Barbara W. *Stilwell and the American Experience in China, 1911–1945.* New York: Macmillan, 1971.

Tugwell, Rexford G. *The Democratic Roosevelt.* New York: Doubleday, 1957.

———. *The Brain Trust.* New York: The Viking Press, 1968.

Ulam, Adam B. *Expansion and Coexistence: The History of Soviet Foreign Policy, 1917–1967.* New York: Praeger, 1968.

Viorst, Milton. *Hostile Allies: FDR and De Gaulle.* New York: MacMillan, 1965.

Ward, Geoffrey C., ed. *Closest Companion: The Unknown Story of the Intimate Friendship Between Franklin Roosevelt and Margaret Suckley.* Boston: Houghton Mifflin, 1995.

Watkins, T. H. *Righteous Pilgrim: The Life and Times of Harold L. Ickes, 1874–1952.* New York: H. Holt, 1992.

Way, Lewis. *Alfred Adler — An Introduction to his*

Psychology. New York: Penguin Books, 1956.

White, Jr., Richard D. *Kingfish: The Reign of Huey P. Long.* New York: Random House, 2006.

Williams, T. Harry. *Huey Long.* New York: Knopf, 1970.

Willkie, Wendell. *One World.* New York: Simon & Schuster, 1943.

Winik, Jay. *1944: FDR and the Year That Changed History.* New York: Simon & Schuster, 2015.

Wohlstetter, Roberta. *Pearl Harbor: Warning and Decision: A National Failure to Anticipate.* Palo Alto, CA: Stanford University Press, 1962.

Woolner, David B. *The Last 100 Days: FDR at War and at Peace.* New York: Basic Books, 2017.

Worster, Donald. *Dust Bowl: The Southern Plains in the 1930s.* New York: Oxford University Press, 2004.

ABOUT THE AUTHOR

Robert Dallek is the author of *An Unfinished Life: John F. Kennedy, 1917–1963* and *Nixon and Kissinger,* among other books. His writing has appeared in *The New York Times, The Washington Post, The Atlantic Monthly,* and *Vanity Fair.* He is an elected fellow of the American Academy of Arts and Sciences and of the Society of American Historians, for which he served as president in 2004–2005. He lives in Washington, D.C.

The employees of Thorndike Press hope you have enjoyed this Large Print book. All our Thorndike, Wheeler, and Kennebec Large Print titles are designed for easy reading, and all our books are made to last. Other Thorndike Press Large Print books are available at your library, through selected bookstores, or directly from us.

For information about titles, please call:
(800) 223-1244

or visit our website at:
gale.com/thorndike

To share your comments, please write:
Publisher
Thorndike Press
10 Water St., Suite 310
Waterville, ME 04901